Like Nothing on this Earth

Tony Hughes-d'Aeth is a Senior Lecturer in English and Cultural Studies at The University of Western Australia. He has published widely on Australian literature and cultural history, including *Paper Nation: The Story of the Picturesque Atlas of Australasia, 1886–1888* (Melbourne University Press, 2001) which received the Ernest Scott and the W.K. Hancock prizes for Australian history. Hughes-d'Aeth was co-editor of Westerly magazine, a literary journal devoted to Australian and Asian writing and culture, from 2010 to 2015.

Tony Hughes-d'Aeth

Like Nothing on this Earth

UWA PUBLISHING

First published in 2017 by
UWA Publishing
Crawley, Western Australia 6009
www.uwap.uwa.edu.au

UWAP is an imprint of UWA Publishing
a division of The University of Western Australia

National Library of Australia
Cataloguing-in-Publication entry:
Hughes-d'Aeth, Tony, author.
Like nothing on this earth : a literary history of the wheatbelt / Tony Hughes-d'Aeth.
ISBN: 9781742589244 (paperback)
Includes bibliographical references and index.
Literature and society—Western Australia—Wheatbelt
Region—History.
Creative writing—Western Australia—Wheatbelt Region.
Wheatbelt Region (W.A.)

Cover image taken from Cowan's wheatbelt scrapbook, c. 1933–1934. Peter Cowan Papers, Peter Cowan Writers Centre, Western Australia
Typeset in 11 point Bembo by Lasertype
Printed by Lightning Source

This project has been assisted by the Australian Government through the Australia Council, its arts funding and advisory body.

 uwapublishing

Contents

CONTENTS

List of Illustrations

Preface: The Clearing Line

Most nights I watch the television news until the end so I can see the weather report. The presenter stands in front of a virtualised image of Western Australia on which appear, in harmony with her prompts, the various data and signs that allow her and us to participate in the narrative of our state's weather. At some point, maybe ten or fifteen years ago, the map of the western half of the continent was replaced with a satellite image which ranged in colour from fawn to forest green. To my naïve eye it seemed that the green portions of this map roughly matched the green parts of our state. I was most struck, and have been ever since, by the sharp line that ringed Perth to the north and east, stretching roughly from Geraldton to Esperance and marking out an area most West Australians know as the wheatbelt. Inside the ring was a wheat-coloured yellow, outside the ring a muted eucalyptus green. The line where they meet, known by analysts as the "clearing line", is the most obvious visible sign from space of humans' effect on the planet. These pixels are abstractions but they are not mere metaphors. They bear a strict relationship to the surface of the land they represent. The pixels are given a colour value based on the degree of "reflectance" measured by the satellite camera.[1] The more light, the brighter the pixel; the less, the darker. The sharp line is

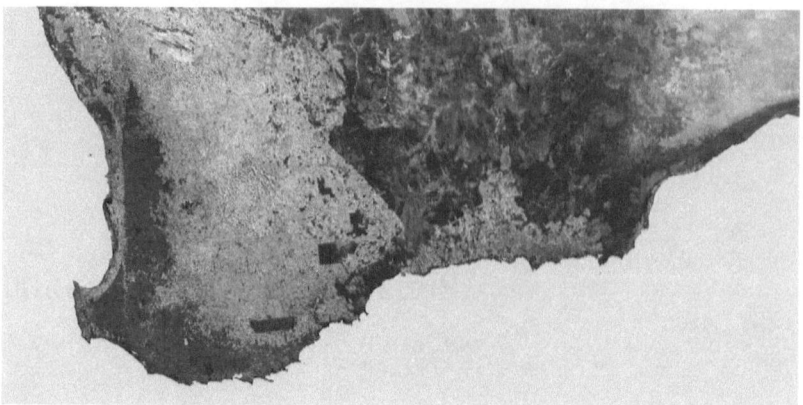

1. The wheatbelt from space.

created by the spectral contrast between native perennials (bush) and the crop and pasture grasses that now predominate in the agricultural areas. It is made sharper by the comparative flatness of the country.

The clearing line follows the rabbit-proof fence which also marks (more or less) the minimum rainfall threshold (the "10-inch line", or after the 1917–18 survey, "Brockman's Line"), below which cropping is unsustainable. Depending on how you look at this line it is either natural or man-made.[2] At first blush it seems overwhelmingly, disconcertingly artificial, if only by its almost perfect diagonal straightness. Yet viewed from its other side it is a line of resistance, the point at which intensive agriculture was no longer able to extend itself. It draws to mind other imperial demarcations, the famous walls that marked the limits of the Roman and Chinese empires. It is this picture, taken every day from machines orbiting in space, that leads us to a central theme of any history of the Western Australian wheatbelt, which is that of radical disappearance. Of the shires and districts that make up the wheatbelt, only 7 per cent of the original vegetation, and thus the animals that depend on it, remains today.[3] Remnants survive only in the form of islanded reserves, large in some terms, but tiny by proportion and without the former continuities that allowed the southwest to operate as a fluctuating bioregion responsive to savage climatic change across aeons.

This book traces the creation of the Western Australian wheatbelt during the course of the twentieth century by considering the creative writing of those who lived in the wheatbelt at various points in their lives and then wrote about that experience. This is what I mean by a "literary history": a history of the wheatbelt as captured in the literary works deriving from it. The book approaches this task by following an "event/witness" model. The event is the creation of the wheatbelt and the witnesses are the creative writers. The creation of the wheatbelt was not felt to be a single event, but instead a gradual and, in lots of ways, "natural" process that took place over generations. But in the deep time of ecological history, the creation of the wheatbelt was sudden and spectacular. Also, from the vantage point of ecology, the event is not the creation of the wheatbelt, but the disappearance of a vast territory of native wilderness with a biodiversity almost without equal on the planet. So, the creation of the wheatbelt and the destruction of the native habitat that preceded it are one and the same, and constitute the "event" that this book is tracing. It took place in two main phases, 1900–1930 (roughly 17 million acres) and 1950–1970 (roughly 20 million acres), with the Great Depression and the two world wars providing hiatuses in the process. Total land cleared by 1970 was approximately 50 million acres or 200,000 square kilometres. To give some perspective, the land mass of Britain is just under 230,000 square kilometres.

Choosing creative writers as the "witnesses" to this event deserves some explanation. My own background is in literary criticism and cultural history and I have gradually come to realise the particular value of creative writing as a document of record. The event of the wheatbelt has been traced through the disciplines of agriculture, economics, social history and ecology. It is significant in each of those domains. Literature, though, offers something different, which is the interior apprehension of how life feels to people. The eleven writers I have chosen to focus on take the story of the wheatbelt from its beginnings in the early 1900s to the turn of the millennium. Each has presented a different problem to me and the chapters spend time introducing each writer. The different wheatbelts that come into view in their writing represent not just changes in historical time, but variations in literary genre and the particularities of each writer's encounter with the wheatbelt. Some grew up there, left and never returned. Others moved there for work in their early adulthood. Others have had family

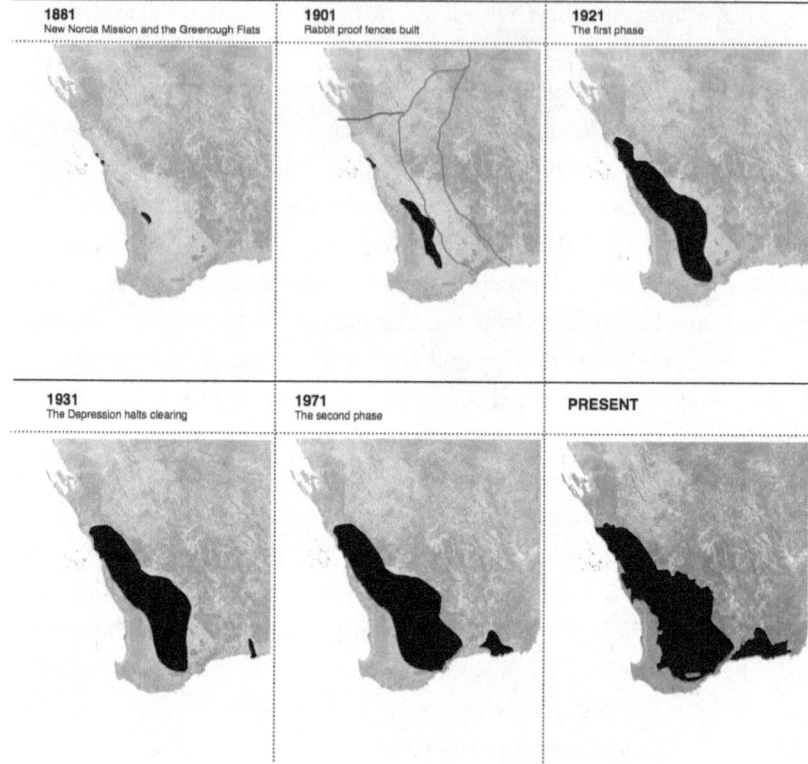

2. The clearing of the wheatbelt.

connections that have seen them return again and again through the course of their life and are able to speak to the changes they have seen take place. It became clear as I wrote that learning about the witness was as important as learning about the event.

Let me briefly introduce the kind of witness that literature offers to the event of the wheatbelt, remembering that what happens is a vast and almost total destruction of the pre-existing lifeworld of the southwest of the continent. Diagrams like the one above illustrate the matter plainly enough, but it is difficult to replicate the sense of shock that such an absence might once have generated. To the acculturated, the wheatbelt will often appear a pleasant blend of fields and trees, an undulating fertile country beneath bright blue skies. One has to imagine a person who did not know what a field was, or what wheat or indeed crops were. Such a person was Ronald Gidgup

Senior, a Noongar-Yamatji man who grew up on a station outside of Carnarvon before moving with his father to Bruce Rock in the wheatbelt in 1941:

> Coming from the station country down to the farming country was different. I never knew what a farming area was until I saw the land was cleared and there were these big haystacks. I thought they were people's homes but they weren't because they were made out of hay. I had never seen a cleared field before and I couldn't work out why all the bush was gone. When you live in station country that's all you see, the bush. I didn't know what wheat was, I had never seen wheat ...[4]

Gidgup's memories retain in an undiminished way the bafflement that ensues when one realises for the first time that something one had thought belonged to the order of permanence has been simply and utterly erased. Another Aboriginal observer remembers a more recent moment of estrangement from the wheatbelt's ordered fields. In his book *Kayang & Me*, Kim Scott describes being sent to a site near Quairading by the Ballardong elder, Ralph Winmar, with Indigenous students from Curtin University on a cultural expedition:

> [Ralph Winmar] sent a group of us to climb the rocky side of that creative spirit, the Waakal, or at least that transformed remnant of it fenced within a small rectangle of the wheat belt somewhere around Quairading and York. On the climb we tasted water running from the wound left by an ancestral Noongar's spear and, standing high on the Waakal's fossilised back, looked out over a tractor describing small futile circles in the paddock below us, and heard the bleating of distant tiny sheep. The breeze in our faces, and the air entering our lungs did not, despite the cleared paddocks and the fences and sheep and tractor, belong to any place known only as "the wheat belt".[5]

For Scott, the moment captured the erasure of Aboriginal presence from the everyday life of the wheatbelt, with its tractors and sheep, and how in its remnant corners the wheatbelt still retains connections to an ancient system of language, thought and human community. Scott's account comes from a point in history where the familiar cleared fields of the wheatbelt become more and more strange. They cease seeming to express the natural historical outcome of agricultural pioneering, and instead represent the violent interruption of a much longer history—the history of Aboriginal occupancy.

In Tom Flood's wheatbelt novel *Oceana Fine* (1989), which we will consider in detail later in this book, we see the wheatbelt—as it is so often experienced—through the windscreen of a motor vehicle. The driver is a young man on his way to work on "the bins" in the eastern wheatbelt in the late 1970s:

> The landscape is so immense, hot and huge like nothing on this earth, that I fear it might swallow me. The heat makes its own horizon, multi-layered and inconstant. Out of this mirage runs a highway ... The car burned along the lonely highway through miles of brown-green bushland and straw-coloured paddocks, the stubble of the wheat blotched with charcoal-green tree clumps and bounded only by the endless miles of fencing strung to the horizon.[6] (3)

More than forty years earlier, in his novel *Men Against the Earth* (1946), John K. Ewers describes a similar scene, one of mesmeric expansiveness, as seen through the eyes of a young girl born in the wheatbelt in the first decade of the twentieth century. She is travelling on a wheat-filled wagon across the sandplain that separated her farm from the railway siding. She is gradually falling asleep, and, tragically, so is her father next to her. She will wake up to his screams, realising with horror that he has fallen beneath the wheels of the wagon:

> She wanted to gaze over the plain to where it joined the sky in the blue, hazy distance. She liked the plain, because it gave her a feeling of distance. It just seemed to go on and on. At home, everything was bounded by fencing. Each paddock was a certain size and shape. But here there were no fences and no shape. The plain seemed to reach right out to the ends of the earth. If you went on across it over its trackless scrubs, with each new rise yielding another illimitable waste, you would come to somewhere, just as you would if you went over the sea. Arvie thought the sea must be something like this plain, although she had never seen it.[7] (121)

While in Flood's novel the driver looks out on a landscape almost entirely denuded of its native vegetation, in Ewers's novel the sandplain appears in its original form. Yet the two descriptions share the quality of sublime awe in the face of a world which escapes limit, and particularly the limits which would signify a "human" quality or scale to the environment. In each case, both the "illimitable waste" of the sandplain in the 1900s, and "the endless miles of fencing strung to the horizon" of the 1970s threaten to overwhelm the viewer.

These examples are all literary in the sense that I will be using this word in this history. In the case of the extracts from Flood and Ewers, the matter seems straightforward. Both are novelists and the words come from novels they have set in the wheatbelt. The quotations from Kim Scott and Ronald Gidgup Senior are less obviously literary. Each is in the mode of memoir, not fiction in the usual sense, but factual, albeit personal, accounts of events experienced. Both Gidgup's reflection on first seeing a land evacuated of bush and Scott's feeling of estrangement on the hilltop near Quairading are literary in the way that they attempt to come to terms with an emotion or memory that somehow resists description in the everyday language that serves to describe reality for most purposes. This temporary failure of ordinary language causes each to search for a way of conveying this experience. For each, what they were looking at was the wheatbelt, but for each the term "wheatbelt" was inadequate to what they were seeing, converting what was strange, profound and drastic into something commonplace, unremarkable and fully completed. In this book, I use "literary" not to designate the line between fact and fiction, but to signal the recourse to the imaginative faculty.

It is this ability for literary writing to suspend the casual (but far-reaching) presumptions of everyday language that provides the basis for the approach I take in this book. One can get a very good idea of the history of the wheatbelt by reading any one of the dozens of excellent shire histories that have been produced since the 1950s.[8] What my study seeks to do, though, is something rather different, which is to try to consider what the wheatbelt *felt* like. This slightly odd way of expressing the matter is meant to suggest that by focusing on literary works we can begin to reconstruct, through the roughly 100-year history of the wheatbelt, a picture of this singular event as a subjective experience, as something which was lived emotionally and imaginatively in the private lives of people's innermost thoughts. The book is arranged chronologically with each chapter based on the life and work of an author who has lived in the wheatbelt and written about that experience. As I have mentioned, I approach each writer as a witness. They are witnesses, along with thousands of others, to a socio-ecological event of planetary significance: the eradication of the lifeworld of southwest Australia. But they are witnesses also of the inner event: of just what it meant to participate in the founding of the wheatbelt. It is in this latter capacity that they hold insights that appear virtually nowhere else, and it is only through understanding the founding of the wheatbelt in this way—as a psychic phenomenon— that we can grasp its full significance.

Introduction: Songs of Wheat

The Western Australian wheatbelt sits on a vast plateau, the Yilgarn block, that dominates the southwest corner of the continent. This plateau is fringed on its western edge by a narrow coastal plain of roughly 40 to 60 kilometres, encompassing Western Australia's only major city, Perth, and running from Shark Bay in the north to the southwest capes. This coastal plain has sandy soils and chains of freshwater lakes and wetlands in the south, and contains the extensive inlets of the Swan and Peel Rivers, as well as the smaller Moore, Greenough, Hill and Irwin estuaries. It absorbs the sprawl of Perth, as people want to stay close to the ocean and its moderating summer breezes. The coastal plain is met on its eastern horizon by the stumpy line of ranges which separate it from the plateau falling away gently to its east. Near Perth, these are known as the Darling Ranges, the Darling Escarpment, or simply "the Hills" or "the Scarp". These hills, forested and with rocky soils, have tended only to be farmed in their valleys and, while logged extensively at various stages, have not been cleared in the way that the lands either side of it have. Thus the Darling Ranges appear as a dark blotch on the satellite photograph. The ranges do not on their eastern side fall back to the level of the coastal plain but taper into the undulating plateau. It is on this country—a mosaic of open woodland, sandplain, and wodjil scrub—that the wheatbelt now stands.

Essentially, the wheatbelt is a rainfall region. Winter storm fronts from the Southern and Indian oceans wash across the southwest corner of Australia and provide sufficient rainfall to sustain forests and woodland and, much more recently, broad-acre grain-farming. (These same oceanic clouds also deposit tons of salt, dissolved in the rain and then sequestered in the soil through which it drains, a fact of some significance in the history of the wheatbelt.) In 1917, a royal commission set up by the Western Australian State Government requested that the Surveyor-General F.S. Brockman produce a map marking the effective safe extent of cropping, and this line is more or less the one that we see in the satellite photograph.[1] On the Great Eastern Highway that heads due east out of Perth towards Kalgoorlie, this limit is reached at Southern Cross, roughly 350 kilometres inland, with an average annual rainfall of 270 millimetres. East of this, the country is used as pastoral rangeland and not for cropping. To the south, the expansion of the wheatbelt was slowed and stopped by more heavily wooded country which, apart from being harder to clear, was more prone to crop rust. The northern limit of the wheatbelt, as with the east, is also a rainfall line, which gradually lessens the further north you go. This has the wheatbelt tending closer to the coast as you head north and becoming more narrow as it is hemmed by the northern and eastern rainfall limits. For grain to ripen, one also needs sun. The generally sunny, warm conditions that prevail in the wheatbelt suit the vigorous growth and maturation of cereal crops, provided there is sufficient rain. Thus, the wheatbelt is bound on its east and north by the 270-millimetre rainfall line and on its south and west, closer to the coast, by the 750-millimetre rainfall line. Land north and east of the former is too dry for wheat; south and west of the latter is too wet. These are rules of thumb but provide the general picture.

The southwest is the traditional country of the Noongar people, comprising some seventeen distinct tribes, but sharing a similar language that distinguishes them from the Wong-gie and western desert peoples further east, and the Yamatji peoples of the Murchison and Gascoyne. Indeed, to the clearing line, the rabbit-proof fence and the rainfall line, we might transpose what early anthropologists

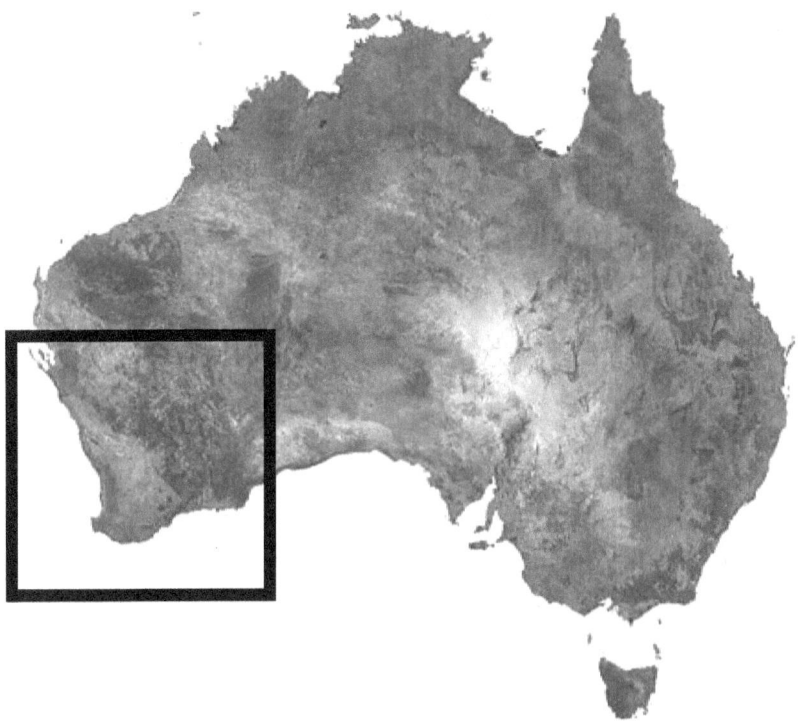

3. The southwest of Australia, with cleared agricultural areas visible.

sometimes called the circumcision line, falling in almost exactly the same place. This line denotes the fact that Noongar men, somewhat unusually in Indigenous Australia, were not circumcised. The wheatbelt is mainly situated on Noongar land and it was the Noongar people that suffered most directly when it was created. It was Noongar people that first met Europeans on the south coast in the early 1800s and when the Swan River Colony was established in 1829. This colony was primarily conceived of as an agricultural colony of free settlers, a relatively novel idea at this point in European imperial history.[2] As flour and bread were staple elements in the British diet, the cultivation of grain for milling was amongst the highest priorities of colonial settlement.

As is generally well known, the colony in Western Australia grew slowly in comparison to the other Australian colonies. Nevertheless, from the outset, wheat was a crucial component of the farming enterprises of the early settlers at, and beyond, the Swan River Settlement. In the early colonial years, wheat was cultivated primarily for domestic consumption, with wool being grown for export. In 1831, two years after the colony was founded, 160 acres of wheat were reaped. In that year, an agricultural society was formed to promote agriculture in the colony. Sufficient grain was grown in 1833 to end the rationing of the first years and self-sufficiency was reached in 1835, but thereafter production really only kept pace with the (modest) increase in the colony's population, and it would be many more years before wheat was exported. By 1837, there were 1,381 acres harvested producing 22,104 bushels. For much of the nineteenth century, the techniques for growing wheat in Western Australia remained unchanged, and were adapted from traditional English methods. The agricultural historian Burvill explains the methods:

> Before crops were sown ... manure was spread and the land ploughed with single furrow ploughs drawn by two oxen or horses. Seed was then broadcast by hand and the sown areas levelled with spiked iron harrows. Cereal crops were cut when ripe by hand with a scythe and the grain threshed out by hand-beating or by horse-treading.[3]

By 1850 the area under tillage for wheat had grown to 4,400 acres. As well as the Avon and Dale valleys beyond the Darling Ranges, wheat was grown on the Swan coastal plain throughout the nineteenth century and into the early 1900s when it was ultimately superseded by the wheat farms east of the ranges. Indeed, as Burvill notes, wheat was grown (and often milled) wherever new farms were established in the southwest, including places not now associated with wheat farming, such as the south coast or the high-rainfall Karri country around Manjimup.

Beyond the coastal districts and the river valleys, the first inland district to be opened up for wheat farming is the area called the Victoria Plains. This was the undulating but wooded country north of Toodyay (known then, on a slightly different site, as Newcastle) and Northam. This land was canvassed in the 1840s as possible grazing country, and a mission was established by Dom Rosendo Salvado on the east branch of the Moore River under the name New Norcia. New

Norcia was also a Benedictine monastery and, under the principles of that rule, was to be as self-sufficient as possible. Thirteen hectares were cleared for tillage in the early part of 1847. From 1860 to 1890, the Victoria Plains "became the granary of Western Australia".[4] Small wheat enterprises continued to be pursued in other areas, usually as an adjunct to pastoral farming, which had the advantage of not requiring either fencing or clearing. The Norrish family had started to grow wheat at Kojonup in the Great Southern in 1849. A small wheat farm of 20 acres (with a mill) was established by A.Y. Hassell in 1861 at the pastoral holding of Jerramungup, inland from Bremer Bay. What is now the northern and eastern wheatbelt—the districts of Kellerberrin, Kununoppin, Nungarin, Doodlakine, Quairading, Dangin, Bruce Rock, Narembeen, and Mullewa—were originally taken up as pastoral leases. For this purpose, the land favoured was the York gum and jam country, which offered better feed for stock and often fresh water in the soaks near granite outcrops. The salmon-gum, morrel and gimlet country was ignored, although this would later become "first class" wheat land. The techniques for growing remained primitive, prompting Anthony Trollope, in his visit of 1872, to judge it:

> Atrociously bad … Men continue to crop the same ground with the same crops year after year without manuring it, and when the weeds come thicker than the corn they simply leave it. Machinery has not been introduced. Seed is wasted, and farmers thresh their corn with flails on the roads after the old Irish fashion.[5]

Yet investment in wheat farming was also hampered, as Bolton points out, by the generally slow growth of the Western Australian population and economy. The latter part of the nineteenth century saw considerable pastoral expansion, but cropping stagnated, increasing modestly from 54,000 acres in 1870 to 70,000 acres in 1890, roughly half of which was wheat.[6] By contrast, these were years of significant crop expansion in Victoria, New South Wales, and Queensland.

During this time (1870–1890) the non-Indigenous population of the colony roughly doubled from 25,000 to 49,000, but still remained tiny by comparison to the other Australian colonies. Very little wheat

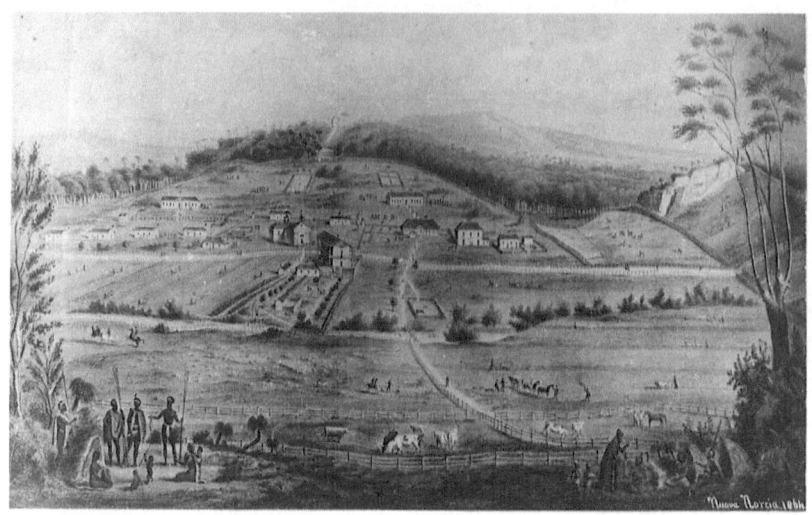

4. An engraving of the mission and surrounding fields at New Norcia, c. 1860. The archives of the Benedictine Community of New Norcia community, 73671P.

was exported, and wool remained the major export commodity. The surveyor-general and commissioner of Crown lands, John Forrest (1847–1918), introduced tariffs to protect local produce at the end of 1887 and he also established a parliamentary inquiry, chaired by H.W. Venn, to map out the future of the agricultural industry in the colony.[7] (Forrest would be appointed the colony's first premier when responsible government came into effect in 1890.) One of the direct outcomes of the Venn Commission was the establishment of Declared Agricultural Areas, including the establishment of the Meckering Agricultural Area, surveyed by George Leeming, for the specific activity of crop production.[8] Fatefully, it was also in 1887 that the movement of rabbits westward along the bight of Australia was recognised for the first time as an impending threat. The Declared Agricultural Areas would become the nodal points in the expansion of the wheatbelt.[9]

The Golden Grain

The watershed year for the wheatbelt would prove to be 1890, when a number of events occurred that would dramatically alter the future of the colony. As mentioned, responsible government was granted, with John Forrest appointed as the colony's first premier. Of even more significance, though, was the discovery of gold, which would transform the colony almost as dramatically as the metal transformed Victoria forty years earlier. The key discoveries were in the semi-arid country some 500 kilometres east of Perth. Gold was found at Southern Cross in the late 1880s, in the Murchison in 1891, Coolgardie in 1892 and Kalgoorlie in 1893. The effects were immediate and dramatic, and are rightly called a "rush". The population of Western Australia trebled between 1889 and 1896 from 44,000 to 138,000. The wheatbelt's most important border is thus not one in space, but in time. The gold rush of the 1890s was the event that funded and drove the expansion of the wheatbelt in its first convulsive period of growth, that is, in the opening three decades of the twentieth century. In the minds of key figures at the time, gold would be the catalyst to the more lasting, and wholesome, economic development provided by agriculture. The influx of people to Western Australia increased domestic demand for grain both as food for people and fuel for horses. At the same time, the newly responsible government saw an opportunity to fulfil the founding vision of Western Australia as an agricultural colony, a pleasant country of farms and villages, feeding the "bread-eating" nations of the world.

The Western Australian parliament passed the Homesteads Act in 1893 (based on similar legislation in the United States) and the Land Act in 1898. These were progressive state-of-the-art bills that were carefully designed to prevent the kind of rampant speculation that had subverted the "Selection Acts" of the Eastern colonies. The parliament also established the Agricultural Bank in 1894 to assist farmers in financing new farms. The completion of the Kalgoorlie rail-line in 1896 and the Goldfields water pipeline in 1902 were central to the creation of the wheatbelt, and initial settlement took place along the axis that linked Perth to the Goldfields, with Agricultural Areas declared at Meckering, Doodlakine and Bainding.[10] At first, the block sizes tended to range between 100 and 400 acres, although this quickly increased. Joseph Placid Stokes's grandfather selected 500 acres near Cunderdin in 1906. It was a small block, but very well situated. Albert Facey's uncle, not a wealthy man by any means, selected 1,000 acres of first-class land near Pingelly in August 1901, taking it up in September the following year. At the other end of the spectrum, in 1912, having made their money as storekeepers at Southern Cross on the route to the Goldfields, Dorothy Hewett's maternal grandparents, Ted and Mary Coade, were able to select 3,000 acres of land 22 kilometres from Wickepin, a holding which made them the richest in the district.

Much of the population increase was driven by internal migration from South Australia, Victoria and New South Wales. The 1890s were Depression years in the Eastern colonies and rural poverty had become chronic. In this context, the incentives offered to settlement were indeed enticing. The legislation allowed an applicant to acquire a "Homestead Farm", which is to say a farm of 160 acres on which they were to reside, for no cost provided certain minimal improvements (fencing, clearing) were completed at annual intervals.[11] In 1897, the Minister of Lands George Throssell (1840–1910) remarked that "160 acres and a wife was all that was required to make the majority of Perth young men happy".[12] Further land could be selected at 10 shillings per acre by conditional purchase. The conditions were a twenty-year repayment period; residence on or near to the land purchased, and that it be fenced within five years. In the years that followed, the sustainable holding of land steadily increased. By the time the wheatbelt began to really operate at the turn of the century, the "thousand acre" farm had become the norm and it was mainly settled on this basis in the first phase (1900–1930) of the wheatbelt's growth. For a while in the years after World War Two, 2,500 acres was considered average. A decade into the twenty-first century the average size of a wheatbelt farm was 20,000 acres. The general rule was that the further "out" in the wheatbelt you were, the more land you needed to ensure profitability. The mechanisation and chemicalisation of the wheatbelt both allowed and demanded economies of scale, which has meant a progressive depopulation of the wheatbelt since about 1950.

While Western Australian land was remarkably cheap, a number of factors still gave prospective selectors pause for thought, and these were matters that were immediately targeted by the government. First of all, the land was remote, in the sense that it was not serviced by ready transportation. It was inland and there were no river systems to ship crops to market. The expansion of rail and road networks was thus a constant ambition for the early developers of the wheatbelt.

5. Land advertisement for the wheatbelt.

The rail link to Kalgoorlie was completed in 1896 and soon lines spurring south and north opened the plateau east of the Darling Ranges to clearing and farming. The Great Southern rail-line was commenced on 20 October 1886 and opened in June 1889. It connected to the Perth–Goldfields line at Beverley and ran south to Albany, creating in its course the future wheatbelt centres of Pingelly, Narrogin, Wagin and Katanning. The goal was to bring most farms within a 20-kilometre radius of a siding or station. The cartage limit was generally held to be no more than 48 kilometres, though some would gamble on carting it further in the hope that a rail would eventually come.[13] In John K. Ewers's wheatbelt novel, *Men Against the Earth* (1946), set in the years before the Great War, one character recalls "how for ten years before the rail was built he had carted to Northam, forty miles [or 64 kilometres] away".[14]

Another major obstacle to farming in the wheatbelt was the non-availability of water. There are virtually no permanent running streams or rivers. The Moore River, mentioned earlier, is a good example. Even in the wet winter months, it is little more than a chain of elongated puddles for much of its course. In the absence of rivers and freshwater lakes, water was obtained from "soaks", which were naturally damp areas adjoining granite outcrops, that could be dug out into small ponds to water stock. The Noongar people had done this, and the early pastoralists had expanded these soaks during the nineteenth century. In the Victoria Plains, the Benedictines dug and lined hundreds of wells, many of which are still intact, though many have also turned saline. In 1902, the famous Goldfields water pipeline designed by C.Y. O'Connor was completed and delivered water from Mundaring Weir in the Darling Ranges to Kalgoorlie some 570 kilometres inland with the aid of six steam-driven pumping stations. Branch pipes were built to water the towns and farms of the adjoining wheatbelt. For districts beyond the reach of the pipe, the government built dams to capture surface run-off from winter rains and summer thunderstorms, and water was carted from them by surrounding farmers, who also built dams on their own land to water stock. Water for domestic use was harvested from rooftops of sheds and houses once corrugated metal became readily available.

From the 1890s, the application of superphosphate as a fertiliser also substantially improved wheat yields and broadened the extent of farming to soils that were not previously arable. James Mitchell (1866–1951), the first Minister of Agriculture would later proclaim of the men leaving the goldfields to take up land in the wheatbelt: "Gold brought these men to Western Australia, and superphosphate will keep them here".[15] The dissemination of new techniques was aided by the establishment in 1894 of the Bureau of Agriculture, which became the Department of Agriculture in 1898. Under all these conditions, areas sown to wheat increased dramatically in the 1890s and early 1900s, more than doubling in the period 1890 to 1900 and again in the period 1900 to 1905. In 1904 Western Australia became for the first time a net exporter of wheat and has remained so, almost without exception, ever since. As M. Barnard Eldershaw declared proudly in 1939, "Thirty years ago Western Australia was importing flour, to-day wheat is her premier product."[16] Today, the output from the Western Australian wheatbelt is crucial to Australia's wheat export. Without the Western Australian wheatbelt, Australia would not, except in good seasons, export wheat.

In all of this the State Agricultural Bank was indeed a crucial, perhaps *the* crucial, institution. The Bank employed people to assess the purchasers of land and establish whether they were meeting the terms of the purchase by making the agreed "improvements". Inspectors conducted due diligence on settler-farmers seeking loans from the Agricultural Bank by auditing them for compliance with the lending terms. Initially, the Bank would make available up to £400 measured against half the value of certain specified "improvements" to the land granted. In 1902, the loan limit was increased to £1,000 and to £2,000 in 1912.[17] The inspector had to assess whether the land and its farmer(s) were likely to repay the loan in due course. This involved measuring the size and quality of the land selected, and recording any "improvements" (especially fencing and clearing) as stipulated under the terms of selection under the relevant Acts. Also, up to 1912, when the rule was relaxed, the inspector checked that residency provisions were being met, so as to prevent the kind of rampant speculative acquisition that had marred the attempts at close settlement in the Eastern colonies of Australia in the previous century. The relaxation of these restrictions saw speculation creep in, with fatal consequences, from 1912 until the catastrophe of 1929.

Along with the Agricultural Bank, the other key government agency was the Lands Department. Eva Braid's study of the "surveyor-explorers" employed by the Lands Department to classify land reveals the considerable energy expended by the Colony, and later State, in the creation of viable farms through commissioning reliable land surveys. She explains that the surveying was closely tied to the construction of railways. For example, as the rail-line was being built east to the goldfields, Agricultural Areas were surveyed along its intended path. Thanks in no small part to its powerful patrons (Forrest, Mitchell, Throssell), the town of Northam became the epicentre of the operation. Just 100 kilometres from Perth, Northam eclipsed its Avon Valley neighbours—York, Beverley and Toodyay (known as Newcastle until 1910)—due to its location on the east–west rail-line that served the goldfields, and later connected to the rest of the country. It was also, as we have noted, the first major axis for wheatbelt expansion. In the late 1890s, it was decided to push the wheat frontier from Northam towards the Goomalling forests, some

50 kilometres northeast of the town. These "forests" were salmon-gum and gimlet woodlands, and doubts remained about the ability of their underlying soil to carry crops. Even if the soils and rains were good enough, farming there would not be viable without a railway connecting it to Perth, so the political argument essentially turned on the necessity of constructing a rail-line spurring north from Northam to service farms not yet in existence. The surveyors were thus tasked with classifying the land so as to assess whether such an expansion would be economic. In effect, the question is the classic one of modern governments in capitalist societies; that is, to what extent infrastructure ought to follow and support enterprise, and to what extent it should stimulate and create it on behalf of interested parties. So, the surveyors were part of a political project as much as a scientific and economic one. The results of government surveys were used by the Midland Railway Company to promote land for sale, granted to them by the government as payment for the building of the rail. This type of arrangement between governments and railway companies was typical of the development of the Northern Prairies in Canada and the United States at roughly this time.

The district around Goomalling, like other districts in the south-west, had been leased as 20,000-acre pastoral runs since the 1870s. Turning pastoral land into cropland was a radical reorganisation of land usage:

> The pastoralists had set up homesteads only where there was permanent water; but for agriculture, men and women would be trying to make farms where they would be fortunate to have even one of those little soaks or gnamma holes. The surveyors would be trying to ascertain rainfall, to find water, to locate and mark the smallest piece of granite, mark out areas of clay where tanks might be excavated and hold water, sink trial potholes to ascertain the quality of the clay. The land differed frequently and suddenly. The belts of forest country were divided by the sand plains of heath and scrub, considered worse than useless for agriculture. Poison country had to be marked, stands of suitable timber for fences and building found, and recommendations made for railway routes and the feeder roads to the railways. Searches had to be made for gold-bearing country, which would be a help for all if found;

but above all the classification was to ascertain soils and sub-soils and the surveyors were to report if they considered wheat growing would be possible. (25; emphasis added)

The Goomalling line, light-gauge and primitive in every respect, was opened in 1902, securing for the district a relatively safe, cheap, reliable transport for both crops and (in the other direction) the materials needed to grow them. From Goomalling, the surveyors pushed out again, this time to Lake Cowcowing, a large salt-pan some 24 kilometres beyond the 48-kilometre cartage radius drawn from the terminus of the Goomalling line. In the spring months between August and November 1903, a surveying team led by Inspecting-Surveyor Marmaduke Terry (1859–1932) classified over a quarter of a million acres (enough, depending on quality, for up to 250 thousand-acre farms) into the four classes of land then used for potential cropland. This land was for a long while known as "Terry's Survey", even after the Cowcowing Agricultural Area was gazetted in April 1905.

Amongst Terry's assistants, both on the Cowcowing survey and the Rabbit-Proof Fence survey, was the young cadet John Aubrey Nunn, whom Eva Braid was able to interview in his bed at Shenton Park Hospital in the 1960s. It is to Nunn that the honour of being the first wheatbelt poet might properly be given. After the entire party contracted dysentery in 1904, some 90 kilometres north of Cunderdin, he wrote a "Bush Ballad", which commences as follows:

> A surveyor's life is the life for me
> It's grand to be in the wild bush, free,
> With axe and slasher, theodolite and chain
> And sometimes working in gales and rain;
> Some days so thirsty, other times so wet;
> And often ½ quart a day is all the drink you'll get
> And it's sometimes filthy water with a snake or emu in it.[18]

And while Nunn's doggerel is written in the conventional irony of the period, the conditions it lampoons were certainly difficult. Indeed, shortly after ascending to the position of acting surveyor-general in

1901, George Leeming was forced to retire due to health complaints attributed to years of poor food and water whilst on his numerous surveys. In 1902, Leeming died in Melbourne, where he had gone to seek further medical help, at the age of forty-three. As well as being physically taxing, the work of surveying could weigh heavily on the conscience, partly because it was the subject of such intense social and political investment. In short, a lot hinged on it. Terry was conscious that people were investing their lives on the basis of decisions he was making. He was acutely aware that his surveys were relied upon, often somewhat optimistically, and at other times quite cynically exploited, for agricultural land development. Giving voice to Terry's concern, Braid writes:

> [These new farmers] would give years of their lives and would acquire debts they could never hope to repay ... Mitchell, in Northam, was telling the world that the land was easily cleared and the only thing needed was men who would go out with their families, take hold of the right end of an axe and get going. (30)

The prospect of individual failure, in the midst of such over-whelming pressure for the wheatbelt enterprise to succeed, must have been horrifying for many, so much so that it was never really discussed, except in a way that converted all the blame of that failure to a source distinct from the plan itself.

The Ideology of Wheat

The account thus far has focused on the material drivers of the wheatbelt, how wheat farming in the twentieth century moved beyond the initial goal of providing grain to the colony of Western Australia to become a major export industry. The pathway from the goldfields to the wheatfields was an adroit piece of social policy that allowed this industry to grow at a rate much faster than it might have otherwise. These aspects of the wheatbelt are generally well known and understood. What is less well documented is the way that wheat existed in the imagination of those who undertook the task of "settling", and in the broader community which supported the enterprise. We use the term ideology to refer to a system of ideas that inhabit a material practice, and in this sense we might plausibly speak of an identifiable "ideology of wheat" operating powerfully in the first three decades of the twentieth century. As much as anything, this book is an exploration of this ideology and the social fantasies that powered it. The work of ideology is complicated, but broadly speaking what it seeks to do is provide imaginary solutions to real contradictions. Many of the contradictions that the ideology of wheat addresses are bound up with the complex relationship that farming has to nature.[19] How, for instance, is an economic scheme for financial gain through the sale of cash crops also meant (and indeed felt) to be a return to nature? What exactly is natural about farming, and how can it be reconciled with its eradication of wilderness in southwestern Australia? Ideology answers these questions where it can, and where it cannot, it offers up methods by which they can be forestalled, evaded, repressed or transmuted into questions which can be more satisfactorily answered.

The creation of the wheatbelt in Western Australia at the turn of the century was not something that happened in isolation. It was in fact part of a far-reaching global phenomenon, amounting in many ways to a second agricultural revolution that spread across the world from the middle of the nineteenth century. In his classic account of the rise and fall of the South Australian wheatbelt, *On the Margins of the Good Earth* (1962), D.W. Meinig situates the emergence of this farming region in the 1860s and 1870s as part of a worldwide agricultural colonisation of "sub-humid, middle latitude, 'open' countries" to granular cultivation. It took place rapidly and almost simultaneously in the latter part of the nineteenth century: "in western Kansas and central Manitoba … in the Walla Walla and the San Joaquin; in the eastern Ukraine and western Siberia; in the inner Pampa and on the High Veld".[20] In Australia, wheat farming first emerged on a large scale in South Australia, which serviced the market created by the gold boom of the 1850s, much in the way that Western Australian wheatbelt was caused by the 1890s Coolgardie–Kalgoorlie gold rush. By the 1870s, Australia switched from being a net importer to a net exporter of wheat. In the ensuing decades wheat spread throughout the colonies, in an intermittent arc from the Darling Downs in Queensland, through western New South Wales across northern

Victoria to South Australia, and into the south of Western Australia by the early twentieth century. Western Australia's was thus the last of the wheatbelts as well as the largest. It corresponded, as we have seen, to a quadrupling of the colony's population and a historic shift in the balance of Australian economic power, integrating the western half of the continent with the east for the first time.

The shift from wool to wheat was a significant economic development and also made small-scale farming profitable in cash terms for the first time in Australia. However, one struggles to find examples in Australian literature in the late nineteenth century where growing crops exists as part of the heroicised work of the nation. If one tries to call to mind the heroes of popular Australian balladry, for instance, such as the poems of "Banjo" Paterson, we find bushrangers and drovers, stockmen and swagmen, boundary riders and billabongs, shearers and prospectors. We do not find many stories or songs about people farming grain. The same goes for the epic nationalist paintings of Roberts, Streeton, McCubbin and the Heidelberg school. The work of ploughing, planting and cropping do not shine brightly in the heavens of our national mythology. Only in the late 1910s, at the very point when horse-drawn agriculture was disappearing, did the era at last find grandeur in the works of Hans Heysen. Perhaps this betrays the restless spirit at the heart of a migrant nation. Shearing and droving were characterised by a romantic nomadology that tapped a fantasy of masculine independence from homely duties and womanly demands. The fact that this mythology has persisted suggests certain continuities in the imaginative requirements that Australia still demands of its national fantasies. But this continuity has eclipsed a period of time, beginning around the time of the Great War, when this was not the case, and when grain farming briefly came to the centre of national celebrity.

With Federation in 1901 there was, in fact, already a perceptible shift in the forms of imaginative investment in rural practices, with a greater emphasis on the productive feats of the grain farmer, and the role this had in nation-building. A new and successful variety of wheat, "Federation wheat", came to be widely used and this points rather literally to the sacramental quality with which wheat came to be invested. Just to give some sense of the scale of the cropping

6. Hans Heysen, *Ploughing the Field*, 1920, Hahndorf, South Australia watercolour on paper 41.8 × 52.3 cm. Art Gallery of South Australia, Adelaide, 816P17.
Hans Heysen, *The Toilers*, 1920, Hahndorf, South Australia watercolour on paper 40.4 × 51.8 cm. Art Gallery of South Australia, Adelaide, 696P29.

revolution in the early twentieth century, in NSW alone the area under wheat production grew from 1 million to 3.5 million acres between 1901 and 1914. And it was at this time that wheat became a subject in literary production. In particular, wheat ballads started to appear in the midst of the traditional pastoral songs in the pages of newspapers, their weekly "country" supplements, and magazines like the *Bulletin* and the *Lone Hand*. The celebration of wheat farming was a significant change in view. Cropping was previously held to be a form of almost shameful drudgery, evoking archaic feudal memories of being bonded to the land and to a master. In this context, one can see the appeal of the figures (drover, shearer, prospector) that populated the national rural mythology at the time. That this could turn so quickly is evident in the new wheat poem's sense of stridency.

Whilst a great many poems could be cited, two poems by Andrew "Banjo" Paterson (1864–1941) and C.J. Dennis (1876–1938), serve to capture the distinctive hopes and visions that wheat farming promised in this era. Dennis and Paterson are near contemporaries, though Banjo came to prominence in the 1890s, while Dennis's fame grew mainly in the years after the Great War. But these beloved national poets meet in the celebration of wheat farming. Dennis's poem, simply titled "Wheat" appeared in his first volume *Backblock Ballads and Other Verses* published in 1918.[21] The first verse and refrain are enough to give the flavour of the ballad:

> Oh! The ways o' makin' money in this world o'
>> Many lands
> An' the means to eke a livin' out are countless
>> As the sands
> There are thousands in the cities gettin' nothin' out
>> O' life.
> But the day-to-day excitement of eternal business
>> Strife.
> Yet a life o' rush and bustle ain't the sort o' life
>> Fer me;
> You can keep yer sudden fortunes, for I'd much the
>> Sooner be

A-growin' —
Wheat, wheat, wheat. It's a game that's hard to
     beat—
Sowin' it an' growin' it—it's what the nations eat.
Tho' it ain't a life o' pleasure,
An' there's little time for leisure,
It's contentin', in a measure, is the game of growin'
     Wheat.

In Dennis's poem, wheat farming is no longer drudgery but the exact opposite, that which frees you from drudgery. The honest toil of the crop farmer is an antidote to the stresses of the urban rat-race, with its ever-present threats of financial and psychological collapse ("You can court your nervous breakdowns, you can slave to make your pile", the poem goes on in another stanza). The "sowin'" and "growin'" place the farmer into a habit of life closer to both the rhythms of nature and the potency of production.

The violent character of the resumption of wooded land for use in the growth of cereals emerges in Paterson's "Song of the Wheat", published initially in the *Lone Hand* in 1914 and republished as the opening poem in his volume *Saltbush Bill, J.P. and Other Verses* in 1917, whilst Paterson was serving in the Middle East.[22] "Song of the Wheat" recounts the transformation of the country west of the Dividing Range from pastoral to crop use. Here is the opening stanza:

We have sung the song of the droving days,
     Of the march of the travelling sheep—
How by silent stages and lonely ways
     Thin, white battalions creep.
But the man who now by the soil would thrive
     Must his spurs to a ploughshare beat;
And the bush bard, changing his tune, may strive
     To sing the song of the Wheat!

The martial tone, in the midst of the Great War, could hardly be accidental, and what for Dennis had been a delicate kind of copping out, becomes for Paterson a call to arms. What is significant, though, is the manner in which the eruption of the war allows, effectively in retrospect, a symbolic context for the agricultural colonisation of the rangelands of southwestern New South Wales:

> Yarran and Myall and Box and Pine—
>   'Twas axe and fire for all;
> They scarce could tarry to blaze the line
>   Or wait for the trees to fall,
> Ere the team was yoked, and the gates flung wide,
>   And the dust of the horses' feet
> Rose up like a pillar of smoke to guide
>   The wonderful march of Wheat.

The shocking speed with which one agricultural moment was being superseded, the pastoral age over whose last years Paterson had so distinctively presided, by a new mode of exploitative, close-settlement, is given a meaning by a war that would soon itself struggle for meaning.

In the ensuing decades of the 1920s and '30s, the wheat poem remained a staple in the *Bulletin*. Charles Souter from South Australia published a series of light-hearted poems in the line of Dennis in 1926, which describe the various stages of wheat farming in metered couplets ("Harvestin'", "W'eat-Cartin'!").[23] R.G. Henderson of New South Wales published an ode to "The Wheat" in which the grain speaks nobly of itself in the first person, revealing how it has shaped human history since the time of the pharaohs.[24] Despite its displacements, Henderson's poem shows a clear sense of the close relationship between the mass production of grain and the reshaping of the world through the mechanisms of globalising capital: "For me they barter their brightest silks and Forge their greatest guns." Such optimism is present but more tempered in subsequent years, often adopting a polite fatalism. Nevertheless, in the wheat song one discerns the formation of a national ideology of wheat-growing which still persists in many ways, encrypted into our imagery and iconography.

If we turn from poetry to prose, we can also see the beginnings of a literature of crop farming nudging into the traditional pastoral stories. In particular, the 1880s and 1890s saw the emergence of a literature of "selection". Selection was the name given to the taking up of smaller parcels of Crown land under the various Land Acts passed by the Australian colonies from the 1860s onwards. They had been specifically passed to encourage close settlement and intensive agriculture, such as the growing of wheat. The "selector" is a notable figure in the stories of *Bulletin* writers like Henry Lawson (1867–1922) and Barbara Baynton (1857–1929). The Drover and his Wife, in Lawson's "The Drover's Wife" (1892) are selectors and so too, Squeaker and his Mate, in Baynton's "Squeaker's Mate" (1902).[25] Both stories reference events some fifteen to twenty years prior to their dates of publication, and in that sense are each tinged with retrospective colouring. But it is not clear in these stories whether either couple is growing a crop; there is no strong consciousness of the task of cultivation, of the kind that was present by the time the Western Australian wheatbelt came to be founded at the turn of the century. The term of the time, that is, in the 1870s and 1880s, and which remains in use, was "mixed farming", and designates all the various agricultural pursuits that were taken up by holders of these smaller lots, including the growing of crops, the keeping of animals on pasture, but also pigs, chickens, potatoes and whatever else might either sustain or turn a profit for the farmer. By far the most popular portrait of the mixed-farming selector was that found in the stories of "Steele Rudd". "Rudd" was the alter-ego of Arthur Hoey Davis (1868–1935) and the narrator of the stories which document the struggles of his family who take up a selection in the Darling Downs in the 1870s. The first of these to appear in the *Bulletin* was "Starting the Selection" in 1895.[26] As their popularity grew, they were published in book form (by the *Bulletin*) as *On Our Selection!* in 1899, selling over 20,000 copies.[27] It was these stories, and their various sequels, along with their countless adaptations as "Dad and Dave" stage plays and radio serials, that forced the image of the small-scale farmer into the national imaginary.

What emerges quite plainly in the "Steele Rudd" stories, to a much greater extent than in Lawson or Baynton, is the particular value given to cropping. Whilst the family turn their hands, often with tragicomic results, to almost every conceivable form of farming, it is clear from the stories that prosperity for the small landholder lay in crops—particularly in wheat, corn, barley and oats. The very first story, "Starting the Selection", documents the family's attempts to sow a crop, beginning with the painful "toil" of clearing an initial four-acre paddock:

> We toiled and toiled clearing those four acres, where the haystacks are now standing, till every tree and sapling that grew there was down. We thought the worst was over; but how little we knew of clearing land! Dad was never tired of calculating and telling us how much the crop would fetch if the ground could only be got ready in time to put it in ...
>
> "Look at the Dwyers," he'd say; "from ten acres of wheat they got seventy pounds last year, besides feed for the fowls; they've got corn in now, and there's only the two."[28]

This "toil" is the basis for the comedy. It is a humour based on poverty, on the ridiculousness that can haunt the desperate. Having cleared the land laboriously and painfully, the Rudds are left with the problem of ploughing it. The problem here was that the family had no horse—and no plough. So they borrowed hoes and turned the land this way, then drilled each grain of corn in by hand. But against this misery is the slow but distinct improvement in finances. The good years were good enough to allow investment in new equipment, and in the bad years the farm at least provided sustenance of a kind, even if a perilously thin one at times. The four cleared acres became, after a season or two, ten cleared acres. The two-roomed "Shingle Hut", becomes a four-roomed one. Fresh years brought fresh challenges, but the trend over time was towards greater wealth, so much so, that by the end of the first book, the Rudds have now gathered sufficient means to buy a "new selection" ("Saddletop"), which was the subject of the next book. There, the family quickly put a "hundred acres of plain-land under wheat" and are blessed with "light showers falling every week" (119). They buy a two-furrow plough, and then a three-furrow one, with new teams of horses to pull them.

The dire quality of the events at the first selection ("Shingle Hut"), the near starvation and extreme privation of the family, is made bearable by the comedy, which is in turn made bearable by the fact that we know from the narrator's first sentence that the events had happened twenty years prior. Published in 1895, this places the taking up of the selection in 1875, roughly when Davis himself, at the age of seven, moved with his family to take up their selection in the Darling Downs. It is this quality of retrospection that gives to these comic tales their mythic dimension. So, by chapter six in the second series, *Our New Selection*, we have this:

> How Time passes! Those days of toil and moil—that weary, up-hill struggle at Shingle Hut—were now thought of only in moments of merriment. Queer old days—wild old ways that all of us loved to remember—none of us wished to forget.
>
> Farming was not the drag—the wretched, murderous, drudgery—it used to be. We were improving every day—climbing rapidly to the lap of comfort. The wheat turned out a success again, and the profit made us all rejoice. (106)

The underlying narrative is one of success, even if most of the incidents document moments of failure. The selection stories of "Steele Rudd" share that sequential, sacrificial typology of phases that were memorably captured in McCubbin's triptych *The Pioneers* (1904).

7. Frederick McCubbin, *The Pioneer*, 1904, oil on canvas, 225 × 295.7 cm. National Gallery of Victoria, Melbourne, Felton Bequest, 1906.

The success of small farming depicted in Steele Rudd's stories is not a dimension often remarked upon, but it is a feature that clearly distinguishes it from the work of his contemporaries, Lawson and Baynton.

The Shores of Cowcowing

How literature dealt with the experience of the small selector in Western Australia is, of course, the subject of this book. The wheatbelt has produced a surprising number of writers, more indeed than I have been able to include. But it is also worth mentioning the writers who did not, by and large, consider the wheatbelt in their writings. Randolph Stow (1935–2010) has been a difficult exclusion from this study, because he grew up in wheat-and-sheep country in Geraldton and its surrounding farms, and wrote about these places in his novels *The Haunted Land* (1956), *The Bystander* (1957) and *The Merry-Go-Round in the Sea* (1965).[29] But, significantly, Stow and the caste he writes about do not consider themselves as the kind of aspirational selector that defined the wheatbelt. In his novels, crops are a distant background, and one sees no evidence of the ideology of wheat. The land had been settled with convict assistance in the mid-nineteenth century and the farmers considered themselves as "station" owners and treated their holdings with the dynastic pretensions that attach to the grazier in Australia. Stow himself was acutely conscious of the distinction between a "farm" and a "station" and apologises in his preface to *The Haunted Land* for confusing the two in his novel: "I have called Malin, Koolabye and Strathmore 'stations', as it is a local custom to give that name to the older and larger properties in this district. They are, of course, not sheep stations, but only very large farms." (vii) In *The Merry-Go-Round in the Sea*, the line between these farms (called stations) and the true stations of the "North" is a source of fascination for the young Rob Coram, where he becomes aware of living on this frontier: "His country was where the small farms ended, where the winter-rainfall ended, where the people ended. Beyond lay the open North: unpeopled, innocent." (69) The farmers in the novel, Rob's various relations, conduct themselves as if they were on stations and his novels have the air of station-romances. Their land is inherited and worked by employees. People ride horses and play tennis. Boys are sent to Guildford ("College") and then to university.

What Stow's case helps illustrate is that the wheatbelt has struggled to be a site of heroic action. Its basic structure is, in fact, a bourgeois one. Despite the immense amount of manual work, the wheatbelt is not, strictly speaking, working-class because the worker actually owns the asset in most cases, albeit under mortgage. Nor, despite some occasional grandiosity, is it really a landed class in the sense that the land held produces sufficient profit to allow a leisured existence for the owners. Instead, a wheatbelt farm is typically a small business, usually family-owned and run, and the people fit most nearly the petit-bourgeoisie, both in material conditions and in sensibility— particularly the quality of aspiration, which defines the middle-class. For this reason, there is something ultimately "small" about the wheatbelt experience which seems to have discouraged writers from locating heroic stories there. The case of Katharine Susannah Prichard (1883–1969) is also instructive in this regard. Despite living in the wheatbelt for two years, Prichard only sparingly alludes to this fact in her writing, including her autobiography. In her novels, she writes instead of the Karri country (*Working Bullocks*, 1926), the Pilbara (*Coonardoo*, 1929) and the Goldfields in her trilogy (*The Roaring Nineties*, 1946; *Golden Miles*, 1948; *Winged Seeds*, 1950).[30]

One of those to select land on the shores of Lake Cowcowing— part of "Terry's Survey" of the Goomalling Forests—was Prichard's husband Hugo Throssell (1884–1933). His father, George Throssell, had been Forrest's Commissioner of Lands from 1897 and a key proponent of the venture. Hugo and his older brother Ric (Frank Erick Throssell, 1881–1917) had taken up the land when it was gazetted before the War. When hostilities commenced, both brothers enlisted, Hugo in the 10th Light Horse. He won the Victoria Cross for valour in the Gallipoli landing, becoming a celebrity in the process. It was while convalescing from wounds from the Gallipoli campaign in England that he met Prichard, who was working as a freelance journalist in London whilst attempting to establish herself as a novelist. She gave Hugo a copy of her recently published novel *The Pioneers* (1915) to read in hospital, a novel that was partially inspired by McCubbin's triptych that had hung in Melbourne's National Gallery since 1905. In 1916, Hugo returned briefly to Western Australia and was asked for his impressions of Gallipoli.

> At about 5.30 in the evening of the 6th August I had the opportunity of seeing in the distance a glorious bayonet charge by the 16th. Line after line charged in the face of fire which seemed impossible for men to live through, and while I was watching it, a man at my side, whom I did not know, called "Hullo Mr. Throssell. How much crop have you in at Cowcowing this year?" It knocked the stuffing out of me, but I told him "240 acres and it's looking well".[31]

This anecdote, with its droll punchline, is the kind of unwitting puncturing of vainglory that is at the heart of Australian humour—a scene straight out of "Steele Rudd". Yet the linkage between the quasi-militarism of the wheatbelt, with its frontiers and surveying teams and a military campaign is not entirely misplaced.[32]

Hugo Throssell survived the War, although both his brother Ric, and Prichard's brother Allan, did not. Returning to Australia, Hugo had two ambitions. The first was to travel to Melbourne to secure the hand of Prichard in marriage, and the second was to recommence the work of building his farm at Cowcowing. Initially, it seemed the former was the greater task. Prichard was reluctant to marry, indeed had sworn she never would, for fear of sacrificing the writing career that was her life's longing. But she acceded to Throssell's proposal, and they moved west to commence married life. Throssell and Prichard (now Mrs Hugo Throssell) spent two years at Cowcowing in 1919 and 1920. They appear not to have been happy ones, according to Braid, drawing on the recollections of friends and neighbours at the time:

> Katharine Susannah Prichard accompanied her husband back to the farm at the end of the War. The living quarters were one end of a large shed, with the stables the other side of a galvanised iron wall. At night the horses made a terrible noise snorting and snuffling incessantly but no one understood her protest if she complained. Her husband and their neighbours all thought the sound of contented horses, well fed, watered and safe, helped them sleep well. (32)

It is doubtful that the noise of horses is what drove the Throssells from Cowcowing, but the insinuation is that Prichard was not used to the privations of frontier life, and complained sufficiently to force her way back to the more civilised if still pleasantly rural surrounds of Greenmount. Braid does add that "both she and her husband were very upset when a bank foreclosed on close neighbours of the area" (32). In a striking omission, Prichard makes no mention of the two years she spent at Cowcowing in her autobiography, *Child of the Hurricane* (1963).[33]

It is difficult to say why Prichard did not use her time living at Cowcowing as the basis for any of her novels or mention it in her autobiography. However, the experience does surface in at least one of her short stories, "Christmas-tree", that appeared in the war-time collection *Potch and Colour* in 1944.[34] The story takes its title from a species of parasitic tree (*Nuytsia floribunda*) that grows extensively through the southwest in the sandy soils of banksia woodland. It flowers a vibrant orange in December just as the rest of the bush dries in the heat of early summer, so the name was perhaps inevitable. In the story, the wife (Minnie Gillard) of a farmer (George) is looking over her farm for the last time, as the bank has called in their mortgage. The rather muted climax takes place later that evening at the end-of-year dance in the local hall, where the vanquished couple put in a rather reluctant appearance, and valiantly try to at least leave with their heads held high. At the dance, flirting with the young women and clapping the men on the backs is the charismatic bank representative, once a storekeeper and now local member, Christopher Tregear, who had just weeks earlier told George that "he could not interfere with the policy of the bank" (168). This is perhaps a nod towards her father-in-law, George Throssell, a former storekeeper and the local member for Northam from 1890 to 1904 and 1907 to 1910, as well as James Mitchell, the former bank manager turned politician, who selected land at Cowcowing Lakes at the same time as Hugo Throssell. Seeing this "old man" at the dance causes a bleak, socialist epiphany in Minnie:

> Pain gripped Minnie with the intensity of her thinking. She understood well enough that there was a rotten financial system at the back of Tregear and this business of mortgages was ruining the

farmers. It was responsible for turning George away from the place he had made; from the cleared paddocks, the house, stables and machinery sheds. All their hope and toil, their years of desperate struggle against misfortune, had gone for nothing. Their youth had been wasted, and now when they were old and weary, they must make another start. What was the use? It would all happen again when they had cleared land and brought it into production. And that old man telling funny stories and laughing so boisterously—everything would go to him and his bank. (168)

This was certainly a view shared by many in the wake of the commodity price collapse that led into the Great Depression. But this explanation does not fit the circumstances of Prichard's own abandonment, with her husband, of their new farm in 1920 in the midst of the post-war boom. There are, however, a number of parallels to the Cowcowing years, such that it becomes clear that this story is narrating a part of Prichard's life that she was unable to bring herself to tell in her autobiography. It illustrates how studying creative literature helps gain a purchase on experiences that are not transcribable without the protection of fiction. Take the following passage, which describes— as a bitter reverie at the moment of their departure—the arrival and early years of the Gillards at their bush block:

And this was the end—the old steel trunk, those cases and her hat-box, under the fig-tree. Minnie's thoughts drifted to the time when she and George Gillard arrived at Laughing Lakes with that trunk and little else besides. They were just married and George had taken up land round the dry lakes which the blacks had called Laughing Lakes. Why, nobody knew. The Lakes had never carried anything but a shimmering gypsum deposit for many years. Not an acre of land was cleared then. George had put up a humpy of brushwood and hessian and added some sheets of corrugated iron later on. They had lived in it for a long time.

He had cut out the timber, cleared the scrub of clay-bush, dead-finish, wodjil and morrell, put a bullock team and log-roller over the thicket, burnt over the broken bushes, ploughed, cultivated and sowed his first crops. What ages ago it seemed! (161)

What this little vignette points to is that beyond the melodrama of the dance and the gloating bank manager, there is also a deeper story at work in "Christmas-tree", and that is the story of the destruction of the natural world. At first glance there seems little consciousness of this, as the whole violent process of clearing the bush for farm land is understood only as a form of thankless "toil". The labour is alienated in the sense that it takes place individualistically, a solitary task in which the settler is pitted against a harsh and unforgiving landscape. The name "Laughing Lakes" is an allusion or quasi-translation of Cowcowing Lakes, a Noongar name of uncertain meaning, but which onomatopoeically resembles laughter. Little thought is spared for their exploitation, for the fact that the land might have indeed been owned by "the blacks" who named the lake without thinking to pass on the meaning of the name. Indeed, the Lakes' laughter is felt as a pitiless sarcasm, and the "shimmering gypsum" a cruel mirage of what a lake is meant to hold.

But then the labour is not as isolated as it has seemed, because Minnie, too, had joined the struggle:

> Minnie had helped him indoors and out, in every way that a woman can help a man when she is young and strong, and as eager as he to tame a wild country and make a home in it. She had lighted burning-off fires and watched them, stooked sheaves, sewn wheat-bags, raised chickens and vegetables, made mud bricks and set them to bake in the sun for the house. It had been a strange, lonely life for her, a city girl. (161)

Here we can ascertain at least the shadow of Prichard's own feelings when thrust into the stark reality of a bush block in the middle of nowhere. That George owes something to her husband Hugo Throssell can be gleaned from an incident early in the story when Minnie remembers her husband's delight at the winter rains coming to moisten his newly planted crop:

> He had sown by moonlight in order to get the crop in, swearing he could smell rain in the air: had just finished when down it came, the rain, in a light wispish shower. George was crazy with joy: stood out in it shouting:
> "Oh, Lord, send it down! Send it down!"

> It was a miracle. The rain had come that year just when it was
> needed, and soaked into the thirsty land. Soon the red earth was green
> with springing wheat. (159)

Prichard's autobiography, *Child of the Hurricane*, recounts an
incident very similar to this, albeit at Greenmount in the Perth Hills.
When the first winter rains fell to soften the soil of their Greenmount
orchard, Prichard described how Hugo Throssell would sing and
dance with joy and say of the moist loam, "You could eat it, couldn't
you?" (256).

In several ways the story of the Gillards certainly departs from
the lives of Prichard and Throssell, most obviously on the matter of
duration. The Gillards had laboured fruitlessly through many seasons,
while Prichard lasted barely two in the years after the War. The longer
time frame of the Gillards' life in the wheatbelt allows the story to
depict the creation of the farm as a process of history and to speak
from a point in time when all has come to pass. But the story also
leaves open the other possibility that I have put forward, which is that
the emergence of the wheatbelt is not so much a product of *human
history* but a violation and eradication of *natural history*. In this sense,
the wheatbelt is something completely outside of this deeper history
and antithetical to it. And perhaps it is this that lends the ambivalent
accent to the fact of financial failure in stories like "Christmas-tree".
The reasons people leave the land must inevitably be as complex as
the reasons people take to it. But in Prichard's story, the point is made
that the arrival and departure are often intimately connected. It is in
departing that Minnie re-experiences all the hopes that were present
in the arriving. In the story, the failure is ascribed to an exploitative
institution—the Bank—as though in it alone resided the operation of
capitalism, and the task of farming was wholly distinct and untainted
by the profit motive. Yet in reflecting on her husband's love of land
in *Child of the Hurricane*, Prichard comes closer to locating the source
of the wheatbelt's intoxicating allure in a certain land-hunger that
is often underplayed. Although she was, in a manner, enchanted by
her husband's Lawrentian sensitivity to the earth's primal patterns,
Prichard also recalls that his "passion for land had involved him in
reckless expenditures and obligations to banks" (260–1).[35]

In some ways what becomes clear is that the story proceeds on the basis of a misdiagnosis. It directs its critique towards a financial system that left the worker—here, in fact, the owner of an asset of production (land)—but out of the corner of the eye something else appears, which is the natural world itself, the subject of so much of this toil as it was systematically eliminated. In many ways, Prichard's story "Christmas-tree" is exemplary of the way that the ecological operates in the creative literature of the wheatbelt. For instance, it is there at the very outset:

> Against the dim blue of the summer sky the Christmas-trees had thrown their blossoming crests; like clouds, raw gold, fluted and curled, they lay along the horizon.
>
> The trees grew irregularly on dry, scrubby land beyond Gillard's fences to the north of Laughing Lakes homestead. Their trunks were scarcely visible from the back door of the house where Minnie Gillard stood. All the year the trees looked dull and sinister standing in the wheat-fields on the edge of the scrub. They were protected by law, and at Christmas time put on their opulent beauty. *Mrs Gillard's thoughts wandered from those trees to the wheat-fields, ravelling and unravelling old hopes, despairs, bitter and sweet memories.* (158; emphasis added)

Also typical in this passage is the extreme ambivalence of the image of nature—the Christmas-tree—ecstatically evoked in the opening paragraph, then taking on a "sinister", brooding quality in the second paragraph. The final sentence links the image of nature to the wheatbelt mythos, making clear that it too is characterised by an occasional, perhaps illusory, opulence which masks a threat. In a later passage, just as the Gillards are pulling away in a buggy containing their worldly possessions, Minnie calls her husband's attention to the Christmas trees:

> "Look," she said.
>
> "What?" he growled, fearing she was going to cry.
>
> "The Christmas-trees." Mrs Gillard's voice shook. "They're in flower. Don't you remember what we read in the newspaper the other day? Somebody has found out the Christmas-tree's a parasite. Its

roots throw suckers round the roots of other trees and draw the sap from them. That's why the trees near it are always so poor and dreary looking—and it's got all that rich yellow blossom."

This becomes the meaning of the image (of the Christmas tree) and the theme of the story—that riches displayed in one place derive from impoverishment in another. But there is a second image of nature that occurs in the story, this time in the form of consolation drawn from wildflowers and the passage of seasons:

> Mrs Gillard remembered how strange and lonely it had been at first. But she had found comfort in the sweep of the sky, the pageant of the seasons on the face of the changing landscape. How she had loved the wild flowers which came up on the soil cleared for crops!
>
> She had never seen any flowers like them. Their colours were so pure and bright. The wild flowers made a vivid fringe—purple, magenta, cerise, yellow, scarlet and blue—to the ploughed lands. Tall, freckled orchids, yellow and brown, grew in places where the fires had been. They were like the eaglehawks which, swooping out of the sky, flew off with her chickens. (161–2)

There is a poignant belief that these wildflowers could persist in the face of continued ploughing. In reality, of course, this would be their last appearance before continued cultivation replaced them with the grain crops in the newly created farms. In this way, the full reality of natural destruction is disguised by the romantic fallacy, Ruskin's term for the imaginary belief that nature might reflect our moods. The final line in the description is something of a *non sequitur*. It is not clear how the orchids are like the eaglehawks, except perhaps that they are the emblems of a nature that will not be colonised, that will continue to do what it has always done. In that sense, the eagle's predation on the chickens is in fact a hopeful image that nature might survive this massive onslaught.

This reading of Prichard's story offers a preview of the method adopted in this history and hopefully suggests something of what is possible when you pay close attention to creative literature as a historical document. Creative writing does not primarily serve history by detailing the emergence of new farming techniques, or the fluctuation of markets, or even the growth and decline of towns and communities. All of these things can be traced in other kinds of documents. What creative writing does is show how people felt, and how often this is at variance with how they wished they felt. In exposing the inner life of the participants of the wheatbelt's creation, we can also begin to grasp something of the remarkable motive force—a desire, and not just a material necessity—that caused a world to disappear and committed thousands of families to a form of life they can have had little preparation to undertake. The literature of the wheatbelt provides a vital bridge between material policy and individual aspiration. In it we often see depicted the arduous expenditure of labour, the kind that George and Minnie did in Prichard's story. And, indeed the kind that Prichard and Hugo Throssell themselves did, along with everyone else who settled in the Cowcowing Lakes. And this process occurred again and again and again, in district after district until the wheatbelt stretched from the Darling Ranges to the Eastern Goldfields, from the Indian Ocean north of Geraldton to the Southern Ocean east of Esperance. But as well as representing the work of creating the wheatbelt, the stories have their own kind of work to do—to try to come to terms with the significance of this grand project; to ask what it might mean.

Chapter One

Albert Facey (1894–1982)

Wickepin (1902–08; 1910–14; 1922–34)

Let us begin our literary appreciation of the founding of the wheatbelt by recalling the story given to us in Albert Facey's *A Fortunate Life*.[1] This book is amongst the most successful autobiographies in Australian publishing. It is also a richly realised evocation of the founding of the Western Australian wheatbelt at the turn of the twentieth century. I am going to dwell in some detail on the picture that Facey gives us of his life in the new settlement of Wickepin in the years before the Great War. Following the War, Facey returned to take up land in the very same district in 1922, which he worked until 1934, when the Depression finally forced him and his family back to Perth. Facey was eighty-seven years old when his book was published in 1981 by Fremantle Arts Centre Press, and he died the following year. *A Fortunate Life* became an instant classic, selling over 250,000 copies over the next decade. The tone of the story is famously understated, its phrasing somewhere between a quite modern reportage and a more ancient form of plainness. As his biographer, J.B. Hirst, puts it: "The style of the book passed beyond plainness into an elemental purity."[2] In *The World of Albert Facey*, Hirst draws a lengthy parallel between Facey and Henry Lawson. He notes the similarity of their upbringing, even though Lawson was born a quarter of a century earlier. Both lived in broken families amidst the hardship of rural poverty, a mixture of mining and small-time selection. But Hirst also finds a similar modest, yet wry, sensibility that sits within their spare, limpid prose. Indeed, Facey narrates the simple facts of his life with a calm assuredness that belies the extremity of the situations he finds himself in.[3] The majority of the book considers events from the first twenty years of his life. Facey's fortunate life draws its singular power from the fact that he was not only present and participating in the foundational moments of Australian nationhood—on the battlefields of Gallipoli and in that other battle to subdue the bushland for agricultural gain—but that he could speak those events into the modern Australian nation like a living relic of moments long thought gone.[4]

Whilst Facey's is by no means the only memoir of a settler-farmer in Western Australia, his is without a doubt the most well-known. Typically the book is cast as a "pioneering" story, yet in the narrative Facey himself does not see his life in this way, but as something much more specific. He is quite meticulous in describing the practicalities and financial conditions that both enabled and constrained this new form of life—the 1,000-acre owner-occupier crop farm, all but given away by the Western Australian Government on the condition that it was cleared and fenced and turned into productive land. The opening of this memoir describes life in the wheatbelt in its earliest years and paints a vivid, child's-eye view of what this meant for those undertaking the task of setting up a farm under the regime that the Western Australian Government had introduced. In 1894, shortly after Albert was born, his father and eldest brothers left their home in rural Victoria for the goldfields of Western Australia, hoping to relieve the family's chronic poverty. It was a calculated gamble, and in the end it failed dreadfully. In 1896, Albert's mother, still in Victoria, received word that the father had died during an outbreak of typhoid fever at Kalgoorlie. The infant Albert was left with his grandparents, while his mother went to Kalgoorlie to be with her elder sons. It was not clear then, but this was the first step in his mother's effective abandonment of her young children. Albert would thereafter be brought up by others. Shortly afterward, the grandfather died and the grandmother, nearly destitute, decided to sell the apple orchard and move west, where along with Albert's mother, the grandmother's eldest daughter (Alice) and husband (Archie McCall) were living.

In 1899 Albert, then five, with two brothers and a sister sailed with their grandmother for Fremantle. The proceeds from the sale of the orchard only got them as far as Northam, roughly 100 kilometres east of Perth. Albert's grandmother wrote to her eldest daughter to send money for the train fare through to Kalgoorlie. While they waited for the money, grandmother and children camped at the Government Reserve. It took three weeks for the money to arrive. A nearby farmer lent them some tools and helped them build a rough camp. The family eventually made it to Kalgoorlie, where they were taken into the care of their Aunt Alice (the sister of Albert's mother) and her husband Archie. Archie was employed chopping and carrying wood for a mine in Coolgardie. It is sometimes surprising to learn that the arid zone east of the wheatbelt supports a vast, open woodland. When one drives east out of the wheatbelt, one does not enter sandplain or flat scrub, but open forest. This is known as the Great Western Woodland and, by analogy, the wheatbelt might be said to stand on the site of the now vanished Great Eastern Woodland. The availability of wood meant that the cheapest way to acquire potable water in the Goldfields was to desalinate the groundwater (via wood-fired condensers), which was plentiful if brackish. The extensive network of light-gauge rail to carry the wood to fuel these condensers and other steam-driven machinery in the Goldfields is one of the many marvels of this epoch of Australian history.[5] But the Goldfields were declining by the turn of the century, and families like that supported by Albert's uncles were casting around for their next opportunity. It was here, as we have seen, that the wheatbelt offered itself.

Albert's uncle, Archie McCall, offers a glimpse into the backgrounds of the settlers of the wheatbelt in its initial phase. He was one of four sons born and raised on a farm in South Australia; the property could not sustain them all and Archie had to go out and find work. Acquiring land in the wheatbelt meant that Archie "had his chance to fulfil the ambition of his life" (16), which was to own his own farm—he was "returning to the land and he and the women were very excited about the venture" (17). Albert recalls his uncle Archie going to Perth for two weeks during August 1901:

[W]hen he returned he had selected one thousand acres of first class land under the Government's conditional purchase scheme, and a homestead block for himself, Aunt Alice and Grandma. The Government was giving a homestead block to any approved person over the age of twenty-one for twenty shillings, and that land, one hundred and sixty acres, became the freehold property of the person concerned. The conditional purchase land could be obtained at twenty shillings per acre for the first class land, and second class land and other land was priced according to its classification. Some of the poor land could be purchased for as low as two shillings and sixpence per acre.

Uncle's one thousand acres were classified first class. The conditions of purchase were that the settler paid nothing for the first five years, then paid so much a half year for the next twenty years to complete the purchase. The Government wouldn't sell land straight out as a cash sale. (12)

The land selected was in a new district southeast of Pingelly and 42 kilometres east of Narrogin. The family left the Goldfields in February 1902 and stayed in York until September when they set out with horse and cart to make the 220-kilometre journey to their Uncle's "dream land" (16). The children, including Albert who was eight years old by this time, walked the 220 kilometres to the new property with bare feet.

The McCalls picked up their final provisions in Pingelly and left the Great Southern Railway line that they had been following down from York to strike off along the road to Pingelly. The Pingelly–Wickepin road was then just "an old bush track" (18; the town of Wickepin was only gazetted in 1908) and they camped the night at Gillimanning before completing the final 13 kilometres to their destination the following morning:

We were all up early the next morning, very excited. We were soon to see this wonderful land that Uncle Archie spoke about so much. We had our breakfast and were soon on our way. About two hours later we arrived, and Uncle took a map out of his pocket and checked the survey pegs. He stood up and said, "That's it, that's my land," pointing to a big belt of tall trees and undergrowth, and I thought, "A chicken would find it hard to get through." (18)

The previous night at Gillimanning the family, under the instructions of Uncle Archie, had made dozens of possum snares. These snares would provide the family's only source of income for the foreseeable future. Possum skins sold for 1 shilling each, and the family would catch hundreds and hundreds in these first months to provide for their existence:

> The first morning Uncle and the boys caught twenty-two possums. They skinned them and pegged the skins out on big trees. Uncle called the trees "white gums". The skins were nailed on with small nails. These skins, when dry, were about nine inches wide and about one foot long, although some would stretch to bigger than this, and some smaller. When dry they were worth a shilling each. They had to be nailed at least six feet off the ground to stop the dingoes pulling them off and destroying them. Aunt, Grandma and we kids used to stand on a box to nail them out. (19)

The family camped until the Uncle and Albert's older brothers could build a humpy. The construction style was that commonly used in the early years of the wheatbelt. It involved cutting sapling poles 12 feet long and roughly 6 inches thick at the base, tapering to 3 or 4 inches at the top. These were set in trenches close together to form the walls of the house. The trenches were 3 feet deep and once the poles were in place the soil was packed in around them. This kind of house was long (50 feet) and relatively thin (12 feet), with a "bedroom" at either end (interior walls were built in the same fashion) and a central living area with a stone fireplace. Clay from a nearby creekbed was packed between the poles to make the walls weatherproof. The roof consisted of a timber frame thatched with "black-boy" (*Xanthorrhoea*) fronds. The doorway was made of a wooden frame covered with kangaroo skin, and the bedroom doors were simply curtains. Water was drawn by bucket from a government well 2 kilometres from the house.

After the house was built, the men began the task of clearing: "They were chopping small trees down and ring-barking the big ones, ready for burning down the next year." (20) On the first of March 1903, after the summer fire-ban was lifted, the Uncle put the first "burn" through. The shoeless children helped with inevitable consequences:

"We got our feet burnt badly at times." (21) Later that year, Albert, still just eight years old, was sent to work for a family some 50 kilometres away. The idea was that they would clothe him and provide him shoes and five shillings a month. Albert was to help the elderly mother of the property owner, whose sight had failed, with tasks around the place. The situation was a good deal worse, in fact, than had been made out. Albert was immediately given an onerous work regime that had him toiling from sun-up to sunset every day. Despite being told he could leave if he was not happy, when he asked to leave he was told: "Get that out of your mind, you're here to stay whether you like it or not." (26) This episode, where the young Albert is, more or less, sold into a kind of slavery, is typical of much of the early phase of the book, in which events transpire in picaresque fashion—with Albert the hapless *picaro*, cast hither and thither by a cruel world. This is not to diminish the actual suffering of Facey, which is profound and deeply moving, but to emphasise that Facey's narration does not take place beyond the governance of genre. The structure of the memoir, built around episodes or incidents, is not unlike the structure of Steele Rudd's "On Our Selection" stories. Like Rudd, there is also a loving attention to the detail of settler-farming—from the precise prices and conditions required to select property, to the construction of bush-houses, the techniques for trapping possums and, time and again, the work of land-clearing. The main difference in Facey, when compared with Rudd, is the tone of the narrative, with the stress falling more towards pathos than comedy.[6]

The family to whom Facey is sent to work are not new farmers and have no crops. Indeed, they are shown to be less a family—like the one led by Uncle Archie—than a kind of primitive clan. They represent, without it being explicitly said, the older order of things. They have built a farm of sorts near a granite outcrop, "Cave Rock", which gives the chapter its title. Granite outcrops had traditionally been one of the only sources of water in what became the wheatbelt. This family drew water for themselves and their animals from a soak dug at the base of the outcrop. They maintain a flock of sheep by penning them each night to keep them safe from dingoes. They have pigs, cows and chickens and grow vegetables. But their main source of income, apparently, is from catching brumbies, breaking them and selling them. At Christmas time they drink heavily and fight openly. They employ in rather loose fashion various local men, including Aboriginal men. One man, Charlie, who was about twenty, befriended Albert and looked after him: "Charlie was a real pal to me ... [he] told me he didn't know who his father was and that his mother had died when he was born, and he had been brought up in the bush with the wild blacks." (29) Another old man in the clan bought Albert two pairs of trousers "from his possum skin money" because he was "pained" at the sight of the boy's neglect. Albert had not been paid and still had no shoes. Life at Cave Rock is represented as an archaic counterpoint to the venture that was being conducted by Uncle Archie just a few dozen miles away. In this way, a certain key element of the wheatbelt is made plain, which is that it was conceived of, almost without exception, as a fresh start. This also introduced a moral component to the wheatbelt project, which was common to settler-colonialism more generally—a belief in the goodness of the exercise, that it was leading to some deeper form of improvement than mere money would be able to measure.[7] The new farms, though certainly primitive in many respects, were nevertheless being run according to the latest land-management philosophies and were "official" in ways that the clan at Cave Rock were clearly not. The old lady, it turns out, was never married and the clan was run by her illegitimate children and their children. Nor does it come as a complete surprise when one day a policeman rides into Cave Rock to inform the mother that two of her grandsons had been gaoled for the theft of horses and cattle from surrounding properties, and this was not, in fact, the first time they had been convicted of such offences.

The climax of the Cave Rock episode is the flogging of young Albert by the current patriarch, known only as Bob in the story. Albert's crime was to remove some of the Christmas dinner alcohol stockpile and feed it to the pigs. The method of disposal was ill-judged, but Albert had done this in the hope of reducing the alcohol-fuelled violence that had ensued the previous Christmas. The matter was dealt with by Bob the next day:

> I didn't speak, just stood looking up at him. He gave me a cut around the legs, then he lashed me three or four times around the shoulders

and body. I jumped up and tried to run out of the stable. As I got out of the doors he caught me around the legs again and I fell to the ground. He continued to whip me. The whip was one he used to tame the horses with and he was an expert. He knew how to use that whip. I don't know how many times he cut me because I must have fainted. (36)

Albert spent a week in bed recovering from this ordeal. Bob had left and the clan had sent for a nurse—the wife of a new farmer—who had bathed his wounds and prevented infection. Albert hatched a plan to escape and eventually made away in February 1905, travelling at night to avoid recapture. Eventually, with the help of a Scottish family of new settlers, he made it back to his Uncle's farm. The picture of the new farm is thus framed by the traumatic exile of the previous two years and this time the McCall's property presents in quite a different light to the initial arrival some three years earlier:

Arriving at Uncle's place I could see the many changes that had been made. They had about one hundred acres cleared and a lot of the land had been fenced. They were all out working, clearing more land for cropping in the winter. This was to be the first crop that Uncle planted. He had bought a milking cow and the women were making their own butter. (44)

None of these details need be doubted, nor the sense of profound relief at having been delivered. Still, it is noteworthy that the farm should present in this way—which is to say, exactly in the form of the dream that had motivated its founding. Albert stayed with his family through 1905, turning eleven in August. His uncle had 100 acres of wheat sown that year, the first in the district to be grown with the aid of an artificial fertiliser known colloquially as "Thomas's Manure" provided by the Government. The Government was also now advancing money to new settlers through a new scheme, which Facey details:

The scheme was that the Government would pay twenty shillings for every acre the settler cleared ready for cropping. Also, they paid so much for fencing and any other improvements that were made. This money was by way of a loan, and a mortgage of the full amount at the end of the year was taken out against the property. This money was free of interest and the settlers were to pay it back over twenty-five years. No repayments were to be made, or interest charged for five years, to give the settler a chance to have his property producing before the repayments started. There was also provision made for loans for stock and machinery. This was how a settler could take up land and settle on it without much or any money. By this time all the land around Uncle Archie's had been taken up so that now he had neighbours on all sides. (49)

The terms, as we have noted, were incredibly generous, and meant to be so, and they had the desired effect. The McCalls, who had trouble locating their block just three years before, were now surrounded on all sides by fellow new settlers. The fact of them all being engaged in the same project led to a particular feeling of common purpose, even if it also led to a degree of envy and competitiveness. Facey's account shows how they would respond to calls for assistance, share or co-purchase equipment for seasonal work such as seeding and harvesting, and work together on tasks that required collective labour—most particularly, the burning off of bushland.

In October 1905 Albert was again sent out to work, this time for an Irish neighbour named Moran. There he worked to clear land and look after the animals, including around 200 fowls. While he was not abused there as he had been at Cave Rock, he wasn't paid the wage that was agreed, and so midway through 1906 he left and tried his luck with a pair of German brothers who were setting up a farm nearby. Again, they did not pay him, despite promising to, and he returned home. In this way, the honesty of the new settlers was also shown to be something that could not be taken for granted: "My experience up to now made me doubt the word of everyone." (53) But the circumstances of the family meant that it was necessary for Albert to keep being exposed to the vagaries of child labour. He was sent again to another family, the Phillips, and this time he was indeed properly cared for and became so valuable and cherished that they eventually sought to adopt him as they were in their middle age and childless. They were wealthier than the typical family and were able to pay him properly for his work: "I had to work hard for a boy not yet twelve years old. I didn't mind this, and I did as much work as I could, as I wanted to please and stay with these people." (57) They kept a paddock with pigs in it and were planting crops and clearing more land for more crops. One of Albert's jobs was to follow the plough and pick up tree roots to be burned as firewood in the house, or simply placed in heaps and burnt for disposal. Phillips also used to fallow the paddocks:

> After seeding was over, Frank used to plough the land that he was going to sow the next year—this was commonly known as fallowing. The farmers used to say that land ploughed for cropping the next year held the moisture better. Should the next season be dry, the farmer stood a better chance of a good crop. If rain came during the summer, the ground so ploughed could be scarified and harrowed, which destroyed any weeds and made seeding easier and quicker. (58)

And while fallowing does confer these advantages, exposing the soil in this way also made it vulnerable to erosion by wind and water and much topsoil was lost through the practice of fallowing.

The "Burn"

By this time, Albert was old enough to take a more active part in the burning off of land. He and Phillips cut firebreaks and ploughed a perimeter around the bush that had been prepared for burning. Fires were then started around the edges and allowed to burn inwards: "That was the correct way to burn off in the wheat-belt in those days." (69)

> Some of the neighbours, and Jack Connor, who was friendly with Frank again, came and helped put the fire through. One very hot day, at about eleven in the morning, they set it alight. We kept walking around the burning patch all day, throwing lighted pieces of wood back from the edge into the burnt part so a spark wouldn't set alight the outside dry grass. This went on until evening. When the danger of a spark had gone, the neighbours and Jack went home. (69)

The strange mixture of isolation and common purpose that fused the settlers together in their disparate existence was never clearer than in accounts of burning. The occasions were marked by excitement and, at the same time, solemnity. On the one hand this was just a natural response to the danger of fire, which could spread with devastating effect. In that practical sense everyone had a stake in everyone else's "burn" and it was useful to have all hands on deck when the fire was lit. But the accounts of burning-off are amongst the most vivid and prominent events in the recollections of settler-farmers in the wheatbelt. The "burn" is often rendered with a certain awful majesty that carries with it not only the sense of danger, but of finality—of decisive transformation and, as well, of utter destruction. The burning was not the only element of clearing the bush; indeed most of the hard work was done beforehand and afterward. But it seemed, in its world-ending fatality, to evoke the process with a particular clarity that was not always obtainable in the tiresome and repetitive toil of many of the other days.

We are now accustomed to the realisation that Indigenous land-use relied on the careful but extensive use of fire, and that this human practice significantly determined the ecological pattern of the Australian continent. Indeed, the bushland of the wheatbelt was very much a product of fire, including the programmatic fires of the Noongar people over several thousand years.[8] But the fires that created the wheatbelt were of a different order. Because the bush was now highly adapted to fire, the clearing fires of the new settlers were artificially prolonged and concentrated so as to permanently kill the vegetation. The ground was then ploughed to prevent regrowth. This overarching purpose, to eradicate as absolutely as possible the native vegetation, seems to lend a distinct mood to accounts of burning-off. We might, in this regard, contrast the descriptions of burning-off land with the way other kinds of bushfires are typically represented. Literary accounts of bushfires, from Henry Kingsley's *The Recollections of Geoffry Hamlyn* (1859) to Patrick White's *The Tree of Man* (1955), were indeed set-pieces of Australian colonial fiction, and they remain a crucial element in the collective imagination.[9] But these fires were (and still largely are) conceived of as events of nature—they are natural and not man-made disasters. In colonial fiction, fires fall upon the pastoral settlers from that same divine arsenal that also supplied droughts, dust storms and floods. The "burns" of the wheatbelt are presented as belonging to a different, decidedly human, order. The first "Steele Rudd" sketch from 1895 gives one of the earliest accounts in Australian fiction of this kind of fire, that is, of the process of "burning off": "With our combined male and female forces and the aid of a sapling lever we rolled the thundering big logs together in the face of Hell's own fires; and when there were no logs to roll it was tramp, tramp, the day through, gathering armfuls of sticks ..."[10] Burning-off is given a Mephistophelean colouration by the presence of human actors as agents of the fire and not merely as victims.

The process of clearing land varied over time and according to the vegetation. Laurie Anderson, a wheatbelt farmer and amateur historian, has given a good overview of land-clearing as the first key action of the prospective farmer-settler. First, large trees—salmon-gum, York gum, gimlet, morrell—were ringbarked and left to die. When they had dried the understorey was fired. In thinner mallee and sandplain country a "scrub roller" was used, which was a large iron cylinder, typically from an old boiler, dragged across the scrub by a horse or bullock team and, in later years, a tractor. After about 1950 the country was generally cleared by two bulldozers dragging between them a length of heavy anchor chain, a process we will see by the time we consider the writing of Peter Cowan. Once the scrub had been levelled the burning would take place. Anderson tells how this was always a "big event":

> The "burn" was usually done with neighbours joining forces all hoping for a good stiff wind to keep the stumps alight, this would save days of labour later in carrying, by hand, wood to stack around any stumps not burned to or below ground level.
>
> I have very evocative memories going back to burns after tea with a shovel—taking coals from big ember heaps and placing them on the up wind side of stumps that had not caught alight. The thousand winking eyes of the coals and the sweet smell of the burning strawberry Jam tree would remain forever imprinted in my mind.[11]

Facey's *A Fortunate Life* is no different from many other accounts in its remembrance of these occasions as special and significant, and indeed pleasurable. With Facey, though, we are given—though at a distance of many decades—the impression the "burn" made upon the mind of a child, as in his recollection of burning with the Phillips family:

> We commenced the clearing the day after the fire went through. I liked this work—it was very dirty. My job was picking up all the small pieces of wood that hadn't completely burnt, packing them into heaps around stumps, and keeping the heaps stacked and burning until the stumps were burnt down to ground level.
>
> When the clearing was finished we had to go back over the cleared ground and fill in all the stump holes. Some of the stumps were highly inflammable trees and burnt down into the large roots under ground for several feet. (69)

Facey's stint with the Phillipses, though, ended on a sour note. They had come to regard and treat Albert as a son, with the wife asking that he call her "Mum". With Albert's permission and that of his Uncle and Grandmother they sought to adopt him, but Albert's birth mother, now living in Perth, refused the request. This changed the emotional texture of life in the Phillips household irrevocably, and Albert became resented and, once again, overworked.

So in 1907, just before his thirteenth birthday, Albert found himself on the move once more. The next family were also a middle-aged, childless couple, although less wealthy than the Phillipses. The Bibbys said they would pay Albert the 10 shillings a week he was paid by the Phillipses, but that they were only able to pay once the bank released money to them based on their scheduled improvements. Unlike others, they kept this promise and Facey retained a lifelong regard for this couple. Again, a major part of the work was the clearing of the land:

> I settled with these nice people who were struggling, like many. My work, for a start, was chopping the small trees and scrub off level with the ground. All trees six inches to a foot thick, Charlie and I chopped down at waist height, then we knocked the bark off the stump and put the pieces around the base. By doing this the stump and bark would dry off, and when the burning season came in February, a lot of the stumps would burn down to ground level. Those that didn't would get

8. Scrub-rolling by horse and tractor. State Library of Western Australia, 015328PD, 66822P and 090410PD.

scorched and would easily burn when we came to them when clearing. The very big trees, from one foot upwards, were burnt down. I liked chopping and burning down. It was hard work and I got big water blisters on my hands for the first week or so, but then my hands got used to it and became tough. (79)

In the early years of wheatbelt farms, the clearing and burning were part of the cycle of work, gradually reducing in quantity as the land was cleared. Even after the land was cleared sufficiently for ploughing, the plough would continue to kick up the roots of the annihilated forest, and it was one of Facey's earliest jobs to pick up these roots for domestic firewood—these "mallee roots" were fondly regarded for their slow and slightly aromatic burning.

Burning became part of the social fabric of early wheatbelt life, the task taking on a communal, almost sacramental quality. Facey describes how the burns were occasions for cooperation, and in 1908 neighbours congregated at the Bibbys' farm to help them put a burn through:

> Burning-off season opened and several neighbours came to help put the fire through the chopped and burnt down timber like they had helped Frank [Phillips] the year before. When one of our neighbours wanted help putting a fire through, we always helped them. This co-operation went on with all new settlers, and they used to meet at each other's places from time to time to discuss and exchange ideas on farming, clearing, fencing and stock …
>
> That burning season, Charlie [Biddy] had what was known as a "good burn". This term was used when the undergrowth, scrub and timber burnt freely and left only the large logs and stumps. We then started on the clearing. Charlie and I worked hard and long hours six days a week from the middle of February through to the end of the first week in April. During that period we cleared the one hundred and thirty acres that we had chopped and burnt down during the previous August, September and October. (88–9)

Another account of burning-off, roughly twenty years after the events in Facey's account, is given in Henry Sherar's memoir of pioneering a farm at Noongaar in the Yilgarn in the eastern wheatbelt in the mid-1920s.[12] (We shall see this district in detail in the next chapter, when we consider the life and work of Cyril Goode.) Sherar moved to the Yilgarn from Perth in 1925 at the age of sixteen, the eldest of three sons. His father, badly wounded in the Great War, was taking up land, the third such venture in his life, having previously pioneered land in Gippsland around the turn of the century and Carnamah in the wheatbelt. After chopping continuously through the end of 1925, Henry, his father and his brothers were excited to commence burning once the season opened:

> Eventually it was time to burn the chopped-down timber. It was all tinder dry with the continuous hot weather. The mallee stumps had suckered up again, but they would get a good scorching as we had packed them well with leaves and wood. There was great excitement this morning, the wind puffing in from the north-east. It was just the day to light up. (26)

The work was risky. In order to produce a "clean burn" one needed dangerous fire conditions: a lengthy period of hot, dry days leading up to the occasion, and on the day itself, hot blustery northeasterly winds for maximum effect. The danger, of course, was that the fire would escape and "burn down the district", so it was done as carefully as possible, with extensive firebreaks prepared in advance. Still, risk was inherent, and this lent to the burn a thrilling frisson, which one sees clearly in the accounts in wheatbelt histories and memoirs. Henry Sherar's account of his life in the Yilgarn is in many ways a fairly sober recollection, but his account of the burn—and this is often true of a settler's first burn—is typical for the exhilaration it conveys:

> Soon there was smoke to be seen down the bottom end of the chopping, followed by huge, angry, red flames with terrific clouds of black smoke.
>
> The wind was getting stronger, but still we waited; us lads being anxious to start lighting. However, Dad kept a strict watch on us. It was not until the fire was well up on both sides that he commenced lighting. We lit a few leaves then took hold of a dry bush as he did

and started lighting. The fire simply roared away with lightning speed. The heat was terrific and it was amazing the way the fire tore along, leaping yards at a time … Gosh it was roaring through! … The fire seemed to set its own draft and draw itself towards the centre. It was very hot … A huge cumulus cloud formed high up in the sky with the dust and smoke.

Now there were huge spirals of dust and ash twisting across the burn. (27)

The two men helping the Sherars with the burn "both remarked what a great burn it was." The intensity of the fire had reduced the piled wood almost entirely to a fine ash and enough heat was left in the stumps that they continued to burn themselves away over the coming days. Just the underground mallee stumps would require a separate effort to remove, the "picking up" that Facey did as a child. Another recurrent memory is the impression of the glowing countryside at night after the burn. Laurie Anderson, many decades later, recalled: "Looking back at the fire from the camp, it looked like a big city in the distance with all sorts of city lights. It was a brilliant sight in the darkness of the night." (27)

The pace of burning and clearing around Sherar's settlement at Noongaar picked up as the land was selected through 1926 and 1927, and in the burning season that began early in 1928 the air was

9. After the "burn". State Library of Western Australia, 21797P.

continuously thick with acrid smoke. Even the preparatory burns to create firebreaks meant that "there was the tang in the air of burnt straw" in the weeks before the burning season opened. Riding with a friend on horseback through the northern parts of the district, Henry Sherar noticed dramatic changes in the landscape: "We were surprised at the large areas of clearing that were being done, acres and acres of the heavy timbered country were cut down and waiting for the match. It was tinder dry, so when the burning season opened, there was going to be a huge conflagration." (53) When the fires were lit that year they created huge dust storms as the soil lost all its binding vegetation and moisture and the hot easterly winds blew remorselessly in: "At the camp it was so hot and dusty lately as almost every day we had a dust storm. Dad said it was because of all the new burns and morrel country to the north ... Some days the dust was thick and choking, and as it was too hot, up would go another fire. Then there would be smoke as well." (54) On one particular day:

> ... there was a strong hot north wind blowing and ... I could see a huge red cloud blocking out the northern horizon ... bearing down on us at a furious rate ... In twenty minutes it was impossible to see more than thirty feet. The choking red dust came inside. It seemed to creep through the tiniest of cracks. It was hard to breathe and this lasted for several hours. It was terrible.
>
> ...
>
> It was now the middle of April, and still it was the same hot dusty weather. It seemed we must be having some kind of punishment as every few days it would be another fierce dust storm. Dad said it would keep like this until we had a good rain. It was caused by all the new burnt country to the north. (54)

It is characteristic that their family's burn was a wonderfully exciting thing, but the same event when practised by dozens of one's neighbours was seen as a catastrophe. The dust was also caused by the practice of fallowing, which, for it to work well, required the fields to be continuously cultivated to prevent weeds from robbing the soil of the moisture that the fallowing process was designed to secure. This was considered best practice and a key principle in "dry land farming",

10. "A huge cumulus cloud formed high up in the sky with the dust and the smoke". State Library of Western Australia, 66823P.

as Henry Sherar recalls: "In this low rainfall region it was said that good fallow was equal to an extra two inches of rain." (84) But the bare fields were also prone to wind erosion, particularly the powdery soils of morrell country.

Contract Work

Back on the Bibbys' farm some twenty years earlier, Albert continued to help with the clearing and burning-off. After clearing 130 acres in 1907, and burning it in the February 1908 burning season, Albert and Bibby cleared another 160 acres in the latter part of 1908, ready for burning the following year. But Albert did not join in that burn because he was contacted, out of the blue, by his mother in Perth who wanted to see her boys again. So, with his brothers Eric and Roy,

Albert travelled to see his mother, who had by this time remarried and was living in Subiaco. The stay in Subiaco was not an especially happy one, and the time with his mother did little to restore his faith in her. Still only fourteen, in 1909 he left Subiaco and travelled north to work on a cattle drive from the Pilbara to Geraldton. During the drive, Albert was lost in remote country for seven days and nearly died of exposure.

By the second half of 1910, Albert was again back in the Wickepin district which he now regarded as his home. He had answered a job advertisement for work boundary-riding on a sheep property at Lake Yealering. It was a 4,000-acre farm protected by a dog-proof fence and it was Albert's job to ride around every five days making sure it was intact and fixing it if it wasn't. He held this job for about a year before relations soured with his manager. He took another job assisting a new settler in the winter of 1911. By now, even though he was just sixteen, Albert's experience in wheatbelt farms was such that his advice was quite valuable to new settlers. His new employers were a husband and wife—the Rigolls—who had selected near Jitarning, just beyond the second (inner) rabbit-proof fence. Together with his brother Len, Dick Rigoll selected 3,000 acres of first-class land in the 12- to 15-inch rainfall band. The drawback was that it was 10 kilometres to the government dam, from which they had to cart water three times a week. However, unlike the prototypical penniless selector (Albert's Uncle, or the Bibbys), the Rigolls had made money in the goldfields and so had working capital to accelerate the transition of bush to productive farmland.

Albert was able to instruct them on what needed doing, as well as assist them in doing it. The first task was to fashion a dam to give on-site water and this took four weeks. This done, they fenced 200 acres of grassland for the horses, using the "lightning fence" method, consisting of two rows of barbed wire strung around trees and any additional posts where suitable trees were not present on the desired line—this took two weeks. The house took a further three weeks to build and, again, because they had money for materials, was significantly superior to the one that Uncle Archie had built. It featured corrugated iron on the roof and on the two windward walls, with the frame from bush timber and white-washed hessian on the leeward walls. The idea was for the house to last ten years and its completion was certainly welcomed by the Rigolls after six months living in a tent. Then the men turned to clearing land for cropping. Over eleven weeks they cleared 140 acres, working six days a week. They chopped down all the small trees and burnt the large ones. The timber was then left to dry out ready for the February burn. Albert finished up with the Rigolls in November, but not before he gave them strict instructions on how to proceed from here. It is worth reproducing the advice in full, as it is a blueprint for how the wheatbelt was cleared by a loosely coordinated army of owner-settler farmers during the initial decades of the twentieth century:

"During the summer months, that is December and January, get as much ring-barking done as you can. That will kill the trees and give the natural grass a better chance to grow freely, increase the feed for the stock and also make the trees easier to burn later. And while you are doing the ring-barking, cut posts from all the suitable trees you come across, for fencing in the winter months after you get your crop in.

"Now you must be ready to start burning off the land we have chopped down, in February. You will want two or three men to help you do this so each time you go to town try and make arrangements for them to start or—if you can manage the finance—get a man just after Christmas. He can work on the ring-barking post-cutting as well as helping the burning—it would be money well spent. (Two pounds a week and keep would be good wages for this kind of work.)

"Now, when burning off, first of all burn all the stumps down to ground level and be careful that you don't burn all the other wood up before you finish this—otherwise you will have to cart more wood to finish burning the stumps. A good idea is to mark out an area, then go over it and pack wood on all the stumps. When all the loose wood burns, shovel the burnt coal off and pack more wood in. Keep doing this until all the stumps are burnt to the ground level, then you can pack whatever wood is left onto the fires and clear it all up.

"Before you start to plough the cleared land, you will have to go over it with a shovel and fill in all the holes that have been caused by some of the dry stumps that have burnt down into the ground.

"Now when the clearing is finished you will have to buy four good, medium draught horses (I advise to buy four young ones and four about four years old). Four horses will pull a three-furrow stump-jump plough. You will also have to buy the plough and you want a drill. A sixteen-run drill is the best and four horses will pull the drill with the harrows behind easily. (196–7)

Facey told Dick Rigoll that if he did "all of these things he would be well on the way to having a real wheat farm" (197). Facey's advice to Rigoll shows up an important feature of the wheatbelt's creation, which was that it took place-along do-it-yourself principles, such that even one not trained in such matters could, by following a fairly simple procedure (though the work was certainly heavy), create a working farm from virgin bush. The advice also shows how the "burn" became almost an art form, one which if done correctly would use the natural combustibility of the local flora to immolate itself out of existence.

From 1912 to 1914 Facey continued to work in the Wickepin district. For much of 1912 he worked for the State Water Supply, building and clearing government dams and repairing government wells. This was a critical part of the infrastructure—along with surveying of land, building the rail network, provision of subsidised

11. Charred timber after the "burn". State Library of Western Australia, 21743P.

superphosphate and financing through the Agricultural Bank—that allowed the do-it-yourself farming model of the wheatbelt. Building dams was, indeed, quite similar work to the building of a wheatbelt farm. The catchment needed to be cleared and fenced against dogs and rabbits before they could be excavated and fitted with pumps and troughs. The government dams were the main water supply for many wheatbelt towns, although gradually the Goldfields water pipeline began to service the towns and districts that adjoined it. When the water-supply work had wrapped up, Facey took on more clearing work, this time some 200 acres for a Louis Smith on a farm near Wickepin:

> The work for Mr Smith was very hard. Chopping scrub and trees down, and cutting logs for burning the large trees down. With a breeze blowing you could burn down a large green tree in a little over a day. We would have as many as twenty trees alight in one day, and while they were burning down we would cut the scrub and small trees down. The job was finished when all the scrub and timber had been felled. For this we were paid fifteen shillings an acre. Working long hours we earned a little over five pounds a week. (220)

The next work that Facey did was on the railways. Again, with Facey, it is easy to slip into a certain archetypal acceptance of the life he led. Of course Facey worked on the railways—just like it seemed the most natural thing in the world that he fought in the trenches of Gallipoli or toured the country as a travelling prize-fighter. But we need to try to preserve constantly the awareness that none of this was natural and that in the case of the railways, as with the government dams, Facey was being incorporated into a coordinated state-sponsored transformation of the landscape. Facey worked on the gang that laid the Wickepin–Merredin line in 1913 (an extension really of the Narrogin–Merredin line which linked the Great Southern line with the Goldfields line). He worked as a "dogger", hammering in the L-shaped nails ("dogs") that retained the rail on the sleeper. This new line from the newly gazetted (1908) town of Wickepin northeast to Merredin, via Corrigin and Bruce Rock, allowed a broad new swathe of wheat farms to be opened up. (In our study, the fathers of both James Pollard and Dorothy Hewett would select farms along this line.) The line was laid between March and October of 1913:

> In time I became quite expert at my job as dogger.
>
> The new line passed through some of Western Australia's best wheat growing country. We had reached a place called Bruce Rock by the end of May, and Corrigin in early August. Our gang was then taken to Wickepin ...
>
> At Wickepin we were to finish the new section, working from Wickepin back to Corrigin. We completed our work on this line by the third week in October, 1913. This meant that I had driven nearly every spike on one rail from Merredin to Wickepin, a distance of about one hundred and twenty miles. (226)

After the work on the railways, Facey got a job as a linesman surveying land in the outer wheatbelt for a surveying firm. He was part of a gang of seven and it fell to him to do the "axe-work" to clear the way for the chain and theodolite. He worked on this through to the end of 1913 and until April 1914. The Great War began two months later and Facey joined up in September.

Communing with Animals

With no schooling, Facey reached his fourteenth birthday illiterate, not even able to sign his name when he had to provide a police statement in relation to some stolen cattle. Nor did he have any friends of his own age that he was able to play with or confide in, having been sent out to work at the age of nine. His care, as we have seen, was haphazard and by most standards abusive. He did occasionally strike up friendships with the adult settlers, including a man named Jack Lander who had also been called to give evidence in the case of the stolen cattle:

> This man was one of the nicest and most understanding men I have ever met. He told me he was from Scotland and that his father was financing him to become a farmer. He was twenty-four years old and hoped that when he got properly settled on the land he would build a house and get married. He told me that he was engaged to a lovely girl. She was willing to come over from Scotland to marry him as soon as

he could make her a home. He also told me that his mother and father were living in Perth and that his father was a businessman. Jack had put two years in at the School of Agriculture to learn how to grow wheat, and also learn all he could about stock and generally equip himself with as much knowledge as possible to be a successful farmer. (100)

In Lander we see a prototype of the model new settler—the kind we will meet again in the next chapter on Cyril Goode. Trained in scientific agriculture, Lander and his parents saw the wheatbelt as a business and life opportunity. He would establish his farm, build a house, marry his girlfriend and settle down to a prosperous family life. This was the script at least. Yet the hardest thing was not the sheer and massive labour that this project entailed but something more intimate, which Lander confesses to the young Facey:

He told me that the hardest thing was the loneliness. He said, "The only time I see anyone is when I go to town for provisions or over to another settler's place. Sometimes I make up an excuse so I can call on another settler just to have a friendly chat." He asked me how I managed. "You haven't had much of a life, always being with middle-aged people and no other children to play with and be with. Don't you get lonely?" (100)

Albert's answer is one that we will see echoed in several of the writers in this study: "I told him that I had at first, when I had to go out to work so young, but I was used to it now and I didn't feel lonely. There was always the birds and the animals in the bush. 'They are like music to me.'" (100) Albert's interest in animals was not unusual. It is a striking fact that that those living in and forming the wheatbelt were often keen amateur naturalists. But the particular circumstances of the wheatbelt's development help explain this. What stands out, historically, is the isolation it involved. The work, as Lander makes plain, was intensely lonely. This marked a difference with rural labour historically, which was communal. The modern wheatbelt farm was based on a model of the owner-occupier-worker. The equipment now available—that is, by the early twentieth century—meant that for the first time in human history it was possible for a single person to farm 1,000 acres. This translated, at the limit, to a population density of one person per 1,000 acres, which means you were on average 2 kilometres from the next living soul. Of course, for the main, and as we have already seen, farms were often worked by couples or families, or co-selected by brothers (although that was also used to double the acreage). There were, too, rural labourers working either on a wage-and-keep basis, like Facey, or as contractors, like Facey's older brothers, Eric and Roy. But even taking this into account, the work was still notable for its isolation.

Ironically, it was clearing that brought people closest to the animals, and as we have seen, clearing formed an enormous component of the early work. Based on the rate at which Facey records clearing, it would take from five to ten years of heavy clearing before a typical 1,000-acre wheatbelt farm was fully converted to farm use. This process put the farmer—often the principal clearer—into direct contact with the profuse natural world of the wheatbelt bushland. It is not surprising then, that many took an interest in the birds and animals they saw. The poignant element is that the farmer's work was to destroy the habitat on which the survival of these creatures depended. It is impossible for a farmer not to have intuited this connection—it was literally happening before their eyes. And yet, there is very little in the way of concern expressed about this fact. Of course, the new settler would have seen the process of clearing as simply inevitable. One can either have a wheatfield or a woodland but not both. The idea that this bush needed to be saved or conserved would have seemed absurd in the light of the development that was planned. Equally, and for quite some time, one would have been able to maintain the idea that one's own personal niche of farmland was but a drop in the ocean of the vast southwest wood and scrub land. It is certainly arguable, too, that the final destruction of the remnant bush is more truly sheeted home to the wheatbelt's second phase (1950–1970), when the advent of better fertilisers and, especially, trace elements opened up the previously neglected sandplain country.

In his account of his life in the emerging wheatbelt, Facey pauses frequently to reflect on the animals and birds he encounters. A number of the most dramatic early scenes involve dingoes, which were prevalent in the southwest in a way that it seems hard to imagine today. Building a government dam near Kulin, he remembers his work-gang being tormented by numerous dingoes at their campsite—"there must have been hundreds of them" (215). There were also various encounters with snakes, including one that killed a neighbour's wife. He also remembers "native cats" (western quoll), "kangaroo rats" (rat kangaroo) and the countless possums trapped for the skins. His journey through the night to escape Cave Rock at the age of nine teemed with native wildlife:

> I hadn't gone very far when my friends the dingoes started to howl. They frightened the very devil out of me. The bush seemed to come alive at night. The possums calling to one sounded like a flat, loud whisper, and occasionally there was a distressed noise, some possum or kangaroo rat fighting for its life. The kangaroo rats only came out at night. They are a small animal, about the size of a house cat, with a body and legs and tail like a kangaroo, and a head like a rat's. When the native cat catches one of these small animals it puts up a real fight. The native cat is the most savage of all the small animals in Western Australia. It is like the dingo in that it won't harm you unless it is cornered. Then it will put up a real fight for its life. A domestic dog won't attack a dingo or native cat on account of their viciousness. (42–3)

But it is birds that feature most prominently and fondly in Facey's account. When he was staying with the Bibbys he would get Sundays to himself and would wander into the bush with his rifle:

> Sometimes I got a shot at a 'roo and many times I would find a quiet spot and sit down and keep quiet and watch the birds and the small animals.
>
> The birds used to fascinate me. There were so many different kinds and most of them were friends of the farmer. The bush in those days was alive with them, their beautiful noises were something you had to hear to believe. (89)

A lengthy description of his favourite birds ensues: the martin sparrow, the willy wagtail, the blue wren, the brown and grey tom tit, the woodpecker, the magpie, the ground-lark, the brown bush quail, the bronze-winged pigeon, the peewit, the plover, the bluebird, the night birds (mopokes and curlews) and the parrots (twenty-eights, rosellas, black cockatoos). Facey uses common names for the birds in the period and his description of their habits are those of a boy, but the fascination is genuine and thorough, and based on a degree of identification. Identification in this context means some felt affinity between the creatures' situation and Albert's own:

> There were, and are, many other varieties [of bird] that are hard to describe. They made the bush a beautiful place and helped one forget about loneliness.
>
> The wild animals were also quite a study for anyone who had to live with them, and sat quietly watching their habits. They lived in a world of fear and danger, always watching, listening and smelling for some scent of trouble.
>
> The birds and animals of the bush were all great company and very nice to see and hear. I loved the bush.
>
> Charlie finished ploughing the new land and then started on ploughing the land that had been cropped the year before. He then did the seeding, finishing at the end of the third week in June. (90–1)

The movement in this passage captures the contradiction between the love of nature and its destruction. Immediately after the contented declaration, "I loved the bush", the next paragraph begins by describing Charlie Bibby ploughing the "new land". And yet this "new land" was, until Bibby and Albert cleared it, the bush that Albert loved. The tonal shift is also significant. Albert's memories of the birds have a distinctly nostalgic tone which most of his memoir does not. Indeed, it is the absence of nostalgia which gives such power and enduring wonder to *A Fortunate Life*; what Hirst called the "elemental purity" of its storytelling. The precision with which he remembers which week in June that Bibby finished his seeding is at odds with the wistful regard for the animals—that they "were all great company and very nice to see and hear." One wonders what has caused the writing to falter in this way—to slacken—when it turns to the animals. There is not one mention of the animals that were driven from their homes when the bush was set alight or chopped to the ground, and yet animals must have been pouring out during such times. We will certainly see later writers, like Peter Cowan, Dorothy Hewett and Barbara York Main, notice these losses, but it is not something that Facey ever mentions. Nor is he alone in remaining silent across this point. Nor, again, is he alone in professing a deep attachment to the bush. This is the situation that prevailed: the settlers both loved the bush and destroyed it.

Returned Soldier

We left the story of Facey with the outbreak of World War One. Facey landed at Gallipoli in May and remained there until he was evacuated due to injury. He returned to Australia in November 1915.[13] Two of his brothers, Roy and Joseph, were killed in the Gallipoli campaign. Facey's injuries were too severe for him to return to service and after further treatment in Cairo he was sent home to Australia.[14] Facey, by his own account, never really recovered from the injuries he suffered. He was declared to be medically unfit for heavy work and instructed to only take on "light duties". In August 1916 he married Evelyn Gibson and she gave birth to their first child in February 1919, with a second arriving in January 1921. For most of this time, Facey worked on the tramways, first as a conductor and later as a driver. In June 1921, Facey contracted diphtheria and spent three weeks in hospital. The doctor treating Facey advised him to leave the trams and go to the country:

> I carried on working with the Tramways while we decided what to do. Then all of a sudden it came to me one day while I was at work. The Government was settling returned soldiers on the land and as I had a lot of know-how about wheat and sheep farming, I thought I stood a good chance of being selected. When I went home and explained the idea to my wife she thought it was the answer to our problem. I had been losing weight and also a lot in wages because of sickness. On a farm I would be my own boss. (296)

So in July 1922, Albert and Evelyn took up a property near the Nomans Lake siding in the Wickepin district that had been his home before the war. It was a plum property in many respects. It was 1,200 acres, 600 of which had already been cleared and boasted a nearly new four-roomed jarrah and iron house. It had belonged to two soldier settlers who had given it up after failing to settle. Because it was too late to put a crop in, Facey decided to fence up the cleared land and stock it with sheep. This proved lucrative, both for the wool-clip and, because the feed was good, selling the sheep at a profit at market. They employed a man to do the heavy work that Facey was no longer able to manage. With his help they put in their first crop the following year, 1923, and commenced clearing some of the remaining bushland for more wheat. Though the barley and oat crop were good, the wheat was only fair that year, so Facey was keen to clear and burn in time for the 1924 growing season: "Land for the best wheat was the new land." (300) That year they put in 300 acres of wheat and got an excellent harvest of fifteen bushels per acre, with good wheat prices as well. Although wool prices were dropping, sheep were still the "mainstay" of the farm. 1926 was also good, but 1927 was a bad year with rain falling at the wrong time and the crop failing, and wool prices continuing to fall. By 1927, the Faceys had five children and they were enjoying the family life on the farm:

> Our evenings were also very pleasant. We'd all sit around and play cards and other games and listen to gramophone records. One day while I was in Wickepin I bought a battery operated wireless. The children were delighted by it. We particularly looked forward to sitting down of an evening and listening to a serial about farm life called *Dad and Dave*. (304)

1928 was another bad year, with too much rain meaning only the higher paddocks could be cropped and the wool price falling even further. The following year was a wonderful harvest, with over 500 acres of wheat cropped and a total yield of 8,000 bags of wheat. But there was a disquieting dip in the price of wheat in 1928 that was being treated for the time being as an aberration. In truth, this was the beginning of a slide in the price that would fall off a cliff within two years. The Great Depression, as it became known, would ruin Facey and thousands of others in the wheatbelt and in farming districts across the country, and indeed anywhere in the world that was exposed to the export market. The wool price also collapsed. And in 1931 rabbits began to appear in plague proportions and there was now no money to pay for netting the paddocks. Facey's health broke down in 1932 and after another year of struggle, and now with six children, they sold up and returned to Perth in February 1934.

What are we to make of Facey's experience? He spent some twenty-four years in the wheatbelt, in two twelve-year stints (1902–14; 1922–34), the first ended by the Great War and the second by the Great Depression. In the first period he worked on contract for other farmers, the Water Supply board, the railways and a surveying company. After the War he returned, this time as a landowner, through the soldier settlement scheme with a wife and young (and expanding) family. He bore physical and psychological scars from his war service and this limited the work he did: "The average man could lift a bag of super or wheat but I used to handle only a four-gallon tin at a time. This took me longer but saved me over-straining myself." (302) The rude health and vitality of his pre-war years were gone, and in the post-war period, at least until the economy collapsed, he employed "a man"—much in the way he had himself been employed in his youth. One feature of Facey's experience is the repeated return to the same corner of the wheatbelt. His earliest work placements were in farms not far from his Uncle's place, but the contracts he found in his adolescence were also all in the Wickepin district, and when it came time to choose his own farm in 1922 he managed to secure a place only 16 kilometres from Wickepin. Facey's working life took him through many of the key activities that caused the wheatbelt to come into being—clearing, fencing, surveying, rail building and water supply.

Of the various activities, though, it is clearing which stands out in Facey's account for the detail in which it is described. There is very little discussion of the other aspects of wheat farming—ploughing, seeding, harvesting. Perhaps this was because he was employed to do the dirtier and heavier work before the war, when he was working on other people's farms. And when he returned, as we have seen, he was not able to do the heavy work and employed someone else to do it. Or perhaps it was just that in the early years, everyone was doing a lot of clearing. The other aspect of Facey's memories that feature especially clearly is his knowledge of how the wheatbelt worked in a material sense. Even though he did not own land before the war, he knew exactly how land was owned and how it could be made to pay. And, after the war, when illness and nerves were affecting him, it was to the wheatbelt that he turned—along with thousands of other soldier-settlers across Australia.[15] Though the land was half-cleared, Facey knew that the "new land" was best for wheat and set about clearing more of it. Clearing the land remained something he both enjoyed and took pride in. It was an accomplishment that he cherished, remembering exactly how many acres he cleared in each year he worked. Clearing will be a theme in the next chapter too, and indeed forms a thread throughout this book. It is not that I wish to say that the clearing should never have happened. I accept the wheatbelt as an economic good and as a path in life for many. I think the question remains open whether too much was cleared and whether a more cautious approach to the matter might have preserved some greater proportion of the natural environment. It is not my place in this study to assess this complex question. What I do wish to document, through the particular archive of creative writing, is what all of this felt like, and what it meant to the people who were involved.

Chapter Two

Cyril E. Goode (1907–83)

Turkey Hill, Southern Cross (1926–32)

Facey's second stint in the wheatbelt, as a soldier-settler from 1922 to 1934, showed us something of the life that was evolving in the post-war years. But by the time Facey returned to Wickepin this was already becoming a well-settled district and the wheat frontier was pushing well out beyond the original "outer" rabbit-proof fence towards the 10-inch rainfall line. This was especially true in the corridor that connected Perth to the Goldfields. This route was well serviced by road (the Great Eastern Highway), rail and, significantly, the water pipeline from Mundaring Weir. From 1917, the Trans-Australian rail was completed and so this corridor now led directly across the Nullarbor and to the east of Australia. Along the road from Perth to the Goldfields, the 10-inch rainfall line fell just to the east of the town of Southern Cross. Southern Cross was settled in 1888 and gazetted in 1890, where it was a centre for gold operations in the Yilgarn—the gold rush spread east from there to Coolgardie (1892) and then Kalgoorlie (1893). By the 1920s, the Yilgarn was being recolonised—this time not for gold but for grain. Although it was marginal country, its nearness to services made it viable, particularly with the emergence of newer drought-resistant strains of wheat.

Cyril E. Goode arrived in Southern Cross on 4 September 1926, one month before his nineteenth birthday. He had travelled across the Nullarbor by train, having boarded at Spencer Street Station in Melbourne on the 27th of August. He was meeting his father to take up land on the fringe of the expanding wheatbelt. Cyril and his father, Henry Francis Good, selected adjoining blocks in the new settlement of Turkey Hill, a satellite district of Southern Cross.[1] Lyall Hunt, author of a history of this region, notes that only in Libya is wheat grown in drier conditions.[2] Goode's father, however, was not without experience of farming in marginal rainfall districts. He had been a wheat and sheep farmer near Grenfell in New South Wales between 1898 and 1911, and Cyril was—like Henry Lawson, some fifty years earlier—born in Grenfell, on 5 October 1907. The family moved to another farm at Frogmore, southeast of Grenfell (towards Yass) in 1911, but lost everything in the drought of 1914. It was a disastrous year in another respect, because Goode's mother, Mary (née Gibson), fell seriously ill and died on 2 May 1915, when Goode was still only eight years old. The father worked on dairy farms through the Great War before moving to the Victorian Mallee district of Buckrabanyule, not far from Wedderburn, where Dorothy Hewett's father, Tom, grew up. Goode and his father stayed in the Mallee until 1920, when they moved to Brighton in Melbourne, where they lived for the next five years. There he attended school and formed a love for Adam Lindsay Gordon who had lived in Brighton. In 1926, Goode and his father crossed the country to take up the land on offer in the West. His wheat-farming experience in the plains of the central west of New South Wales and the newer, dryland farms of the Victorian Mallee meant Goode's father had a background that would have prepared him, to some degree, for the challenges of founding a farm in the far-eastern wheatbelt of Western Australia.

The Diaries

Spending the night in Southern Cross, Goode and his father drove in a Ford car to their adjoining blocks at Turkey Hill on 5 September 1926. The dates are known because, upon embarking on this adventure, the young Goode commenced a diary, initially just haphazard notes, in a pocket-sized account book. Goode became a meticulous diarist over

12. Goode on the Nullarbor and arriving at Southern Cross. Goode's personal photographs courtesy of Cathy Culbard.

the next sixty years, and his record of life at Turkey Hill is preserved in the ten "Southern Cross Books", which open a diary set stretching to over a hundred volumes.[3] Goode's mother had been a music teacher and, though she died when he was still a boy, he seems to have inherited from her a literary sensibility, and in particular a love of reading, which we see emerge gradually but forcefully during the course of Goode's Turkey Hill diaries.[4] At their beginning, the diary entries are little more than notes of daily activities, hastily scrawled in the pages amongst the record of outgoing expenses. With each book there is a growing attention not just to tasks done but to Goode's own feelings about his strange, lonely and quixotic life in the wilderness of the outer wheatbelt. In this sense, Goode is a unique witness to the event of the wheatbelt. His diaries, poems and newspaper columns for the *Southern Cross Times* not only give a contemporaneous account of the life of a "new farmer" in the formative years of the wheatbelt but, crucially, reveal the imaginative investment that attended the material transformation of the land. Goode is almost unique in the remarkable coincidence of two processes—the founding of a wheatbelt farm and the formation of a writer's mind. In no other writer in this study are these two operations so intimately united. No other writer invested more of his heart in the dream of the wheatbelt. Goode, just eighteen, and with nothing else in the world, had staked his future in the unpromising country north of Southern Cross and threw his body arduously and relentlessly into making a farm that would sustain a future as a land-owning farmer.

Raised in the settled farming districts of Victoria, Goode was shocked at the primitive conditions that confronted him: "*District very backward, only 1 crop.*" Nevertheless, he immediately started the work of clearing: "*Between 5th and 14th Sept as tools had not been sent on, I started ringing* [ringbarking]. *Very awkward without camp gear etc.*" On 19 September 1926 he was at last able to pitch a tent on his block (No. 531) and he would live in this tent throughout the next months:

> *Often I used to stay for some time in tent. Outside cooking and tent life not very romantic after a few days of it. The water supply was in kero tins ... a great draw to the ants wanting to drown themselves in it ...*
>
> *Once when Dad was building house for Teal* [a friend and fellow settler] *I only had 2½ kero tins of water for 1 week; nearly did a perish.*

13. Tent life. Goode's personal photographs courtesy of Cathy Culbard.

The early diary entries document the initial work of clearing and setting up the block, and occasional social visits to (and from) neighbouring farmers, mainly single men, and to the town of Southern Cross. The Goodes had a Ford motor car and this allowed them to travel fairly freely through this remote country, although the car was still considered a luxury and used sparingly. Much of the internal movement about the large acreage was on foot. As we saw in Facey's memoir, the clearing work started immediately. In Goode's case, it continued, year on year, until Goode was eventually driven from the land in 1932 as the Depression began to grip. Reading his diary brings home the protracted, at times almost maniacal, nature of clearing the wheatbelt. Perhaps it is a difference in temperament, or perhaps because it is being described in real time, but unlike Facey, Goode found the work of clearing monotonous and dispiriting. It was arduous work: the timbered country was felled by axe, and the scrub was "scrubbed" (called "scrubbing"), while "suckers", the re-growth of mallee roots, were "bashed". The devastated vegetation was then organised into piles and burned in February and March when the hot northeasterly allowed the burn to proceed most efficiently. A typical entry from March 1927 reads:

> *Got straight to burning off 40 acre patch (west of 70 acres stubble) when I drove down from 531. The weather was good for clearing, with plenty of NW winds and we got about 10 acres finished the 1st week. The 1st 10 acres included some of clean burned scrub; but the next piece of morrel and salmon [gums] was harder and we had about 8 acres of thick salmon left when March rains came.*

Occasionally, the heavy, unrelenting nature of the work got the better of Goode, as it did in the winter of 1927:

> *The latter part of July and into August I was chopping on 56 acre strip near Turkey Hill which H.G. started on Wed 13th. The 1st week I wasn't feeling too good because of strain which had got a bit worse chopping on H. Lee's. Joined medical fund July 25 and went into SX [Southern Cross] on Sat 30th. Advised to give up axe which I had to do the last few days of the preceding week.*

But he kept clearing the scrub country, where the axe was not so necessary: "*During October and into November I was sucker bashing on mallee belt above 30 acres; also cutting and burning out clump in centre and 5 acre patch along E. boundary.*"

Another major difference to the experience related by Facey is that Goode was working for long periods on his own. Facey always worked with a partner or as part of a gang. Goode's isolation was taking a psychological toll and many entries attest to sleepless nights in spite of the heavy work. Nor was Goode the only one to suffer from challenges to his morale. On 25 October 1926, after he had been in the district for over a year, he attended a lecture in Southern Cross by George Sutton (1872–1964), who had been appointed the first Director of Agriculture in Western Australia and held the post from 1921 to 1937. Though born in Lancashire, Sutton had come, like Goode and his father, via the wheat-growing districts of NSW west of the Dividing Range. There, he was a close friend of William Farrer who developed the revolutionary "Federation" strain of wheat that opened millions of marginal acres to cropping. Sutton had run his own experimental farm in Cowra, and had produced the rust-resistant variety "Nabawa", which Goode and others were using at Turkey Hill. Sutton's speech *"about wheatgrowing and the progress of the district … seemed to brighten the outlook considerably."* At the end of 1927, Goode harvested the first crop from his block, a mere 20 acres. That more could not be got off in this season was a shame, and in fact, more than that, a disaster, because 1927 was a bumper season in the Yilgarn with very favourable rains (too much, indeed, for Facey at Wickepin), and it would have provided Goode with a crucial buffer against the catastrophe that lay ahead. No one knew then that 1927 was as good as it ever would be for the new farmers of Southern Cross, at least for the next quarter of a century.

Into 1928 the clearing continued. January and February were particularly productive. Generally, the pattern was: *"Scrubbing in morning, burning in afternoon."* On 29 February 1928, Goode writes: *"Finished 20 acres (bad scrub and mallee) … looks very different to the wall of suckers there a few months ago."* The burning continued through March, almost every day. On 28 March he walked to meet a fellow farmer on the clearing: *"Bush opening up well and looking very different to when I was chopping here last July ('27)."* Everyone else was clearing as well and on occasion they would help each other, taking turns on each other's blocks. There were also dedicated clearing teams at work under contract, including a Welsh clearing team that were camped nearby to Goode during the first few months of 1927. Goode notices on more than one occasion that the extreme isolation affected people in different ways. On 11 April 1928 he was returning from working his block when he *"noticed that old Fiz.P was nearly finished* [his] *burn and as usual was in skirts"*, adding in the margin to this: *"Queer sort of chap is a great clearer, but wears skirts."* Also, along with his diary, Goode also kept a record of his activities with a camera. These photos reveal the conditions of the land in its original state, and the changes made—the building of sheds, the clearing, the purchase of machinery, and so on. One photo records an Aboriginal mia-mia, which he captioned *"Black's Camp on Dad's clearing (or what became a clearing)"*. The fact that the mia-mia is made on land cleared shows the continuance of Aboriginal habitation in the face of the land's reassignment to the agricultural purpose of yielding grain crops.[5]

14. "Black's Camp". Goode's personal photographs courtesy of Cathy Culbard.

To assuage his loneliness, Goode found solace not only in his diary and camera, but also in reading, obtaining books from town, occasional visits to Perth, and through the mail. Goode was a serious reader, betraying a hungry intellectualism that also set him apart from his fellow farmers. On 3 May 1927 he writes: *"I started to read 'His Natural Life' (Marcus Clarke) was just one century later than the date in the opening line of the book."* From 1927 onward he kept a note of all the books he read at the end of each diary booklet. Apart from Marcus Clarke's great novel of convict life, in 1927 Goode read books by Bergson, Voltaire, Anatole France, Balzac, Poe, Schopenhauer, Mark Twain, Molière, de Quincey, Thomas Paine, Samuel Pepys, T.H. Huxley, and he also began to read Thoreau. Most of these were obtained through an American book service called The Little Blue Book Company, which promulgated classical literary works as well as studies in contemporary issues (along the lines of 1940s "Pelican" books) bound in characteristic cheap blue paper. Even so, one sees a marked interest in philosophy and also in the literature of the continent, especially French and German masters. In early January 1928, whilst building the "super shed" (superphosphate), he read *Jane*

Eyre. Later that month, in the midst of a particularly intense phase of clearing and burning, he read *Hamlet.* In April he was reading Lawson's poems, the same month he sowed 100 acres of "Nabawa" with a tractor he bought with a neighbour.

Goode and his father, and the other new settlers, had little romantic attachment to the horse team, and in any event feed and water were not easy to obtain this far out. So, they quickly went down the path of "power farming", buying machinery on hire-purchase and betting that the cost would be met by the quicker attainment of higher yields. Certainly, in the late 1920s there were considerable grounds for optimism, particularly in the eastern wheatbelt. The "3,500 Farms Scheme" was an arrangement between the British and Australian governments in which £34 million was to be set aside to develop some 8 million acres of "virgin land" in an arc sweeping south from Southern Cross through Newdegate and east to Salmon Gums, and a full survey was commenced in 1929.[6] Five hundred of these farms were to be north of Southern Cross in the Yilgarn where Goode had settled. In 1928, a rail-line had been completed to Bonnie Rock in the far north of the Yilgarn, and farms allocated there. So, for Goode in 1929, progress would have seemed to be everywhere in evidence.

15. Power Farming. Goode's personal photographs courtesy of Cathy Culbard.

As we will recall from Facey's account, 1930 turned out to be a record wheat harvest, and the Yilgarn, even though it was a brand new district, and on land once thought marginal at best, had led the way. As the agricultural historian G.H. Burvill notes:

> In the Yilgarn area, after only three years of wheat-growing, nearly 80,000 hectares of wheat were harvested in the year [1930] for a yield of over 82,000 tons; and at Moorine Rock railway-siding, 20 km west of Southern Cross, a stack of bagged wheat contained about 250,000 three-bushel bags (over 20,000 tons). It was said to be the largest stack of bagged wheat ever built in the state.[7]

Unfortunately, though, Goode never quite caught up with this boom, and by the time he was able to get his land into a productive state the Depression had crippled the industry.

Campfire Reflections

Yet, in the late 1920s, the times still held considerable promise. In any event, a new ambition had come to Goode—he wished to be a writer. He later noted that he was inspired to write by a Little Blue Book with the title *Hints on Writing Poetry*.[8] His diary records the beginnings of this in the autumn of 1928, where he mentions writing a story called "Riddle" on the 13th of April. Then, on June 1st, he writes: "*Very cold showery morn. Jack went out and after washing up, settled down to writing. Too cold for good penmanship; but got about 10 pages written by dinner finishing later – Story – 'The New Overseer'.*" By this time, nearly two years had passed since he had first arrived at Turkey Hill. Goode was still only twenty years old, but he was beginning to get some perspective on his life, and the writing became a valued part of his weekly activities. Writing helped calm Goode's anxieties: "*When I am writing I notice that the feeling of wander-lust or the impatience to be out doing something subsides somewhat; but last year in the bag humpy the wet days seemed intolerable.*" He was particularly fond of Continental philosophy. He found Schopenhauer "*very instructive*": "[E]*very maxim seems to fit my case exactly, and the writer holds a high place in my esteem because of his keen insight.*" On the 28th August, Goode reports his "*first attempt at verse*", and the poem, titled "Evening", is copied into the diary. The writing was filling Goode with confidence and hope: "*In afternoon in elated frame of mind—thinking of possible publication of poem and future scope for short stories in the setting of the Yilgarn.*" On the 12th of September he composed two further stanzas and sent the revised poem to the *Southern Cross Times*, a two-sheet newspaper edited by Archibald "Bullant" McIntyre, an old Sydney journalist.[9] McIntyre published the poem, now called "Campfire Reflections", signed Cyril Everard, on 12 September 1928:

Old friend! Give the glowing fire more wood.
    Tonight, the wilful wintry winds are howling
Around this camp, where salmon-gums once stood,
    And dingoes in their lonely way went prowling.

On nights like these, how often I recall
    The primitive days that passed so slowly by,
When I lived in tent amongst the timber tall,
    In solitude, beneath Westralia's sky.

By the broken brown of the beetling breakaways,
    With axe I worked to fell the thickets dense;
That in the future there'd be better days,
    And crops, that might o'ertop the boree fence.

From Turkey Hill, or on the Wheatley side
    The Yilgarn tourist now-a-days observes—
Past fields and lakes and camps where men reside—
    Koolyanobbing Ranges' "Rugged curves."

The poem's form is that of the pastoral elegy. It contains the wheatbelt's dream: that arduous toil would lead to "better days" with bountiful crops replacing the wilderness. But it also speaks wistfully of "primitive days"—of prowling dingoes and dense salmon-gum forests—that were too wild and wondrous to be imagined by the contemporary "Yilgarn tourist". Yet the passage of time is but three years, and hardly the work of nameless aeons, even though it may have sometimes seemed that way to those doing the work. Moreover, it is not entirely clear what is being mourned in the poem. Is it the ancient world that has been eradicated? Or is it the fact that the work of eradication is now invisible, the suffering unwitnessed, behind a screen of tamed fields and obedient crops? The tourist can only see the shadow of this labour—and the wilderness it was pitted against—in the "rugged curves" of the distant Koolyanobbing Ranges.

This accelerated historicism is a distinct feature of the accounts of the wheatbelt. The barrier-gate of history seems to be erected almost immediately, so that no sooner does something happen, then it is already a quaint memory from a distant time. It is as if, in the writing at least, there is no present tense, no time in which the moment is being experienced. The month before he wrote this poem, Goode records a visit from a friend which shows that even in conversation there was a marked need to historicise:

> Had dinner and read short stories in <u>Western Mail</u> and then went out burning off. Nearly finished when Norman Haynes came in motor truck. He was slightly drunk and in a very philosophical mood. We had tea and sat around stove yarning about the early days of pioneering and mining in Yilgarn and the [Gold] Fields.

The moods that Goode records in his diary swing significantly between hope and despair, and the crops seem to confirm both states—elated confidence that the world is all right and that it has not all been for nothing, and then brutal confirmation that everyone is but a plaything of fate. But even the sight of a healthy crop tends in Goode's diary to call immediately to mind the world—the "bush"—which it replaced. On 13 August 1928 he notes: "*My crop is looking splendid and I feel more contented to be back this time than when I used to when I only had chaff bag camp. Then the bush used to be all around the camp and this end of the settlement seemed to be quite 'out of it.'*" Again, five days later: "*Pleasant aspect now when one views the green crop where last year a terrible tangle of dead timber lay—no! not last year; but just last burning season. Feb, Mar, Apr.*" Here, Goode catches himself pushing events further into the past than they in fact were, as if shocked by how suddenly and totally the world is changing—even though he is the agent of that change.

The cause of this gradually becomes clearer. As the obligation to meet adversity with good cheer expires, Goode's journal begins to confess more openly the terrible nature of the conditions that he endured on his arrival. On 23 September 1928 he writes: "*Glad to be back at my old camp again as old man's humpy always seems to cast a gloom over me. Perhaps it is because of my awful ordeal camping there for about 2 years under the most depressing times this settlement ever went through. 2 years of absolute Hell!*" And despite a promising start to the season, the 1928 crop did not come on. As Facey mentioned, rabbits were becoming a major problem and Goode had to start netting the fields, a considerable additional labour and expense. On 15 July 1928 he attended a Progress meeting in the district: "[T]*here was a good deal of attendance ... Very unruly discussion on question of fencing Lake System against the rabbits.*" This part of the Yilgarn is encircled by a vast chain of salt lakes—Lake Baladjie, Lake Deborah (East and West), Lake Julia, Lake Seabrook—and the rabbits were thought to be breeding there. Goode later named his farm "Lake-Range", an allusion to the fact that it lay between the Koolyanobbing Ranges and the shores of these lakes.

By the end of September 1928, the confidence of August had evaporated and the district was looking at a failed season. On his regular Saturday visits to Southern Cross, Goode notes: "*Town not nearly so busy as previous Saturdays ... All talking of failure of wheat crops, etc. One ray of hope showed when I saw that my poem about Turkey Hill—'Campfire Reflections'—had been published.*" Nor did Goode's poem go completely unnoticed. In the next issue, F. Jackson from Turkey Hill published his own "Camp-fire Reflections", sending up his earnest neighbour. It begins: "I'm a heaven-sent poet, a consummate liar— / And I'll tell you my tale of woe." It continues:

I, too, have chopped of trees a few,
    And there's corns on either hand.
Mighty quandongs, how they flew,
    For I slogged to beat the band

Alas, the crop will not o'ertop,
    The rotten tea-tree post,
The beastly thing has gone the flop—
    A one-bag yield at most

For the rain has followed the axe,
    (A theory that gives us mirth).
The reason for our sad climax
    Is—that it fell on a wood-yard in Perth.

From Turkey Hill, or the Wheatley side,
    If a traveller shall fare,
Quaint tales he'll hear, both wide and wild
    Of a mighty rabbit scare.

I have no beetling breakaways,
    To make my farm romantic,
But, still, I'm broke in other ways—
    In fact I'm nearly frantic

Dingoes may go their stealthy way,
    And continue on their prowling,
But be it known, and sad to say.
    It's me, not them, that's howling.

Against the elegy of Goode's poem, Jackson chooses satire, no doubt trained to a keen edge by the *Bulletin* writers so popular at the time. Like Goode's poem, though, there is a double object. On the one hand it is teasing Goode for the ponderous sincerity of his plea, but also it is targeting the boosters of dryland farming. He takes the theory, popularised in the settlement of the Great Plains of North America in the late nineteenth century, that "the rain follows the plough" and gives it a new inflexion—"the rain follows the axe"—which allows the droll punchline: to "a wood-yard in Perth". The theory had fallen into general disrepute, but was periodically revived whenever local circumstances offered the slightest support for its possible truth. By the 1920s, this theory was a kind of joke, and, at the same time, a tantalising possibility for farmers of marginal land.

Goode was not put off by Jackson's ribbing. On 3 November 1928 he reports getting his first haircut in Southern Cross: "*While there the barber was greatly impressed with my latest verse in 'Times' and I was glad I took the trouble with it.*" In fact, Goode joined the ranks of the district boosters by taking on the role, late in 1928, of "correspondent" for an occasional column, "Turkey Hill Notes", for the *Southern Cross Times*. Other correspondents would report for other districts, such as J. Keightley's "Noongaar Notes" for the township of Noongaar, just west of Southern Cross on the Goldfields rail-line, mainly being settled by soldier-settlers. (It was in Noongaar that Henry Sherar, whom we met in the last chapter, was farming and burning off.)[10] There was a lively sense of rivalry between the wheat-growing settlements, and exchanges took place in the pages of the *Times*. On 12 November 1928, Keightley wrote in the *Times* to "rebuke your Turkey Hill correspondents", whom he called "sheiks and immature poets":

> In the settlements furthest out there are always misfits, misanthropes and dreamers associated among the more work-a-day kind of settler. All have little tragedies in their lives, perhaps only known to themselves, and all have some finer points than are shown on the surface. Country correspondents should attempt their best thoughts, bringing wit, satire and friendly criticism into play, but carefully avoiding personalities. The "Times" offers a fine avenue for the interchange of different views from different districts and for the improvement of such talent as at least one of your correspondents possesses.

Goode answered in his next column, with an attempt to correct the impression some—such as the Noongaar correspondent—may have of the "Lake Country" that "Turkey Hill is essentially a resort of misanthropes and poets."[11] Goode was keen to paint Turkey Hill, though still a "bachelor's settlement", as a "progressive" district. Land was being surveyed, roads built and "more clearing has been done this year than during any other year in the past." Like his poem, but this time in the form of positive corroboration, Goode invokes the mythical Yilgarn tourist to convey the picture of the district:

> A tour through this progressive area will dispel the current illusion that the bad season and the resultant poor crops have turned some settlers' heads. On every side one hears the purring of tractors and the whirring of headers or harvesters, as the busy farmers hurry to get the golden grain safely away before it gets damaged by hail or fire.

In the quiet of his diaries, though, Goode was not as ebullient. The entries through 1928 are often quite desperate and he reports finding sleep difficult, waking too early or waking too late, spending days inside reading and struggling with motivation, interspersed by periods of manic activity, usually clearing. As we have seen with Facey, clearing was financially essential to the new settler, as the loans made by the Agricultural Bank were advanced on a "progressive" basis. At the time, the Bank paid 25 shillings per acre for clearing, half when the timber was cut, and the other half when it was burned.[12] But more than this, clearing occupied the status of a pure good in the universe of Goode's life, and, in large measure, in the world of the emerging wheatbelt. If nothing else could be done, then at least clearing promised the possibility of a future happiness. Clearing was coterminous with progress, and progress was the motto of this social experiment.

But Goode's mood often remained intransigent. He continued to read philosophy, both European and Eastern, not so much for the enjoyment of the ideas but for spiritual consolation and out of a deep need to find a way to understand his position. On the 6th of October he wrote: "*I am frequently calling to mind the rather sad verses of 'The Rubaiyat' which seems the only system which offers freedom from worrying over the complex schemes around us.*" Omar Khayyam's twelfth-century religious poem functioned in the late nineteenth and early twentieth centuries as a kind of precursor to existentialism, popular among young poets for its beguiling mixture of agnosticism and fatalism. Edward Fitzgerald's ubiquitous English translation ran through five editions between 1859 and 1889, and the various quatrains, or even lines within them, operated as epigrams that could be cited to account for life's limits in an age that was wedded to progress. Suggestively for Goode, Khayyam's imagery, like the parables in the New Testament, frequently referenced the experience of grain farming that occupied the lives of those in the Middle East's fertile crescent. How sweet the invitation would have seemed, when the poet called out: "But come with old Khayyam ... With me along some Strip of Herbage strown / That just divides the desert from the sown." There could hardly be a more fitting description of Turkey Hill than this. Khayyam proposes a pastoral retreat from the maddening cycle of day-to-day life amongst one's fellow citizens, but also realises that even this is not enough:

A Book of Verses underneath the Bough,
A Jug of Wine, a Loaf of Bread—and Thou
Beside me singing in the Wilderness—
Oh, Wilderness were Paradise enow![13]

It is from Khayyam's *Rubaiyat* that Goode takes the expression (translated by Fitzgerald), the "Golden Grain". Certainly, the expression had a popular valency at the time, and in particular the association (both a material one and metaphorical one) between the Goldfields and the wheatfields around the unifying concept of gold. This was particularly true of the Yilgarn, which was the transitional zone between the wheatbelt and the goldfields.[14] But Goode imbues this phrase "Golden Grain" with the specific importance that it garners from the *Rubaiyat* as the embodiment of earthly hope. As Khayyam writes (in Fitzgerald's translation):

And those who husbanded the Golden Grain,
And those who flung it to the Winds like Rain,
Alike to no such aureate Earth are turn'd
As, buried once, Men want dug up again.[15]

The Golden Grain is thus, in Khayyam's *Rubaiyat*, a symbol of human vanity, and of the earth to which we will all once more be cast in the end. This depiction of wheat as a false and futile god is one that increasingly came to take hold of Goode's imagination.

The Grower of Golden Grain
After turning twenty-one earlier in the month, Goode reflected in a lengthy diary entry for 24 October 1928 that he found himself now in "*a mood something like I used to be when I used to go over this ground about this time last year*": "*Reflecting on the toil it took to clear the tangle of suckers and scrub off this very land which appears as a nice undulating paddock; alas! it will not yield very high this year—not that it did otherwise last year (owing to the rabbit plague).*" As the diaries become bleaker, the newly created landscape of cleared paddocks take on a strange and melancholy complexion:

When I happened to see the ½ moon over East a peculiar sense of unreality swept over me—a feeling quite familiar to people who live long on their own.

It is closely allied to the mood wherein everything (even life) seems rather futile and calls to mind the sad reflections of Omar K.

His main consolations continued to be reading and writing. On 15 October 1928 he wrote "Ode to the Growing Period, 1928" as a reflection on the opening of the Ghooli State Farm, near the No. 6 pumping station on the Goldfields water pipeline. Ghooli is now the end of the wheatbelt as you travel towards Kalgoorlie on the Great Eastern Highway. The State Farm opened in 1928 but did not survive the Depression. Even in 1928, with (relatively) high prices, the message to local farmers was received with some scepticism, given the dry year they were enduring. Goode's poem captures the mood of local farmers on a sunbaked October day:

> Now Yilgarn farmers stare askance, at the bright sun overhead.
> Their sunburnt brows in black despair are knit.
> The heat waves on the meadows beat and turn our hearts to lead—
> We seldom now around our paddocks flit.

But Goode's poem was also keen to emphasise, even allowing for irony, that the science of farming would see them through in the long term:

> Ghooli State Farm is indeed, an institution great,
> Whose methods will assure our future bliss
>
> Oh Farmers! Round about the 'Cross' be careful how you sow,
> On scratching methods you must not rely,
> The fallow-wheat-and-pasture system will make the district glow,
> And Southern Cross shall blaze again on high!

On New Year's Day 1929, Goode completed a poem, "The Grower of Golden Grain", which was published in the *Southern Cross Times* on 19 January. Its tone was decidedly melancholy and is written with the full realisation of the failure of the previous year's crop and in genuine uncertainty about the future viability of the district. The poem depicts the arrival of a new farmer to the district who has laboured for "years" and has nothing to show for it. The role of humour is diminished and bitterness and anxiety prevail:

> Where some broken rocks are rising from a shallow salty lake,
> There's a wretched little humpy that the breezes often shake;
> And a worried settler paces in the hut below the rock—
> Thinking hard upon the subject of a thousand acre block.

The poem thus begins from the present state of anxiety and the imagery evokes only a precarious, barren and forsaken landscape. There is little in the way of mitigation and the situation is sobering, as though all jokes have now been cast aside, and it's time to confront the dilemma as it really is. The next stanza casts backward from this point to the moment when it all began, with high hopes:

> Years ago with hope uplifted he settled in the West,
> Picked a site to hoist his canvas 'neath the mossy granite crest;
> Then he said with voice emphatic—eyes upon a distant goal:
> "*Some*one has to do the bushwork as the seasons onward roll!"

Again, it is worth noting that the "years" in question were in fact three years, although the poem seemingly suggests the passage of countless years. His difficulties came to be registered as a historical process grounded in the deeper time of generational labour, when in fact, by most historical measures, the activity was sudden and violent.

> Buried in the lonely bushland with the everlasting flies,
> There for years he swung the hatchet long before the sun would rise;
> And in Nineteen Twenty Seven when the crops were fine and tall,
> Planted he five hundred acres—Brer Rabbit ate it all.

The poem reverses the connotations previously given to machinery in Goode's "Turkey Hill Notes" for the *Southern Cross Times* just one month earlier, where he had spoken of "the purring of tractors and the whirring of headers or harvesters, as busy farmers hurry to get the golden grain safely away." Now, in this poem, the "whirring 'header' wanders round to find the yield" and "the tractor grates upon his jaded nerves". The poem comprehensively recants the words Goode wrote as the Turkey Hill "Correspondent", comments which he seems to consciously allude to:

> Once he claimed the local scenery held a certain vivid charm,
> Swore that life was just a picnic on a West Australian farm.
> When in lighter mood transported, talked of fields of "Golden Grain,"
> Never thinking for a moment that it might forget to rain.

Goode's writing through this time (1928–29) is not a single narrative of hope falling gradually and reluctantly into disillusion, but rather a concerted oscillation between fervid optimism and dire pessimism. These bipolar mood swings reflect a genuine uncertainty about the enterprise—neither Goode, nor anyone else, knew how the story would end.

Later that year, Goode published "The Grower of Golden Grain – Part II", which attempted to redress the despondency of the first poem. Rather poignantly this sequel is "Dedicated to Mr G.L. Sutton, Director of Agriculture". The dedication is not in any way made jeeringly, but in quite earnest gratitude. The poem begins with the forlorn figure of the settler by the granite boulders: "Still the settler worries sadly / On the money that he owes." But the mood is lifted by

16. Cyril E. Goode's father, Henry Francis Good, in his wheatfield at Turkey Hill. Goode's personal photographs courtesy of Cathy Culbard.

the arrival of the local bank inspector. In new settlement farms, there was a close involvement of the Agricultural Bank in the activities of the farms they were funding.[16] The inspector, a Mr Edwards, consoles the settler on the disappointment of last season and counsels a more scientific approach:

"You must work your fallow better
If success you would achieve—
Follow Mr Sutton's doctrine!
Make your rate of seeding light.
Follow these rules to the letter
And your chance of failure's slight."

The settler listens carefully to "the rules concerning wheat" and carefully follows the instructions, and …

Though the season wasn't normal.
In the wheat lands of the West
And the scratched in crops were withered—
Yet the fallow stood the test!

The poem ends triumphantly for the settler, where "Olympic voices cheered him / From the broken granite rise: 'Hail thou faithful son of Ceres / You have justly earned your Prize'". The sequel poem recuperates the failure that had occupied the original. The distinction between methods discussed in the poem—fallowing versus "scratching in"—was a major issue in the eastern wheatbelt at the time.[17] Fallowing, a method thought to have been brought across from South Australia and Victoria at the end of the nineteenth century, was designed for low-rainfall areas and sought, essentially, to use two years of soil moisture to grow one crop by eliminating weeds. It was promoted widely in Western Australia after the drought of 1914 and was proved successful during trials at Nangeenan (Merredin) Research Station, though the drawback, as mentioned in the previous chapter, was potential soil erosion. "Scratching in" was the name given to crops planted without fallowing, particularly in recently cleared fields.

The year 1929 started favourably with heavy rains in early May and good rains through June. In the 3 July issue of the *Southern Cross Times*, Goode reports that the Yilgarn farmers had managed to seed widely and the hope was for a season like that of 1927 that would allow the previous year's disaster to be forgotten. There were worries, though, over the seemingly inexorable increase in rabbits, and also the depredations of "wandering bands of dingoes" which were devastating poultry and preventing any attempt to introduce sheep or cattle into the new farms. Under the sub-heading "Improvements" he writes: "Most of the settlers who have been here for the last five or six years have their farms well opened out. Mr W. Forrester has 800 acres under crop and about 600 burned up and ready for fallowing." This led to Goode feeling it was "incumbent to pay tribute to the clearers", who:

> In burning season during day or night,
>> Were long hours burning off amid the head
> Of smoking fires or their flickering light,
>> Preparing for the fields of waving wheat.

After smuggling this poem into his column, Goode points out, as if the credit might fall elsewhere, that "it will be understood that the settlers have done as much of the clearing themselves as possible under the circumstances." But 1929 would also prove to be a bad year for the district, with low rainfall again the major factor. And while 1930 started ominously dry, it proved in the end a record season, at least from the point of view of yield. Of course, in the meantime, Wall Street had crashed in October 1929, although the effects were not immediately realised in the rest of the world, including the Western Australian wheatbelt. Although there was some general inkling that the international financial instability would have consequences, no one understood just how bad it would get, and the effects of the Depression were not widely felt in rural areas of Western Australia until the middle of 1930.[18] So the irony, noted by Facey as well, was that 1930 delivered a record season, reversing the failures of 1928 and 1929, only to have prices collapsing by the time they reached market.

But the mood in 1930, judging from Goode's columns in the *Southern Cross Times,* was not unhopeful. The financial crisis was troubling, but the crops were looking good and, after two dreadful years, seemed to offer considerable hope that the district was turning around. His poems also took a more hopeful note. "Yilgarn Madrigal", a sonnet from July 1930, invokes "Gay spring" who "has robed the fields that stretch around, / With verdure green a-waving in the breeze" and points cheerfully to "pleasant ordered waving wheatfields ... On rich clay slopes and flats." Another poem from 1930, "By Mine and Field", is written as a reply to a correspondent's ("Boomerang") "pessimistic reflections" earlier in the year. Goode's poem nostalgically recalls the history of the district as a goldfield. The miners had come and gone,

> But to these men who went before
>> And paved the thirsty way,
> We owe a debt that's rather more
>> Than we can e'er repay.
>
> For soon the great bushland awoke
>> From age-long, useless sleep.
> When settlers struck with measured stroke
>> Into the heart-wood deep.
> And now where leagues of timber lay
>> In hazy stretches drear,
> Are fields where sheep and cattle stray
>> And pleasant homes appear.

The poem is unusual in that it does not mention wheat, and it suggests that the collapse in wheat prices was starting to cause genuine fear. In his "Turkey Hill Notes", Goode relays a joke then doing the rounds of new wheat farmers: "When you've saved up enough money to get married, buy a flock of sheep or cattle and start farming properly." Another poem, "Yilgarn Optimist", published in April 1930, attempts to make light of ominous developments, placing the falling prices into the general run of adversity that any farmer worth his salt will cope with:

You might have gambled all you've got upon this season's crop,
And then have seen your wheat wilt off and watched the prices drop.
Perhaps you've turned and called yourself a fool for coming here.
But just over once or twice: "Well, what about next year?"

The sand has blocked your roadway up and smothered all your fence,
But still the Road Board's only young—and old age teaches sense;
And anyhow the wind may come and blow the stuff away—
Don't let a bit of sand like that disturb you for a day.

Your stock have picked your stubble bare, your dams have given out,
And starving sheep pollute the air by dying round about.
Trustees are hanging on your heels and driving you stone mad,
But calm yourself and say "Ah well, it might be twice as bad."

Unfortunately for the farmers of the Yilgarn, the situation was indeed twice as bad, probably more, than it seemed to be, and the soil erosion and the wilting crop were the least of the problems. Goode continued to read voraciously, though, again with an emphasis on the Europeans—Gogol, Chekhov, de Maupassant, George Sand, Ibsen—but also Henry James, Upton Sinclair, Coleridge, Dickens. As in previous years, he read Thoreau, this time his essay "On Walking". The only Australian writer mentioned is Steele Rudd, whose adventures might at least have given some comic relief to Goode struggling on his own selection. The major difference one notices in Goode's life as compared to those of the Rudds—and even the Faceys—is the absence of familial support. Goode mentions his father but only very sparingly and one comes away from reading his diary with an overwhelming sense of loneliness and isolation, which is not at all what one sees in Steele Rudd.

"Poems of the Depression"

By 1931, the situation in rural Australia—and across the globe—was no longer in dispute. The Depression had arrived and it was clear that the drop in prices was not bouncing back to 1920s' levels. As a consequence, the viability of many farms, particularly in the newer, marginal areas, was doubtful at best. As late as August, Goode was trying to put a brave face on the matter, at least in his Turkey Hill Notes for the *Southern Cross Times*. The year had improved with good soaking rains and sun in August and the crops were looking promising. The Turkey Hill farmers were making the best of the crisis, and were determined to stay on their land:

> The "Great Depression" has caused very few of the settlers here to depart and the way they are struggling to regain the enormous losses occasioned by the collapse of the wheat market,—is indeed commendable! The flagrant injustice of the situation is without precedent and one wonders how much longer the "man on the land" will bear the yoke.

Goode offers his readers a rather ambiguous consolation from one of his favourite authors: "But, in these depressing times … remember Thoreau's maxim—Enjoy the land but own it not!" This appears to be the last time that Goode wrote his Turkey Hill Notes for the *Southern Cross Times*. For him, the season did not end well, and the failure of the crop coupled with the further collapse in price spelled the end for him. In February 1932 he writes bitterly in his diary: "*Crop a decided failure so there seems nothing for me to do but to walk off as I said I would if the crop was a failure!*" The next entries are heartbreaking. On 11 February, under the heading, "Impressions on Being Wound Up" he writes:

> *They told me that they were winding me up as much for my own good as their own and Evans from bank said that SX should never have been opened up as a farming district and that eventually it would drift back to station country … I know I would be much better off away from the awful existence; but it will take some time to get used to the idea of recasting my whole mode of existence and leaving sun scorched Yilgarn perhaps for ever.*

On 12 March 1932, in one of the last entries for his time in the Yilgarn, Goode titles his reflections, "Picking up Odds & Ends at 'Lake-Range' Farm", and details the mournful task of going back to his farm-hut and packing up his few, precious belongings, and with them all the hopes he had clung to for nearly seven years:

Two chaps here when mailman and I arrived and I gave him several cupboards to take into Perth for me. Glad when they all went and I got on with wrecking all fittings and taking books out of shelves ... I had collected around me for last 6½ years ... Straightening up things ... and thinking of the glow of ambition with which I came to the place and comparing it with my outgoing after all these years I felt utterly miserable ... Ah! What heartbreak after all these years of loneliness

It is at this point, when for Goode and many of his neighbours the game was up, that he becomes especially eloquent. Hitherto his poetry had to pose awkwardly between competing futures, by turns wildly optimistic and bitterly pessimistic. With the end clearly in sight, the poetry deepens and begins to move beyond the country-town doggerel that he himself had understood it to be.

As early as January 1929, Goode was beginning to imagine his verse as a book, and by the end of his time at Turkey Hill he had accumulated enough poetry to compile a small volume of poems which he had privately printed by the Southland Press in Melbourne in 1932 titled *The Grower of Golden Grain, and other Inland Ballads*. Goode explains their genesis in a short foreword, which also apologises for their sombre mood:

> These verses were written during the course of seven lonely years spent in clearing, farming, and prospecting, and are intended to portray the life of a part of Australia in the making.
>
> Most of the characters are taken from real life, and are still living around the places mentioned in the verses. It is regrettable that this also applies to the melancholy vignettes of the depression—these are only too true.
>
> Owing to lack of space, a number of pieces of more hopeful outlook have been omitted; they may shortly appear in a separate volume.

The volume is prefaced, too, by a verse "Prelude", also in an apologetic vein, "For these rhymes were with carelessness strung, / Mere doggerel at best."

The Grower of Golden Grain is divided into two sections, with the later poems grouped under the title, "Poems of the Depression", as

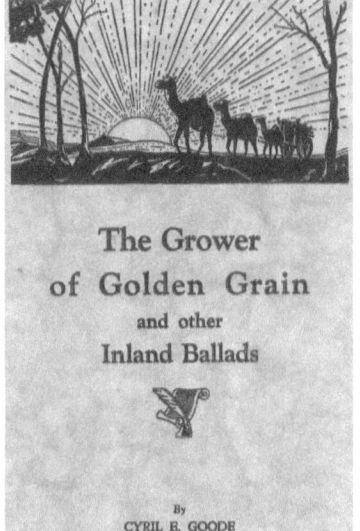

17. *The Grower of Golden Grain* (1923) and author's photograph for *The Bridge Party at Boyanup* (1944).

if to formally acknowledge their distinct status. These poems are confessional in a way that his poems in *The Southern Cross Times* prior to the Depression could not be, although the diaries reveal that the doubts they express existed well before the Depression. What the Depression introduced for Goode was the concrete reality, as opposed to the long-feared possibility, that everything he had done and was doing was for nothing. Goode was wound up in January 1931, but not before he published a "Part III" to his poem, "The Grower of Golden Grain", with the subtitle "Exit" and a preface addressed "To the thousands of settlers who will doubtless be forced to suicide, starve to death—if wheat does not reach 4 shillings per bushel." In January 1931, the wheat price bottomed at 2 shillings and 2 pence a bushel.[19] It remained below 4 shillings for most of the next decade; its average during the 1930s was about 3 shillings, which was well below the cost of production for many areas.[20] Goode was correct about the effect it would have on farms. The number of males recorded as farming in Western Australia peaked at nearly 24,000 in the years 1929 and 1930. By 1939, the number was 14,609.[21] The poem takes up the profound disillusionment caused by these events:

Once again has come the harvest
   And the crops are yielding grand
But, the price is disconcerting
   For the man upon the land
And the grisly spectre, Hunger,
   Roams the wheat-belt near and far,
While our "helpless" politicians
   Booze around some private bar!

Goode's poem was part of what Bolton describes as "a lot of lively versifying among the Yilgarn farmers during these frugal months of early 1931" (139). Bolton cites not only Goode, but also "Boomerang", from the pages of the *Southern Cross Times*, who used poetry to protest their situation and the growing sense that they had been sold a lie and now politicians in both Perth and Canberra were running for cover.[22] Bolton notes that the Yilgarn farmers had for some time exhibited "a lively sense of grievance" (91) at their plight. But Goode's poems focus less on the uncaring politicians than on the sheer heartbreak of the exercise; the hours, days, months and years of toil that had led, at the end of the day, nowhere at all. His poems now stand as records not just of a sense of injustice in the face of economic crisis, but of the action of creating the wheatbelt, an event both systematic and radically personal. Once again, Goode puts forward in his poem the ingenuous settler, who is guilty of nothing other than believing the government in its promises. In doing so, he creates a micro-history designed to contradict, by hard-lived experience, the narrative of progress:

Through the years with hope and patience
   Worked a man with heart aglow,
On a virgin bush location,
   Felling trees with mighty blow;
Til the clearing spread before him,
   And he sowed it down with corn,
Watched the rabbits fatten on it,
   With expression half forlorn.

Then he cleared the timber faster,
    And prepared a spacious mead,
Which would keep the rabbits busy,
    And perhaps return his seed;
But an extra arid season
    (With a minimum of rain)
Perished off the live stock early—
    Shrivelled up the golden grain!

Followed then a year of plenty,
    When the fallow pulled him through,
And he burnt his wretched humpy—
    On the rise a cottage grew!
Pride and gladness filled his bosom
    For a few short months or so—
Then the prices fell to zero,
    Dealing him a mortal blow.

The poem recapitulates the years between 1927 and 1930, its roller-coaster of seasons and adversities. It ends with an image of suicide that exceeded the tastes of the poem's genre:

Then our grain-producing hero
    Offered up a futile prayer
(For starvation joined with worry
    Breeds the madness of despair);
Then he seized a hempen halter,
    And retired to his shed,
Where you'll find him fast suspended,
    Quite inert, and rather dead.

Australian balladry, and literature more generally, had exhibited since the colonial period a certain grotesque or macabre dimension, often clothed in bitter, droll humour. But the severity of this image—the farmer who has hung himself—is not properly restrained either by humour or maudlin sentiment, and so survives to deliver a shock. It was moments like these that prompted Goode's warning preface when he published *The Grower of Golden Grain*. The brief notices the book attracted, which Goode gathered in a scrapbook, in papers such as the *Benalla Standard* and the *Brighton Southern Cross* tend also to note the mood of the poems.[23] The *Shepparton Advertiser* offers the opinion that "Depression is not a good subject to write verse about unless one has a keen sense of humour", and hoping that the author "turn his attention to brighter subjects" in the future. The poems did garner approval in the West, where the *Sunday Times* praised the more cheerful poems, such as "Yilgarn Madrigal", but also found that "[s]everal of the poems are spoiled by a little too much introspection and unconstructive (poetically) cynicism."[24]

Another poem, "The Settler", first published in the *Southern Cross Times* on 1 June 1931, relates plaintively the hopelessness of the situation, and reflects on all the wasted work, particularly the back-breaking clearing work:

> Alas, it was I who toiled in the sun
> long buried away in the forest deep;
> nought farmer can do have I left undone,
> and you see my harvest what I reap.
> My agricultural race is long!
> I gaze o'er the field that I know needs
> the axe and plow on the weeds entwined;
> at the desolation the heart night bleeds,
> for the place is ruined now it's assigned—
> assigned not because of my misdeeds.
>
> …
>
> Thus entered I Yilgarn, and thus I go;
> for such failures people have dropped down dead;
> ah, thus am I paid for the wheat I grow,
> I might have paid, too—but now, instead,
> I owed the lot: oh, why is it so?

The theme is continued again and again, in poems like "Song of the Bankrupt Wheatgrower", "The Aftermath (A Settler's Lament)" and "Whither Bound?". The cluster of poems by Goode about the onset and consequences of the Depression are an eloquent, more or less contemporaneous account of the emotional effects of the collapse of rural commodity prices. And in the profound disappointment of the loss of his farm, what flows out in the poetry in a very direct and sharply delineated form is the ideology of wheat. This ideology, as we have already seen, unites an economic scheme for financial gain through the sale of cash crops with a complicated fantasy whose elements include both self-sufficiency and collective action, masculine labour and a celebration of fertility, a return to nature and its thorough eradication, and, not least, a forgetting of markets and the dictates of the world that led directly to a thorough dependency on world markets.

Clearing and Burning

Goode is a prized witness because his profound disillusionment revealed just how totally he had invested in wheat's ideology. But his life and work are valuable beyond this. In particular, he provides a vital account of the wheatbelt's founding action, the clearing of native vegetation. The land that he cleared, mainly salmon-gum and morrel, is part of the Great Western Woodland that extends from the eastern wheatbelt into the Goldfields.[25] Goode's diaries, as well as his poems, reveal just how staunchly this flora resisted the onslaught of axe and fire. In 1950, Goode was interviewed by the *Williamstown Chronicle* and recalls that for the seven years he lived in the Yilgarn, "Half of the year was spent chopping down timber and scrub, the other half in burning off."[26] Facey (as we have seen) and Jack Davis did their fair share of this work, although mainly on a contract basis for other people, and they only wrote about it many years later. For Goode, clearing was the main work he did, and the sowing, cultivating, harvesting, and bagging seem simply footnotes to the principal task. Of course, it needs to be remembered that the system at the time effectively paid land-selectors to clear, in that they were lent money on the basis of it being done. In a certain sense, the money from clearing was much more reliable than the money from cropping, even if it was technically still a loan. For Goode, it is highly probable that he obtained more money from clearing than he did from the sale of wheat.

In Goode's poetry, particularly his later lamentations, clearing—as actual work—is often derided and treated as a kind of purgatory to which he had been unfairly condemned. True, there was, as time passed, and more and more of the land "opened up", a feeling of pleasure at what had been achieved, but little pleasure was seen to attach to the task itself. Again, Facey's pleasure in the work of clearing stands in stark contrast to Goode's loathing of it. Nevertheless, "The Clearer", which appeared in *The Grower of Golden Grain*, is a ballad that celebrates, albeit slightly ambivalently, the work of clearing. Although it is prefaced with a line from Omar Khayyam—"Here with a loaf of bread beneath the bough"—the poem seems to owe little to the mystic who turned away from the turbid claims of society and towards a life of contemplation. Goode's ballad is in the Australian tradition of heroicised depictions of rural labour, and the poem clearly places "the clearer" into the same masculine pantheon as the shearer, the stockman, the drover and the boundary rider. In this, one can see a careful shift away from the figure of the selector—the struggling, slightly pathetic, occasionally comic figure from Steele Rudd and others in the *Bulletin* school. In this poem, "the clearer" emerges in bold, declaratory lines with a healthy smattering of exclamation marks and pounding Tennysonian iambs to emphasise the epic, world-creating nature of the clearer's mission:

> Surveyors have lately cut up the land,
> > And the slumb'rous forest is waking,
> As eastward farther the field expand,
> > Where settlers their homes are making.
> 'Tis a lonely life and a hard one too,
> > For those in the bush-land clearing,
> For the rough bush camp has comforts few—
> > E'en fewer than first appearing. (15)

Civilised life seems to spring directly from the clearer's axe. The poem, like others of its kind, was a plea for admiration and gratitude, because the suffering of these men was for us. But the tone of the poem is not entirely convincing. Certainly, we know from Goode's other work and from his diary that his own interior life was not exactly marching to a drumbeat of pioneering passion. There is also a bass-note in the poem which wishes to express that the work is, in the older sense of this word, *terrible*:

> As from the horizon the world's great lamp
>   On a new day brightly flashes,
> From out of the timber nearby the camp
>   Come sounds of heavy crashes,
> As the axeman, with many a measured swing
>   (That set all the echoes waking)
> Does soon to destruction the largest bring,
>   With a crashing of limbs and breaking! (15)

This awesome quality—such a contrast to the repeated descriptions of clearing in the diaries as dreary, boring and mind-numbing—reveals a hidden scene in the psyche of the clearer which powered the activity at the ideological and imaginative level. The work is described as "primeval", an elemental struggle with the primary forces of life. This sublime dimension is exposed with an even greater clarity when the poem turns from the axing of the forests, to the "burn":

> In the midst of Summer the fire will sweep,
>   With a smoke-wrack dark unfurling,
> Through the clearing, and higher the flames will leap
>   In a vortex madly swirling.
> Like a carnival city viewed from a height
>   (Whose lights are a changing medley),
> Will the burning timbers appear at night,
>   With their embers glowing redly. (16)

The surreal quality of the embers burning in the heart of the assembled pyres at night lends a diabolical glow to the destruction wrought. Until the final stanza, the poem is equivocal on just who "the clearer" is—is it simply the settler, like Goode himself, clearing his own block? But the poem's conclusion, which also develops the association with Hell, makes it clear that the clearer is itinerant and that he will move on to other work when this is done:

Then for weeks, on oppressive awful days,
    Ere the final stumps are level,
The clearer will work in the smoky haze
    Like a mediaeval devil.
He then may canvas and blankets fold,
    And hoist to an able shoulder,
And drift away to prospect for gold,
    Or work on the mines at Boulder. (16)

Clearing teams were part of the method by which the wheatbelt was expanded so rapidly. We have seen Goode mention the "Welsh clearers" camped near him, and Facey and his brothers both worked as contract clearers.[27]

The Power Farmer

As well as being a writer who was a first-hand participant in the mass-clearing of the wheatbelt's vegetation, Goode was also an example of a new age of mechanical farming. The paucity of water in the Yilgarn made keeping horses difficult and made powered machinery economical, at least for as long as the high wheat price of the 1920s held. It is a rather different picture of the wheatbelt to that given in Facey's memoir, where even when he returned to take up land as a soldier-settler after the war he still worked the land with a six-horse team.[28] In other writers who we will meet, like James Pollard and J.K. Ewers, there was an active resistance to the encroachment of powered machinery, with its din and clatter contrasted with the serene, primeval intricacies of the horse-drawn age. Later writers such as Peter Cowan and Dorothy Hewett also tend to evoke an image of the wheatbelt that occludes its radical industrialisation. Goode seems to have apprehended that the kind of farming he was now doing was not exactly consistent with the pastoral images of the popular mind. In "The Power Farmer's Soliloquy" he depicts the start of the power farmer's day in a way that is far more suggestive of the factory than the field:

When the roar of an engine and clatter
    Breaks in on your dreams,

Reluctant you rise for its freezing
    In the bare iron camp;
Then go on with the oiling and greasing
    By acetylene lamp.

Ah, the shift will be ten or twelve hours—
    The same as before!
There'll perhaps be "occasional showers,"
    And break-downs galore.
The stumps and the roots in the clearing
    Cause many a jar;
And harsh sound the grind of the gearing
    That echoes afar.[29]

Goode's experience was also not that of a family farm, something that prevailed in spite of the most primitive (even brutal) conditions, in the world described by Facey. The farmers of Goode's Turkey Hill were a "bachelor settlement" and the work they did much closer to that typically associated with prospecting. The men helped each other work their land in the same way that the men clubbed together to work adjoining claims in the prospecting era, so memorably captured in a story like Lawson's "The Loaded Dog". They lived on tinned meat in bare camps, and ameliorated their loneliness by working together or yarning or, on occasion, drinking at each other's camps or on visits to town. The rudiments of this life comes through in the diaries, poems and photographs that we have already seen in this chapter. But for a detailed picture of life on his camp-farm at Turkey Hill we have to turn to the stories that Goode wrote in the 1930s.

Unlike the poetry, it appears that these stories were written mainly after Goode had left his farm at Turkey Hill. He had tried for a couple of months to find work in the district—he worked briefly as a tractor driver—but the Depression was, if anything, still worsening and no one had money to pay workers. With his last £6 he boarded the SS *Karoola* for Melbourne.[30] There, he managed to get 500 copies of his volume *The Grower of Golden Grain* printed, which he then hawked door-to-door, sending copies to every newspaper he could think of. This path to publication left a lot to be desired, particularly in the midst of a severe global depression: "don't try it when one in every six people in the country is out of work."[31] He then took work in country Victoria, in "Kelly country" around Glenrowan, before returning to Western Australia to take up work in a large goldmine at Wiluna. He worked in Wiluna from 1934 to 1939, when the mine started to wind down. These were good years for Goode, in marked contrast with those in the Yilgarn, and he felt a previously unknown financial security and appreciated the social cohesion that factory life offered after the isolated toil of Turkey Hill. He also became a communist, not unusual for a working man of an intellectual bent at the time. It was during the Wiluna years that Goode began to produce short stories that remembered the time at Turkey Hill, and it is from these that we gain a sharper sense of the lived detail of his life, and that of his class of wheatbelt farmer-settlers. These stories appeared in his later collections, *Yarns of the Yilgarn* (1950) and *Stories of Strange Places* (1973).[32]

One of the first of these stories "White Ants: A Tale of the West" depicts a "settler" at his bush camp with details that correspond to those that Goode gives of his own camp at Turkey Hill. Like the "settler" in the poem "The Grower of Golden Grain", this settler has also camped "close to a great upheaval of sprawling conglomerate boulders", but we now get to see this camp in simple prosaic detail:

> The usual camp requisites lie about the inside of the place; bush-bed, kerosene box table and box seats—and more boxes nailed to the crazy walls to hold the settlers [*sic*] few private effects. These consist chiefly of a number of battered volumes—some leather bound—which are somehow strangely reminiscent of more comfortable habitations ... Coming perhaps from a polished book-case in some modern sub-urban home.[33]

The books are the unusual feature of the camp, as the narrator notes, and set up the settler as slightly at odds with his environment. As the settler awakens to his day, he is greeted by butcher-birds chirping happily and "hopping expectantly from the over-arching salmon gums or gimlets, eager to see what this strange invader of their sanctuaries will throw them at breakfast time" (64). The subtle shift to the position of the bird, and how strange this might all look to it, reinforces the sense of this scene being somehow outside the order of nature, and the settler as an alien agency—"this strange invader". Moreover, what might have been the restorative rhythm of this simple life in the woods, is met by the settler with a certain eerie derangement characteristic of the eccentric hermits in Lawson's tales:

> The lone settler rises and stirs the ashes of the galley fire, a little distance from the camp …
>
> The eternal frying-pan is soon sizzling over the flames and after the tinned meat is sufficiently warm, the settler breaks his fast. The butcher birds seem to take a greater interest in the process than he does … fits of abstraction are common to one living in the bushland. (64)

The story is significant because it depicts the settler (in later versions of the story "the man") involved in clearing work, and after breakfast, "he sharpens his axe before setting out to wrestle with the wilderness which rolls in unbroken miles on all sides … trying to carve a home out of the chaos" (65). The narrator provides a commentary on this settler's state of mind, which we learn has taken a melancholy turn, perhaps as a consequence of the essays he is reading by Schopenhauer, or borne down by "his uncongenial toil" (65). In his distraction he does not notice the birds, butcher-birds and magpies, who "sing in their raucous notes and flutter about near him apparently half tame and perfectly unconcerned" (65). These birds provide a cheerful juxtaposition to the grim and distracted settler and set up the story's central dynamic, which is to situate human activity inside the ironic gaze of "nature". The animals in the story exist on a simpler, wiser plane than the hapless humans suffering through their alienated work. It shows an interest in nature that was not evident in Goode's poems nor in the diary, where the only encounter with an animal that is recorded is the shooting of a wedge-tailed eagle, whose hung carcass he also photographed.[34] The birds in the story "White Ants" were interested spectators when he felled a tree or set it alight: "Numbers of little creeping things are then driven from their homes only to be devoured by their more intelligent feathered cousins." Later, when the mail cart visits, it is again described from the point of view of the animal (a horse this time), with the settler once more absent of mind: "The pre-occupied clearer hears neither the rattle of the cart nor the recriminations which its human burdens hurl from time to time at the unfortunate quadruped which hauls them back to the bush." (66)

The story's climax is in fact delivered by this fateful cart in the form of a letter from his girlfriend in the city he had once lived in. The thought that all this work might one day pave the way for their union had sustained him even as his hope has slowly dissolved with each passing day. The letter to "Dear Jimmie" ends:

> At a party the other night, I met a lovely chap … and oh, what a divine dancer. I think I'll marry him. Excuse me ringing off, but he has just blown the tooter of his sports model out in front and I'll have to rush out. It might be just as well if I didn't write again.
>
> Cheri-o.   Babs. (66)

It is not clear whether a more tactful letter from "Babs" would have changed the outcome for Jimmie as his "ambitions, which had almost become obsessions by now, came crashing down around his camp" (66–7). He takes a length of rope and scales a nearby breakaway:

> After adjusting one end of the rope carefully around the stout limb and the other end about his neck, his eyes wander across the awful chaos of scrub for a final admiration of some splashes of crimson fast dying to grey. His eyes seem to hold an expression embodying the sadness of all the ages.
>
> "Ah, Nature! What mockery to flaunt your mysteriously beautiful garments in puny Man's face!"
>
> With this enigmatic remark he steps out into space. (67)

Jimmie does not die, though, but wakes up half an hour later, bruised and confused, gradually realising that the white ants of the story's title had thwarted his suicide. The droll coda to the story functions to partially anaesthetise the aching hopelessness of Jimmie's plight, which in turn must be taken to, in some measure at least, reference Goode's own experience at Turkey Hill.

The theme is taken up again, even more explicitly this time, in "A Matter of Morrels".[35] The story begins with the now-familiar figure of a young settler ("Bill") arriving at his block and feeling a wave of disappointment at seeing what lay ahead of him. The settler has made, it turns out, a fatal mistake by selecting morrel country, rather than the heavier salmon-gum and gimlet country that Goode himself had chosen and which, at least in these early years, proved more resilient. It turns out that Bill "had always been a nature lover" (51) and almost immediately becomes entranced by a praying mantis that fell onto his chest as he stretched out under his makeshift tent for the first time. He notices how well adapted it was to its environment, how utterly its body matched the bark of the pole it had fallen from. Its tiny forearms seemed first to have adopted the attitude of prayer, but on further provocation started to box out frantically, so that Bill christened him "Jack Dempsey":

> Being a stranger to the Eastern wheatbelt, Bill just marked out the hundred acres of bush nearest his camp and started chopping down. In these early stages the relative value of soil covered by different timbers had not been proved, so he could scarcely be blamed for choosing morrel country.
>
> During the dreary routine of these months he spent a lot of his spare time studying the various forms of insect and bird life in the surrounding bush. Writing descriptions of them helped to pass the long and lonely evenings. (52)

In time these descriptions are published as a series of nature articles in "a city journal" written under the pen-name, "The Mantis", and leading him to become known by his neighbours as "Bill the Mantis"—"his long, spare, frame and benign expression making the name peculiarly apt" (52). Bill continued to chop and burn, clearing 100 acres in the first year, followed by another 200 the next, and even though the season was a "howling failure", he pushed to clear 200 more, till within three years he had a total of 500 cleared acres. With a supply of water from a nearby soak he was able to push ahead without the tractors his neighbours were all buying. But, after a good start, the next season was again a failure, particularly for anyone on the looser morrel soil.

With nothing left to lose he tried dynamiting some quartz outcrops on the off-chance they were auriferous. They were not: "Then as a way of using up the last packet of gelignite and of giving expression to his pent-up feelings, he started boring and charging the big, ant-eaten morrells near his camp. After all, he had every reason in the world for hating those accursed trees." (54) But the fuse had "run" and the charge exploded before Bill had time to get clear. When he awoke he was pinned under the tree, not in any great pain, but knowing that his back was broken. As he lay there dying, a praying mantis fell once again onto his chest, first swinging its tiny fists, then bringing them together, apparently praying: "He watched it awhile smilingly, then whispered faintly: 'Ah, that's more appropriate!'" (54) Of all Goode's stories, this is closest to that of his contemporary James Pollard, whose career we will consider in the next chapter. Not only does it document a settler-naturalist of the kind that Pollard had been in the 1920s, but the closing scene, wry but still sentimental, calls upon Nature—exemplified by one of its tiny "denizens"—as the agent of grace. But where Pollard's stories are coy on the obvious and direct

18. "Eagle I shot". Goode's personal photographs courtesy of Cathy Culbard.

relationship between a farm and the bush that it replaces, Goode's story makes no secret of the fact that this nature lover, Bill, is also a thorough and ardent nature destroyer. Whilst it would be too much to say that this story espouses a conservationist ethic—we need to wait for Cowan for that—it is hard to displace the idea that Bill's death is an act of revenge on the part of Nature. And if not revenge, exactly, then certainly there is the same note of mockery that was sounded at the end of "White Ants", where human anguish—even the gross finality of suicide—takes on a slightly ridiculous complexion.

Another story from around this time, "The Power Farmer", was published in the 1935 edition of the rural annual *The Golden West*.[36] The story recollects the Yilgarn wheat adventure of the previous decade, and especially the move to "power farming" in the 1920s, which took off in the Yilgarn at a time when water for horses was harder to obtain than credit for machinery. There had been talk of water being piped up from the main goldfields line, but this had yet to materialise, and "owing to the water being delayed so long, nearly everyone was going in for tractors" (30). The central figure in this story is not, this time, a young settler loosely modelled on the author, but a man who in his 60s, stood out against the youthful cohort of Yilgarn settlers, and who seems to be at least in part modelled on Goode's father. When *Yarns of the Yilgarn* was published in 1950, Goode dedicated the book to "my Father Henry Francis Goode, Pioneer of Three Australian States". Like his father, the veteran farmer in Goode's story had farmed in both New South Wales and Victoria. In the story, "The Old Man" (as he was known) had mortgaged a failing farm over East and "decided to try his luck in the new wheat areas of Westralia" (28). His habit of constantly referring every experience in the Yilgarn to these other places was the source of both mirth and solace to the younger men around him:

> The "old hands" of that settlement will remember the "Old Man's" peans [*sic*] of praise about the fertility of the newly cleared paddocks.
>
> "It's equal to the richest soils I've seen in New South Wales and Victoria!" he often remarked … "I had a place in the Northern Wimmera once and I maintain that we could grow similar crops here if we employ the right fallowing methods." (29)

At the Old Man's purchase of a new-fangled tractor, his younger colleagues were able to gain a measure of revenge as, flummoxed, he needed to again and again call for their help to get his machine working. In the background we see the fateful procession of years that had led Goode and others to ruin. The "wonderful harvest" of 1927 that had put the Yilgarn "on the map", although "we all regretted that the areas under crop were so small—mostly under a hundred acres" (29). Followed, then, by the drought years of 1928 and 1929, before the whole game was ended by the collapse of prices in 1930. The humour of the story, and the pathos, derives from watching this man—a pioneer of three states—humbled by this wretched machine sold to him, by one of the many eager salesman trawling the area, as "a hundred years ahead of anything else on the market" (30). In due course, the tractor arrived at the siding, "freshly painted and with a suggestion of sinister power about it" (31). The machine transformed the Old Man's camp into a chaos of broken and spare parts, old copies of *Power Farmer* magazine, bills for oil and other signs of the dominance the tractor had now assumed in the farmer's life. The story casts the arrangement in Faustian terms: "For several months the 'Old Man' looked upon the roaring monster with a feeling akin to awe." (31) The mixture of pride and frustration caused by the machine is described with mild comedy, as the man struggles to start the tractor each morning and bears the mounting costs of repeated breakdowns. Lending an urgency to the narrative is the continual deferral by the Old Man of a trip back east to see his family. Eventually, the other men club together enough money to buy him a trip home and he reluctantly accedes. By now the markets had turned and the settlers were, more or less, all waiting to be wound up. The departure of the Old Man seemed to signal the end, and it emerges that he had, for all the jibing, been something of a talisman:

> For a couple of years there had been a kind of belief lurking in our minds that, when he went, it would be time for all of us to pack up. So it caused some surprise when he landed back from Perth and talked about "giving it another fly." (32)

Like many of Goode's stories, this one ends with a macabre twist. On the autumn day when the Old Man was due to start work with his tractor, his younger friends decide to see how he is getting along. They were surprised to find the tractor stationary in the middle of a field, but with its engine "roaring away" (33). The Old Man lay dead on his cherished fallow several yards from the tractor's engine, killed either from the exertion of cranking the handle or, as one of the onlookers suggests, from the shock of it starting first-time.

The "Power Farmer" is written in the mode of the stories of Henry Lawson, who took his style from Bret Harte and Kipling. Lawson's genius was to balance his stories evenly between satire and something more profound, something that escapes the mitigation offered by the humour—a muted horror in the face of a man disintegrating at the edge of civilisation. This is what gives Lawson his modernist edge and situates him, like Joseph Conrad, as a transitional figure in the newer, bleaker sensibility that would take hold in the twentieth century. Goode's stories fall short of Lawson's—hardly a criticism— but share his laconic power. The "Power Farmer" also makes use of the technique favoured by Lawson (in a story like "The Union Buries Its Dead") where the events are narrated by an unnamed member of the community in which the events transpire. This narrator acts then as a kind of spokesman—a social "voice" akin to the classical Greek chorus—who is able to mobilise a double sympathy for both the tragic figure (the "Old Man") and those who have to persist without him. In this way, the lonely death of an old man in an empty field (or, in Lawson's story, an itinerant worker drowned in a billabong) is recouped on behalf of those around, who have now become, in a sense that is both simple and profound, survivors.

The major difference between Lawson's world and Goode's is that Lawson, even in his famous journey from Bourke to Hungerford in the drought of the early 1890s, never seems to have imagined the dilapidated back-blocks could actually disappear or revert to wilderness. In this way, Goode's story of "The Power Farmer" is emblematic, not just of life on the western wheatbelt, but of a deeper conflict with nature, in which nature is both the victim and uncanny judge of human hubris. The irony it dramatises is the fact that the man who emblematises pioneering freedom had ended his life enslaved by an uncaring machine. In this sense, the wheatbelt itself takes on the first blush of a complexion it would acquire at the close of the twentieth century; not the patchwork of yeoman farms serenely placed outside the hectic cares of modernity, but the extension of industrialised modernity into the sacramental task of growing food. In Goode's story, the tractor does, for the most part, remain just an instrument, playing the role that stubborn animals have played in similar tales. But in its "sinister power" and particularly the eerie final image, where it continues to roar in the empty field with its erstwhile driver dead beside it, Goode insinuates into his "yarn" a spectre that will haunt future wheatbelt literature. The Old Man, for his part, represented the wheatbelt in positive form, the fact that it was not entirely novel and had been tried successfully in other parts of Australia: "We all liked the Old Man. A yarn with him was a tonic to cure our attack of morbid discontent. Right through, he 'maintained' that the place had a great future." (30) The Old Man hovers towards a status—the status of tragedy—that the wheatbelt would not fully occupy until the work of Dorothy Hewett in the second half of the twentieth century.

Goode's stories, written in retrospect, even though only by a few years, offer a closer picture of his life at Turkey Hill than the earlier poems. It is a picture corroborated in the diary, albeit in a rawer, more impressionistic form. The stories are written by a more mature man—Goode was now in his mid-twenties—than the one who was enduring the difficulties, uncertainties and disappointments of Turkey Hill. Many of his stories re-tell, from only slightly different angles, the experience of those years, and seem to produce an ever-clearer picture of a time that was, despite a façade of good cheer, almost unbearably chaotic for Goode. One of the more poignant accounts takes place in "Making Adjustments (A Character Sketch)", which is to all intents and purposes a memoir and the "character" in question—Jason Smith—a version of Goode himself.[37] The major difference is that Jason takes a wife, a good woman, who supports him through the difficulties that mount in the end to the point that the farm is lost. Unlike the other stories, this one has neither a patina of grim humour nor a sudden twist in its tail. Instead, it recalls with a calm fatalism the passage of Jason Smith through the Yilgarn, from the granting of 1,000 acres of second-class land to the winding up of the farm seven years later. We see him ride the 25 kilometres through unmarked bush tracks to his property on a bicycle in the hot sun, and

chased into a tree by dingoes on the trip back to town. He returned
to pitch his tent, where he would live for several months, before he
could build a humpy out of saplings and superphosphate bags that
constituted the more permanent housing of the settlers at this time:

> Then the real struggle began … months and months of chopping
> down and then more trying months of burning off, carting water from
> native soaks called 'gnamma holes,' and, when they dried up, bringing
> it from the stand-pipe at the siding; seeing no one all the week and
> living on tinned foods only.
>
> …
>
> After a while he found the lonely life was driving him mad. Not
> merely talking to himself—that is nothing—most people in the bush
> yarn away to themselves; but to take both sides in an argument and
> always defeat oneself, is going too far. (37)

Fortunately for Jason—Goode himself was not so lucky—he was
rescued by his new wife, who kept his spirits up even though the
promised prosperity never quite came:

> Followed four or five years of chopping down and burning up …
> and no holidays either! One good season [i.e. 1927] had brought the
> district into prominence and everyone seemed to be talking about
> it. The "Western Review" of the time broke into lengthy eulogies
> about "Prosperous Yilgarn" and the "extraordinary crops." It ended
> one article by saying: "The Yilgarn crops are superb. It is doubtful if
> any district in the State has ever been able to show such magnificent,
> uniform crops. The Agricultural Bank inspector who handles the
> north side of the main line expects the average yield for his district to
> exceed twenty bushels per acre."
>
> Other journals spoke glowingly about the "iron horses of the
> man on the land" and among other puerilities stated: "The Yilgarn
> district is being chiefly developed by tractor power for which the land
> is admirably suited." (38–9)

When the next good season finally arrived in 1929–30, the price, of
course, had collapsed and Jason brought off "over four thousand bags

of wheat at quarter the previous year's price." By this stage, Yilgarn wheat was costing 4 shillings per bushel to produce and fetching less than two at market. The story ends with Jason announcing to his wife that they had to walk off the farm, but that this was just one more "adjustment" and life was all about adjusting. The story seems to acknowledge, too, that the final truth of the time might never be captured—missed both in the adversity of the first instance and then, again, in the perversity of the recollection:

> Time and that unconscious poetic fancy which we all possess seemed to invest those times with a veil of romance. In looking back across the arch of years at his hard experiences, the setting seemed more glamorous ... an elusive beauty entwining itself into recollections of things that in the long ago seemed too prosaic for a second thought. (40)

Goode, indeed, did continue to make adjustments in his life, eventually turning away from the "land" that had always been at the heart of his father's wishes. During his five years at the large goldmine at Wiluna, Goode met Jessie Morrison, who was nursing there. The two were married in Melbourne in 1940. Goode had been rejected for military service due to dust on the lungs, a legacy of the underground mining at Wiluna. He was manpowered to work at the Government Ordnance Factory in Maribyrnong which manufactured high explosive munitions for the war effort. He stayed there until 1947, when he moved to work on the turbines at the Spencer Street Power Station, where he worked for the next twenty-five years until his retirement in 1972. He passed away ten years later, in 1982. Goode continued to write throughout his life, with little overall recognition. During the war years he managed to publish a collection of his verse, including several poems from his earlier volumes, under the title *The Bridge Party at Boyanup* (1944). In 1950 he launched an ambitious venture to start an annual series called "Western Yarns" that would meet the contemporary interest in American pulp western novels and tales, but with Australian content: *"That there is a market here for this type of adventure magazine is evidenced by the twenty or thirty American 'westerns' appearing regularly on our bookstalls ... many of them written by Australians who have never been out of their own country!*" Goode financed the printing of 5,000 copies of the magazine, complete with advertisements for radios, bicycle tyres and fountain pens. In the end he managed to sell 2,000 copies and at least break even. The first issue was called "Yarns of the Yilgarn" and was entirely comprised of stories by Goode, all from his Turkey Hill years. Subsequent issues were expected to be made up of stories by different authors, but in the end there were no subsequent issues of the magazine. Significantly, Goode also saw his set of stories—"along with writers like Katherine [*sic*] Prichard, Gavin Casey, John K. Ewers and Peter Cowan"—as "creating a literature of Western Australia". Although the claim is part of a puff for the publication of *Yarns of the Yilgarn*, it is significant that Goode was reading both Ewers and Cowan by this time. Nor was it entirely without foundation to push the claim that bit further and suggest that what "London and Service did for the Yukon and Harte did for early California, this little band of writers is doing for our own romantic West." Though it is also true that Cowan, at least, would have cringed at this characterisation.

The salutary facts of Goode's life indicate a short-but-intense intersection with the history of the wheatbelt, just seven years in a life that spanned seven-and-a-half decades. Goode's continual return to those years is not so unusual in the sense that people often do return to their formative years in their writing and reminiscences. Goode was eighteen when he arrived at Turkey Hill and twenty-five when he left. The years there seem to have permanently marked him, leaving a scar that is akin to that left by a war. But, equally, Goode left his own mark on the Yilgarn. His farm at Turkey Hill is still the edge of the wheatbelt. It did not revert to station country or get "swallowed up" again by the bush, as people ruefully suspected would happen when they walked off their farms in the early 1930s. Nor did subsequent generations push out any further, even when high prices and new agricultural science drove further expansions, especially in the south through Ravensthorpe to Esperance and beyond. Goode's life at Turkey Hill is thus signed into the landscape in graphic fashion. Even after he slowly melted back into a typical post-war suburban life in Melbourne, the land remained etched with his effort. It lends a certain piquancy to a brief reflection from his story "The Power

Farmer": "How the place had changed. One could see for miles in every direction. When we had first taken up our blocks there was no such thing as a 'skyline' – just the nearer dark green bush." (33)

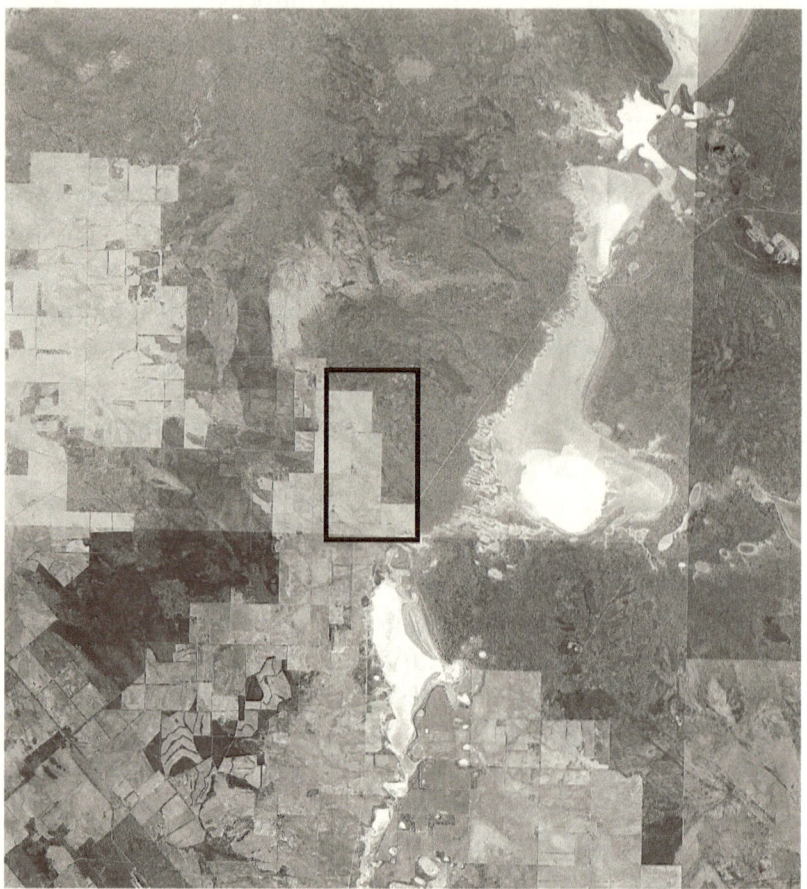

19. Turkey Hill in the Yilgarn, 2013. LandSat photograph supplied by Landgate (WA).

Chapter Three

James Pollard (1900–1971)
Calingiri (1918–24)
Babakin (1924–27)

James Pollard was born in Yorkshire in 1900, six years after Facey, and seven years before Cyril Goode. In 1910 his father, also James, migrated to Western Australia in the hope that the climate might improve his health. He worked initially in Bridgetown and then in an orchard near Mount Barker in the Great Southern region. There, with a friend, James Senior obtained a contract to clear land. The family joined the father in 1913 and Pollard, fourteen at this time, assisted in the clearing work. The conditions in rural Western Australia were primitive, as we have already seen in the lives of Goode and Facey. The Pollard family camped in tents, drew their water from a nearby stream and cooked over an open fire. Pollard then found work caring for a farm near Katanning before enlisting in the AIF in 1916. After the war, he took up land as part of the soldiers' settlement scheme, which sent over 5,000 men into the wheatbelt to start farms.[1] He spent nine years in the wheatbelt, from 1918 to 1927, where he wrote both a popular nature column for the *West Australian* newspaper, and a series of "Bushland" romances, that were partially set in the wheatbelt. The "Bushland" trilogy of novels—*The Bushland Man* (1926), *Rose of the Bushlands* (1927) and *Bushland Vagabonds* (1928)—were published by Hodder & Stoughton in London. This alone makes Pollard a significant Western Australian writer and one of the first to publish overseas. Moreover, his writing contains the first sustained literary treatment of Western Australian rural life and the natural world in this region.[2]

As a literary witness to the wheatbelt, Pollard's experience of soldier-settlement, which we can glimpse through his fiction, makes a useful counterpoint to Facey. When James Pollard died in 1971, his younger sister, Alice Powell, recalled in a letter the circumstances surrounding his enlistment in the AIF in 1916. The letter, found in Pollard's papers in the Battye Library, is headed, "My Brother, James Harvey Theodore Pollard, Jr., An Unsung Hero":

> I know this won't be published but will swear in front of the highest judge this is true. By this time the war had broken out. Then is when we're all so true to our mother country, and everyone was at a fever pitch. Recruiting mass meetings everywhere and the Girls B____ Stupid (forgive the language but I idolised my brother) handing out – thinking they were so clever – white feathers to the boys. At this time Jim (an idealist all his life) only 16½ found a white feather under his [pillow].[3]

Pollard served with the 51st battalion of the AIF in the Third Battle of Ypres, also known as the Battle of Passchendaele, which lasted from June to November of 1917. In this archetype of attritional warfare, the British forces succeeded, at the cost of 140,000 of their soldiers, in capturing roughly 8 kilometres of marshy land and control of the Flemish village of Passchendaele. The very same land was regained by the Germans, without resistance, five months later. Pollard was severely wounded in these hostilities. He suffered a bullet wound in his left shoulder and lung damage as a consequence of poison gas. A piece of shrapnel was also lodged into his neck. Unsurprisingly, his convalescence was protracted. Even after being discharged from Lemnos Military Hospital (in Perth) the shoulder wound remained open and required continuous re-dressing when Pollard returned to his father's home, now in Wongan Hills in the inner wheatbelt. As with Facey, the injuries precluded Pollard from most of the work he had done before the war. His sister recalled that he was unable to do any heavy lifting and indeed that she had been drafted in to be the "rouseabout" in his stead. After his discharge from the army on 27 May 1918, Pollard was granted land at Calingiri in the Victoria Plains under the soldiers' settlement scheme.[4]

It was at Calingiri in 1922 that Pollard started publishing in *The Listening Post*, the official newspaper of the Western Australian branch of the RSSILA (now RSL). He produced a series of vivid, even shocking, accounts of life in the trenches. The most startling of these, "Annihilation's Waste" (1923), described the impressions and thoughts of "Johnnie", a young messenger moving between the advancing front and the command centre several kilometres behind.

> The waste of life was appalling, and where many would have hurried along, afraid to see, Johnnie traveled slowly, calmly, for there was nothing there, to him, in any way appalling … Dead men, literally in hundreds and thousands, were sown over this field of stagnation; and Johnnie sought vainly for the answer to a question which mocked his ears as he walked: "What shall the harvest be?"[5]

20. James Pollard. State Library of Victoria.

The story ends with Johnnie watching a labour battalion engaged in the task of "cleaning up" the battlefield, in particular burying the dead men and horses. Watching this grim task Johnnie hears "a haunting, murmuring whisper coming from the far-away: '*Will they ever catch up? … Will they ever catch up?*'." Pollard's sketches for *The Listening Post* pushed the boundaries of tolerated directness in their post-traumatic readership. "Annihilation's Waste" (the title comes from the *Rubaiyat*) contained a warning from the editor about its graphic nature. But the magazine's editor also wrote and thanked

21. *The Listening Post*, 2 April 1922.

Pollard for his contributions by saying how his writings "portray a very faithful picture of trench life, and bring back to diggers memories of old time experiences."[6] The word "old" here betrays the need to push what were in fact quite recent experiences into a more distant past.

Pollard worked the farm at Calingiri, with his father, for six years from 1918 until 1924. Eventually, though, Pollard concluded that he "was not cut out to be a farmer".[7] No doubt his war injuries played a part, his gas-damaged lungs and the bullet and shrapnel wounds. He also, it is clear, suffered from "exhaustion", and that range of effects that this term covered at the time, and which in a later era we would not hesitate to name post-traumatic stress disorder. It is worth remembering that when Pollard was invalided out of the AIF in 1918, he was still three weeks shy of his eighteenth birthday.[8] In 1924, Pollard relinquished his farm at Calingiri, in the relatively well-settled mixed farms of the Victoria Plains, and moved to Babakin near Bruce Rock along the corridor of new farms opened up by the Narrogin–Merredin rail-line that Facey had helped build before the war. Pollard's father had set up a wheat-agency in Babakin and Pollard joined him there.[9] He stayed for three years until—"tiring of bush-life"—he moved to Perth in 1927. He lived initially in West Leederville, then in Kalamunda, before moving, ultimately, to Cottesloe. There he lived for the remainder of his life, except for a period in Darwin during World War Two.

"Denizens of the Bush"

In 1923, while still at Calingiri, Pollard commenced his popular weekly nature column, "Denizens of the Bush" for the *West Australian* newspaper. Pollard had developed, in the years after returning from the war, a deep interest in local flora and fauna and had become an accomplished amateur naturalist. "Denizens of the Bush", which Pollard wrote under the *nom de plume* "Mo'poke", ran in the *West* from 1923 to 1937. The column, often just a few short paragraphs, fostered an interest in native animal and plant species that proved popular and sustained. The significance of the column lay in the manner that it mediated amateur observation and expert opinion. The column contained the author's own observations of the natural world—insects, birds, animals, plants—and reproduced those of readers, who were encouraged to write to Mo'poke, care of the newspaper, with questions and comments. The column was written in an often playful style, where the native creatures discussed were like characters in children's stories. Nevertheless, nature for Pollard had a distinctly spiritual quality in which he found solace, particularly in the wake of his experience in the Great War. In 1927 he wrote that he had been "moulded … in the bushland close to Nature's heart" and that this had imbued him with "an instinct to seek for the best and the most beautiful in Nature."[10]

Pollard's career points to the coincidence of popular nature study with the clearing of the southwest for agriculture, and the founding of the wheatbelt. This is something we have already glimpsed in untutored form in Facey, and the more literate Goode, whose later stories feature the farmer-naturalist on several occasions. Pollard's column shows the widespread nature of this phenomenon. From its beginning in 1923, Pollard's column quickly drew a stream of letters from readers who offered further observations, questions and clarifications. Thus, from 10 January 1927:

> Mr D.F. Petek of Moore River says he has never seen me refer to "that useful and harmless bird, the kite." I think I have at times mentioned the kites, usually when discussing other hawks, but not to any extent. "I hope you will give these birds a good word in your notes," says Mr. Petek. I have a fair knowledge of the smaller kind and have never seen it molest any bird. My friend says the bird is too often confused with those hawks that prey on chickens and the small birds of the bush.

Or, from the same column:

> "J.S." (Merredin) awakes a new interest in writing of trees. "Why is it," he asks, "that in grassy timber country the grass does not grow close up to the white gums? In the red gum and jarrah country you find the grass growing so close to the trees that it frequently hides the butts … But when you look at white gums, you find a space for a yard or so around the tree quite bare."

Mo'poke's response in this case was simply: "I don't know. But I should like to know, so perhaps some botanical friend will volunteer an explanation." In this way the column became a forum for the exchange of information concerning natural history. The column can be seen in the context of other movements towards amateur field observation during this time—and Pollard joined each in succession—such as The Naturalist's Club, the Royal Australian Ornithologist's Union (RAOU) and the Gould League.

Partly through these organisations, Pollard developed a network of expert associates to whom he would refer enquiries. In his column, from 8 October 1927 he reports being sent a flower specimen from "Erdna" in Marvel Loch on the eastern fringe of the wheatbelt and, not knowing the flower, takes it to Charles A. Gardner, who identified it as *Lachnosineys dempsteri* (not, as Erdna had suspected, a form of flannel flower). Gardner was then an assistant botanist at the Department of Agriculture, but was promoted in the following year to the position of Government Botanist and Curator of the State Herbarium. Pollard also wrote frequently to Leslie J. Newman, Government entomologist with the Department of Agriculture from 1918 till his death in 1938, and to Ernest Le Souef, founding director (1897–1932) of the Perth Zoological Gardens. The latter, the middle of the three remarkable Le Souef brothers who dominated zoological collections in three states, wrote to Pollard in 1924 regarding a reader's conviction that swallows have been seen to hibernate in the winter. Le Souef felt that this was unlikely, as nowhere else were birds known to hibernate, but that nature is prone to spring surprises and overturn one's most treasured views: "I am sorry I am not able to give you anything definite on the subject which you ask, but the older one grows the more one shrinks from giving a positive opinion about anything of this nature."[11] Pollard's particular passion was for birds and he commonly turned for advice to Dominic Serventy (1904–1988), the seminal figure in Western Australian ornithology. Serventy was one of the few naturalists to develop an international reputation, and yet remain in Western Australia. Serventy was also, in the late 1920s, the Honorary Secretary of the Naturalist's Club and had nominated Pollard for membership to the RAOU.

As well as featuring responses to letters in his column, Pollard maintained an active private correspondence with his readers, debating the finer points of animal behaviour. One of his early correspondents was Bruce W. Leake, a noted pioneer of the Kellerberrin district, and long-time amateur naturalist, who wrote to Pollard on 3 September 1923 concerning the habits of the pipit (ground-lark):

> Your letter of the 27th to hand. I have been very interested in your articles, and am still of the opinion that what I wrote is quite correct.
>
> In regard to the Pipit's eggs, of course these vary a good lot, but they are always almost an inch in length, and thickly marked with spots. The nest is built in a depression in the ground ... [12]

A J.W.H. of Manjimup writes on 24 April 1924 to Mo'poke that he reads "Denizens of the Bush" with considerable interest and that "some people tell me that they regard it as the most interesting column in the paper."[13] W. Matson of East Wagin responds in a letter from 25 February 1924 to a column about black cockatoos:

> ... Well I have one here. He is now over two years old and is talking well. I was told that they could not be reared, but this one is in good health and looks good enough to live for a long time yet. I let him run about the yard all day too, and put him to bed in a box at night.[14]

Matson goes on to note that in clearing the salmon-gums from his property he invariably found a "young one" in each tree he cut down. This detail, presented as incidental, is a reminder of the close connection between clearing land and observing animals. Pollard continued to write "Denizens of the Bush" until 1937, as well as publishing articles in periodicals such as *The Australasian* and the Western Australian annual, *The Golden West*.[15]

In the mid-1920s, a separate correspondence, also concerned with nature but on very different terms, emerged between Pollard and an H. Mervyn Jones. Jones first wrote to Pollard early in 1925, after overhearing his name on a Perth tram.[16] Taking this chance unveiling of Mo'poke to be a favourable omen, he ventured to write to Pollard directly. Jones confesses that he is "English, Homesick and a Book and Nature lover" and that he hoped, without quite knowing why, to have found a kindred spirit in the man who wrote each week as Mo'poke. "I imagine you like 'Thoreau'," he writes, "your writings bring

'Walden' back to me." He then urges Pollard to help him understand the Australian bush, which feels alien to him and so distant from the English countryside of his youth. He longed "to have the Australian bush introduced to one. I just fear it now." He continues: "Why do I fear the bush? It's rather difficult to explain just why. To me the bush is strange and unfriendly. I am an alien. The unseen spirits know one not. I feel utterly alone. I need a bush lover to introduce one."[17] The tone of Jones's letters changes when he discovers that Pollard is many years his junior. Solicitousness gives way to a wry mixture of melancholy and ennui in which Jones apostrophises Pollard as "Youth", beginning one letter, "Dear 'Youth' in the Bush" and signing it, "from 'Age' in the City."[18] It is not possible to overlook the distinctly homoerotic complexion of the correspondence. Pollard and, especially Jones, have recourse to a certain code of the period by which these affections were, in part at least, sublimated; namely, the imaginary world of fairies. This language of fairies had been given enduring form by the phenomenal success of J.M. Barrie's play, *Peter Pan*, first performed in the Christmas pantomime season of 1904. Indeed, Jones writes on New Year's Day of 1926 of seeing and very much enjoying the 1924 silent-film adaptation of *Peter Pan* in a Perth picture house.

In an earlier letter (15 November 1925), Jones wrote to Pollard: "So you saw Fairies at Kalamunda. In such a night and in good company it would be dull indeed not to see Fairies. Oh 'Youth' no one knows better than I the Glamour of the Moon, Titania, Oberon and all the

22. Sydney Long, *Spirit of the Plains*, 1897, oil on canvas on wood, 62 × 131.4 cm, Queensland Art Gallery, Brisbane.

following Queen Mab and Robin, Elvin Gnomes and Brownies. I know them all." Pollard tells Jones: "You write comforting words in every letter, and your earnestness is a thing pleasing to me, who finds so few people earnest."[19] Jones, for his part, is often beset with an acute sense of his own failure, embarrassed by his agedness as well as his infantilism, and asks that the correspondence be kept confidential: "Please never discuss 'old Jones' with anyone."[20] At other times he pleads desperately for letters: "Please write to me any old way that suits you. So long as it gives you pleasure to write, it will give me pleasure to read. I often have bad moods and black moods, but while I can keep the Peter Pan alive, I am fairly safe and sound."[21] Jones clearly idealises Pollard, investing him with the deepest hopes of humanity: "While we have young men with poetry in their souls to write Fairy Tales and Nature Studies there is hope for the coming generation."[22]

The letters from Jones also offer an insight into Pollard's writing for children. Generations of Western Australian school students were introduced to Pollard's writing through the numerous nature stories and sketches he contributed to the Education Department's monthly *Our Rural Magazine* (1920–51), which was sent to every correspondent student and country school in the state. On 3 January 1929 J.M. Drew, Minister of Education under the Collier Labor government, wrote to thank Pollard for contributing to the love of nature in children:

> It seems to me that these articles should do much to stimulate inquiry and to encourage the children to take a sympathetic interest in the native plants and animals of their own districts. In a new country like ours the field of research is boundless, and to awaken in the child a desire to investigate the wonders about him is to start him upon a task that must yield rich returns in both pleasure and knowledge.[23]

Drew, as journalist and politician, had long advocated close settlement, especially in his tenure as Minister for Lands (1904–05) and Minister for Agriculture (1905). In June of the following year, Clarence Eakins, the Head of Correspondence Classes, wrote to Pollard:

> Of all our nature writers you are, I believe, the most popular with the children, and I sincerely hope you will find it convenient to continue

to help us. My immediate chief, Senior Inspector Miles, has desired me on the first opportunity to tell you how greatly he esteems what you are doing for our school. Our magazine is now playing an important role in our education scheme and is greatly appreciated not only by correspondence pupils, but in schools also. The circulation is now 10,000 and its remarkable success is due to the generous assistance that has been forthcoming from my big list of helpers.[24]

Pollard's ability to connect children to nature through his stories and sketches did not go unnoticed beyond the Nullarbor. In 1940, T.L. Harris, the editor of *The School Magazine* (first published in 1916) in NSW asked for permission to publish—"How Birds are Useful to Men"—suggesting that if he could do so they "would be doing something for the cause of the birds and the Gould League in this State."[25] Harris confides that "for a long time I have read with enjoyment the nature study articles" published in *Our Rural Magazine*: "You attack the subject in such an original and interesting way that I am sure they are popular with children."

It seems that part of Pollard's particular popularity with students and teachers was that he maintained the sentience of animals without a direct appeal to fairytale folklore. His animals were thus a mixture of scientific fact and anthropomorphic projection. In Pollard's story, "When Wings Make Magic", published in *The School Magazine* in March 1948, the viewpoint shifts subtly between the two young children who discover "a lady leaf insect" and the insect herself, "Poda."[26] Poda is caught and consumed in the end by "Ophian ... a beautiful lady wasp, a slender, graceful creature who, with her slim legs dazzling and her gauzy wings reflecting the sunlight, seemed like a fay in the sunny air." The crucial distinction here is between sentient animals beholden to the laws of science—wasps do indeed use the paralysed bodies of insects to incubate their young—and creatures, such as May Gibbs's gum-blossom babies, who are the avatars of fairies and act accordingly. Indeed, the tide turned against fairies in the 1930s and by the 1940s, Doris Chadwick, editor of *The School Magazine*, found it necessary to inform her contributors that: "We have found that many children nowadays do not like fairy stories, but prefer stories with keen

—Drawn by JOHN ANDREWS.

Ophion Pursues Foda.

[Drawn by W. M. ROLLAND.

23. Illustrations from Pollard's children's stories.

human interest. Stories about animals, either natural or humanized, are suitable if they are really well written. Inanimate objects do not often provide interesting subjects."[27] This didactic strain in Pollard's writing, where he sought to educate the reader both scientifically and sentimentally, was something that also carried over into his writing for adults.

The Bushland Man (1926)

At the same time Pollard was writing his nature column for the *West Australian*, he was also writing novels. The "Bushland" trilogy was written at the farms in Calingiri and Babakin and brought out by Hodder & Stoughton—leading publishers of popular romantic fiction in the early part of the twentieth century, who published the likes of John Buchan, Edgar Wallace, Baroness Orczy and the westerns of Zane Gray. It was with the latter that Pollard was most closely aligned, at least from the publisher's view, and in the mind of an English readership. Pollard's novels were not written in the rollicking style that characterised pre-war adventure romance, but in a more measured, reflective register. Hodder & Stoughton were also the British publishers of the American nature writer and novelist, Gene Stratton-Porter, one of the key influences on Pollard's writing.[28] Stratton-Porter was immensely popular in the early part of the twentieth century, writing "nature novels" that blended romantic adventure with detailed botanical and zoological descriptions and drawings. Pollard took from Stratton-Porter this combination of romance and amateur naturalism.

In *The Bushland Man* we see the wheatbelt for the first time in the pages of a novel, albeit at the edges of the action. *The Bushland Man* is centred on Pete Rodon (the "Bushland Man") employed as a "ranger" to protect the timber in a parcel of land owned by the Western Stock Company. The land is in the fictional locality of Binrinni, which in name and other respects appears to allude to the Calingiri that Pollard lived in at the time he wrote the novel. There are farms in the region as well as bushland. Rodon's job was to live on the Company's property and to make sure that no one logged it, or set fires that might endanger the wood. The arrangement seems, in historical terms, an odd one, and so too does the expression "ranger".

Little distinct value was ever placed on the timber of the wheatbelt woodlands, except for immediate local use. No one would ever think to guard it. Essentially, everyone had their own stands of timber, and the main problem was trying to get rid of it, so the land could be put to more productive use. The scenario of the ranger employed to "guard" the wood demonstrates the direct debt that Pollard had to Stratton-Porter, and particularly to her famous novel *Freckles* (1904), where the titular hero is given custodianship of the Limberlost forest of central Indiana owned by a certain Grand Rapids Lumber Company.[29] The "Freckles" of Stratton-Porter's book was a classically picaresque character, a plucky invalid (he had only one hand and was not much larger than a child) who proved his worth to the world in spite of adversity. Stratton-Porter's novel was also picaresque in the sense of it proceeding by a series of incidents, a little in the manner of *Huckleberry Finn* or, indeed, the early chapters of *A Fortunate Life*. Pollard's hero, Pete Rodon, was not outwardly disabled, although he does in the course of the novel undergo grave injury, hospitalisation, and prolonged convalescence. Rodon had the solitude and the laconic habits of the typical bush hero of this era, but lacked the central trait of wit that typified the *Bulletin* tradition. Pollard's novels are almost impossibly earnest and it is in this, as much as the direct evasions of the subject, that one can hear the deafening silence of the Great War resounding through Rodon's otherwise idyllic life. It is likely for this reason, too, that the novel seems almost deliberately depleted of history so that one cannot place it very easily in time, except that it appears to take place in the present (the early 1920s).

The novel commences with an encounter between Pete Rodon and Rene Neil. Rene is accompanied by Dick, the son of a local Binrinni farming family, the Stroners, and their meeting is used to establish an important contrast the novel wants us to understand between the "bush" and the "land". Pete is protecting the natural woodland (the "bush"), if only for later exploitation, while the surrounding wheatbelt settler-farmers are "on the land". In this novel, the farmers are *on* the land, but Pete is *of* the bush:

> He had lived so long in the bush that something of its mystery had grown upon him, and a part of himself he had given to the bush. The

strange secretiveness of the forest was his, and its quiet; and the forlorn
loneliness of the plains had influenced him so that often he was wistful
and humble of soul. His moods varied as the moods of the bush varied.
The land had the power to call him. (49)

The point is drawn out by a comparison between the affable and
honest farmer Dick Stroner, and the lean, spare Pete Rodon: "Dick
Stroner was perfectly agreeable. He worked hard, early and late, on
his farm, and saw little of the real bush. And Pete Rodon, whose
nights and days were spent in the virgin lands, was a man whom he
admired" (11–12). It is striking in this novel that the rapidly emerging
farms of the wheatbelt are cast decisively on the other side of nature.
We saw no real consciousness of this in Facey. Even the urbane Cyril
Goode, who in a story like "White Ants" had pitted the settler against
a fickle and ironic nature, stopped short of seeing the wheatbelt as
the enemy of nature. In Pollard, the conflict between nature and
man is played out socially in Pete's interactions with others, and also
internally as a conflict within Pete himself. The key word in almost
every description of Pete is "natural", where the word is used to
contrast Pete's character with the affectations of false human society.
Indeed, even Pete's inarticulacy and social phobia are signs of his
naturalness: "He had failings surely, as every man had, but they were
a man's failings, natural failings—he was a natural man" (145). Pete's
quiet vitality is also addressed by reference to his horse "Tess" and his
dog "Flyer", who function as alter egos of the hero:

> Pete studied [Rene] as she looked down at the dog. She leaned forward,
> her hands tense on the reins. Her face was slightly flushed.
>
> "The savage!" she whispered, then relaxed, and her colour deepened.
> She turned to him. "I could love him! He's magnificent! Yet he's
> natural," she continued more slowly. "He belongs here." Her gesture
> took in the whole wide virgin bush. (29)

Later, when Pete is camping in the deep Karri forests of the
southwest, he knows instinctively that he must hobble his beloved
horse in such a wild and atavistic environment: "Tess was a horse
who would soon revert to the primitive; there was that in her nature,

in her blood, that was always the beckoning of the silent, invisible, indefinable, yet powerful forces of the wild" (281). In the continuous invocation of Pete's affinity to the wild, the natural and the untamed, he is shown to be outside the encroaching social proprieties of the wheat farms of Binrinni. He helps the farmers from time to time but is not bound by their incessant worries, and monotonous drudgery. His mind is not weighed down by the endless fretting over wheat prices and new equipment.

The romance between Pete and Rene is also refracted through the opposition of pure nature and false human conventions. Rene is a city girl, and is brought into the country by the Stroners during one of her holidays. At Binrinni, she is captivated by rural life, and loves to ride horses and to spend time in the company of a different variety of man—Dick, Pete—to that she meets in the city. Like Pete, though, she is placed on the side of nature and experiences the upwelling of nature's "forces" as a result of her encounter with Pete: "She felt that strange forces were coming into her life, forces she was powerless to arrest, and she had no desire to stay them; and she felt that they were bringing big changes for her" (72). For his part, Pete, though enchanted by Rene, does not want to surrender his manly life in the forest with his horse, his dog, his camp fire and tent. He scorns the settled life of the farmers and their endless toil and worry. Yet he is also painfully conscious that he has nothing to offer Rene, that even if she did love him and he her, he had not made anything of himself, and could provide nothing for her were they to marry. The impasse is resolved through the appearance of an antagonist, Dake Maxton, whom a contemporary reviewer described as "a thoroughly 'bad man' of the American type."[30] Maxton is also from a Binrinni farming family, and when he sets his sights on Rene it exacerbates a pre-existing rivalry with Pete. The matter comes to an early head when Dake recklessly causes Pete to fall from his horse. Pete is seriously injured and taken to hospital in Perth, and a significant portion of the early part of the novel takes place there. It is a strange move in a romance novel of this kind to so singularly immobilise its hero. It leads to a kind of *negative* action, where the emphasis is placed on Pete's stoic endurance in the face of his injuries, and with an acutely felt humiliation at the deprivation of his capacity to act. When Rene brought her girlfriends with her to visit Pete at the hospital, they saw "that he was a man, and approved because he bore inaction and suffering with never a sign of weakness" (92). To make matters worse he must hear, during these visits, about the apparent courtship between Dake and Rene. Again, though, the jealousy he bore Dake was kept secret, even from himself, and this too was part of his being highly "natural". Thus, even though he was "among the shrewdest and most discerning of men", he was also, "of course, blind to his own senses, unknown to himself—and he never tried to know himself" (95).

Once Pete regains his health, he returns to Binrinni, because "the call of the wild was strong in his soul" (95). The phrase, made famous by Jack London's *Call of the Wild* (1904), provides a guide to the moral universe that "Nature" was for early–twentieth-century masculinity, and helps us to understand the mentality that prevailed in the early decades of the wheatbelt. The wheatbelt becomes, like the war had been, a test of manhood. One might contrast this with the comic accounts of failure in Lawson and Steele Rudd. Pollard's work has the quality of being deadly serious, and failures are total and cannot be shrugged off with a droll punchline. On his return, Pete discovers that a large number of jam trees—some 10,000 in all—had been logged for use as fence-posts. The crime is not a major one, jam trees were plentiful and were extensively used for that purpose because of their resistance to termites, but nevertheless it needed to be reported back to the Western Stock Company, and Pete cannot help but feel that it was his failure even though he had been in hospital at the time. He resolves to investigate and find who is responsible.

Returning to the bush also allows Pete to recommence his study of nature, collecting caterpillars and butterflies, and observing the behaviour of the birds, reptiles and small marsupials in his allotted stretch of wheatbelt woodland. He wrote long letters to Rene describing the habits and traits of these animals. The lessons in turn gave each of them an acceptable forum to play-act their courtship via the intimate lives of animals under discussion. He takes Rene and her sister Grace on a bushwalk and points out a stick insect:

> "A shy creature," said Pete to the girls as they stood near and watched the inoffensive insect, whilst it surveyed them with great eyes staring

from a small head on a thin, elongated neck, "always hiding in the shadows. It feeds on leaves and is otherwise harmless. It has many enemies, though, and is aware of them. That is why it is always fearful, as you see it now, lurking among the foliage, of which it seems a part." (131)

If his horse and dog stand for Pete's understated virility, these shy bushland creatures stand for his fragility. Indeed, Pollard's Pete Rodon is the first in what becomes a distinct wheatbelt type—the amateur naturalist, a version of which we have already glimpsed in Goode's stories. The figure of the naturalist recurs in Ewers, and continues in Peter Cowan, Barbara York Main and John Kinsella. "I was always interested in natural history", Pete tells the avid Rene, "and roaming most of the west I have learned much about its bushland creatures" (99). He tells her how he sends specimens to "scientists in the East." In his rough bush camp, he keeps a small library of books on natural history and works by Kipling, Conrad, Ruskin and Henry Kendall. Rene is shown a room in Rodon's hut lined like a museum with insects in cases and specimens in bottles. The scientists he works for supply him with "collecting-boxes, killing-bottles, nets, cases, and other paraphernalia of the active entomologist" (173). His activities are related in letters to Rene:

> "I captured an interesting fellow this morning," he wrote once, "one of the 'wanderers,' a fine big fellow with golden-feathered wings, the veins forming a mazy black pattern. It had brushy feet and a downy body, and the most inquisitive eyes you could wish a butterfly to possess." (227)

A contemporary review of the book suggested that the native animals and insects were "labelled and catalogued by a man who knows more about science than about the technique of fiction", and that the "atmosphere" was "of the laboratory, and not of the open bush."[31]

Pete's reclusive life, studying nature and protecting the forest, is directly contrasted with the lives of those pursuing wheat farming in the same district. Pete's position outside of the wheatbelt project is not something the novel can pass over without comment. This is because Pete is actually defying a powerful association between work, land and masculinity. The charge that Pete is not a proper man because he refused to work the land in the service of production is put to Rene by Pete's rival Dake:

> "Peter Rodon is a waster," he declared brutally. "Does he ever work? What is it but play, looking after that land at Binrinni? What is it but play, hunting insects? He has been offered work. He will not take it. He could take a farm. Why does he not go on the land? He does not like hard work. He prefers to ride about the bush." (152–3)

In this way, the decisive question in the novel becomes why Pete refuses the wheatbelt life. Logic, convention, expectation all point to this as the correct, indeed enviable, path for a young man, and yet he refuses the invitation. These are not abstract sociological questions for Pollard and take place in the direct context of his own war injuries, and his decision ultimately to leave the land at Calingiri that he was granted as a returned soldier. These experiences help us to understand why the novel takes the form of an elaborate and impassioned apologia for its hero. In particular, it is a defence of Pete's refusal to be a man in the way that society—instanced here in the shrill voice of Dake Maxton—insisted he ought to be. In this respect, the "opportunity" offered by the opening of the wheatbelt also became a kind of scourge. If anyone complained of not being able to get ahead, they were simply told to "go on the land", and any who did not were loafers, wasters, and idlers.

The central debate in the novel is, therefore, set up as one between a duty to the world (work, production, reproduction, filial love) and a duty to Nature. What was at stake in this debate was in fact the basis of masculine being. The narrator and the angelic Rene patiently advocate the case that what may seem, to the callow onlooker, like a life of dissolution, was instead one of profound meaning:

> Yet Pete had never idled. Indolent moods he knew, even as most men of excessive energy know them; but those moments of quiet relaxation had played no small part in moulding the industrious man he was. His

so-called loitering, his hours of apparently profitless watching of the wildfolk's ways, his rides through the bush seemingly without object, had helped greatly in keeping him natural. (183)

But the wheat farms all around Binrinni keep contradicting Pete's stance and even Rene wonders what would be so wrong with taking up this life: "But you seem so interested in wheat-growing, and know so much about it, that it seems strange now that you never think of taking a farm yourself" (248). Pete's answer is instructive insofar as it gets to the heart of the ideology of wheat, and the careful way this ideology placed crop-farming as the opposite of wage-slavery. Pete punctures this myth in a conversation with Rene that takes place on a hill overlooking a wheat farm being worked:

> He was silent for a few moments and she could not read his thoughts. "I think I could never get used to the monotony of it," he said at last. "Think of the harvesting. This fellow here, for instance"—nodding to where across the field on his left a harvester was crawling along the farther edge of the area of unstripped wheat—"has been driving that harvester every day excepting Sundays since the middle of November. When he finishes at the end of this month he'll cart his wheat into Binrinni, driving a wagon every day for more than another month. In April he begins seeding, and the whole perform-ance has to be gone through again—cultivating, drilling, ploughing, cultivating, hay-cutting, harvesting, and carting. In between he has to attend to a thousand and one odd jobs," he finished, "though many of those have to be done with a frequency that becomes monotonous." (248)

It is notable in this summary, incidentally, that the work of clearing is not mentioned. This suggests either that it had already been completed, or was omitted from the description of the yearly cycle because it was not quite consonant with Pete's main point about the rigid cycle of the farm-year. But leaving it out does alter the impression somewhat. For, even though in the 1920s these farms were very new, they appear in the novel as if they were an ancient and integrated part of the landscape. Moreover, the drudgery and "monotony" of the work on a wheat farm is exactly what Ewers, two decades later, when imagining the lure of farming the wheatbelt, conceived of as a rhythmic attachment to the cycles of life. The novel wrestles with this contradiction in this hilltop conversation. After hearing Pete's thoughts, Rene answers:

> "You're a strange man, Pete. Thousands of men are wheat-farming and leading happy lives."
>
> "Yes. I've only mentioned the unattractive side, and only as I see it. The life is hard, clean, and healthy—a man's life."
>
> "And a woman's," said Rene gently.
>
> "Yes," he agreed quietly, adding after a slight pause, "together."
> (248–9)

This is an important concession in the context of the novel, because it is clear in other elements of Pollard's work that wheat farming is not dismissed out of hand as a pursuit without merit. Indeed, Pollard maintains a hope for reconciliation between grain farming and nature. But in doing so he is also recognising that the opening of the wheatbelt created a fundamental antinomy between these two orders.

The climax of the novel is the burning of Pete's forest by Dake. Rene and Pete are riding through the forest when the fire is started. The fire moves quickly, and Pete watches helplessly as the precious wood, which he has spent his recent life protecting, burns out of control. Neither Pete nor Rene feel especially threatened by its progress, however. On their horses they are quickly able to ride out of its path, and from the safety of an adjoining ridge they witness the conflagration:

> Rene had never before seen a bush fire. In the shadow of the billowing smoke of this one she was awed, yet not afraid. It stirred and thrilled her. Pete looked at her once and she did not notice his glance. He saw that for the time being she was fascinated by the scene, and he smiled wanly … even now he felt impelled to watch the working of the forces sweeping the forest away in smoke and flame. He had never seen a forest fire rage as this one raged. No forest he had known in the wheat lands had escaped the fiery destroyer for as long as this forest had; no

other forest had been allowed to become so densely crowded with undergrowth. (257)

The fire here is not the kind that we saw in Facey. It is not a burning off of bush to clear it, but a wildfire lit by arson. The fact that it is met with fascination does resemble the "burns" described by wheatbelt settlers. But this fire takes on an additional quality that is suggestive, not just of wheatbelt burns, but of the author's war experiences on the Western front. We are drawn to this interpretation by a number of features in the description, but also by the sheer circumstantial proximity of the writing to the events that so gravely damaged Pollard's body and psyche. The description, in particular, emphasises the unprecedented nature of the conflagration: "He had never seen ... No forest he had known ... no other forest had been allowed ..." Positing this description of the fire as a disguised recalling of the high explosive barrages of trench warfare helps to account for the immobility of the witnesses—the fact that they seem glued to the spot as the fire explodes around them—because it is a mark of traumatic recall that one is unable to move, frozen and forced to see again and again the traumatising scene:

> They felt the heat even here, but did not move again. Pete saw that several other fires had started among the trees. Soon these merged with the greater body; and the whole forest appeared to be burning in mass. The roar grew louder, wilder; and many voices seemed to the girl and the man to be rushing back and forth and swirling through the trees. They heard the crashings of falling branches, the crackling of swift-scorched limbs and twigs and foliage; now and again a muffled report as a tree split open. Above the timber the fire-voices ascended far with the eddying smoke, smoke speckled with smuts and flakes of charcoal. (257)

One need make few transpositions to make this the scene of Pollard's war experience. The passage itself already holds a vocabulary of human dismemberment and screaming placed anthropomorphically into the suffering trees and the shrieking flames, and when it is over their "skeletons" (258) are all that remain. Then there are the "reports" of the trees splitting open.

In the midst of this fire, Maxton tries to kill Pete with his whip, just as he had nearly done at the outset of the novel, but this time without the pretence of accident. But Pete is saved by Nature. First, in the guise of his dog Flyer who drags Maxton to the ground. Even after this, Maxton tries again to kill Pete, this time with a smouldering branch, but once more Nature intervenes and drops a burning bough on Maxton. Rene and Rodon rescue him and return him home, where he survives and repents. In the aftermath, Pete takes a new view of Maxton, after hearing from his parents how dedicatedly he had helped them build their farm and how assiduously he had devoted his life to their security. In other words, how he was able to consistently perform his "duty". Indeed, Pete feels, in spite of himself, a certain shame in the face of his rival. When Maxton has been returned home, injured but destined to survive, Rene asks how Rodon is feeling, and he assures her he is "sane once more" (271). This admission points to the fact that the fire was traumatic not just because of the loss of the forest, and the failure of Pete in his role of forest guardian, but because it unleashed within him, with Rene present to view it, the desire to kill. Again, we can see a key element of war-time experience (the breaking of the taboo against homicide) in this depiction.

In the novel's *denouement*, Rodon, having lost the forest he was employed to protect, feels he has no alternative but to resign. He takes up an offer from a scientist to capture and kill a number of marsupial specimens in the Karri forests around the Kalgan River. Much to Rene's disappointment, she sees Rodon once more take refuge in his nomadic isolation. But this time, Pete loses his appetite for the work he is given, which involves killing two dozen tiny possums. Apart from the brutality of the act itself, Rodon worries that his specimen hunting might be contributing to the dwindling of native species. He also voices a concern for the fate of the Jarrah forests, and tells Rene about the necessity of preserving areas of the state on behalf of Nature: "They are needed because so many of our animals are restricted in their homing instincts to certain localities" (296). And the killing of possums once again takes on a complexion that is difficult to divorce from the events that had so decisively conditioned Pollard's life and the millions who fought in the Great War:

That Melbourne professor wanted a dozen honey-mice and a dozen pigmy 'possums, dead and preserved in spirits—the cold-blooded sinner! I have captured six of each, and with these he'll have to be satisfied. I've committed murder twelve times for him—and felt a murderer twelve times ... I'd have less on my conscience to-day if, instead, I'd brained twelve scientists each with a brand new nail-spiked club! (293)

He goes on to decry the fact that "so many men the world over should wage ceaseless war on Nature's fold", how the demands of scientists were "without end", and that this work was even "more wasteful and stupid than wars between men" (293). This final letter acts in the manner of a confession to Rene, who is endowed throughout with the power of his absolution. Realising that Pete wanted to return and live with her, she contacts the Great Western Stock Company and explains that the fire was not the fault of Pete. The director of the company offers Pete a thousand acres on which to grow trees for commercial exploitation, in particular Jarrah. The novel ends with Rene and Pete looking forward to their new life in this new forest.

Rose of the Bushlands (1927)

The next novel, *Rose of the Bushlands*, differs from *The Bushland Man* in that it takes place on a wheatbelt farm not in the adjoining woodlands. In other words, the wheat farms that had been so disparaged by Pete Rodon in *The Bushland Man* now become the centre of action. Where *The Bushland Man* had seemed to take place almost in a never-never land, outside of time and place, *Rose of the Bushlands* is directly framed within the events of the War and of Western Australia's development. Indeed, *Rose of the Bushlands*, in a way that would predict the later novels of Pollard's friend J.K. Ewers, undertakes to historicise the appearance of these farms, to turn them into legitimate property that can be owned and passed down.[32] The legitimation of property is also directly linked to the legitimation of men, as we will see. In keeping with this more evident history, the effects of the war are much more prominent in this novel than the earlier one.

The farm, "Elouera", had been purchased by Joseph O'Meare with the aid of the soldiers' settlement scheme, "four thousand acres of mixed country" at "Birkalla". It was cleared but not in very good shape, as the original settlers had lacked the capital to put it in good order. Having secured the land, the next problem for Joseph was that he was in absolutely no condition to work it. At the repatriation hospital, Joseph "went close to death" (35) several times, and his health remained fragile once he had been released. Joseph (like Pollard) had been badly gassed and was a "nervous wreck". Like Peter Rodon, Joseph found solace during his painful and frightening convalescence, writing letters, mainly to his niece, Rose, in Melbourne. Rose had agreed to join him at the farm once she had finished her study in Melbourne. Her father, Joseph's brother Michael, had been killed early in the War, but before that had also farmed in the wheatbelt, where Rose grew up:

> In-between-whiles he wrote to Rose, sometimes from his bed where, after suffering the agonies of a body that burned with the poison-gas that had inflamed his whole system, he sought comfort in penning for the girl pictures of the life she would live when she joined him; sometimes from his chair on the veranda where, relieved for a time of his sufferings, and with a panorama of bush and farming lands stretching before him, he conjured visions in which the fairies of his native sod revelled among the bushes and the trees and the flowers of the bushlands. Rarely did he allow the girl a glimpse of the torture he endured. (35)

The work on Joseph's farm—the clearing and fencing and so on—was done by employees, in particular Steve, who managed the affairs, and the slightly older Ben. Joseph attempted to supervise as much as his health allowed, but many days he was confined to his bed.

The opening of the novel narrates the arrival of Rose at Joseph's farm. She arrives late one night in early winter, after a long journey by rickety wheatbelt train, at the small hamlet of Birkalla. From the rail siding she was conveyed by buggy to her uncle's house by his manager, Steve Morgan, who lets her know that her uncle would have come himself but had not been well lately. The moonlit journey of some 15 kilometres took her through the mixed vegetation of the wheatbelt country, through sandplain and gimlet forest, and the cleared paddocks of the settler-farmers springing up through the district. The novel remains focalised through Rose's apprehension of her new environment and we learn that this trip was taking her back into the Western Australian bush after several years in Melbourne:

> She used to be a better judge of distances than she was now, she reflected. She had been a girl of the bush before. How long ago it seemed. This return to the land, this long drive, was revealing to her that she had changed greatly since those days. She wondered if she would get used to the bush again. (18)

The reverie is broken by Steve, who abruptly stops the buggy to shoot a dingo that had started to follow them:

> "How did you know?" she questioned in a whisper.
> Morgan shook his head. She wondered why he did not answer. She knew nothing of the hunter's instinct; and this man had hunted dingoes up and down the backblocks during many years. In the darkness he had grown to feel that a dog was following. But he himself could not have explained that feeling, could not have explained how he knew. (20)

Steve Morgan is thus in the mould of Pete Rodon—even their names are assonant. Like Rodon, Morgan is a solitary figure who is most at home in the elemental universe of Nature. Here he operates on the kind of natural, instinctual basis that those of us who live in cities and in settled areas have long forsaken. And, like Rodon, Morgan is to be brought in from this condition by the arrival of an innocent, feminine angel, who will understand and admire his naturalness, but also find a way of reconciling the call of the wild with the insistence of social duties. When they reach the homestead, Rose sees him in the light of the kitchen, "his overcoat thrown open, he stood revealed as a man of the out-of-doors—big in the chest, wide-shouldered, his body tapering slightly at the loins; squarely and lightly poised; strong, healthy robust … Instinctively she judged him a man of men." (25)

Rose, for her part, is also given a mythic quality via the quaint device of a picture that hangs in the bedroom she is given in her uncle's house—*The Return of Proserpina*—which causes her to wonder if her Uncle knows that this picture (one might assume, given its popularity at the time, Frederic Leighton's 1891 painting of this name) is her favourite. Rose, as Persephone, is cast as the classical agent of fertility. In Leighton's influential version of the scene, Persephone's return from the underworld is imbued with the sentimental tones of the ascension that followed the tastes of Victorian Christianity. Casting Rose in the role of Persephone is indicative of the fact that in the wheatbelt, fertility is often in question. We have already seen this in the poems of Goode, but it becomes a strong theme in later writers like J.K. Ewers and Dorothy Hewett, and into the present, with Tom Flood and John Kinsella.

24. Frederic Leighton, *The Return of Persephone*, c. 1891, Leeds Museum and Art Galleries (Leeds Art Gallery) UK / Bridgeman Images.

The shift in narrative perspective corresponds to a more sophisticated psychology in the male hero. Whereas Pete seemed primarily at war with the abstract demands of society and civilisation, Steve Morgan struggles with his own conflicting instincts. Riding home from town with Rose he decides to detour through some woodland to shoot a kangaroo for dinner. Rose admires the way that he immediately acquires the keen qualities of a hunter, but at the key moment the kangaroo happens to glance up and Steve decides not to fire. He explained: "I think I must have grown soft-hearted … Once I used to think nothing of shooting kangaroos. But now I can never kill a sitting 'roo, and even when I shoot one running I feel sorry for the brute" (138). But the motivation for the change of heart remains opaque to him and it is Rose who narrates the internal drama on his behalf:

> Something had fallen away from him … Hitherto he had ridden as a hunter, with thought mainly for the game he desired. Now he rode simply as a bushman, a man wholly in sympathy with the bush and all it contained. In the moment when he sighted the kangaroo a strange battle he had fought, and swiftly. The man was far from the bush then; but how swiftly he had returned to it! Just the inquisitive glance of a sitting kangaroo to turn him in one instant from a hunter to a bushland man, loving the animal he had hunted. Strange! (138)

Rose, too, is shown to be at one with the natural world. And Steve is the one to notice this, as he teaches her how to shoot a rifle:

> There was a gentle sway of her body, a lithe swing of arms and shoulders, and as her cheek nestled the butt of the weapon and she glanced along the barrel he saw her for a moment or two quiet and motionless, and the background of great bronze trunks and gleaming green leafage, red-brown earth and dead leaves and maturing grass, seemed in those moments no longer a background. She merged with it all. Down through the aisles of the trees the lights and shadows were dreamy, growing together in the distance. Here they were around the girl, and the shadow of one tall tree caressed her every time she took aim. Steve saw no contrast. Rose was part of it all; she fitted the scene; she belonged to it. (160)

In this moment, Steve realises that he is in love with her and was "destined" to be so, for she was "as wholly of the bush as he was" (160).

> The narrow creeds he had half learned in his youth and had glimpsed in after years had been swept from him by the bushland winds he loved; and in the heart of the free, virile lands he roamed he had developed a mind and soul that allowed of but one creed, one God. Wandering the forests and plains with the sun and the clouds, the winds and the rains, the trees and flowers, the wild folk, for company, he had grown nearer by far to God than he could have done in the cities, living the life of his fellow-men. (160)

The romance in the novel is thus allied with a harmonious and transcendental nature, which exceeded the "narrow creeds" of men. Contradictions and discord are the products of the social world; the natural world is free of them and it is this which Pollard invokes in his term "bushland". As Steve muses: "A bushland girl she had been born, and a bushland girl she was now fast reclaimed, and must remain" (161).

> [Rose] had thought of him that way as a bushman, as a man of the bush. Now she saw him in the same light as a man of the land. Somehow that gave him an added value. He was not merely a quiet, serene man of the backwoods, of the aloof bushlands. He was a son of the soil. She glimpsed something of what has been written. She knew how the man had lived and grown, alone with the wild. She felt that destiny had led him to this place of his in the life of the land. He was Nature's man yet, and always would be, but in the service of Nature. (171)

So where did the conflict in the novel arise? If Steve and Rose were both natural and living in nature, how could anything go wrong? The novel introduces three sets of problems. The first of these is the problem of their immediate neighbours, the Nestors, who were sabotaging their fences. This bears a close resemblance to the scenario in *The Bushland Man*, where Dake operated as a continuing menace to Pete Rodon. The second, not unrelated, problem in *Rose of the Bushlands* was that of invading vermin, both plagues of rabbits and the depredations of wild dogs. Lastly, there was the problem of class. The O'Meares, including Rose, were a distinguished aristocratic family, while Steve was an orphan, with an unknown father. If "Nature" represents harmony in this novel, each of these antagonisms is to be understood as a crime against nature. One might add a fourth problem, which has the effect, in some ways, of uniting and internalising the other three. Like Pete Rodon, Steve struggles against his own violent impulses, suggesting that the true battleground of nature lies within the human psyche.

In any event, and as with most of Pollard's work, the movement in this novel is towards reconciliation. His fiction tries to dramatise the settling of antagonisms, and this novel is no different in undertaking to find solutions to the problems it raises. On the question of class, the novel situates the matter in Victorian terms, in which the issue of socioeconomic difference is displaced into the matter of legitimacy, of one's "name". Steve, as an orphan, has none. The importance of class would have to wait for the next generation of writers, Peter Cowan and Dorothy Hewett, to be seriously addressed. Nevertheless, Pollard's novel is significant in that it is representing the newly disclosed social space of the emerging wheatbelt. Where *The Bushland Man* had looked askance at the wheat farms that surrounded Pete's woodland, *Rose of the Bushlands* is set squarely on a wheat farm. As we have seen, it is the first Western Australian novel to do this and so is the first sustained treatment, in prose fiction, of life in the wheatbelt. Because it is a romance and not a realist novel, the picture Pollard provides is not suffused with the finely grained details of daily life that give the reader the texture of wheatbelt experience. It must be said that in all wheatbelt fiction there is paucity of realism in this strict sense, and a preponderance of romance. Certainly, in Pollard's novel we do not get a detailed social matrix which documents the interaction of lives. Instead, there is a schematised "society" which consists on the one hand of the quasi-family built up around Joseph O'Meare, and on the other, of their scheming, embittered neighbours, the Nestors.

But the novel is also, in marked contrast to *The Bushland Man*, interested in the methods and processes of farm life. There are detailed descriptions of pickling seed wheat (washing it in copper sulphate to prevent rust) and drilling the wheat into the field.[33] Moreover, because

Rose arrives in early winter, the novel's action spans the growing season, and the action closes with the harvesting of the wheat and the hay. With Rose as the newcomer, the novel is able to follow her as she is instructed in the various work going on about the farm, as Steve, Ben and Joseph explain their tasks to her. The farm is still run by horses, even though Joseph does now own a car, and the distant sounds of tractors can be heard on neighbouring properties. In this sense the novel depicts the transition years of farming's mechanisation, where the age-old reliance on horses was still at the heart of much of the work done. It is the disappearing world of horse-drawn farming that Hans Heysen captures in his works of his era, and Colin Thiele, his biographer, remembers from his early childhood. The horses in the novel are known by name and are given attributes and personalities. When faced with the choice of going to town by car or by buggy, Rose chooses the latter, even though it means getting wet in the drizzle. The novel is not necessarily nostalgic, as the modes (mechanical and horse-drawn) were coexisting at this point, and although there is a preference in general for the horse over the internal combustion engine, there is also a grudging acknowledgement of the utility of the latter. Joseph declares at one point: "Henry Ford is a man we have learned to venerate because he has given us a car that will go anywhere" (63).

In *Rose of the Bushlands*, we also get a view of the wheatbelt from *within*. Where *The Bushland Man* surveyed the wheat farms from Pete's position outside the enterprise, looking down from his horse in nearby hills, in the second novel the farms are the centre of action and the bushland is the margin. Early in her stay, Rose is brought out on the verandah by her uncle Joseph and they watch the sun rise over the property:

> From the front veranda they looked out over miles of farmland. A few giant salmon gums stood about the yard, their tops swaying in the wind. Beyond, the land sloped down and up in clean, red, smoothly tilled soil. To the left it rose to a line of gum trees. On the right a patch of smaller trees stood, beyond them other fields. The view extended forward for perhaps ten miles, and most of it was cleared and tilled land. Slope followed slope till they appeared to run together

where earth and sky met. Here and there a field showed grey with
the old stubbles of the last harvest. Patches of timber darkened the
landscape in places and lines of trees revealed the direction of roads.
Three miles away the roof of a house showed dully through scattered
trees. (54)

The view from the verandah is the archetypal settler's view, the
point from which the property is surveyed in prospect with the
security of the home behind the viewer. From this position we already
have, in a novel of the 1920s, the wheatbelt in the form by which it
would come to be known, a "landscape" of rolling fields with belts
of vestigial timber amongst the spread of farming properties, roads
and homesteads. The effect of the description is to render the land as
a long-achieved, settled, indeed natural, state of affairs. One has no
sense of this period being one of frantic and large-scale expansion,
where even the well-settled regions were little more than twenty
years old. The wheatbelt that Pollard describes in this novel from 1927
has already emerged, and contrasts strongly with the sense we get
from Facey and Goode of a dynamic, almost frenzied, conquest of the
wilderness. There are no descriptions of land-clearing and burning,
which were such an important part of establishing the wheat industry.

Only occasionally does the novel give voice to the eradications that
founded the wheatbelt. The scene described above, neutral enough in
its elements, paints a very deliberate scene for the reader, one of the
settled, productive land that was the animating vision of the wheatbelt.
But the description is also one which depicts a certain state of mind in
Joseph and Rose as they contemplate what lies before them:

> Looking at her uncle she saw that his face was still. The man hardly
> moved. He was lost in contemplation of the scene. She turned back to
> the view, feeling the lure of it. She had strange thoughts. She tried to
> picture the great stretch of tilled land as it was in the virgin state when
> man first looked upon it. (55)

It is only a minor moment in the text, but it does provide a
glimpse into the existence of a dissonance between the wheatbelt as
idyllic farm landscape and the memory of what it had so recently

been. These thoughts are described as "strange" and this word is a recurrent one in Pollard's work, where it usually marks an uncanny moment or point of emotional confusion. Its usage here reveals a direct origin for the oft-remarked strangeness of the wheatbelt, which becomes such a marked feature of wheatbelt literature after the 1970s. At last her uncle turns to Rose and says, simply, "It is a picture made by men" (56).

In spite of the novel's concern to depict some of the processes of wheat farming, it is not ultimately the main fulcrum of the novel. The grain does not have that semi-mystical quality that J.K. Ewers will claim for it in his work, and which was such a strong element in the ideology of wheat in the opening decades of the twentieth century. Instead, the action subtly shifts the focus away from the growing of wheat as a positive process, and towards defending the wheat from attack from malevolent outside "forces". In this respect, even the pickling of the seed wheat can be seen as a prophylactic exercise, guarding the wheat from fungal infection. Indeed, it is the vermin that afflict the wheatbelt that command the greater part of the novel's attention. In the first half of the novel the focus is on rabbits, whilst in the latter half it is on dingoes and wild dogs. The primary boundaries in the novel are the fences that surround the paddocks of Elouera. The cheap manufacture of fencing wire in the late nineteenth century transformed the pastoral industry of Australia by removing the need for shepherds. Yet, while farm fencing evolved primarily to keep sheep enclosed, the key fences in Pollard's novel are not of this kind, but rather are "barrier" or "vermin" fences designed primarily to keep things *out*. The key incidents in the novel are the breaching of these fences by their neighbours, the Nestors. In the first case, a stretch of the rabbit-proof netting protecting the wheat paddock was pulled up by the elder Nestor; in the next case, a stretch of dog-proof fencing was removed from the sheep paddock by Nestor's son Ray, allowing the sheep to be mauled. In this way the novel's basic structure is a defensive one, and the wheatbelt emerges as a place in constant need of defence and protection from external assailants.

Within this defensive structure, Steve Morgan adopts the role of guardian. In this sense we see the strong continuity with Pollard's earlier novel, where Pete was employed to protect the forest of his employer. Morgan's role is much more consistent with the path of history, but it does compromise Steve's position as a "natural man". The novel does not take aim at wheat itself, in the way that modern critics might, seeing it as a monocultural invader sweeping all biodiversity before it. Instead, the unnatural element of the wheatbelt in Pollard's fiction is the endless cycle of daily work that grain farming demands. Steve Morgan is ill at ease with the drudgery of wheatbelt work. Significantly, he is not primarily shown as an agricultural worker. Instead, he is most often pictured in active pursuit of wild dogs, hunting, tracking, laying traps, or surveilling the terrain, as if his true lineage lay with the nomadic heroes of Australian literature and folklore, especially the figure of the "boundary rider" prevalent in Lawson's stories. The matter is given contrast by a second employee of the farm, the older and doggedly faithful Ben, who is shown to be contented with the drudgery of farm life, and who thereby frees Steve to undertake his chivalric role. As with Pete Rodon, though, we are constantly reassured that Steve is anything but lazy—even his contemplative periods are characterised by quiet intensity.

Certainly, the threats posed by rabbits and dogs were far from imaginary. We have seen in both Facey and Goode that, by the 1920s, rabbits were starting to affect the viability of wheatfarms even before the Depression struck. In his novel, Pollard uses Rose to show the shock caused by the sheer quantity of rabbits:

> She saw millions of them ... Birkalla farmers had never known them worse. Trappers were busy in the district, and every train that went through the siding on its way to Perth picked up hundreds of carcasses and skins. Thousands of rabbits were killed every day, but those that lived bred so that no appreciable lessening of the pest could be marked ... Their warrens were everywhere along the roadsides; every unfenced field had its multitude, and in neglected paddocks she saw warrens several acres in extent. (173)

The control of rabbits also becomes the basis for social action as the farmers realise that only a concerted approach can hope to make a difference. There is a lengthy account of the attempt to clear rabbits from the property. It is not glamorous work and does not fit readily within the romantic tenor of the novel. Rose is brought along to watch the men. The methods of controlling rabbits at this time included shooting, trapping, netting and fumigation, as well as digging in the burrows. The one depicted in the novel was a variation on the fumigation method, where piping was fitted to a car's exhaust and fed into the warren. In addition, as a "finishing touch", rags soaked with bisulfide of carbon were stuffed into the holes and then covered with soil:

> "This is not the orthodox method of fumigating," remarked Joseph, as he and the girl stood watching the operations, "but it is efficient and economical."
>
> "But—I hardly understand," said Rose, looking puzzled.
>
> "The fumes of the burnt petrol and air are poisonous," her uncle explained, "so much so, in fact, that men sometimes succumb to them. You can imagine the effect on rabbits."
>
> Rose nodded, her face clearing. (68)

Rose is a little taken aback by the clinical destruction of these creatures but her uncle explains: "I suppose it does look cruel, Rose … But when you realise that the rabbits ate about a hundred pounds of the crop in this paddock last year, I think you'll admit it's not cruelty. It's a kindness we're doing, really, to ourselves and other folks, for they must have wheat." (70–1)

On later days they returned to the fumigated warren with shot-guns to take care of any surviving rabbits. The casual manner in which Joseph explains the necessity of this eradication belies the close parallel it has with his war-time experience. There, too, a network of tunnels was subjected to poisonous gas-attack, with the hapless inhabitants powerless to escape. Indeed, Steve had earlier said to Rose, when asked what was in store for them tomorrow: "To carry war—poison gas and stink-bombs—into the enemy camp" (60).

By contrast with the control of rabbits, the control of dogs is a project of a distinctly more intimate nature. Where the rabbits were attacked with industrial methods on a mass scale, the dogs are pursued on almost personal terms. Steve uses his experience to profile the nature of the predator in question, determining that it is not a

25. Rabbit fumigation.

"pure" dingo, but a deadly mix of dingo and kangaroo dog, and he pursues the animal into the Marai Hills, an open bushland adjoining Elouera. In the account of Steve hunting the dog, he is time and again described as being at one with nature, where the natural world is perfectly legible to him and his heightened senses quickly discern the movement of his quarry. But the narrative pauses to give a more general account of the problem:

> The dingo was never a greater menace in Australia than it is today ...
> The annual count of dingoes destroyed in Western Australia alone

runs into thousands. Every wild dog in the country has a price on its head. Many owners of big flocks employ men simply to trap and poison on their runs. The dog penetrates the close settlements and is found throughout all agricultural areas. (207)

In this editorial mode, the novel also draws attention to the "ironical" relationship between the growth of pests and the expansion of farming, "that man in the process of establishing himself and his industries on the land always breeds trouble for himself and those industries" (208). The grain and cleared fields provide ideal conditions for the rabbits, who themselves provide fodder for the wild dogs that are also sustained by the availability of sheep. The working dogs used in farming and in hunting breed with their "wild ancestors", the dingoes:

> So we get a wild dog possessing all the cunning and the vice of the true dingo … his vice is to kill sheep and to go on killing out of what appears to be a sheer, wanton lust for the taste and reek of blood—a wild dog made more menacing by the addition of the knowledge and sagacity and the high intelligence of the domestic animal.
>
> The greatest curse is the dingo-kangaroo-dog cross, and it was a killer of this type that Steve Morgan had to match himself against. (209)

This discussion of dingoes is reminiscent of the opening chapter of Xavier Herbert's *Capricornia* (1938), "The Coming of the Dingoes", where the arrival of dingoes on the continent was used as a metaphor for the arrival of white man into northern Australia. As an iconic Australian animal, the dingo nevertheless occupies a border zone between a native and an introduced species, and is often imbued with characteristics that evoke a paradoxical mixture of atavism and invasion. In Pollard's novel, the dingo is on the side of nature and indigeneity, but is susceptible to corruption and admixture. Moreover, Steve's pursuit of the animal also invites a parallelism between hunter and hunted, in which Steve is beset by contradictory instincts, at once a part of the pattern of nature and an instrument of its conquest.

These matters are brought to a head when Nestor's son Ray is spotted by Rose attempting to dynamite a tree so it will once again break the dog-proof fence that protects the sheep paddock. Ray Nestor had unsuccessfully pursued the affections of Rose and realised that he had lost out to Steve. Rose pleads with him not to destroy the fence, but Ray responds: "What you don't know is that I want Morgan to realise I'm on the side of the dingoes" (216). In the ensuing struggle, Ray attempts to rape Rose, but she is saved by Steve, who appears with the impeccable timing of melodrama. Steve defeats his adversary but the more important drama is once again the one within himself, where he battles against a primal violence: "He stood watching Nestor, and though his face was dark and twisted, and his eyes aflame with the light of primitive feeling, there was yet something of his manhood with him, a slender bond yet controlling the savage" (218).

The tussle with Ray also strips away the inhibitions that had prevented the open declaration of mutual love between Rose and Steve. Yet when Steve broaches the subject with her uncle and guardian, Joseph cannot bring himself to approve the match:

> Steve remained silent.
>
> Joseph sought his eyes. He spoke very slowly.
>
> "I am an O'Meare, Steve—you will allow me something for that." He paused a moment, then went on. "Rose, too, is an O'Meare." He paused again. "And you—?" His voice dropped on that unfinished sentence. (230–1)

Thus rebuffed, Steve takes himself into exile in the Marai Hills. In doing so he comes to occupy a position quite similar to that of Pete Rodon in *The Bushland Man*, in the untrammelled wilderness just beyond the borders of the farm. Joseph's refusal to endorse his niece's marriage to Steve becomes the culminating event of the novel. Joseph struggles with his decision and his health deteriorates almost immediately, suffering a "severe breakdown" (281), as if it were the direct consequence of his bigotry. The war injuries, particularly his gas-damaged lungs, relapse and it seems he is on the verge of death. The anguish over the match seems a little at odds with the setting of the novel, as though the wheatbelt were really the place where the future of the British aristocracy was being determined. This particular development seems a peculiar Victorian anachronism for a novel of the late 1920s. Indeed, Rose tells her uncle that she is an Australian and does not need to be beaten about with talk of "breeding" and "name". She refers the issue of legitimacy to the court of Nature. When Steve admits that perhaps, after all, he was not worthy of loving Rose, she responds: "Steve, you must not think like that. The mystery of your birth may remain a mystery, but you know, don't you? You must know, must feel, that your parents were natural, human folk" (240).

As the permission to marry comes to dominate the conclusion of the novel, the other issues are hastily put to an end. Steve captures the wild dog by mimicking the call of its dead mate, a pure dingo, and brings the pelt to Elouera so that Joseph may know he has once again saved the property from harm. The problems with the Nestors are quelled when it turns out that Rose held the mortgage over their property and Steve purchases that mortgage. They realise that any further misdemeanours would see them sold up by Steve. So the entire passage of the novel contracts to this one decision that rests on the shoulders of Joseph, who is still torn: "God knows, he's a man— all man; but he has no beginnings; he has only himself" (267). In a remarkable coincidence, the doctor who comes to treat Joseph at his farm was the very doctor that had treated him in the fields of Ypres. The fact that Joseph is clearly at the end of his life allows the two to remember the terrible events of that battle. They recall a young man in the field hospital who had "been blinded with shrapnel, and there was a hole in the back of his head" (295). The verdict was that he "ought to have died an hour before" but his suffering continued pointlessly until he eventually died. As Joseph's state worsens he falls into a delirium in which the memories of the war erupt:

> "... Twenty-eight hours of solid shelling, and men smashed to pieces all around me ... that blasted mule as it died wailed like a banshee. It was ripped clean through ... Gas! Gas-shells with the barrage, and the gas-alarms were all blown to glory – and a thousand demons were running loose in the night and lighting a thousand fires every minute! My God! Gas ..." (286)

In extremis, Joseph prays for guidance and is answered by a set of words "writ in pale radiance against the opposite wall" which read: *PRAY*

TO NATURE, MY SON! This call leads him at last to the epiphany that his objections to the marriage of Steve and Rose were *unnatural*: "And ever the conviction grew within him: that they who lived most true to Nature were most blessed in the sight of God and man: they who recognised Nature as the mother eternal had the greater nobility, were the truer to Life, and stood the nearer to Heaven" (302). The marriage goes ahead with Joseph's blessing. Joseph survives his ordeal to live one more contented year and see the birth of Josephine, the daughter of Rose and Steve, "whose name ... stood for the fulfilment of many dreams, and an acknowledgement of Nature's supreme gift" (312).

"Servants of the Fields"

We can conclude our portrait of James Pollard by moving ahead some twenty years to a story he wrote that appeared in the *The Golden West* annual of 1947–48. "Servants of the Fields" concerns the pipit (groundlark), whose nesting habits he had debated with Bruce Leake in the 1920s. In the story, the pipit's name is Teepo. The device of naming animals in stories is one he had used extensively in his children's writing, but it is less common to find in a work for adults:

> Teepo the groundlark looking level across the grass observed the distant approach of a five-horse team, against a background of homestead treetops and blue sky. The bird watched the team haul a plough through the gateway into the field; and flicking its white tail feathers it flew low and swiftly to a fencepost near the gate.[34]

Teepo observes the farmer—named Joe's "mind's eye"—and the horses with the same kind of loving attentiveness that Mo'poke and his readers had observed the species they encountered. Significantly, these "small grey-brown birds living close to the soil ... were not always easily observed." On the following day, the startled birds stop Joe's team in its tracks and he finds the small ground-nest of Teepo directly in the path of the plough. He relocates the nest to a stone cairn in the centre of the field, thus sparing it the fate of countless similar nests in the wheatbelt. But the danger does not end there. The story's work is not, in other words, completed by the kind gesture of an aged farmer towards an animal. The next day Joe finds fox-tracks and realises that by placing the nest in the cairn he has saved the birds and the eggs from the plough but deprived them of their natural camouflage, indeed has put them in the very nook where a fox will forage for lizards and mice. That night Joe and his son wait for the fox to come—and shoot it just as it is making its way to the cairn at the centre of the field. The story concludes from Joe's viewpoint, although in a way that suggests that the true scene is elsewhere:

> And as he turned the garden gate, the old man stood for a moment looking across the night-dimmed valley, picturing in his mind's eye a pipit returning in the night's peace to its frail treasure beside the stone-pile.

It is clear, even from this synopsis, that the story unfolds through a series of observations—Teepo observing Joe and the horses; Joe observing the horses and Teepo; the horses observing Teepo and Joe; Joe's son observing Joe and the horses; the fox observing Teepo and Joe. The story can largely be boiled down to a conflict between benevolent and malevolent observation. The place of this fraught complex of gazes is taken by a picture in Joe's 'mind's eye' of the nest in the cairn. In some ways this is the very action we all perform when we replace the conflict and contradictions of life with a soothing image, and the wheatbelt is no exception.

In the story, Joe and the birds share common purpose as "servants of the fields". In this pact, Joe protects the pipits from the dumb plough and the sinister fox, and they protect the crops from the insects and larvae that might infest them. This pastoral myth, however, is upset by the detail that Joe is an "old man, older than his field." Only a very specific order of things permits a farmer to be older than his field.

> ... but Joe as he followed the ever-lessening spiral of his day-to-day journey often saw them come and go between ploughed land and grass; and because he habitually took much the same personal interest in the wild, free denizens of his fields and timber paddocks that he took in his domestic animals, Joe as he watched the pipits knew what they were about.

This reparative image, in which the farmer looks after the land and the land's creatures, concludes the story. Nevertheless, the story remains in the minor key, as if this is a very small consolation in a very large catastrophe. It is reminiscent of the portrait Pollard painted of Flanders in "Annihilation's Waste" in which a Labour Battalion is "cleaning up"—burying the dead, removing live ordnance—the devastated battle fields that have so recently been conquered, and would just as soon be ceded. They, too, were "servants of the fields".

Chapter Four

John Keith Ewers (1904–78)

Arrino (1920–21)
South Tammin (1924–26)

J.K. Ewers, "Keith" to his family and friends, was born in Perth in 1904, the second child of Ernest and Annie Ewers. His parents had migrated from Ernest's father's Gippsland orchard to Western Australia the previous year, arriving on 2 December 1903, with very little in their pockets. They arrived, according to Ewers, on the very same boat, the *Woolowra*, that had seven years earlier brought home a disillusioned Henry and Bertha Lawson after their stint in Western Australia. In 1910, Annie Ewers died of heart disease at the age of fifty. She had been forty-four years old when she gave birth to Ewers, and thirty-eight when she bore his older brother, Don. Ewers's father, widowed at forty, was ten years younger than his first wife. Ewers spent his early years in Subiaco, before his father remarried and the whole family moved to the newly forming suburb of Carlisle, southeast of Perth, in 1914. During the early years in Subiaco, it was his eccentric, but much-loved, Aunt Lisbeth who led Ewers to books and literature:

> She introduced me at an early age to a diverse range of writers like Emerson, Tom Paine, Henry Lawson, Joseph Furphy, Francis Thompson, James Whitcombe Reilly, Oscar Wilde, Jack London, not

to mention a whole stream of lesser lights, fragments of whose writings she had collected and stored in a number of scrapbooks.[1]

After moving to Carlisle, Ewers attended James Street Intermediate School in Perth. In 1916 his elder brother Don came of age and immediately enlisted for service. The following year, 1917, Ewers won a second-tier scholarship to Perth Modern School, which still left the family with the considerable cost of providing the necessary books. In April 1918 the family received the devastating news that the eldest son Don had died from shrapnel wounds to his head received on 30 March in the Battle of the Somme. The death of his beloved elder brother deeply affected Ewers. He became an ardent pacifist in later years, and for this was denounced in the letters pages of the papers as a writer who did not understand patriotism. Ewers reveals in his memoirs that the most difficult element of Don's loss was his own memory of the unrestrained pride he had felt when his brother had joined, bragging to all his schoolmates that his brother was now a soldier.

Born and raised in the city, Ewers first saw the wheatbelt during August vacations spent at a relative's farm at Dumbleyung (east of Wagin) in the Great Southern. Then, in the summer of 1920–21, having just finished his fourth year at Perth Modern, Ewers worked as a rouseabout for six weeks for a family at Arrino (near Three Springs), in the northern wheatbelt. After finishing at Perth Modern at the end of 1921, Ewers commenced his career as a teacher the following year by accepting the position of Monitor at Thomas Street School. His family, by this stage, needed his contribution to their limited finances, and he felt a sense of debt for their supporting him this far. With this in his mind, he decided against attending The University of Western Australia after matriculating and applied instead for teacher training at Claremont Teachers College. He missed out on the two-year program and so he accepted a place in the one-year training program. This abbreviated training was designed to meet demand for teachers in the single-teacher country schools that were proliferating rapidly at this point with the growth of the wheatbelt. In the one-year college there were about a dozen men, and approximately twice as many women. The men were all returned servicemen, and somewhat older than

Ewers. Many were missing limbs and others were, in Ewers's opinion, "psychologically affected by their war experiences" (79). Ewers was too young to serve in the War, being just fourteen when it ended. The cohort in the one-year program felt like the "poor relations" in the College, and the idea of giving less training to country teachers in single-teacher schools seemed driven by a desire for economy more than anything else. As Ewers pointed out to his instructors: "It was a curious system that sent men and women out to such solitude with only one year of training, whereas those who would become assistants in large schools with daily contact with others on the staff were given two years" (78). In subsequent years, very few remained as teachers. Ewers's friend John Ewing, also a war veteran, was "the only man in that short-course to graduate to the headmastership of a large primary school in the city":

> One by one, the others dropped out, taking other jobs. One became a grocer, another entered the commonwealth public service and did well there. One went off his head and had to be put into an institution. I lost track of most of them but all, including John, must have found it difficult to come from soldiering to a year of study … The problems they faced when they went to their lonely schools in the bush must have been particularly difficult for them. (80–1)

Nevertheless, when asked for his preference for country placement at the end of the year's study, Ewers had no hesitation in saying "anywhere in the wheat-belt" (83), and he was posted to South Tammin in the eastern wheatbelt, some 190 kilometres east of Perth.

"The Wheat Men" (1926)

Arriving in the town at the beginning of 1924, Ewers was given the rather disturbing news that the previous teacher had abandoned the school after being accused of indecently dealing with one of his female students. The consensus had been that the teacher, a war veteran, had been in a fairly fragile state and this allegation had been the last straw. In time, it was the father of this girl who was eventually charged with sexual abuse, and although he escaped conviction, the children were removed from his custody. The district of South Tammin was, in the mid-1920s, newly emerging, expanding southward from the town of Tammin. Tammin was built on the main rail-line to Kalgoorlie, and so also enjoyed the significant benefits of the Goldfields water pipeline. Once the better land to the north of Tammin had been taken up, new farmers started selecting blocks to the south, which was considered a lower grade of land due to the preponderance of sandplain soils:

> The country was predominantly sandplain with belts of timber, mainly salmon gum and gimlet, running through it. To the north of the line was the better country. It had been longer settled, the farmers were more prosperous and all had cars. The railway cut the district in two socially and there was little mixing between those of the north and those of the south. When I visited twenty-five years later [i.e. around 1950] all this had changed. Subterranean clover and trace elements had come into use and the sandplain was carrying fine flocks of sheep. Farmers from both sides of the line met on terms of equality, playing bowls on the green which had been established since I was there. Money had become the great equalizer. (86)

The eradication of the sandplain was one of the significant ecological events in the history of the wheatbelt. Initially, it was saved from clearance because it was found that the "gutless" soils that sustained this low vegetation were not fertile, either for crop or pasture. But, as Ewers notes, the introduction of "sub-clover", which fixed nitrogen and trace elements that were crucial to a sheep's wellbeing, suddenly made all the tracts of sandplain available for productive agricultural use. And so they went the way of the wooded country, only much faster as the land was so much easier to clear.

The school to which Ewers was sent in South Tammin was nicely situated in the countryside, and as he prepared for the return of the students from summer holidays, Ewers gazed out over the vista that the school offered:

> ... I stood for a long time near the front fence gazing at the panoramic view over about six kilometres of undulating country, some fallow, some pale yellow with the previous season's stubble and some still under timber. Thomson's farmhouse was the only building in sight,

across about a kilometre of paddocks, with more paddocks beyond it and the backdrop to the scene was a lofty granite outcrop or tor known as Mount Stirling. It was a view I never tired of, a pattern of colour that changed with the seasons as fallow gave way to green crop which in turn became golden as the wheat ripened. Like Dorothea Mackellar, I loved its far horizons. (87)

In Tammin, Ewers also became interested in his spare time with the natural world and bushland that remained amidst the cleared farms. As we have already seen, this was a not uncommon pursuit, and it was in Tammin in 1924 that Ewers first made the acquaintance of James Pollard, although at this point he simply knew Pollard by his pen-name, "Mo'poke", whose column he followed avidly in the *West Australian*:

It became a habit of mine when I observed some interesting phenomenon of nature to send a letter to "Mopoke" and occasionally he would quote me in his column and add his own comments. Gradually, "Mopoke" revealed himself as James Pollard who was then living at Babakin, a small country town really not so very far from South Tammin. In fact, it was only some sixty-four kilometres as the crow flies ... but in 1924 good roads were scarce ... So Babakin was another world and, anyhow, I had no transport of my own. (102)

"If I remember rightly," continued Ewers, "my first letter was about the extraordinary acrobatics of the gossamer spider."[2] On 19 December 1924, Ewers sent four insect specimens to Pollard to identify—"I am sending down a few insects which happen to have come to hand during the last week or two ... [because] you seem to have your finger on the pulse of life."[3] Indeed, Ewers's passion for insect collection remained strong in the ensuing years. He corresponded with George Lyell of Gisborne, Victoria, whose lepidoptery collection of over 50,000 specimens was donated to, and still comprises the bulk, of the National Museum of Victoria's holdings:

[Lyell] was then working for Cherry & Sons, manufacturers of entomological supplies, and through him I obtained killing bottles, setting boards, rustless entomological pins, an insect case and even a butterfly net ... I sent him many specimens, not only from the wheatbelt but also from my later schools in the forest-country of the southwest.[4]

The description of Ewers's entomological activities tallies very closely with those of Pete Rodon as described in *The Bushland Man* (1926). With the study of nature forming the initial bridge between the two men, Ewers eventually confesses his secret wish to be a writer and Pollard makes his own emerging writing career known to Ewers. In December of 1924 he wrote to Ewers with these words of cautious encouragement:

> You have a pretty hard row to hoe, and though I'm only a little way along my own row yet I've gone a little farther than you and may be able to offer some little tips. Anyway it would please me if I could; I guess there are a number of things you want to know ... and if we can help one another that will be very good. (102)

The intimacy of a correspondence like this is easy to underplay, yet it was on the strength of their letters alone that Ewers was invited as best man to Pollard's wedding in January 1928, the first occasion the two had actually met. Although Pollard was only four years older than Ewers, the gap was significant for the simple reason that Pollard had served in the War that had also taken Ewers's older brother, Don. The difference between serving and not meant everything to men of that era. On 26 March 1926, Ewers wrote to Pollard:

> Tell me ... was the War just one long horror, or did the happy times dominate over the unpleasant ones? ... I look upon it as one of the greatest calamities of my life that I was too young to participate in that great outing ... I would selfishly welcome another war for my own personal ends, for I think I have missed a great deal by having been born in 1904 instead of 1898.[5]

Ewers's subsequent pacifism is seemingly at odds with this sentiment. But it is also an understandable tension in a young man of this time.

Ewers's first published works were written whilst still at teachers' college, but his writing career really commenced after he moved to Tammin. In the three years he was in Tammin, Ewers published over thirty stories, poems and articles in various newspapers and journals.[6] He published stories in *The Western Mail*, *The Australian Journal*, *Triad*, *The Australasian*, *The Australian* (based in Perth) and the *Aussie*, often under the *nom de plume* "J.K. Waterjugs". The latter two magazines, *The Australian* and the *Aussie*, both derived their readerships from returned soldiers. *Aussie: The Australian Soldiers' Magazine* was published "in the field" in France under the editorship of Phillip Harris.[7] Harris had brought the printing press with him from Australia and, sanctioned and supported by the AIF, the magazine's circulation rose to 100,000 by the end of the Great War. It followed the *Bulletin* style of jocular nationalism, and met the desire in Australian soldiers for a publication that spoke in the distinctive vernacular made famous by that magazine and which it now called "Diggerish". The magazine continued publishing after the War from Sydney, changing its name to *Aussie: The Cheerful Monthly* and specialising in humorous sketches, articles and cartoons.

Also during his years in Tammin, Ewers composed a short-story sequence that would eventually be converted into his breakthrough novel *Money Street*, published by Hodder & Stoughton in 1933. It is this novel, focusing on the lives of the residents of a small North Perth working-class street, for which Ewers is now most remembered. When he left Tammin in 1926, Ewers was still only twenty-one. His ambition was to be a writer who could live solely on the money generated by writing, but at this stage, and in fact throughout his life, Ewers found that this work was neither steady nor lucrative enough to constitute a living, and he worked as a teacher for many years, indeed most of his adult life, to pay for his writing. After the three years in Tammin, Ewers was posted to Group Settlement schools, first in Collie, and then in the Vasse region, southeast of Busselton. The closed-in sensation of these heavily timbered townships was a great contrast to the horizons of the wheatbelt—and not an especially agreeable one. After two unhappy years in the south, Ewers applied for and received a posting back to the city. At this time, returning to the city also meant sacrificing one's prospects of promotion. Ewers taught for many years at the primary school at Beaconsfield, a suburb of Fremantle, until his partial retirement in 1947. Of course, teaching was not only a matter of money, and it is clear that through a long and varied career Ewers was a committed and gifted educationalist.

Ewers is an important figure in the literary history of Western Australia, indeed in many ways one of the most important, particularly for the way he helped professionalise literature and develop an active and engaged community of writers in a city and state where this had not previously existed. Modest about his talents, and never imagining himself a great writer, he was willing nevertheless to entertain his ambitions, and he formed friendships and alliances of mutual assistance, and respect, with fellow writers. He was prolific and possessed an admirable work ethic. He sought to promote his own work nationally by assiduously visiting editors and writers in Sydney and Melbourne. His memoirs often candidly recite the rebuffs he received at their hands. "Furnley Maurice" (Frank Wilmot) looked bored; "Banjo" Paterson told him to speak to his agent, when he sought out the poet in 1929 with the idea of making a film based on *The Man from Snowy River*; a young Kenneth Slessor did not snub him but, then again, it was before Slessor had gained much fame.

In the following decade, Ewers worked with Walter Murdoch at The University of Western Australia to develop an "Australian Reading Circle". Begun in 1930, it was a venture designed to promote the increased reading of Australian literature. Whilst this organisation collapsed in 1931, its activities were preserved in many ways by the Adult Education movement that was gathering force in Perth at this time, and included the activities of UWA's "Summer School", at which Murdoch and Ewers lectured to the wider community who were free to enrol in the courses at modest cost. In 1929 Ewers began contributing a weekly column to the *West Australian* newspaper called "Pioneers of the Pen" devoted to classic Australian writers. Here, Ewers was indebted, no doubt, to the newspaper literary criticism which had brought Murdoch to notice in Melbourne—particularly Murdoch's "Books and Men" column for the *Argus* under his pen-name, "Elzevir", which had begun in 1905. It was this column, perhaps more than Murdoch's own work in the night classes at Melbourne University, that gained him sufficient prominence to win the foundation Chair of English at The University of Western Australia, when it opened in 1912. When Ewers's "Pioneers of the Pen" had run its course, he convinced the editor to start a new column called "Australiana" devoted to current Australian works of literature, which ran for over two years. After a falling out with the *West*, Ewers began publishing a weekly Saturday column in the *Daily News* (a competitor of the *West*) called "The Australian Bookman", which ran from 1932 until 1933. The following year, 1934, *Walkabout* magazine was launched by the Australian National Travel Association, and Ewers would publish frequently in its pages during its long life (it ceased publication in 1974).

Ewers's writing was by no means confined to works about the wheatbelt, but it significantly intersects with the history of that region. From the point of view of a literary history of the wheatbelt, we can draw on his experience as a young man at a single-teacher school in the emerging district of South Tammin. In this, he is a key witness of the wheatbelt. Amongst the works that appeared during this period in his life, that is, between 1924 and 1926, perhaps the most telling is a poem, "The Wheat Men", that was published in the *Bulletin* in 1927. Ewers was proud of this poem because it was the first and only work of his to have been accepted in "The Bushman's Bible".

There is no maiden. Our song
Dies for the want of a lover—
Dies like a wind in the wheat
    Dies at our feet.
Nay, there is a lover. Her heart
Pulses our own with its beat;
We of the open spaces,
    We of the wheat!

There is no home, for our lips,
Speaking it, raise but a shadow—
Raise but a story of years;
    Raise not our tears.
Nay, there is a home. Without ending
Incense shall burn at our feet,
Heaven a temple above us;
    We of the wheat.

The virgin of slenderest grace
Dances, the wind for her music;
Lo! Like a fay at our feet
   Dances the wheat!
Mellows the sun, and maturing,
Pour us the offering sweet;
We shall be loved in the evening,
   We of the wheat!

At first glance it seems that this poem might be one of the wheat ballads that proliferated from the turn of the century and peaked in the years either side of the Great War. But the poem is not a ballad, at least in the usual sense, because it lacks a consistent rhythm that would allow it to be sung. It is rhythmic—particularly the final stanza—but the rhythm is fractured and arrested for most of the poem, and the enjambed lines also confuse the metre. This makes it a little mannered for the *Bulletin*, and also distinguishes it from Goode's poems for the *Southern Cross Times*, which were occasionally introspective, but never arrhythmic.

The poem is, in effect, a fertility ritual. In this respect it does share something with the wheat songs of the era, but also with the mythic concerns of modernism, and notably with T.S. Eliot's usage of the fertility myths recorded in James Frazer's *The Golden Bough* (1890). This mythic aspect of the wheatbelt is one that will come to the fore some years later in the work of Dorothy Hewett, who was heavily influenced by Eliot in her adolescence. Ewers's poem resembles a fertility ritual both in its structure—a movement from desolation and impotence to fruition and potency—and also because of the animated image of the wheat. The poem is actually about the men who grow the wheat, but these men are unable to speak. This is, in fact, the basis of their lamentation—that their words are unrequited: "Our song / Dies for want of a lover." Later, what is missing is not a lover but a "home". But again, it is a failure of speech: "Our lips ... raise but a shadow." And also, that the story that is spoken is "one of years" but does not "raise ... our tears". This echoes the critique offered of wheat farming by Pete Rodon in James Pollard's *A Bushland Man* published the previous year, which is that the farming is but a numbing and endless cycle of tasks, and not a moving and redemptive expression of life. The poem's major gesture is to rebut this grim possibility. It does this in two ways. Firstly and implicitly, by the existence of the poem itself. In this way, the poem is a performative remedy to the unsung work of the wheat men. The second and more overt way is to place against the loneliness of having no one hear one's words, the shimmering image of the wheat *dancing* in the field. The wheat becomes the erotic substitute—"the virgin of slenderest grace"—for the missing lover of the opening line. In this way the poem grasps the intimate connection between the image of wheat, its personal significance, and the wish for love and home.

During the 1930s, Ewers began to conceptualise a major new work of fiction, which would span several novels and tell the story of the wheatbelt in all its historical grandeur. In many ways, this project was predicted by his early poem "The Wheat Men", which lamented that no one was telling their story. With the idea of giving these wheat men a voice, Ewers resolved to narrate the novel in their own plain language. In November 1938, he commenced writing a book he called "Avea Lea", which drew on his experience in the wheatbelt a decade earlier. The manuscript ran to 500 pages when it was completed in 1941. Failing to find a publisher, partly due to the war-time embargo on paper, Ewers broke it in two. *Men Against the Earth*, the first in the planned series, appeared in 1946, and the sequel, *For Heroes to Live In,* was published in 1948. He wrote a third volume with a grant from the Commonwealth Literary Fund in 1949, but was unable to secure publication and abandoned plans for writing a fourth volume. The two published volumes—*Men Against the Earth* and *For Heroes to Live In*—encompassed the founding of the wheatbelt in the early 1900s through to the onset of the Depression. The third, unpublished volume, written nearly a decade later, took the story forward to the outbreak of World War Two. Ewers would come to regard these novels as his most important works, and hoped they would one day be republished in unified form under the title "The World of Avea Lea", after the novel's heroine. The project was ambitious in its conception and, more self-consciously than any other literary work before or since, sought to tell the history of the wheatbelt as a human saga. For Ewers this was a human history but was also at some level an "environmental" history. The word *environment* was not then what it would become for us, but was beginning, in the interwar years, its semantic migration toward its current usage. The title "Men Against the Earth" was taken from M. Barnard Eldershaw's *My Australia* (1939), in a passage that neatly encapsulates the agonistic proto-environmentalism of the late 1930s: "Man against the soil, the soil against man, the adjustment of one rhythm of life to the other, the going on together, which is the only final victory." It was in the wheatbelt, wrote Ewers, that he learned "the real rhythm of Australia", which was one based on a dry static summer, and a wet frenetic winter. Significantly, these seasons, the inverse of the northern European pattern, were for Ewers "epitomised" by the wheat, which was in sympathy with the southern Australian cycle by living in winter and dying in summer. The concept of "environment" as something localised and specific was a major focus of mid–twentieth-century thought in Australia and Ewers was actively involved in this intellectual project.

In the late 1930s, Ewers had formed a friendship with Rex Ingamells, the founder of the Jindyworobak school of poetry in South Australia. The Jindyworobaks were an Adelaide-based literary coterie led by Ingamells that sought to found a school of Australian poetry based on the unique *essence* of Australia. They sought this essence in the distinctive natural features of the Australian continent, but also, and more problematically, by invoking the culture, language and dreaming rituals of Aboriginal people. The word Jindyworobak was said to be from the Victorian Woiwurrung language and means "to join". Other Jindyworobak poets included Ian Mudie, Roland Robinson and Nancy Cato, and they published their work in a series of Jindyworobak "Annuals" that appeared between 1938 and 1953. Judith Wright and Dorothy Hewett both published in these annuals, although they would later distance themselves from the more naïve aspects of the Jindyworobak project.

Ewers, too, published in the Jindyworobak annuals and enthusiastically took up the nativist principles of their movement, especially the idea that Australian literature needed to speak to Australian experience and, furthermore, that this needed to be evident in the form of the work, its language, imagery, characterisation and setting—even its metaphysics, though it was not always clear what an Australian "spirit" should look like. Nevertheless, Ewers took from Rex Ingamells's manifesto *Conditional Culture* (1938) the key analytic of "environment" as the criterion by which Australian literature ought be assessed. In early 1944, Ewers gave a series of ten lectures on Australian literature for the Adult Education Board at the encouragement of the elder Kim Beazley (then Tutor-Organiser for the Board). The substance of these lectures was published the following year by Georgian House as *Creative Writing in Australia*, a short introductory account designed for use by students that showed the strong influence of Ingamells and the Jindyworobaks. In these lectures, it is made abundantly clear that the success of a work was ultimately, and sometimes rather peremptorily, decided by the extent to which it demonstrated a harmonious relation to the "environment". For Ewers, the "real problem that faced creative writers in a new land" was "the problem of harmonizing themselves and their works with their environment" (28). It was also Georgian House, a press closely associated with the Jindyworobaks, that finally published Ewers's novel *Men Against the Earth* in 1946. Thus, though written before World War Two, it only appeared after it, and the publishers were at great pains to emphasise that Ewers's novel was, above all, a picture of utter normality, as they write in their flyleaf:

> It is the story of a farming community, a healthy, normal group of people, their joys and sorrows, their struggles through bad seasons, their quiet gratitude for the occasional bountiful harvest. There is no psychological problem, no sexual degeneracy, no case for the amateur psychiatrist. The publishers feel that *Men Against the Earth* presents a faithful picture of Australian country life as it is lived by the ordinary everyday people who form the great bulk of our population ...

The imperative toward normality is the great ethos of post-war reconstruction. People were just getting on with things, not dwelling "morbidly" on the past, or the contradictions offered by the life of the instincts to which the two world wars so horrifically attested. But despite the assurances on the flyleaf, the novel is far from offering a settled picture of pioneering, rural existence.

Men Against the Earth (1946)

Men Against the Earth, written in the late '30s but not published until 1946, covers the years from 1907 to 1914, and is set in the fictional township of South Yorallin in what was then considered the eastern wheatbelt. South Yorallin is a rendition of South Tammin, where Ewers was posted as teacher between 1924 and 1926. The events of this novel thus reach back to a period before Ewers's time in the wheatbelt, most significantly to the time before the Great War. The weight of this event on those who lived through it and its aftermath tends to imbue the time that preceded it with a strange prelapsarian glow. Writing in 1938, in the looming shadow of the new war, Ewers's novel opens with an air of fateful innocence. A group of new farmers, including the future patriarch of this saga, Tommy Lea, are drinking in a pub and talking about the price of crops, wheat yields and varieties, farming methods and the general run of things that farmers would talk about when they catch up. We are told, indirectly, that the year is 1907, and that Tommy's first crop had been eight or nine years earlier, at the time of the birth of the first of his four children (a fifth was expected). Tommy and his wife Bessie had taken up land in the late 1890s, in the wheatbelt's very earliest years. Tommy emerges as the most bullish of the group at the pub, particularly in his enthusiastic advocacy of superphosphate and the potential for cropping the sandplain country hitherto thought to be of dubious fertility:

> "You're not tryin' to grow wheat on sandplain, are you?"
>
> "You're a bigger fool that I thought you was, Tommy, if that's what you're thinkin' o' doin'."
>
> "Fool, am I? Well, we'll see." Tommy paused before going on. "Listen, you blokes. I was readin' the other day about some bloke, I forget his name, but he was a scientist or something. An' he said back in ninety-eight—that's nine years ago—he said there was goin' to be a world shortage of wheat, see?
>
> …
>
> He went on to say that if all the bread-eatin' countries in the world went on increasin' their populations at the same rate as they was doin' then, that by nineteen hundred an' thirty one there wouldn't be enough wheat in the whole world to feed em …" (3–4)

Whether it was plausible that such a conversation took place in 1907 is open to question, but the sentiments were certainly present as the idea of the wheatbelt was vaunted. The exchange captures the book's early tone, and its attempt to put into the mouths of the participants something of the economic assumptions that underwrote the wheatbelt as a private and public venture. The passage makes clear that it is not just the ignorance of the approaching war that taints Tommy's hopes with dramatic irony to an audience in the late '30s, but his inability to foresee the Great Depression. But Tommy's optimism is generally shared by those around him, and in a later meeting with the bank manager (Ted Graham) to discuss a loan to build a house on his property, he is surprised by the enthusiasm of their support:

> Tommy couldn't quite get over the way the bank seemed anxious to make him spend more than he wanted to. Graham explained it by saying,
>
> "We've got faith in wheat, Tommy. We regard wheat as the basis of this country's future prosperity. Gold's slipping back. But wheat's going to be the biggest thing the West has ever seen. You see if it isn't."[8] (83)

In Ewers's novel, Ted Graham reiterates his optimism at a later point in the story, this time to Tommy's wife Bessie, telling her that "wheat's going to stay good for a long time" and that it was not possible to grow too much because there was going to be "a world shortage of wheat in ten years" (149).

It is significant that Ewers's wheatbelt saga begins, literally, in a drunken haze. Later, as Tommy rides home from the pub where he had made his animated pronouncements and with a dray full of superphosphate, he reminisces about the birth of his first child, Avea ("Arvie"), who will become the heroine of the saga. This young girl, we are gradually given to understand, is the symbolic embodiment of the wheatbelt, a character who is the emblem of the synthesis that Eldershaw posited in the passage quoted earlier: "the adjustment of one rhythm of life to the other, the going on together, which is the final victory." The birth of Avea is depicted with surprising frankness in Ewers's novel. Tommy had been "ploughing in the burn for the first crop at the time" (6) and had dismissed his wife's pleas to be taken to the neighbours. By the time he returned for lunch, his wife had already commenced labour and, in a panic, Tommy had loaded her onto the dray with some cushions for the rough, slow journey to the next farm. At the gate, the baby appears to have already crowned: "When Tommy climbed up again after opening [the gate], he saw what had happened. God, how the sweat broke out cold all over him! He didn't dare look again." (7). In the end, the baby was born without complications and with the assistance of his neighbour's wife.

Tommy appears in these events as a rather diminished patriarch. His slightly buffoonish qualities make him good sport at the pub, and his ignorance of the needs of the situation were painfully exposed at the moment of Avea's birth. Indeed, in the course of rushing his wife over to his neighbour's house he managed to leave the gate open causing the escape of 100 sheep, twenty of which died from eating poison bush. When he reached the neighbours, the wife who took charge, "made him feel small, hanging about waiting" (7). So, inasmuch as the fortunes of the Leas are meant to be an allegory of the wheatbelt, the founding father, Tommy, inspires little confidence. Indeed, the novel appears to suggest that the wheatbelt happened as much in spite of its Tommy Leas as because of them. The novel gets around this difficulty by investing Tommy's daughter with a mystical significance, naming her as the animating spirit of the wheatbelt adventure. And the birth of the wheatbelt is thus shown to be a miracle, akin to the miracle of birth:

> When he said goodbye to Bessie, he thought how pretty she looked lying there with the youngster in her arms. Looked sort of different, somehow. And that bit of a bundle at her side was hers and his. It didn't seem possible. But there it was. That morning there was nothing, and now ... (7–8; original ellipsis)

There is thus a tension between two forms of causality in the novel—a material one based on markets and the increasing demand for wheat, and a magical one based on the miraculous appearance of something where there had been nothing, in other words the fulfilment of a fantasy. Tommy's own seduction into the life of the wheatbelt had begun, we are told, in the early 1890s, when he was walking his way, with thousands of others, to the goldfields in Kalgoorlie. On this journey, Tommy notices the soil and vegetation and begins to muse:

> Sometimes of an evening Tommy would dig with a stick into the earth, turn it up and examine it. It looked good stuff. There was more body to it than the light loam round the Vasse. It ought to grow things. There was wheat growing at Northam. It was green and lush when they left. Why shouldn't it grow here? (31)

In Tommy's case, he never actually made money from gold-prospecting, though he spent two years attempting to do so. In the end, he found work on the rail-line that was pushing out towards Kalgoorlie from Northam, even as the fields themselves began to peter out.

The early stages of the novel consist of advances and setbacks for Tommy Lea and his family. The house is destroyed in a severe winter storm, and Tommy's only son—also called Tommy—drowns whilst drawing water from a nearby dam. Tommy's father turns up out of the blue, having sold his dairying farm in the Vasse, and wishing to join his son in semi-retirement. Bessie is not pleased with the situation, arguing they already had too many mouths to feed and nowhere "proper" to sleep. But these events transpire quietly, haphazardly, as if to suggest something of the periodic chaos that interrupts, but can never quite break, the rhythm of country life. In the midst of the reality of this life, Tommy plays an important role in the narrative—he is the agent of "dreams" in the novel, which is to say the daydreams and fantasies that animate people's lives and direct them in their aspirations. The importance of Tommy's daydreams are that they are in fact those of the wheatbelt, those that drove it into being at least at the subjective level. He dreams of owning his own land and growing crops. He dreams of one day having a family. Once he has this family he dreams of improving the home they live in, replacing the rough-built shack with a proper house. An important element to these dreams is that they are often opposed in dialogue by other characters, such as the ridicule he suffers in the bar when he dreams of growing wheat on the sandplain. Such opposition turns Tommy's daydreams into a contest of wills, into a quest for vindication.

> Mrs Duncan had sold out after [her husband] Jack's death, and George Collins had walked off his block. Perhaps they expected him to do the same. After all, he'd suffered more than either of them—first the house, then the kid. But he was damned if he was going to let his troubles drive him off the farm. He'd see them all in hell first. He had roots deep in the district. With the Duncans gone he was the oldest settler in South Yorallin. (107)

In this contest, the land (the weather, the soil and so on) is a treacherous friend to Tommy, working at times for him, before double-crossing him and joining forces with his doubting, jeering enemies—the "they" in the passage above. His constant refrain through the novel is "we're gettin' on".

26. *Men Against the Earth* (Georgian House, 1946).

The pivotal event in the novel is the death of Tommy, who is killed in bizarre fashion. He and the twelve-year-old Arvie are carting the wheat from their home to the Yorallin siding, when they both fall asleep. Tommy slips from the front of the wagon and is run over by its wheels. Arvie manages to flag down a neighbour and her father is rushed to hospital, first to Northam, and then to Perth. Tommy survives, though his leg must be amputated, and he commences a long convalescence in Perth. The mother (Bessie) keeps the farm going with help from Tommy's father, the elder children, and neighbours. But Tommy never fully recovers; the wound never quite heals, and he eventually dies in hospital later that year of pneumonia. The main result for the narrative is a transfer of the focus of thoughts from Tommy in the early chapters to his daughter Arvie in the latter chapters. But in terms of the lives of the surviving Leas, not much seems to have changed. The father's death should provoke a crisis, but somehow does not. In the end, the evacuation of the position of patriarch is rendered not as a singular catastrophic conclusion, but as part of the sequence of set-backs that are part and parcel of pioneering life. A year after her husband's death Bessie muses, "how everything went on just the same" (163).

The cycle of cropping was the metonym for this continuity, even if its introduction was marked by a radical discontinuity with what went before. This is how wheat attains its paradoxical position, a symbol of stability and regeneration, yet built upon the eradication of an ancient pattern of life that it now comes to represent:

> The wheat was thrusting its roots into the soil, its leaves were beginning to curl now and would be blowing softly in the night wind. Soon the days would grow warmer, the wheat stalks stiffen, then turn pale; the binder would cut them and tie them and throw them aside; the new harvester Tommy had bought the year before would strip and thresh and bag the grain; the waggons would churn up dust on the road to Yorallin. All the same, except Tommy.
>
> Far away to the west a curlew cried.
>
> Bessie sighed and turned and went in. (163)

The publishers were right to emphasise the stoicism of the folk in this novel. It is as if the whole point of the narration is to convert terrible tragedy into ordinary misery. The exercise would be almost plausible if there was not one missing element, which is the operation of grief. In place of actual grief, there is the transmutation of present suffering into the hope of a future. It is here that the novel pivots from Tommy, the flawed father, to Arvie, the ideal daughter.

When Tommy dies, he bequeaths to the family not only the cleared land and the beginnings of a profitable farm, but a fortifying purpose, which is to fulfil his dreams—the dreams of the wheatbelt. With the tragic early drowning of young Tommy, it is Arvie who assumes the mantle of bringing the hopes of her father to fruition. The bank manager decides to support Bessie, and arranges for her to employ a man to carry out the heavy labour on the farm. However, when this man, Ted Barnes, begins to make advances toward Bessie and the daughters, he is let go. The threat posed by Barnes is felt primarily through Arvie, who has taken over from Tommy as the organising consciousness of the story. Barnes is a threat to her—he gropes her when they are alone—as well as to her mother and to her young sister. Both the latter two are flattered by Barnes's attention, which, from Arvie's point of view, is part of the threat he poses. Barnes is cast as a crafty and manipulative suitor, and his place is much better filled, according to Arvie, by the memory of her father. But the situation is kept in motion by Arvie's ascent into womanhood. This event is paralleled by a social transformation in South Yorallin that is brought about by the establishment of a school, and the arrival of its first teacher, Ross Daniels ("Danny"). This is the part of the novel closest to Ewers's own life, with the idealist Ross Daniels acting as something of an avatar for the author, albeit more than a decade prior to Ewers's tenure at Tammin in the mid-1920s. Avea, although only thirteen when Danny arrives, develops a strong affection toward the young teacher. The novel concludes with Danny leaving for the War, being farewelled at a dance in the school hall.

There are a number of crucial ways in which *Men Against the Earth* is an exemplary wheatbelt narrative. The novel is eager to represent the somewhat feverish passion with which the wheatbelt was settled. In Ewers's novel, the land is taken up with great gusto, but then

27. Ethel Spowers, *The Plough*, 1928, linocut printed in colour, 17.3 × 36.6 cm. National Gallery of Australia, Canberra.

endured, almost as a kind of penance, as it punishes its occupants with disaster upon disaster. Occasionally, although the focus of the novel is on the individual struggle, the characters—Tommy, in particular—are struck by the pace of change in the broader surrounds.

> Tommy Lea had come back from his visit to Fred Martin's full of the way the country north of Yorallin was going ahead. It was some years since he had been out that way. He knew from the increasing number of waggons at wheat carting that the district was growing, but he wasn't quite prepared for what he saw out there. He told Bessie about it.
>
> "Never seen nothin' like it! Clearing everywhere. Mind you, it's better land out north, takin' it all round. More heavy stuff and not so much sandplain as we've got on this side." (73)

Tommy acts as the register of development in this novel, carefully keeping track of new settlers, and the activity on the land around his. His attitude is one which mixes competitiveness against his new neighbours, with pride—and occasional awe—in their collective achievements and the rapidity with which they were occurring.

The new settlers filled up some of the empty patches that stretched from Bristowe's to Maguire's along the road to Yorallin. After Maguire's were eight miles of sandplain and no one was likely to settle there. It now only wanted someone to take up Collins's and the line would be unbroken. Tommy pictured in his mind what it would be like in another ten years. It would be just as it was out north now. Mostly cleared, here fallow, there crop or last year's stubble. Only the worthless bits of timber left standing—a patch of scraggy white gum where the soil was hard, sour, grey clay, or of york gum or morrel where it was fine red powder like talc that you couldn't do anything with. And, perhaps, bits of sandplain where it cut in, although as Tommy had proved, sandplain had its uses when farmed together with the heavier country. (109)

This passage, focalised through Tommy and expressing the mentality of the moment, displays the emotional drivers that partnered the material forces in the wheatbelt expansion. The land that was not cleared was thought "empty" and, paradoxically, could only be made full by emptying it. The "useless" parts of the land were put up with, provided they did not overwhelm the useful parts. When land was not taken up and settled, the "line" was broken, and when it was occupied, the line was complete. These metaphors are consistent with the poems and diaries of Cyril Goode and other settlers.

This passion for land acquisition, the sheer exuberant joy of it, is not always an easy quality to square with the quiet, stoic endurance so praised in the valuations of Facey's *A Fortunate Life*. Part of the way that this tension is reconciled in *Men Against the Earth* is through the intersection of generations that is at the heart of the literary saga. Tommy's unbridled, slightly uncouth, demand for land and material advancement is ultimately made palatable by the fact that he is himself sacrificed in the service of his dreams. That he fell asleep carting his beloved wheat to the siding, and dreaming of future agrarian conquests, only to be run over by that very cart is a poignant, if slightly bathetic, correction to his insatiable land hunger. Arvie, as the heroine of the next—*native*—generation, is able to exist in a certain purity of relation to the land, having not had to participate in the more grubby moments of its acquisition. Even in Facey's account there is a division between the ardour of his uncle Archie, in acquiring his "dream land" from the government, and the aching reality experienced by young Albert, working on a neighbouring farm to alleviate the family's poverty. In that sense, Albert was on the side of sacrificial cost—like the two Tommys (father and son)—and not on Arvie's side, the side of the heir and beneficiary. Of course, Facey, was able, as it were, to change sides after the war, becoming the beneficiary of a farm largely cleared by others.

As well as the generational pattern in *Men Against the Earth*, there is also a pattern of socialisation, whereby the hardships of the family become the hardships of the community, the "district". The process is crystallised in the petitioning for the creation of a school. Just as Facey's story recalls the exact legislative requirements for the acquisition of land, Ewers's novel represents the process by which a district might apply for a school. Typically, the novel articulates this government scheme in the vernacular of its users, whose canny sense of how to "work the system", somehow renders the system less programmatic, less forced. Tommy discusses the matter of a school with his neighbour, explaining that he had been wanting one for some time:

> "Been wantin' one ever since I come out here. But there's never been no kids, except mine. Let's see, there's your three. How old's the youngest … Four … That's too young. Thompson's got one of school age. That's three. I got three. That makes six. Maguire's two makes eight, Carroll's two ten, an' Taylor's one makes eleven. That's any god's quantity. The Govmint only wants eight to start with. We better see the others an' do somethin' pretty quick. They take a hell of a lot of shiftin', them Guvmint blokes." (111)

One can picture the scene well enough, Tommy's fingers and thumbs keenly at work, calculating the figures. It is a feature of Tommy's approach to the world that he is always in something of a rush. Time seems to be slipping away from him, opportunities only knocking briefly at his door, before sailing away forever. In some ways this echoes the personality of the author, who, in his early years, was very much a young man in a hurry. Yet it also matches the haste of the wheatbelt's settlement, which appears in historical time as a striking, rapid transformation on a massive scale, but in the personal time of lives lived, this speed is only visible as an underlying, muted urgency—indeed, the initial working title of the novel was "The Urgent Years". After writing to the Education Department, Tommy receives the following reply, dated 27 November 1911:

> T. Lea, Esq.,
> "Eden Vale,"
> SOUTH YORALLIN
>
> Dear Sir,
>
> In reply to your request for a school to be established at South Yorallin, will you please ask the parents of children of school age to fill in the particulars on the enclosed forms. Upon receipt of these forms, should the number of children be sufficient according to the Education Act and Regulations, the Inspector of Schools for your district will make a personal visit for the purpose of selecting a school-site. (113)

The centrality of schools, and also of distance education, to the experience of the wheatbelt is not to be underestimated. The historian of education in Western Australia David Mossenson notes that the pre-war years were a time of rapid increase in the state's student population, which went from 30,000 in 1908 to 40,000 in 1913.[9] In this five-year period, 300 new schools were established in the agricultural areas, mostly in the wheatbelt:

> Most of these schools consisted of between ten and twenty pupils spread through all or several of the grades, with one teacher in charge. Because of their size and isolation, the rural schools were expensive units per pupil, but the Moore and Scaddan governments were determined to sponsor land settlement, and access to schooling was an inducement they advertised at home and in Britain.[10]

In the period leading up to the Great War approximately twenty new schools opened each year. To cope with the staffing requirements, six-month rural training programs were offered at the teachers' college, and there was a variety of on-the-job training and support, though inevitably the standard of rural education continued to lag behind town-based classes. Resignation rates were high amongst the teachers in this challenging environment. For Mossenson, though, "those who remained in charge of remote schools for any length of time pioneered the wheatbelt in perhaps as true a sense as the parents of the children they taught".[11] Teachers themselves sought to mitigate the effects of isolation by forming, in 1908, the Country Teachers' Association, which then published the monthly *W.A. Teachers' Journal*, to which Ewers was a frequent contributor. In these circumstances, it is not surprising that the school occupies such a prominent place in *Men Against the Earth*.

However, even before the desire for schooling galvanises the farmer-settlers of South Yorallin, ties had been loosely formed around the practice of their work. When Tommy is injured whilst carting wheat, neighbours join together to complete the harvest for him. This reciprocity acted as a primitive social security, and helped curb the competitive nature of the enterprise. But, as we have seen, the task that, more than any other, bonded neighbour to neighbour was the burning of land for the purpose of clearing it:

> After harvest, Tommy should have done some scrub-cutting, but there wasn't time. All he could manage was to put through the burn of fifty acres of timber he'd felled during the winter. Arvie helped him snick the heavy logs together with old Baldy hitched to a chain. He levered the lighter logs into position with a crow-bar. Together they picked up and moved over the ash-strewn ground. The smoke hung heavy in the air. Their new neighbour George Collins, was having his first burn. Tommy had promised to help him, but except for a day or two showing him how to make the most of the wind and keep his fires burning, he had to leave him to himself. (57)

Later in the novel, as the settlement increases, the "burn" becomes a more concerted social activity, tinged with real danger, and takes on the metaphysical quality that we saw in the accounts of Facey, Goode and other farmer-settlers. The description in the novel is utterly consistent with the mood of these accounts:

Burning season started on the fifteenth of February, but a fortnight earlier isolated fires broke out and smoke ringed the horizon. But when the fires went up from the new clearing out South it seemed as if the whole world was ablaze. All four new settlers had clearing ready for the burn. Jim Carroll and Paddy Maguire were the first. Working together they blackened the northern sky with the smoke they sent up. (114)

Later, as the fire breaks away and threatens to burn across the stubble toward Tommy's house, the excitement becomes inflected with genuine fear, and the participants feel that they are battling, not just for their livelihoods, but for their very lives:

The stubble aflame crackled like a thousand stockwhips. The heat, borne on the north wind, wrapped itself about the house. In no time the paddock was changed from golden stubble to a stretch of grey, smouldering ash. Here and there roots that had worked up to the surface sent up streaks of smoke ...

All that day and the next the sky was grey with smoke. The homestead at Eden Vale was bathed in a half light. When the sun did for a brief spell discover a thin patch in the smoke, it shone through like an angry red ball. (114–15)

As with Ewers's mentor, James Pollard, the language used to describe the conflagration in the novel appears to take its terrible overtones from Great War reportage. These reports were read avidly by Ewers as a boy, particularly in the heady early days of the War, when the event had the quality of a grand and epic sporting contest in which every Australian soul was invested, not just in its outcome, but in its deep, elemental play. And as we saw in the writing and life of James Pollard, the War was for those living in the '20s and '30s, both the source and the conceptual mode of life *in extremis*; in short, of what the end of the world looked and felt like.

Certainly, there is in Ewers an intensified consciousness that the wheatbelt had instituted a primal discord in the order of nature. This was something already raised in Pollard's novels in the 1920s, for instance, in the distinction between Pete Rodon, "of the bush", and the farmers, "on the land". For Pollard, though, the wheatbelt still existed as a place of regeneration—this was indeed one of the premises behind soldier-settlement, that a closeness to the earth would heal the wounds of battle. But the antagonism in the wheatbelt in Pollard's fiction is still mainly carried by external villains (Dake Maxton in *The Bushland Man*, the Nestors in *Rose of the Bushland*), or by pests such as rabbits and dingoes. There is little sense, as is certainly floated in Ewers's work, that the venture might have been fraught from the very outset. The simple answer to the difference between Pollard's novels and Ewers's, is that Pollard's were written before the Depression had decimated the wheatbelt and arrested the open-ended optimism of the '20s.

Yet in *Men Against the Earth* it is not just the knowledge of the Depression that is conditioning the writing, or if it is this knowledge, it seems that it has forced a new attention on the costs of the wheatbelt. In Pollard and Goode, Aboriginal people are all but invisible, and they are in Ewers as well, but their absence is at least noted. Aboriginal people, as they do in the work of Lawson, hover at the edge of the wheatbelt farmer-settlers in *Men Against the Earth*. Because the first half of the novel is focalised through the character of Tommy Lea, we see the Noongar through his eyes. In that sense, his prejudice—which Ewers would certainly have seen as such—is representative of the feelings of the time. Tommy's casual racism does not meld quite so readily into the voice of the narrative as such sentiments do in Lawson, though neither is it subjected to any moral correction, as would come to be required in later generations. In an early conversation with his neighbour Jack Duncan, Tommy is told how "the blacks" had helped deliver his wife's first child.[12] Tommy then asks, "Any nigs there now?" Duncan explains: "They come and go. You can't hold 'em for long" (38). Later, in the new consciousness offered by his daughter Avea, the Noongar appear refracted through Ewers's Jindyworobakism as embodiments of an ancient, but disappearing, wisdom. This supernatural sentience lives on, whether it is in spite or because of their absence, and is available to the new inhabitants, if only their sensibility is sufficiently attuned. That Avea is able to sense the value of these people, where her father only saw nuisance, is part of the dialectics of the generational saga in which she appears in the position of a more modern ideal. She remembers that there "used to be a tribe of blacks camped in the district and sometimes one or two of the men came around asking for food", and had once stolen a pair of her father's pants drying on the line. She remembers that her "mum was afraid of the men". But they seem to have disappeared when Avea was still a small child and she had asked her father, one day, what had happened to them: "Goodness knows. Inland, I suppose. And good riddance, too. You can't trust 'em about a place" (51). She pushes him for more answers:

"Where do they live?" Arvie asked her dad one day.
"Nowhere in particular," he said. "They just travel about."
"Haven't they got houses?"
"No. At any rate, not what you'd call houses. Just bush humpies."
"Where did they come from?"
"Why, they were here before we come, Arvie. They used to be the only people living here." (51)

But whilst they disappear from the district, apparently, they do not disappear completely from the narrative. In fact, they reappear at a signal moment, the very moment at which the story transitions from Tommy's story to Arvie's story, that is, at the moment that they both fall asleep and Tommy falls beneath the wheels of his own wagon. Before Tommy falls, Avea had begun a dream in which Aboriginal people feature:

But presently the smooth grinding of the wheels on the sandy track lulled her into half-sleep. She could still hear [the flies], still feel the movement of the waggon, but she seemed to be chained down. She couldn't move even a hand to brush away a fly. It was a pleasant, far away sort of feeling.
She began to dream. It was a strange dream about the sandplain and there were niggers on it, like those who used to visit the farm when she was little. And somehow the schoolteacher was in the dream and Molly Maguire. But the teacher wasn't teaching. He was listening to a big nigger wearing the pair of her dad's pants that had been stolen off the line. Arvie couldn't tell what he was saying, although she tried.

And then he turned quickly towards her and it wasn't a nigger at all. It was Oliver Bristowe. She screamed and woke up. (122)

In a mostly conventional realist novel, this event is surprisingly weighted with symbolism. The derogatory word "nigger" is Avea's father's and in reality Tommy had taken the land traditionally owned by the people he now derided. But in the dream her father has gone, and the only sign is the repetition of the word "nigger" and his stolen trousers, now worn by a large Aboriginal man who is teaching the teacher (her future husband, Ross Daniels) in words Avea cannot hear. The second substitution, which turned the man presiding into Oliver Bristowe, is the one that wakes her up. Oliver is a boy the same age as Avea from a neighbouring farm, who she detests for his incessant bragging.

The dream is remarkable not just in itself but because it is happening at the same time that her father is sustaining his fatal injuries. The scream that Arvie issues when waking up hangs in the air after she awakes, and she feels a slight bump, and notices her father is no longer on the seat next to her. Her scream then becomes her father's scream as he lies on the track behind the cart with a shattered leg. So the dream and the accident are fused and the novel delivers the strange eventuality of an occurrence that takes place simultaneously in the imagination and in cold, hard reality. This sense in which the dream is in fact somehow authoring reality is sustained by the fact that Oliver Bristowe, the braggart who appears at the end of the dream, goes to war later in the novel only to return with a paralysed arm, in an injury which echoes the father's ruined leg. The symbolic calculus of the scene (incorporating both dream and reality) occurs along an axis of possession and dispossession. Outside the dream, the land is lost by the Aboriginal men to the father, but they steal his trousers. Inside the dream, the father has disappeared and a large Aboriginal man is now wearing his trousers. Still inside the dream, but following the "but now" logic of a dream's succession, the person now wearing the trousers, and holding court, is a bragging boy. It is this prospect—the reality that the father is a boy in man's trousers—that terrifies Arvie into awakening. When she does awake, it transpires that what she had dreamed had been made real. Her father undergoes symbolic castration under the wheels of his own precious cargo.

Because Avea embodies the wheatbelt, her dreams can be understood as a reference to what is left unconscious in the wheatbelt story. What I have been calling Tommy's "dreams" are more properly termed fantasies or daydreams. Tommy's dreams of agricultural prosperity and the triumph of production over an antagonistic nature are not exactly unconscious, although they were not necessarily the substance of everyday conversation. They seem innocent enough and are ratified more generally in the ideology of wheat. Avea's dream is an authentic dream in that it is motivated by thoughts that are repressed. In Avea's dream there are two thoughts that seem the subject of repression: that the land is truly owned and to be spoken for by the Aboriginal people who have "disappeared", and that her father is a tiresome and puffed-up self-aggrandiser. Of course, we are dealing with a work of fiction and one might reasonably argue that this is the author's own judgement and not that of his character's unconscious thoughts. Nevertheless, what fiction allows is for the introduction of such thoughts into the wheatbelt's drama. In this way, they become visible and operative in a way that may well not have been permitted in the public speech of 1930s Western Australia when the novel was written.

The issue of ecology is also traversed in the novel in ways that suggest the matter was subject to repression. The severe drought of 1914 is shown in the novel as reviving the old fear that the district could not sustain cropping. It is significant, though, that the fear is given in ecological terms, emphasising environmental change as a consequence of destabilising a homeostatic system, rather than simply a "drought":

> Everyone was worried. They couldn't talk about anything else. The Jonahs said it all come of clearing so much land. Trees brought the rain, they said. Cut down the trees and the rain went away. The district was done for. They might as well pack up and go now. (189)

Another purpose of novels is to allow language to function in dialogue. In that sense, the positions of the characters of Yorallin can be taken as representing positions in a debate. Though the position of those who feel that trees attract rain is given here as occurring at the margins, it is nevertheless given, and the significance is not so much whether this view, or indeed the opposing notion, also popular at the time, that "rain follows the plough", is correct, or proved correct, but that under the conditions of crisis, the basic premises of life can be drawn into question. Indeed, no one seems the least bit concerned about the removal of trees in this novel—with the possible exception of Tommy's father—until there is a drought, when it suddenly becomes an issue. What this shows, paradoxically, is that people had all along been concerned that the removal of trees would have consequences, and were suppressing that fear and that their silence, indeed, was evidence of this fear, not of ignorance.

The historical coincidence of the terrible drought of 1914 with the outbreak of the Great War is an example of how events in the broader world can be amplified or caused to take on new significance by the patterns in the wheatbelt. Thus, every wheatbelt enlistee in 1914 was not only joining in to defend the empire, but also fleeing the drought. We have already seen something of this incongruity in the lives of Hugo Throssell, A.B. Facey and James Pollard. Ewers, in the shadow of the next war, paints the general mood in Yorallin:

> Then they got the news that England had declared war on Germany. It was like a sudden thunderstorm, the way it shook them. War! It was just as if it had come to take their mind off things. They couldn't talk of anything else for a while ... The two Clarkes [English migrant brothers], who reckoned this was a poor bloody country, anyhow, didn't waste a minute. They were off like a shot to Perth ... Some of the young lads out north slipped down to the city one week-end. Fred Martin's boy, and Barney Crow's. Young Moore from Barden's store went off. (190)

The government stepped in with loans to farmers to meet the twin events of drought and war, and prevent a mass exodus off the land at the very moment when the production of grain had gathered the status of a security issue—"Feeding the soldiers was one way of beating the Germans." (206) Ewers's own pacifism, inspired by the waste of his brother's life, is visible in the novel as a quality of circumspection. But the tone of the novel is not beset by finger-waving; there remains a genuine sympathy for the forces that drive people into action—particularly radical action, whether it is to grow wheat in the wilderness or to risk one's life in a foreign war. Ewers's novel also keeps a keen eye on the interplay of events at times of upheaval. For instance, the once-respected German migrants, the Schmidts, are arrested and interned at the outbreak of hostilities. Their erstwhile neighbours wasted no time in, one by one, looting their property of anything valuable: "By turns, one after another of the farmers visited the camp and took whatever was lying about. These were the spoils of war. They were glad the Germans were gone." (192)

The emerging hero of the novel, the schoolteacher Ross Daniels, does not enlist immediately, partly out of duty to his students. But by the summer he announces he has joined up. He is given a rousing farewell, as were the other men in the district, and the mood of the novel in the midst of war, as it draws to a conclusion, is oddly upbeat. The appearance of the Great War toward the end of *Men Against the Earth* shows how the wheatbelt, as well as being an event in itself, was also a medium in which events of the wider world are registered. This is a notable feature of the shire histories which record, with little variation, the impact of the two world wars and the Great Depression on the respective shires, districts and towns of the wheatbelt. In this, the wheatbelt is shown to be simultaneously a place beyond the troubles of the world and also urgently involved in them.

In *Men Against the Earth*, which concludes in 1914, we see only the initial stages of the Great War. The effects on the community at South Yorallin are mixed, but on the whole the inhabitants seem pleased, indeed excited, by the news of war. The young men mostly join up, and are happy to do so. Their families are sad to see them go, but this is balanced by pride. Moreover, the fact that the farms are able to keep going without the men who have joined up in droves exposes the underlying process of mechanisation, which is the constant attendant to wheatbelt life. The ambivalences around mechanisation pervade the wheatbelt, and for good reason. On the one hand, it was technology that made the wheatbelt possible, as we have already seen. Certainly, in the "bachelor farms" of Goode and his neighbours, the work would have been nearly unthinkable without mechanisation. The generative dimension of technology is present in a certain techno-fetishism of agricultural shows which celebrate each new device, each new model of motor-tractor and combine harvester, and sees in all of this the wonderful march of progress. On the other hand, there is the inevitable conclusion that all of this would lead in the end to less and less people. It is not possible to isolate gender from this ambivalence, because the threat it posed—even though it was rarely admitted—was primarily to masculinity. The poignant historical irony of 1914 is that the men of the wheatbelt fled their increasingly mechanised farms for an increasingly mechanised war. Of course, these matters were more than an irony for the participants, and the facts of this were certainly in Ewers's mind when he set out to write the Avea Lea saga. It is at the level of irony, however, that they appear in *Men Against the Earth*, because the author and the reader know that the adventure of wheat that took place in the first decade or so of the century would soon meet the events that would define that century.

For Heroes to Live In (1948)

The sequel *For Heroes to Live In* continues the saga commenced in *Men Against the Earth*. The title is drawn from British prime minister Lloyd George's slogan during the elections of 1918 that Britain, after the War, must be "a land fit for heroes to live in", and Ewers draws on both the hope and the irony that attach to that statement. The novel opens in 1918 with Ross returning home to the arms of Avea, who had waited for him throughout the War. At first, Ross is just visiting to renew acquaintances within the community, although the suspended, and now blossoming relationship, with Avea does not escape the notice of anyone. A further desire that Ross confesses to holding is that he might "go on the land", and indeed the winning of Avea's hand is not fully divorceable from this wish. As the reader is often reminded, Avea *is* the land:

> He saw her before she saw him. She was leaning on the fence, gazing over the distant paddocks with which she seemed always so closely identified. That was how Ross had thought of her while he was away—a girl who had lived close to the earth, who was familiar with every detail of the life, the seasonal changes, the sheep, the wheat, the warm friendliness of the people. (7)

Avea sees that the War had made Ross thinner and harder, stripping him of the youthful bounce he had in his previous life as a teacher. Yet the War had not made Ross decisive, and he dithers over whether farm-life is really for him. He tries to make his hosts decide the matter for him and they each cautiously demur. When he puts the same matter to Avea, she turns on him:

> "Tell me, could I … do you think I could … be a farmer … be a good farmer, I mean?"
>
> …
>
> "I've no patience with … you if you cannot make up your mind for yourself. You said I knew you. Of course, I knew you. Or I thought I did, and the you that I knew, Ross, could do anything—anything that he set his mind to do. Why have I got to tell you this? … Why have you not been able to tell yourself? You must answer the question. I cannot help you." (19–20)

Avea is annoyed by the contrast between Ross's uncertainty, and her father's utter conviction. This, in effect, is the essential change in modality that the new novel brings. Ross labours under the burden that his attempts at farming are the subject of an inheritance. Where Tommy's primary motivation was to prove his doubters wrong, Ross is driven by the desire to be esteemed as a farmer, as though his manhood depended on this judgement. In short, Ross is a modern man in a way that Tommy is not. This is a theme that Peter Cowan would develop much more insistently in his fiction, which begins to appear around this time.

The judgement that so overawed Ross as he sought to establish his farm reflects the fact that the saga had reached its next moment of generational passage. While, in the end, Ross does take up farming and marry Avea, something of his personal ambivalence is captured in the provenance of the land he acquires. Wishing to stay in the district of Yorallin, where he was known from his teaching days, he passed up the chance at land offered in the soldier settlements "further east". Instead he applied for and received the land that had belonged to the Schmidts prior to their internment at the outbreak of the Great War. Ross's land thus exemplifies the idea of a complex inheritance, which is to say, an inheritance that, if legal, is not entirely proper. Ross views the rumours about the Schmidts with some scepticism, but considers this part of the sad brutality of war. He is also delighted by the amount of work the two brothers had done and how this would get him and Avea off to a "flying start" (24).

Against the unseemly quality of the land's acquisition, and in many ways in expiation of it, the novel details Ross's emotional investment in the process of farming—of growing grain to feed the hungry. The novel lovingly details the way in which this work was infused with these gratifications. So, even though much of the heavy work of clearing had been done by the Schmidts, there was a further 400 acres remaining to be cleared and "[t]hat would be his own work, his own pride" (25). And after the clearing had been done, he "looked forward to the time when he would drive the first furrow in that patch of heavy red earth" (25). This essentially romantic attachment to the work of farming is diametrically opposed to the view of farm work in "Steele Rudd". Rudd's "Dad", the comic everyman who unites the enterprise of the clan, is never shown to enjoy his work. He works like a demon, certainly, while the boys are always dreaming up ingenious methods for skiving off, but there is no suggestion the work might be enjoyable in and of itself. Instead, the pleasure of the exercise is reserved either for the achievement of a plentiful harvest, or, in a slightly different register, pulling off a sly deal. He also, as the sons all see, takes pleasure in the work being done in the service of his goals by others: "Zeal was what Dad wanted on our new selection. He told us so often. He liked to see people zealous—people who took pleasure and pride in working—for him. We could never work too hard or too long for Dad." (115)

The pleasure that Ross is shown to take in his work belongs to a different species. He helped others on their farms and, when using the plough, "marvelled at the feeling it gave him to turn up the red earth as fallow for the next year's crop" (11). Once he gains his own farm, he is enchanted, almost obsessed with the tasks of cultivation:

> After every shower during the summer, Ross ran the cultivator over the ploughing. He bought seed-wheat from round about—Gluyas Early, Canberra, Nabawa and Federation—and pickled it in bluestone.

> In April he started drilling. The first winter rains came early and the drill got bogged a couple of times. He came home muddy and tired with balancing on the back-board of the drill. But he was so happy, he was always whistling or singing. (50)

As in the earlier book, *Men Against the Earth*, we have the burning of the native vegetation depicted with a mixture of pleasure and awe. The real pleasure occurred when things burnt well:

> They had a good burn. The weather favoured them. It was so hot that even the trees that were green because of the delay over the clearing burnt away nicely, leaving long thin corpses of grey ash upon the earth. Salmon gum and gimlet burnt easily, green or dry. But if the weather wasn't right, if the air was at all damp, they often charred and went black. (74)

Immediately after the burn had reduced the timber to ash, it was possible to drill the seed directly without ploughing. The freshly cleared land felt as if it belonged to Ross in ways that the land cleared earlier (by the Schmidts) did not. The barely submerged metaphor in the scene where he describes his pleasure in this task would seem to be that of virginity:

> ... Ross began drilling on the burn. It made him feel good inside to see the grey ash-strewn earth turning up chocolate brown and red. He hadn't felt the same about last year. That was another man's job. He had only taken it up where they left off. But this was his own. No one else had ever made this bit of God's earth grow wheat before. (75)

This scene shows how immediately destruction is replaced, at the level of the image, with creation. The ideological work, reduced here to the most intimate of actions, consists in the replacement of natural fertility with human fertility. I have sought in this study to treat the wheatbelt as an event, which although it lasted a century, was felt in the deep time of ecology as a sudden devastation. But for those inside the event, this was not generally visible—the particular fascination of the "burn" derives perhaps from the fact that in this act the event did become visible. In all of this, and in spite of its ill treatment, the land is determinedly retained as a redemptive agency, inverting the whole habit of thought, and material reality, in which it was something to be cleared and exploited: "Ross felt he wanted to be part of this richness, sharing with others the experience of growing crops the earth grew, becoming part of it" (15). Avea is, for Ross, the emblem of joining in nature's rhythms, someone who was at one with "the elemental soil" (15) and somehow belonging to it in a way that he did not: "She was at home in this environment in a way he could never be until he, too, shared the life with them. He had lived on the earth. But now he wanted to live with it and by it, drawing sustenance for both body and soul from it." (15)

In such ways, *For Heroes to Live In* is more expansively pastoral than *Men Against the Earth*. Unlike the raw community in the opening novel, the sequel depicts the district of South Yorallin prospering, with more and more soldier-settlers and high wheat prices. The farms are crawling with cars, machinery, and insurance salesmen quick to find uses for the farmers' money. With time, Ross and Avea join in this prosperity. They have children, two boys and a girl, buy a car, and then a tractor. The primitive quality of the life that Avea had lived with her family in the years before the Great War ebbs away before the tide of progress. The image is one of a good life, with good, simple people, getting on with their plans and their futures. Miss Armstrong, who had replaced Ross as the teacher at South Yorallin, muses on these matters as she prepares to attend the wedding of Ross and Avea:

> They were not rich people; they were not clever people. They had little of this world's goods and they seldom uttered a profound thought. Living from day to day, they had their petty differences which now and then flared into sizable feuds ... But on fundamental issues they were held by bonds of good fellowship and elementary decency. (31–2)

The novel places these kindly, if slightly condescending, remarks in the mind of a stranger because they might not fit well as thoughts in the characters of Yorallin, but the novel supports this essential view.

One of the key elements of this purer country life was a freedom from self-consciousness, so the characters are not often in deep meditation. In this sense, Ross is already at odds with his "environment". The fact that Ross had to choose the farming life at all, rather than having it given to him by birth, already situates him—according to the logic of the book—in a structural illegitimacy. We are continually reminded that, unlike Avea, he is not "of" the land. In this matter, Ross's experience of the Great War stands in the place of this disruption. The impasse the novel starts to trace is between his hope that the "earth" will heal him and the creeping realisation that it will not, and perhaps at the most profound level cannot. The ambiguity in the novel is over whether this failure to heal was a matter of circumstance, or that the healing capacity of living "close to the earth" was a fundamental misconception.

The turning point in the novel is the onset of the Depression and the collapse of wheat prices. But Ross's problems pre-date this catastrophe and are shown in the novel, mainly from Avea's point of view, as a gradual worsening of mood—a sullenness, a surliness even—that she as the good wife sets about trying to soften and mitigate. Against a backdrop of post-war prosperity, Ross is shown, after his initial pleasure with his new life in the country, to be never quite settled in it. The implication is that this is to do with the War. Ross, like Ewers's friend James Pollard, suffered injuries to his lungs as a consequence of poison gas. Early in the novel, this causes Bessie (Avea's mother) to doubt Ross's suitability to the farming life:

> Ross was a good, steady lad. She could see that. But he wasn't used to the land. Sometimes Bessie doubted if he were strong enough. He had been gassed at the war, and there were times when he was seized with a fit of coughing that nearly choked him. (22)

Ross's cough worsens from time to time, particularly in winter, leaving him unable to work for periods. When moves are made to hold an Anzac remembrance service in Yorallin, or to build a Memorial Hall, or to rename the local hospital the Kallaning District Memorial Hospital—Ross opposes them bitterly: "That's their idea of a memorial. Having dances and socials in a hall with dead men looking on" (52). He feels all these moves were aimed at giving a false generality to the experience of the war, "so that those who can't possibly know what it meant will think they do" (52). Because Avea is on the side of the earth, it falls to her to heal the broken Ross, as she reflects: "He had seen much pain and brutality, seen men slaughtered and suffering. His faith in man and man's work was not destroyed. But it was shaken. She must help him to rebuild it." (95)

For Heroes to Live In, however, seeks to be sociological as well as psychological, and the plight of Ross is meant to exemplify that whole generation bisected by the Great War. The history of the founding of the Western Australian wheatbelt cannot be fully separated from this event. Apart from the temporal coincidence in which the War fell in the middle of the first phase of the wheatbelt's establishment, there were also the many soldier-settlers, who between them opened over 6 million hectares of land for agriculture in the years after the war. Ewers's novel records this influx[13]:

> The papers were full of settlement schemes away out east. Districts were being settled that no one had ever thought would grow wheat because they were too dry ...
>
> They were mostly soldier settlers that were going out. Their lives ripped in two by a war that had consumed their youth, they were hungry for something to do to fill the uneasy vacuum of peace. (100)

War and wheat were united, also, by the quality of hope. The sustaining hope of the war was that it would yield a better world, that somehow the sheer insanity and scale of the killing would remake the human constitution in ways that would make a repetition of this event impossible. The wheat farm then became the image of this restitution of humanity to those who lost it. It was in this context, for example, that Hugo Throssell recalled his conversation about Cowcowing in the heat of the Gallipoli landing.

In the novel, the problem of War extends beyond the manner in which it conditions Ross's character. The War, so optimistically greeted in the first novel, now lingers as the spectre of the final futility of human action. In this sense, the War spreads into the hopes for the wheatbelt and opens up a fundamental question over whether the wheatbelt is best regarded as a natural or an artificial creation. Even the ever-sanguine Avea is troubled by such thoughts as she drives across the sandplain that separates her farm from the railway line and the town. She remembers the dreadful day that her father and she fell asleep carting wheat along this very stretch of road and he fell beneath the wagon's wheels. But her thoughts turn to the sandplain and the designs of farmers to bring it under cultivation when science allowed: "I daresay this country will all be under cultivation one day," (65) remarks Ross. Part of Avea would welcome this:

> In a way she would be glad when it was [cleared]. It would take something of the cruel loneliness out of that stretch of scrub-land. Never again would a girl of twelve, or anyone else for that matter, be faced with disaster and have to make quick decisions far from human habitation. (65)

Yet in spite of the improvement that cultivation and habitation would bring, it was also this exact quality of isolation from the modern world that was at the heart of the gratification of wheatbelt life. She ends her reverie by saying to Ross: "I hope they leave a corner of it uncleared ... so that we'll still have wildflowers" (65).

In parallel with the inexorable clearing of wild land, there is the gradual mechanisation of the farm work. The contradiction here is between the earlier tactile pleasure of turning the earth and working the horses, and the new fetish for the efficiencies of machinery. As we saw in the poems of Goode, such as "The Power Farmer's Soliloquy", the introduction of machines divided the farmers between those who saw merit in the equipment and those who felt that their cost could never be fully recouped by the labour they saved, both for humans and for horses. Outside this economic argument, a more metaphysical argument is allowed to transpire about the damage that machines do to the experience of the work—in short, their alienating effect, something which Peter Cowan's writing takes up explicitly. Not surprisingly, because she is "of the earth", Avea opposes Ross's wish to buy a tractor, and, when he gets one anyway, she resents the constant and infernal clatter introduced to her once peaceful world. Even before this, the sounds of others' tractors were intruding:

Ross wouldn't be happy ... till he got a truck and a tractor. It was extraordinary how he became machine minded all of a sudden. There were two tractors out south already ... one at Bristowe's and one at Barnes's. When the wind was from the south they could hear Bristowe's tractor quite plainly. When it was from the east, it was Ted Barnes's they could hear. (110)

But for Ross, the fact that Ted Barnes had a truck meant that he had made four or five trips to town with his wheat in the time that Ross had taken to cart in just one load, and each time he was overtaken he was left choking on the dust and feeling "as if he wasn't moving at all" (113).

The novel also links, by focalising such associations through Ross, the mechanisation of farming with the mechanisation of war. In particular, it parallels the introduction of tanks to the muddy fields of the Great War with the arrival of tractors in the wheatbelt's muddy fields:

He had seen the military machine becoming mechanized after thousands of years of individual campaigning. God, the way those tanks had slithered over the mud of Flanders! Horrifying things, but grimly capable and efficient. They were going to make a difference in future wars, he reckoned. And tractors were much the same in farming. (132)

The presence of horses on farms, and the closeness of farmers to their horses, is seen by Ross to be simply "an accident of history" (131), and his own position as one outside this tradition was in this case a distinct advantage. He started to identify with the newer generation of "scientific" farmers, who were untrammelled by tradition.

We have already seen from the poetry of Cyril E. Goode how the Depression caused an abrupt reversal in hope. The Depression ripped the veil of nature that had been used to shroud the economics of cash-cropping. The catchcries that peppered the wheat paeans of the 1910s and '20s—that the farmer was feeding the people of the world and so on—came sharply up against the brutal moment when the market offered a price for this commodity that was below the cost of production. There are many memorable accounts of what this experience felt like, as the price of wheat, which had already been down on earlier years, fell off a cliff in February 1930. The wheat price had peaked in the 1920s at 9 shillings a bushel, and anything around 5 shillings still yielded a healthy profit. If it stayed at or above 5 shillings, then Ross thought he might have gained free-hold possession of his farm within another five or six seasons.[14] Bolton's magisterial account in *A Fine Country to Starve In* details the political and social repercussions of this event as the genuinely terrifying reality of a market with no *bottom* started to settle into the minds of a State which had staked almost its entire prosperity on the steady increase of this market. In Western Australia, the problems of the economic crash were compounded by the fact that the majority of farms were held under finance, and so the collapse in prices forced the immediate prospect of foreclosure. The loans were designed to take a few incidental bumps, the odd poor season and so on, but the whole arrangement could not cope with the ongoing removal of the cash that wheat had systematically generated, especially in the boom years of the '20s, and which had led to greater and greater leveraging. In the novel, Ross and Avea are not at the very sharp end of the crisis, having at least had a number of years to pay down their loan—Avea's sister Connie and her husband, on the other hand, walk off their farm in the northern wheatbelt, as both Cyril Goode and Albert Facey had.

Not everyone was forced off the land in this time, though, and in Bolton's account of the Depression, a complex picture emerges of how different people, groups, sectors and districts fared during these years. Even though the Depression was a very serious challenge for Ross and Avea, it is not represented as being the death knell to their farming lives. They were in a position to survive, albeit under much straitened circumstances. But it functions as a trigger to Ross's collapse, and with some ambiguity, his death. Ross's death takes place—in the mode of classical drama—off-stage. He excuses himself from dinner to go and shoot some rabbits that had gotten into his wheat paddock. A shot is heard but Ross does not return. When the farmhand Ikey goes to check on him, he brings the grim news that Ross is dead. He had shot himself, apparently accidentally, while climbing the paddock fence. But there remained an understandable doubt over whether it had, after all, been an accident. Avea, even though she accepts Ikey's account and the police had not deemed an inquest necessary, is concerned that in the circumstances "people might think …" (246).

In fact, the rabbits that Ross had gone out to shoot on that fateful evening are the metonym for his mental decline. Very early in the novel, the increasing prevalence of rabbits is noticed as a slight blemish on an otherwise rosy picture of rural advancement. They had appeared, tellingly enough, whilst Ross had been away at War:

> There had been very few in the district when he went away. Already the farmers were beginning to complain. The fringes of the crop were eaten into and before long they would be getting the lot. Some seemed to think they would never be really bad. A dry summer would kill them off, they reckoned. (14)

But as the '20s progressed, the rabbits continued to increase—something noted by Facey, Goode and Pollard. Yorallin (that is, Tammin) lay between the two rabbit-proof fences, the outer one that crossed the rail-line at Merredin (the No. 1 Fence), and the inner, No. 2 Fence that crossed at Cunderdin (called Cundin in the novel). The second fence was built when it was clear that the first fence had failed and in order to protect the Avon Valley and the very richest of the agricultural land. This left those between the fences with the idea that the rabbits were now "fenced in" between these barriers, making this zone a *de facto* breeding ground for the pest. Government inspectors travelled around the districts to make sure that farmers were doing everything possible to prevent rabbits from breeding on their farms. Ross's more established neighbours, Ben and Oliver Bristowe, led the way in fighting rabbits:

> Ben and Oliver were busy all that winter fencing around their block. They buried the bottom of the wire six inches below the ground, so that the rabbits could not scratch under it. They were going to poison all the rabbits inside the fence and after that they reckoned there would be no trouble keeping them down. (79)

Ewers himself was in South Tammin at this time (1924–26) and experienced firsthand the problem. In fact, he bought a set of traps and lay them each morning and night to supplement his teacher's income. His diligence led to him acquiring the nickname "Rabbit" from his pupils, but this soon caught on more generally amongst the people of the district. As the novel progresses, the rabbits are seen to get ever worse, so that "Ross was beginning to wonder whether he was growing wheat for himself or to feed the bunnies" (157).

In the scenes leading to Ross's death, the rabbits represent the mocking frustration of his every ambition. Wheat was now selling at 2 shillings and 1 penny per bushel and still heading down. For Ross, the sheer cost of bringing it to market was 3 shillings and 3 pence and the venture was not really safe over time at anything less than 4 shillings. The appearance of the rabbits inside his expensively netted field was, for Ross, a signal that the whole project was a joke at his expense: "This was what he had worked for all these years ... This was what he and thousands of others had gone to the war for ... Millions of hungry mouths crying for food on the other side of the world and millions of bushels of wheat right here that no one wanted to buy" (239). He is suddenly overcome, though it had been brewing for some time, by a feeling that the terrible suffering of the War had been for nothing. At this point, marching out to shoot the offending rabbits, he begins to hallucinate, somewhat in the manner of a photographic negative, the inverse of the ideology of wheat. Instead of the fields of grain representing the meeting of the world's need and hunger, and affirming his own procreative potency, he sees the fields as a pitiless and mocking enemy, a literalisation of the "no-man's land" in which he had fought and suffered:

> The thought stung him to a sudden passion. The stubble and the standing wheat become transformed into all the things he had ever fought or wanted to fight against ... row upon serried row of Germans advancing grey-green over no-man's land ... ignorance and prejudice standing in the way of understanding ... privilege and vested interests holding up the world, starving millions, crushing others in an attempt to safeguard themselves, reducing labour to a pittance, killing dreams, smashing ambitions, stifling hope ... (240)

Thus, at this fatal moment, Ross's despair yields the repressed counter-narrative to the heroic story of wheat. The ideology of wheat was based on feeding the world, on giving bread to the hungry, and in this it was imagined outside the capitalist machinery disfiguring the lives of those in the city. Of course, the reality of the wheat industry was that it was entirely enabled by the rise of global capitalism and its concomitant mechanisation. The collapse of prices in the Depression brought this home and punctured the sustaining mythology that had also kept Ross afloat in the midst of the incomprehensible carnage of the trenches.

Where once the wheat lands had produced a visual and "natural" affirmation of life beyond the city, now they seemed to hold only recriminations. Presciently, in other parts of the wheatbelt Ross has heard that blocks are being lost to salinity: "The more they cleared, the more the salt came up" (218). He questions why the government settled it at all. In all of this Avea is positioned as a source of optimism and simple faith in the future of wheat, but at the same time acts as a kind of ecological conscience, as in the following line of thought:

> But they slashed the earth, they made it their servant, they set their seal upon it – a seal of straight fences, a lattice of straight roads. They disturbed nature's laws of life and made things grow in straight lines because it pleased them to do this, because it was economical to do this. (169)

Avea's is the most naked critique of the wheatbelt that we have yet seen. It casts the whole venture as a crime of human pride against the order of nature. Of course, Avea is also a wheat-farmer herself and the lines on her farm were presumably just as straight as those of any of her neighbours. Indeed, Ewers' novel is part of an emerging ecological consciousness in the 1940s, captured in the poetry of Judith Wright's *The Moving Image* (1946) and paintings such as Russel Drysdale's "The Crucifixion" (1945)—and in the writing of Peter Cowan.[15]

An Interrupted Nature

Ewers's two wheatbelt novels—*Men Against the Earth* and *For Heroes to Live In*—quite conspicuously portray two distinct moments in the founding of the wheatbelt. The first moment is the ruthless, naïve conquering of the land by Tommy Lea. His actions are understood to be elemental, and if not dignified in speech, then certainly dignified by their utter conviction. Tommy's reign spans the years from the turn of the century to the outbreak of the Great War. The second moment is that of Ross Daniels and encompasses the returning soldiers and the prosperous years that culminate in the catastrophe of the wheat price collapse in 1930. Unlike Tommy, Ross is an uncertain king, even though in material terms he enjoyed levels of wealth well beyond his predecessor. As important as the depiction of each era is the relationship between them. The two eras pivot at two points. The first and most obvious is the War itself, operating as historical *caesura*, that element necessary to history by which it organises events between a before and an after. Indeed, it is the traumatic weight of the War that complicates Ross's attachment to his project. But the second point of pivot between the two stories is the one that connects both Tommy and Ross to Avea. Avea is the innocent in each case even as her role folds from daughter to wife and mother. She is also the avatar of the "land", an ambiguous designation which modulates between the natural world that precedes the wheatbelt's settlement and the cycle of activities that farming introduces. Like her father, she is—despite constant assurances about her intelligence—rendered in the manner of an untutored, noble savage. She does not comprehend Ross's worries and retains a simple faith in her life and world.

In these ways, Ewers's novels provide a moral constellation of the wheatbelt constituted in terms of historical fatality (the settlement of districts, the War, the Depression), but also in terms of a metaphysical discord between "man" and "earth". This latter relation articulates, moreover, the problem of gender as one in which the primary crisis exists in the field of masculinity. The women in Ewers's novels suffer, but they do not suffer from the thought that maybe they are not fully functioning as women. But the men are troubled, and the key elements of the drama in these books revolve around their potency. The crisis reaches its crescendo with Ross feeling that his every action has been futile, that he has fought man and the earth and been left with nothing. That he produces wheat that no one wants, that his seed is worthless. At the heart of these contradictions is the concept of "nature". The wheatbelt was and is, by every measure, a traumatic interruption to the natural world. Of course, the southwest of the Australian continent was profoundly shaped by Indigenous people over at least 40,000 years of settlement, so it is wrong to think of the tapestry of wheatbelt ecology as pre-human. Yet, equally, the systematic eradication of native vegetation and the fauna that depended on it during the twentieth century was an extinction event on a grand scale, one of the more far-reaching ecological erasures of recent human history. The novel both recognises and disguises this process. In this it is exemplary of all ideology, which in its purest terms rests on the enlistment of social fantasy to cope with traumatic reality. Thus, Ewers's novels never finally put in question the properness of "man" living with the "earth", nor that the wheatbelt can achieve this utopian *rapprochement*. The novel depicts the Depression as a "man-made" catastrophe, and yet the idea that wheat has a "natural" price, which magically fits the amount required to keep a farmer in first-world comfort, is not questioned. The traumatic quality of the Depression consisted not so much in its wide-scale impoverishment, but in the stripping away of the veil that masked the naked operation of an economic system which had no "natural" valuation of human life.

28. *Harvest* (Angus & Robertson, 1949).

Chapter Five

Peter Cowan (1914–2002)

Kondinin—Mount Kokeby—Waeel (1933–34)
Beverley (1935)
Benjaberring (1940–41)

In terms of wheatbelt writers, Peter Cowan belongs to the generation of writers that follows Ewers and Pollard, even though their writing careers overlapped by many decades. More than anything else, Cowan is separated from his predecessors by the incursion into his work of aesthetic modernism. He was not just a new voice in the writing of the wheatbelt, but a distinctly new voice in Australian fiction when his first story "Living" was published in John Reed's modernist magazine *Angry Penguins* in 1943. Cowan was born in Perth in 1914, the son of the solicitor Norman Walkinshaw Cowan and Marie Emily Johnston. The family lived in the quiet suburb of South Perth, which was then connected to the city primarily by a ferry, although it was possible to travel the long way round across the causeway to East Perth. Cowan's paternal grandmother was Edith Cowan, who in 1921 became the first woman to be elected to an Australian parliament. When Peter Cowan was eleven his father died suddenly and the family were forced to move to a smaller home and take on boarders to make ends meet. In 1930, at the age of sixteen, Cowan completed his secondary education and commenced work in an insurance office, initially as a delivery boy, which he enjoyed, and then at a desk, which he found utterly miserable: "I mean offices then were replicas really of Dickens' day ... sort of sitting at a little desk, playing with bits of paper."[1]

29. Cowan in Perth in 1930. Peter Cowan Papers, Peter Cowan Writers Centre, Western Australia.

The experience led to what he later thought of as "a good deal of psychosomatic illness" which took the form of intense migraines that affected his vision. With no improvement in his health or mood, Cowan, now aged eighteen, decided to leave the office job and go and work in the wheatbelt. This decision was made in 1932, at the very worst point in Western Australia's Depression. The collapse had arrived a little later in WA than the rest of Australia, where unemployment amongst registered trade unionists, for instance, peaked in the April–June quarter of 1932 at 30.3 per cent.[2] However, Cowan seems never to have regretted this decision and, indeed, looked back upon the years between 1932 and 1938 (after which he returned to Perth to recommence study) as amongst the best of his life:

> I became a farm labourer and in the social scale there was nothing lower than a farm labourer. You were indeed nothing, and some of the employers hardly spoke to you and you didn't go near their families or anything like that; though that varied. The conditions were such that today it would be laughable. There was often just a section of the machinery shed where the one or two employees slept ... But none of

that mattered. I enjoyed that. I liked working there and I think I just liked the physical work. It was exactly right and what I needed at the time.[3]

Cowan's picture of the wheatbelt comes, therefore, from this vantage point—that of the itinerant worker who was also an urban refugee.[4]

After Cowan had resigned his job as an insurance clerk in 1932, he started work in the country in November the following year, working at five different farms in the first twelve months—Kondinin, Mokine, Kokeby, Coolup and Waeel. Cowan's own work and reflections are often rather depleted of details, but it is possible to gather a sense of his movements during the 1930s and '40s from correspondence he maintained with his mother, friends and his future wife, Edith Howard.[5] The letters to his mother, Marie Cowan (née Johnston), are particularly instructive as they report candidly the details of his life in the country. They also come closest to anticipating, and indeed refining, the prose style for which he would eventually come to be known. On 11 November 1934, then aged twenty, he wrote a review of the preceding year from the farm he was working on at Waeel, just north of the Great Eastern Highway, between Meckering and Cunderdin, which he titled "Mr Cowan's Bumper Agricultural Anniversary" in "8 volumes":

> 365 days – long days – short days – dull days – days crammed with incident – days when the game didn't seem worth the effort – days when there is no place on this earth just like the good old farming areas of Western Australia. It is on the latter days that the unshakeable spell of the country is laid upon one. An irresistible lure which lifts one above the often weary and heartbreaking toil and allows a glimpse of things which a city dweller cannot aspire to – is not privileged to realise. Thus it is that I do not regret that day one year ago when I left, with a suddenness which has characterised most of my decisions since, the world I knew and set off into the unknown.

He gives a brief portrait of each place, where a certain premature wistfulness is already a feature of his reflections. Of Kondinin, his first job, he writes that it was "a place of such vast spaces as I knew not existed untill [sic] I became all to [sic] familiar with them. The loneliness of that place however comes back to me even now with a recall which is hard to resist – why I know not." The Kondinin job ended in a way that Cowan knew was typical of him. His boss was oiling the harvester when Cowan confronted him: "Then suddenly something, perhaps a couple of months of bag-sewing, forced me against my will towards that harvester – where I delivered my ultimatum. The rest is ancient history – I was in Perth two days later."

From one farm he wrote a letter ("8 page issue all about Mr. Cowan. Don't miss it.") to his "Dear Ma" where he gives the return address as "The Hovel, Hell's End."[6] Here, the accommodation "is one or two worse than Kondinin" and causes him to exclaim to his mother in mock resignation: "Mrs Cowan I surrender – I'm undone – nerve gone – morale routed." Four farms and less than twelve months later, Cowan was working on a wheat farm at Waeel, "a finishing school so to speak", where "I have been taught everything up to a leaving standard – it remains now to get out and apply it for myself." He spent much of the next six years working on farms in southwestern WA, mainly in the wheatbelt, where the farms were, even in the difficult times of the Depression, slightly more affluent. But despite declaring his education "finished", he never goes on to buy his own farm. Of course, the Depression completely changed the viability of much of the industry and there were no longer loans to allow farmers to buy the equipment needed to convert virgin bushland into working farms. But it is not even clear, and this comes through in many of the stories, that had this opportunity still been present, Cowan would have pursued it. He was tempted, though. In his personal papers there is a copy of the 1930 "Short Guide to the Conditions of Land Settlement in Western Australia" with the relevant rules concerning the taking up of land marked-up, although such a guide became almost laughably useless the moment it was printed thanks to the Depression.[7]

Cowan's letters to his mother also show the beginnings of a particular mode of landscape description that would mark his fiction throughout his career. He proposes in one letter to try an "innovation" and take his mother, in words, along with him on "my sheep feeding round" and uses this to paint a picture of the farm as a landscape. It represents a distinct shift out of the joking, self-effacing register of his early letters to his mother:

30. The Young Cowan with his two sisters and a land settlement guide from his personal papers. Peter Cowan Papers, Peter Cowan Writers Centre, Western Australia.

We reach the main road and turn to the right up a long gradual rise. To the left are about a thousand acres of fallow stretching to timbered hills on the horizon – to the right, as we climb, more and more miles become visible – undulating multicolored country – chocolate, brown, & red fields of fallow mingle with yellow and straw colored stubble, here and there black patches of burnt grass intervene – and the tops of the ridges and rises are green with timber.[8]

At the end of the day's work, Cowan describes the softening of the landscape under the gathering dusk and a "sunset whose glory of changing colors must bring inspiration to anyone possessed of the faintest imagination – a sunset peculiar to the wheatbelt." After writing this lyrical passage he asks his mother if she might keep this and other letters "in which I've tried a dash of descriptive effort" that he might use them later as "rough copy." But shifting registers again he also tells his mother that the home block is in bad repair: "Completely barren & the creek I mentioned is salt – dead trees stand in silent mockery along its banks. I tried to have a wash in it but could get no lather up – more silent mockery ... Even looking at the wheatbelt as I have endeavoured to – to see the best of it – it takes a

31. Cowan's wheatbelt scrapbook, c. 1933–1934. Peter Cowan Papers, Peter Cowan Writers Centre, Western Australia.

lot to make it pleasant." Noticing the salinity of the creek is an early sign of the ecological consciousness that Cowan adopted ever more forcefully during the course of his life.

An undated letter to his mother from a farm 14 kilometres north of Beverley begins: "Well, I've done it again — sold myself into this blasted slavery. This time I seem to have hit the ends of the Earth. For unattractiveness and stark barrenness this place has even Kondinin knocked rotten."[9] The letter from Beverley is even more despairing than the earlier letters and Cowan wonders if he will even last a month at this farm. What is clear from the letters is an extraordinary ambivalence in Cowan about the country. The shifts in his mood allow for quite markedly different impressions to appear in sequence, often in the same letter. He is also struck by the almost surreal juxtaposition of life in Perth, mere hours away on a train, to life in the wheatbelt:

> These quick changes are a never ending source of wonder to me. To think that in a few hours one can step so completely from one world into another. From a world of streets & houses, comfortable chairs and beds, a wireless & Crosby — not to mention a bath, into a world of amazingly barren open spaces — a few kero boxes to keep things in & an old frame as a bed, no amusement or recreation ... & a small bowl to wash in. Ye Gods — why do we do it! The only thing to remind one that it's not all a dream are one's own belongings in a suitcase ... The quickness & completeness of the change brings an extraordinary sense of unreality ... & one is left at the dreary tasks, surroundings, & outlook of a typical wheatbelt B___ farm — and just an average one at that.

Despite the unquestionable isolation that existed in the wheatbelt, and which Cowan's fiction beautifully evokes, his letter here also points to the fact that there had emerged by the 1930s a road and rail network through the rural southwest and the wheatbelt that allowed transit back and forth to the city. From many parts of the wheatbelt you could get to Perth within the day, or, at the worst, overnight. Along with this, what is palpable in Cowan's early letters is the simple fact that by the 1930s the wheatbelt is already there; it is not—as with Facey, Goode, Pollard and Ewers—a thing which is coming into being. While Facey was in the wheatbelt before the War, these last three writers were all in the wheatbelt mainly in the 1920s. The change in the felt sense of history when you move to Cowan just a decade later is very marked. Indeed, many of Cowan's stories begin with someone arriving either by train or by car into a rural district to start work. They do not commence with a farmer setting out to pioneer a farm, and in this sense they represent a distinct departure from the battler-farmer tradition of Steele Rudd. The farms in Cowan's fiction, even the newer wheatbelt ones, are usually already there and in full production. In his stories, farms are not foundational projects that organise the life of the family or community, but are almost taken for granted, regarded with a mixture of indifference and occasional resentment. The founding of the farms does not feature in the narrative, except ruefully in the light of a later, bitter harvest.

Drift (1944)

Cowan finally gave up country work as a serious proposition at the end of 1937. But the nearly six years he spent working as an itinerant labourer in rural Western Australia would form the basis of Cowan's first two collections of short stories, *Drift* in 1944 and *The Unploughed Land* in 1958, and colour his writing ever after. Returning to the city, Cowan enrolled at The University of Western Australia in 1938 at the age of twenty-four. With the outbreak of war, he was sent to Melbourne and came into contact with John Reed's modernist coterie. He married Edith Howard in 1941, though they had been together for some years before this, having first met in 1935. After the war, Cowan taught in Melbourne for a couple of years before he and Edith returned to Perth. There, he taught initially as a "prep" teacher to students around twelve years of age at Guildford College before, in 1950, going on to a specialist English and Geography position at Scotch College. He taught at Scotch until 1963, when a Commonwealth Literary Fund Fellowship allowed him to turn to writing full-time. In 1964 he was appointed Senior Tutor in English at The University of Western Australia and in 1965 joined the editorial staff of *Westerly* magazine, a literary quarterly based in the English Department at UWA. He served as Senior Tutor for many years, eventually retiring in the 1980s. He would remain an editor of the magazine until 1994.[10] Between the stories in *Drift* from the early 1940s, and his final story "The Room" published in *Westerly* in 1997, Cowan's writing career spanned six decades. Whilst there is a clear aesthetic trajectory in his work—it becomes ever sparer in its scenic detail—there is also a striking sense of unity in Cowan's stories and he has an almost painterly commitment to his own style.

Cowan's pre-eminent critic, and long-time friend, Bruce Bennett, identified Thomas Hardy amongst his early influences, but it was the "American moderns", especially Faulkner, Dos Passos, and Hemingway, that captured the attention of the young writer. One might also add John Steinbeck. Writing to his future wife, Edith Howard, on New Year's Day in 1941 from the small wheat bin where he was working at Benjaberring, he complains how he had lent "Mice and Men" to another young woman, "who said yes it was good, but that it depressed her, and so did not finish it all."[11] The incident would be good preparation for his later career as a teacher and tutor. But it was Hemingway's stark, yet lyrical, prose that, more than any other writing, gave the young Cowan an alternative to the dominant tradition of bush realism associated with the *Bulletin* school. Hemingway provided a means for the author to be earnest without being romantic, at least not in the sentimental Victorian vein, which appealed to ideals that had so dramatically failed in the Great War. By stripping the prose of any ironic distance, and adhering to a spare, often monosyllabic diction, Hemingway brought his readers into a direct relation to language, which is then experienced as an almost primitive force. It would be wrong to suggest that this was a form of writing that was "fitted" to the wheatbelt alone, for the style remained the same whether Cowan was writing about 1950s suburban Perth or the ruthlessness of war-time Melbourne, and yet there does, too, seem a correspondence between the attenuated form of the writing and the kind of wheatbelt that becomes visible when this writing is employed.

The other decisive element that Cowan took from both Hardy and the Americans—especially Faulkner and Steinbeck—was the concept of a literary region. Hardy and Faulkner pioneered the literary region in the form of a densely realised fictional rural setting. But it was a particular kind of rural locale, one that lives in the hinterlands of nations undergoing modernisation. Indeed, Cowan's views on the matter, which he wrote in a letter to Edith in the 1940s, are amongst the earliest statements on this subject in Australian letters.[12] It is not that regional writing had no precedent but that it was not seen in these terms. Instead, rural localities in Australia had been conjoined in the service of the unifying ideal of "the bush". Defending his plan to write a regional novel, he writes:

> I can see what you don't want me to do, You don't like the idea of a regional novel, and I am quite determined to write only regional novels until I have a quite different type of experience. I will probably never have this, but that will also probably not stop me trying regional novels. Look at the American regionalists – definitely successful. I think that regionalism is something the Australian novel needs.[13]

He goes on to write that he is "not Ernestine Hill or Frank Clune, or Ion Idriess" and does not want to try to depict a typical, true or general Australian "scene", but "to use a small section of a country and the people in it to shew up the general trend of economic and social conditions." But there is also something of a tension in Cowan's declarations, even here at the outset of his career, because he is not concerned with the depiction of *background*: "I don't want here to fill in the background, it's not necessary. I'm saying in effect – this is what this place is like – what do we do about it."

One sees something of Cowan's regionalist ambition in his first published story, "Living" (1943), although it quickly becomes plain that a region, for Cowan, was characterised as much by its psychic conditions as by its geography. In the story, a young farmer is in the middle of his harvest. One expects, in the manner of a short story, that some incident will now take place—a fire, a visit from a neighbour, or perhaps even a stranger. In fact, something does happen, but the event is entirely an internal one; or, viewed another way, the event has already happened, and it is only here, in the middle of the harvest—the wheatbelt's triumphant moment—that it catches up. The decisively modern, or modernist, element is that things are narrated as consciousness. In other words, we do not see events and *then* hear the protagonist's reactions and thoughts, we see things happen *as* events inside the protagonist's consciousness. The character speaks, but he is speaking to himself:

> He sat in the car. Across the yard he could see the crop, the paddock to the left stripped, a pale colour, with the forms of the sheep in it. The other paddock had only about three rounds done. All along the side and behind the wheat he could see the flat foliage of the jam trees. Might have time for a couple of rounds, he said. The dog strained at the rope. Time I've harnessed up wouldn't be worth it. He looked at the wheat, and all at once there were tears in his eyes, and it welled up in him, all he had forced down through the hot unbelievable morning and afternoon. I can't stand this, he said aloud. I can't stand it. I can't stand this. His hands twisted heavily on the wheel. No, he said. No. Well, it's done. I can't believe that. I can't see it. She's gone. Alright. This doesn't help. It's work, see. The wheat. Get it off. Get it carted. This is no good. (35)

The whole passage would make more sense if we only knew what "it", "this" and "that" were referring to, and yet it is their ambiguity which animates the fictive scene. It is not clear, in the end, whether the woman—"Lois"—who has departed has died, or simply left. She has been sick, but in the stream of consciousness to which we are made privy, she is treated as having betrayed the farmer—"Oh Christ, that she could lie like that" (37). It does not seem to matter, as the primary sensation is one of abandonment. Her departure has rendered the entire enterprise, the whole life of the farm, meaningless. There were moments like this in Goode, Pollard and Ewers, where the wheatfields, which were the symbol of a meaningful and integrated life, suddenly became the exact antithesis of this, staring back with hostility and mocking. But significantly, on those occasions, the men were defeated by outside forces—the collapse of prices in the Depression, the return of war-time trauma, the depredations of drought or rabbits. Cowan's story makes no reference to such assailants; indeed, the farm seems a picture of success. The wheat stands dry, full and ready to be taken off … but the farmer cannot do it. He thinks about carting a load instead, but it seems it is too late in the day for that too. He thinks then of milking the cows, and it is too early for that, but then he decides to do it anyway. But bringing them in, he finds that they have little milk and, anyway, "there's the tinned" (38).

This is a new kind of wheatbelt, no longer socialised (as economic saga, by Ewers), or the subject of metaphysical hopes (and unity with Nature, as with Pollard), but one that has become thoroughly subjective—utterly prone to mood, and, thus, incapable of offering consolation. The notable feature in this new wheatbelt is a certain quality of silence, fused with menace. Cowan's literary critics, and he himself, have singled out silence as central to his prose style, an insistent unsaid weight that hangs over the sparse dialogue that lace his stories and novels.[14] The wheatbelt did not become any more silent between 1920 and 1940—indeed with mechanisation, as we saw in Pollard and Ewers, it became much noisier—but in Cowan's work one feels the silence acutely for the first time. In his stories, the silence is there waiting for you, waiting for the moments when the routines of life come apart, or start to stutter: "He looked at the clock again. He wanted to talk. The silence would do the things again it had done then. And it was all too clear in the silence. There's no reason he said" (35). The silence in Cowan's stories is repeatedly declared, but it is also brought about by the staccato rhythm of the prose, in the untethered impersonal pronouns (it, this, that), and in the *non-sequitur* leaps between thoughts, leaps which in their turn bear witness to a psyche at war with itself as to the basic terms of its being. One also finds in the story an extension of the fears that beset Pollard's characters, notably Pete Rodon, and those in Goode's stories, in which the wheatbelt is experienced as a kind of hungry machine which consumes those lured into its vision of rural freedom. The whole range of farm work stops looking like an idyllic enactment of nature's rhythms and presents instead as a repetitive series of soul-destroying actions.

In "Living", the unnamed farmer keeps staring at his alarm clock in the rudimentary house: "He had wound it up last night. Carefully, one of the mechanical things" (35). He also looks at the calendar, some of the months having been marked off, but even that had been abandoned. He looks again at the crop, the image of his ambivalence: "It's been a good crop, he thought. The rest'll go a bit better, if anything. Be late getting it off. The bin probably be closed.

Well, they can flamin' well receive the wheat. That's what they're there for. It would be a good crop, he thought." (37) The repetition of the phrase "good crop", modulating between nostalgia (*has been*) and hope (*would be*), contains a sudden flaring of anger towards those who are receiving the wheat, as though pre-empting the possibility of rejection. The flickering of this rage, though, is abortive, as if even *that* will not find a place that will take it, and the silence forms in the place of that hatred: "He didn't think anymore of the wheat. He let his hand rest on the bags and he looked out across the paddocks to the dark line of the jams behind the wheat without seeing. The long emptiness of the afternoon seemed to close about him. Nothing, he thought. There's nothing there now." (36) Cowan's work thus introduces a credible psychological intensity to the wheatbelt. His landscapes are less innocent than those of his predecessors and hold their human inhabitants uneasily. One does not feel, as one does with Goode, Pollard and Ewers, that his characters are marionettes acting out a foundational drama, but rather that the wheatbelt is, for Cowan's anti-heroes, almost beside the point.

There is also a markedly different ecological consciousness. Certainly, in the earlier writers we saw an admission that the wheatbelt had been won at the expense of "Nature." But there is no Nature of this kind in Cowan. Pollard and Ewers believed in a late-romantic version of Nature, one that was both vitalist and agonistic. For them, Nature was imagined as feminine and there was a longing for unity with it, and for an end to the "war" against her. Moreover, Ewers's Avea Lea and Pollard's Rose operated as the avatars of Nature in her maternal guise and sought to reconcile the estranged male heroes. Cowan's stories of the wheatbelt render a nature that is much closer to Lawson's bleak vision, even if the writer throughout his life felt he was working against the tradition that Lawson spawned. Cowan shared with Lawson a particular aversion to the romanticising of nature in Australia. Like Lawson, he typically describes it as "scrub", and it tends to appear either as a dark grey line *encroaching* from the horizon, or as an abstract "pattern" of light and dark shapes. The emotion that is directed towards the natural world, when it does spill out in "Living", is angry resignation: "He looked over at the jam trees. Suppose he didn't take it off. Let the sheep have it. Well, he thought,

the jam trees win. All the years, he said aloud, they've been there ...
Let the sun bake the soil and let the jams come back on it. Let the
scrub have it." (38) It makes a contrast with the careful preservation of
the jam trees by Pete Rodon in Pollard's *The Bushland Man*. But the
anger is not so much directed at the trees as at the farm which he had
set up in spite of them.

After its initial publication in *Angry Penguins*, "Living" reappeared
in Cowan's first collection of stories, *Drift*, published by Reed &
Harris in 1944, though the stories were written between 1930 and
1942.[15] Printed on cheap war-time paper, *Drift* featured a garish cover
by Albert Tucker, part of his series of paintings of drunken soldiers.
The stories are set mainly in the southwest of Western Australia—
in Perth, in the wheatbelt, and in the cooler, wetter forest country
further south. The collection was prefaced by a blurb on the dust-
jacket, probably by Max Harris, which made cautious reference to
Lawson: "The name of Henry Lawson is a dangerous one to use as a
criterion when speaking of another Australian Short Story writer; but
it was Henry Lawson who established the Australian tradition of short
story writing, and it is important to make it clear that Peter Cowan
upholds that tradition among the younger writers today." The book
was dedicated to Alec King, the English lecturer at The University
of Western Australia who had introduced modernist poetry to
Cowan's generation—which included Dorothy Hewett—and exposed
them to the influence of Joyce and Eliot.[16] It is in this context that
mentioning Lawson was "dangerous" because the publishers—John
Reed and Max Harris—were desperately trying to loosen the grip of
the *Bulletin* school on Australian fiction. Interestingly, though, they
could see that there was also, if you like, a "modernist" Lawson, one
whose exquisite prose style and existential unease was not entirely out
of step with modernist taste. Cowan's achievement, in the eyes of the
publishers, was his fitting of the rural setting to a modernist ethos.[17]

The story "Harvest" begins a little like Pollard's *Rose of the Bushlands*,
with a rickety wheatbelt train rattling into a deserted siding at night.
On board is George, who we discover is on holiday from his desk-job
in the city, a holiday he had been ordered to take by his employers.
His friend Jim waits for him and drives him back to the farm he works
by himself. As in "Living", the farm is in the midst of its harvest, but

32. A copy of *Angry Penguins* from Cowan's papers along with the cover of *Drift*. Both feature artwork by Albert Tucker.

unlike the unnamed farmer in that story, Jim is coping quite well with the task, and has enough in reserve to tactfully accept George into his care. As the story follows George and his thoughts we get glimpses of his life in Perth, which we learn had reached a dead end. He is drinking too much, cannot sleep at night and has lost his appetite. He is plagued with a feeling of overwhelming futility, which he struggles to express to Jim, when the latter gently prods him on the matter:

> "I never wanted to do anything but live the ordinary city life—you know, work regular hours, have your bit of fun and your comforts. That sort of thing."
>
> "That never did go too well for me."
>
> "No. Well, now it doesn't seem too good for me. Where am I going? Sometimes when I've got the guts to look and see where—well, you can't look at it, that's all."
>
> Jim nodded.
>
> "I don't fit," George said. "And I don't know why."
>
> "You can't fit into that kind of life any more."
>
> "Well, what's the solution?"

"Don't know," Jim said. "I don't think there is one."

George moved his hand. "No. It's full stop." (119–20)

George is not saved by the wheatbelt, it does not provide him with a spiritual epiphany or sense of direction, but it does grant him a degree of space. In this, the story itself does exhibit its own quiet endorsement of the work of farming. George, as a less than eager new chum, helps Jim with the harvest. He drives the truck to the weigh-bridge and helps unload the bags. We see in the story, incidentally, a number of material changes to the wheatbelt, such as the shift to bulk-handling, with the wheat being placed in open bags, which are emptied at the bin. It is now a time of cars and trucks, although the harvester is still horse-drawn. Unusually for Cowan, the story has a quite definite location, albeit in a fictional town ("Nukerin") said to be not far from Koorda and the Cowcowing Lakes in whose vicinity Hugo Throssell and Katharine Susannah Prichard farmed briefly in the early years of the Depression.

If there is an enduring affection in "Harvest", it is directed towards the simplicity of the relationship between George and Jim. Jim asks few questions and makes no demands on George. On his side, George is a modest guest, and helps as best he can, but conscious, too, that he is a little in the way. Cowan writes openly about loneliness, a quality which one never actually sees expressed in the work of Pollard or Ewers, although it is present in Goode's diaries and in certain moments of Facey's early life. In each of these other writers, loneliness is not something that seems quite proper for a man to admit feeling. Pollard's outsiders exist in dignified isolation, apparently content in their woodland hideaways. Cowan's anti-heroes, by contrast, have lost faith in the ideal of self-sufficiency. Rather than rescuing George, the privations of the wheatbelt seem instead to reflect back at him the inconsequentiality of his own life in the city. As with the farmer in "Living", George feels time painfully, and compulsively looks at his watch:

> Inside, he looked at his watch and noted that the alarm clock in the kitchen was a quarter of an hour fast … Looking at his watch he saw there was more than an hour … Well, he thought, you came. Here's the place. How's it going to help? He lay there and the flies still

228

worried him. He seemed to have no energy. Nothing to keep him in his body. The room seemed to be strangely lighted. He felt heavy.

He woke and jerked upright. He looked at the watch. (112)

There is, though, something of the ambivalence of Pollard's characters when it comes to the descriptions of work. Work ends up being seen by George as the saving grace of farm life. He comes to see, and Jim agrees, that the wheatbelt's primary value is its ability to host meaningful masculine work. George realises this in a moment where once again the silence "suddenly" assaults him:

> Suddenly, but as though all along it had been waiting to come, he felt the silence. He stood still, listening. There were cicadas outside. Through the window he could see the trees, a light greyish colour under the heat, and the hard-working fallow across the road by the dam. He thought, how does he stand this. And then he said it loud and he said, well, he works. Yes. And that looks like what I'd better do. (115)

The matter does not quite rest there. Certainly, there is a realisation that work is integral to happiness, but the story does not answer the problem that had arisen in "Living" in which work itself loses its meaning. Nor does Cowan find in work the cure to alienation that the Marxists were advocating at this time and which was affirmed more hopefully, if not always convincingly, in the social realist stories and ballads of Dorothy Hewett. The Marxist critic John McLaren, a perceptive reader of Cowan, notices the futility of action that pervades the lives of his characters. "Cowan shows", writes McLaren, "how the scrubby anonymity of the bush offers brief refuge to those who find themselves at home nowhere" (107).

Indeed, the work is not quite the soothing balm to George's jangled nerves that he had hoped it might be. As he begins to lead the horses with the harvester he "felt a queer irrational fear" as "the machinery came to life" (110):

> Then as they moved into the crop the wheat began to come through the machine, and the sound of it changed. He watched the steady even

stretch of the wheat heads and how they met the iron bar of the comb and were drawn into the beaters. Like something irresistible the iron moved and out behind sprang the stiff stubble. (111)

Again, there is something quite novel in the sensation that Cowan describes, the operation of the machine inspires in George a form of awe which seems much closer to the industrial sublimity of factories than it does to the heave of human agricultural labour. Even the horses disappear in Cowan's account, as if they too were being driven by the machine rather than drawing it. They are nothing like the named, personalised creatures that appear in the earlier writers, or even in the more nostalgic descriptions of contemporaries such as Colin Thiele. Later in the story, George experiences again this same uncanny fear in the face of the harvesting machine, where "it" seems to be moving as if by its own will: "It pulled out and swung in to the dump. As the horses came in close and the machine he felt for a moment nervous as he had done that morning. But then the harvester stopped and Jim got down slowly, and it went in the air of ordinariness." (116) The machinery harvesting the wheat with its whirl of irresistible blades both entrances and revolts George. In this story, and in direct opposition to the ideology of wheat, the harvester is an engine of pure loss. Its violent, relentless operation seems to open up an abyss in the otherwise ordinary work of the farm that is connected to the menacing silences that haunt him.[18]

Jim seems oblivious to such things and works steadily in his tasks. George quizzes Jim about his life and half envies, half fears the radical difference it presents from his desk job in the city. At odd moments he falls into reveries that are tinged with fear and melancholy but also hover towards a certain tantalising transcendence. In spite of Jim's homespun simplicity and steady sense of purpose, the farm never seems fully settled, and Cowan's close focalisation through George keeps the landscape in a state of disquiet:

There was a wind, and he could hear plainly the leaves of the shade trees and the crickets. The scrub was darkening and seemed queerly remote. He began to be conscious of an extraordinary loneliness. It was as if quite suddenly the bush and those cleared acres of crop and fallow had become withdrawn from him and he was looking on something that had no place for him and that he could not reach. (119)

Even so, George feels that the isolation and ambivalence of the life at Nukerin might still be a more viable path than the emptiness of his city life. He even half-heartedly suggests to Jim that they might take on the land together, but Jim suggests that this won't work, and George knows he is right. The story ends on what is, at least by Cowan's standards, a hopeful note, with George looking out from the verandah towards the half-harvested field. In a way typical of Cowan, the conflict in George's thoughts is presented almost as an optical illusion, as though paradox itself had been displaced into the visual field, and feeling becomes a kind of trick or pattern:

George stood on the verandah and he looked at the square of the stripped wheat about the wheat in ear. The wheat lay in shadow and that which had been stripped did not show out with the clearness it had under the heat. The two were more nearly unified into the one they had been before the stripping. The shade trees and the line of timber about the far boundary were dark and back of the rise the hard colour of the sky was reflected in thin scattered clouds. George looked from the wheat to the slow scrub covered rise and the deepening colour of the sky and the clouds. He looked at the pattern of the scrub and the fallow and the stubble and the wheat, and it was a pattern that seemed to have extended itself to his days in the time he had come to work with it. (125)

This is the closest Cowan comes to reconciliation. Unlike Pollard, there are no glowing letters on a wall asking the characters to pray to Nature. Instead, things which were hard and stark become a little less so, not so as the edges are lost, but so that they are allowed to interplay. The shorn stubble is brought back into relation to the unstripped wheat it had so recently been, and the scrub is integrated into a *pattern* with the fallow and the stubble and the wheat. In this way, Cowan's stories anticipate very closely the atmospheric visuality of Howard Taylor's abstract paintings of the 1980s and early '90s.

Like Taylor's late paintings, Cowan's landscapes appear as a shaded Rorschach of tonal variation—there is almost always a dark belt of timber on the horizon that is growing darker.[19] Or the sky will be scrubbed clean of clouds that will then suddenly reappear, banking menacingly with an approaching storm. It is also a remarkable fact that the three leading modernist landscape painters in Western Australia—Guy Grey-Smith, Robert Juniper and Brian McKay— were all born in the wheatbelt. Grey-Smith was born in Wagin in 1916, Juniper in Merredin in 1929 and McKay in Meckering in 1926. Another major modernist painter to hail from the wheatbelt was John Perceval, who was born on a farm at Bruce Rock in 1925 and lived there for the first ten years of his life. Perceval met Arthur Boyd in the army and moved to Melbourne, where he married Boyd's younger sister Mary.

Ambivalence best characterises the emotional quality of Cowan's wheatbelt, an ambivalence that turns around the idea of isolation. Cowan has spoken of how he quite enjoyed the isolation, indeed the silence, that rural work gave. He noted with annoyance the appearance of transistor radios on wheat bins after the war, and how that introduced a baleful din to what had once been a tranquil world. The opening story in *Drift* is called "Isolation", and as well as being probably the finest and richest in the collection, it is in many ways a prototype for much of Cowan's work—because it sets out the specific

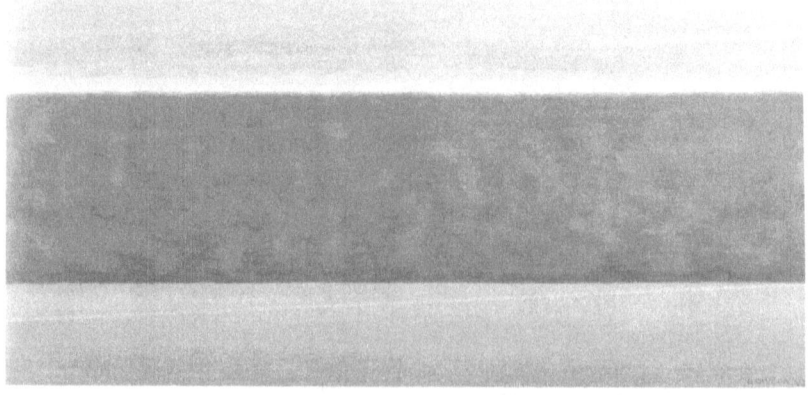

33. Howard Taylor, *Tree Line*, 1996, oil on marine ply panel, 60.7 × 121.8 cm. Douglas and Magda Sheerer Collection, Perth.

drama that isolation instils. It is set in the timber country to the south of the wheatbelt, on two adjoining properties, carved out of the forest. In the stories of the timber country, the forest is used as an image for the silence that operates in the wheatbelt stories. Cowan's writing helps us to see the wheatbelt as against the other, often earlier settled, agricultural districts in the southwest—the orcharding and dairying of the south coast and the Capes regions. Cowan mainly worked in the wheatbelt during the '30s because those farms were more likely to have money to employ him. The wheatbelt was the growth region and even in the Depression, with the collapse of grain prices, it maintained an economic superiority over the smaller southern farms. These smaller, older farms carved from the great forests are not, though, considered to be fundamentally different to the wheatbelt farms, except perhaps in the way that they concentrate action by more efficiently bracketing off the outside world. "Isolation" opens, rather strikingly, by viewing these two farm properties from above, through the eyes of a wedge-tailed eagle:

> To the eagle swinging well up the two clearings were as one, and only a dot of lighter colour in the spread of undulating forest. But in the great bird holding the air with its stretched, taut wings there was an awareness that this light patch of colour was a new thing in its timber covered domain, and something not in the natural, unchanged order of things it knew ...
>
> For the two men who had carved them from the forest the clearings meant life, and the wedge they had driven to form a split in the forest did not appear to them, as it might have done had they been able to view it from where the eagle was, a minute chink which might have closed in on them at the will of the forest.
>
> The wedge-tail planed lower. The clearings took on distinctness, individuality; the small buildings showed as dark blots ... the dead ring-barked trees twisted strangely above the cleared land, contrasting with the living wall of forest pressing in on the cleared space. (9)

The adoption of an animal as the sentient point in the story was a device that Pollard used from time to time, but not quite in this way. Here, the eagle represents a form of vision that sees a deep ecological time, that recognises within the welter of individual acts, the intrusion of something unprecedented, "something not in the natural, unchanged order of things it knew." This passage keeps alive a double-vision. To the men who had cleared the forest, the clearings were hard-won achievements to which they clung with no certainty as to their ultimate reward. Their whole world was wagered on the hope they would one day be able to sell the produce that could be grown once the trees were gone. But seen from *above*, what one sees is the incursion of nothing, emptiness, into what was something. These men had formed something which had never previously existed, a "split" in the forest. In this sense, the story works very much like an allegory for the wheatbelt itself.

We learn that the two farms had belonged to two men who had formed a partnership to share the costs of clearing and fencing.[20] They had then each taken separate ownership of the adjoining farms they had together created. The younger, more ambitious of the two, Jim, had provided the impetus for this venture, with his older friend Morris content to follow his lead. But even though Jim is the more successful farmer, he envies Morris, and particularly he covets Morris's wife Jean. Jean had come from the wheatbelt and had initially felt hemmed in by her husband's farm, in a manner reminiscent of Ewers when he was transferred from South Tammin to Collie and then the Vasse:

> Jean ... missed the distances of the wheatbelt, the wide acres broken only by the small ridges and rises, and the scattered, irregular belts of scrub. The forest depressed her, there was no horizon, vision ended at the clearing's limits, at the dark wall the timber made about each cleared space. She had felt shut in, bound to the routine of existence almost visibly by the ever-present line of trees. (13)

Time passes and Morris is killed by falling timber in a storm; Jean decides to continue to work the farm alone, resisting the offer of Jim to buy it. Jim is angered by her stubbornness, and the story follows his torment.

> The solitude that had become habit had marked Jim. He was now sufficient unto himself. In a queer way he did not seem to live in the

present at all. His farm had every modern improvement that could prove itself better than that which had been in use, but he himself was apart. (17)

One is struck, more than anything, by the hermetic isolation of the participants in the drama, the quality which gives the story its title. This idea of silent dramatic juxtaposition—a kind of Mexican stand-off—is an important qualification to Cowan's concept of isolation, and perhaps even all isolation. What appears to be a reclusive reduction of one person to his or herself, often conceals the fact that this person is in the most intense possible relationship with someone in the life of their mind. When Jim's friend and older unwitting rival, Morris, is claimed by the hand of fate, Jim fully expects to "inherit" both his land and his wife. Instead, he is forced to learn the bitter lesson that she will never be his. Cowan's story, typically, does not end with any great transcendent moment. Instead, it fades gently, with Jim and Jean agreeing to coexist separately but together. The main work of the story was not in the service of some romantic need to bring forbidden lovers together, but in reconciling Jim to the facts of life.

The interesting thing is how this sad, elegant fable is brought into relation with the story of the land itself. The land becomes the medium of human, in particular masculine, desire:

> For [Jim] the land was something vital, something into which he projected his own hopes and fears, and whose indifference or hostility had not only to be met by constant, unremitting labour, but by a kind of inner resolution, a dedication of oneself wholly to the service of that more powerful element, the land. By such an attitude hostility or indifference might, if they could not be turned to benevolence, at least be allayed, kept, as it were, unaroused … [He had only] a slender hold on their new soil. (13)

Like many passages in Cowan, this one is marked by crucial ambiguities. First and foremost, it is not at all clear whether Jim is working for ("to the service of") or *against* the land. Next, we are not sure if the land epitomises "hostility" or "indifference", yet the consequences of either are quite distinct. Lastly, it is ambiguous whether Jim's ultimate goal is to tame the land (to prevent it hurting him) or, on the other hand, to possess it, to make it serve him. The matter is complicated by the sense that the land was what he and Morris had worked for together, until Jean had ruined their idyll: "And the cause of his divergence with Morris, and the consequent readjustment, was the woman. She stood for that which he had lost and what he might lose and for what Morris might lose in the future, so that already she seemed as a symbol of failure." (14)

What is significant for the literary history of the wheatbelt is how Jim's suffering is linked in Cowan's fable to the clearing of land for farm use. In his acute perception of the subjective component of "agricultural expansion", Cowan is dramatically different from any writer before him, and most writers after him. During the long, frosty coexistence of Jim and the widowed Jean, history—in the general sense—unfolds, and the world takes shape in the form that we, in a later generation, accept as necessary:

> During these years the district was changing … War began against the trees, the jarrah and karri valuable commercially, and against those that were given no value but which covered the soil the farms took; war against the trees that brought men there and kept them there. There was no consideration of what might happen when the trees were gone, the trunks passed out unrecognisable from the mills or standing stripped and dead over the cleared land, and such a day seemed remote, even impossible. (16–17)

This idea of a war "against the trees" was something which both Ewers and Pollard had recognised, but for them the matter was metaphysical, part of a historical fatality that man would eventually learn from and seek reconciliation. But in Cowan, the process of ecological destruction is thoroughly personal. The story is reminiscent of fairy stories where the troubles of a king and a queen can cause the whole land to slide into infertility and ruin. It is as if the impasse between Jim and Jean somehow created the conditions for the deforestation of southwestern Australia.

In a story like "Isolation" we can also see a major difference in Cowan's ecological consciousness to that of his predecessors. This is the realisation, not ever fully present in Ewers and Pollard, that the natural world that was making way for the expansion of farming was really and truly disappearing. Cowan's fiction, in a way quite unlike Ewers or Pollard, is open to, and perhaps even founded on, catastrophic loss—the irrevocable disappearance of something of deep value. In Pollard and Ewers, one feels that if only certain stupidities or bigotries could be let go of, then the reconciliation would surely happen. That once the cruel effects of wars and societal inequality were laid to rest, then a brighter, fuller future will emerge. It is hard not to connect this idea of a total destruction of nature with the actuality of total war that engulfed Australia, especially after the Pacific theatre opened in 1941. Cowan speaks of the war years as a time—very difficult to conceive of later—where the citizens of Australia had their lives controlled, censored and monitored to a very high degree. The Great War defined the lives of Facey, Ewers and Pollard, gave to them all their crucial coordinates, conditioned their sense of what it was to be—and to fail as—a man, and more generally what was at stake in the world. It shaped their sense of time, of loss, of future, and the horizons of what was natural. The impact of World War Two has a similar centrality for Cowan, although the effects are quite different. The first War had ripped away the veil of heroism that had initially masked the wholesale human slaughter of warfare in the industrial age. Where the Great War had begun as a grand adventure with much fanfare, World War Two seemed to come about slowly, inexorably and with a sense of deep dread, as if it was all only a matter of time. Cowan's stories published in *Drift* were written between 1939 and 1941 and capture the strange sensation of Australia being drawn into war for the second time in just over a generation.

The Unploughed Land (1958)

Following the War, Cowan returned to Western Australia, in part because of the severe shortage of housing in Melbourne and the difficulty of finding an adequate home for his wife and young son. It would be fourteen years between the publication of *Drift* in 1944, and the publication of Cowan's next collection, *The Unploughed Land,* in 1958.[21] The most significant new story to appear in *The Unploughed*

Land was the long title story which concludes the collection. At fifty
pages, it is nearly a novella, especially by Cowan's standards. Yet
Cowan's papers show that the story had started life as a much shorter
sketch originally composed in the middle of 1944 under the title "In
the Midst of Life …"[22] It was revised and added to the following
year and retitled "Williams' Farm", where it acquired a new framing
scenario, which Cowan recorded in July 1945 as follows:

> *Arrive in the fog – same as before – except sees expression of pain on woman's
> face*
> > *next day – follow old story up to night in kitchen*
> > *accent loneliness during talk* [23]

Following this basic structure, "The Unploughed Land", as it
appears in its final form for the 1958 collection, begins, as many of his
stories do, with a man—Lee Davis—arriving to work on a property.
It is a winter's night and the wheatbelt district is enveloped in thick
fog when Lee arrives. After some difficulty, he finds the house of his
new employer. Through the lit window, he sees an elderly woman
and a younger one, who must have been her daughter—she, like her
mother, was large and plain—and he was watching them when he
was surprised by the father returning from a nearby shed:

> He stood as though he had not realized that he had stopped and was
> looking in the window. The two in the room made no movement.
> In their stillness, and with the silence, it was as though he looked on
> something halted in time. He paused as though it held some significance
> that evaded but must come to him. Then he heard the heavy tread
> behind him and he turned quickly, guiltily, and the big shape was
> curiously like the fog, grey, unclear. He felt a quick unreasoned fear,
> like a child. The man close to him did not say anything.[24] (153)

After the introductions, Lee is shown to his lodgings, a section
of the machinery shed partitioned off by corrugated iron. Cowan
recounts how this was often the quarters when working on a farm,
and a similar accommodation was given to Ewers when he boarded
with a farmer when teaching at South Tammin. The action has the

sensation of exile, from the warmth and unity of the family kitchen, to the cold transience of the shed. Lee seems to savour, even if a little bitterly, the sense in which he belongs to no one:

> On the floor were old wheat-sacks for a mat ... He would never know how many others had put in time in the room, sleeping in this bed to be ready for the next day. For it was always the next day. Never now. But this was not a good time to think like that, tired, and in a strange place ... The place and the walk from the turn-off and the fog and the people were mingled in his mind, and he thought of the woman, and the girl, and she did not take any prizes, and the man ... He lay in the bed in the small room, and there was the heavy stillness of the fog, and he began to feel warm and he was tired. (158–9)

In the morning, the fog has gone and Lee sees the property. He is pleased that the house and sheds are surrounded by trees, which was unusual in his experience, "where so many of the homesteads stood on bare rises as though their owners hated the sight of a tree" (159). Having arrived during the seeding, Lee is set to work with the drill. Again, it is a partially mechanised world, so that while Lee had arrived courtesy of hitching a lift in a new Bedford truck, on the farm the machinery is still horse-drawn. The world is clearly that which Cowan had experienced during his years on farms in the '30s: "At the far end of the shed a black utility stood, but he thought it did not seem to figure prominently in the day's work, and there was no tractor. He had been told by the agency he might be required to drive a team. 'Might' seemed a careful evasion." (160) Cowan himself graduated through the tasks of rural labour to the driving of horse-teams, and came to like that work. One could expect more money if one drove a team. But in this story, the horse-team is already something of an anachronism, and to Lee, "it suddenly seemed like a long time since he had worked with anything but tractors" (161). The girl later tells him that they are the last ones in that district to be still using a team.

Lee comes to enjoy working for this family, and they treated him—unlike many he had worked for—like one of themselves. The girl gradually warms to him and they speak occasionally when she brings his lunch or tea out to where he is working in the paddocks.

The work of the farm is rendered in plain but gentle terms in Cowan's story. The narration is unhurried and the tasks seem to follow each other in simple succession. However, this idyllic mood is not allowed to sit unchallenged. The girl, we eventually discover her name is Vera, and Lee find themselves together in town on a Saturday night. He had spent the afternoon in the pub and she was picking him up before collecting her parents at a neighbour's.

> He said, "First time I've been in this town."
> She was looking along the road. She said, "You're lucky."
> "How's that? It's not such a bad place. No worse than others, I suppose."
> "No better, either."
> "Well, that might be right."
> "It is." (165)

In the relationship that begins to evolve between Vera and Lee there is a dramatisation of the collision of ideals that takes place in the heavily invested terrain of the wheatbelt. We are not told why Lee has come to the kind of work he now does. He tells Vera that his father had worked in the railways, and that he himself had started out working as a clerk in a timber mill but had not liked it. The farm work he had done since is almost the exact kind of work that one does when one does not wish to explain one's choice of vocation. The patient rhythm of the prose echoes the meditative isolation that grants Lee a degree of solace, which he traces in his daydreams that inflect the landscape that surrounds him:

> He thought, working in the upper paddocks away from the house, that the property was certainly well out of the way … He became used to the view from the rise where he was working, the wide expanse beyond the newly sown paddocks, the scrub and patches of timber that made a dark border along the other ridge, far over, and that formed the limit of vision, except for the sharp outline of the hill pushing up behind the ridge. He used to watch the hill, and the way the colour changed on it as the day advanced, and how sometimes it seemed so close that he could walk to it. (166)

But again, the idea that somehow the work yielded perfect contentment for Lee is undercut in the very next sentence when we learn that he "was not sorry when Saturday broke the week and they went in to town." And then, seeing Vera in town with a couple of her friends, he "felt suddenly his own isolation and [that] he was tired of being by himself, there was the sudden need for someone just to speak to, and she was the only person he knew in the town."

It is characteristic of Cowan's fiction that his characters do not properly know themselves, and their own contradictions often take the form of "sudden" impulses that appear to directly go against their avowed positions. Lee had almost convinced himself of the fact that he could exist in noble isolation, independent of any need to call upon another, and the unbearable indebtedness that this seems to imply. But Vera put the lie to this. For Vera's part, she is in the wheatbelt, born to it, and seemingly bonded to it. All she can think about is wanting to leave. On a whim, Jim asks Vera to see a movie playing in the local town hall. This in itself is an odd moment in the fiction of the wheatbelt. There is no suggestion of movies existing in the work of Pollard and Ewers, even though the medium was alive and well in the 1920s and '30s. Even when it is mentioned in the work of Cowan's contemporary Dorothy Hewett, one gets a slightly romanticised, childlike sense of Hollywood as a completely immersive fantasy space. In Hewett, there is at times—though it does falter—an almost total identification with the stars of the silver screen and the sense that these wondrous stories and characters merged seamlessly with her own febrile fantasy world. The experience of cinema in Cowan's fiction is quite different, even as his own work became increasingly cinematic in its use of montage. What is felt by Jim in the cinema of this wheatbelt town is not the pleasure of being transported elsewhere, but estrangement and confusion:

> The newsreels filled the screen, and it was like looking at other worlds, at events that were a long way from the flat acres of the wheat, and the scrub, and the small town, so far as to deny any point of contact and these reflections of another world held no more reality than one of the animated cartoons. And the supporting film, when it came, was of a world as remote, one which had invention and convenience and ways

of living taken for granted by those who watched it, so long as it was something reflected on a screen, but unrelated to the fabric of their own living, and the fact that some features of it could be translated to that fabric with advantage was unconsidered. (167)

Even the locution of the description becomes a little tortured here, as if to reflect the scrambling of reality that the film effects in Jim. Pollard hardly mentions the existence of towns in the wheatbelt. While in Ewers's work towns appear as signs of the growth of settlement, in Cowan's writing the towns sit oddly in their landscape. As Vera and Lee walk along the main street of the town, there are houses on one side of the street and on the other, "the low scrub and, farther down, the open paddocks, dark and flat, and as though all unrelated to the houses, the road like a division between things different in time" (185).

The episode in the cinema does show something not seen in other wheatbelt works, perhaps not even until Kinsella takes the stage in the late 1980s, which is a mediated wheatbelt. This is a wheatbelt that is shot through with modern, mediated life, and not distinct from it. Pollard's heroes keep private libraries of books in their bushland hideaways and perpetuate a mythology of the withdrawn nature-intellectual, in the mould of Thoreau. By contrast, Cowan's characters, particularly in this earlier period of his writing, are notably untutored—they are not bookish, and are not usually able to express at any length their feelings or thoughts. The isolation of their lives is not mitigated by dynastic metanarratives or family sagas, and instead the characters seem, to use Cowan's own word, to *drift*. Some have drifted, like Lee, into the wheatbelt, and others—like Vera—are hoping to drift out. Neither of these types sees the wheatbelt as part of a narrative, and it is, in fact, part of the slow painful work that they undertake in Cowan's fiction to make a story of their experience, to find in their fragmentation and isolation, a viable plot for their lives.

Cowan was a great admirer of Kenneth (Seaforth) Mackenzie's coming of age novel, *The Young Desire It* (1937). Indeed, the novel, set in Guildford Grammar and the hills south of Perth, gave Cowan courage to write about his own locations in a modernist fashion and also to write frankly about sexual desire.[25] In "The Unploughed Land", it is under the force of their loneliness that the wheatbelt landscape becomes suffused with desire for Lee and Vera. A certain aching hunger is also driven by the accumulation of Cowan's understated sentences. Driving home with Vera and her parents after the cinema, Lee "thought how you could feel the empty cleared spaces spreading out from the dark road, the flat expanse of the wheat and the fallow paddocks, just as in the day time you could see them" (168). In spite of himself, Lee becomes more and more attracted to plain, taciturn Vera. Something in her sullen defiance captures his interest. Nevertheless, he suggests that she should maybe just leave, if that is what she wishes. But she cannot leave, she says, either out of duty to her parents, or because it does not seem that another place might be any better. When Lee expresses his frustration with her fatalism, she is able to point to his own restlessness. He says that he has of late been thinking he will "find a place and settle down somewhere" (171), but Vera doubts it:

> "Well," he said, something in her tone forcing him to a personal issue, "you don't want to stay here yourself. Or so you reckon. Why should someone like m'self? Only way you can keep at this kind of thing is by moving on. When you get a cheque go down to town or the beach somewhere and have a spell."
>
> She said, "Now you know why I hate that town." (171–2)

In classical fashion, the romance between Vera and Lee follows the advance of the season, and interspersed between the scenes of their awkward lovemaking we see the seeded fields blush slowly to life, "the green stain of the new grass, the patches of timber and scrub seeming deeper in colour" (174). Again, in spite of himself, Lee finds that he actually cares about the place he is now working in:

> And he began to think of the work and the week ahead, and he thought that in many ways it was a good place, he was left alone and it was as if he had a personal interest in the work, as if it had been for himself, and he knew that he did not want to leave it now, and that he wanted to see the harvest that was the tangible result of all they had done, to see it finished. But it never finishes, he thought, there is never an end. (179)

Lee's train of thought runs as if he were resisting a seduction, terrified that if "you began to think like that you became caught up in it." The work and the girl are conjoined in his thinking, and it is now less clear that Cowan does indeed take a different line to that of Ewers and Pollard, whose fiction is powered by an idealised female figure that stands for the land to which the men commit their lives. The major difference, of course, is that Cowan's characters are not saints. Their main virtue is a truculent, spasmodic honesty that makes them vulnerable and, occasionally, at least in their own eyes, humiliates them. As Lee thinks again about getting his own place, instead of drifting about and working for others, he thinks of Vera:

> And he thought of the girl, and how they had walked up to the hill where the salmon-gums were, and he remembered vividly her bare legs and how he had felt that he should touch them, as though his hands moving on her flesh with its warmth and vitality were a need beyond that which was personal, and he thought, If it is to go like that it will involve us like the place and the work and the seasons. And there is no end. (179)

The shadow of Hemingway hangs heavily over this passage with its undulating run-on sentences and melancholy combination of fatality and eroticism. Even the slightly mannish Vera recalls Hemingway's heroines. In these moments, Cowan also prefigures the lush sexual nostalgia of Hewett's memoir of this same period, *Wildcard*. The sexual hunger at the core of human motivation is what distinguishes the fatalism of Cowan's and Hewett's work from that which reigns in Pollard and Ewers. In the older writers, the wheatbelt came about through metaphysical and material necessity—Man must conquer Nature, it has always been thus. In Cowan, there is something of this, but the relationships are much more tightly drawn into the intimate play of love and hatred. They share something with the rural tragedies of John Steinbeck, his characters raw and inarticulate, yet somehow elevated, like noble savages who refuse to succumb to the lure of the dramatic irony that makes life bearable to the jaundiced modern eye.

Cowan writes quite beautifully, and delicately, about sexual attraction.[26] In "The Unploughed Land", the unlikely pairing of Vera and Lee is consummated on a rainy afternoon in Lee's makeshift accommodation in the shed. The passage concludes one section of the story and is immediately juxtaposed by the opening of the next section, describing the budding wheat. The two passages are united by the repetition of the word "curve":

> … The light from the fire was on the curve of her strong shoulders and her arms and her breasts firm and drawn down under their own weight.
>
> In the paddocks that had been seeded the wheat came on, it rose from the stiff new shoots till it had fullness and the leaf broadened and drooped in its characteristic curve. (190)

If this had been a film, then one could imagine a slow dissolve from one image to the other, from the breasts of the girl in the firelight to the curving leaves of the sprouting wheat stalks. It is, like the manifold photographs of children standing, smiling in the fields before harvest, a direct connection of the wheat to human fertility.

In parallel with the ripening of the fields and the passage of the love affair, a third arc is introduced into the action of the narrative, involving the gradual succumbing of the mother to illness. Here, again, we can draw a sharp contrast with the work of Pollard and Ewers, where the paternal figure was the sacrificial element—Tommy Lea in *Men Against the Earth* and Joseph O'Meare in *Rose of the Bushlands*. The woman—we never hear her name—dies quietly in a desert of understatement. She dies in the springtime and the family keep going, accepting this event as they do all events. The whole dynamic of "The Unploughed Land" is given by this kind of gradualism. Everything occurs slowly, imperceptibly, and by degrees—only to then be punctuated by sudden, unexpected moments of decision or realisation. These convulsive moments often erupt out of dialogue that starts innocuously before one or the other participant strikes, intentionally or accidentally, the raw nerve:

> She said suddenly, "Is that what you're going to do?"
> "What?"
> "What you said. Get away from it all."
> "You're back to that."

She did not say anything.

"Why should I?" he said.

"You always have."

"I don't know."

After a time he said, "We could go away for a while. Go down the beach or something. There won't be much to do after the harvest."

"And come back?"

"Well, I suppose."

"You wouldn't."

"Well," he said, "do we have to, come to that?"

"I do."

"No."

"What about my father?"

He did not say anything. Ahead of them there was the shape of the scrub that closed in about the culvert.

"I don't know," he said. "I can't work it out." (197)

Here, again, Cowan's fiction credibly locates these moments in the texture of ordinary activity. There is a strong contrast between his dialogue and the set-piece speeches of Pollard or the folksy idiomatic musings of Ewers. The romance at the centre of the story is strung tautly between a man and a woman who both think they want to leave. Lee has always left, but has become tired of it. Vera has never left, and wishes she might. But there is also a contrast between their respective escape fantasies and a wish for something that each, without quite realising, feels or fears they are not entitled to, which is that they might marry each other and have their own lives together. The ebb and flow of their progress towards this realisation is dramatised partly through the contrast that Lee notices each evening as the blinding brightness of the day sinks away. At this point he would become "aware of the stillness, the quiet, that seemed to reveal the vitality of the earth around him, the pulse of it, something that was dormant in the light as though the sun were inimical to it, suck it to dryness and listlessness, but that was revealed now in the darkness and was like a negation of the age and sterility that seemed to lie in the flat distances and the dull-coloured scrub and the hard sky, like a landscape exhausted by the long movement of time and now old, drying and indifferent" (178).

34. *The Unploughed Land* (Angus & Robertson, 1958).

As Lee starts to contemplate a future where he might own his land, and a life with Vera, he becomes more drawn to the figure of the father, who had always appeared, to him, a little odd and aloof. Lee is fascinated by what seems to be an almost automatic quality in the man's pursuit of his tasks:

> ... he thought it was as if the man was himself regulated by the seasons he understood so well, responding automatically, this year sowing more, this less, without will of his own. His existence seemed almost a routine devoid of human qualities, as though he had become absorbed in the land and the movement of the seasons until he was a part of it. (193)

The qualities he had once found strange and even a little off-putting become, as the story progresses, the subject of Lee's admiration and even emulation. With the mother gone, a new trio emerges which now includes Lee. But he finds something sad in the father's singularity, his wordless movement through his work. Lee wonders whether he could bear it, and in some way his vacillation over whether to offer himself to Vera is bound to this question. The marriage of the old couple is an enigma to him. He knows they must have loved one another at some point but does not see the evidence of this in their late years. He fears that marriage would bring about some similar, slow death. But he is also not sure that their marriage was dead. In the midst of an argument, he asks Vera whether her father even misses the mother.

> She did not answer at once, and then she said, "It's hard to say. In a way."
>
> "I wouldn't say he'd even noticed."
>
> "You don't know," she said. "You don't know about it all. And why do you worry about that? You've come round to that before."
>
> "Perhaps I have," he said. "And you won't answer. Anyhow, what difference does it make?"
>
> "It seems to, to you."
>
> "Well, it doesn't."
>
> "I know what you think."
>
> "Yes?"
>
> "Yes."
>
> "It might go like that for everyone. How do I know? So why worry?"
>
> "You think it would for us."
>
> "No, I didn't say that. How do I know? It's what I said, maybe it goes that way for everyone. But it's not good worrying about it."
>
> "It's you that does."
>
> "Let it go," he said. (198)

Not for the first time, Vera gets the better of her older, worldlier lover, able to more precisely pin down the source of his fear.

At the end of such skirmishes, the narrative re-enfolds the combatants into the pattern of the season. The work on the farm seems to provide a necessary shelter for people from each other. When they reach an impasse and do not know where to go, they simply restart their work, and interact on that basis. It is a slightly more hopeful vision than that offered in "Living", where the man's life falls apart when his wife departs, or "Harvest", where George cannot quite be steadied by his sojourn on the wheat farm of his friend Jim. The work of this farm comes to bond Lee, Vera, and her father together in a manner that does not depend on their moment-to-moment feelings towards one another:

> The three of them seemed to become gathered into and inseparable from an existence that was linked to the acres of wheat, the high standing growth of it and the sun on the innumerable heads massed thickly over the shape of the land, the hard smooth grain that fattened the dumps of bags, hot and bleached, the bags pointing inwards across the widening stubble, an existence linked to and having no end beyond these factors, robbed of human qualities, as though for a time they were inanimate, automatic, as much mechanical and directed to the single end as the harvester with its own complicated inner working and pattern. And as though, when they stopped and the task was completed, they would be as devoid of purpose as the idle machine. (200)

The interesting element of this passage is that it draws on what is now a familiar metaphor of farm work being automated and machine-like, but here it is painted in positive terms. The machine is a good thing, an image of integrated human conduct, able to offer itself in the service of something beyond the immediate wishes and even knowledge of its individual members.

The solution to the story, though, is not left solely to the work of gradual adjustment. It does not depend entirely on the kind of slow and hard-won détente that reconciled Jim and Jean in "Isolation". The situation is short-circuited in an age-old fashion, because Vera falls pregnant. That in itself is not remarkable, and as soon as they commence a sexual relationship one more or less expects that there will be consequences in the story. The striking thing is that Vera admits she did it deliberately, somewhat exceeding the limits of what one can accomplish purely on one's own in these matters. But it is a confession of love in its own tortured way:

"I know what you're trying to say. We don't need to blame each other. I'll tell you—I don't want you to think what I've done is anything to stop you going. It's not. I've thought about it. I did it on purpose. It's not a trick I've played on you. You won't understand, but it was for myself. I wanted a child. I guess I wanted that kind of life, too, but that's one of the things it's not good wanting different. Anyhow, I didn't do this for any of the reasons you'd probably think." (203–4)

Nor does Lee fall into predictable masculine resentment, and instead takes the pregnancy as the confirmation of his suppressed wish to stay and start a farm of his own. He tells Vera: "Things settle themselves, and that's about the only way." The final scene of the story fast-forwards to the following season and Lee is ploughing the field that gives the story its title, and where the winter rains "had begun the whole movement and rhythm again" (205). As he ploughs, Lee thinks of his pregnant wife and "he thought of another life entering and becoming involved in this, in the timeless persistence, and the slow movement."

> And he thought if, perhaps suddenly, perhaps with a slow awareness, it would ever see this, the land, the different-coloured soil, the long slow slope of the hill and the timber that covered the rise, the salt-pans and the unceasing mirage of summer, the sheds and yards and the break of trees that was about the small unchanging house, and the people whose lives were centred in these things, if it would ever see them as a stranger might, as he had himself once looked upon them, seeing them perhaps as inexplicable, or perhaps as holding an interpretation it had no wish to encompass.

The slightly uncanny element to this elegiac conclusion to the story is that the future baby is referred to as "it", a necessity to which we are often rather uncomfortably driven on such occasions. But the embryo rather disappears under this pronoun until "it" becomes almost an objective, other-worldly sentience that must come to terms with "this"—the farm embedded into the world of the wheatbelt. The last phrase—*holding an interpretation it had no wish to encompass*—is enigmatic. The baby, it is conceded, may come, in spite of its

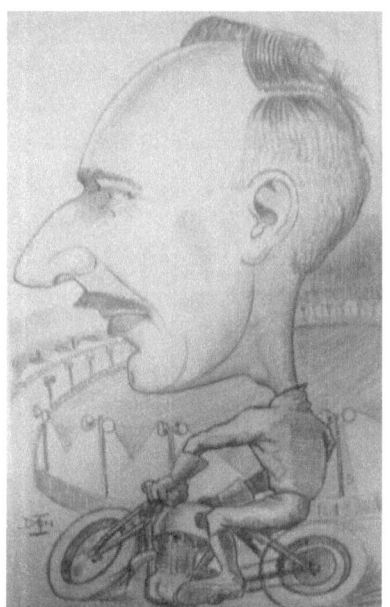

35. Caricature by one of Cowan's Scotch College Students. Peter Cowan Papers, Peter Cowan Writers Centre, Western Australia.

being conceived in this very place, to see "this" as "inexplicable". But even this inexplicability is not allowed to end matters because perhaps the truth is that the farm and its people *are* explicable but the "interpretation" was not palatable, that is, in accordance with "its" wishes. This moment troubles the otherwise quietly optimistic tenor of the story's conclusion, because it points to a founding repression. The fact that this child was conceived out of wedlock will of course become plain to "it" at a certain point in his or her life. The child, in this sense, will share with the wheatbelt the quality of being retrospectively legitimated.

Summer (1964)

Having made his name as a short-story writer, Cowan's debut novel appeared in mid-career—and mid-life, he was now fifty—with the publication of *Summer* by Angus & Robertson in 1964. Cowan had been trying unsuccessfully to publish novels since the mid-1930s, and a very early version of *Summer* had in fact been rejected by Angus & Robertson in 1952, whom he had contacted at the suggestion of the writer Henrietta Drake-Brockman. Both literary agents and

publishers indicated that the works proposed and submitted were less
novels than expanded short stories, which, if one looks at Cowan's
manuscripts, was exactly what they were. The breakthrough came
with the winning, at the end of 1962, of a Commonwealth Literary
Fund fellowship which funded him to write full-time in 1963 and to
resign his position at Scotch. The novel follows the passage of Henry
Simpson, a middle-aged Perth businessman, into the wheatbelt to take
up seasonal work on a remote wheat bin. In Cowan's collected papers,
the first notes for the novel date from 21 May 1960, and indicate the
basic scenario of the novel, which was then called "The Tree":

> *Job clerk and bin —*
> *arrives station waggon — sets up machine —*
> *first day quiet, pleasant, as he had expected*
> *cameras for birds, will get time weekend*
>
> *...*
>
> *In weekend sets up cameras — sees dead tree — meets her*[27]

A manuscript was completed the following year, still with "The
Tree" as its title.[28] As the novel was redrafted a new beginning was
added to the manuscript which provided the back-story to Henry's
arrival. These kind of initiating events had always been kept to the
barest minimum in Cowan's stories. Occasionally, details would be
introduced about how a character's life had reached the point at which
we meet them in the text, but often these are sporadic and almost
evasive, as if they were embarrassed or running from something that
is contained in these facts. Cowan's stories uphold this secrecy and,
indeed, are built upon it.

The opening three chapters of *Summer* take place in Perth more
or less in the present day—that is, the early 1960s—of the novel's
publication. The city, despite its isolation, is marked by a post-war
suburban passivity, with evidence of material comfort in the lives
of Henry and his wife. He seems to be a successful businessman—a
partner in an importing firm—and supports his wife comfortably in a
leafy suburb of Perth, with two cars and a gardener to trim the shrubs.
They have an adult daughter who has left home, and the illusions that
had supported the marriage have clearly faded. The novel is narrated

in the third-person and with a certain hard-bitten cynicism suggestive of *film noir*. The comparison is borne out by the evolving situation in which Henry suspects his wife of having an affair and follows her one night in his car. When, instead of meeting a girlfriend at the cinema, she climbs into the car of another man, he engages a private detective to compile the necessary evidence. The resulting scene is straight from 1950s cinematic melodrama. The couple are watching television, which, like the cinema in "The Unploughed Land", was a site of blaring unreality:

> He watched the suddenly meaningless movement that steadied to other faces, other facades, other actions, which were soon blended to a like anonymity.
>
> She said, "I'll be going to Rosemary's tomorrow evening."
>
> "Why don't you ask him here?" he said. All through the meal words had waited that he could not force himself to utter.
>
> "Ask—you mean Rosemary? She's having an evening—"
>
> "No."
>
> "I don't know what you mean?"
>
> "Just—why not ask him here?"
>
> "I see," she said. "So you know."
>
> "At last." (13)

Henry's fatalistic acceptance of his cuckolding is related rather explicitly to a childhood of being bullied, particularly because he wore glasses. His failure to "see" that his wife had long ago given up on him was symptomatic of his congenitally "defective sight", and his wife's abandonment of him for a brighter and better rival fell, in his own self-recrimination, into a pattern of such things for as long as he could remember.

His departure to the wheatbelt was a strange decision for someone in his position. He was no longer young, and he had no real background in country life. But he had a residual attraction to the wheatbelt from childhood holidays, and he thought, as he explained to his daughter, that it might also be a chance to pursue his interest in bird photography. This hobby is also, in a slightly skewed way, connected to the problems he has in seeing, and perhaps more to the point, in being seen. In the wheatbelt he constructs a hide from which to photograph a nest of rare smoker parrots. The wife's complaint, once finally caught out, was to ask him where on earth he had been all this time, and Henry himself concedes that he had not really been present in the marriage for many years: "You're not human ... You can always go and work in your dark-room" (18). In the midst of this domestic misery, the wheatbelt looms in his memory as a place where things were otherwise:

> Sometimes he thought the year he had spent at his uncle's farm in the wheat belt had been a turning-point, after which his sight had remained constant instead of declining, and, coincidence though it had no doubt been, he had, almost superstitiously, built for himself a pledge of security, that if ever his eyes did begin to fail him he would go back to that life which had so attracted him. Its power took him still for holidays to the farm, though the woman he had tried now to follow in the grey car had never liked it or the country, had spent no more than a week-end there, her air of martyrdom ensuring it was not repeated. (9–10)

In other words, the wheatbelt had already existed in the recesses of his mind as an escape strategy if ever life got too much. One does not have to press too strongly to find a connection here with Cowan's own life. After spending much of the '30s in rural Western Australia, and the war years in Melbourne, Cowan recommenced life as a teacher with a young child and wife in suburban Perth. The years at Scotch (1950–62), where he taught English and Geography, were clearly quite fulfilling ones, although it is also a period where Cowan's writing was not pursued with the same regularity that it was in the '40s and again in the '60s. When he commenced study at The University of Western Australia in 1938, he worked on the wheat bins to help support himself, which he enjoyed. That was normal enough for a student in those days, and indeed the practice of UWA students being employed to staff the wheat bins continued into the 1980s. Less conventional was Cowan's decision to work on the bins during his time as a teacher at Scotch and he took this work following a break-down after ten years of teaching: "[B]y the end of the '50s, after I'd been, say, ten years at it, I felt I'd really begun to have enough and I did, in fact, suffer what people now call 'burn out', teachers' burn out … Nobody had ever heard that word before."[29] A sympathetic headmaster, Dr Maxwell Keys, helped to make it possible for Cowan to go back to the wheatbelt where he felt less oppressed by life:

> For a few years, three or four years I think, I used to go up and work on the wheat bins, coming down at the weekends, but something I'd done in the 30s, and this kept me going. I mean it simply was what one needed, a complete change somewhere away, back, in my case, in the country which had always revitalised me. Though it wasn't always approved by some of the other senior masters there, there was headmaster [Keys] who could see that that kind of thing was necessary and probably would be a good idea … to let people go away. I didn't get out of any school time. I did it in the holidays. They were late-opening bins.[30]

The result of Cowan's pre-war, student experiences and the post-war repetition of these journeys is the emergence for the first time of the "wheat bin" into the imaginative literature of the wheatbelt.[31] The shift to bulk-handling was already visible in Cowan's story "Living" (1943). But the full bulk-handling of wheat—grain placed directly from harvesters into trucks, then measured at weighbridges, transferred to corrugated iron bins, and automatically lifted into trains—is what we can see by the time *Summer* is published in 1964. Bulk-handling had been recommended as early as 1913 by the Grain Advisory Board, and there had been a failed attempt at co-operative bulk-handling in 1920, but it was not until 1932 that five experimental bins were built in the Wyalkatchem district on the Dowerin–Merredin line.[32] In some ways, the turmoil of the Depression gave co-operative bulk-handling, which had languished in the too-hard basket for decades, an economic necessity and occasioned the political will to start the expensive task of automating grain delivery from field to port. In 1933, fifty-three receival points were built, which grew to 103 in 1937 and 234 by 1940–41. The number of points peaked at 305 in 1965, when a process of rationalisation led to fewer, bigger bins being used in the '70s and since.

The introduction of bulk-handling in the 1930s gradually transformed the wheatbelt in the ensuing decades. The bins at the receival points became the largest structures in the landscape and, at the level of iconography, recoded the image of farming into something much more industrial. This had the effect of making quaint and anachronistic the vision of farming as a timeless marriage of mankind with the soil. Cowan was the first writer to see the bins as having a certain industrial sublimity, somewhere between a cathedral and a factory, marked by vast interior space that remained closed and empty for much of the year, before springing to life in November with the commencement of harvesting. The bins were monuments to functionality and made no concessions to form, but, even so, they were captivating in their sheer size and the incongruity of their sharp geometrical lines, as if they were cubist follies introduced into the landscape:

> As he stepped into the long, high bin the glare of the late afternoon light was shadowed. Near the far end, from the open gap sheet in the roof, the sun cut sharply though the dust haze above the pile of wheat that sloped upward like an inverted funnel, as neat, as smooth-sided. From the elevator nozzle the wheat, brown liquid through the dust, poured solidly onto the heap, sliding, settling, the dust rising thickly in the shadowed air. He watched the steady flow into the empty bays of the bin that seemed wide and unthreatened by the slow spread of the grain, until the engine note lifted, and the rush of the chute slackened. (32)

In parallel with the belated industrialisation of the wheatbelt, the city of Perth was entering into the beginnings of what might be called the post-industrial consumer age. With this, the sense of the artificiality of modern life had also become much more palpable by the late 1950s, the feeling that we were somehow living simulated or facsimile existences, and the corresponding longing for "authentic" forms of being that was at the heart of existentialist philosophy at this time. Cowan, indeed, felt that 1950s Western Australia was doubly imprisoned by the seductions of modern mediated living, and a complacent and conservative intelligentsia:

> I was involved in discussions with people high up in the writers' society, Australian Fellowship of Writers in Western Australia [FAWWA], who

vehemently argued that Western Australia and Australia did NOT need, for instance, the influence or really to be much aware of the French writers who were coming through at the time. So obviously people like Sartre and so on, they didn't want them in here. One of them said to me, "Do we want that kind of thing here?"[33]

In some ways what the wheatbelt gives in Cowan's novel *Summer* is a correlative to the passage of modernity. The wheatbelt is both outside and inside modernity because it was beyond the ambit of many urban conveniences but also subject to the very processes— technologisation, internationalisation, economies of scale, advances in agricultural science—that were changing the face of cities. The opening chapters of *Summer* not only emphasise the sterility of Henry's marriage but the aseptic withdrawal of life beyond a screen of artificial substitutes. In his lounge, Henry lives surrounded by falsity—a living room devoid of life:

> In the lounge he lit the heater. He did not want to eat, he took a drink and went to sit before the growing warmth of the heater in the fireplace in which they no longer lit fires, and the stains from the smoke had been painted over. The round core began to glow, he thought it curious he should watch it as he might have watched the flames about a log. (4)

The room was decorated with photographs and he had the television on although he did not watch it, conscious only of the "curious unreality" of the figures on its screen. All of this is contrasted with his primitive new life at the wheatbin, where he lives in an iron shed that is hot during the day and often cold at night. He lives off simple rations and the room is heated by a wood-fire.

Henry's arrival into the wheatbelt is not narrated. We hear him telling his daughter that he is going to leave and the next chapter opens with a sketch of the siding, which we come to realise is his new home. The sketch that opens chapter four and introduces the wheatbelt to the reader is, in fact, a relic of a much earlier period in Cowan's writing, and had originally been published in *Ern Malley's Journal* in 1952.[34] In this sense, this image can be thought of as the

36. The "A-Class" Bin.

seed of the novel, the fulcrum around which the whole tortured love triangle will come to turn. Viewed thus, Cowan's calm, almost formulaic, descriptions of the wheatbelt landscape can be seen as themselves a kind of screen, behind which we must suppose churn quite lurid passions, so that these images are formed as objects of meditation, designed to stop the ceaseless flow of thought and anxiety. A peculiarity that also lends an element of dullness to Cowan's descriptive passages is that he does not, like most novelists, invoke the reader's full range of senses by introducing sounds and odours. The sound and smell of a scene are the means by which an image is made immediate to a reader, yet Cowan's writing studiously avoids this, and reading his descriptions one gets the impression that he is analysing a picture of the landscape rather than trying to convey to his reader the full sense of being in it:

> The light came slowly, like a hardening of the sky, the colour striking upwards from the deep band above the horizon. The patches of scrub and timber showed without distinctness, dark about the lighter squares of the cleared land, the fallow like broken scars, and the pale colour of the wheat. The tops of the scattered trees, the upper leaves, pale, and moving in the cold early wind, began to reflect the light, their dark greyish colour lifting. (28)

At the bin, due to the fall of his work mate from the bin's grain elevator, Henry is left in sole charge. It was an eventuality that Henry seemed to welcome, even though it meant more work, because it absolved him from the necessity of having to talk to someone all the time. But, even so, the move to the wheatbelt does not remove from Henry the burden of desire. Having left a wife who had come to despise him, one is led to surmise that he has sought—in the wheatbelt—an end to the turbulence of love. The time on the bin is a retreat of Henry into himself, along the lines of Pollard's Peter Rodon, where his life is given just by his work and he can avoid the hell of other people. Like Pollard's heroes, he has his books and his camera and his interest in wildlife, and these can be counted on to not tarnish his being with the unbearable condition of wanting something (someone) that might not want you.

Henry finds himself in a situation that is classically Cowanesque—alone with another couple. Apart from the desultory parade of wheat-laden trucks, Henry's only contact with other people is with the Everetts—Tom and Jill—a married couple who run the nearby shop that services the surrounding farms. It quickly becomes plain that the husband is abusive towards his wife and Henry is drawn into the fatal conflict by a mixture of loneliness, pity, attraction to the stoic Jill Everett, and hatred of the bullying Tom Everett, who stands in for the bullies of his childhood:

> This jest of his fellows at the end of the day was especially bitter, delaying what had become the hour of escape, and sent him away finally with a conviction of his impotence and futility. And a bitterness for which he could find no outlet ... He developed the defence of never intruding or asserting himself, of hanging at the edge of groups, of finding corners of the ground likely to be deserted, as if he might turn attention or notice by his very insignificance. (14–15)

Everett is a new kind of villain, distinct from the caddish late-Victorian antagonists that operated in Pollard's romances. He is more blatant than the scoundrels that tormented Pete Rodon and the O'Meares, with a boorish sexuality and a constant threat of physical force. And the matter is made complex because he is married to Jill, rather than making designs on a woman that is not yet committed to another. He is loud and overbearing, drives too fast and seems to enjoy frightening and humiliating people.

Jill Everett is a typical Cowan heroine, whose cool, wary exterior barely conceals an underlying terror, and whose outward character displays a mixture of furtiveness and ruthlessness. The relationship proceeds in the midst of inarticulacy, as both Jill and Henry are habituated to keeping their thoughts to themselves. It is Cowan's major aesthetic achievement to successfully represent dialogue between people who do not really wish to speak. The mutual shyness provides, paradoxically, the conditions for stunted revelations. Jill asks Henry the obvious question, which is why on earth someone like him—middle-aged, educated—has come to work on a wheat bin in the middle of nowhere; what was he looking for?

"Oh—a kind of freedom. Away from building and people in masses. Where I could look at things, do some photographing, things like trees and birds. Landscape. I suppose silence."

"You can photograph silence?"

"Yes."

"You'll find those things here, if they are what you want."

"It would be called escapism, I suppose. I don't see why, except that any removal from the mass, from the hive, must be branded. But I want to spend some of whatever time is left with these things, anyhow." (71–2)

As in other Cowan stories, a distinct value is placed on physical work. Although we see little of Henry's day-to-day tasks, and these do not seem to matter in themselves, Henry's appearance begins to change, the sun tanning his skin and the work sharpening his body. And the growing pile of wheat in the bin "was like a tangible statement of the week's work" (36). The work at the siding restores Henry's depleted masculinity and prepares him for the inevitable conflict with Everett. At the same time there is a tension between the cleansing physicality of Henry's labour and the eerie loneliness of the siding where he works. In the novel, the wheat bin remains a looming presence in the narrative, a distinct element that broods on a horizon that is otherwise marked only by the patches of remnant timber in the cleared landscape. Even nearing night, "the roof of the wheat silo" stood "black and sharp" against the last, faint rays of the sun (35). Jill tells Henry that she is terrified of the bins and that she "could never go into one of those wheat bins at night" (48). And often, in the narrative, the sharp angles of the metal sheeting are paired with the sharp angle of the light that falls through the open sheet—the "gap sheet" used to fill and empty the bin—of the roof to lend an expressionist angularity to an otherwise rural scene.

The bin carries with it the suggestion of danger at the hands of something inhuman in its scale and operation. The fact that the story opens with Henry's intended co-worker having already fallen from the grain elevator adds to this element of suspense. On another occasion, Henry is on the roof when a willy-willy in the nearby paddock threatens to swerve over the bin:

Watching, he was aware sharply of fear, as he thought of the loose
iron sheets he had been tightening. There was no time to secure them,
or to reach the ladder. The spiral came directly at the silo, then, as if
deflected by the open bulkhead beyond it, the swirling dust and leaves
darted out across the road, the chaff from the edge of the wheat pile
scattering like the dust itself. (99)

The sudden, capricious intrusion of danger lends a climate of menace
to the world that Henry has come to occupy, and subverts his fantasy of a
rural escape, pointing to the conditioning of his existence by still deeper
fantasies. The presence of the bin also transforms the natural quietness
of the wheatbelt into an uncanny silence. After lunch one day, Henry
suddenly becomes aware of the silence, how the "siding was deserted,
the movement of the trucks, the chatter of the engine and the elevator
forgotten", and how it "seemed all an infinite distance from anything,
as if he existed in a curiously complete isolation" (38). Significantly, it is
at this very moment of uncanny silence and sudden anxiety that Henry
sees the smoker parrots for the first time and determines to try and
discover their nesting place in the neighbouring bush. Another trigger
for the sense of aloneness that afflicts Henry is the presence or absence
of Jill. When she is not there, he feels desolate, even though if she were
there he would not in all probability be talking with her:

Along the road the shade was scrawled thinly upon the red earth.
The building was silent, the car gone from the garage. He was aware
of sudden loneliness, of existing against some endlessly alien and
indifferent landscape, the trees silent in the heat, away beyond them
the paddocks of stubble and unharvested grain, the thin dark lines of
scrub; it was as if he found himself in some long-deserted and unused
place, where he, solitary, was without significance. (85–6)

The drama that unfolds between Jill and Henry is as much an
existential one—not too far removed, indeed, from Camus or Sartre—
as an emotional one, and when they do speak their concerns are
rather metaphysical for lovers. Their flirtation seems to be mediated
through philosophical speculations about the nature of solitude, as if
desolation were a perverse aphrodisiac:

… she said, "I like it at this time. If it were not so lonely."

He was reminded of what she had said before. "It's something I've tried to think about," he said. He lifted his hand in a gesture to indicate the paddocks, the lines of scrub and timber, the stillness. "This has a kind of reality that dwarfs other places. But it's so remote you can scarcely associate yourself with it at all. Like existing by sufferance. And for most people that's not possible."

"Yes. But what does one do, if it is like that?"

"Humanize it with our ghastly buildings. Our housing slums. Flood people all over it. Destroy it so we need never be faced with what it is … Somewhere in the beginning, in whatever early groups we had, we developed with the fear of silence and of ourselves. It is in us. As the impossibility of solitude is in ants and bees … In a clash of environment this must go, of course. For tomorrow's people it will scarcely be remembered." (88–9)

Everything in the novel seems threatened with a crushing futility. Even the pictures that Henry takes he regards as almost empty gestures, "no more than conscience, as if man erected a brief memorial and felt his duty done, his sanctimoniousness redeemed" (93). The critique of the hubris of civilisation borders on a more generalised misanthropy, and a revulsion at the way "men spread in a low greyness across the earth." The sentiment bears some resemblance to Robin Boyd's denunciation of suburban sprawl in *The Great Australian Ugliness* (1960), but Boyd's work did offer the hope that the matter might be redressed by re-educating Australians in the field of taste.

Again, it needs to be emphasised just how different Cowan's sense of loss is to that of Pollard and Ewers. The intrusion of World War Two, and most particularly, the advent of the nuclear age, seems to decisively mark writing in Australia in the 1940s and '50s. For the first time, when something is gone, it seems to be truly and utterly gone. The loss of a species or a habitat was once lamentable, but, in this era, such a loss becomes truly terrifying, signalling the possibility—such a feature of existentialist writing—that anything could now be thought, and anything that could be thought, could be done. Existentialism was a kind of moral vertigo that was not imaginable in writers such as Ewers and Pollard, even though they had seen the horrors of the

Great War and watched the basic assumptions of material life crumble before their eyes in 1929. It is in this crucial respect that Cowan is the first modern writer of the wheatbelt.

But *Summer* is not only a novel of ideas. We also get a glimpse of the broader community—beyond the three figures at the siding—when Henry is invited along to a party at the Rileys', neighbouring farmers and friends of Tom Everett. The Rileys stand in for the landed interests of the district, with two generations—the father Harry and his adult son Stan—occupying the stone, iron and asbestos house that "sprawled lengthwise along the slight rise of bare, long-cleared land" (56). The Rileys are a long way from the salt-of-the-earth pioneers that founded the district of South Yollarin in Ewers's novels. They in some ways resemble the cunning, destructive Nestor family in *Rose of the Bushlands*, but the Rileys' malevolence is not innate, just uncouth and ruthless. Stan's clothes "had an air of flashiness" and the party that they are hosting is depicted as debauched. Both Henry and Jill are ill at ease amongst the heavy drinking and opportunistic sexual predation that abounds. Tom has sex with the Rileys' teenage daughter, May, a relationship which is an open secret amongst those gathered. After the encounter, Tom is called in to talk to Harry Riley, May's father, to discuss the sale of a parcel of uncleared land belonging to Tom that the Rileys want to clear for a dam so they can stock an adjoining paddock. Tom, for reasons not clear, does not wish to part with it, but Riley raises the matter of his daughter:

> "How's May?"
>
> "May?" Everett saw his hand, the thick chapped fingers resting on the papers. "You should know."
>
> "Don't see much of the little sod now she works in town."
>
> "That'd be more than I do."
>
> "It would?"
>
> "What do you mean by that?"
>
> "You've known her for a while now, Tom. I've never objected. Never made any trouble. She's only a kid, y'know." (63)

Under the veiled threat of a prosecution, Tom is forced to agree to sell the land. The deal, repellent enough, is essentially a rental

PETER COWAN

agreement with Tom paying with land for the sexual use of Harry's underage daughter. This dirty arrangement provides a sub-structure to the overt love triangle that ensnares Henry, Jill and Tom. The linkage between the two imbroglios is the land, for it is on this very piece of land that Henry has been photographing the smoker parrots. It is this linkage through the uncleared woodland that gives to the novel, which is otherwise a crime thriller, albeit a sophisticated and subtle one, the quality of environmentalist allegory.

The character of May, Harry's daughter, though a victim of larger forces, is also surprisingly resilient. She accepts the advances of Tom Everett with resigned contempt and quickly apprehends that out of this relationship, and the awareness of her sexual attractiveness to men, has sprung a new power. Once the land is acquired from Tom, the Rileys move quickly to get it cleared and a young man—Ted Yates—is brought in to do the bulldozing. May attracts Ted's attention and their relationship progresses in a kind of generational parallel to that between Vera and Henry:

> "What will you be doing," she said, "when you come back?"
>
> "Clearing," he said. "I work for an earth-moving contractor. Anything in that line, dam-sinking, clearing, levelling. I've been working out Hyde Rock way. Small job down the line a bit from here, and then I'll be down in the south-west." (84)

One would think Ted would be a more unattractive character than he in fact is, that he might emblematise the callous destruction of life that his work calls him to do. Certainly, he is not in the slightest bit sentimental about the task—quite the opposite. He is young, self-employed and knows there is "good money" in what he is doing, and he enjoys the carefree move from job to job and, it is implied, woman to woman. Yet May is drawn to his decisiveness and self-confidence, and his heedlessness is cast as refreshing rather than overbearing. May and Ted make an unlikely source of hope in the narrative, offering a more authentic alternative to the corrupt destructiveness of Tom Everett and the Rileys. When the novel ends, they seem to carry the promise, albeit a faint one, of a new beginning, of something rising from the ashes. Ted's brutality—in contrast with Everett's—seems uncalculated and, for this reason, forgivable. The fact that he is able to now protect May from Tom's advances—this is made clear in a showdown at the milk bar in town where May works—also casts him in a favourable light. He puts to an immediate end the dirty arrangement that seemed part and parcel of the way people like Everett and the Rileys did business.

The fatal step in the action occurs when Henry and Jill commence a sexual relationship. Not long after this, Tom discovers them and after beating his wife comes to look for Henry, whom he finds setting up his cameras near the dead tree he has been using as a hide to photograph the nesting smoker parrots. In the ensuing struggle, Henry kills Tom, choking him and smashing his head against the tree. The tussle does not take place with the customary choreography and the men fight awkwardly and desperately clutching at each other's faces and throats. For some reason, Everett was trying to grasp Henry's glasses—the symbol of his impotence, myopia and masochistic self-abnegation:

> He knew that work had given his own body strength … With sudden clarity he saw that if he could will it he need not be easily crushed, the simple defeats and endless humiliations of that other time need not rise now to the sense of impotence. His fingers held. (128)

After killing Everett, Henry hides the body in the trunk of the tree, in the cavity he had previously been using as a bird-watching hide. The final third of the novel is a taut psychological suspense story where the reader is kept on edge over how the consequences of this crime will be settled. Jill and Henry decide to stay quiet and hope that Tom's own well-known flaws would make the possibility of his simply abandoning the store without word a plausible one. The Rileys are the first to notice Tom's disappearance, mainly because they are wishing to push ahead with clearing the land. They suspect that Jill, whom they hate, has something to do with it. In this way the novel also has an element of class with a distinct dynamic not visible in, for instance, Ewers's work. Here, Jill and Henry belong to an educated class that finds the conduct of the Rileys and Tom Everett distasteful. The term "red-neck" has only recently been imported from the United States, but one sees in Cowan's novel the beginnings of the de-romanticisation of country people, also visible in Kenneth Cook's *Wake in Fright* (1961) and its 1971 film adaptation.[35]

At the crux of the story is the hollow bough of a dead tree and the novel was originally simply called "The Tree". This tree, "once bigger than any of its living fellows" (39), serves two functions in succession, both opportunistically seized by Henry. In the first instance, he sees that it is close enough to the nesting smoker parrots to serve as a vantage to photograph them. Not only that, the cavity was perfectly suited to hiding a standing figure. It thus literalises Henry's place of refuge, where he can conduct his photography perfectly hidden inside the tree. This tree is thus a version of the hideaways that Pollard's characters liked to occupy. But like Pollard's heroes, Henry cannot keep his hideaway hidden—the turmoil that he is running from follows him unerringly to this exact place. When Everett discovers his affair with Jill, he marches directly to the tree. The tree then conceals the murder that Henry perpetrates. In this sense, the tree foreshadows the function of the well in Elizabeth Jolley's famous novel of that name—and the more elaborate Gothicisation of the wheatbelt by Kinsella and Flood which involves imbuing sites within it as places of forgetting or repression.[36] The future use of the tree as a form of coffin, or indeed, an instrument of compost, is in fact anticipated in the text quite deliberately, when Henry slips one afternoon while photographing and partially falls into the space deeper inside the dead tree:

> The suddenness of it had shaken him, and he looked down into the hollow. A man might have fallen, and with an injured leg stayed there till the thin endless streams of ants and the flies that would swarm with the heat had levelled him to no more than the charred wood, the dead leaves and broken twigs, the remains perhaps of some more minute lives, that had come to cover the shadowed base of the trunk. It was something he had not thought of before. (113)

But the tree is not left to dissolve the human body it would come to host. After Henry stows Everett's body in the tree, the entire woodland is levelled and burnt. Neither Henry nor Jill had known that Everett had sold the land to the Rileys and had no idea it was slated for clearing. In fact, they decide in the end to confess their crime, only to find that the body and the tree, indeed, the whole world of that bush had been systematically reduced to ash. It produces a very strange sensation because one crime—the destruction of the bush—eradicates the other crime. In some ways, following Henry's own logic, the mere lives of people should really be as nothing compared to the ecocide of one of the district's remaining vestiges of wheatbelt bush. It is an ironic compensation that Henry and Jill are saved from the consequences of their crime by Everett's crime against May, which put him in the debt of the Rileys, his only friends, who inadvertently, but as a direct consequence of this transaction, bulldozed the evidence of his murder. The crimes all seem to implode upon one another. Even Henry's adultery with Jill repeats the humiliation for Everett that Henry had suffered at the hands of his own wife, and which was the reason that he had fled the city. In simple terms, Henry flees adultery in the city so as to commit it in the country.

From this we can see that the plot of *Summer* is essentially concerned with the capture of a resource—the parcel of uncleared land owned by Everett and sought by the Rileys. But the matter is complicated by the emergence of this land as a subjective force in its own right. The uncleared land becomes uncanny in the sense that it seems to be existing independently of the tawdry human dramas that surround it. The land cannot be reduced to a single status. In an economic sense it is the means by which the Rileys might earn more money by watering stock once they build the dam. However, the land is not purchased with money alone, but by Harry Riley, in effect, charging Everett for the sexual usage of his underage daughter. In this quite literal sense the land has been prostituted. Then Henry arrives and the land becomes a place of refuge, where he might find peace far from the madding crowd. But even here, Henry's pleasure carries an erotic, voyeuristic overtone, as he spies and photographs the nesting parrots hidden within a hollow tree. The land then becomes the scene of Everett's killing by Henry, which while deserved and done in self-defence, nevertheless carries the spectre of patricide, as the direct result is that Henry now obtains Everett's wife for himself. At the end, all of this is annihilated, as the bulldozer crushes the forest beneath it, and the remnants are burned. To narrate the end of this woodland,

Cowan reverts to a technique first seen in the story "Isolation", which is to have the event witnessed by an animal—not an eagle, this time, spying warily the appearance of a gap in the forest, but a goanna in the path of destruction:

> Like a pattern of the dry brittle leaves stirred by wind, the goanna shifted forward. The sound might have been behind it, loud, insistent, punctuated by the crash of metal. The body of the small reptile held the ground, only a stiffness in the carriage of the head suggestive of life, of uncertainty. Then, with a faint undulation of its short body, the legs thrusting as if sideways, the brown armoured shape moved over the soil that time had mated it to in a seeming perfection. Hard, dry, plated, it might have been invulnerable. As it was harmless, its ugliness like jest. The treed soil and the spiny undergrowth in the hot silence of sun, meaningless. Near by, the grey smooth log base curved to shelter the heavy body. The head moved only slightly.
>
> The crash of metal destroyed time and meaning. The ground moved, the soil quivering and breaking. Beside the log the legs jerked grotesquely, the body thrust forward, the blunt head lifted, wide jaws split to reveal the purple-starred tongue that thrust in menace towards the wall of scoured steel. Then the log rolled, the soil climbed, and the eyes of the reptile saw without interpretation the tops of the broken bushes, the log still shifting beneath, the tussocks of scrub it had crawled among, higher to the boughs of trees it had never seen, then the metal crashed, and with the sticks, broken roots, and debris its body twisted and was crushed, dumped to the long row of smoothed soil that filled its jaws and the slow eyes. (176–7)

No passage of writing before or since more graphically articulated the moment of ecological destruction upon which the wheatbelt was founded. Cowan's understated prose, so often criticised for its surgical coolness, is able to bring into relief the sheer enormity of the destruction that occurred with banal repetition across the entire southwest in the decades of the twentieth century. The meeting of the goanna and the bulldozer so perfectly captures the uncomprehending collision of incommensurable realities—"the reptile saw without interpretation"—and the terrible efficiency of the exercise.

The terror of the destruction of the natural world is amplified in the novel because it takes place off-stage, at least in terms of the main action. Jill and Henry wrestle with the consequences of Everett's killing, and agonise over whether it will be possible, even if they escape capture, to live with themselves, or whether Everett, in death as in life, will always stand between them. Stan Riley, always resentful of Jill, suspects that she and Henry may well have had a hand in the disappearance of Everett. The local policeman, without much enthusiasm, interviews Jill and makes some initial investigations. All of this is happening in the foreground and yet, in the background, the bush is being cleared by Ted Yates and his bulldozer. As Henry continues to receive the last of the grain he is dimly aware of a sound he cannot quite place, but it never really fully forces itself into his consciousness, nor could he know that it meant his crime could now never be traced:

> He could not place the sound, he had not thought there was wheat still to be stripped in the direction from which it seemed to come. In the afternoon the sound held distinctness, clarity, and he knew that it was of a tractor, but not with a harvester. It puzzled him, in the periods when the siding was so deserted and silent that he might have wondered if anyone had ever come there or whether the squat silos and the iron hut, the elevator jutting stiffly against the sky, the wheel tracks about it, were not the symbols of some dream from which he would wake to another time but partly remembered. Of the sound there seemed no explanation he could find, and he waited impatiently, with a kind of fear, for the darkness. (177)

The novel ends eerily. Henry, who had decided to give himself up, had gone to retrieve Everett's body from the tree only to find that the whole bush had been levelled. Nothing now could be done, and Henry and Jill, so prone to doubt, feel that for the first time in their lives they had been given a reprieve and that, after all, they might be entitled to happiness. Ted, the bulldozer driver, now finished with his work, invites May to come with him, and they leave in his car and caravan to head back to the city. The final scene is not of any of these people, however, but of the cleared land, where the wrecked trees had been bulldozed into piles and set alight. It is the close of day, and as the sun retreats the glow of these pyres starts to become visible:

> Behind the belt of trees lines of colour grew across the scarred slope of the paddock, the glow gaining until the small store by the road stood out black against it. The heat held the logs and boughs, the stumps that became hard, hot pools of light, the wood no longer recognizable. (189)

The glow of this destruction silhouettes the house that had been the scene of the calamitous affair between Jill and Henry. In this way the novel concludes by decentring the human anguish, leaving it somehow inconsequential in comparison with a more complete decimation of a world.

"The Tractor"

More than anything that Cowan had written to this point, *Summer* is a study of destructiveness. The novel is a precursor to the increasing concern that Cowan developed for matters of conservation in the middle years of his life. In 1966 he wrote to Judith Wright to ask for permission to quote from her poem "At Cooloolah" in his novel *Seed* (1966), and to express his admiration for her work: "I find it lies very close to my own thinking – only always it seems to have just that edge of crystallization my own thoughts lack."[37] Wright wrote back happily permitting Cowan to quote from the poem and adding: "I feel you work in the line of my own thought, too: but perhaps we're the last that can think in that way. The bulldozers will turn us in before long, and they'll plant a bed of petunias on top of us."[38] Many of the concerns of *Summer* are repeated in one of Cowan's more widely anthologised stories, "The Tractor", which appeared in his collection *The Empty Street* (1965), but was first published in *Meanjin* in 1964. The story is set on a wheatbelt farm and, like *Summer*, concerns the plans to clear and burn a patch of remnant bush. The main character, Ann, is a schoolteacher being courted by the farmer, Ken, who plans to clear the bush. The distinguishing feature of this story, however, is that the bush is occupied, not this time by a family of nesting smoker parrots, but by a mysterious man living a fugitive existence over ten or more years in rough bush camps. The story begins with the report that the two tractors that were going to be used for the clearing had been "interfered with", indeed sabotaged with sand in the oil. Suspicion falls immediately on the man in the bush, who has also been suspected of myriad other misdemeanours over the years, from breaking fences to running water tanks dry. Previous attempts to apprehend him had come to nothing, though, and the incident with the tractors had brought about a resolution to finally deal with him by setting fire to the bush and driving him out that way. Unlike *Summer*, where it occurs without the opportunity for opposition, the actual decision to clear the bush is debated, with Ann challenging Ken on whether it must, after all, be done:

> "Clearing with those tractors and the chain," she said. "Everything in their path goes—kangaroos—all the small things that live in the scrub—all the trees—"
>
> He looked at her as if her words held some relevance that must come to him. He said, "We clear the land. Yes."
>
> "You clear it," she said. "It seems to be what is happening everywhere today."
>
> "I don't know what you mean, Ann," he said.
>
> She got up from the chair by the steps. "Perhaps he feels something should be left."
>
> "Look," he said, "maybe you teach too much nature study at school. Or you read all this stuff about how we shouldn't shoot the bloody 'roos—so that when some crazy swine wrecks our property you think he's some sort of a—"
>
> "Some sort of a what?"
>
> "I don't know," he said, aware she mocked him. "Better than us." (54)

The story seems an attempt to give the bush an actual personality in the form of this man who lives in it—a figure familiar from literature and folklore as that of the "wild man". Significantly, although when he finally appears he is black, he seems to have been burnt so by the sun, and is not Aboriginal. He seems to be a white man, indigenised, and carries something of the primitivist wish for a person who is the direct expression of nature, not unlike the kind of metaphysical Aboriginal people that appear in Australian writing of the mid-twentieth century, not just in the Jindyworobak movement, but in novels from *Coonardoo* (1929) to *Voss* (1957), and who continue to live on in the fiction of Tim Winton.

> His movement was somehow liquid, unhuman, and then she thought of the natives she had once seen in the north, not the town natives whose movements had grown like her own. But with a strange inevitability he moved like an animal or the vibration of the thin sparse trees before the wind. (65)

The man is in the end shot by Ken and the other farmers because, they say, he had shot at them first. In that sense, the story shares a similar grim fatality with the novel *Summer*, but the major difference is that the introduction of the wild man allows the clearing of the bush to enter into the dynamics of human drama. Cowan also explores with some sensitivity the wish to preserve the natural world. That Ann does care for Ken, and that Ken is by no means a monster, keeps the environmental plea from assuming a too simplistic colouring. The major imaginative work in the story is on the part of Ann, who is trying to *picture* this man, but cannot quite seem to do so because the contours of his life are so fundamentally other to hers and those she knows. In this sense, the radical difference of nature from culture is preserved in the impossibility of picturing him. When Ann wanders into the woods with the intention of warning the man, she stumbles into the wilderness like Ellen Roxburgh in White's *A Fringe of Leaves* (1976), completely unequipped to meet its demands. The open woodland is like the heart of darkness, except it is suffused with brilliant sunshine that pours through the brush, with only the barest of shade:

> She stood in the patch of shade, and she tried to reason that she could not have come far, that she could find her way back if she was careful. And in the silence she thought again, as she had the night before, of the man she had come to warn. It had seemed that if she could explain to him, he must understand, and that perhaps he would go.

She had relied on there being understanding between them, that at least in these things they must feel alike. So that it had seemed her words would have effect. Now, in the heat and the silence, it was a dream, holding in this place no reality. It was like nothing she could encompass." (63–4)

The turn in Cowan's fiction to environmental themes was part of a broader shift in both national and international ideas, and his own writing career. In the late '60s and into the '70s he became a strident voice for environmental preservation, particularly taking up the issues of suburban sprawl in Perth's ever expanding metropolitan area. Cowan's work after the mid-1960s did not focus again on the wheatbelt, though it is there in the memories of characters in his late novel, *The Hills of Apollo Bay* (1989), one of whom had grown up in the wheatbelt and brings his girlfriend there on their university holidays:

> But all of this is a kind of battlefield. It's broken enough people. You just fight the land. And look at it. I'm not sure it's not being destroyed. The timber gone. The salt spreading on the flats. Dust storms. I feel strongly for this country. I don't want to work at a kind of destruction.
>
> I can see that, she said. If that is how it seems. And there is a sense of that. Destruction. I could feel it just looking from the train. I think it frightened me. (53)

One can see the evolution of Cowan's style, here, from the Hemingwayesque lyricism of his earlier stories to the uncompromisingly jagged impressionism of his late work. But one also sees the theme of destruction still living in his late works, and which his works during the '40s, '50s and '60s brought into the imaginative consciousness of the Western Australian wheatbelt.

Chapter Six

Dorothy Hewett (1923–2002)

Yealering / Wickepin (1923–34; 1956)
Corrigin (1934)

Dorothy Hewett is the most significant writer to come out of the wheatbelt, and the first to have grown up there.[1] A major and complex Australian author, Hewett's poetry, plays, fiction and memoirs indelibly mark the terrain of national letters.[2] Hewett lived the first eleven years of her life on "Lambton Downs", her grandparents' farm at Malyalling, a railway siding on the Narrogin–Merredin line that Facey worked on. The farm had been selected by her maternal grandfather, Ted Coade, in 1912. Coade, with wife Mary (the acknowledged financial mastermind of the pair), had made money running a store in Southern Cross during the years of the goldfields boom. The farm consisted of 3,000 acres of prime land, 22 kilometres northeast of Wickepin. It was a large and prosperous holding at a time when thousand-acre farms were the norm. The Coades could afford to employ people to work the land, and also to open up goods stores in the towns of Wickepin, Corrigin and Yealering. Their daughter Doris Irene ("Rene", *Ree-nee*), Dorothy's mother, was postmistress at the Corrigin store and it was here that she met her future husband, Tom Hewett.[3] Originally from Wedderburn in Victoria, Tom Hewett had come to the wheatbelt with his brother after serving in the Great War, attracted by the cheap land on offer in the West. Upon his marriage to Rene, Tom Hewett moved into the Coades' farmhouse and formed a partnership with his in-laws. Hewett himself selected a further 1,000 acres, albeit largely sandplain, bringing the total family holding to 4,000 acres. The venture proved successful and even in the dark years of the Depression, both the Coades and the Hewetts would remain comfortably well-off. In 1934, Tom and Rene, with their two daughters Dorothy and Lesley, moved briefly to Corrigin to run the family store there, but after three months they moved again, this time to Perth, where they would remain thereafter. In Perth, both daughters finished their secondary schooling, a rare thing for girls of the time. Dorothy initially attended Perth Girls School in East Perth during 1935 and 1936 and then the prestigious private Perth Ladies College (now Perth College) in Mount Lawley from 1937 to 1940.[4] Dorothy enrolled in a Bachelor of Arts degree (majoring in English) at the University of Western Australia in 1941.

Although they died in the same year, Dorothy Hewett was nearly a decade younger than Peter Cowan. They just missed each other at university. Peter Cowan finished his degree at the end of 1940, having enrolled as a mature-age student in 1938. They are united by the shared influence in their work of aesthetic modernism, although the influence could hardly be more disparate in its effects when one compares their respective oeuvres. Similarly, the influence of the wheatbelt in their writing is almost equally pronounced, but their relation to it is quite different and rooted in a contrast of experience. Hewett grew up, from her earliest days, in the wheatbelt, leaving on the cusp of puberty. Although she visited the farm in holidays after that, as an adult she returned only briefly, and disastrously, in 1956 when a plan to work the farm with her parents and her then partner, Les Flood, fell over almost as soon as Flood saw the property: "'Christ!' he says. 'What the fuck have you brought us to?'"[5] Despite this, the wheatbelt remained the site of Hewett's imagination and fantasy, a constant companion in her writing, even as she moved back and forth across the continent between Perth and Sydney. Cowan grew up in South Perth and only came to the wheatbelt in his late teens, a refugee from the difficulties of his life, and with a hope of becoming either a farmer or a writer or both. Hewett, on the other hand, apprehended even as a child that she would need to leave the enchanted remoteness of rural life if she ever wanted to achieve her literary and theatrical ambitions. Their writing styles are also a study in contrasts, with Cowan's quietism and carefully conceived studies in isolated life, and Hewett's vivid phantasmagoria and baroque larrikin humour. Even within Hewett's work there is a dizzying amplitude, ranging from the modernist force of her early poems under the influence of Tennyson, T.S. Eliot and Edith Sitwell, to the socialist realist stories of the late 1950s and early '60s, to her expressionist musical farces of the '70s and '80s, as well as a late return to poetry, this time responding to the experimentation of American poetry of the '50s and '60s. Lastly, there is her great memoir of her early life, *Wild Card*, published in 1990. As we will see, the wheatbelt is refracted differently through each of these modes.

37. Dorothy and Lesley; Dorothy with her lessons at Lambton Downs.

Lambton Downs is in many ways coterminous with Hewett's childhood. The wheatbelt we get through her writing is a combination of her own childhood memories and fantasies, and the family mythology, particularly that running through her mother's family. These join to imbue Hewett's wheatbelt with a distinct sense of enchantment.[6] In the mesmerising first chapter of *Wild Card*, Hewett describes, sensation by sensation, her experience of her childhood home, which becomes a kind of gingerbread house, filled with wonder and terror, seduction and danger:

> The first house sits in the hollow of your heart, it will never go away. It is the house of childhood become myth, inhabited by characters larger than life whose murmured conversations whisper and tug at the mind. Enchanted birds and animals out of a private ark sail out on tides of sleep, howling, whistling, mewing, neighing, mooing, baaing, barking, to an endless shimmer of wheat and cracked creek beds. (1)

This kind of Proustian reverie, dense with both fantasy and recollection, typifies Hewett's memoir. Her description mingles memories with smells, and sounds with feelings and images, to evoke a pulsing world which seems to be both full of potential and outside of any normal rules. It seems to happen in an alternative universe, beyond time and history.

Hewett wrote from an early age, including poems and plays, which she would stage with the assistance of her younger sister, Lesley, for the grown-ups on the verandah at Lambton Downs. Her family cooperated with her precocious talents: "I compose poems in bed and wake my parents in the middle of the night; patiently they write them down, marvelling, no doubt, that they have produced a swan" (19). Nor was Lesley safe from the demands of her precocious older sister:

> Now I make up my poems to the drone of the separator out in the wash house, mesmerized by the underground rhythm. But sometimes they flash upon me out in the paddocks miles from home, words, images, lines tumbling out in a frenzy so that I have to run back, gasping for pencil and paper. If my sister is with me she has to remember the lines as I say them, over and over, and pity help her if she doesn't. (19)

Some of her writing was also done as part of her schooling. Lambton Downs was too far from the nearest school and the girls were educated via correspondence lessons. Correspondence students were encouraged to write poems and stories to submit to *Our Rural Magazine* (1926–46), a monthly journal prepared by the Education Department and sent to all correspondence students and country schools. (Both Pollard and Ewers were frequent contributors over the years.) Hewett's earliest published poem appeared in *Our Rural Magazine* in 1933.[7] It was called "Dreaming" and was written when Hewett was ten years old:

I'm sitting up here in the old gum tree,
And a dear little robin is singing to me.
I'm dreaming of dragons, princes and kings,
Of fairies, gnomes, elfins, goblins, and things.

Sometimes I hear the fairies pass,
Perhaps it is only the wind in the grass.
I am not frightened, I couldn't fall,
Sitting up here in my armchair tall.

I dream that I'm a cavalier bold,
Rescuing princesses in times of old.
But of course I'm only pretending, you see,
And my castle is just the old gum tree.[8]

Hewett's "Dreaming" is, like many of the children's poems in *Our Rural Magazine*, a fairy poem. But the striking aspect of the poem is that it does not internalise the fantasy in the way that almost all the other children's verse does. The fairy fantasy is made to appear as fantasy: "But of course I'm only pretending, you see, / And my castle is just the old gum tree." "Dreaming" is a cheeky poem that exhibits something of Hewett's trademark swagger ("I am not frightened, I couldn't fall") and is a premonition of the wheatbelt her later work gives us. At its heart is the characteristic double-gesture of Hewett's writing, the colouring in of an entire spectacular and romantic fantasy world, followed by its immediate erasure by irony, cynicism or ruefulness. By the time of her late adolescence, this doubled quality to her character had become an eerie, indeed frightening, feature of her personality for Dorothy Hewett:

> I can't remember the exact moment when I became conscious of the divided self. There is the girl who moves and talks and rages and loves and there is the writer who watches and writes it down, who even in her most passionate moments is saying, "Remember this".
>
> This cold, detached consciousness that always writes it down afterwards without fear or favour, who is she? Does this mean that I will never be able to experience anything fully with sincerity and passion? Whoever she is, she has come to live with me for the rest of my life – analysing, taking account of, describing everything ... a monster? (90)

Of course something of this division exists in everyone, but Hewett's sense of separation is unusually acute, and the coexistence of the licentious, daring, scandalising actions of her public self with the meticulous need to record the consequent agonies is also, at least at first, somewhat surprising. Moreover, even at this point, Hewett had a keen sense of her rivals, particularly a certain Alice Bland, whose poems are heavily featured in *Our Rural Magazine*, and a subsequent anthology *Brave Young Singers* (1938), edited by the Director of Distance Education, J.A. Miles:

> ... every year I win second prize for illustrated stories and poetry at the Royal Show. Only Alice Bland always beats me. We both have our poems published in a Correspondence School publication called *Brave Young Singers*. I despise Alice Bland's poetry. It's all about helping her mother and being a domestic treasure. At the Royal Show I am introduced to her in the Agricultural Pavilion. She is a wholesome-looking brunette with short bobbed hair, several years older and taller than I am. Impossible, though, to see her as a rival. It doesn't make sense. (39)

Hewett correctly assesses the distinct difference between her and the unfortunately named Bland. Bland's poems articulate, without irony, the belief in the enterprise of the wheatbelt, while Hewett's see the world ironically and sceptically.

In 1934, the family left Lambton Downs for Corrigin, to run the store they owned there. Although this was a temporary move, in fact they never returned to Lambton Downs, moving instead to Perth, where the two girls could complete their secondary education. Her sister Lesley remembers how deeply the loss of their childhood home affected Hewett: "it was a great wrench for her at the age of twelve to move to the city, leaving every known, loved part of our lives".[9] Hewett was sent to Perth Ladies College which had been founded in 1902 by the Anglican order of nuns, the Sisters of the Church, and where she mingled with the daughters of wealthy Western Australian families. Here, she continued to foster her literary ambitions, capturing the eye of sympathetic teachers and like-minded students, including Lilla Harper, for whom she developed an intense infatuation. Hewett's father, in particular, also continued to support his daughter's wish to write. In 1939, he arranged for sixteen-year-old Dorothy to meet J.K. Ewers. At this time, Hewett was in her sixth form at Perth Ladies College and Ewers was enjoying a period of relative success, following the publication of *Money Street* (1933) and his regular columns in The *West Australian*. Unbeknownst to Hewett, he had commenced writing his wheatbelt saga, under the 'working title *The World of Avea Lea*', in November of the previous year:

> A sheaf of my new poems clutched in my hand, I am taken by my father to see my first live writer … Keith Ewers, the West Australian novelist. We sit in his dim little study and he tells me my poems are "quite extraordinary for a sixteen-year-old", but to, "forget about being a writer. There's nothing in it, except heartbreak … I've had to work as a schoolteacher all my life".
>
> I leave, dancing on air, because this bespectacled thirty-year-old with the long, kind face has praised my work. We stand awkwardly on the porch.
> "Do you still want to be a writer?"
> "Yes."
> He grins wryly. "Then I suppose you will be." (77–8)

Hewett matriculated and enrolled at UWA in 1942 in the Bachelor of Arts with a major in English Literature. There, she encountered Ewers again, when he delivered—along with Henrietta Drake-Brockman and Mary Durack—the Commonwealth Literary Fund lectures on Australian literature. Hewett remembers Durack as "the first writer who doesn't tell me to forget about it" (89). The CLF lectures were inaugurated in 1940, to promote the study and appreciation of Australian literature. As we have seen, Ewers had been involved, as far back as 1930, in the promotion of Australian literature, both through Walter Murdoch's Australian Readers Group at UWA and through his columns in the *West Australian* and the *Daily News*.[10]

In her English major at UWA Hewett was taught by Alec King and Alan Edwards. Hewett had entered UWA in the immediate post-Murdoch era.[11] Peter Cowan had dedicated his first volume *Drift* (1946) to Alec King, and King influenced a generation of students to the value of the English romantics and their modernist successors. Alongside King, Hewett was also taught by the "new professor",

38. Hewett near Gingin in 1940, aged 17.

Alan Edwards, appointed to replace Murdoch in 1941. Edwards had studied with F.R. Leavis and I.A. Richards at Cambridge in the 1920s and, with King, set the tone of the study of English for the war and post-war years at UWA.[12] Hewett remembers Edwards lending her the banned novels of Henry Miller (87). Katharine Brisbane, who commenced at UWA in 1949, remembers King as "lovable", but Edwards as "an acerbic Leavisite".[13] At university, Hewett was drawn to the radical politics of communism, a commitment she shared with her future husband, Lloyd Davies, and a small coterie of fellow university students. She also wrote and staged the one-act play *Time Flits Away Lady*, with herself and Lloyd Davies in the leading roles (90). But Hewett's formal education was not proceeding smoothly. She failed her first year of study at UWA and in the following year, 1942, enrolled in teachers' training college, with a view to becoming a kindergarten teacher. However, she did not complete the year. She worked as a sales assistant at Albert's Bookstore and as a junior reporter for the *Daily News* before also losing that position. She also started selling the Party paper, *The Workers' Star*, on behalf of her local Victoria Park branch, canvassing door to door and infuriating her long-suffering parents. Then, in December 1943, Hewett attempted suicide by drinking from a bottle of Lysol in her bedroom at her parents' home in South Perth.[14]

"Testament" (1945)

Surviving her suicide attempt, Hewett, still only twenty years old, tried to put her life back together. In 1944, she married Lloyd Davies, then still on active service. In Davies, Hewett chose the most stable of her several suitors. Despite his radical leanings, Davies offered a bourgeois pedigree and a professional income as a solicitor: "My salvation will be politics and marriage, in that order" (111). After Lloyd Davies concluded active service with the end of World War Two, Hewett and he bought a run-down property in the Darling Ranges outside of Perth and she bore her first child, Clancy. Hewett became a reporter with the communist *Workers' Star*. At university, Hewett had been strongly influenced by T.S. Eliot and Edith Sitwell, eventually siding with the latter. She compares Sitwell's "Gold Coast Customs" to Eliot's "The Waste Land": "But Edith Sitwell's

Waste Land is a world of bright objects suddenly hurled against the eye balls, to the accompaniment of a screaming jazz band" (36–7). And, in a comparison that would work equally well between her and Peter Cowan, she notes how Sitwell's poem is a "hectic drunken orgy compared to Eliot's quiet bitter portraits of contemporary life" (37).[15] But with her increasing involvement with communism, Hewett abandoned the modernists as decadent and bourgeois. In one of her columns for the *Workers' Star,* she states that: "The aim of the writer should be as social interpreter, his realism the realism of the people working, fighting, living, struggling."[16] Having joined the Party in 1945, Hewett remained a committed and fiercely loyal member for twenty-three years: "I need order in my life. I need a pattern, a systematic view of the world – and Marxism would give it to me".[17]

Hewett's artistic formation thus took place in the contest between modernism and Marxism, both of which had a particular emphasis on history and struggle. But Hewett, like Ewers, and probably at least partially through Ewers, was also influenced by the Jindyworobak movement in South Australia. As we have seen, the "Jindies" were a syncretic movement which co-opted a pan-Aboriginal spirituality and a proto-environmentalism into a unique brand of radical nationalism.[18] In artistic terms, it is best understood as a variety of modernism, with its accent clearly on the primitivist strain of that aesthetic movement. Hewett's first publications in an adult magazine were her poems "My Love" and "Suicide of an Architect" which appeared in the third *Jindyworobak Anthology* in 1941. She won the *Meanjin* Poetry Prize in 1942 for her poem, "Dream of Old Love".[19] Further poems appeared in the 1942 *Jindyworobak Anthology* and she continued to publish in the *Meanjin Papers* and *The Black Swan* until 1946. Hewett read and admired Cowan, especially his "new book of modernist short stories, *Drift*" (112) published in 1944: "*Drift* made me realise that even then it was possible to be a modernist in Western Australia, the most isolated state in an isolated continent."[20] She had also seen the possibilities of the "poetic novel" (86) in Christina Stead's *Seven Poor Men of Sydney* (1934), Eleanor Dark's *A Prelude to Christopher* (1934), Kenneth "Seaforth" Mackenzie's *The Young Desire It* (1937), and Eve Langley's *The Pea Pickers* (1942). Hewett also remembers reading Judith Wright's *The Moving Image* (1946), "which bursts on me like a

39. Dorothy and Lesley, with Ralph Lang.

bombshell" (122), and for which she has a "secret" preference over the Jindyworobak publications, such as *Harvest Time* (1946), by her friend Vic Williams, who worked on the Fremantle wharf.[21] This tension between modernism and communism would be an important feature of Hewett's life over the next two decades.

In May 1945, Hewett's poem "Testament" brought her to national attention: "A miracle happens. 'Testament' wins first prize in the ABC Poetry Competition. I have arrived. I am interviewed on the ABC, my poems are broadcast on the Young Artists' programme, my photograph is in the ABC Programme Guide." (105) Although she had won the *Meanjin* poetry prize in 1942, the ABC prize in 1945 was significant because it brought recognition beyond the narrow confines of Australian poetry circles. With "Testament" she felt that "maybe this is a real poem at last" (110). It consisted of three long stanzas and narrated the family history of her parents (the Hewetts) and her maternal grandparents (the Coades) in the wheatbelt. It is stridently critical in a way that is different to the criticisms of Goode, Pollard and Ewers, and reflects the fact that Hewett is a second-generation wheatbelt resident. Those other writers criticised the wheatbelt as an enterprise, but Hewett's poem criticises the wheatbelt as an inheritance. Indeed, the particular power of Hewett's critique arises from the fact that the wheatbelt enters the intimacy of the family home. The title "Testament" signals the theme of inheritance, because a testament mandates the distribution of property amongst the heirs of an estate. As well as testament, the poem is also a testimony, in which Hewett testifies against her own history, where her ancestors are called to account for their conduct, and the pioneering glow of their achievements is ruthlessly dispelled:

> They carefully translated their whole way
> And pride of living to a hangman's land,
> Ploughed the dark soil, wrenched order from its chaos,
> Its sullen, hostile hatred of their hands,
> Subdued it, mixed their coolness with its hunger,
> Never gave up, or ceased to plough and sow,
> Because it was their only living passion,
> These cold-eyed men with honour in their hearts:
> The passion for the land, to feel the soil
> Ache through their thin loins, it was like
> Another man's hunger for a wanton woman[22]

While "Testament" evinces contempt for the male pioneer, the cool hatred of the poem still elevates them to the status of gods by addressing them in this mythic register. The poem is at considerable pains, though, to blight these heroes with a certain desperate, even mad, hunger; to daub their passionless conquests with needs they hypocritically wish away or put onto others. It deftly uses repetition of key words and phrases—"wanton", "stiff-necked", "mad-eyed", "nodding"—to give the solemn weight of historical judgement a corona of seething anger.

Hewett's wheatbelt, which appears for the first time in "Testament", is a mythopoeic union of the poet's childhood and the more general Australian pioneer narrative. It does share elements with each of the writers we have already encountered. With Facey she has in common the fact of an unhappy childhood spent in the wheatbelt, even though perhaps neither of them would describe it as such. It must be said, though, that Hewett's hot-housed, quasi-middle-class upbringing in the 1920s seemed a universe away from the stark, primitive and plainly abusive years that Facey spent working as a boy on the virgin farms of new settlers before World War One. With Cyril Goode, Hewett shares both a political affinity, and a sense of the wheatbelt as a kind of capitalist fraud, a trick at someone's expense. And yet she also shares with James Pollard a fundamentally romantic conception of the wheatbelt, even though her risqué sexual frankness seems utterly incommensurable with Pollard's prim heroines. Pollard's "Bushland" novels (1926–28) appeared when Hewett was still a small child, but she seems not to have known of them, even later in life. With Ewers, whom, as we have seen, she met as a sixteen year old, she shares a conceptual commitment to the wheatbelt as a place made by history. Interestingly, despite Hewett's deep commitment to communism, it is Ewers who maintains the much sharper sense of the material determinants of the region, though his writing is far duller. And lastly, with Cowan, her closest contemporary, she shares—despite their deep tonal contrast—both a commitment to modernist aesthetics and the apprehension that sexual hypocrisy lies very near to the heart of regional life.

Contemporary with the early poems of Judith Wright (1915–2000), first collected in *The Moving Image* (1946), Hewett's "Testament" shares Wright's distinctive tonality, the same sombre biblical diction and the same bitter fatalism. Wright's early poetry, like Hewett's, was published in *Meanjin*, which also published in 1943 (although it had been written in 1939) A.D. Hope's "Australia". Hope's classic sonnet of ambivalent celebration—it is both a stern telling off and a closeted paean to the national "spirit"—can be seen to presage both Hewett and Wright, offering a mode that allowed them to eventually outgrow the naïve nationalism of the Jindyworobaks with whom each was also briefly associated. But it is Wright's reworking of the settler story, and her unsparing assessment of her pioneering forebears, that captures the quality of existential crisis that was so palpable in Australia with the advent of the Pacific War and is the hallmark of the early *Meanjin Papers*. Hewett exhibits the same controlled alarm that Wright so brilliantly mastered, the terror of one who has inherited the earth at the very moment they realise that the earth is under the gravest threat.

Like Wright's poems, Hewett's "Testament" is suspended between archetype and ancestry, at once the account of a location and of a nation. The particularity of Lambton Downs, with its "tattered salmon-gums in rags / like gaunt beggar women" and "the she-oaks / Dripped and murmured with an aged / Dim loneliness", only gradually emerges against the allegory of the colonial backdrop:

> An old house lying silent in the Summer,
> Haunted by children, flowers, and orchards,
> Days that seemed a dim and golden
> Heritage of dream; then all the years
> Moved in a liquid sunlight on the grass. (38)

And the critique of the pioneer in "Testament" is also an indictment of her father's dour Protestant family. Their ascetic need for order and control acted out in the clearing of trees: "Building their red board churches in the clearing, / Puritanical among the ringbarked gum trees." (36) In "Testament", the land of the wheatbelt is depicted as devastated: the final stanza works as a kind of calendar, with the seasons assailing the farm with dust and heat, and then eroding rains. It is not quite the ecologically attuned apprehension of destruction that would come later in Hewett's work and the "salt" which appears in the later works is not mentioned here. Instead, Lambton Downs appears in "Testament" as a modernist wasteland directly influenced by T.S. Eliot's, in which the land is a metaphor for spiritual emptiness.

"The Wire Fences of Jarrabin" (1957)

Hewett's marriage ended in early 1949 when she abandoned Davies and her son Clancy, and drove over the Nullarbor with Les Flood, a boiler-maker, ex-RAAF pilot and communist Hewett had met through the Party. She spent the better part of a decade in Sydney with Les Flood, with whom she had three sons, the youngest of whom, Tom Flood, we will meet again in this history. Hewett had already stopped writing poetry in 1946 and did not write again, creatively, for another ten years. It is not easy to say exactly why Hewett stopped writing. Later, she stated that she had been "[s]ilenced by political activism, the deep-seated anti-culturalism and socialist realist dogmas of the

Australian Communist Party, plus the terrible struggle to survive."[23] Certainly, Flood was not a supporter of his wife's writing and appears to have been threatened by her substantial talents, often bullying her with jibes about her writing being evidence of her bourgeois vanity. It is not without significance that as his fits of paranoia worsened, they culminated in his building a bonfire in the back garden and casting Hewett's manuscripts into them, with the children gathered to watch. Nevertheless, the last two years in Sydney marked the re-emergence of Hewett as a writer "after ten silent years" (246). The most famous outcome of this period was *Bobbin Up* (1959), a novel based on her experience of working at the Alexandria Spinning Mills when she had first arrived in Sydney a decade earlier. It was also in this period that Hewett wrote the first eight chapters of a novel she was calling "The Wire Fences of Jarrabin", set in the wheatbelt of her childhood.[24]

If it was communism that ended Hewett's literary ambitions in 1946, it was also communism that resurrected them in the mid-1950s through her association with the Realist Writers gathered around Frank Hardy. The first Realist Writers Group was started in Melbourne in the years after the war by members and sympathisers of the Communist Party, in particular Hardy, Stephen Murray-Smith and Ian Turner. The Melbourne group nurtured writers like Judah Waten and Alan Marshall. Hardy, who had become famous with the sensation caused by his novel *Power Without Glory* (1950), had moved from Melbourne to Sydney in 1954 and started a Sydney Realist Writers Group. It was in this group that Hewett found the support to recommence her writing career, even if in later years she was somewhat qualified in her gratitude, describing them as "a beleaguered little group in a philistine Communist Party in a philistine Australia" (248). But she concedes that they had been the "the necessary support system for a new left-wing writer struggling to survive in a hostile environment" (248). Hardy recalls meeting Hewett as early as 1950, when he was still living in Melbourne:

> When I met [Hewett] first in 1950, she told me quite pugnaciously that she had given up writing poetry in favor of political activity (she had joined the Communist Party in 1945). It took me and other communists a long time to convince her that the greatest contribution she could make to the Party was her poetic gift.

The Realist Writers adhered, more or less, to the Stalinist rules for creative writing laid down by Andrei Zhdanov in his address to the Soviet Writers Congress in 1934, the year that Hewett's family had moved to Corrigin and then to Perth. The key element in socialist realism, as it came to be known, was the depiction of the working class as a revolutionary agency. Hewett had already been won over to this view of literature but this had caused a paralysis in Hewett's own creative writing, which she could not reconcile with a strict vision of socialist realism.

From the drafts that Hewett read to Hardy's Group in 1956 and '57, she developed the short story "The Wire Fences of Jarrabin". Ironically, the story was first published in that bastion of bourgeois femininity, *The Australian Women's Weekly*, on 6 November 1957, titled—"My Mother Said I Never Should". Hewett ultimately published the full version of "The Wire Fences of Jarrabin" with the press, Seven Seas, in an anthology of radical Australian writing—made up of the Realist Writers congregated around Frank Hardy—titled *The Australians Have a Word for It* (1964). "The Wire Fences of Jarrabin" is a coming-of-age story about an eleven-year-old girl living in Jarrabin: "Two streets of red gravelly roads and one asphalt, a glimpse of corrugated-iron roofs under a clump of spindly gums—that was Jarrabin."[25] It is narrated from a future

40. *The Australian Woman's Weekly,* 6 November 1957.

point in that girl's life, and the unmistakeably rueful quality of the retrospection speaks to the ending of an innocence. In the story, it is not always clear whether the suppositions are those of the young girl, or the grown woman who is narrating. Nevertheless, the narrator is conscious of the privileged position her family held in the town and the consequences this had for the social life of her and her sister: "My parents owned both the stores and the garage, and a good quarter of the corrugated-iron roofs straggling up the slope, and, as they charged top rents and never did any repairs unless the local Roads Board summonsed them, I can understand why my sister and I were not exactly popular among the residents of Jarrabin." (53–4)

The girls were relieved when they were befriended by two Aboriginal girls, Irene and Edna McKenna. These Aboriginal girls are based upon Irene and Edna McLimmens, whom Dorothy and Lesley had met on their arrival in Corrigin in 1934.[26] In the story, the narrator is immediately smitten with Irene, the elder of the two, who had an intoxicating sense of her own independence. The McKenna girls rescued the narrator and her sister from their gilded cage as the daughters of the town's most prosperous residents and opened them up to the games and pastimes of the other side of town. They played together with the navvies' (railway workers) kids and for the first time enjoyed life since moving to town from their farm. But this classless idyll could not go on forever. At the climax of the story, the mother of the narrator unfairly accuses Irene of trying to steal a small bottle of perfume. The mother was throwing things out anyway, and giving things to the girls as she was doing so, and Irene had helped herself to the bottle. The mother calls her a thief and demands an apology, but Irene refuses. The mother responds by forbidding further contact with the McKenna girls:

> "You can't have Irene and Edna back again to play," said my mother, turning and thrusting her broad hands viciously into the flour bin. We could see the ugly red flush on the back of her neck. "I can't stand stealing. All niggers are the same. Give them an inch and they'll take a mile. The minute your back's turned, they're shoving things into their pockets. Don't ask to have them again. I can't stand liars." (63)

It seems a minor event in the scheme of things, a mixture of a mother's petty indignation and the casual, endemic racism that prevailed in wheatbelt towns.[27] Irene seems to have been fairly untroubled by the kind of telling off that was doled out to her at regular intervals. But the narrator is traumatised by the incident, losing in the same moment both her only friend and the residue of any faith she had in her mother. Life, thereafter, the story explains, could never be the same:

> We still played with Edna and Irene at school, but it wasn't the same. We couldn't join the gang of kids at the railway yard. We had to come straight home. Edna and Irene couldn't call for us at the shop or come round to our place any more. My father started asking the daughters of the local aristocracy in to play, providing little afternoon teas and a dolly tea-set, a gramophone with lots of children's records, and other bribes guaranteed to make us popular. It worked, of course, and the bank manager's daughter, the doctor's daughter, and the daughter of the agent for Dalgety's farm machinery all came round to play in the dim weatherboard rooms behind the shop.
>
> Now I realise they were the only ones in Jarrabin not on a landlord-tenant basis with my parents or grandparents. They had less reason to hate them, and more reason to keep with them. Between them they fleeced the town, enjoyed the proceeds, and had an understanding not to poach on each other's preserves. (63–4)

A short time after the perfume bottle incident, which ended the friendship with the McKenna girls, an industrial dispute broke out with their Aboriginal father, Big Jim McKenna, at the centre. (The *Women's Weekly* version omitted this second part of the story concerning the strike.)[28] This episode has the effect of translating the perfume bottle incident from the interior shame of family tyranny to the heroic exterior realm of class struggle:

> He had been sacked for standing up to the new manager when he was bounced for taking an extra day off to visit this old mother at Kunjin. The real reason was that the manager wanted to put on another driver. The sight of Big Jim with his muscled self-confident body and soft,

easy manner irritated him like an itch. He had come from up north where niggers stayed in their camps and knew how to talk to a boss. Big Jim compounded the injury by being married to a white woman. His kids topped the class at school. He got on well with all the drivers. Far from hiding his Aboriginal ancestry, he always referred to it with pride, and treated his old mother with respect and affection. (65–6)

The dispute split the town and those who supported Jim were ostracised, but in the end, with the solidarity of his friends and fellow workers, he wins back his job. The manager who had tried to sack him was sent back up north and "the town settled back into the red dust of summer" (68). The strike echoes less the experience of Hewett in the wheatbelt, than her experience with Lloyd Davies in 1946 visiting the Pilbara Station Strike of 1946–49, led by the Aboriginal men Clancy McKenna and Dooley Bin Bin, and the trade unionist and communist Don McLeod, events which she celebrates in a number of her poems.[29]

The strike episode in "The Wire Fences of Jarrabin" rather romanticises the linkage between the workers (the "navvies" who built and maintained the railways) of the wheatbelt and the Aboriginal people, but the two marginalised groups were integrated in her socialist vision. Yet this vision of unity is, in turn, broken by the plaintive note of the girl's exclusion from it, trapped on the other "side of the fence". The story ends on the image of the narrator, on the brink of her departure from the town, staring forlornly at Irene McKenna playing with the navvies' kids at the railway yard:

> "Irene, Irene," I called. The trailing strands of the snapped wire on the railway fence stopped me as I ran forward.
>
> ...
>
> "Irene," I called. "Irene, come back." But she was too far away. The tears dripped between my fingers, glistened for a second on the strands of the wire fence, and dropped slowly, bitterly into the green grass of Jarrabin.
>
> ...
>
> I never saw Irene McKenna again. It took me ten years to learn that the future lay on her side of the fence, ten bitter years to pass through that fence to Irene and Edna and the navvies' kids of Jarrabin. (69)

The fence thus becomes the symbol of both social division (black and white, workers and capitalists), and a temporal division which marks the end of a certain kind of innocence. For the narrator, the events in the story thrust her (but only after "ten bitter years") into a life of reparation for this injustice, and a realisation that her common cause would be with those on the other side of the fence to the one that she was born.

The coexistence of two separate determinations—one based on family (mythological) and the other on class (materialist)—is an important split in Hewett's writing and affects the way we interpret the wheatbelt she gives us. Certainly, we see class and race in the wheatbelt for the first time as actual political fault lines in Hewett's story.[30] With Ewers, there was a broad sense of the epic transformation of the land, and how this was driven by large economic forces, but the politics in his novels were generational, not based on present-day material disparity. With Cowan, we did see the wheatbelt from the vantage point of the rural worker, but these figures did not identify themselves as part of an exploited class; Cowan's anti-heroes felt marginalised, but it was a metaphysical marginalisation, and the path forward was an existential one and not one of concerted political action. Moreover, one looks in vain for mention of Aboriginal people in Cowan's work. Indeed, the presence in the wheatbelt of Aboriginal people is the subject of a quite comprehensive amnesia. With Hewett we are suddenly, and belatedly, confronted with a wheatbelt that as much as it thought of itself as being founded by yeoman farmers, was clearly marked and sustained by a division between the propertied and the dispossessed, those who owned land and those who had nothing but their labour to trade.

"Legend of the Green Country" (1965)

By 1958, the situation in Sydney with Les Flood had become unbearable. Suffering paranoid schizophrenia, Flood's behaviour was becoming ever more belligerent and dangerous. Hewett packed up her things and took her three sons back to Western Australia, some nine years after she had left. Here she rebuilt her life, returning to complete the Arts degree at The University of Western Australia. Hewett began to publish in *Westerly*, the journal founded in 1956 by the Arts Union, but later run by the English department at UWA. In 1959 she published "Once I rode with Clancy" in this magazine, part of her return to the poetic form, which she had abandoned in 1946. Still under the influence and patronage of Frank Hardy, the poems now were rhythmic ballads, demotic in their appeal, but infused with the lush lyricism of Hewett's adolescent work. The wheatbelt emerges into this new format, reanimating the Hewett-Coade family mythology, but set into a rollicking ballad form that blends the mood of the arch, Gothic declarations of her earlier modernist phase with the blunt muscularity of her socialist phase. The result in "Once I rode with Clancy" is the invocation of a form of revolutionary nostalgia:

> Once I rode with Clancy through the wet hills of Wickepin,
> By Kunjin and Corrigin with moonlight on the roofs,
> And the iron shone faint and ghostly on the moonlit siding
> And the salt earth rang like crystal underneath our flying hoofs (44)

The same "dour, and sardonic Quaker men" that dominated "Testament", recur in this poem some sixteen years later, but now they are swept aside by the flying hooves of the romantic Clancy, with each repetition of the chorus:

> Let the old men clack and mutter, let their dead eyes run with rain.
> I hear the crack of doom across the scrub,
> For though I ride with Clancy there is much of me remains,
> In that moonlit dust outside the Kunjin pub. (45)

The wheatbelt is no longer a place of utter perdition, borne down by the sins of the father, but a time-marked region, pregnant with wicked, daring, tragic potential. The poem's narrating voice internalises this deep drama, and sees a future in the past:

> My golden hair has faded, my tender flesh is dark,
> My voice has learned a wet and windy sigh
> And I lean above the creekbed, catch my breath upon a ghost,
> With a great rapacious nose and sombre eye. (45)

The hurt is not gone, but somehow the bitterness is. This is the work of a writer in command of her suffering, and it puts into being a wheatbelt still in contest, rather than impotent and condemned. This wheatbelt is the one that will dominate Hewett's mature work, which emerges in rich variety throughout the remainder of her life.

Hewett finished her Bachelor of Arts degree in 1961, and then undertook, after completing a preliminary program (with a dissertation on the novels of Randolph Stow), a master's degree on the novels of Vance Palmer, supervised by John Barnes. During her postgraduate study she was employed as a part-time and then a senior tutor, before finally abandoning the academy in 1973 to return to Sydney and to write on a full-time basis. During these fifteen years spent at The University of Western Australia, between 1958 and 1973, Hewett forged her way from relative obscurity to the front rank of Australian poets and playwrights.[31] In the late 1950s and '60s, the major outlets for her new poetry, stories and criticism were UWA's *Westerly* magazine, the left-oriented *Overland* magazine published in Melbourne, and Frank Hardy's journal, *Realist Writer*. In Perth, Hewett met and married Merv Lilley, and they had two daughters, Kate (named after Katharine Susannah Prichard) and Rozanna, to go with the three sons Hewett had with Flood. Merv Lilley had been a gardener at UWA, but had had a long and varied life as a labourer and unionist, and had even worked with Frank Hardy in his younger years. A part-time poet as well, Hewett and he co-authored *What About the People!*, a collection of political poems and ballads that was published as a stapled paperback by the National Council of Realist Writers in 1963 with an introduction by Frank Hardy. The book was also a means for Hewett to reclaim her earlier poetry. "Testament" is included in the volume along with other poems from her young adult years which had seemed, in the strict grip of Hewett's earlier communism, as romantic indulgences or bourgeois regressions. Now such poems were seen as answering the kind of broadened political imperative that Hardy had introduced to Hewett, which emphasised the importance of "her own emotional and personal experiences".[32]

Something of the sense of renewal that the return to Perth initiated is captured in the final lines of Hewett's poem "My Fortieth Year" published in *Westerly* in 1963 (September, no. 3):

41. The 1959 *Westerly* issue in which Hewett first published "Once I Rode with Clancy" and *What About the People!* published by the National Council of Realist Writers in 1963.

All must now be fired
From the heavy lump of clay, to the glowing girl,
Into this green wood, this enchanted ring,
Where all the lessons must be learnt again,
The books re-read, the tongue stumble
In the sweetness, and the spell recast.

I gather at my knee the children of my spirit,
Old as a legend, new as milk from heaven,
In the round green wood of the world. (67)

This poem signals Hewett's returning to the wheatbelt through the optimistic eyes of her own childhood wonder. Where "The Wire Fences of Jarrabin" had centred on the experience of disillusionment, this new mode that emerges in Hewett's poetry of the 1960s depends on the strategic re-enchantment of this childhood world. It allows the brilliant, wicked interplay of innocence and knowingness that typifies her greatest works, and infuses her wheatbelt with a sparkling ambivalence that no writer before or after her quite saw, at least not in the way she did. Hewett's definitive wheatbelt is one that interweaves psychology, fairytale, social history and family romance in a beguiling, almost taunting, pantomime, in a manner pioneered in the drama of Bertolt Brecht.

The emergence of Hewett as a writer rather than a wunderkind or polemicist is marked by the publication of perhaps her greatest poem, the autobiographical "Legend of the Green Country", in *Westerly* in 1966 (Summer, no. 4). Like "Testament", twenty years earlier, it won the ABC poetry prize and was broadcast to the nation in 1965. The poem is also the pivotal element in Hewett's first solely authored volume of poetry, *Windmill Country*, published by *Overland* in 1968 with assistance from the Commonwealth Literary Fund. This collection included many of the poems published in *What About the People!*, but this time in a frame that specifically spoke to a literary audience. Although it appears next to earlier Hewett poems that recycle the family mythology, such as "Testament" (1945) and "Ancestors" (1945), "Legend of the Green Country" supersedes these earlier treatments. In 1965, Hewett was forty-two years old, had commenced her M.A. and was working as a tutor in the English Department.[33] David Brooks has noted the poem's indebtedness to T.S. Eliot, particularly *The Waste Land*, with a number of allusions, but also its cadences and its ghostly ensemble of characters parading through the verses like spirits in a séance.[34] Also, the world-weary, teasing narration of this seething universe owes a good deal to the influence of Eliot. This was a slightly different Eliot to the one that Hewett had fallen in love with in her late teens and then abandoned in her early 20s. Eliot in the 1930s was a radical modernist, upsetting not just the long-held precepts of literary form but the very nature of what it was like to be in the world—to be *modern*. By the 1960s, Eliot was routinely taught in universities and was the key modern master (along with Yeats) in poetry.[35]

Moreover, Eliot's allusive, mythic form allowed Hewett to depict her Yealering childhood with the wry linguistic play and restrained agony of high modernism. It is not an easy match. The drab countryside of the wheatbelt seems to fit more readily into Peter Cowan's spare sentences than the rampant and baroque action of Hewett's work. The famous opening lines of Eliot's *The Waste Land*—"April is the cruellest month"—are consciously echoed by Hewett in the opening lines of "Legend of the Green Country": "September is the spring month". The poem produces a wheatbelt unlike anything that had yet been written. In its sense of epic history, of a place built and transformed, it is unlike Eliot's haunted modern wasteland; but in the way that it presents to us a universe wrecked by venal hypocrisy it is utterly attuned to Eliot's vision of the modern world. It is an audacious transposition in many ways, for Eliot's image of modernity was the heaving metropolis of London, the epicentre of industrial revolution and the nodal point of the world's first industrial empire. Hewett's wasteland was the stretch of land between Wickepin and Yealering, the centre of nowhere in particular, except of two things, the family saga of her own childhood, and the transformation of one small corner of the globe into a devolved grain-growing mega-farm. Hewett borrows, again from Eliot, who famously borrowed it from Frazer's *The Golden Bough*, the mythic trope of a land desolated.[36] The particular version of this story owes much to the Arthurian cycle and the figure of the Fisher King, whose impotence pervades his kingdom.

The crucial importance of "Legend of the Green Country" to the wheatbelt's literary history is that for the first time we see the wheatbelt as a tragedy. We have already seen sadness and hardship. The forlorn, embattled men and boys that figure so prominently in the work of Facey, Goode, Pollard, Ewers and Cowan have yielded a gallery of defeated masculinity. We have seen how intensely the growing of wheat, the fields pregnant with grain, represented the image and ideal of masculine potency. But it is in Hewett's hands that the wheatbelt first becomes endowed with the tragic stance. Hewett's "Legend of the Green Country" infuses the family narrative with the regal dimension that is necessary to tragedy. It tells the story of the defeat of her father by her mother and her maternal grandfather by her grandmother. The war fought is one between the sexes, and the men lose. But it is not a simple feminist reversal, because in the end it saves its deepest criticism for the matriarchal empire to which Hewett (at least her poetic persona) was heiress: "Mother to daughter the curse drops like a stone" (78):

The women were strong and they destroyed their men,
Lying locked and cold in their sexless beds,
Putting greed in their men's fingers instead of love,
They drove them from the earth, left them derelict,
Dead mutton hanging on hooks on the verandas. (77)

Both the men and their wives share in the guilt of this defeat, and their children's bitter harvest is that their lives are rendered futile. The poem inverts one of the wheatbelt's iconic structures, the windmill. Before the advent of solar pumps in the twenty-first century, windmills dotted the paddocks of the wheatbelt, replenishing the sheep troughs with artesian water. In Hewett's poem, the windmill is the sign of emasculation and "windmill country" is the land presided over by a castrated king.

The windmill head hangs, broken-necked, flapping like a great plain
    Turkey
As the wind rises ... this was my country, here I go back for
    nurture
To the dry soaks, to the creeks running salt through the timber,
To the ghosts of the sandalwood cutters, and the blue breath of their
    fires,
To the navvies in dark blue singlets laying rails in the scrub. (72)

Hewett also gives us an entirely new and much fuller sense of the feminine than that of her male predecessors. She has absolutely no interest in the idealised femininity offered by Pollard, Ewers and Cowan. Hewett's women are not always attractive, but they are powerful. What Hewett also gives us for the first time is the sense of someone *returning* to the wheatbelt. This allows it to be seen not just as a place that has sprung into being (as in Facey and Goode), or that seems always to have been there (as in Cowan), but which has appeared, flourished and then fallen. This gives a completely different sense of history to the wheatbelt.

In "Legend of the Green Country", the narrating voice is very close to that of the hermaphroditic Tiresias in Eliot's *The Waste Land* and Sophocles's *Oedipus, the King*; in other words, someone who sees all, suffers all, who cannot do other than bear witness and ache and testify. The speaking voice in the poem, the "I", acknowledges their deep complicity, the fact that whatever outrage is described is integral to the fact of their existence. From Perth, this persona "listens" to the cries of the suffering land of her childhood:

> There is no end to it and I stand at the mole watching the sea run
>   out
> Or hang over the rails at the Horseshoe Bridge and listen to the tide,
> Listen to the earth that pleasured my grandfather with his flocks
>   and acres
> Drowned under salt, his orange trees forked bare as unbreeched
>   boys.
> Only the apples, little and hard, bitten green and bitter as salt,
> They come up in the spring, in the dead orchard they are the fruit
> Of our knowledge, and I am Eve, spitting pips in the eye of the
>   myth-makers.
> This is my legend.[37] (73)

42. *Windmill Country* (Overland, 1968); Photograph attached to Hewett's application for position of Senior Tutor at UWA in 1965.

Whereas the idealised women of Pollard, Ewers, even Cowan, were harking back to an Eve before the fall, Hewett's Eve is fallen and under no illusions, "spitting pips in the eye of myth-makers". All the images in the poem are of infertility: the dead orchard, the rising salt. Only the bitter, hard apples that persist offer a small image of hope in a landscape of destruction.

This "Eve", who stands outside of time and judges the actions of the ancestors, is caught between admiration and revulsion. There is, in particular, an ambivalent regard for the grandfather in "Legend of the Green Country", who gallops across the countryside like a wheatbelt lone ranger: "The great horse reared and he sang and swore and flung his hat at / the sky". Yet as we saw in the opening images of the poem, the grandfather is also, literally, stripped and upended by the salinity he helped cause: "my grandfather with his flocks / and acres / Drowned under salt, his orange trees forked bare as unbreeched / boys". By contrast, the grandmother embodies the obdurate mercantilism of the wheatbelt as enterprise. She is pictured as a joyless witch, embittered by the foreclosure of her hopes in life and determined to exact her revenge on the world by foreclosing on them:

> My grandmother had a bite like a sour green apple,
> Little and pitiless she kept the till,
> Counted the profits, and stacked the bills of sale.
> ...
> Her barometer; crops and wool and railway lines.
> Each night she read the news by the hurricane lantern,
> While the only child wept for love in the washing-up water.
> ...
> She balanced the ledger and murmured, "God is love",
> Feeling like God, she foreclosed on another farm.
> ...
> She cackled and counted a mythical till all her days. (73)

Like those written of her maternal grandparents, the pen-portraits of Hewett's parents are also drawn in contrast with one another. They do not have quite the same level of caricature as the grandparents, their sins slighter but somehow sadder:

My father was a black-browed man who rode like an Abo.
The neighbors gossiped, "A touch of the tarbrush there".
He built the farm with his sweat, it lay in the elbow
Of two creeks, thick with wattle and white ti-tree. (74)

But the fact that the farm was built by him did not stop him
from being, in the end, "the mendicant, who married the store-/
keeper's daughter" (74). Hewett's mother bleeds more openly than her
grandmother, and repeats the giving up of hope that seems to be the
central pattern and unlearnt lesson in this poem and others:

She wept in the tin humpy at the back of the store,
For the mother who hated, the father who drank
And loved her; then, sadly, she fell in love
And kissed the young accountant who kept the books
...
She hated the farm, hated the line of wattles
Smudging the creek, kept her hands full of scones,
Boiled the copper, washing out sins in creek water,
Kept sex at bay like the black snake coiled in the garden (74–5)

What becomes apparent, however, is that the heart of the poem,
indeed "the green country" of its title, is the desire of the father. It
is he who holds the key, it is his crushed hopes that determine the
health of the universe, and are in need of rescuing and not merely
consolation:

But never a word of that far green country of his spirit,
Where the trees grow greener than the Gippsland grass.
All this is locked away in grief and salt.
Maybe, in death, his lips will whisper it,
And the green vision that gave sap to all his days
Will rise again and give him back his country. (57)

Another unusual feature of the poem is that its lament is not one
against material failure, but against material success. This creates
an odd tension in the poem, which echoes a broader tension in the

wheatbelt itself. This is that in its own terms, measured by yield alone, the wheatbelt was (and remains) a roaring success. It does, in some real way, continue to "feed the world". In amongst stories of struggle and failure, there have also been many wealthy farmers. Thousands of children (not least, Dorothy Hewett) have been put through Perth's finest private schools on the back of farm profits. Hewett's charge is not that they (her grandparents, her parents) have failed as farmers, but that they have ruthlessly succeeded.

> They breasted it all, the waves of drought and depression,
> Of flood and fire ...
> Their haystacks burnt as gold as their money bags, their till
> Was full of horses drooling on oats and rock salts, of cows
> With udders streaming white milk in the frost mornings,
> Of roosters crowing their triumph from the stable roof ... (55)

In this respect, Hewett's version of the wheatbelt is close to Cowan's. Cowan, too, does not present the wheatbelt as a failed experiment. He takes its ongoing success, in financial or productive terms, more or less for granted. Both he and Hewett, though, view the wheatbelt askance, and find a fundamental emptiness in the lives of those who have found material success in farming. One can certainly find a correspondence between Cowan's novel *Summer* (1964) and Hewett's "Legend of the Green Country" (1965), even if they are speaking in quite different registers. The most marked feature of each of these major wheatbelt works is the intrusion of an environmental consciousness. In each case—Hewett and Cowan—this is a notable change in key from their earlier works. And it points to a crucial way in which the wheatbelt would come to be regarded, and which will be an important part of the picture that emerges in the remaining writers of this study.

The paradox of Hewett's work is that by making it so intensely personal, by equating without hesitation the garden of Eden with the humble homestead orchard of the family farm in Yealering, she mounts a vision of the wheatbelt that is capable of holding its deep historical import. Drawn into this family armature are the two central catastrophes of the wheatbelt's emergence, Aboriginal dispossession and ecological destruction. The matters fret at the edges of the works of her predecessors, but in Hewett they appear boldly and without apology. The issue of Aboriginal dispossession is more muted, though, in this poem than it had been in the story, "The Wire Fences of Jarrabin". In the poem, the father is repeatedly described as "riding like an Abo", a term of derision, but in the poem an epithet used to mark the man's former vitality, destroyed by the family he married into. The other image, deliberately confronting, is the figure of the land as an abused Aboriginal woman:

> No wonder I cannot count for the sound of the money-changers,
> The sweat and the clink, the land falling into the cash-register,
> Raped, and eroded, thin and black as a myall girl on a railway
> siding. (72)

Such an image would no longer be tolerated. Aboriginal people today will not accept any further work as metaphors in the service of colonial guilt. But in 1965, such an image was deeply offensive to middle-class Perth. It directly linked the ongoing sexual exploitation of Aboriginal women—a dirty, open secret at the time—with the blameless, wholesome renewal of the wheatbelt's "country life". No one had yet had the courage, or bad taste, to say that the land that was so revered in the wheatbelt had been "raped", and not only that, but it had been raped just as Aboriginal people had been, and still were, literally and figuratively. The authority to level such charges, crimes of the utmost enormity, was purchased by Hewett at the expense of family loyalty.

"Legend of the Green Country" also shows a much sharper sense of ecological crisis than "Testament" had twenty years earlier. In particular, the problem of salinity dominates the poem, with the word "salt" or "salty" recurring ten times. Section V of the poem relates the efforts of her father, the poem's Fisher King, to fight the problem of salinity:

> He saw the salt of its death rising.
> He said, "I have a plan", and rode with it into the cities,
> A plan for trees, acres of trees blowing by creekbeds,

Forest marching in long green lines to save a country,
Picking up their roots and digging them into the earth,
Holding it fast against the salt and the wind tides.
But the laughter rose in gales from the men in cities.
Their desks shook, their papers scattered like almond blossom in
    storm,
"Visionary"... "Dreamer ... go back to the bend in two creeks,
Thick with wattle and ti-tree you have grown to love,
Go back and wait for the trees to wither, the creek to run,
Drowned in salt, for this is your heritage ..." (76–7)

Both Ewers and Cowan had mentioned salinity in their writing. The problem of salinity is as old as the wheatbelt itself. It was recorded almost immediately, and first became a problem with the Great Southern rail-line, where it was noticed that the water sources used to refill the boilers on the locomotives were turning salty if they were in cleared land.[38] The salt led to rapid corrosion in the boilers and the rail authority's solution was to only draw water from non-cleared areas. Continuous scientific advice, notably at Royal Commissions in 1917 and 1933, warning of the dangers of over-clearing, was ignored in the push to settle the wheatbelt and expand agricultural production. This pattern continued after World War Two, when a huge new expansion of the wheatbelt occurred, driven by high post-war commodity prices and further advances in soil science. Even the passage of the Environmental Protection Act in 1971 did not finally alter the prevailing view that salinity was a minor problem. The matter could not be said to have gained widespread public, industrial and political support until the 1980s, when at last the full magnitude of the problem was admitted.

The issue of salinity reveals a change in ecological consciousness that had occurred not just in Hewett but the Australian imagination more generally. We can see this clearly if we compare her two poems, "Testament" and "Legend of the Green Country", written twenty years apart. Both poems put the colonial myth on trial, and find the pioneer-heroes guilty of various crimes. But "Testament", written in 1945, casts the failures of her forebears in moral rather than ecological terms. In "Legend of the Green Country", the same ancestors are tried again, but the charge sheet reads differently. They stand alleged of the same cant, hypocrisy and meanness, but this time they are also charged with ruining the environment, with salt as the irrefutable proof. This shift shows how environmental consequences are now part of the language of responsibility. The emergence of an ecological consciousness, in the contemporary sense of this term, is something that we have already seen in Cowan. For Cowan, the issue, like it was for Pollard, was primarily one of habitat loss and species destruction. Hewett is less concerned with this than with the concept of a ruined land. Thus, the extinction of a species figures less prominently in her work than does the death of the family orchard. Both Hewett and Cowan were admirers of Judith Wright, and although several of the poems in *The Moving Image* (1946) specifically address the issue of soil erosion, it was Wright's poem "At Cooloolah", first published in the *Bulletin* in 1954, that can be said to be the seminal moment in Australian literary environmentalism.[39] As with Wright, however, there is a crucial tension in Hewett's work between the urge to decry the crimes of her ancestors and an equally strong attraction towards the vitality of these figures.

The Man from Mukinupin (1979)

The "Legend of the Green Country" gave the Lambton Downs years their distinctive treatment, one that was reworked in each of her next volumes; blended artfully with the Lady of Shalott in "Memoirs of a Protestant Girlhood" from *Rapunzel in Suburbia* (1975); detailed again in "Father & Daughter" from *Greenhouse* (1979); dominating the opening sections of the sublime autobiographical "Alice & Nim" poems from *Alice in Wormland* (1987); featuring in some of the finer poems in her late collections, *Peninsula* (1994) and *Halfway up the Mountain* (2001); and, of course, erupting in the lush lyricism of the opening sections of her memoir, *Wild Card* (1990). But in the late 1960s and throughout the 1970s, Hewett turned increasingly to drama, the literary form in which she gained pre-eminence. Her first play, *The Gipsy Dancer*, was written at Lambton Downs and performed on the occasion of her eleventh birthday to those members of the family not involved as cast.[40] Her mature dramatic work first appeared in 1967 with *This Old Man Comes Rolling Home*, a realist play about working-class Redfern in the 1950s staged at the New Fortune Theatre at UWA. The New Fortune is a theatre built into the "New" Arts building (completed in 1963), which approximates the scale, dimensions and properties of the Elizabethan stage. For much of the year it is home to a scattered brigade of peacocks and students biding time between classes, but is used as a theatre through the warm summer nights. It is an "open" theatre, formed in the courtyard of the three-storey Arts building, and Hewett's early plays were shaped by its distinct properties, including her feminist classic, and expressionist *tour de force*, *The Chapel Perilous*, which debuted at the New Fortune in 1971. In 1980, she wrote: "I am haunted by its size, its atmosphere, its flexibility, its infinite variety, so that whenever I sit down to design another landscape in my head, it is always there, posing questions, creating problems and forcing me to find solutions ... If I was asked to name the greatest influence on myself as a playwright I would say it has been the design of the New Fortune theatre."[41]

Hewett's plays had struck a completely different note to that seen in her realist fiction and modernist poetry. They were earthy, surreal, and effervescent, distinctly *à la mode* with Australian counter-culture. In some ways they were similar to Patrick White's expressionist plays of this era.[42] They certainly seemed to be written by a completely different Dorothy Hewett than the one who had written "The Wire Fences of Jarrabin" or "Legend of the Green Country". Yet none of Hewett's early plays, though all in varying degrees autobiographical, were set in the wheatbelt. It was not until the late '70s that Hewett's dramatic oeuvre incorporated the wheatbelt, with the staging of her most famous play, the musical drama *The Man from Mukinupin*. The play was commissioned in 1978 by Stephen Barry of Perth's National Theatre Company (1956–84) and staged at the Playhouse Theatre in Pier Street in 1979.[43] It was commissioned as a festival play in honour of the State's Sesquicentenary, but the play introduced a wicked irony to the triumphalist tone of the celebration of the 150 years that had elapsed since the founding of the Swan River Colony in 1829. Hewett was living in Sydney by this time, but her notoriety in her home state remained. Barry noted in his introduction to the original published playscript that "my announcement of this commission met with vociferous and considerable opposition ... I had quite innocently stirred a hornet's nest even before Dorothy had committed a word to paper: people stopped me in the street to enquire why I had asked 'that woman' to write for the Playhouse in Perth".[44]

Hewett's musical play is amongst the greatest works of Australian literature. It is set in the fictional town of Mukinupin in the years between 1912 and 1920. According to the stage directions, Mukinupin is "a typical West Australian wheatbelt town east of the rabbit proof fence".[45] The setting of the play in the years before and after the Great War, and the centring of action on the marriage choices of a young woman—"Polly Perkins"—at a general store, echo elements of the experience of Hewett's mother, Irene Coade. Katherine Brisbane called *The Man from Mukinupin* an "atavistic play" bubbling with "tribal memories", but it is worth adding that the medium of these memories is the matrilineal mythology Hewett had imbibed in her infancy. In this sense, Mukinupin might be thought of as the "choral" embodiment of her mother's memory. Describing her own time in Corrigin in *Wild Card*, Hewett superimposes her parent's mythological past (from thirty years before) on the contemporary town's dreary shops and streets:

> This is the main street where my father rode, the Black Prince on his black horse, home from the war, and saw my mother in a rage kicking a flaming primus stove across the road. She was the local postmistress and the primus stove, used for heating the sealing wax for the post bags, kept exploding and was almost useless.
>
> This is the shop where he called for her on their first date; the black horse prancing and flighty in the shafts of the sulky, they drove hell for leather out to Kunjin and Vale farm, where she had to endure a family prayer meeting. (45)

It is this Corrigin—beset by a double consciousness (of both "now" and "before")—that is made use of by Hewett in her great play. It becomes the setting and vehicle of an encompassing celebration and critique of not only the wheatbelt, but Australia too, inasmuch as so many of the patterns and problems of the wheatbelt express broader colonial practices.

The play begins in a dream-space in the dry creekbed at the "back" of the town. It is night and the audience is subjected to eerie and interweaving voices, sounds and chants. The world is not at all that of the wheatbelt as it wants to be known, but an unsettling, enchanted admixture of hidden wishes and lost souls:

ACT ONE

In darkness the weird night music begins on the sound track, continuing until the mood of night and eeriness has been well set. The music is interspersed with a line of dialogue, an occasional giggle, scream, shout of laughter or a coo-ee.

ZEEK'S VOICE: (*chanting*) Water … Water … Water …
WIDOW TUESDAY'S VOICE: (*chanting*) Moth and rust … Rust and moth …
TOUCH OF THE TAR'S VOICE: (*calling*) Coo-ee … Coo-ee … (*a high giggle*)
HARRY TUESDAY'S VOICE: (*calling imperiously*) Lily! Lily Perkins!
TOUCH OF THE TAR'S VOICE: (*mocking, fading out*) Harr-ee! Harr-ee! Harr-ee!
EDIE PERKINS' VOICE: (*moaning*) Wash your hands … put on your nightgown … don't look so pale.

(*The background music rises to crescendo as, against the back scrim palely lit, and back to audience, is spread-eagled the shadow of the FLASHER in raincoat and felt hat, flashing.*)

FLASHER: Look Polly! Look Polly! Look Polly!

(*Wild laughter, a scream, blackout.*) (5)

The scene continues as the various "night people" are gathered into a "Morris Dance", each carrying pitchforks and wearing gumboots. They are also stuffed with wheat sheaves, "so that they look like moving haystacks." And they begin the first of the play's many songs, "The Five Man's Morris", a demented harvest song:

Bringin' in the sheaves, bringin' in the sheaves
We'll bless all Mukinupin bringin' in the sheaves.

The bells will toll and gold will roll
Around us in a ring
We'll bless all Mukinupin
When we bring the harvest in. (6)

In this strange way, the play displays the agrarian impulse beneath the wheatbelt, a drive that has its origins, however displaced, in the northern European agricultural patterns of the pre-industrial era. In particular, the unique symbolic value of the harvest, whose ancient festivals are preserved to some degree in the annual Royal Agricultural Shows in Perth and other Australian cities. Katherine Brisbane is right to say that the play is closest in spirit to *A Midsummer Night's Dream*, because it takes directly from Shakespeare the intersection in the dramatic universe of the planes of romantic comedy and divine caprice.[46]

Once the night figures conclude their festivities, the stage brightens and the audience makes out the stylised backdrop of a country town, with "Mukinupin Town Hall" emblazoned on a cardboard portico, "Perkins General Store" blocked in stage left, and at the right, the aged spinsters, Clarry and Clemmy Hummer sitting perpetually on their verandah observing the action askance from the corners of their glimmering eyes. The Misses Hummer function as the story's narrators, half in the action, half out of it, like the chorus in Greek tragedy. In quick succession, we meet the rest of the cast, the middle-aged storekeeper, Eek Perkins; his "deaf as a post" wife, Edie, who communicates mainly by reciting Tennyson; and their daughter, Polly, the play's heroine, bursting with youthful innocence. Next, Polly's two suitors: the young, gormless Jack Tuesday, who works in her parents' shop and fumbles forlornly after Polly; and the travelling underwear salesman, Cecil Brunner, whose mature years and steady income make him the preferred candidate in the eyes of Polly's parents. Cecil sings:

I'm a knight upon the road,
flogging lingerie
I sell the stuff of romance

in a corset and toupée

...

As I move about the country,
the saltlakes and the scrub,
there's a mirage that haunts me
in every country pub.

When I fold up my corset,
and take off my toupee,
there's little Polly Perkins
in my lingerie. (39)

The dreamy otherness of Mukinupin lends it the antebellum charm of the long Edwardian summer, where domestic dreams and municipal improvement fully occupy the worries of the town. Its inhabitants live at quiet cross-purposes to each other and the concerns of the outside world come through with a certain faintness that depletes them of their urgency:

EEK: The line's going through to Jiliminning.
EDIE: What's that father? Speak up.
EEK: *Jiliminning ... Line's through!*
EDIE: (*proclaiming*) "The mighty bush with iron rails is tethered to the world"; and our daughter is singing like ... Jenny Lind.
EEK: Make a good wife for a steady feller. Says here some Archduke's been assassinated at ... some outlandish place.
EDIE: Where?
EEK: Sar-a-jevo.
EDIE: Never heard of it.
CLARRY: Thank God we live in Mukinupin.
CLEMMY: Nothing ever happens here.
POLLY: Summer's ending. I've put my 'air up and lengthened my skirts. (21)

Of course, this sense of nothing happening is itself a kind of daydream. We will see this when we turn in the next chapter to consider the life and work of Jack Davis. One might point, for instance, to events in Moora, Katanning, Quairading and Mount Barker in the years immediately prior to the Great War, where significant conflict surrounded the issue of whether Aboriginal children should be permitted in local schools. Also, as Anna Haebich points out, from 1911 "Aborigines were increasingly denied access to normal hospital facilities" in wheatbelt towns.[47] Such conflict, a direct result of the municipal aspirations of the new wheatbelt towns, led to the opening and expansion of "Native Settlements" at Moore River and Carrolup during the war years—institutions which would incarcerate Aboriginal people for the next three decades. But these things are nowhere mentioned in any of the writing before Hewett (Facey, Goode, Pollard, Ewers)—it is as if they never happened.

In Hewett's play, the town's equilibrium is disturbed in the first act by the arrival of a husband-and-wife theatre troupe, Max and Mercy Montebello, who are touring the countryside performing scenes featuring Shakespeare's great heroines. The character of Max Montebello seems loosely based on the veteran stage and screen actor and director Max Montesole. Montesole had played Cassio opposite Paul Robeson's Othello in the famous London production of the play at the Savoy in 1930 and toured Western Australia in 1934, the time when Hewett first moved to Perth after the three months in Corrigin.[48] In Hewett's play within a play, at the climactic moment when Othello (Max Montebello) moves to strangle Desdemona (Mercy Montebello), the comically naïve Jack Tuesday jumps onto the stage to defend her safety and honour. Amongst this vaudeville, news arrives about the commencement of hostilities in Europe:

(*EEK stand and reads aloud:*)

EEK: August the third, 1914. Should the worst happen after everything has been done that honour will permit, Australians will stand beside our own to defend her to our last man and our last shilling.

(*No one takes any notice of him. There is a roll of drums. Enter MAX MONTEBELLO, very Italian, with a sweeping moustache, wide-brimmed black hat, and a cloak. He stands at the Town Hall entrance and strikes an attitude. There is a breathless hush.*)[49]

The announcement of war and the visit of the travelling theatre change the fortunes of Jack Tuesday, the "grocer's boy" whose advances towards Polly were coming to nothing whilst his prospects had seemed so modest. His bounding onto the stage caught the eye of Mercy Montebello, who tells him that he is a "natural" for the theatre and that if he ever wanted to, he could join their travelling troupe. Emboldened by this, he presses his claim on Polly, only to be rebuffed. He then threatens to enlist: "Lovely Pol, if you don't marry me I'll enlist in the W.A. Light Horse and go to Palestine." It rather backfires when Polly simply clasps her hands together and exclaims: "And be a hero. Oh, Jack!" In the interim, Cecil Brunner returns to woo Polly and Jack decides to join up: "Better than a grocer's boy. Or a nightie traveller." (42) Jack's decision, though only distantly patriotic, is nevertheless celebrated by the town as they all join together to sing him off to war, waving an Australian flag:

> Your country needs you in the trenches,
> Follow your masters into war,
> And if you cop it we'll remember you
> At the Mukinupin Store.
>
> Economic domination
> That's what we're fighting for,
> Join up and save the Empire,
> We've got to win the war. (42)

Jack's departure makes Polly realise she does really love him. Polly, looking desperately for Jack, leaves the store and enters the night. This is the signal for all the alter-egos of the townsfolk (played by the same actors) to appear: Zeek, the mad twin brother of Eek, stumbles onto the stage with his telescope and divining rod; Harry Tuesday, the bad twin of Jack, returns, drunk and surly, from two years' hard labour in Fremantle Gaol; and Lily Perkins ("Touch of the Tar"), the Aboriginal half-sister of Polly (unbeknownst to her), makes her appearance. They bring with them the town's back-story, the foundational traumas that have been quietly swept under the carpet. Each of them carries an improper knowledge and no longer holds an incentive to keep it secret. The drunk Harry tells his mother, the Widow Tuesday, with bitter humour: "Yeah. They reckon ol' Eek spent a lotta time down in the creekbed with them gins, before he took up murderin' em, an' become a lay preacher." (55) This revelation answered an earlier taunt the Widow Tuesday had made to Eek, when she was pressuring him for a second mortgage: "Some 'as got skeletons in their cupboards … and they're not white ones." (37)

Hewett's story is quite scandalous here and moves beyond even her condemnations in "Legend of the Green Country" and "The Wire Fences of Jarrabin" because now the massacres and the miscegenation are located *inside* the Perkins family. Within Australian literature, the precedent for such admissions had really been set by the poetry of Judith Wright, and one might parallel the increased prominence given to Aboriginal massacre in *The Man from Mukinupin* with Wright's revisionist family history, *The Cry for the Dead* (1981). In the play, the "night sounds" are now clearly tied to a massacre in the creekbed in the "old days" that was led by the storekeeper, Eek Perkins. Once again, the Misses Hummer operate as the repository of the town's forbidden memories:

> (*The night sounds begin as the stage darkens … A last crow calls, a dingo howls, an insect begins tapping; there is a wolf whistle, a coo-ee, then a wild scream.* CLARRY *starts up.*)

> CLARRY: What's that?
> CLEMMY: Don't be a fool, Clarry. It's only the Flasher down in the creekbed.
> CLARRY: (*relieved*) And the girls giggling under the pepper trees, holding hands.
> CLEMMY: (*darkly*) The blacks like wild ducks crying under the guns.

> (*There is change of tone now which* CLARRY *has been fighting off.*)

> CLARRY: (*faintly*) The sky was full of crows … wasn't it?
> CLEMMY: And arsenic in the waterholes.

> (*There is a quavering voice a long way off.*) (45)

The aging sisters Clarry and Clemmy speak, at times, not to each other but in substitution of each other, finishing each other's sentences or lines of thought in a way that acts as commentary to the notional action of the story. Later still, Edie, the storekeeper's wife and Polly's mother, wanders onto the stage, sleepwalking and quoting (anachronistically) from Mary Gilmore's poem, "The Aboriginals" (1930):

> EDIE: Where fled the quarry, leaping
> By the hill and creek and plan,
> They lie together, sleeping,
> The hunter and the slain. (59)

In this example, the suggestion of an earlier massacre is given a sudden gravitas by the eruption of Gilmore's poetry. This allusion to a massacre is referencing less a specific history of the wheatbelt, than a broader history of colonial violence in Australia and Western Australia. The new farmers of the wheatbelt were not, by and large, dealing with violent Aboriginal resistance when they cleared their farms in the twentieth century. This direct violence, still a feature of contact history in the northwest until at least the 1920s, was not the main mechanism for Aboriginal dispossession in the southwest at the time the wheatbelt was being formed, although it was a feature in the southwest until late in the nineteenth century.[50] Perhaps the best way of reading this act of genocide is to do so in the spirit of the play, which is to simultaneously accept that it really did happen, and that "it" (violence, dispossession, appropriation) also *continues to happen*. This is the key political innovation of Hewett's form. It is not a realist play and is not bound to historical detail; but it is a historical play in the sense that it consciously puts history into play.

The play reflects the author's conviction that no authentic account of the history of Western Australia since colonisation—the reason why the play was commissioned after all—could fail to address the central fact of violent dispossession. Detailing the individual acts was not the concern of the play; it sought to assert a history of violence, rather than provide it. The slightly incongruous location of genocidal action in the bumbling storekeeper Zeek captures the confusion that many Australians feel in the face of our history. The incredulity comes partly from the fact that there seems no evidence, no visible sign in daily life, that this terrible action has taken place. There is no cenotaph, such as the one that is erected for the war dead and which conditions the space of the stage in the second act. The crime scene has been wiped clean, as it were, and the murder now resides—in Shakespearean fashion—in the neurotic psyches of the characters. The creekbed thus acts, in effect, as Mukinupin's unconscious, and its denizens act out in the form of hallucinatory dramas the events that have been erased in the civic and domestic orders of the Town.

Polly is, initially, the only innocent in this parade, but her innocence is soon called into question. Clemmy chides Polly when she continues to plead her innocence: "Polly Perkins, you've strayed down the wrong end of town after dark, so now you're going to get more than you bargained for." Polly's purity is also impugned by the existence of her half-sister Lily (the same actress plays both), known as "Touch of the Tar". Lily is, in that sense, the "knowing" half of Polly: "'ear 'em, cryin' an' screamin', y'know. They reckon they was done in, down the creekbed, fulla bones. Me bastard Daddy was in on that." (58) When Jack wanders onto the stage, missing Polly, he finds Lily instead, and she draws him away to the creekbed: "Come on Jack, I'll take care of you. It's nice … in the creekbed. Warm an' dark an' soft, she-oak trees: real nice for us. You'll see." (59) So in this same way, Jack, too, loses his innocence and confronts the dual realities of sex and race. The opening act of this two-act play thus ends in the same way as it began, with a seemingly chaotic carnival of figures, indecently acting out or speaking out, a layer of truth that is excluded from the primary drama in the blended domestic and public spaces of the play's main setting—the shop and the town hall. The site of this forbidden action is the creekbed, which we never actually see but is constantly alluded to.

Act Two begins on the other side of the War, a train whistle playing "Yankee Doodle Dandy" to announce the armistice.[51] The Great War occurs, as it were, in the intermission. One moment, we are in the simple, eccentric universe of Mukinupin, and the next, four years have passed by and everything has already happened, the catastrophe has run its course. But in some way this dramatic structure does reflect the basic reality of what the War must have felt like for those in the wheatbelt, because it was an event that was both intimate and impossibly distant. In the play, the reality of what has occurred in the War is marked by a change in the focus of dramatic action. In Act One, it had been the Perkins's shop, and the romantic intrigue surrounding the affections of the young, maidenly Polly. In Act Two, the action is overshadowed by the dull presence of the memorial to the town's dead ("EEK: Ninety-seven enlisted men and twenty-four died. Not a bad record for Mucka", 92). Everything now takes place beneath this obelisk, which in turn points to something which cannot be spoken (the horror of war) but is everywhere apparent. Instead, there is this almost manic public memorialisation. The town fêtes Jack as a returning war hero, showering him with bunting and floral tributes, patriotic songs and speeches. Eek announces: "Yes, Australia was there, Mukinupin was there, to crush Germany and re-divide the world. At one stride our young Commonwealth put on the toga of nationhood, vindicated the rights of man, and maintained the moral order of the universe." (67) But Jack cheerfully explains he is no hero. In fact, it was his brother Harry who had won the Victoria Cross, although he had since gone AWOL and was back to his bad old ways. Eek offers Jack his job back, but he declines this and also the offer of his mother's land mortgaged to Eek. Instead, he will become a shearer:

> EEK: I'll make another offer. What about … the land?
> JACK: Ma's dead of gallopin' consumption, so you can keep the lousy farm. It's only stinkwort and poison bush anyway.
> POLLY: Oh, Jack, you'll never get on.
> JACK: Get on! Be a farm labourer, workin' sun-up till dark six days a week, live in a tin shed with a stretcher in it for a quid a week and me keep. Come off it, Pol. No, I'm goin' shearin'. (70)

Clearly, Jack has returned from the War with a sharpened sense of perspective, and is disinclined to re-adopt his earlier servility. He then confesses to Polly that his true ambition is not shearing, but acting, recalling the encounter with the Montebellos before the War. He goes off to join Mercy's acting troupe.

From there, the action unfolds with the elegant precision of a Shakespearean comedy, as the pieces are moved around the board until each marriageable character finds their "true" mate. Jack leaves with Mercy to conquer the stages of the world, but not before reuniting with Lily Perkins. He goes to great effort to dress her up in the finest clothes that Mukinupin has to offer, even after Edie declares: "We don't serve blacks in here." (91) Later, Edie tells Eek: "I've never been so humiliated – serving your bastard." (94) Polly, having lost Jack, agrees at last to marry Cecil Brunner, the underwear salesman. Cecil had been put on Polly's trail by Mercy as she bid to secure her alliance with Jack. But it is Mercy in the end that sorts out the mess. A kind of Blanche Dubois but endowed with wisdom instead of mere pathos, Mercy's fading charms remain sufficiently intact for her to enchant the men of Mukinupin. She brings back Jack, now a successful actor, in time to interrupt the ill-conceived marriage of Polly and Cecil. Jack marries Polly and she joins him on the chorus line. The jilted Cecil becomes a useful catch for Mercy, who decides—like the theatrical sisters Clarry and Clemmy—that this is where she will retire; the two will open "the best fish and chip shop in Mukinupin." (120) The play ends with a double marriage—Jack to Polly, Cecil to Mercy—conducted by Eek. Nor are the night-people forgotten. Harry Tuesday, who has spent the second act lurching drunkenly about the stage—an ironic counterpoint to the town's new War Memorial—saves Lily Perkins, who tries to drown herself in the flooded creek, and the two are married by Zeek in a carnivalesque wedding in which a popular edition of Shakespeare—"merry, tragical, tedious and brief" (110)—stands in for the Bible and the prayer book.

The paradox of *The Man from Mukinupin* is how such a manifestly ridiculous scenario still manages to capture, better than any other work, the contradictions of the wheatbelt. The answer lies in the grasp that Hewett has of theatre and theatricality. In "Legend of the Green Country", the poem is narrated by a timeless "Eve" who has seen the tragedy of history play itself out beneath her. In *The Man from Mukinupin*, this narrative role is taken on by the "Sisters Hummer", who watch events transpire from the verandah of their house at the side of the stage, hovering wryly over the affairs of the town, and articulating between its day and its "night" activities.[52] We learn that Clarry was a *costumière* for the J.C. Williamson theatre company. Clarry had "dressed the divine Sarah", and the banter swirls with talk of Lillian Russell, Gladys Moncrieff, Jenny Lind and Nellie Stewart.[53] Clemmy, meanwhile, had been an acrobat for Wirth's Circus: "But then His Majesty's burnt down on a Palm Sunday and I fell from the high-wire and ended up ... in Mukinupin."[54] (20) These theatrical ladies, with their theatrical memories, lend a Brechtian air of serious-farce to the events of the play. As Clarry says: "In the theatre everything is possible" (19). Their very staginess means that the action in the play always takes place inside quotation marks. This delimits, and also enables, the "open stage" that Hewett prefers. It also makes plausible the staging of the play within the play by the travelling theatre group, The Montebellos. The play's dramatic irony emerges in the contrast between the glamour of the golden era of the stage (before it gradually lost its prestige to cinema), and the utter ordinariness of the wheatbelt town. The wheatbelt is thus both "the open stage" of possibility, and its rude undoing.

More than anything else, Hewett introduces doubleness as an organising conceit to the wheatbelt. Where Pollard, Ewers and Cowan had maintained a more or less consistent social order, albeit one that faced threats both internal and external to it, Hewett presents a wheatbelt that is beset by incommensurable realities. It is neither the embodiment of the utopian rural paradise, nor the wasted remains of nature and culture, but both of these things at once, existing in permanent superimposition. This fundamental conception repeatedly insists itself at every level of *The Man from Mukinupin*. In some ways, this play is the perfection of Hewett's work because it most fully realises the idea of duplicity. The most obvious, and in many ways most telling, technique is Hewett's use of doubled characters. That is, of using a single actor to play twinned (usually polarised) figures. In the play, the fair Polly is twinned with the tainted Lily, the bastard daughter of Eek. Eek, a doddering shopkeeper by day, is replaced at night by his disowned twin brother Zeek, a visionary and water-diviner. Lastly, there is the eager Jack Tuesday and his anti-social twin brother, Harry. This doubling technique was developed in *The Chapel Perilous* and used in other plays such as *The Golden Valley*. In *The Man from Mukinupin* the doubling indicates the line of repression which separates the positive wheatbelt image from its negative.

The brilliance of *The Man from Mukinupin* derives from its simultaneity, from the fact that several layers of the world happen at the same time. This is brought into being through the fact that only certain characters actually speak to each other. The central romantic triangle of Polly, Jack Tuesday and Cecil Brunner are involved in fairly conventional exchanges of speech, but as we have seen with the Sisters Hummer, conventional dialogue is often replaced by other forms of locution. A more obvious case is the simple fact that the play is a musical. The musical numbers provide the occasion for the outbreak of concerted "social" speech, as when the town unites in song to call for Jack's enlistment. The fact of everyone knowing the words to a song, suddenly underlines that these words are fundamentally shared, that there is a common script at such moments and thought seems to occur in unison. Other songs, like Polly's lament on her marriage to Cecil, express a subjective protest against this same social script, or ironically quote the script back to itself. A song by Jack's outcast brother, Harry, is used to refute the wheatbelt's pastoral dream:

> New Holland is a barren place,
> in it there grows no grain,
> nor any habitation
> wherein for to remain.
>
> She is my gold, my darling,
> she gives me drought and rain,
> when I plough and sow her
> upon the saltbush plain.
> ....
>
> I'll plant her and I'll rape her,
>   I will not run her down,
>   upon her gold and torment,
> I'll build my shanty town ... (62)

In such ways the songs in the play not only express the sentiments underneath the action but also cut across the action, opening it up to critique and irony. This is the kind of wheatbelt that now can be made visible by the time we reach 1979, although it still took one of the nation's most gifted writers to capture it.

Hewett's Wheatbelts

It should by now be clear that a number of wheatbelts came to life in the major works of Dorothy Hewett. Most particularly, we can contrast the social realism of "The Wire Fences of Jarrabin" (1957) with the modernist lamentations of "Legend of the Green Country" (1965) and the expressionist effusion of *The Man from Mukinupin* (1979). What Hewett seemed to apprehend, or at least what her work would seem to suggest, was that the wheatbelt was not susceptible to a single rendition. Her work is of unique value for the way that it not only describes but exemplifies the contradictions of the wheatbelt. This crucial aspect is closely related to the fact that the wheatbelt was utterly personal to Hewett. The wheatbelt cannot be fully reduced to either a material phenomenon (global capitalism) or a mythic one (the

43. Lambton Downs, 2015.

yeoman dream) but these two forces met in the intimate confines of the farming family. Hewett's upbringing within such a family make her a crucial witness to the event of the wheatbelt.

Like Cowan, Hewett could see that the wheatbelt was not just a beginning, but an ending as well. Each saw the wheatbelt as bearing in its history a fatal determination, a basic loss. Hewett explained how the eleven years she spent growing up at Lambton Downs continued to grip her, and asks what does "it" (the wheatbelt, Lambton Downs, childhood itself) stand for?

> In the years since, I have often returned to this landscape as if haunted by it. It stands on the horizon of my mind, a dream landscape of childhood, unchanged, inhabited by ghosts larger than life, passing like shadows under a huge sky. What does it stand for? A child's Eden with a black snake coiled waiting under the African Daisies. For there is often in these [wheatbelt] poems, along with the apotheosis of place, a sense of foreboding, of the sinister inevitability of time and ruin. As a myth it is therefore interchangeable—it is the life/death myth out of which the human consciousness is formed.[55]

The answer to the basic question of the wheatbelt existence— "What does its stand for?"—is thus glued to her own subjective history. When she looks back at Lambton Downs, she realises it is no longer there. One of the most poignant renderings of this moment occurs in the epilogue to *Wild Card*. While the memoir had concluded in 1958, with Hewett's return to Perth, the epilogue takes the reader forward to a moment in 1987, just prior to the release of *Wild Card*, when Dorothy, with her sister Lesley, returned to visit the farm at Lambton Downs:

> The roads were grown over, the gates wired up. Desolate, treeless except for the hardy York gums and jams, the crossing over the creek was barely distinguishable, but lying in the hollow were a scatter of corrugated-iron sheds and a single brick chimney.
>
> "Oh God!" we cried. "Oh God! Is that the house?"
>
> Two almonds, a few figs and one quince survived. No she-oaks, no wattles, no tea-tree, no paperbarks, no bottlebrush, no salmon gums,

no stables, sheds or post and rail sheep yards, only the concrete dip left like a scar in the home paddock, littered with iron and rusty machinery. Day's timber all gone—a denuded landscape. (271)

The image is true, the things she remembered were not there, but it is not those things that are missed. They are the sign of what is missed. Hewett's desolation is recorded in a fantasy image she sees in a hand-mirror she remembers from "the first bedroom":

In the tarnished glass there is a card house made of fibro, weatherboard and corrugated iron bowling over and over through the empty paddocks, torn apart and scattered across the sunstruck miles with nothing left to show that once a family worked and loved and quarrelled here, planted orchards, gardens and crops, raised animals and children, grew angry, sentimental, passionate, proud and sad. (271–2)

Perhaps, then, more than anything else, the contribution of Hewett's literature to the wheatbelt is the institution of a new form of tragic time. Indeed, apart from the intensity of its scenes, the other key way of coming to terms with Hewett's writing is by an understanding of its sense of time. The preferred tense of her memoirs, for example, is not the conventional past tense, but a curious mixture of the present ("We go to Yealering for the last time", 47), the "perfect" future ("I'll write poems and plays and stories full of ghosts", 49) and "perfect" past ("Lou has been sent away", 47). The effect is disconcerting. It causes a narrative style that is continuously at war with its narration (its sequencing of events), flashing forward and flashing backward, until the sense of a timeline becomes a shimmering field of things that *have happened* long ago or *will happen* with solemn inevitability in the on-rushing future. Hewett's writing continually alludes to a set of stories that took place prior to the commencement of the time that we live in now, but whose effects in every way determine us.

I open the gate for the last time ...
I close the gate. When the azure blue summer bird migrates back to the dry creek bed, I won't be here. We drive away through Day's paddock into the future. (*Wild Card*, 49)

324

Chapter Seven

Jack Davis (1917–2000)

Mogumber (1932)
Brookton (1933–36; 1946; 1955–62)

Jack Davis, the Aboriginal writer, activist and intellectual, is not usually thought of as a wheatbelt writer, but he lived and worked for at least eleven years in the wheatbelt, mainly on the Brookton Reserve with the relations of his mother's second husband, Bert Bennell. His poetry, and especially his plays, show us a wheatbelt that we do not first realise is the wheatbelt. We see little in the way of the iconography and aspirations of the ideology of wheat—no sense of an epic struggle to turn "virgin" bush into productive farmland, no waving fields of wheat, and no lyrical descriptions of landscape. Instead we see life, to cite Hewett's closing image from "The Wire Fences of Jarrabin", from the other side of the fence—the Aboriginal experience. As well as Brookton, Davis also lived in the timber town of Boddington for nine years after World War Two, which is in close contact with the wheat and sheep country around Wandering and Williams. The mill at Boddington, unlike the Jarrah mill at Yarloop where his father had worked, was set up to process the timber from York gums, which were uniquely useful in the packing of munitions during and after World War Two. He also spent the first fourteen years of his life in and around Waroona and Yarloop and a year at the Moore River Native Settlement at Mogumber, in the sandplain country near Gingin. Davis thus lived in the wheatbelt for as long as Hewett, and longer than Ewers, Pollard, Goode or Cowan. In outlook, his was closest to Cowan's in the sense that he was an itinerant labourer for much of his time in the wheatbelt. Like Cowan, he also worked on the wheat bins after World War Two. But being Aboriginal in Australia, particularly before 1967, was an experience that is difficult to reconcile or make commensurate with the experience of those who were non-Aboriginal. It is this experience which, from a literary point of view, Davis was the first to deliver into the public domain. In this chapter I want to consider Davis's literary work for the way it documents the Aboriginal wheatbelt. But I also want to use the facts of Davis's life to open up a picture of Aboriginal experience. With this in mind, I will also be introducing other writers and figures to a greater extent than I do in other chapters in order to help document this complex picture.

Davis understood the close relationship between farming and Aboriginal dispossession: "Where the white man had turned the soil whole tribes were completely obliterated." One of the things lost is language. For Noongar people, wrote Davis, of the "fourteen tribes which inhabited the southwest of Western Australia", each with a distinct language, now "[o]nly one language … remains, a composite of the fourteen languages, and that is the Nyoongah tongue, and I regret to say that if by some miraculous means our people of the eighteen-thirties were to return, they would find it difficult to understand and speak the Nyoongah language of today."[1] Before looking more closely at the literary works of Jack Davis and what they say about the wheatbelt, it is useful to examine the intersection of the history of the wheatbelt with the history of Indigenous people in the southwest of Western Australia. The historical circumstances of the founding of the wheatbelt meant that, by and large, its expansion during the twentieth century was not along a frontier in the classic sense. It was a re-usage of land that had been settled, albeit "lightly", during the course of the nineteenth century in the form of pastoral leases. Before that, of course, Aboriginal people had been living in the region of the wheatbelt for tens of thousands of years. At the time of colonisation in the 1820s, the southwest was occupied, as Davis has pointed out, by an interlinked series of tribes that have come to be known as Noongar.

The word simply means "man" in the language that they shared.[2] The Noongar tribes were distinct in language and ritual practice from the Wong-gie and Yamatji people to the north and east. Interestingly, the lands of the Noongar correspond in their boundaries quite closely to the outer limits (10-inch rainfall line) of the wheatbelt, although they also populated the wetter and coastal country inside the 20-inch rainfall line. Noongar people worked in the early pastoral stations of the southwest as shepherds (necessary due to the prevalence of dingoes and poison shrubs) and other general station work. They also farmed their country before and after colonisation in ways that were reported extensively in the early survey and exploration accounts. Not only "fire-stick" farming designed to increase native pasture for the sustenance of game, but extensive aquaculture in rivers, lakes and coasts, and the harvesting of native yams in yam-fields.[3] In his recent fiction, the Noongar writer Kim Scott has explored the relationships that existed in the early contact period between Noongars, sealers, whalers and colonists on the south coast.

Even though the direct violence and disease epidemics of the nineteenth century were less marked in the twentieth century, the emergence of the wheatbelt had a devastating effect on the remaining Noongar people of Western Australia. At the turn of the twentieth century, the area that would become the wheatbelt was home, in Anna Haebich's estimation, to some 1,500 Noongar people:

> Their economy and lifestyle were built around employment on pastoral stations and hunting and camping on the vast tracts of uncleared land in this area. They were exploited for their labour, but these adaptations also provided them with a degree of economic independence and enabled them to retain their ties with the land and certain elements of traditional Aboriginal life. With the development of the wheat belt the Aborigines were forced off the land, their existing way of life was destroyed, and they were ultimately left trapped in a life of poverty in small camps on the fringes of the wheat belt towns.[4]

Aboriginal people had been involved in crop-farming since the 1840s at the Benedictine Mission at New Norcia in the Victoria Plains, which were developed intensively during the wheatbelt's expansion in the early 1900s. Rica Erickson describes how the mission's founder, Dom Rosendo Salvado (1814–1900), had at an early point seen the owning of farms as a key to Aboriginal survival in the post-contact environment. After winning a large lease from the colony—at their peak, in 1885, the Mission held 975,000 acres—Salvado "proceeded to parcel out the land among the Aborigines who helped the missionaries", giving it to them "for their exclusive use".[5] Erickson continues: "Although funds were not available to build homes for them on these lots, his object was to establish a village of native proprietors, who should become husbandmen and artisans, as well as real Christians." (19) She later explained that: "The experiment of settling natives on their own farms succeeded with a few families, but only if they stayed near the Mission under the benevolent supervision of the priests." (54) Erickson makes it clear in her account that as the wheatbelt expanded into Mission-held leases at the end of the nineteenth century, there was considerable resentment that foreign Catholics had been given valuable land and in turn had made land available to Aboriginal people for agriculture. "It is little wonder", she writes, "that men complained that the Mission had 'picked the eyes out of the country', and that some disputes arose over rights to waterholes." (49) The fact that the land actually belonged to Aboriginal people, and so was not "given" to them at all, is not given any weight in Erickson's account. Beyond New Norcia, a small number of Aboriginal people applied and were granted land in the 1890s and 1900s, but these did not in the main lead to long-term holdings. Erickson writes that, in the early 1900s: "A few [Aboriginal] families settled on farms and even bought small locations, but few persisted in ownership." (88) She does not go into the reasons why these farms did not succeed, but the matter was investigated by Anna Haebich who found that Aboriginal-owned farms were severely hamstrung by uncertainty over their tenure since Aboriginal people could have their land resumed at any time. This in turn made it impossible to borrow against the value of the land in the way that was the central element of the business model for the "new farmers" of the wheatbelt, as we saw with Cyril Goode and Albert Facey.

At the same time as Noongar people were being forced from the land as the old pastoral system made way for the new close settlement, and the unalienated Crown land was sliced up to create homestead farms, Aboriginal people in the pastoral regions to the north and east were becoming subject to the provisions of the Aborigines Act of 1905. This Act, replacing earlier Acts from 1886 and 1897, vested a right in the state to remove children of mixed Aboriginal descent ("half-caste") from their parents. It also created the office of Chief Protector of Aborigines, along with a system of local Protectors (usually the local policeman). The legislation in the 1905 Act started the widespread transit of Aboriginal people across the length and breadth of Western Australia. The nodal points in this vast network were the Carrolup (1915–22; 1940–51) and, to a much greater extent, the Moore River (1918–51) Native Settlements.[6] Carrolup is near Katanning in the Great Southern, and Moore River is halfway between Bindoon and Moora in the Midlands district of the wheatbelt. The Native Settlements were the key institutions in the implementation of Aboriginal policy during the long tenure of A.O. Neville, appointed as Chief Protector of Aboriginals in 1915. He held this post until 1936, when he was made Commissioner of Native Affairs until his retirement in 1940. The Native Settlement on the banks of the Moore River near the Mogumber railway siding became a multiethnic Aboriginal centre, with Aboriginal people from the Goldfields, Pilbara, Kimberley, Murchison and Gascoyne all ending up there along with Noongar from the southwest. From Moore River, Aboriginal people were sent to work on farms as general labourers (men) and domestic servants (women) on wheatbelt farms, but also on dairy farms further south and onto pastoral stations in the more arid zones.

The full extent to which the formation of the wheatbelt was built on the back of Aboriginal labour has not been finally assessed, although Anna Haebich's work gives a detailed treatment of Aboriginal life in the southwest during these years. It is certainly not at all apparent from the many shire histories of the wheatbelt that Aboriginal labour was an important feature of the "pioneering" of these districts, and as we have seen it was something completely absent from the writing of Goode, Pollard and even Cowan. For Ewers, who does mention Aboriginal people, they feature only as a nuisance and as magically "disappearing" into "the interior". It was Hewett, with her story "The Wire Fences of Jarrabin" published in 1957, who actually confronted race for the first time in the literature of the wheatbelt. Robert Bropho, born in a camp at Toodyay in 1930, has written of life on the Moora Reserve in the Midlands of the wheatbelt: "Aboriginal people of the Moora district are responsible for many farms in the Moora district today, such as burning off, stone-picking, fencing. Aboriginal people are the foundation stones of the new police station, the new swimming pool. They did a hell of a lot of contract work in Walebing, New Norcia Mission, Dandaragan area, Coomberdale area, Watheroo, Miling."[7] Even as fine a history as Rica Erickson's *The Victoria Plains* (1971) is virtually silent on the topic of Aboriginal labour. Another history of this district, commissioned by the shire, R.R.B Ackland's *Wongan–Ballidu: Pioneering Days* (1965), in a chapter on "Native Place Names", asserts that "very few natives have been in evidence in the Agricultural era". He relates that Aboriginal people had been employed by local pastoralists in the 1880s in horse-breaking, shepherding, shearing and ringbarking, however: "The new settlers never favoured natives, as whenever one was engaged, all the relatives gathered around and became an embarrassment." In particular, "the native community spirit of sharing" was found to be "foreign to our way of life." Ackland continued:

> When dingos were plentiful, natives were paid ten pounds per certified scalp, and a small tribe was camped near the townsite.
>
> An interesting sidelight occurred in 1940.
>
> The spokesman from the native's camp approached the Road Board with a request that water be laid on to their camp and sanitary facilities established.
>
> This was referred to the Department of Native Affairs, which replied that the number of natives did not warrant anything being done.
>
> The camp soon dispersed and it is a very rare sight to see a native here. Most have congregated round New Norcia and Moora.[8]

The extreme passivity of this description, which treats the matter as a mere curious incident, is utterly typical of accounts in the shire histories. In this example, the "natives" were used when they were needed, but when they asked for water and basic sanitation, they were referred by the town to the Department of Native Affairs—the most underfunded of all state government departments, who predictably refused to intervene.

Alice Nannup

To gain an idea of what life was like for Aboriginal people during this time we can look briefly at the life of Jack Davis's contemporary, Alice Nannup (1911–95). Alice Nannup's story, which she tells in *When the Pelican Laughed* (1992), offers an insight into the way that Aboriginal people went in and out of the wheatbelt during its formative years. The wheatbelt was a place of exchange, bringing together the Noongar indigenous to the region and Aboriginal men, women and children from much further afield, particularly from the north of the state, in the Pilbara, Gascoyne and Kimberley, where pastoral stations created the conditions for the so-called "half-caste problem". In 1911, Alice was born to fifteen-year-old Ngulyi at Abydos Station near Port Hedland. Ngulyi herself had been born at Pilbara Station, between Roebourne and Marble Bar. Ngulyi spoke five languages—Nyamal, Palyku, Kariyarra, Ngarluma and Yindjibarndi—as well as English. Alice's father was a white stockman named Thomas "Tommy" Bassett and she took his name—Alice Bassett. While Alice was still young, her mother and her siblings moved to another Pilbara station, Mallina, owned by the Campbell family. It was here that Alice, because she was "fair", was caught up in the new system codified in the 1905 Act, and which was being interpreted, more and more, as addressing the issue of children of mixed descent. This issue had become the subject of considerable anxiety; indeed, it is fair to say, it had reached the stage of moral panic. This "problem", like all moral panics, actually harboured a range of social fears, but most particularly the basic question of whether Australia really was a white country. Of course, there were base material motives such as the cost and inconvenience of providing for unwanted children, not to mention the embarrassment they caused. In any event, the result of this need to address the "half-caste problem" was decisive in the life of Alice Nannup and thousands of Aboriginal people over the next decades, including, as we will see, the parents of Jack Davis. For Alice, the matter was decided between the station owners and a government representative:

Then, this one time, and I remember it as clear as daylight, the Aboriginal Affairs man ended up staying the night. He stayed up at the station house with Mr and Mrs Campbell. They had a conversation together and that must have been when they made all the arrangements.

After his visit the Campbells talked to my mother, my aunt, and my Uncle Paddy about me and Doris. Doris was another fair one like me, and they told them they were going to take us down South to educate us, then bring us back home to our family. I was really excited about going, it sounded like a real adventure. Besides, I thought, it was a good way for me to get out of marrying that old fella I was promised to. But I didn't know, I never even thought of it really, that there were other plans for me. (39)

In 1923, the twelve-year-old Alice and two other children travelled by boat from Point Samson in the Pilbara to Fremantle with Mrs Campbell. They were accompanied by Alice's father, Tommy Bassett, although Alice did not yet know him as such. In Perth, the party reported to the Aborigines Department in Murray Street, before travelling to Beeginup in the Great Southern. Whilst transiting in Perth, Mrs Campbell made it known to Alice that Mr Neville (the Chief Protector) had forbidden further contact between Tommy and Alice. It was at this point that Alice found out that Tommy was in fact her father. It was a feature of the Act that Alice could not see Tommy *because* he was her father. The idea was to break the bonds of parenthood and any "confusion" this might cause. She never saw him, or her mother, again.

In this way, Alice Nannup, along with many others from the widespread station country of Western Australia, found her way into the wheatbelt, working on farms. At Beeginup (near Broomehill), Alice worked milking sixteen cows and separating the milk: "Looking back, they didn't have us there as kids, they had us as slaves." (53) They were paid 2 shillings a week, but that was frequently withheld on the grounds of some misdemeanour or another. They had no shoes and on the freezing winter mornings would warm their feet in fresh cow dung whenever they could. After Beeginup, which the Campbells had been minding for another family, they moved to Pallinup (near Gnowangerup) and worked there, mainly clearing and fencing: "We had to go out sucker-bashing too, because the Campbells decided to put a crop in. They bought us three little axes and we'd go out chopping down the scrub." (54) At Pallinup the school had closed, so after a year there A.O. Neville informed the Campbells that the children should be sent to Moore River (Carrolup had closed by this stage) because schooling was mandatory.

Alice and the two other children (Doris and Herbert) arrived at Moore River in August 1925. She spent two years in this institution before, towards the end of 1927, and at the age of sixteen, she was informed that she was to go out to work. She was sent by train to the wheatbelt township of Williams, on the Albany Highway, where she worked as the housekeeper for the local policeman (named Larsen), and in particular, as the carer for his invalid wife. It was arduous work and there was little gratitude shown, but Alice was determined not to be sent back to Moore River. At Williams she was paid 5 shillings a week, half of which was given to Neville to bank on her behalf. As at Beeginup, whenever her employers felt like doing so, she was sent off to work elsewhere, for friends and neighbours. When Larsen's wife went to hospital, Alice was sent to work for a time at a farm at Kojonup that belonged to Larsen's sister:

> I worked in the house and as soon as the housework was finished I went down to the farm to help with the harvesting. They were cutting wheat at the time. They take the heads off and put them through a thing called the winnower. The winnower throws all the cocky chaff out and all the seed goes into a bag. I had to stand there and do that from about ten o'clock in the morning, through to about five in the afternoon. (93)

As the wife's health deteriorated, the Larsens moved to Perth and Alice with them. Mrs Larsen died on the last day of 1928. At the end of January 1929, Alice was sent out to work at a wheat farm in Wyalkatchem owned by a family called the Cashmores. She worked both inside the house and on the farm, particularly at busy times such as harvesting, when she would bag the wheat and stitch up the bags. The stint at Wyalkatchem ended after four months, when Alice was sent back to Perth for treatment for a severe case of mumps. After recovering, instead of being sent back to the farm, Alice was asked to work as a maid to the Neville family, at their Darlington home in the Perth Hills: "I used to call Mr Neville Sir, and his son I called Master John. But I called his wife Mrs Neville and the girls by their names, Anne and Cynthia. This was a cap'n'apron job, you know, you've got to wear a uniform. Mrs Neville used to buy material and I'd make them up for myself." (121)

The job at the Nevilles was only temporary, and Alice was returned to the farm at Wyalkatchem. She recalls being threatened as she disembarked at the train station in the town by local men and having to take refuge in the police station. Mrs Cashmore explained to her that Aborigines were not allowed in the town after dark: "Wyalkatchem was a very prejudiced town. It was a real colour bar place, no Aborigines were allowed there. All the people who were working on farms out there – like Muriel Ugle, Minnie Darby, Alma Bell, Charlie Sandstone – all of them would just go into town to do their bit of shopping, then they had to go straight out again. That's what it was like, not a soul allowed after dark." (127) After falling out with the Cashmores, Alice returned again to Perth, and once more served in the household of A.O. Neville, before an altercation with Mrs Neville led to her being dismissed and sent back to Moore River. From Moore River, Alice was sent to work on a station near Leonora. Here, the owners lived a high life of tennis parties and had their servants in cap'n'apron. The white servant that worked there earned 25 shillings a week, while the Aboriginal servants were notionally paid 5 shillings a week. In fact, though, at this station, Alice was never paid. The rule at the time was that if you were sent to work, you could only apply for a transfer after twelve months. But after four months, Alice and two others decided to abscond. They made it as far as the town of Leonora, and from there Alice wrote to Mrs Cashmore, who in turn wrote to Neville. Alice then went back again to Wyalkatchem, where she stayed until 1932 when a letter arrived announcing she was to be married to Will Nannup, a man she had met during her last stint in Perth. Marriages involving Aboriginal people needed the approval of Neville. Alice Bassett and Will Nannup were married at the Church of England chapel at Moore River in May of 1932. In the three months that they were forced to stay at Moore River before their wedding, Alice stayed at the compound and noticed how much worse everything seemed since the last time she had been there, between 1925 and 1927. The marriage was, more or less, an arranged one. Will applied to Neville to marry Alice, and when approved, notice was then passed to her. Speaking of Will, she writes: "We got along all right, but we didn't really know each other that well because we'd never got the chance. In one way I got married to get away from the government, and I think a lot of women did that." (148)

Apart from two years at Mullewa in the early 1960s, Alice Nannup never lived in the wheatbelt again. Being married did mean a reduced subjection to the whims of the Protection system. Will and she had moved after their wedding to take up work at Meekatharra and ended up in Geraldton, where they spent the best part of thirty years. During that time Alice Nannup had thirteen children, ten of whom survived. Nannup's story is exemplary because it shows how closely linked the wheatbelt was to the system of Aboriginal Protection formalised under the 1905 Act. The life-stories of Aboriginal people, which have been published in increasing numbers since the 1980s, recall lives spent in wheatbelt farms and towns.[9] The remarkable thing is how rarely the life-stories and local histories of farmers and districts mention Aboriginal people. The work of recent historians, most particularly Anna Haebich, has substantially filled in this silence and also helped explain it. The situation was a complicated one, and the experience of Aboriginal people varied considerably. Nevertheless, certain patterns were repeated and at the heart of the process was the program of State Government intervention which controlled Aboriginal lives in the years between the 1905 Act and the 1967 referendum which led to full citizenship rights.

Jack Davis, *A Boy's Life*

Jack Davis was born six years after Alice Nannup, not on a Pilbara station, but at King Edward Memorial Hospital in Perth on 11 March 1917. His parents, however, were both originally from the Pilbara. His mother was removed from her people in Marble Bar when she was seven years old and "given" to a white family in Broome to become their servant. At the age of fourteen she became a servant to the local bank manager and followed him south when he was transferred to Pingelly in the wheatbelt. It was there that she met her husband, William Davis. He too was taken from his mother and given to a white family, who raised him. After working as a stockman in the Pilbara and Kimberley, Bill Davis had, by the age of twenty-five, moved to Northam. After their marriage, Bill Davis, with his wife, settled in the district of Waroona in the southern Darling Scarp, where he raised a family that eventually included five boys and six girls. As well as Waroona, the family lived for a time in Lake Clifton and, from 1923, the timber town of Yarloop, where Bill worked at Millar's Timber Company. Jack and the other children attended school and were a part of the community, his father being a noted cricketer and footballer. His father kept his job when the Depression hit in 1929 but the prospects for his children were not bright. In 1932, A.O. Neville wrote to Bill Davis offering to teach farming skills to Jack (then fourteen), and his older brother Harold, at Moore River. Crucially, Bill Davis had citizenship and his children were not subject to removal under the 1905 Act. Thus Jack Davis entered the Moore River settlement under different auspices to many there, that is, not as a child removed from his parents because of their mixed ancestry, but as—at least so they thought—government-sponsored apprentices in the field of agricultural work. The reality fell rather short of this.

Between Yarloop and Moore River, the two Davis youths stayed at Bennett House in East Perth, an Aboriginal hostel where Alice Nannup had also stayed.[10] It was here that Davis met other Aboriginal people for the first time and experienced the "first stirrings" of racial prejudice as they dined separately—with the Aboriginal kitchen staff—from the manager of the hostel. The train to Moore River Settlement stopped at the Mogumber siding, where they were met by the camp's notorious superintendent, Arthur Neal, and they were driven the 12 kilometres to the settlement in the back of a ute. Jack and Harold Davis were to spend the next nine months at Moore River, from January to September 1932. The settlement consisted, at this time, of a "compound" of some 450 children and, to the west, a "camp" of some 750 adults. The compound housed boys and girls of school age, roughly between the ages of six and fifteen, in segregated dormitory accommodation and under a strict regime. Jack and his brother spent their first three months at Moore River in the compound, before requesting (and being granted) leave to live in the camp under the guardianship of a woman named Mary Noble. The squalor and chaos of the camp was, for Davis, a considerable improvement on the institutionalised cruelty and misery of the compound.

The "education" that the two boys were given in farming techniques was half-hearted at best: "I had imagined that we would be taught to set up a team of horses and drive a harvester or a plough. Tractors were the future and I had hoped that we might be taken to see one and perhaps learn to drive it."[11] In fact, they were parked in the nearby Clark Road paddocks with some rudimentary equipment and told to do clearing work. Given that clearing work was typically one of the tasks that Aboriginal labourers were given, there was a brutal logic to this, though it was certainly not what had been held out as the purpose of the boys attending Moore River:

> No attempt was actually made to teach me and my brother farming. One day Harold asked Mr Neal why.
>
> Mr Neal's cryptic reply was, "You're learning about all you'll ever learn about farming here." So as one was not supposed to question the Superintendent, we came to the conclusion that stabbing Zamia palms and picking roots in a paddock was to be the sum total of our knowledge of farming at the Moore River.[12]

That education was rather a subsidiary consideration was pointed up by the fact that the "lesson" corresponded exactly with the general labour that was given to the men in the camp. The able-bodied men of the camp gathered each morning to be given their work orders—generally picking roots and stabbing palms.[13]

Davis is a crucial witness to the experience of Moore River because he was resident in both sections of its community: the structured regime of the children's compound, and the unstructured, informal but still heavily regulated life of the camp. Also, he arrived late enough and his stay was short enough that—together with other mitigating factors such as his education and literacy and the fact that his father was a citizen—he was able to survive the experience without succumbing to it. Narrating these events in later life, he remembers being *bemused* by what he saw at Moore River, on his arrival at the superintendent's house at the top of the small "avenue" which contained the main buildings in the compound:

> We walked outside and stood on the verandah, the crowd milling around us. I was somewhat bemused by the scene. I had never seen so many Aboriginal people before in my life. I was to learn later that the population of the settlement was 450 people, consisting of Aborigines from all over the State.[14]

Bemusement is, in the context of this study, a distinctly *literary* feeling in the sense that it imports a crucial distance—the space of irony—into Davis's observations. There is now a substantial archive of memories of Moore River on the public record. Susan Maushart's book, *Sort of a Place Like Home: Remembering the Moore River Native Settlement* (1993) drew on seventeen separate informants (including both Alice Nannup and Jack Davis) to piece together life at Mogumber in the three and a half decades of its operation. A range of memories—sad and joyous—are visible, and a clear picture emerges about elements of life in the settlement; but it is only Davis who expresses bemusement upon arriving on this "scene". This specific quality is invaluable in understanding the experience of Aboriginal people in the wheatbelt—caught in a world of limited literacy—from the point of view of a literary history. It is an element of the character of Jack Davis that would appear spectacularly in the form of his first collection of poems, *The First-Born* (1970), and the great plays he wrote over the ensuing two decades. Many people have recollected life at Moore River, but Davis, more than any other, was able to *represent* it.

After nine months, the Davis brothers were advised that their father had sent for them, and though they had made some good friends during their stay, they were more than happy to be saying goodbye and returning home. Back at Yarloop the father had gone, along with everyone else at the Mill, onto a reduced work schedule as demand fell with the effects of the Depression. The family was able to supplement their food by hunting and gathering, and though there was not a lot of money, the situation did not seem especially dire as everyone else in

Yarloop, and the rest of rural Australia, was in more or less the same boat. The Davis family were obviously Aboriginal but Davis recalls no particular discrimination from the local community, where they were very much involved in its affairs and life. A sudden catastrophe was to change all of this, however. Their father, walking back in the evening from a hunting expedition, slipped while jumping across an irrigation ditch—he broke his neck and died instantly. Apart from the devastation of losing a much-loved father, the family were now without a source of income, and there were no jobs for the elder sons in the district. The family were told they were, as Aboriginal people, entitled to rations, and they were forced to take these to survive, but the mother decided after a period to move with the seven youngest children to Brookton to be with her tribal sister Maude.

Jack stayed in Yarloop for some months, then he too went to Brookton, a wheatbelt town on the Great Southern rail-line between Beverley and Pingelly: "For the first time, we were forced to live in a camp made of hessian and thatched up with blackboy fronds."[15] Davis got a job on a nearby farm working up to sixteen hours a day for 5 shillings a week plus keep. It is one of the intriguing parallels in this literary history that Jack Davis and Peter Cowan (who was three years older) were working in wheatbelt farms during roughly the same years, namely from around 1932 to around 1936 or '37. The nature of the experience is noticeably different, though. Cowan was employed through an agency and was accommodated usually in a workman's quarters created by walling in a section of the machinery shed. Cowan also mainly describes situations where he worked alone or just with the farmer himself. Davis seems always to be working with others. After a brief period in Brookton, Davis threw in the farm job and headed to Kalgoorlie. But no sooner had he arrived when, owing to a riot on the main street, he and ninety-two others were packed onto a freight train and sent to Narrogin. At Narrogin, the police took immediate exception to a now hungry and unruly consignment of men looking for work—Davis was the only Aboriginal man. The events paint a picture of life at the peak of the Depression where gangs of the unemployed were flung from town to town in the vain hope of finding a living. After Narrogin, Davis found his way to Corrigin, where he got a job loading wheat:

The farmers at the time were not much more wealthy than any of the itinerant workers or unemployed that constantly flowed by. It was the first year of bulk-handling.[16] Corrigin had a very small bulk bin and the rest of the wheat was bagged and stacked. In those days there was no wheat pool and the buyers bid for and bought their wheat at the siding, marking their purchases with chalk and arranging the shipping themselves.

Farmers would go out and plough up a patch of sandplain, ground completely undeveloped, and grow some wheat there and live in a camp, or a hessian hut, and hope that they could get their two-and-sixpence a bag, somewhere around ninepence a bushel, for their wheat. They would take a couple of bags of wheat over to the flourmill and exchange them for flour. They were poor and lived on mutton or wild game, and flour.[17]

Davis was in Corrigin just a year or two before Hewett, six years his junior, briefly lived in the town in 1934. Camping on the Corrigin siding, he was literally one of those on "the other side" of "The Wire Fences of Jarrabin". The farmer that employed Davis had a truck—"the first truck in the district, a battered wreck"—and Davis and he used it to cart wheat to the siding, twelve bags at a time, twelve loads a day.[18]

During this time in the early 1930s, Davis returned often to Brookton, where his mother lived, following the seasonal work around, along with all the others in these Depression years. His mother had re-married a local Noongar man named Bert Bennell and she lived with him and the kids at Brookton Reserve, which was like many other reserves on the outskirts of wheatbelt towns. Town reserves needed to be near enough to towns so that they could distribute rations, but far enough to spare the sensibilities of the new farmers and townsfolk. Davis explains:

Reserves were small, useless parcels of land left over from the great land-grab. Once the property needs of a farming community and its town had been met, a few discarded acres would be set aside as a reserve for Aborigines. It seldom had any economic value and certainly never had sufficient natural resources to support a traditional

Aboriginal lifestyle. Itinerant labouring work was the only means of support an Aborigine could expect …[19]

The usage of reserves continued until at least the 1960s, and Davis himself would live at the Brookton Reserve both before and after World War Two. In the 1930s, Davis's mother, who supported her family by washing and ironing in the district, successfully fought to keep her children in the local school. Whilst attending the local school had never been an issue in the timber town of Yarloop, it was a major issue for Aboriginal people in wheatbelt towns.[20] Davis noted that: "In Brookton there was a general resistance to the admission of Aboriginal children into state schools, but my mother was adamant. Of course, the objection was never expressed in race terms. There was always a reason given: the Aboriginal children were dirty, or their hair was nit-ridden, or they were covered in scabies." After some other Aboriginal kids were excluded from the school, Davis's mother marched her children down to the police station and demanded the policeman strip them down and search them thoroughly. But the sergeant demurred:

> "Look, Mrs Davis, as long as your kids are clean and tidy and well-behaved, they can stay at the school as long as they like."
> She then went up to the school and informed the head-master, and through him the community. "My children are going to school and that is all there is to it," she said.[21]

His mother's pluck would serve as a crucial inspiration for Davis as he met discrimination at various (and numerous) moments in his life.

Davis also became close to his stepfather, Bert Bennell, and the two travelled the district from York to Pingelly, which was the traditional Bibbulmun country of the Bennell family. They did the usual run of casual labouring work—fencing, clearing—that employed Aboriginal people in the era of wheatbelt expansion in the days before widespread mechanisation. A little surprisingly, for a district that was settled very early in Western Australia's colonial history, the Noongars of this middle part of the Avon Valley had managed to avoid the worst excesses of government and mission interference. It was from Bert and his relations that Davis learned the Noongar language and lore that would feature in his later writing.[22] Bert was born around 1886 and grew up at a time when the language was still widely spoken and traditional rituals were practised in the southwest. Later, Davis came to regard these years, from the age of fifteen to seventeen, as the happiest years of his life.[23] It was the depths of the Depression, and no one had any money, but he never wanted for food or company.

Davis left the wheatbelt in the mid-1930s to go and meet his brother, who was living in Carnarvon. Carnarvon, at the mouth of the Gascoyne River, lies some 900 kilometres north of Perth. There is enough water beneath the usually dry bed of the Gascoyne, fed by summer cyclonic rains, to irrigate banana plantations, which were the town's main industry. Carnarvon also served as a port for the surrounding pastoral stations, which stocked both sheep and cattle.[24] In the late 1930s and through the war years, Davis worked on stations in the Gascoyne. He worked initially as a drover, droving stock to Carnarvon from Lyndon Station, and then, for a much more extended period, as a stockman and boundary rider at Williambury Station, in the catchment of the Minilya River. Davis was unusual in that he was genuinely bicultural in this highly segregated world. Educated and literate, and the son of a citizen, he did not suffer from an innate sense of difference from the white owners of stations: "I was always treated as one of the white stockmen and I ate and slept with them and not in the camps on the rivers or on a bare piece of red earth." (*First-Born*, vi). Station life brought Davis into direct contact with the interface between tribal Aboriginal people and pastoral commerce:

> The stockmen's quarters were also of stone, and comfortable. I was sometimes invited to eat in the station dining-room and often gathered, with the boss and other station-hands, to listen on the crackling radio to the news of the Second World War. The whole atmosphere of the station was one of relaxed refinement.
>
> Down by the banks of the creek, living in shanties they had constructed from discarded sheets of iron, were about a dozen remnants of the local tribe.[25]

At Williambury he spent a good deal of time posted on his own at Kimber's outcamp, maintaining fences and windmills and water troughs, three hours' ride from the station. For company, Davis started to spend time with the Aboriginal people at the station, who in the seasonal break of work, would gather with other groups at a place known by the derogatory name "Pinkeye Camp" which was about 18 kilometres from Kimber's outcamp.[26] Davis was given the name "Jagardoo" by the people, which would become the title of his second volume of poetry, published in 1978.

In all, Davis spent some ten-and-a-half years up north, mainly in the Gascoyne, before returning to the family at Brookton just after World War Two. After a short period of rural labour, Davis found a job at the Boddington sawmill, where a number of Noongars worked, including members of the Kickett family. Davis decided he wanted to operate the steam-saw, but this job required an engine-driver's certificate. This, in turn, required that Davis obtain citizenship. That his father was a citizen did not make Davis a citizen. Davis was a good candidate for citizenship, but it came at a significant cost. In essence, taking citizenship drove a wedge between the citizen and other Aboriginal people. Citizens were no longer allowed on reserves, and though they could drink in a hotel, other Aboriginal people could not, and indeed any sharing of alcohol was deemed "supplying" and constituted an offence. Nevertheless, Davis took citizenship, and ignored these strictures.

Davis worked for nine years in the Boddington Mill, before it closed down in the mid-1950s. He then returned to Brookton, once again:

> I undertook fencing, clearing, burning-off and well-lining. Rabbiting was also a steady source of income, and I set myself up with a horse and cart, and a stack of rabbit-traps. It was a job in which I could engage my nephews and other relations, and I came to know many of the younger-generation members of my large extended family.
>
> Brookton was quite unlike Boddington: the Nyoongah population existed as an entity quite distinct from the white population of the district. At that time the Aboriginal population was a fringe group living on the reserve or camping on the properties of the few farmers who utilized the cheap labour that an Aboriginal family made available.[27]

By the 1950s, though, a long and irreversible decline in rural labour was beginning to take effect, the consequence, in the main, of mechanisation, which dramatically reduced the manpower required to perform the multitude of farm tasks. From clearing with bulldozers, to large-scale planting and harvesting, to bulk-handling of grains—everywhere, there were just less people needed than before. And yet, for those with farms, this was a time of unprecedented prosperity in the wheatbelt. High post-war prices and high demand for wool driven by the Korean War, along with the evolution of new farming practices (especially subterranean clover and trace elements) all substantially improved the profitability of the land. But the costs of this revolution fell particularly heavily on Aboriginal people, who had depended on the tasks of rural labour for subsistence, as Davis points out:

> Many Aborigines were beginning to find conditions very hard. Employment, always seasonal, was becoming more and more difficult to obtain. Contractors using bulldozers and tractor-driven equipment were starting to replace unskilled Aboriginal labour. Myxomatosis had robbed Aboriginal rabbit-trappers of their livelihood, and there was still no form of social welfare to support those out of work.[28]

These conditions led to a revival in the importance of Christian missions—both Catholic and Protestant—in the southwest. Under Neville, the missions were tolerated, but there was a strong preference for government-run settlements (Moore River and Carrolup). Carrolup was taken over by the Baptist Union in 1952, and re-named Marribank.

And yet, as well as being a party to continued cultural interference—the missions were instruments of assimilation—the Church, after the war, was also a vehicle for an increasing politicisation of Aboriginal rights. In 1949, Mary Jones, the daughter of an evangelical Presbyterian minister, set up the Brookton Aboriginal Church. This church became a meeting place for the Aboriginal community of the district and began to take up issues that were affecting the lives of Aboriginal people: "There we would collect, and discuss politics, religion, and Aboriginal affairs, with Miss Jones herself joining in.

Ours was an Aboriginal voice in an early stage of development."
(Chesson, 125) It was the beginnings of the Civil Rights Movement
and Aboriginal disadvantage was taking on a new complexion and,
into the 1960s, a decisive momentum. Davis taught in the Sunday
School at the Brookton Aboriginal Church and eventually became a
lay preacher, developing skills of advocacy and communication that
would serve him in his later life as an activist and public intellectual.
After two years with the Church, Davis left Brookton to work on
the wheat bins further afield, but the general paucity of work in
rural areas forced him to Perth by the early 1960s. There he got a
job with Co-operative Bulk Handling, weighing wheat, and was able
to buy a house in the modest, then semi-rural, southeastern suburb
of Maddington. In Perth, Davis became involved in the Nyoongah
Church, and, through them, the Aboriginal Advancement Council
(AAC; formed in 1963, formerly the Western Australian Native
Welfare Council). Thus Davis joined the emerging national advocacy
for Aboriginal rights that was becoming more and more serious,
particularly with the formation in 1958 of the Federal Council for the
Advancement of Aborigines and Torres Strait Islanders (FCAATSI),
which brought together the various state-based advancement councils
and which would become instrumental in the campaign that led
to the successful citizenship referendum in 1967. Davis became the
Western Australian state secretary of FCAATSI in 1969 and, also in
that year, the director of the AAC.[29]

The First-born (1970)

Whilst they were integrated into society to a greater degree than many
other Aborigines at this time, neither of Jack Davis's parents could
read, and it had been Jack's job as a boy to read them the newspaper.
Davis had, in the end, some eight years of schooling, which was
much more than most Aboriginal children, and indeed many white
children at this time. He loved school, but was also prone to illness:
"I was inclined to have horrible dreams, nightmares, and I was told
that I was a very sensitive boy."[30] He formed an early love of words:
"I used to go to bed with a dictionary because I loved words and
wanted to understand words."[31] At Moore River Settlement, he was
introduced to Aboriginal languages for the first time. One older man

from the northwest came from the same tribe as his father: "I used to spend many hours talking to him: he used to sing aboriginal songs and I used to write down the aboriginal words ... He had a beautiful voice and to hear him sing in his own language was something which I am afraid is lost because he has been dead for many years."[32] In Brookton in the early 1930s he learned Noongar from his stepfather, Bert Bennell. It was not a written language and one of Davis's vital functions, one of his lasting legacies, is the way that he formed a living bridge between the spoken Aboriginal experience and the writing of the modern world. At least as far back as this time (after Moore River, before the Gascoyne) Davis had already commenced a life of writing poetry:

> Throughout all this time I had been writing continuously. It was an impulsive habit, invented by a restless mind to relieve the boredom of a camp bereft of very many other resources. My materials were nothing more substantial than a lead pencil and a few scraps of paper. The audience was generally myself, although I often read my work to George Stack and a few other friends. Before I could present them to a wider public, my poems had to remain locked in my mind for another three decades.[33] (Chesson, 63)

Davis continued to write poems to pass the time when he worked on stations in the Gascoyne later in the 1930s and through the war years, where one fellow stockman nicknamed him the "Black Banjo".[34] He also submitted his first poem for publication during this period, at the age of twenty (c. 1937), to the *Northern Times* (1905–52), a Carnarvon newspaper. The poem was accepted, at least Davis received a letter to this effect, but was never printed and Davis felt that this was due to racial discrimination. Wounded by this, Davis did not send any more poems to newspapers, but continued to write them "for my own amusement".[35] These poems, recollected in later life, would form the basis for the first two collections of Jack Davis's poems, *The First-Born* (1970) and *Jagardoo* (1978): "A lot of the poems that I wrote were lost, as old lunchpapers are apt to be; but I have been able to recollect many of them, and they form the bulk of my published poetry."[36] The poem submitted

to the *Northern Times* in 1937 provides a window into the sensibility
of Davis at the age of twenty, and an early glimpse into his subdued
lyric power:

> I built a boat of dreams
> I set it sailing on a calm, blue sea
> With silver sails
> The fabric of my schemes
> Floating on a sea of unreality.
>
> The storm clouds gather fast ahead
> Too late to care
> My silver sails are torn to shreds
> I am left standing forlorn and in despair.
>
> I cannot build a boat again
> My eyes are dim with age of old
> Far too soon I have reached my mount of pain
> My eyes grow dim, my flesh grows cold.

The poem is remarkably similar in effect to the poem "Dreaming"
that the eleven-year-old Dorothy Hewett wrote for her correspondence
classes. It is a poem about the collapse of a fantasy, but Davis's poem
does not have Hewett's cheeky humour. There is a hint of wry irony
(and self-recrimination) in the phrases "silver sails" and "fabric of my
schemes", as if there were a certain callow blindness in this setting out
into the world on "a boat of dreams". But overall, even though this
poem is one of desolation, its tone is resigned and there is a calmness
to its declarations.

In the post-war years, returning from his decade up north, Davis
"started to write a lot more seriously than [he] had in the past" and
"started to save lots of pieces of verse" (*First-born*, vii). In 1970, by
which time Davis was running the Aboriginal Centre in Beaufort
Street, he was encouraged by the Australian novelist Richard Beilby
to consider publishing his poems. Beilby had seen the poems posted
on a board outside Davis's office when he had visited the centre:
"'All right, Dick,' I said. 'If you want to you can post them away.'"

(Chesson, 145) The poems were published by Angus & Robertson in 1970 as *The First-born and Other Poems* with an introduction based on a transcript of a recording that Beilby had made of an interview with Davis. There was also a lengthy Bibbulmun vocabulary compiled by Davis. The publication of Davis's poems was preceded, and perhaps made possible, by the sensational success of Kath Walker's poetry, *We Are Going* (1964) and *The Dawn is at Hand* (1967), the first books of poetry by an Aboriginal person.[37] Walker's books sold more copies than any Australian poet since C.J. Dennis. Walker had been writing poetry since the late 1950s when she had been encouraged by Stephen Murray-Smith and the Realist Writers.[38] It was Murray-Smith who introduced her to Brian Clouston, the owner of the Brisbane-based Jacaranda Press. Her manuscript was read by Judith Wright, and Wright immediately grasped the significance and power of Walker's verse. With the assistance of the Commonwealth Literary Fund, Walker's *We Are Going* was brought to press, a landmark moment in this history of Aboriginal writing. Walker's was a political poetry, often directly addressing the "white man" and speaking with an imploring, pan-Aboriginal "we", which directly challenged the political status quo.

44. Jack Davis, *The First-born* (Angus & Robertson, 1970); Kath Walker, *We are Going* (Jacaranda, 1964).

Davis and Walker were good friends by the time he published *The First-born* in 1970. Although neither were founding members of FCAATSI (formed in 1957), each had joined shortly afterward (Walker was Queensland State Secretary in 1961) and met regularly at the annual conferences during the 1960s.[39] Davis recognised that Walker's poems were "the beginning of modern Aboriginal literature" and that she herself "must be regarded as the forerunner of modern Aboriginal authors".[40] The early reviews of both Walker and Davis ranged between patronising faint praise and outright dismissal. Philip Roberts of the *Sydney Morning Herald* found "the often stilted diction" of Davis's poems to be "not without charm", and at moments even possessing "a fine intensity".[41] It needs to be remembered that poetry was enjoying a particular privilege at this time and was felt to be the medium of culture at its most serious and sophisticated articulation. An anonymous review in *Southerly* notes that Jack Davis, echoing the stock-characterisation of Namatjira, lived "uneasily between two worlds".[42] The reactions of Australian reviewers to the poetry of Walker and Davis (and Kevin Gilbert, whose volume *End of Dream-Time* appeared in 1971) betray a category mistake that would take some time to rectify.[43] Judith Wright was the first critic of note to understand that the critical handbook that had served other occasions did not meet this one.[44]

The poems in Jack Davis's *The First-born* are generally short, rhyming lyrics, often in the elegiac tonality that was one of the key-notes in Walker's poems, although they did not follow hers—at least not yet—down the path of political manifesto and into, as they were characterised at the time, "protest poetry". Walker, although the more trenchant, was also the more comic of the two poets. Her poems often mugged a version of Aboriginal English that drew its critical edge from the lineage of bumpkin-philosophers in Steele Rudd's *On Our Selection*. Perhaps the most brilliant of these comic poems was Walker's "No More Boomerang" which ends a series of deft contrasts between the "then" of tribal life and the "now" of modernity by offering this suggestion: "Lay down the woomera, / Lay down the waddy. / Now we got atom-bomb, / End *every*body." (33) The italics she places in the word "*every*body" gives the word its Aboriginal English cadence. Davis's poem "A Eulogy for Peace—by an Old Aboriginal" is the one poem in *The First-born* which mimics this kind of speech: "Why don't white man sit down quiet by fire? / Not stand up and call other country-fella liar." (39) But, for Davis, this exploration of Aboriginal vernacular would come about later, when he turned to theatre.

Davis's poetry was quieter than Walker's and also, by and large, more personal. He shared, though, Walker's painful sense of the lost world of tribal life. The title poem of the collection, "The First-born", answers the same implicit question that Walker's famous poem "The Past" answers: how does an Aboriginal person today embrace a legacy that is both devastatingly real and tragically lost?

> Where are my first-born, said the brown land, sighing;
> They came out of my womb long, long ago.
> They were formed of my dust—why, why are they crying
> And the light of their being barely aglow?
>
> I strain my ears for the sound of their laughter.
> Where are the laws and the legends I gave?
> Tell me what happened, you whom I bore after.
> Now only their spirits dwell in the caves.
>
> You are silent, you cringe from replying.
> A question is there, like a blow on the face.
> The answer is there when I look at the dying,
> At the death and neglect of my dark proud race. (1)

The poems in *First-born* touch on the various points in Davis's life, his childhood at Yarloop ("Retrospect", "The Boy and the Robin"), and his life on the Gascoyne stations ("The Aboriginal Stockman", "Dingo Dingo"). Others speak to the kind of life Davis was living by 1970 in the suburbs of Perth ("My Dog") or crossing the country by plane ("Day Flight") and to the politics of Aboriginal life as it was still being played out both in the city ("The Accident", "Slum Dwelling") and in remote Western Australia ("Yadabooka", "Laverton Incident"). Like Walker, he plays a careful game with the images of traditional Aboriginal society, invoking them, but also decrying the museumisation of Aborginal culture. Poems like "The Artist" and "Skeletal" reflect wryly on the fascination that white Australia has with dead Aboriginal people, with Aboriginal culture as a trace of what has gone. Each of these poems animates the Aboriginal person as a living presence; in "Skeletal" an Aboriginal skeleton in a museum is apostrophised:

> Yes, Old One, you knew how to live.
> You had no need of white man's legislation.
> What you could see was yours, supreme,
> The earth and sky out of a dream
> Was your Creation.
>
> Fancy is gone, my dream of you is broken
> By children rushing in the dim-lit room.
> I touch the show-case gently as a token
> And I hear him whisper: "Courage",
> Through the darkness and the gloom. (26)

Most of the poems in *First-born* are not linked to specific places and are not really directed at their remembrance. Instead, they try to articulate Aboriginal experience "today" (i.e. 1970) as a metaphysical plight. The placenames and explanatory notes that are included in certain poems stitch them, almost accidentally, into place. So, for instance, the poem "Camped in the Bush" ends:

> Over the campfire
> The bat cries shrill
> And a "semi" snarls
> On the Ten Mile Hill.
>
> And the lonely whistle
> Of the train at night,
> Where my kingdom melted
> In the city's light. (5)

The Ten Mile Hill is just outside Toodyay above the course of the Avon. The train to Kalgoorlie follows the Avon Valley through the Darling Ranges to Northam. The presence of semi-trailers snarling up the Toodyay Road could place the event on either side of the War, but more likely after the War. The country at Ten Mile Hill begins, to the east, to open out onto the wheatbelt, and to the west, to the hinterland of Perth. Davis was the first to express a distinctly Aboriginal sense of the interface between country and city that characterises the Western Australian wheatbelt. It was not just a distinction between production and consumption, or nature and civility, or the rural and the urban—but a fundamental difference in the kind of history one, as an Aboriginal person, could inhabit. The dilemma had simply not been described before, at least not from the *inside*.

Also emerging in Davis's poems is a poetry of the mission, the native settlement and the reserve. In Walker's poems, and in many of Davis's too, the contrast is typically between tribal life and modern life. The poems of tribal life paint a picture of vitality and balance and draw on traditional stories. Powered by this, other poems attack the forces that ripped Aboriginal culture apart, and the laws and hypocrisy that continue to oppress Aboriginal people today. Less visible in Walker's poems is the reality of life in the institutions and reserves that Aboriginal people lived in for much of the twentieth century. The stated policy in Walker's first two volumes of poems is "integration" (based on multiculturalist pluralism), contrasted with "assimilation", which had been the goal of post-war Aboriginal policy. By 1970, when Walker's two volumes were released together as *My People*, the dedication was to the new policy of self-determination that would govern the aspirations of Aboriginal people over the following decades. In the title poem of Walker's *The Dawn is at Hand* (1967), the refrain that is repeated throughout is "Fringe-dwellers no more." It is the life of fringe-camps that, for Walker, represented the collapse and decay of Aboriginal culture and, naturally enough, the concern was to turn this situation around. Davis, too, addressed the cultural collapse that was a feature of the camp-life, as in the plaintive poem "Aboriginal Reserve":

They stir a fire that is dying,
The sparks fly upward blending
With night and a people crying.
O where, O where is the ending? (34)

And poems such as "The Drifters", "Desolation" and "A Nightmare of Reality" express a deep distress at the hopelessness that was
devastating the lives of so many Aboriginal people, one that Davis was
dealing with every day in his job managing the Aboriginal Centre in
Beaufort Street in the late 1960s:

We stumble along with a half-white mind.
Where are we?
Who are we?

...

> The tribes are all gone,
> The boundaries broken:

> ...

We are tired of the benches, our beds in the park,
We welcome the sundown that heralds the dark,
White Lady Methylate!
Keep us warm and from crying.
Hold back the hate
And hasten the dying. (36)

The term fringe-dweller had been popularised by Nene Gare's
novel *The Fringe Dwellers* (1961), which followed the story of a teenage
Aboriginal girl—Trilby Comeaway—who returns from a mission to
live with her family in Geraldton. The Comeaways then move from
their corrugated iron humpy to new housing at "The Wild-Oat Patch"
set up for Aboriginal people, as Trilby's mother tells her family:

"Them houses are goin up special fa coloured folk," she told the sisters.
"All scattered about, too, not in a heap like we was rubbish. That's what
  they call discrimination."
   Mr. Comeaway laughed. "Ya got that arse about," he told his wife.
"*Ass*-imilation, that's what you mean."[45]

Nene Gare's husband, Frank Gare, became a district officer with the Western Australian Department of Native Affairs, first in Carnarvon (1952–54) and then Geraldton (1954–62), and Gare's novel draws mainly on the time in Geraldton, where, amongst the families she met through her husband's work, was that of Alice Nannup's, and the two became friends.[46] The term fringe-dweller would be reclaimed for Aboriginal experience several decades later by Robert Bropho in his radical history *Fringedweller* (1980), which documents his life in the camps of metropolitan Perth, as well as the wheatbelt and goldfields, and further afield.

Davis himself does not use the term fringe-dweller, but his experience living on reserves at Brookton, Northam and elsewhere, and the attendant institutions—for him, Moore River—are a feature of his writing, particularly his later plays, but also visible in his early poems. The poem "Family", as a footnote explains, "was inspired by the sentencing of two aborigines to three months' jail for leaving a country reserve without permission, to visit a brother in the Allawah Grove housing settlement." Allawah Grove was established as a "Transitional Housing Scheme" by the Department of Native Welfare in 1958 and reflected a shift in policy from segregation to assimilation, at least for Aborigines of mixed descent.[47] It was an important part of the policy and practice of the scheme that the families resident there were tightly controlled. The last thing the Department wanted was for it to become another reserve. Davis's poem is written from the point of view of those on the country-town reserve, and in this it recapitulates his own life experience in and around Brookton in the 1930s, '40s and '50s:

> We would like to visit our brother today.
> We're new here, fresh from a country town.
> We would like to talk of folks far away
> And the life we led as children.
>
> How we gathered the tails at lambing time:
> They sizzled and curled on the open fire.
> We followed the plough at seeding time
> And screamed at the plovers, wheeling. (33)

Other experiences of these years—rabbiting, shearing—are recounted before the poem concludes:

> This is the pattern your ordered mind
> Has forgotten, this way of perceiving
> That survival through sharing and sharing, my friend,
> Was a Carpenter's way of believing.[48] (33)

Davis's poem emphasises a view he formed later in life that the Depression years, though marked by profound poverty, were not as miserable as they seemed because people felt an authentic solidarity.[49] One would not wish to overstress this point or to romanticise poverty, but the poem expresses an ambivalence about assimilation—apostrophised here as "the pattern of your ordered mind"—that echoes Davis's own anguish over electing to take citizenship in the 1950s, conscious that this step introduced a clear division between himself and many of his relations, indeed his brothers and sisters. But glimpsed through this poem is the life of mixed seasonal work—"We followed the plough at seeding time"—and living off the land that helped Aboriginal people in the southwest survive the Depression years. The importance of rabbits, both to the diet, and as a form of income is touched upon: "We circle the rabbit, crouching low, And he fled from our do'aks flying." The inclusion of the Noongar word "do'ak" (throwing stick) emphasises the adaptive dimension of life in the early years of the wheatbelt for Aboriginal people. The traditional hunting tool's continuance in a world transformed by agriculture and introduced animals is linguistically registered by the intrusion of a Noongar word into an English poem. In this sense, the poem speaks against, at the level of its own diction, the process of assimilation.

The book of poems is unusual for the length of its preface, a transcription of a biographical interview of Davis by Richard Beilby, which detailed for the general public the experience of an Aboriginal person through the course of the twentieth century. The preface was an important document in this sense, and it is notable that it is in Davis's voice, and displays his own deep thinking on the remarkable facts and forces that conditioned his life. Davis's autobiographical reflections make it abundantly clear to the reader that he is, in every sense, an intellectual and not just an activist, a member of what Nugget Coombs described as the emerging "Aboriginal intelligentsia" that were profoundly altering the terms by which Aboriginality was being addressed in the broader Australian public sphere.[50] Just as important as the introduction is the lengthy appendix of Noongar words that accompanies *First-born*. The appendix is an extensive and autonomous Noongar dictionary and not just a glossary of the occasional Noongar words used in the poems. Walker noticed this in an early short review of *The First-born* for the University of Queensland poetry journal *Makar* (edited by Martin Duwell): "To me the writer [Davis] seems to be saying, 'these spoken tribal words are dying fast and my duty, therefore, is to record as best I can, what I can.'"[51] In other words, Walker understood Davis to be undertaking what is sometimes termed "salvage ethnography", the grim task of capturing culture at the moment of its disappearance. Davis was, indeed, seriously occupied with recording a comprehensive list of Noongar words, conscious that the language was gravely imperilled, and that his own knowledge of the language from his stepfather was a not insignificant repository. In this sense, Davis was the first Noongar linguist, the first person equipped to navigate the archival record of Noongar words preserved in the writing of early colonists, as well as the modern anthropological and linguistic study that emerged in the post-war period, with experience of the language as a user.[52]

Kullark (1979)

While Davis's first creative writing was in verse, he seems also to have understood, at an early point in his writing career, the possibilities of theatre. His concern with the play of language, with the rhythms of Aboriginal English and the gestures of contemporary Noongar life, along with a realisation that cultural survival depended on the reclamation of history, all led Jack Davis towards the stage. In particular, he became interested in the way theatre directly involved and addressed its audience. He was also conscious of how theatre, through its collective nature, led to something living via those who produced it. Theatre thus enabled Davis to circumvent the limits of poetry as a form, as well as its policing by strict cultural guardians who could only bring themselves to say, when confronted with the historic appearance of Aboriginal poetry in English: *well, that is all well and good, but it's not poetry.* The Aboriginal poet and playwright Kevin Gilbert wrote his play about Aboriginal seasonal workers, *The Cherry Pickers,* in prison in 1968, where he was serving a life sentence for the murder of his wife in 1957. When it was staged in August 1971, it became the first play written by an Aboriginal person to be performed. Gilbert's script and the ideas around the social impact of drama—a post-Brechtian sense of dramatic praxis—led Bob Mazza and others to develop the Black Theatre movement in Redfern in 1972.[53] Davis's experiments also date from that year, although once again he credits Kath Walker with suggesting the move into drama:

> As early as 1972 I had been experimenting with theatre ... I had seen the script of a short play by Kath Walker and I was extremely interested in the prospects the medium presented. Theatre offers an opportunity to use all the talents of speech and body-movement present in Aboriginal oral literature and dance since time began. It was an exciting way to reach an audience.[54]

Davis wrote a script for a play which he titled "The Steel and the Stone", but which "turned out to be too long" and became a kind of seedbed for all his future dramatic works.[55] The first play to emerge from this draft was a play called *The Dreamers*, which was staged at the Bunbury Arts Festival in 1972.[56]

This early performance in Bunbury was the herald of Davis's great trilogy of plays—*Kullark* (1979), *The Dreamers* (1982) and *No Sugar* (1985).[57] These plays were framed by two jubilees, the Western Australian Sesquicentenary of 1979 and the Australian Bicentenary of 1988, and it is evident that the plays are, in a significant way, an answer to these celebrations of the success of Australian colonisation. The first of these plays, *Kullark (Home)*, appeared in the Sesquicentenary year alongside Hewett's *The Man from Mukinupin*—and the two plays share a similar subversive spirit. Both plays, Hewett's and Davis's, were produced by the National Theatre, though Davis's play was performed in an offshoot of the main theatre called Theatre-in-Education, which produced drama for school children and was run by Andrew Ross. Ross directed *Kullark* and staged it at the Titan

Theatre in Perth. The collaboration of Davis and Ross was a key ingredient in the success of *Kullark* and of the later plays.[58] The 1979 State Sesquicentenary was an event which, like an Olympic Games, called a particular form of historical consciousness into being, and it is notable that both *Kullark* and *The Man from Mukinupin* are plays which have the form of a historical pageant. Because such anniversary celebrations mark the passage of time and community since "the beginning", how this initiating event is characterised is important. In a settler colony like Australia, the event was either the beginning of "settlement", from the settler point of view, or the beginning of the "invasion", from the Indigenous point of view. Certainly, by 1979 it was no longer possible to ignore the glaring tension between the celebration of Western Australian achievement and the plight of Indigenous Western Australians—in fact, it was increasingly difficult to not see the obvious and unavoidable way in which those two things were connected. Hewett's *Mukinupin*, with its teasing, deft satire, drew attention to the process of repression that sits underneath a wheatbelt town. This repression of the facts of dispossession and discrimination in *Mukinupin* allude to a broader denial of this history in Australia. But Davis's *Kullark* does something wholly new in Western Australian creative literature, which was to represent the experience of colonisation from, in Henry Reynolds's phrase, "the other side of the frontier". Whereas in Hewett the Aboriginal characters perturb and destabilise the white town's sense of itself, in Davis we see the perspective reversed for the first time—how white people and, in particular, white history looks to the Indigenous.

Kullark has a primary setting inside the household of an Aboriginal family, the Yorlahs, somewhere in "Southwest Australia" in February 1979. The Yorlahs live in a town, which from certain references appears to be in the Avon Valley (Northam, perhaps, or Brookton) where Davis had spent his formative years. The Yorlahs live in a rented house not far from town and in this sense—that is, because they do not live on a reserve—are partially assimilated. Their son is training to be a teacher and the family typify the moves (and opportunities) that by the late 1970s were allowing Aboriginal people to occupy more educated positions in mainstream society. That, at least, is the starting position for the play, the place from which it commences a careful and devastating dissection of the historical forces and crimes that have brought the Yorlahs to where they are. It is not that the Yorlahs are mired in hopeless despair and social failure; they have their fair share of problems, though they are managing as best they can. The play does not present a world in crisis or mobilise itself as a Royal Commission into a disaster. In fact, it is the very normality of the Yorlahs, the everyday nature of their squabbles, that the play sets about unpicking. Its effect is to take everyday disadvantage and locate this inside a matrix of deep historical dislocation. In this, Davis's play does share something with other wheatbelt writing—even as far back as Cyril Goode's poems written in the Yilgarn in 1920s—which attempts by various means to fracture the image of a "settled" rural landscape. In his great history of pastoral writing in Britain, *The Country and the City* (1973), Raymond Williams spoke of how the pastoral mythology of the English countryside veiled the conditions of its creation, the generations of invisible agricultural labour, the profound inequality in the distribution of work and wealth across these estates.[59] Creative writing has the potential to both mystify and demystify a rural life imposed by a very recent colonisation.

The play opens with Alec Yorlah nursing a hangover and fending off the consequent criticism of his wife Rosie. A funeral has just taken place and he has been drinking with relations from Gnowangerup and elsewhere, and Rosie is worrying that this might jeopardise their lease. The man who has died is not named, but the Yorlahs had first met him at Moore River, when they were children. This is the first mention of Moore River Native Settlement and foreshadows its importance in this play and future plays. The old man who has died was Noongar and is a link to the pre-enclosure period, before the wheatbelt was created, when the southwest was sparsely occupied with pastoral leases. As Alec explains: "Well 'e used to tell us when we was kids back at Moore River 'ow 'e was brought up shepherdin' sheep before any fences was put up. An' that wasn't yesterday." (10) The scene ends with a recollection of the story of *Wahrdung* (crow) and *Koolbahrdi* (magpie) that is repeated at various points in Davis's work. The story, a version of a Noongar dreaming story, tells of how each of these birds— originally white—gained their distinctive plumage after fighting in black mud. Wahrdung was completely coated, but Koolbahrdi was only covered in patches, leading to its piebald appearance. In Davis's work this story alludes to the racial consequences of colonisation. The story is a kind of "fall" narrative in which pride is the catalyst, the main purpose of which is to manifest the consequence of action—to announce that reality has been caused. As the story ends, didgeridoo music "crashes in" to signal a jump from the Yorlahs and present-day reality to the beginnings of colonisation 150 years before. These events are narrated by the Noongar leader, Yagan, who lived on the Swan coastal plain at the time the colony was established. Played by a young Ernie Dingo, Yagan addresses the *Warrgul* (rainbow serpent) and relates the story of his people's decimation.

The action in Act One of *Kullark* adroitly shifts between the events in the Yorlah household in 1979 and the incremental deterioration of relations between settlers and Indigenous people in the Swan River Colony in the 1830s. These events in the very early life of the colony are situated sympathetically within the household of a modest settler-family who had maintained good relations with Yagan and his father Mitjitjiroo before the clumsy intervention of colonial law. The assassination of Yagan and Mitjitjiroo and the decimation of the Bibbulmun people at Pinjarra in the 1830s are the climactic events of Act One. These killings encapsulate the trauma of invasion and signal the defeat of Noongar independence in the nineteenth century. Act Two is organised around another traumatic event, the wholesale removal of people to Moore River in the 1930s. The latter event is the one which is most intimately associated with the wheatbelt. The action centres on the expulsion of the Northam Aboriginal people, a calculated piece of ethnic cleansing, and one of the most notorious events in the progressive incarceration of Aboriginal people in Native Settlements and missions during the first half of the twentieth century. The Depression had an immediate and devastating effect on rural Aboriginal people in the wheatbelt by drying up the seasonal work on which they had come to depend. The increased unemployment had the effect of concentrating more Aboriginal people in town reserves, and coincided with a new intolerance in wheatbelt towns, themselves now under financial duress. At the time the "susso" paid to the unemployed was worth around 70 cents and the Aboriginal ration around 22 cents.

On 16 January 1933 a group of roughly ninety Aboriginal people, consisting of at least eleven families, were forcibly rounded up at their camp near Northam and sent by train to Moore River Native Settlement. The town camp at Northam was, Haebich tells us, "typically situated one and a half miles from the town, in a river bed opposite the sanitary depot and the rubbish dump."[60] The ostensible reason for removing the Northam group was a concern for public health and the incidence of scabies was cited. This was a recurrent pretext in such matters. Scabies is not life-threatening and was readily treatable. Nevertheless, it became the grounds for the removal of the Northam Aboriginal people. When they were finally examined at Moore River, only four people were found to have the condition. The Northam group were made up of various families whose history of periodic callous eviction is a crucial element in the story of the wheatbelt. Many were, according to Haebich, originally from New Norcia, but were "pushed off" the mission at the turn of the century. They took up camp at Moora "until the early 1920s when, following a sustained and vicious campaign by the white town residents, they were forced out of the town and into surrounding districts." (304) From there, many moved to the Northam town camp. There was a strong suggestion that the removal order of 1933, which had a dubious legality even under the extensive powers of the Act, was motivated by the fear that premier Mitchell, the member for Northam, might lose his seat in the coming election if he did not act to appease aggrieved townsfolk. In the end, Mitchell did lose his seat in the general annihilation of the conservative parties in 1933.

In *Kullark*, the Northam expulsion of 1933 marks the point at which the social history of colonial dispossession intersects directly with the Yorlah family. Alec, who we meet in middle age in 1979, was part of this removal of the "Northam mob". His father Thomas Yorlah (played by the same actor) introduces himself directly to the audience, saying he lives in Northam now but was born on the reserve at Narrogin: "You know I been workin' 'ard on farms all me life. Sun up till sun down. I don't make much money, but me kids always get a full belly." (46) This modicum of self-sufficiency, itself a minor miracle of cultural survival, is then torn cruelly from the family by the peremptory action of the government. Even though Thomas

Yorlah is "quarter caste" and thus did not fall under the Act, and he was not living on the reserve, nor in the receipt of rations, he still got caught up in the dragnet. The second act of the play documents life at Moore River and Thomas Yorlah's determination to get his family out at all costs. He petitions Neville directly who drily responds that while Yorlah himself might not fall under the Act, his wife, a "half-caste", and their children did—in effect offering him the solution of abandoning them. The family absconds four times, and Yorlah is gaoled for six months each time in Fremantle as a consequence, before the Department eventually lets them go to save themselves the continual expense of chasing him down.

Davis's play violates a significant taboo by introducing both Neville and the superintendent of Moore River, Arthur Neal, as characters in the play. Their portraits are far from flattering and the effect of placing them into a fictional story, albeit one based on historical events, is to situate them in a public moral register—the register of narrative—in which their conduct can appear as not merely misguided but plainly, now that it is inside a play, villainous. These officials, Neville and Neal, were of course themselves simply instruments of public policy, put in place by politicians who were in turn elected by Western Australian voters. As with Hewett and her treatments of massacre, Davis undertakes a complex engagement with history. In some ways, what both were trying to do was to dehistoricise history, to rescue events from that exculpatory form of history in which responsibility for wrong actions tended to dissolve into a multitude of well-meaning mistakes.

The play continues the slow drawing together of the historical present with its antecedent causes by introducing a young Alec Yorlah in 1945, just returned from active service in New Guinea, and officially "classified white by the Commissioner of Native Welfare." (60) His father, Thomas, welcomes him home and welcomes, too, the prospect of finally being able to give up begging for work at a pittance at the gates of wheatbelt farms. Thomas had just finished a "clearin'" job: "There was eight hundred acres all together; us *Nyoongahs* did four hundred for a quid an acre, *Wetjalas* did the other four hundred. Found out later they got thirty bob an acre, and it was the same sort of country." (61) Alec, now equipped with citizenship rights, moves himself and his wife Rosie to a rented house outside town. The policeman tells him to make sure his relatives stay away, and to remember he is now forbidden on the reserve. The matter was close to Davis's heart, no doubt, since he took up citizenship in the 1950s. When the police leave, Alec tells his mother: "Well, did you hear him tellin' me to keep on the straight and narrow? Can't have 'lations visitin', can't live on the reserve. Citizenship don't sound much like freedom to me. I seen a lot of blokes die in the war for freedom. None of 'em would call this freedom, none of 'em." (63) But Alec is still happy, thinking that his children might actually get an education and a job "with a bit of dignity", adding: "They've been servants and farm hands for too long. Far too long." (64)

The method in *Kullark* of intersecting historical moments directly with the realist frame of the present day is one that Davis and the director, Andrew Ross, would continue to develop in their future collaborations. A key device in uniting past and present is the use of backdrops. In *Kullark*, the backdrop is formed by a panoramic mural of the rainbow serpent (*Warrgul*). Revolving doors in this screen allowed actors to enter, as it were, from differing time periods. Each door was painted, on the reverse side, with a picture to indicate the period of the character. So, for instance, when the future Governor Stirling and the botanist Charles Fraser are shown on their surveying expedition in 1827, they enter "*through a revolving screen, revealing a watercolour of the Swan River in 1827. This picture cuts the Rainbow Serpent near the tail.*" (13) It is a simple device—the play after all was designed to tour to schools—but this aspect of the stagecraft effected a profound reversal of the colonial narrative. The colonial history that was the occasion of the 1979 celebration, and was dominating the airwaves at the time *Kullark* was staged, now appeared as a small rectangular excision in a sprawling cosmology. In this sense, we have a more-than-apt metaphor for the rectangular excisions of the wheatbelt paddocks that now extend across the entirety of the Western Australian wheatbelt.

The Dreamers (1982)

It was the success of *Kullark* in 1979 that allowed Davis and Ross to rework the one-act version of *The Dreamers* that Davis had staged in Bunbury in 1972 into a two-act full-length play. *The Dreamers* debuted at the Dolphin Theatre at The University of Western Australia in February 1982, before touring nationally the following year. It may sound obvious, but the key to understanding *The Dreamers* is ascertaining who is dreaming. In its basic substance, the play—like *Kullark*—is realist, and like the earlier play is set in the present-day household of a Noongar family, this time the Walltitches'. Again, their exact location is not given—just "South-Western Australia"—but the youngest son, Shane, plays for South Midland and it seems that they live in the outskirts of Perth, in what is optimistically known as the Swan Valley. The dynamics, though, are distinctly those of a country town, with a local hospital, local policeman who knows them well, complete with a lock-up (also well known), and local shops, and a pub named The Exchange Hotel. Even if they live on the fringes of the metropolitan area, the wider circle is clearly that of the wheatbelt, particularly that axis of it that follows the Avon into the Great Southern, with relatives and events scattered through towns along it—periodic visits from the "Northam mob", fights at the "six acre reserve" at Williams, footy games at Wagin, trips to the Katanning Show, cousins in Gnowangerup and so on. Perth itself is hardly mentioned.

The action of the play takes place in two acts, the first in summer ("Beeruk" in the cycle of Noongar seasons) and the second in winter ("Moorga") later that same year. The main drama surrounds the slow death of Uncle Worru (played by Davis in both the 1972 and the 1982 versions).[61] In Act One, Worru is picked up from the hospital and brought home to the Wallitch house, where he immediately starts drinking again with the layabout men—Roy (the father), his cousin Eli, and the elder son, Peter—who live there. The house is managed by the family's matriarch, Dolly, who keeps the fragile finances together as well as looking after the indolent men and the two high-school age children, Shane and Meena. In Act Two, Worru is seen to have gotten steadily worse, and more prone to the hallucinations that were sporadically occurring in Act One. He is forced back to hospital against his wishes, and dies there. The play ends with a eulogy to Worru by Dolly.

Underneath this arc, the gradual death of Worru, the various activities of Wallitch life transpire. The daughter Meena is trying hard at school, and battles her family's chronic disorderliness as best as she can. She has also started seeing a boy and is staying out later. Shane is less academically minded, but not yet a victim to the shiftless ways of his elder brother Peter, his father Roy and Uncle Eli. It is this roguish constellation of Aboriginal men that carry the main action of the play. Their first move is to take the money that Dolly has given them for the children's lunch and buy a flagon of wine, and much of the rest of the play is them engaged in a cat-and-mouse game with Dolly in which she is trying to get them to help her run the house, and they are trying to scheme their way towards more alcohol. Though the situation seems dire, the overall mood is never especially bleak, and one instead finds, beneath the hopelessness, a certain knockabout resilience in the Wallitch family. The fact of imprisonment seems to be borne almost too lightly by the men, as if it were just in the nature of the world. They certainly hold the *Wetjala* responsible for their plight, but equally point the finger at themselves.

> PETER: Look, *Nyoongahs* buy their grog from *Wetjalas*, they break the law and they git judged by *Wetjalas*. The lawyer's white, the cops are white, the magistrate's white, the warden's white, the whole box and dice is white. Put a *Nyoongah* against all them. I tell you we ain't got a bloody chance.
>
> ...
>
> ELI: Look at this eye, broken nose, busted eardrum [pointing to his head] thirteen stitches. You know who done all that? Not *Wetjalas*, but *Nyoongahs*, me own fuckin' people! (83–4)

Their drunken debates around such matters provide, indeed, a refreshingly honest assessment of the social problems that mar their world. Despite the difficulties of their life, there is also a kind of spirit of adventure born out of the hand-to-mouth quality of their existence. Each day presents a new, even if familiar, challenge to their wits and resources, and the family seems to be sticking together rather than falling apart.

The basic social realism of the play, however, is crucially framed by the appearance at key points in the play of an entirely different time-scheme. So, before being cast into the bustle of the Wallitch family's chaotic breakfast, with the kids on the way to school, the audience is firstly treated to a vision of the past—a past which bears ambiguously on the present-day travails of the Wallitch family. The play begins as follows:

> Dawn. We hear the distant echoing voices of children singing a tribal song.
> A tribal family walks slowly across the escarpment silhouetted against the first light of dawn. The men lead, carrying weapons, the women and children follow with bags, kulumans and fire sticks. As they disappear the voices fade and a narrow beam of light reveals WORRU alone downstage. (73)

As these directions make clear, it is Worru who is going to function as the bridging character between this silhouetted past and the vivid social realism of the main action. The play thus delivers the central dialectic that we saw in Davis's (and Walker's) poems which opposes the nightmare of Aboriginal life "today" with the image of Aboriginal life before colonisation. It is, of course, an impossible comparison. No living person spans the two realities and even those who might—and Albert Namatjira was the archetype for this doubled figure in the post-war years—seem to also emblematise the impossibility of this reconciliation. The problem is exposed, in fact, by the act of writing and goes to the heart of what changes when a community constituted through oral knowledge enters a universe where lives are determined by documents. Davis was conscious of this antinomy; indeed, he was perhaps more sharply aware of it, through the unique circumstances of his life, than anyone had previously been. Born to illiterate Aboriginal parents, Davis was the first in his family to write and the last in his family to not write. But knowledge inside his nuclear family was not primarily oral. Both his parents had been removed from a very early age from their tribal families on Pilbara stations and had grown up in white homes. At Moore River, at the age of fourteen, Davis came face-to-face with the kind of tribal people that his parents had been taken from, dragged into Mogumber's net by some bureaucratic vicissitude. The memory of these aging tribal Aboriginal people is a crucial element in the poems and plays of Davis. Then, after Moore River,

at Brookton on the reserve, Davis was immersed in the adapted life
of Noongars, especially of his stepfather Bert Bennell, which existed
in the blended world of oral tradition and modern rural life. In his
early twenties he went to the Gascoyne, where he spent the next
decade, experiencing life both as a fringe-dweller in Carnarvon and
a stockman on the stations.

In all of these ways, Davis is a pivotal figure, exposed to
Aboriginality in many of its key variants: from the assimilated life
of his father's timber town at Yarloop, to the annihilationist brutality
of Moore River, to the reserves of Brookton and Carnarvon, to
the segregated world of the cattle station, and finally to the political
life of Aboriginal advocacy in metropolitan Perth. In the apparent
simplicity of Davis's poems and plays, we see, in fact, a concatenation
of each of these systems of Aboriginal being. This is not always
obvious in the gentle lyricism of the poems or the earthy realism of
the plays, but it is impossible to understand them without also being
exposed to the intersection of epochs which they dramatise. Uncle
Worru in *The Dreamers* is the embodiment of the irreconcilability of
Aboriginal history and it is significant that Davis cast himself in this
part. As the silhouetted Aboriginal family disappears from the ridge
in the opening image of the play the spotlight falls on Worru, who
delivers an opening soliloquy. It is in the form of an elegiac poem,
reminiscent of those in *The First-born* which dwell on the bitter irony
of Aboriginal survival:

> I walked down the track
> to where the camp place used to be
> and voices, laughing, singing
> came surging back to me.
> …
> Now we who were there
> who were young,
> are now old and live in suburbia,
> and my longing is an echo
> a re-occurring dream,
> coming back along the track
> from where the campfires used to gleam. (73)

The "re-occurring dream" in this poem initiates the inference that it is Worru, and others of his generation, who are the *dreamers*, condemned to dream of times that are now lost. There is thus a pathos attached to the concept of dreaming in the very first scene of the play. As the play unfolds, Worru is retrieved from his latest visit to the hospital, vowing never to return come what may, and brought into the house of his niece, Dolly Wallitch. There, he joins seamlessly into the drinking and banter of the men. In time-honoured fashion they gently rib their old uncle, calling him "Pop" or "Popye", but also retain a certain reverence for his knowledge about the old ways and days. The younger men wind him up, and he tells them stories while they drink and play cards. The stories are as important for the way he tells them, particularly the Noongar words and expressions that pepper his speech, as for the incidents they relate:

> WORRU: Well, they was gitten old fellas, them two, Cornell and Milbart, they was stayin' in Wagin an' they wanted to git to Katanning Show, see? And they was *wayarning* [scared] of the train, real *wayarning*. [Laughing.] Anyways, they got in a railway carriage and that train was goin' *keert kooliny, keert kooliny* [quickly] rounds them bends and them corners. An' – an' – they was... they was...(84–5)

As the play progress, Worru seems to fall increasingly back into Noongar speech, until several of his speeches in the second act are entirely in Noongar. At the same time, and concomitantly, Worru begins to address less the people in the room than the figures in his memory. One can certainly see a resemblance here to the dramatic structure in Hewett's *Man from Mukinupin*, where the traumatic history exists in uncanny fashion in the form of a doddering elderly figure speaking at telling cross-purposes to the main dialogue. Worru performs a function not unlike those of the "night people" in Hewett's play—the Sisters Hummer, Zeek Perkins, Touch of the Tar, Harry Tuesday—by importing a history that is conditioning the overt drama but excluded from the consciousness of those caught in it. The key difference, however, is that in Hewett's play the white wheatbelt town occupies the foreground and the traumatic remnants of contact are in the creekbed behind the town. But in Davis's play, the ramshackle Wallitch house is the locus of action.

What Davis brilliantly succeeds in dramatising is the fact that the Wallitch clan is actively repressing not just its history but the present reality of their lives. In this sense, Davis is a writer somewhat in the mould of Toni Morrison, whose novels depict black American families through America's traumatic history. White oppression exists in Morrison's novels as a background condition, rather than as the substance of the overt action. Her novels do not gloss over racial injustice, but they are not occupied with dramatising it directly. Instead, Morrison's novels focus on the more insidious effects of the history of black America, the way that its extreme conditions have produced a certain terrifying morality of the defeated. Davis does something similar. Certainly, we see a family who has virtually nothing to show for themselves, they live hand-to-mouth, dependent on "SS" (Social Security) payments, which they typically gamble or drink as soon as they collect them. The eldest Wallitch son, Peter, is clearly already going off the rails in the first act, and has to be bailed out of the local lock-up after being caught riding in a stolen car. In the second act, he is in gaol at Wooroloo, and Dolly has to visit him, though the audience never sees him after this. The fact that Peter is now in gaol does not preoccupy the family and the drama is not built around this young man's wasted life, or the system chewing up yet another young Noongar. The real tragedy, in fact, seems to be that no one treats the matter as a tragedy. It is here that the title of Davis's play begins to invert. It is not Worru who is beset by dreams of an earlier, better time, it is the modern-day Wallitches who are dreaming away the disaster of their daily lives. Indeed, Worru's visions speak more clearly to the current predicament than do the angry disputations and petty recriminations of the Wallitch family. Not that the play condemns the family utterly. There seems a genuine warmth and rough-hewn affection that makes up for their many failings. But, nevertheless, the presence of Worru frames their squabbles in a grander, more tragic confrontation.

The men in *The Dreamers* represent the struggle of modern Aboriginal life and the different strategies that have evolved to survive the challenges in it. Roy, the father and notional head of the family, is a pragmatist, wanting to do the right thing where possible, but not always succeeding and not often trying very hard. But he never abandons his family and though he wears his sense of duty lightly, he tends to shirk rather than fully abdicate. Of course, his indefatigable wife Dolly manages to keep things going even when he is skiving off. But as the play folds into the second act, Dolly loses the sheen of ideal matriarch, and more often than not is joining in the drinking too. The two children, while not "going bad", are also gradually being caught up in the tribulations of teenage years. Eli, Roy's cousin, has survived through a mixture of appeasement and con-artistry, begging money in the local town with the assistance of a fake eye-patch. Dolly's nephew Robert appears in the second act, with a car and education. He lives in the city and is resented by Eli, for the implied slight on his life.

Throughout all of this Worru wanders, neither neglected nor particularly noticed. His role in the play is to act as a living window into the history that runs through the Wallitch family in ways they are not able to comprehend. Worru's connection is a double one because he contains both the direct link to Moore River—where he was incarcerated—and to the place before the catastrophe "where the campfires used to gleam". When Worru returns from hospital and gets drunk with Roy, Eli and Peter, the scene ends with him attempting to dance before falling over and then being replaced by another dancer who is young, vital and connected to his culture:

WORRU rises and begins a drunken stumbling version of a half-remembered tribal dance. PETER turns the volume up and continues his own disco dance. WORRU pushes him aside and dances to the amusement of ELI and ROY, until his feet tangle and he falls heavily.

The scene freezes, the light changes, and the radio cuts abruptly to heavy rhythmic didgeridoo and clap sticks. An intricately painted DANCER appears on the escarpment against a dramatic red sky, dances down and across them, pounding his feet into the stage. Finally, he dances back up the ramp where he poses for a moment before the light snaps out on the last note of music. (86)

The same pattern occurs several scenes later when Worru, after reminiscing with Dolly about Moore River, lies down and drifts away, mumbling to himself, then calls out to his old friend Milbart, long dead:

> WORRU: Milbart, Milbart, Milbart! *Gitji wah*, Milbart. Make a
>   spear, I wanna catch a *kulkana*. Make spear, Milbart!
>   *Gitji wah!*
>
>   *Didgeridoo crashes in, the lights change. The* DANCER
>   *appears at front of stage in stylised rhythmic steps, searches*
>   *for a straight stick, finds it, straightens it, pares and tips*
>   *it before sprinting up the ramp onto the escarpment and*
>   *striking the* mirrolgah *stance against a dramatic sunset as*
>   *the music climaxes.* (99)

One can see how the dramaturgy of the play depends on the continued intrusion of this other scene, this determining prior moment. All the elements of stagecraft are used to bring about its existence, the challenge being to portray autonomous (pre-colonial) Aboriginal culture as a present absence, something which is there, but not there. This pre-existing culture is built into the play's setting via a backdrop that encircles the rear of the stage and also features an elevated walkway. This backdrop works as a stylised escarpment, approximating the image one gets of the Darling Ranges from Perth and the coastal plain. In this sense it is the sign, from the metropolis, of the interior—and, so, also the insignia of the world before colonisation. In the opening of the play, the Aboriginal tribal family marches quietly across this escarpment, silhouetted, like a shadow-play. At the end of the first act they march in the other direction, again silently, but this time in chains. The lighting changes and so does the music. The DANCER functions as an emissary for these people, entering the foreground of the stage to embody the culture that is chained in the background.

In fact, the play constructs a lineage that runs from the social reality of the Wallitch family in present day southwestern Australia, through the mediating figures of Worru and the DANCER, and finally to the lost tribes of the Noongar and the spiritual origins of the Dreaming. At the beginning of the second act, the family appear once again, this time in bedraggled clothes indicative of the years after colonisation, spent on the fringes of white settlement. The key element in the dramatisation is the layering effect that Davis achieves—the existence of multiple moments, traumatic and excluded from present reality, but also constituting it:

> *A cold wet winter afternoon. The kitchen/living room is shabby and untidy, dirty dishes piled up on the sink, rubbish, bottles, cigarette packets on floor. Clean clothes are draped over a chair in front of a single bar radiator.* WORRU's *bed has been turned around, his room is squalid.*
>
> *An eerie traditional chant as the family of Scenes One and Nine of Act One trudge across the escarpment against a bleak, wintry sky. The women lead carrying an assortment of boxes and bundles. They are inadequately dressed in blankets and shabby period clothes.*
>
> *As the sound fades and they disappear, a light builds on* WORRU *lying on his bed moaning and mumbling a mournful litany, half English, half* Nyoongah. *He coughs painfully, raises himself and staggers feebly into the kitchen.* (110)

As the figures on the escarpment gradually come to meet one another—each in their "shabbiness"—the effect is to invest the Wallitches tumble-down lives with historical dignity. At the same time, Worru's gaze deepens, now looking past the colonised family in their "shabby period clothes" towards the very thing that had vitalised them in their first serene, proud march across the scarp. In the second act, Worru begins to see and sing about the Featherfoots (*Tjena guppi*), mythical creatures that prey on the unsuspecting. He sings a song in Noongar:

Allewah! Tjenna guppi nyinanliny,	[Watch out, featherfoot there
A nyinanliny, a nyingnanliny,	There, there, there
nyinanliny.	
Mundika nyinanliny,	There in the bushes
Mundika nyinanliny,	There in the bushes
Ngunyinniny kaka woorniny,	I'm laughing

A koka woorniny	Laughing
Thenna guppi nyinanliny,	Featherfoot there
Tjenna guppi,	Featherfoot
Tjenna guppi,	Featherfoot
Tjenna guppi,	Featherfoot
Woolah!	Hooray!]

Shafts of cold light fade in revealing the DANCER as featherfoot at the front stage. He is heavily decorated with leaves and carries two short sticks. He dances slowly across the stage and up on to the escarpment and off as the music and lights fade. (130)

One should not underestimate the achievement of Davis in introducing Noongar language into European theatre. As Davis pointed out, the language was gravely imperilled by the second half of the twentieth century, and it remains so. By the late twentieth-century few, if any, spoke the language as a primary medium of expression, although the language persisted in hybrid with English as a variegated Noongar pidgin used by Noongar families throughout the southwest. The featherfoot song sung by Worru contains only nine Noongar words, but in its particular cadence, repetition, and sense of humour bespeaks a whole set of relations. It is like a tiny cell of living culture. Its presence in a contemporary Australian play is more or less a miracle.

Unlike *The First-born*, with its reliance on an anthropological apparatus, *The Dreamers* brokers Noongar culture and language without hesitation or apology. What becomes apparent as the play reaches its climax—the death of Worru—is that this language emerges as the true hero of the play. Noongar language, initially experienced as ethnic colouring, insists itself ever more strenuously into the action. Its residue in the speech of the Wallitch family turns it into a kind of long-lost relation—joining them as they argue, reminisce, debate, joke, tease and insult each other. In Worru it gradually overtakes him as he dies. In other words, he literally dies into language. This reverses, once again, the concept of dreaming. It was initially thought that Worru was the one dreaming—of olden times, difficult times, more painful but more real. Then it seemed that it was the present generation of Wallitches who were dreaming their reality away, sleepwalking through the wasteland of their cultural holocaust. But the play ultimately posits something much more hopeful, which is that Noongar culture continues to dream its subjects even though they have forgotten it. Worru thus becomes not the last of his tribe, but a sacrificial carrier of culture's continuance. As Worru lay dying in the hospital, Shane, still in the Wallitch house, sees "something" in Worru's room. His father Roy tells him to go back to bed:

SHANE: I'm not goin' till I find out how Popye is.

                ROY *walks slowly out to* WORRU's *room.*

ELI: Aw, stop worryin', boy, you couldn't kill that old fella with the back of a sleeper axe.

                ROY *stands still in* WORRU's *room, then walks back with slow measured steps, all eyes are on him.*

         What's the matter?

                ROY *looks at him, doesn't reply but sits and stares blankly ahead.* (137)

We never know what Roy sees, the audience is not privy to the sight, nor is it reported. The implication, though, is that in this one moment at least, the Wallitches have woken up. The scene concludes with the DANCER, not dancing this time but singing "sorrowfully", cross-legged on the escarpment:

Nija Wejula, warrah, warrah!	[The White man is evil, evil!
Gnullarah dumbart noychwa.	My people are dead.
Noychowa, noychwa, noychwa.	Dead, dead, dead.
Wejala kie-e-ny gnullarah dumbart.	The white man kill my people.
Kie-e-ny, kie-e-ny, kie-e-ny,	Kill, kill, kill,
Kie-e-ny.	Kill.] (137)

This simple threnody is then taken up by Dolly, who delivers the play's closing soliloquy, a eulogy to her dead uncle.

Stark and white the hospital ward
In the morning sunlight gleaming,

But you are back in the *moodgah* now
Back on the path of your Dreaming.

I looked at him, then back through the years,
Then knew what I had to remember:
A young man, straight as wattle spears
And a kangaroo hunt in September. (138)

In moving from poetry to drama, Davis found a form that was able to capture the complexity of the Aboriginal situation in the southwest, the almost impossible dilemmas faced by the Noongar. The dramatic form allowed something more than the then-and-now of the poetry. In *The Dreamers* what is brought out so electrically is the actual problem, which is that, in so many ways, "then" is now.

No Sugar (1985)

Davis's most ambitious play, and the culmination of his partnership with Andrew Ross, was *No Sugar*, a four-act play commissioned in 1984 and first staged in 1985. It is a play well known in Western Australia, where it was extensively taught in high schools throughout the 1990s. It is based around an event that we saw represented in the second act of *Kullark*, the removal of the Northam Aboriginal people in 1933. The play opens at the Government Well Aboriginal Reserve outside Northam in 1929 and we see the life of the reserve depicted through two intermarried families, the Mundays and the Millimurras. The hero of the play is Jimmy Munday, who is the brother of Milly Millimurra. Milly is married to Sam Millimurra and they have three children—Joe, in his late teens, and the slightly younger pair of David and Cissie. The group is rounded out by Gran Munday, the mother of Jimmy and Milly. This play is the most purely realist of Davis's works and there are no intersecting historical phases appearing to disrupt the central action. But by starting the play in 1929, Davis is not only able to note the beginnings of the Great Depression but also to subtly introduce a longer view of history by adverting to the celebrations of Western Australia's Centenary. The eldest son, Joe, reads haltingly from a newspaper account of a parade "commemorating the pioneers" that featured a float of Aboriginal men dancing on the back of a truck as "a reminder of the dangers they [the pioneers] faced". Jimmy Munday, hearing this, is disgusted: "You fellas, you know why them *wetjalas* marchin' down the street, eh? I'll tell youse why. 'Cause them bastards took our country and them blackfellas dancin' for 'em. *Bastards!*" (16) In this way the historical pageant of the Centenary is framed by a rather different consciousness than the one being paraded. As we have noted, the target is not just the 1929 Centenary but the recently celebrated 1979 Sesquicentenary and the approaching 1988 Australian Bicentenary:

> JOE: "The pag...page...page-ant pre-sented a picture of Western Australia's pre-sent condition of hopeful optimum-optimis-tic prosperity, and gave some idea of what men mean when they talk about the soul of the nation."
> SAM: "Sounds like bullshit to me ..." (17)

The onset of the Depression is marked by reductions in the rations given to Aboriginal people. At the police station, Milly and Gran are told that they are no longer issuing soap. Later, they are told that meat and dripping have been cut from the ration, too. But the poverty is also an occasion for fraternity as the Noongar camp take in an unemployed farmer, Frank Brown, and give him food and company. Brown, an ex-serviceman, had been a farmer at Lake Yealering, a part of the wheatbelt already familiar to us from the work of Hewett and Facey. But like Facey and Goode, Brown was forced off his land when the Depression hit: "... between the rabbits and a couple of bad seasons and the bank, the bloody bank, I lost it; the lot, even the crop in the ground." (29) Brown's presence at the camp is noted by Sergeant Carrol of the Northam Police Station who suspects (correctly) that Brown has been supplying the group with alcohol:

> SERGEANT: [*intimately*] Listen, mate, don't try being smart. This time I sent Munday back to his camp with a warning; next time I'll nail him and the bloke that buys wine for him. The last bloke I nabbed for supplying is doing three months hard labour in Fremantle.
> FRANK: Thanks for the tip.
> SERGEANT: Why don't you think about movin' on?

FRANK: Where to? I been on the road already for six months. Kondinin, Merredin, Kalgoorlie: no work. Headed up the Murchison, Mullewa, Northampton: nothing. I got a wife and two kids staying with her parents in Leederville. I can't even raise a train fare to Perth to go and see them. (18)

In the first two acts of the play, the action moves between three distinct but interrelated settings: the family's camp at the Government Well Reserve, the Northam Police Station run by Sergeant Carrol, and the Native Welfare Department in Perth where we see the Commissioner, A.O. Neville, at work. One of the elegant dimensions to this play is the way that these three "scenes" are shown to be connected. This is the key element in the drama, in fact, and at the very heart of what the play is able to graphically show. Namely, that the lives of the Mundays and the Millimurras—and beyond them, of all Aboriginal people living in Western Australia—were being determined by an alliance between a government bureaucracy and the police. In one brilliant early scene, we see A.O. Neville simultaneously dictating a letter to his Minister protesting recent budget cuts to his department, while talking by telephone—on a very bad line—to Sergeant Carrol at Northam Police Station, who is himself being besieged by the Millimurras and Mundays because it is ration day. The scene swirls between these moments, showing the two overworked men both struggling to communicate in challenging circumstances.

The purpose of the phone call between Neville and Carrol is to discuss the opposition of Northam residents to a new site for the reserve. In essence, they opposed any site at all, and in the end they get their wish when the Aboriginal population of Northam is expelled. But what Davis captures, in this comic collision of demands and imperatives, is the interplay of forces and voices. In point of fact, neither Neville nor Sergeant Carrol actually want the group removed. The Sergeant sees the white complainants as half the problem, while for Neville the intransigence of the Northam residents will ultimately mean a significant influx to the already overcrowded Moore River Native Settlement. In the letter to the Minister, Neville notes, amongst other things, that of eighty girls sent for domestic service from Moore River Native Settlement in the past year, thirty returned pregnant.

What Davis's play exposes are the patterns of hypocrisy. Aboriginal policy was driven, as we have seen, by the wish to address the "half-caste problem", but the policymakers seem to see no contradiction in sending young girls out to isolated farms where they were highly vulnerable to sexual exploitation. In these ways, Davis integrates the history of Noongar people into the play. In the banter between Gran Munday and Sergeant Carrol, the policeman suggests that if she doesn't like the flour then she could go back to grinding wattle and jam seeds in the old Noongar way. She shoots back: "Where? *Wetjala* cut all the trees down." (22) The play is also consistent with the fact noted by Anna Haebich that many of the Northam mob had originally lived at the Catholic mission at New Norcia Abbey. Jimmy Munday had been a "choir boy" at New Norcia and Sam and Milly had been married there. The play agrees, too, with Haebich's assessment that the removal of the Northam mob was driven by premier Mitchell's fear that he faced defeat in his own long-held Northam seat if he did not appease the residents on this matter.

The first act of the play concludes with the arrest and transportation of the Northam mob to Moore River. The remainder of the play takes place mainly at Moore River, where the Northam group is initially held separately in quarantine to assess the level of scabies. Again, the play is broadly consistent with Haebich's account in that of the eighty-nine removed from Northam, only four were found to have the skin condition. The superintendent, Arthur Neal, is nonplussed by the fact that he has to now care for another eighty-nine residents at the underfunded and overcrowded settlement.[62] The climax of the play has Jimmy Munday and the others subverting the ceremonial visit of A.O. Neville to Moore River on Australia Day 1934. Jimmy confronts Neville and Neal, jeering them about the defeat of Mitchell in his seat of Northam:

> JIMMY: Did you vote for Jimmy Mitchell's lot?
>
> ...
>
> Yeah, you must done, eh?
>
> ...
>
> Nothin' to do with the bloody scabies. And that's why we got dragged 'ere; so them *wetjalas* vote for him.

...

So he could have a nice, white little town, a nice, white little fuckin' town. (99)

These turn out to be Jimmy's dying words as he collapses with a heart-attack. But Jimmy's dying words do find Neal and Neville and derail their carefully choreographed event. This is the essence of the play's motivation. It is not a play that seeks to stage a history that is better than the one that took place, but rather it is a play that wants the full truth of this history to be registered in the face of those who would wish to whitewash it.

It is impossible to underestimate the influence of Davis's depiction of Moore River, A.O. Neville and Arthur Neal. The film *Rabbit-Proof Fence*, through which a great number of people in Australia and internationally come into contact with the story of the Stolen Generations, takes its picture of Moore River and A.O. Neville almost directly from Davis's *No Sugar*. Neville's dialogue often consists of direct quotations from published writing by Neville in a technique that is sometimes called "verbatim theatre".[63] In the play, and since, Neville has become the face of Aboriginal Protection, and his character is used to dramatise the essential contradictions of the Protection policy. Of course, the key ambiguity is in the word "protection".[64] Notionally, the Aborigines Act of 1905 was to protect Aborigines. Protect them from what? The somewhat embarrassing answer, although little embarrassment is betrayed, is: *from the colonial society that was issuing the order of protection*. Certainly the Act did contain legislative protection from the worst excesses of colonial violence. But finally, as the sergeant himself grasped, the major beneficiaries of the "Protection" offered in the Act were the mainly white citizens of Western Australia, particularly those living in rural areas. In the emerging towns of the wheatbelt, the provisions of the Act were used to institute a form of apartheid in which Aboriginal people were kept out of the towns through curfews and other forms of soft or hard police power. We have already seen how the wheatbelt was the product not just of thousands of enterprising settler-farmers, but of a very significant governmental program which marshalled the resources of the state to fund land surveys, roads, railways, water provision, mass lending, fertilisers, scientific advice and research, and dozens of one-teacher schools. The work of Davis shows that there was another bureaucratic regime that was also intimately connected to the wheatbelt and that was the system of Native Protection. This regime dealt with the Noongar and other Indigenous peoples that lived in the lands being taken up by the wheatbelt, but also funnelled Aboriginal people from far-flung pastoral districts through Moore River and into the wheatbelt as labourers and domestic servants.

No Sugar is remarkable for the dramatic concision with which it captures this complex situation. It is also a delicately poised picture. Davis does not pull any punches when it comes to the venal hypocrisy that was at work in the treatment of Aboriginal people. This is not simply something that Davis had read about in a book or heard stories about from older relatives, this was the substance of his early life, and the play relates the texture of reserve and settlement life with a richness that comes from lived experience. But the white protagonists are not the cardboard villains that they could so easily be in a play like this. Neville, for all his faults, was concerned for Aboriginal welfare—and so was the police sergeant at Northam and Matron Neal (the director of the hospital at Moore River and wife of Superintendent Arthur Neal). It is perhaps only Neal himself who is presented with no redeeming qualities. Again, Davis dealt directly with Neal in his short stay at Moore River, so his portrait was, so to speak, drawn from life. What Davis is able to do, better than anyone before or since, is to capture in a single story the complexity of Aboriginal policy as it affected the lives of thousands of people during the twentieth century. No account of the wheatbelt can be complete without understanding this dimension of its history.

Chapter Eight

Barbara York Main (1929–)

Bungulla / Tammin / Northam (1929–47)

With Jack Davis we had, rather belatedly, the literary reappraisal of wheatbelt history from the perspective of Aboriginal people. The issue was presaged in the late 1950s by Dorothy Hewett's work, but it was not until the 1970s that Davis won the cultural space to express this as lived Indigenous experience. If we turn to the issue of environmental destruction we have seen that this fact was registered by James Pollard in the 1920s, in some of the earliest creative writing to emerge from the wheatbelt. The proto-environmentalism in Pollard, and also Ewers, noted with regret the loss of species, the disappearance of trees and bush, and—in Ewers at least—the appearance of salt in the country of the wheatbelt. In the later work of Cowan and Hewett, a much more modern sense of the environment begins to appear in which the environment is fragile and woundable, capable of being destroyed not just here and there, but *in toto*. This change corresponds more broadly with the birth of modern environmental consciousness. One can see this beginning fairly clearly in the 1930s and '40s, where there was, for instance, a strong reaction to the massive soil erosion that had occurred through North America and Australia.[1] This caused a new awareness of the function of topsoil—as nature's generative substance—and that it could be "lost" and was not inexhaustible. In

Australia, Elyne Mitchell's books *Speak to the Earth* (1945) and *Soil and Civilization* (1946) captured this new sensibility.[2] In Western Australia, the Parliament passed the *Soil Conservation Act 1945* which set up the Soil Conservation Service to address topsoil erosion by water and wind. The word "environment" was also beginning to replace "nature" as a way of describing the natural world in its entirety as can be seen, for instance, in the CSIRO's handbook *The Australian Environment* (1949).[3] The effect of this new word was to emphasise the interdependence of organisms upon one another.

A decisive moment in environmental consciousness was the publication in 1962 of Rachel Carson's *Silent Spring*, which documented the insidious effect of chemical pesticides—DDT in particular—on the natural world.[4] The title of Carson's book referred to the discovery that organochloride pesticides like DDT, when ingested by birds, fatally weakened their eggshells, leading to a decimation of bird species in North America. This demonstration of the invisible effects of human action was a sudden and shocking revelation because it pointed to the way that humans were interfering not just with the overt elements of nature—flora and fauna—but with its secret interior mechanisms.[5] Nature became alarmingly vulnerable in a way never before imagined. In Australia, this new mood was seen in Vincent Serventy's best-selling book *A Continent in Danger* (1966) which documented the plight of Australian mammals.[6] He reminds his readers that in 1927 there were some 10,000 licensed koala trappers in Australia and in that year alone over 600,000 koala skins were sold. (53) Today, in 1966, he announced, 40 per cent of native mammals were at risk. It was time to act: "Tomorrow will be too late". (13) The matter of environmental destruction was given apocalyptic urgency by the dawning of the nuclear age. Accounts of the effects of the attacks on Hiroshima and Nagasaki, notably John Hersey's chilling accounts for the *New Yorker* in 1946, left no doubt that an unprecedented form of destruction had been unleashed. The invisible and often delayed effects of radiation and radioactive fallout—new words in the modern consciousness—prepared the public for the case Carson was to make against DDT. But it was the advent of thermonuclear hydrogen bombs in the 1950s with their massively increased destructive power that suddenly made human-authored planetary annihilation—absolutely unthinkable hitherto—an actual possibility and, as the Cold War deepened, a terrifyingly realistic scenario. It is not without significance that Carson's *Silent Spring* was published in the same year as the 1962 Cuban Missile Crisis. This was also the year in which James Watson and Francis Crick received the Nobel Prize for their discovery of the molecular structure of DNA.

This pivot in the late 1950s and early 1960s transformed what had been a general concern and regret that specific animals and plants were being lost, into a fear that "the environment" itself was being destroyed. As we have already noted, it was the work of Judith Wright more than anyone else that brought about this paradigm shift in Australian letters. She took the proto-environmentalism of the Jindyworobak writers and infused it with an ecological specificity. One sees this emerge ever more sharply as her poetry moves from the metaphysical accents of *The Moving Image* (1946) into the fully-fledged eco-poetry of "At Cooloolah" (1954) and *Birds* (1962).[7] A similar sea-change can be traced in the movement from Xavier Herbert's *Capricornia* (1938) to his *Poor Fellow, My Country* (1975).[8] In the wheatbelt the birth of environmental consciousness is best seen in the work of Barbara York Main, a zoologist by training, but a writer of rare power and subtlety. Two works by York Main, in particular, *Between Wodjil and Tor* (1967) and *Twice Trodden Ground* (1971), made the full ecological consequences of the creation of the wheatbelt hauntingly clear.[9] That these consequences now seem all too familiar can easily rob York Main's works of their radical import, but they remain classic studies of the environmental price of the wheatbelt's success. As the daughter and sister of farmers who had cleared the decimated land she now studies, York Main is conscious that the people who have done this were ordinary human beings who responded to the conditions they found themselves in and were motivated by the normal aspirations of people everywhere to provide a living for themselves and their families. And yet, even so, the land which had withstood the severity of nature's elements for millennia, and even hosted quite equably human society for more than 40,000 years, was eradicated in two generations during less than sixty years of the twentieth century. This is the central moral fact of the wheatbelt and it impinges on every writer we have encountered. It is the magnitude of this calamity that is brought to light in York Main's account.

Barbara York Main was born in Kellerberrin in 1929. Her father, Gerald Henry "Harry" York (1891–1973), emigrated from Yorkshire in 1909; his brother Herbert York, two years his senior, had come out two years earlier. They selected land at Bungulla in the east–west corridor that connected Perth to the Goldfields. The farm was roughly halfway between Tammin and Kellerberrin on the Great Eastern Highway and some 15 kilometres north, near Yorkrakine Rock. It was good land in many ways, well situated both in rainfall terms and in proximity to major transit arteries. It was not far, in fact, from John Ewers's school in South Tammin and one might recall Ewers's assessment that the land north of the highway was the better land; it was settled earlier and sustained wealthier farmers than the poorer country south of the highway where he was located. In the years leading up to the Great War, the two brothers worked with professional clearers to clear the block and get the crop in. In 1915, Harry York enlisted and served in France where he was wounded. Herbert stayed home to look after the farm. After a period of convalescence in England, Harry returned and selected another block of land through the soldiers' settlement scheme. It was immediately adjacent to the existing block and Harry set about clearing this next tract of virgin bushland.

York Main's mother Gladys York (née Tobias) was born in Coolgardie in 1895 where her parents had run a goods store selling supplies—everything "from frying pans to flour"—to prospectors in the Goldfields.[10] After selling up and moving to Perth in 1903, Gladys's parents returned to the country to take up land near Yorkrakine just prior to the War. According to Gladys, they had taken up the land to give work to her intellectually impaired brother. She recalled, in later life, the circumstances:

> There was a lot of unemployment and Jimmy Mitchell was Minister for Lands (I don't think he was Premier at that time). Well he decided to open up a new area and place people on it and they had 300 applications and they were balloted. A lot of the men were unemployed, quite a few lumpers and different walks of life. A man named Gray he had taken up land due north of Tammin but was west of Yorkrakine and

45. Harry (Gerald Henry) York, 1912, and doing clearing work in Wodjil scrub. State Library of Western Australia, 021813PD.

contracted to bring a lot of new settlers out on to their blocks. The families came out together and there was hessian humpies put up for them [and] they had a dam centrally. That would have been 1908 I think. These fifty people were settled on the blocks.[11]

In fact, the Tobias family and the York brothers both took up land as part of the same 1908 Yorkrakine land release. Gladys remained at Claremont Teachers College and after finishing her qualification was posted to the two-teacher school at Yorkrakine in 1917 so that she could live with her parents. The school catered to about twenty-five children when Gladys arrived, but this swelled to forty-eight children as word spread that a "fully trained" teacher had been appointed. Gladys travelled 9 kilometres to school and back each day from the family farm.

Harry York married his neighbour Gladys Tobias in 1921. They had five children in all, four sons and Barbara, all born at the hospital in Kellerberrin. Barbara, in 1929, was the fourth child. Because of the abundance of older brothers, she was not required to help very much on the farm, except to look after the chickens and help her mother around the house. For long periods, in fact, she was left to her own devices and she would spend these moments either reading or wandering around in one of three patches of bushland which her father had kept on the property to supply timber for fencing, firewood and other needs. This included a 20-acre patch of bushland around the farmhouse which had been the site of the original camp during the farm's infancy. Here York Main developed an early fascination with the plants and creatures of the native bushland, particularly the insects, which she would collect and keep in old shoeboxes. She first noticed trapdoor spiders in this bush at the age of seven or eight, not realising then that these creatures would become the centre of her eminent career, but she formed an early desire to be an entomologist and to work in a natural history museum. Since the farm was beyond the easy reach of a school, York Main studied, like her close contemporary Dorothy Hewett, through correspondence classes. Her teacher recognised in Barbara an able and avid student and encouraged her to pursue her interest in natural history by sending her books from the school's lending library. As well, from her days as a teacher, her mother Gladys had accumulated a number of books that her daughter read hungrily. York Main was particularly drawn to those books about nature and animals, such as Gladys Froggatt's *The World of Little Lives* (1916).[12] Froggatt's "little lives" were a series of insect studies originally published in the children's pages of the *Stock and Station Journal* (NSW). What stays with York Main from this book are the illustrations which were able to unite in a single picture on, say, the life cycle of a mosquito, each stage of its life and its habitat. These pictures, in their diagrammatic unity, held the ecological sense of the organism they depicted.

York Main also remembers enjoying the works of May Gibbs, who grew up on the edge of the wheatbelt in Harvey, west of the Darling Scarp, about 100 kilometres south of Perth. Gibbs's *Gumnut Babies* (1916) initiated a series that would capture the imagination of Australian children for much of the remaining century.[13] For the child-naturalist York Main, Gibbs's work appealed as providing, despite its anthropomorphism, accurate and detailed pictures of

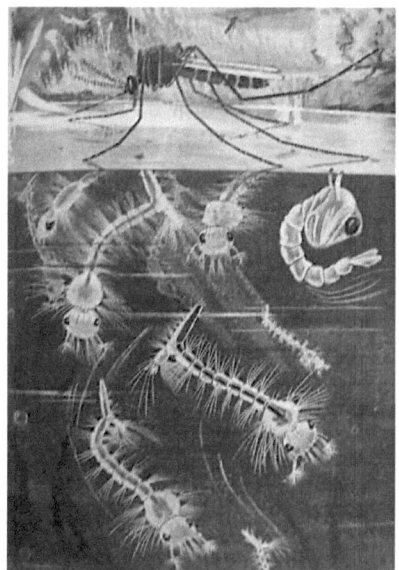

46. Gladys Froggatt's *The World of Little Lives* (1916); Frontispiece and the lifecycle of the mosquito.

native flora. They answered not just her need for stories steeped in wonder, but her deep desire to find names for the intimate wilderness in which she spent her time. For this reason, perhaps, York Main also found particular delight in another of her mother's books, Alice Clucas's *Behind the Hills* (1926).[14] This children's book was published in Perth and set in the town of "Wylakatchem", a thinly disguised version of Wyalkatchem, the town and district immediately to the north of Tammin. *Behind the Hills* tells the story of a girl, Carol, who lives an isolated existence on a farm with a busy mother who only seems to notice her when she needs something done. Carol is running yet another errand for her mother when she befriends a magpie, Mrs Maggie, who offers her some magic seeds. These cause Carol to shrink down to the size of a fairy, allowing her to climb atop Mrs Maggie and fly with her to the "Golden Land" beyond the hills. In this Golden Land, Carol meets King and Queen Leschenaultia (who recline in gum-leaf hammocks in Bushingham Palace) and begins a series of adventures. The Golden Land is attacked by the evil Calosang Tribe but it eventually prevails thanks to the help of the Tuarts. "The Tuarts", the book explains, "were a very progressive race, and had recently perfected a powerful machine-gun, known as the Tuart Cannon" (54). The story concludes with Carol waking up. Was it all a dream? No, says Carol, even though she knows this is just what her mother will say: "Mother does not believe in fairies, for she has never been to the Golden Land Behind the Hills in the Land of Imagination; but I do, and I hope to go there again some day" (66).

We have already been introduced to the enchanted world of children's writing, both for children and by children, in our consideration of James Pollard and Dorothy Hewett. In broader cultural terms we can find in these stories by Gibbs and Clucas that late-Victorian sense of childhood so enduringly evoked in the writing of J.M. Barrie, Lewis Carroll and, particularly, Rudyard Kipling. Kipling is significant not just because of his popularity in Australia, but because in works such as *The Jungle Book* (1894) and the *Just So Stories for Little Children* (1902), he linked indigenous knowledge,

47. Illustration from Alice Clucas's *Behind the Hills* (1926).

naturalism, and the occasioning wonder of childhood into a kind of corrective universe, one that registered a muted apology for the violence of empire, if not for its goals.[15] A close friend of Baden Powell, Kipling wrote children's stories that became, through the Scout and Guide movements that flourished in the twentieth century, a pseudo-religion of initiatory myths and practices, advancing the virtues of imperial citizenship and self-growth. Victorian children's writers such as Kipling often made a child the perceptive centre of their stories in order to anchor the stories in a domain outside of the fixed adult order. One senses in these "stories for children" an effort to remake the stark symbolic terrain of modernity by calling upon the fairies and pixies of a disappearing oral folk tradition. Thus animated, the stories became a forum for playing out the world's adult struggles in disguised form.

The distinctive dimension of Australian children's authors such as Gibbs and Clucas was the way that this fairy-world was mapped onto Australian animals and plants, sometimes invoking a vulgar appeal to Aboriginal creation myths. This was particularly visible in the period of popular nativism in the decades following Federation. "Wattle Day", first celebrated in 1910, was popular throughout the 1920s and '30s, and Australian motifs drawn from nature—lyrebirds, kookaburras, emus—began to adorn the mass-produced furnishings and window fittings of this period. It was during this time, for instance, that kookaburras were introduced into Western Australia by Eastern states migrants who felt the bush here was lacking their distinct aural contribution. Barbara York Main's childhood bears the imprint of this phase in Australian nationalism, and this is evident in another children's book published in Perth, *Granny Smith's Book: Verse and Legends of the Bush* (1941), which Barbara received as a gift for her twelfth birthday.[16] *Granny Smith's Book* was a series of poems, fables and sheet music thematising native flora and fauna. In "The Wildflower Chorus" and "The Dance of the Gum-Nuts", plants and animals take the form of fairies, elves and sprites, while in "The Carnival of Spring" we hear the story of the kangaroo-paw, the Western Australian state flower that blossoms in late winter and early spring:

> The little Elves then raised their heads, and seeing the smiles around
> them, were very relieved; but when they saw the Kangaroo-Paw

Flowers, they were astounded to see such a wonderful sight, they could hardly believe their eyes; so they caught hold of one another and danced and sang through the Bush in great glee.

Another Spring had come and the Fairy was pleased with their work. (35)

Granny Smith's Book emits in a juvenile register the nativism we have already seen in the Jindyworobak movement that influenced both Ewers and Hewett. But York Main was to turn away from these more fanciful treatments of native wildlife towards a more direct apprehension of this world through the discipline of science.

In 1942, at the age of thirteen, York Main was sent to Northam High School. She had won a scholarship to the high school from the Distance Education School. She boarded, with a number of other girls, in the house of a woman, Mrs Porter, living in the town. York Main remained at Northam High School for five years. During this time she was tutored in natural history by Vincent Serventy (1916–2007), who taught maths and physics at Northam but ran an after-school nature club for students that would go on field trips to local bushland. Vincent Serventy was the younger brother of Dominic Serventy, the noted ornithologist who was in correspondence with James Pollard during the 1920s and '30s. Vincent Serventy would become a nationally famous popular naturalist during the 1950s and '60s, with a series of best-selling nature books and pioneering television programs. As we have already noted, Serventy's book *A Continent in Danger* (1966) brought the modern sensibility of environmental threat to a wide audience in Australia. Serventy was also the host of *Nature Walkabout*, which aired in 1967, and was Australia's first environmental television program. Another amateur naturalist that York Main became close with during her high school years was Chris Jessup, a locomotive driver on wheatbelt trains who was based in Northam. Jessup's father had been a sandalwood cutter so Jessup knew the wheatbelt bushland from the years before the mass clearing. Jessup, like Pollard and Ewers, was part of the informal army of amateur naturalists that served museums and universities by collecting and sending specimens for identification. Jessup was in close contact with Ludwig Glauert (1879–1963), the director of the Western Australian Museum. It was

Jessup who urged York Main to matriculate from high school so that she might study science at university. It is also worth mentioning that York Main viewed education as "the way to escape the life of farming", one which she had found, as a girl and a woman, held no real place for her, certainly not in the way that it did for her brothers. Many years later she reflected that "the last thing I wanted to do was to become embroiled in the life of a farming community."[17]

As well as wanting to be an entomologist working in a museum, York Main also wanted to be a writer. Having gained entry to The University of Western Australia in 1947, she thought carefully about whether to pursue a degree in arts or science. Eventually, she enrolled in the science degree with a major in zoology. She reasoned that while she might, after all, be able to teach herself to write, zoology required a formal training. In any event, she wished to be a writer of general natural history and so science was essential. At UWA she resided in the University Women's College (later renamed St Catherine's College). She was introduced to entomological fieldwork by Dr Ernest Hodgkin, and also gained experience during vacation work with the entomological branch of the agriculture department. But she did not wish to follow the path into the growing field of "economic entomology", which was the study of pests and how to control them. Her interest lay firmly in the taxonomic study of insects, spiders and crustaceans and, as it would turn out, her local environment was teeming with an almost unrivalled degree of speciation in this order of creatures, many of which remained completely unclassified. Indeed, this became the work of her lifetime. Her honours project was a study of freshwater crustacea in the ephemeral ponds of the wheatbelt, whose eggs would persist in a dry state through the long summer months to hatch again when the winter rains fell and the ponds replenished. After honours, York Main worked for two years at the University of Otago as a junior lecturer before returning to UWA in 1952 to commence a doctorate. She completed her PhD in 1956 on the eco-evolution of trapdoor spiders in southwestern Australia, and was one of the first generation of doctoral degrees to be awarded at UWA, and only the second woman to receive the degree from this institution. During the course of her PhD she married Albert Russell "Bert" Main (1919–2009), also a zoologist, who was appointed to the zoology department of UWA and became an internationally recognised expert on frogs. Marrying Bert was to cost York Main any chance of a formal appointment at UWA, but she was appointed an honorary researcher in zoology in 1958, which gave her access to lab facilities and the opportunity to apply for grants. Winning grants allowed her to finance her research and even be paid an occasional salary in the ensuing years.

Between Wodjil and Tor (1967)

By the early 1960s, York Main's life was divided between her young children and her scientific research. Her growing reputation as a naturalist led to the publication of *The Spiders of Australia* (1964), illustrated by the author.[18] Her publisher, Jacaranda Press, was founded by Brian Clouston in 1952 to publish educational literature. Clouston was something of a visionary, and is notable for publishing Kath Walker's seminal volume of poems *We Are Going* (1964) on the recommendation of Judith Wright, who was then employed as a reader for the house. In 1965, Bert and Barbara took their family to Brisbane for sabbatical in order to do fieldwork on the frogs and spiders of Queensland. York Main took the opportunity to meet with Clouston and to propose another book—one of a quite different character to her field-guide on spiders. York Main said that she had been working on a children's book based on the animals in the wheatbelt bush she knew so well. Clouston's response surprised her. He said, why not write the book for adults? The work then conceived was to be a detailed account of life in the bush through the course of one year.

So it was that in 1967 York Main, at the age of thirty-eight, published *Between Wodjil and Tor*, a natural history of an area of remnant and partially regrown wheatbelt bushland bordering her family's farm. The book is illustrated by the author with simple pen and ink drawings, a habit of the field-naturalist. The bush being described is to most eyes an unremarkable stretch of open woodland and wodjil, a barely perceptible valley that abuts and extends westward from Yorkrakine Rock, a large granite outcrop, or "tor" to use York Main's word. Yet in the central wheatbelt of York Main's family, where less than 5 per cent of the original bush remains, this patch of scrub encompassing the granite outcrop of Yorkrakine rock, a neighbouring rise of wodjil woodland, and the "swales between" of salmon and gimlet gums and jam trees is sufficiently intact for York Main to undertake a natural history. Wodjil is the local name for the scrub that predominates on the deep sandy soils and is also known as "light land" or "sandplain":

> It is here in a small area of the plateau, somewhere around the "middle" of the Wheatbelt...in this patch of wodjil, the granite tor some miles away, the timbered clay flats between, and their surrounding countryside, that we shall observe the unfolding of a year's life of an animated landscape...(4)

Between Wodjil and Tor is written in the form of a calendar, beginning in the hot, late summer, where the countryside is bunkered down against the scorching easterly winds that prevail in this season and where not a drop of rain has fallen for several months. The chapters then take the reader forward through the cooling trend of autumn as the days draw in but remain dry and clear and into, at last, the rainy months of May through to August when the precious store of annual water is deposited and husbanded by the plants and animals adapted to this pattern. Then the days start to lengthen and the weather warms and the cycle begins again.

The idea of constructing a natural history around a yearly cycle is a venerable one. York Main had in mind both Thoreau, particularly his *Walden* (1854) and *The Maine Woods* (1864), and Gilbert White's *The Natural History of Selborne* (1789).[19] White's *Selborne* comprised a series of letters, delightfully observant and rich, written to his friends Daines Barrington and Charles Pennant concerning the natural history of his native parish of Selborne in Hampshire where he had long served as parson. A "Naturalist's Calendar" compiled from these letters appeared in editions following White's death in 1793. The letters span a period of two decades and bristle with reflections on the local species and habitats. In Australia, a nature calendar of this kind was published by the amateur ornithologist Jack Hyett (1915–2001) in 1959 under the title *A Bushman's Year*.[20] It is this kind of ecological calendar that York Main began to write for the country between wodjil and tor, melding an "ideal year" out of the many years she

South-east slopes + shelves of granite 'tor'.

48. The tor, the wodjil and the timbered "Swales Between", *Between Wodjil and Tor.*

had spent in this place as a child and as a scientist.[21] By tying her observations to that of the life-forms of the wheatbelt, York Main produces, in effect, a radical rewriting of the seasons. Indeed, though she would not have known it, the seasonal activity she describes fits almost exactly the six Noongar seasons of Birak (Dec–Jan), Bunuru (Feb–Mar), Djeran (Apr–May), Makuru (Jun–Jul), Djilba (Aug–Sep) and Kambarang (Oct–Nov). Like the Noongar calendar, York Main's calendar begins in the height of summer. This season corresponds with the dead of winter in Northern Europe. Animals and plants have retreated into a survival mode to make their way through the long dry summer. Aestivation—the hot-climate equivalent of hibernation—is employed by certain animals. When the temperatures begin to reach the summertime maximum of around 40 degrees Celsius, aestivating trapdoor spiders lie in a deep torpor in underground burrows safe from the searing heat.

As well as the yearly cycle, which works subtly against the assumptions of a culture founded on the rural habits of Northern Europe, *Between Wodjil and Tor* mobilises the deep time of geology to situate the profound quality of what is actually present in these seemingly drab remnants of scrub. The southwest of Australia has few parallels—perhaps only southwest Africa is comparable—in terms of its longevity as an integral eco-sphere. It is, for example, forty times older than the landscape of eastern Australia.[22] The effect of this longevity, and several related factors, has meant that speciation in southwest Australia is amongst the highest in the world.[23] This is now well recognised, but York Main was amongst the first to make this absolutely remarkable situation known to a reading public:

> The whole great wide rolling landscape has, since the close of the Pre-Cambrian, retained its compositional integrity and its topography is the outcome, not of accumulated, invasive, marine material—but of continual wear—or reworking, alteration and surface shift of its own inherent substance. There is no landscape more ancient than this anywhere and, because of its age, it has been able, for aeons, to receive and support a fauna and vegetation, limited in variety and density only by the rigorous requirements set by the relatively barren nature of its soils and hazardous, climatic conditions. The climate, since the Miocene, has become progressively more inhospitable with brief, wetter periods. At the same time this apparently progressive, deleterious environment has been the impetus for the adaptive radiation or expansive evolution of numerous smaller animals and countless plants. (42)

The book's structure is tied temporally to the yearly cycle embedded in deep geological time, but also topographically to the three zones of the rock, the wodjil and the valley woodlands. A third movement in the story is up and down the orders of life—from microbial plants and animals through to the shrubs, trees, insects, reptiles, birds and mammals. Each of these organisms takes on a new complexion depending on the yearly cycle, and often their patterns are closely related to each other. This movement through the activities of the life-forms in a given moment of the cycle means the narrative dwells noticeably in the present tense. Here is a description of a lizard—the mountain devil—using its skin to drink the rain falling onto it during a summer thunderstorm:

> Exposed to the shower, into which they had emerged from their retreat in the sand and rocks, were some mountain devils. As the rain fell, the skin of each lizard, like blotting paper, soaked up the drops. This absorbed moisture passed by capillarity through special channels in the outer, keratinized layer of the skin towards the mouth. The animal opened and closed its mouth continuously thereby allowing the moisture to pass over its lips, where its passage into the mouth was facilitated by mucus secretions. Thus, although the water 'catchment' is the outer layer of the lizard's skin, it is not absorbed directly through the skin into the internal organs via this route but imbibed through the normal route—the mouth. (44–55)

49. "Mountain Devil", *Between Wodjil and Tor.*

For us, what is significant is the observation of a world completely outside the transformed landscape of farming colonisation. We saw this briefly in Cowan's writing and, in a slightly more domesticated form, in the writing of Ewers and Pollard. Yet, York Main's ecological vision makes available, for the first time, the dynamic and interrelated character of the wheatbelt's natural world.

Between Wodjil and Tor overwhelms with the intricacy and sheer marvel of the adaptations made by life-forms to the rigours of the environment. In another case, we learn of a particular weather phenomenon that only occurs occasionally in very late spring or early summer, where moist tropical air can wander down trough lines across the central wheatbelt and Goldfields bringing sultry overcast conditions and occasional heavy localised showers. This rare combination—for the wheatbelt—of air that is both warm and humid, allows animals to move quickly but without the risk of desiccation:

> Often and often the southern ridge bordering the valley will witness, away to the north, the gradual build-up of dark clouds which may cause the fall of a few points of rain along the extent of the tor and its high surrounds, or at least a rise in the local humidity at ground level. Such change in the air is sufficient to cause a close muggy atmosphere over the summer dry landscape. Under such conditions the underground galleries of termites "erupt"—those of some forms above the litter and parched soil into conical "flight towers". On one such summer evening at dusk, from the openings in the soil, alate termites (*Coptotermes*) took off into the air; off to form the great nuptial clouds. After mating in the air each pair, on falling to the ground and detaching its wings, would form the nucleus of a new colony. (130–1)

The nuptial theme is continued with a description of the frenzied courtship of a species of trapdoor spiders which can only mate when this humid early summer weather prevails, even though it does not occur every year.

> With the falling dusk, rising humidity and finally a rain shower, combined with the high temperature of 88°F or more, recently moulted male spiders (Dekana) of the family Dipluridae emerged and vacated

for all time the burrows in which they had lived out their four or more years of development. Like dry, wind–blown leaves they rushed across the ground, some eventually during the evening to find the burrows of females, which they would enter and where mating would take place. Only the combination of high temperature and humidity can ensure the wandering of males and mating of these spiders. But due to the longevity of females it is not essential for reproduction to occur every season. (131)

In this way, York Main's *Between Wodjil and Tor* is not just an elegantly written natural history of a piece of remnant bush; it is also a powerful counterpoint to the world of wheat and mixed farms. Ewers saw the wheat as being in harmony with the natural pattern of seasonal life. There is indeed a general accordance in the growing seasons of both the introduced crops and the native vegetation. But the complex interrelationships that define the natural bushlands mean that they are functionally quite distinct and of a different order to the monocultural regimes of sown paddocks.

In writing *Between Wodjil and Tor*, York Main avoided the didactic exposition followed by popular naturalists since the nineteenth

50. Crop, with bush in the background, *Between Wodjil and Tor*.

century, which had also entered the television era in Australia via the programs of her former mentor Vincent Serventy. Such popular educational documentaries tends invariably to address us as if we were overeager students, keen to follow the camera into nature's hidden corners. York Main's approach in *Between Wodjil and Tor* is quite different. Hers is a mode of lyrical evocation, dense with metaphor and musicality, which also takes seriously the fundamental alterity of the non-human organic systems. From the point of view of the wheatbelt's literary history what we get here is something like the parallel world that Davis introduced with Aboriginal experience. A world which is both before and beyond farms and farming. In York Main's writing, the bush is not something existing at the edges of farms, but an alternative universe, one which was capable of initiating a profound transformation:

> To climb through a wire fence, out of a ploughed and sown paddock, into a wild, wind-raked stretch of bushland is to tumble into an order of life, unmoulded by man, but one which can jolt his mind into a deeper wonderment, not only of this ungarnered territory but of the whole natural world. (Preface)

She compares the remaining bushland vestiges to museums, calling them "islands of yesterday". In this way they take on a quality of deep pathos, infused with the loss of their former continuity as a mosaic of connected natural systems.

Between Wodjil and Tor is a narrative perched between two determining regimes—the ancient and the modern. We see all the ways in which the life in this stretch of bushland is conditioned by intricate, primordial patterns. But we also experience how the ecosystem's existence has been made precarious in a way that it has not been for 250 million years—since it formed part of the Permian ice cap of the Gondwanan supercontinent. Animals and plants which had survived the vicissitudes of continental drift and climate change that took them over the millennia from Antarctic winters to the wet tropics and into the current dry, temperate oscillations—these highly evolved organisms were no match for the instruments of European farming. One of the ways in which York Main responds to this catastrophe is to speak on behalf of unity and interrelationship. This is a particular change in scientific paradigm that marks the formal evolution of ecology in the mid-twentieth century. So even though we encounter many diverse forms of life in *Between Wodjil and Tor*, the account avoids merely listing elements as is, to some extent, intrinsic to the process of scientific classification. Nor does she take the alternative route offered by the kind of popular nature study that we saw exemplified in James Pollard's "Denizens of the Bush" column for the *West Australian* in the 1920s and '30s. There is certainly a similarity to the latter style, and York Main's own induction into nature study through Chris Jessup and Vincent Serventy in Northam belonged to this tradition. But what York Main created in *Between Wodjil and Tor* was an expository form of writing that functions as a living tissue in which animal and plant life can transpire, not simply as the quaint animal figures of a children's story, but with the full dignity of an existence won in the radical contingency of evolutionary life.

Thus, what distinguishes the natural history that York Main writes is the way that it tries to connect things back together, to link them. This entails an impulse that moves dialectically against the classificatory method of the life sciences. Scientific classification has the side effect of alienating life-forms, and rendering what had been a complex of interlinked patterns as a hierarchy of classes. For this reason, York Main emphasises at various points the crucial function of soil algae in wheatbelt ecology. Soil algae lives in the top-soil and binds it. If undisturbed by hooved animals, this crust is quite capable of retaining nutrients in an integral upper layer that can withstand both dry wind and sheeting floods without erosion. In this way, the humble algae, an organism one might imagine as anathema to the dry, dusty woodlands of the wheatbelt, acts as a glue that holds life together, and is the foundation for the "higher" plant and animal species. A similar function is observed in other life-forms whose role is hardly given a moment's thought. There are the leaf-litter mats that mulch and feed tiny organisms, providing fodder and habitat. The termites and ants work industriously to break down organic material—work which in wetter climates would be done by fungal activity. The tunnels and galleries of termites and ants also aerate the soil and make it amenable to plant growth. Flies and spiders and moths all operate in this integrated network of interdependent life.

As well as these specific examples of interconnection, York Main's account connects the diverse life-forms by their differing responses to climatic conditions through the annual cycle of seasons. Their shared dependence on the yearly changes in atmospheric conditions offers a material unity to the story York Main tells. This points towards a distinctly modern sense of the term "environment" to mean not just the "Mother Nature" that Pollard invoked, but a sober sense of shared predicament. York Main also gives to the material unity of climate a rhetorical life. This emerges in her poetic evocation of the winds that prevail in the wheatbelt. By and large, the southwest of Australia is a land of wind. There are still days—particularly in the transitional seasons—but more often than not a wind will be running over the landscape, either the hot, dry easterly winds of the summer pattern, or the cool southwesterly winds and occasional violent storm fronts of the winter configuration. What York Main's account makes us realise is how this means that the landscape is almost never silent, but undergoing a constant rustling and sighing as the wind shakes the vegetation—rustling the dry leaves of the mallee gums, and the stripping bark on the boughs, or shifting the dry leaf litter. In the casuarina woodlands there is a constant sigh of the wind running through the needles. This provides an aural background which is punctuated by the sounds of bird, insect and reptile life.

The wind is the sound-image that opens the account of this bushland in the first chapter, where it appears in the form of the powerful easterly that typifies summer nights in the wheatbelt. As the desert from where it comes cools, this wind becomes a gentle balm and relief to the scorching heat of day:

> Out of the east it came; into the silent stillness of the night there came a cool rustling waver of air. At first softly, with a stirring and shaking of leaves, then with a roar and a rush, the wind came tumbling and rolling over the whole, wide, night-shrouded landscape. It rolled westward in gusts and rushes, finally to form a steady front of rushing air which at last swept strongly across the indented edge of wilderness, across farmlands and broken, ragged stretches of timber. (1)

One can see how the passage of this wind is indifferent to the land it sweeps across, touching everything—bush and farmland alike—and, under the cover of darkness, gathering the entire landscape into its embrace. The image is languid, even erotic, as the wind's "cool caress" (1) moves over the plants and elicits from them sounds which are distinctive of their modes of growth:

> Softly, it brushed the flat hanging leaves of eucalypts until they quivered and tapped lightly against one another. Gently, ruffs of bark were loosened to chafe upper lengths of trunks, dry twigs grated against turgid branchlets until as the wind strengthened, crisp fragments of bark were freed and twigs snapped, all falling to rustle amongst the hummocks of dry litter heaped at the butts of trees. A pale wash of moonlight lit bark hummocks and intervening bare areas of hard pebbled ground, and slid silver lines around the curves of smooth upper boughs of mallees. The wind moved through the thickets of mallee, whirred in the sheokes, bottle brushes, tea trees and hissed in the long dry grass heads from the spiny cushions of spinifex.

York Main uses the wind—apostrophises it as an active agency—to represent a land in dynamic connection with itself. The ululating language, composed of assonant and alliterative phrases and figures—"slid silver lines", "summer-fulsome scents"—make the wind a musical vector for the contiguity of the natural world which by day was marked by violent estrangements wrought by just two generations of intensive agriculture. The wind is both an agent of grace—a holy spirit—and an erotic tide that brings everything it touches into a kind of orgiastic crescendo:

> Locked boughs groaned together, ribbons of bark unravelled and were plaited and unplaited by the fingering wind. On and on the wind rushed; on through the timber and bush, on and over the wide rolling landscape; over dry salt lakes, through wooded flats, over sandy rises and gravelly hillocks; sometimes it lifted over granite domes which rose above the general level of the countryside. Up and over these rocks the wind would whine, to break into shrill cries in clefts and gouges and between huge lumpy boulders. (3)

What distinguishes York Main's work from conventional popular natural history is a recurrent gesture towards that which is beyond the elucidation of scientific discourse. This is done by diverting from the process examined and towards the feeling that it instils, from effect into affect. Here I do not mean the melodrama that pervades most nature shows and in which we function as pantomime audience, but a deepening of the perceptive faculty that transports the reader into the scene:

> All was still and quiet…twigs crackled, bark flaked softly, a dry leaf fell with a sigh from a mallee…the last of the wattle pods cracked open and the seeds fell to the woven mat of brown and yellow phyllodes on the ground. The acrid smell of the cypress pines (*Callitris morrisoni*) rose and permeated the surrounding bush and mingled with the tannic scent of drying bark and the volatiles of eucalypts. The only persistent sound was the deep, muffled murmuring of bronze-wing pigeons. (16, original ellipses)

What occurs in this passage and many like it from *Between Wodjil and Tor* is the reuniting of the senses. Scientific description is biased heavily towards the visual, not just in literalising the practice of observation, but in the more general way that knowledge itself is deeply wedded in Western culture to the faculty of seeing. To suddenly smell the "acrid" cypress pines and the bouquet of scents released by the eucalypts has the effect of reanimating them from their stultification in the classificatory regime. Likewise, to hear the "murmuring" of the pigeons brings them into an immediate relation that no degree of analysis can yield. In doing this, York Main tactically forgoes the semantic precision of scientific language in order to set in motion associational trains—the pigeons murmuring into the dry still evening—that make us *there* in the landscape as sensate, memoried organisms rather than disembodied analytical eyes. Yet York Main's writing does not forsake the scientific paradigm so much as hybridise it with the sensual or creative mode that we associate with literature. In so doing, she avoids the obverse of pure instrumental knowledge, which is aestheticism—a romantic record of sensory affects (aromas, sounds, plays of light) which trigger moods and memories. Instead,

51. A stormy sky over patchwork fields, *Between Wodjil and Tor.*

Between Wodjil and Tor retains as one of its central objectives the understanding of—to put it bluntly—*how it all works.*

Having a great sense of how the landscape worked made York Main acutely aware of just how much had been lost and how difficult it would be to repair it, even if the will to do so could be mustered. Of the fires that are an essential part of the reproduction of plants and the regeneration of bush, she notes that now that the landscape is fragmented it is not able to recolonise itself from unburnt portions. And, equally, the fires could now be occurring too frequently to allow the next generation of plants to reach a seed-bearing age before it too is burnt, causing an "irreversible decline" (49). The watercourses that once formed an integral part of the wheatbelt bushland are now degraded into little more than drainage channels, prone to gullying:

> Little more than a generation ago this creek passed the whole of its route though virgin bushland and its flood course was impeded by trees and litter and its wide flow, rather than scouring the ground, had an aggrading effect, depositing silt and debris as it flowed past slowly. But now for the most part its flood spills out over bare paddocks or stock-grazed timber country, where it gathers surface soil into its stream, thereby eroding and guttering. (66)

Nor is there to be any comfort in the thought that it might just "grow back" if we let it, a point she makes clear in the discussion of a patch of land once farmed, then abandoned. It had the appearance of the original bush at first glance, but key elements were missing, most particularly the soil structure, which through the mechanical effects of hooved stock had been loosened and lost the protective mulch of the litter mats and the binding of the soil algaes (which also fix nitrogen to the soil) and surface lichen: "And because of the unbound, unstable soil surface there were none of the terrestrial creatures which are part of a mature bushland—there were no trapdoor spiders." (109) The breakdown of soil structure meant regeneration was a much more difficult task than simply allowing grazed or cropped land to "go back to bush":

> The reclamation of cleared, ploughed ground is far, far slower than regeneration following the natural catastrophe of fire. Colonization of cleared ground is by a process of immigration. There are no remnant stocks of mallee, melaleucas, Petrophilia in the ground ready to sprout new growth. There are no tubers of orchids to send up seasonal blooms. There are no fibrous butts of Ecdeiocolea tussocks or tubers of yams or bases of flax lilies to shoot new rush-like leaves. There are no seeds or spores sheltering in the soil. Nor is the open, broken, tilled ground receptive to bush seeds in the way that an ash bed following fire is.[24] (110)

And in the lower ground a separate problem emerges with the incursion of ground salt into the surface layers. Ground which once boasted eucalypt woodland and acacia-sheoke thickets was now home to the salt-tolerant samphire ground cover found in the salt lakes of the wheatbelt and Goldfields.

York Main's writing—in its metaphorical density, its complicated forms of narration, and lyrical sense of language—is indisputably literary and is amongst the finest environmental writing to have been written in Australia. *Between Wodjil and Tor* was the realisation of her ambition to write detailed natural history for a wide audience. It is a form of writing which is remarkable for finding a certain very distinct poetry in the precise verbs (*aestivate, metamorphose, exfoliate*), adjectives (*keratinized, pupal, uterine, alate*) and nouns (*capillarity, spiderling, rejectamenta*) of scientific description. York Main is also significant for being the only writer in this study who both grew up in the wheatbelt—she went to Perth only at the age of eighteen—and then continued to spend a significant portion of her life there as an adult. Not to live, that is true, but to visit family and study it intensively as a scientist. The importance of this is that York Main has a distinctive double vision—one of childhood immersion and another of adult detachment. The achievement of York Main is that she does not abandon the wonder that animated the child's experience, even though maintaining a connection to these memories became exceedingly painful as the natural world started to disappear before her eyes. It is the fact that York Main's eyes are kept open during this process which yields, almost in real time, the crucial tipping point of wheatbelt consciousness, which is the transformation of a landscape framed by bush into one in which there are suddenly only islands of remnant bushland, fragmented and highly prone to decline as a consequence. Even Cowan and Hewett seem not quite capable of capturing the enormity of the loss. For Hewett, the fact that the bush is gone seems to be just an extension of the fact that her childhood is gone. Cowan was a committed and early environmentalist, he certainly understood destruction, and he was a keen birdwatcher and photographer, but he was not a trained ecologist and could not know the networks of relationships that underpinned an ecosystem. So, with York Main, we get this icy paradox: we finally see the wheatbelt bushland in its true complexity and we suddenly see that it is gone.

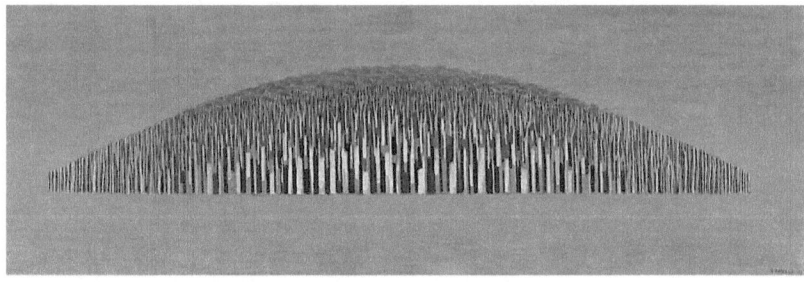

52. Howard Taylor, *Tree Island*, 1991, oil on canvas, 66.7 × 198.5 cm. The Kerry Stokes Collection, Perth.

In this regard, York Main is the wheatbelt's Rachel Carson and the image she provides of the collapse of ecosystems is every bit as affecting as the "silent spring" that Carson evoked with devastating effect five years earlier. One can understand the simple, though profound, effect of clearing and ploughing bushland. But York Main showed the insidious devastation that could result from sheep grazing in bushland—upon the soil structure and everything that depended on it. What York Main reveals is the destruction that has occurred even in those precious few places where it seems the bush has been preserved:

> Down along the flats were stands of timber—of gimlets and salmon gums and morrel—which had been exposed to grazing for over forty years. The trees still stood as magnificent trees, with burnished bark and crowns glistening in the early summer light, but there was no understorey, no strata of acacias and sheokes or bottle brushes and no clumps of sweet herb-scented underbrush. The ground brushed clean and barren by the wind. Orchids and ephemerals no longer sprouted from the earth in their season. The crisp fronds of ferns no longer unfolded above the cold damp earth in winter; their resistant rhizomes had been exposed and broken long ago. (137)

The bark humps and litter mats that dot the floor of the ecosystem in its integrated state are gone and with them everything that lived in them: "the litter humps that had been habitat to a whole assemblage of Cryptozoic creatures—crickets, centipedes, beetles, silver fish, cockroaches, trapdoor spiders—and had provided food for others— termites, which indeed helped to return it slowly to the soil." (137) In winter, the litter mats prevented erosion by water, they "channelled the falling rain into the soil through the colander of its structure." Then, in summer, "the litter matrix insulated the soil." (137) And yet, despite being witness to a devastation that she was singularly equipped to perceive, York Main writes *Between Wodjil and Tor* with an almost complete absence of bitterness. There is certainly a sorrow in the writing, although for the most part the tone is one of subdued wonder. It is not, moreover, written by someone who is outside the wheatbelt's dream—she is, as we have said, a child of this dream. Indeed, she has a farmer's eye for weather and her acute consciousness of the importance of seasons and of soil owes as much to a childhood spent on a farm as it did to her university training in the natural sciences. It is this placement both inside and outside the wheatbelt's economic and ideological motives that makes York Main such a significant figure in the literary history of this region.

Twice Trodden Ground (1971)

Four years after *Between Wodjil and Tor*, York Main published *Twice Trodden Ground*, also with Jacaranda and also illustrated by the author. It consists of seventeen short, semi-fictional stories which depict encounters with the countryside of the wheatbelt. The title refers to the fact that the land of the wheatbelt had first been "trodden" by the bare feet of Indigenous Australians and, much more recently, had felt the far heavier tread of European boots. For York Main, these first people have departed at some point prior to her arrival and are never to return.[25] Aboriginal people only exist as a trace: "They left only signs and artefacts on camping grounds and around waterholes— apart from that the countryside was left in its natural state." (1) This view of a "nomadic" Indigenous population that evaporated as the Europeans arrived is one that rather bypasses their concerted and violent displacement, but it was one which it was still possible for a sensitive intelligence to hold in 1971. It would become harder as the decade progressed, as we have seen. The work of Jack Davis and other first-wave Aboriginal authors, as well as activist-writers like Hewett, pushed Aboriginal experience into the public sphere. Moreover, Sylvia Hallam's study of Aboriginal fire-stick farming in the southwest, *Fire and Hearth*, published in 1975, made the dramatic claim, since accepted as correct, that the Aboriginal people were significantly responsible for the character of the "natural" bush they were supposed to be a part of.[26]

Yet, despite the fact that York Main relies rhetorically on the myth of the evaporating indigene, *Twice Trodden Ground* is not a triumphalist account of progress. In this her book represents a significant shift away from the shire histories of the wheatbelt that had started to appear in the decade or so prior to *Twice Trodden Ground*. Indeed, York Main's book is partly written as an answer to these histories, which were commissioned by wheatbelt shires to provide a "story" which would encapsulate the arduous work and radical changes of the last half a century. The first of these shire histories was in fact J.K. Ewers's *Bruce Rock: The Story of a District* (1959), quickly followed by Frank H. Goldsmith's *The History of Morawa District: The Story of Progress* (1961) and F.A. Law's *The History of the Merredin District of Western Australia* (1961).[27] Further accounts were produced over the next few decades, until almost every shire in the wheatbelt had its own history. York Main sets her own reflections apart from these shire histories, acknowledging that they are directed to a different register of effects:

> The following essays do not amount to a shire history. They hint rather at the effect of place on human emotions as much as the effect of man on place. Or is it only my own response to locality that I present? I do not think so. The potency of place—of landscape—is sometimes of lifelong recurrence, even though the response to its influence may be unformed, unvoiced. (2)

Despite this typically modest characterisation, it quickly becomes clear that York Main's work is not just a slightly more personal version of the story given in the shire histories, but a radical counter-history of the wheatbelt, one which opens it up to a searching and far-reaching critique. Where the theme of the shire histories is achievement, what has been gained, the motif of *Twice Trodden Ground* is decimation, what has been lost. Indeed, in relation to the vanished Aboriginal people, the secret intuition of York Main's book is this: *and we are going too.*

Twice Trodden Ground is, in fact, built upon this basic tension, one that we already saw in *Between Wodjil and Tor*, between a recognition of catastrophic loss and a deep hunger for continuity. York Main concludes her preface by asking: "But what … [happens] when one returns to find on the original substrate only fragile remnants of the former landscape!" In this she anticipates the moment in Dorothy Hewett's *Wild Card* where the author returns to find the home of her childhood, Lambton Downs, completely destroyed. York Main shares with Hewett the fact of having grown up on a wheatbelt farm. For both, the wheatbelt is coterminous with their infancy and bears all the ambivalences that flow from this. York Main's "revisits" to the wheatbelt, now as an adult (mother, zoologist), become both the analogy and the experiential means of seeing the wheatbelt as doubled—or split—by the effects of its agricultural colonisation. The word York Main uses to describe this uncanny doubling is "superimposed":

> I spent my early childhood in an environment which to a large extent still showed the imprint only of the first human tread. It was a landscape primarily of virgin bush. On my subsequent revisits the countryside has exhibited the full impact of the second tread—all the modifications wrought by settlement superimposed on the slight signs of the earlier tread of nomadism.
>
> Throughout the following sketches this double image is implicit: the broader one of a landscape touched by two cultures and the personal one of this same landscape, first embracing my early life, and later re-entered by my adult self. (1)

The wish that the stories evince is that this gap might somehow be closed, that the childhood world be recovered, that the bush that has now vanished be restored. Or at the least, that these losses find some adequate form of symbolisation: "In countering despair I have searched for a *continuity* in such change, thereby attempting a reconciliation." (2, original italics)

The concern for what has been lost—most particularly the bush itself—along with the desire for continuity, reveal a significantly different inflection to York Main's conjuring of Aboriginal absence than was first apparent. In the shire histories, the Aboriginal people are the past, and the settlers are the future. In *Twice Trodden Ground* the Aboriginal people are still the past, but, in fact, so too are the Europeans. This is a position that gradually emerges in the stories of *Twice Trodden Ground*.[28] These are split into three sections, "Disillusionment", "Retrospection" and "Reconciliation". The divisions are reminiscent of the tripartite structure favoured by Peter Cowan in his short-story collections *Drift* (1944) and *The Unploughed Land* (1958). Certainly, too, there is something of Cowan's quietism in the spare quality of York Main's prose and the steady, almost topographical way the landscape is described. But the writing is punctuated by moments of childlike enthusiasm and occasional passionate exclamations—things almost wholly absent from Cowan's writing. The opening essay, "Farmhouse", relates an episode in which York Main has brought her young children for the first time to the house that she had grown up in. "Farmhouse" is just two pages long, a vignette that depicts a dialogue between the young children and their mother. It is a stormy autumn night, and the children are frightened by the sound the wind is making:

> From their beds the children cried out, "What is it? What is that noise?"
> "It is the wind. It is the wind outside in the trees, in the paddocks, in the sky."
> "No. It is here. In the house. In the walls."
> "That is the house answering. It is the wind and the house."
> "But do all houses talk?"
> "No. Only old ones. Old ones grown up from the ground."[29] (5-6)

Like Hewett, York Main is *returning* to the wheatbelt and experiencing this as loss. Hewett's 'Legend of the Green Country', which had been published in *Westerly* in 1966, introduced the tragic dimension to the wheatbelt's image, and the disconcerting idea that it was the very strength of its founders' hopes that had bequeathed a heritage of disappointment. But York Main's sense of alienation is much sharper, more personal and, one might also say, at least at first glance, less political. It takes place in the domestic wildness of a mother's dialogue with her anxious children. The children's anxiety transports their mother back to her own childhood tribulation, so that the scene of this earlier childhood is *superimposed* on the present one. The dialogue is taking place simultaneously in two moments: in the present as the children are being placated, and in the re-enactment of an ancient dialogue played now with knowledge of what is to come.

The narrator's children insist that the noise is not coming from outside but inside—"No. It is here. In the walls." Indeed, the wind that rushes through the roof-space of the author's childhood home indicates that what was taking place "inside" the farmhouse was inseparable from what was taking place "outside". The wind becomes

53. The farmhouse and the bush that was kept at Fairfields, *Twice Trodden Ground*.

the emissary and sign that the farm and its surrounds are connected by a "surging":

> Pushing open a door and out into the night, there beyond the shrubs and garden are the moving spokes of the mallees, with above, bands of darkness sliding against the clouded sky—and there is everywhere, a surging. It comes and scratches against the old walls and plucks at the vines along the east wall and prises at the seams in the iron roof and here and there it rushes in at the join of a window sash or a door. And the solid walls, the warm fire of smouldering mallee roots, the sparks in the still, grey-white ash, the little warm shut-off hollow within that old, gnarled, rough-walled bastion: it is entered by a draught from without and that house is part of its surroundings. (6)

The seething lyricism of this description anticipates the lush opening passages that begin Hewett's *Wild Card*, published sixteen years later. The wind is an ambivalent agent inasmuch as it is both a chill draught that disturbs the cosy interior warmth, and an umbilical cord that connects the house to "its surroundings". This ambivalent connection of inside to outside is captured in the image of the mallee root burning in "the little warm shut-off hollow" of the fireplace. Recollections of life in the wheatbelt are almost universal in their fond memory of mallee roots in the fireplace. Invariably, the gentle aroma and the deep, slow burn of these roots is associated with the comfort of hearth and home. Yet as we saw in the life of Facey, these roots were the by-product of clearing. The main "burn" conducted in March each year removed the visible mass of vegetation and, with a little luck and skill, the larger tree stumps. But with trees in mallee form, a clump of thinner boughs—beautifully imaged by York Main in the description above as "moving spokes"—emerge from a common subterranean trunk, and it is this submerged trunk that is called the mallee "root". In recently cleared paddocks, the plough would continually strike these mallee roots and we might recall that it was Facey's job as a boy to pick these up and bring them back to use within the house. In this direct way, the cosy interior warmth of the house was a product of the destruction of the bush, and a microcosm of a broader relationship that tied together the outside and the inside.

In "Farmhouse", the dialogue between the children and the mother becomes echoed, but also driven, by that taking place between the house and the wind. Indeed, the meeting of wind and house takes on an almost passionate, or erotic complexion, reminiscent of D.H. Lawrence:

> Again the wind flings against the house and into the deep gape of its verandas, grasping it to itself. And the house, too, reaches out through the binding base of its earth walls to the roots and life of those tangled mallees, and the creak of the wind is the answering creak of the house. (6)

Now the house, in whose fireplace glows the burning mallee root, reaches out through its earthen walls towards roots of the still-living mallee trees beyond. This union of the house's foundation with the underground roots of the mallee is then given an auditory life by the "creak" of the wind answered by the "creak" of the house. It is a complex and highly charged conceit and yields an image of the life of the wheatbelt farmhouse rather different from that which emerges in the orderly narratives of progress delivered by the shire histories.

The other significant dimension of the dialogue in "Farmhouse", and this is true of *Twice Trodden Ground* more generally, is the appearance of the third generation. If we look back at the literature we have considered thus far it is, for the most part, a literature of either the first or the second generation to have arrived in the wheatbelt. York Main and Hewett are the only two writers in this study to have been born and raised on wheatbelt farms by parents raised themselves by settlers. In them, we get the full effects of the strange seclusion of family life on an isolated farm in the years between the wars. Facey arrived in the wheatbelt in childhood but there is no sense of isolation, at least not that charmed sensation of life lived in a bubble that comes from both Hewett and York Main. Goode, Pollard, Ewers, Cowan and Davis all arrived in the wheatbelt as young men. Most of them also left the wheatbelt while still young, although Cowan and Davis returned in their middle years. In their respective work, it is Ewers who is most interested in the generational dimension of wheatbelt life, although Cowan, too, considers the matter. In Ewers, there is a generational exchange between Tommy Lea on the one hand, and his daughter Avea and her husband Ross Daniels on the other. Avea and Ross inherit the wheatbelt from Tommy's generation, who had toiled against the virgin earth and brought it into being. The children of Avea and Ross—the third generation—play little part in the two published novels *Men Against the Earth* and *For Heroes to Live In*. In Cowan, we see something of the generational tension in his long story "The Unploughed Land", where the aging farmer's grown daughter Vera can think of nothing more than leaving the farm that she feels trapped in. In the end, another solution is reached by her falling pregnant to the protagonist of the story, Lee Davis. The conception of this child acts as a sacrament, re-binding Vera and Lee to the country. In that sense, the baby in Cowan's story fulfils a similar role to that played by Avea Lea and, for that matter, Rose in Pollard's *Rose of the Bushlands*.

In this context, "Farmhouse" begins a new dialectic by asking the question, what is it we give to the next generation? It is no longer the farm itself that is in question, but what was framing and holding the farm—the environment. In Pollard, the matter was set up as a contrast between Pete Rodon and Steve Morgan who were "of the bush" and the farmers who were "on the land". In Ewers, Avea Lea

54. Clearers employed by Harry and Herbert York. State Library of Western Australia, 021792PD.

was symbolic of a procreative synthesis that married both the growing of wheat and the bushland that surrounded the farms. By the time we reach Cowan though, especially his novel *Summer* and his later stories, the bush is the subject of a ruthless extermination. In Barbara York Main, this stark reality is confronted for the first time: it's gone. The bush is no longer a frontier, it is not even a frame, it is a vestige, tiny pockets of a once-vast bushland—"islands of yesterday". Barbara York Main knew the bush more thoroughly than Pollard's Rose or Ewers's Avea, but it was no longer possible to sustain the illusion that she was somehow emblematic of it. Her work on trapdoor spiders bespeaks a particular identification with the withdrawn, the fragile and the overlooked—the qualities that now characterise what is left of the bush.

A new historicity emerges in *Twice Trodden Ground* in which there is a past that is quickly being forgotten and a future which has suddenly arrived—a future that was there before its inhabitants even realised. In "Headstones of Settlement" the narrator ruminates on the ruined homes of earlier settlement, where often the only sign of lives spent fighting the earth were the dilapidated remains of chimneys and hearths:

> Often and often again I find these chimneys, each guarded by some relic of a garden—a lofty palm, a never-dying pepper tree, a kurrajong, tangle of lantana, or perhaps a few straggly trees of bush. Most are isolated in paddocks, some crept around by concealing scrub, a few obscured by the asbestos and tile mask of 'new' homesteads without chimneys of their own, the universal electricity and gas having usurped the rite of the hearth. (8)

It is this sense of vanquishment that pervades York Main's *Twice Trodden Ground*. Like many of her conceits, the motif of the chimney is characterised by ambivalence. It is both a link and a loss. The remnants of homes are reminders of what has passed before and in this sense serve the cause of continuity that was one part of York Main's stated aim. But they also declare an unreclaimable loss and this sets a bleak limit to the horizons of the future. As the title of the story makes clear, the wheatbelt is a graveyard:

Tombstones now of homes, of families, monuments to settlement—
they were once each the living core of a pattern of life. Some have
always been to me no more than nameless headstones, growing each
year a little more derelict, sinking deeper into the submitting soil.
Others evoke recollections—dim memories of iron roofs and latticed
verandas strung with honeysuckle, dolichos or tecoma, shadowing
small-paned windows which in turn did not seem to open to the
inside, but reflected in their dust-darkened glass a shadowy external
world shot through with ephemeral shifting images of what lay beyond
each house. (9)

This evocation of the vanished farmhouses that once surrounded
the crumbling chimneys is consonant with that given in the story
"Farmhouse", where the fireplace with the burning mallee root
reached down through the foundations of the house—built from
local clay—so as to connect with the still-living roots of the remnant
mallee bush. These vanished homes were, the description continues,
"dark secret places, as though connected to the outside not through
blatantly open doors but by some subterranean system of tunnels—or
roots, for they were as impenetrable to an outsider as a tree." (9)
Once again, there is a complicated conceit at work which links the
disappearing—but lingering—homes to the bush that their owners
destroyed to create their farms. The chimneys, like the remnant
islands of bushland, "were once each the living core of a pattern of
life" (9). And there is also, this time in the form of a visual trick, the
intimation of a doubled or split existence in the description of the
darkened, dust-covered windows which, instead of yielding a glimpse
into the "inside" of the home, gives back "a shadowy external world
shot through with ephemeral shifting images of what lay beyond each
house" (9).

The dialogue with the third generation that emerged in
"Farmhouse" is continued in other stories in *Twice Trodden Ground*,
most explicitly in "A Third Generation Farm", which follows a boy
as he helps his father feed the stock, turning out bales from the back
of a ute. The boy is not, like the children in "Farmhouse", fearful or
anxious, in fact he is enjoying his work and thinking "how he liked
it here":

He would be a farmer too, when he grew up, and plough and plant crop. It was fun in the winter running after the drill along the fresh-made channels in the moist brown earth. And in the summer, when it was hot and there were mirages coming back and forth across the stubble after the crop was harvested—chewing wheat, hot from the grain bin. (16)

As they go about their work, the boy asks a series of innocuous questions, but which all result in the same answer.

What are those big trees? Those are salmon gums—we used the hollow ones as feeders when we chopped them down … there used to be a lot more. And those smaller ones. Jam trees, we cut those for fence posts, but now we use steel ones as the jam trees are getting scarce. Would there be any kangaroos in this bush? "Not here, boy. The scrub's too sparse. The stock have been in it for years. And anyhow it never was much good here, not since ages ago. We used to cut the brush sheokes to make the bough sheds and make the thatched roofs for the pigsties and the first sheds," the man said absently. (16)

As they head home again in the ute, the boys asks a question that tries to get behind the answers his father had given to each of his previous enquiries. He realises that in the past things seemed to have been rather different—fuller—than they were now:

"When Grandpa came here it was all bush, wasn't it Dad?"
    "That's right, boy."
    "How did he make a farm?" the boy went on.
    "Oh, he cleared the bush. Cut down the big timber, burnt and ploughed. It took years. The scrub here was tough, and they didn't have the big machines—scrub-rollers and bulldozers like now. But, yes, he made a farm," was the nonchalant reply. (17)

The boy then pushes his father just a bit more: "'Tell me Dad,' and the boy's eyes dilated with wonder and he began to get excited, 'tell me, Dad, what did it look like, all bush.'" (17) The father is finally caught in the fullness of this question:

The man looked down into the boy's face, into the bright questioning eyes, and then glanced up through the windscreen, out over the staves of telephone wires as they flipped past, across the furrowed paddocks, the hatch lines of fences, the few, wind-warped, broken, dying trees—across the wide farmlands roped down with S.E.C. copper strands, and said hesitantly, "I can't remember, boy." (17–18)

This story is one of several in *Twice Trodden Ground* that takes on the shape of an environmental fable. The particular significance of this story is that it makes the actions of the wheatbelt—yesterday and today—answerable to the reasonable expectations of the future, represented here as the farmer's boy. This specifies the conditions of a new form of environmental ethics. Hewett took her ancestors to task for ruining the wheatbelt, but there was no room, and in fact, no real wish, for reparation: the establishment of guilt was an end in itself. York Main's introduction of a third generation who want to know why the bush that had been the joy of the previous two was now gone, creates an ethical space for present change and reparatory action. While Hewett's guilt is static and permanent, indeed baroque in its extravagance, York Main motivates a much humbler but more productive emotion, which is shame:

The man looked down at the boy and felt a sudden smouldering shame. He'd never thought about it like this before—what they'd done. His father and himself and all the others. In their single-minded anxiety to make their farms, this other they had done too. But was it too late everywhere? In the areas being opened up now, where they were scrub-rolling and bulldozing and making new farms, where they were also filching from the earth something which could never be planted back to be as it had grown over thousands of years? Too bad that it was easier to make something new than something old! What if they realized—now? Maybe if every district kept untouched a big tract of their bush, and if every farm had wide closed strips along their fencelines and a fenced-off park perhaps? Would their grandchildren then ask as the boy asked again, "What did the bush look like, Dad?" (17)

This missing bush has the qualities of Carson's "silent spring"—a gaping void where one had expected to find, to use York Main's expression, "the living core of a pattern of life". Also, York Main's story no longer accepts unquestioningly the pioneer alibi in which those who went before did what they had to do to survive. No doubt this was true, one need only look at the poverty in Facey's life to realise that at least in many cases the farm was a means to survive in a world where such a thing was far from guaranteed. But York Main's story pushes the point to the present. What about the clearing that was being done now?

The story "The Scapegoat" is just as pointed. It describes the denuding of a wheatbelt granite tor that had once been clothed in rock oaks and hosted kangaroos and rock wallabies who drank at the pools fed by the granite catchment. It begins with a picture, now familiar to us, from 1920: "Clearing, for the first few months, was the prime task. Pyres criss-crossed the bare, tufted openness until thicket and timber gave place to oats and wheat." (19) It then skips forward forty years to 1960:

> The farm was settled. It was a success.
>
> A stone house replaced the hessian shack. It stood, a part of the rocky landscape, to the west of the big humps and in their grip. Sheep trekked up the low slopes into the gorge to the dam. They made trails below the trees. Year by year a toll was taken of these trees—they vanished, and the rocks bulked higher into the sky.
>
> What had once been a tumulus rising from the woodland was becoming a heap of grotesque tombstones in a bare, open graveyard—of prosperous farmland. (20)

The final, sepulchral image again gives the wheatbelt a rude new figuration, as "an open graveyard—of prosperous farmland." The wheatbelt is a pyrrhic victory. The destruction of the whole life of this outcrop takes place slowly enough that it can be put down to some gradual shift in the pattern of things, perhaps even nature itself, which is prone to change after all. But it also takes place with sufficient speed that it can be witnessed in the living years of an author of just thirty-eight years of age. The death of a mountain had happened

55. Illustration from "The Scapegoat", *Twice Trodden Ground*.

before the eyes of a still young woman. The question that the story asks is why no one has raised an objection. Like the farmer quizzed by his son in "Third Generation Farm", the locals fall back into a semi-truth to mask the shame that sits at the edges of consciousness—they blame the rabbits: "It was the rabbits, the deuced rabbits that ate everything, crop and scrub alike." (21) The rabbits are the "scapegoats" of the story's title.

York Main takes a significant step in this story by shifting the narrative position to the landscape. We saw some hints of this in Cowan. His "Solitude" began from the viewpoint of a wedge-tailed eagle watching the settlers carve a clearing for their farm; and in the climactic moment of *Summer,* when the bulldozer clears the remnant bush containing the body of Tom Everett, the narrative position shifts to that of a lizard in the bulldozer's path. In "Scapegoat", York Main moves the story to the perspective of the rock itself: "The rocks protested", she writes, as they are stripped of their covering:

> And gradually as the trees withered and fell and rotted at the base of the rocks, they stood out—bold, stark, dominant. Defiant. The whole landscape was changing. And as the soft veils of the rock oaks were

drawn away the rocks became fiercer, aggressive, hostile; they almost grew larger—at least the perspective of the landscape had altered. And they were aloof. The heart and life of the land which had dribbled away as the bush was destroyed retreated into that massive rocky core and boiled there, seething beneath the stony skin. (20)

The moment in which these rocks begin to represent outrage at their treatment is reminiscent of Aldo Leopold's famous essay on "Thinking Like a Mountain" that was published in his *Sand County Almanac* (1949). In that essay, Leopold describes a mountain that is denuded by deers whose numbers had mushroomed since local farmers had eliminated their predator, the wolf. The phrase "thinking like a mountain" was Leopold's shorthand for a position from which ecological balance might be understood—that is, from the *mountain's* point of view. To the mountain's "mind", the loss of the wolves was catastrophic. York Main's vignette shares with Leopold's the mountain's point of view, as well as the startling central image of a mountain once covered but now, thanks to human intervention, utterly bare.

Twice Trodden Ground needs to be understood in the context of the massive clearing of the wheatbelt that unfolded in the post-war decades. As we have noted, the wheatbelt's clearance had two main phases. The first phase of clearing took place between the turn of the century and 1930, by which time roughly 6 million hectares were cleared for farming. The Depression brought land-clearing to a sudden halt and comparatively little was cleared in the next two decades. When commodity prices finally recovered in the years after World War Two, clearing resumed to the degree that between 1949 and 1969 the total area cleared for farming more than doubled to nearly 14 million hectares. In the same period, wheat production and the number of sheep trebled.[30] However, the massive growth in wheatbelt clearing did not, by and large, involve an extension of the wheat frontier. The rainfall lines still governed the wheatbelt's overall extent but attention now fell on the "light land" which had been left untouched because it was not fertile according to the techniques and economics that prevailed before 1950. Indeed, about half the land in the wheatbelt was "light land", and it was this which was cleared in the post-war period. As previously discussed, this was made viable as

farming land by the development of pasture crops—new cultivars of
lupins and subterranean clover—which could sustain sheep, and of
new fertilisers containing nitrogen and trace elements (zinc, copper)
which were added to superphosphate. The quantity of superphosphate
was also increased and applied to sown pasture as well as to cereals.
A second wave of soldier-settlers joined in this new land expansion,
particularly in the scrub and mallee country around Jerramungup,
inland and east of Albany.[31] There was, though, one major new
expansion to the previous boundaries of the wheatbelt, and that was
the development of the Esperance sandplain from 1965, where over
300,000 hectares were cleared over the next decade.[32]

Once the fertility problem had been solved by the agricultural
scientists and post-war commodity prices changed the economic
landscape, the advent of bulldozers meant that the land could be
quickly and cheaply cleared. Despite the elegiac tone of York Main's
book and her quaint pen-and-ink drawings, it is the faint drone of
the bulldozer, as much as the wheatbelt's winds, which provide the
background noise of the book—becoming audible only occasionally,
as it had for Henry working alone on the wheat bin in Cowan's
novel *Summer*. In Cowan's writing, a new machine—the bulldozer—
becomes the ominous emblem for unstoppable mechanised eradication.

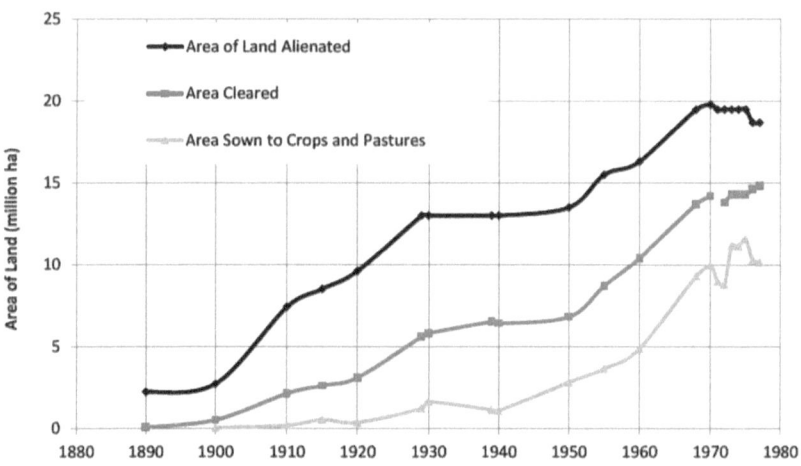

56. Area of land released and cleared in Western Australia 1890–1980, adapted
from Burvill (1979).

Bulldozers were first used to clear wheatbelt land in 1946 and quickly took over as the major method of clearing land, capable of flattening trees up to 10 metres high.[33] They replaced the axe and the manual toil involved in clearing land in the years before the war. The wheatbelt was now being cleared by machines as much as by men.

Where "Scapegoats" had taken the position—the ecological position—of the mountain, "The Betrayal" attempts to go inside the mind of the farmer. It was a view familiar to York Main as the child and sister of wheatbelt farmers. The story is about the clearing of residual bushland, the typical action of the second, post-war, phase of wheatbelt clearing. Apart from the economic advantage, the clearing of residual bushland seemed, at least this is the suggestion of the story, to be motivated by a desire for complete mastery. In this, the remaining bush was not just useless in its current form, but an affront to the ideal of productivity:

> He looked out from the deep shade of the veranda into the dazzling light, gazing from where the house stood, high up on the slope, down across the organized paddocks and the wheat crop to the flat beyond where the stretch of timber still stood, and even farther to the white glare of the sky. This land he held, this land of merging paddock and unploughed bushland. He held it with his purse...and sometimes with his heart.
>
> But it would not be his, really his, until he had cleared it all, until he had routed every acre of bush and tined the soil with his machines. When it—every acre—produced what he dictated then and then only would it be really his. (30)

The claim that the clearing of land was driven by more than money, and even that money itself was not quite the simple "food on the table" necessity that it was casually assumed to be, is one that was still quite impolite in 1971, in an era in which the Depression and war-time austerity still cast a forceful shadow. What York Main was insinuating was that the country had subtly passed out of a mode of survival and into a form of avarice to which no one was owning up. Perhaps even more shocking is that the wheatbelt was starting to reveal itself as a place that was governed by economics in ways few had guessed, even after the devastating collapse of prices during the Depression. Because now the wheatbelt was once again successful, and yet as the farms grew and succeeded, the towns were shrinking and dying. What became evident now was that there was nothing in the economic motive of agricultural production that necessitated family life, vibrant communities or regional identity.

"The Betrayal" contains one of the most vivid accounts of second-phase mechanical clearing, as chilling as Cowan's in *Summer*:

> And so scrub-rolling began. The bulldozer grunted its way through the bush, rushing at the boles of trees, nuzzling their scaly bark until they quivered and the bark began to flake and the whole trunk shuddered so that the branches trembled their leaves. The timber would split and then shatter, long fissures running upwards until the trunk cracked open and the wetness came out and trickled into the dust and bark. Then the tree would lose its hold on earth and sky and life and tumble over, its branches thumping to the ground: it would break up, stiff, waxy leaves flying and fallying, and finally the keeled trunk lay still. On and on, tree after tree splintering and toppling for days until the whole landscape was torn and dishevelled—until scrub-rolling was done. (31)

Like the farmer in "Third Generation Farm" though, this one begins to be disquieted by his actions, conscious of some violation of an order that he thought held no claim upon him. But with this farmer, and with no child asking awkward questions, this misgiving does not get so far as a conscious thought, just a feeling of unease and faint disorientation:

> Late one afternoon, when the job was at last finished, the man climbed down from the bulldozer and began to walk back through the debris towards the truck. Inevitably he had to scramble over jumbled trunks and push past broken boughs. At one point as he forced his way he half fell against an oozing, splintered trunk and his arms were smeared with its wetness. The sap stuck to his hands as he struggled free of the branches. He stood and looked for a moment, down at his hands and the crushed sprawling tree at his feet. (31)

The smear of sap on his arms bothers the man and he is briefly overcome with a vague horror and disgust by how it "congealed on the inside of his wrists...sticky and horrid in the web of his fingers." It would not rub off but clung to his skin and stuck to the hairs on his arms. He stared at his hands, which he could not seem to clean:

> And it seemed that he had not just looked for one moment at the sap of a single tree oozing away through a wound too big and awful to heal itself, but into a timelessness where the life of the entire earth was running out into space through the awful gashes made over the whole span of growing and dying civilizations. (31)

Certainly, with this last conception we seem to have departed from the probable thoughts of this farmer and into the emerging agenda of the worldwide environmental movement. But depicting the farmer as being tripped up by his action, finding himself, however fleetingly, at odds with his productive ideal, is a significant moment all the same.

Once the bush has been cleared, the farmer burns it and eventually brings it into production. Removing this last bush opened up the farmhouse to the winter wind. It was completely surrounded by open paddocks now. The crop grew well in the first year. But summer rain and an early winter turned the low-lying ground into a bog and no crop could be planted. That summer, as the ground dried, a "silver scum" encrusted the surface, which is the punchline of the story: "He had betrayed the land for silver—but the silver was ground gone salt." (34) This is the closest that York Main comes to the mood of Hewett. Not only does the story feature soil salinity, Hewett's favourite symbol for the ruined land, it also casts the matter in the mode of an original sin—a primal crime whose consequences we are all now inheriting. But York Main is also clear in this story that, unlike in the previous generation, the relationship between clearing and salinity was known. Indeed, the farmer was conscious of the risk of clearing this land, but cleared it anyway, regarding the existence of such thoughts as a sign of weakness. In this, the resilience of the farmer, his determination to prove—like Tommy Lea—the doubters wrong, folds from a virtue into a vice, and the clearing of the land is turned from a sacrament into a betrayal. York Main underscores this with a reflection delivered after the farmer first seeds his newly cleared land. In time it would produce a crop of grain: "the grain which time and time again with all the faith of a germinal civilization has been set in some ground, binding earth and man together, or driving both into the desert." (32)

This devastation of the remnant land, that had been preserved by the Depression and the lack of trace elements, provides the note of quiet rage in *Twice Trodden Ground*.

"Marginal Country" (1972)

The motifs that appear in the sketches of *Twice Trodden Ground* find their most developed expression in the long short-story "Marginal Country", published in *Westerly* in 1972.[34] The story is the longest and most complexly realised fictional work that York Main wrote, and resembles the early stories of Peter Cowan in the way that it tracks the effects of isolation on the lives of those living in the wheatbelt. The action takes place in the present moment with the second-generation farmer Wilton Workman, who had inherited his farm—"The Pines"—from his father Will Workman. The father had taken up the land decades before in the (fictional) wheatbelt district of Noongulin. Will and his wife had recently retired, as was customary, "to the city", and while the wife was enjoying the advantages of city life, the old man had found himself at a loss: "The empty glare of windows, the absence of familiar and moving shadows of trees and creepers, threw him into confusion." (24) In Noongulin, the older Will Workman had been a figure of some importance, but "on the green-edged suburban pavement, he was become no-one at all." (24) On the farm, his eldest son, Wilton, had slowly edged out his younger brother Kim, who had accepted the farm could not support both brothers' families and bowed to the primacy of Wilton's claim, though not without some understandable resentment. Wilton thus finds himself in command of a successful farm and becomes one of those destined to remain and grow in this era of rapidly rising cost-structures. He acquired, one by one, the farms of his neighbours and relatives as they sold-up, "small-time farmers, who one by one had dropped away from the countryside as Wilton's hold on it had hardened." (36) In the face of this, Wilton would mouth the slogan—"Get big or get out!"—as a reassurance that this process was inevitable and he was simply joining the future on the only terms being offered. He was a realist who was not diverted by the sentiments that seemed to fog the minds of those around him, and whose ebbing profitability gave the true picture of their worth.

The figure of Wilton, and the successful Workman property, is counterpointed by their neighbours the Hudlestons. This lazy and rather dreamy couple—as they were perceived in the district—had gradually let their property run to ruin: "The Hudlestons ran a few pigs, fowls, turkeys, a couple of cows and subsisted at some kind of level incomprehensible to their now younger neighbours. They persisted anachronistically along the clump of salmon gums and gimlets, the knot of mallee and thin dejected sheokes." (25–6) Ivy Hudleston lived absorbed in this isolated world, devoting herself to her wild, bedraggled garden, where she prized above all else her flowering bulbs. Tending them each year—lifting them, separating them, storing them and giving them out to people through the district:

> Through the eruption and recession of bulbs ran threads of continuity. Through each brown bulb Mrs Hudleston would see *all* life regenerated; she would see dry, brown paddocks awakening in an autumnal greenness, and feel most keenly new life throbbing in old, bush trees scattered across the countryside and tremble with joy at the sudden resurgence in heath and thicket. The bulb had become Mrs Hudleston's emblem. In Nungoolin bulbs were tradition. (26)

This image of the lovingly tended bulbs, even though they are in no sense native to the wheatbelt, stands nevertheless for the continuity that was disappearing from it. Ivy Hudleston's bulbs are a metaphor for the native bushland that persisted on their property through their benign neglect. They are emblems, too, of a certain faith that life, given space, was capable of invisible forms of resilience. All of these sentiments were anathema to Wilton and to the new generation of farmers who could see only self-indulgent delusion and soft-headed mismanagement.

Ivy Hudleston is the surprising heroine of "Marginal Country", partly because she does not try to understand or "reduce" the landscape to any other need. Her straggliness allowed and accepted the disorder of nature and its right to be:

> From her ramshackle house on the stony hill, Mrs Hudleston would embrace the countryside. The great squares of paddocks, green or brown, the shaggy clumps of mallee, the contoured slopes and the straying creek courses, the last few root-heaps humped like strange tumuli here and there beside the distant fences, all the wide country stretched out and down below. It was all here, she willed it so. Even that knot of trees hiding the Workmans' place the other side of the gully, down from the watching pines on the rubbly hill. (Those Workmans with their grand house and ordered gardens and orchard trees, them with their style.) It was all spread out below her, the paddocks and trees and tracks and the moving colours of the cloud shadows, all settling into place just for her. The shape of the landscape belonged to her. That young Wilton Workman could think what he liked. Sweating his body and soul out, day and night. For more crops, more stock, more pasture, more land. He would tire the soil. It would turn on him in the end. The country would turn on him in the end. It is a strange irony that sometimes it is the lack-a-daisical farmer who, in the long run, is kinder to the landscape! (27)

But the Hudlestons do leave their property, which Wilton acquires, resolving to remove the "hundred acres of wodjil the Hudlestons had never bothered to clear" (27). When Ivy and Clem Hudleston are eventually forced off their land (where they had lived "like natives"), they end up buying a house in the town to see out their days.

But the real sadness of the story does not belong to them. They accept life's changes and defeats with a dignity that is not apprehended by the prim community that sees them only as a ridiculous failure. The story's pity is reserved, in fact, for Wilton, whose successes leave him feeling empty in ways he is not able to fathom. He has reaped the rewards of agricultural science and his land was more productive than it had ever been—and far more profitable. He had seen neighbours leave and their houses fall into ruin but had only concerned himself with bringing this next new tranche of land into the productive orbit of his expanding empire. This compensated for the land that was being lost slowly but surely to salt and erosion. That the sandplain country was now able to be cleared had come at just the right time, as the older cleared country began to suffer. As he explains to his friend, Cedric:

> "Twenty years ago you wouldn't have considered clearing it [the sandplain country]. Just so much useless land. Not many places are ever without some poor ground, either saltlake or sandplain or gravel ridges. But now, this is prime country. With the low ground going salt, the sandplain if fertilised is fine country. Less than half our cleared ground is really any good now. Either gone salt or eroded and cut about with the creeks." (30)

Instead of seeking a lesson in the degradation, Wilton finds only that grace appears to be on the side of the farmer, yielding up new land for use as the old land perishes. No thought seems to be given to what might happen if the new land suffers a similar fate. Cedric pushes him on some of these matters, and the poignant decay of the old homes—at least this must touch Wilton in some way: "Wilton remained unperturbed. The people? They were no more than phantoms which stayed briefly and passed away, no matter where— that was no concern of his—availing the land for what he considered its proper use, intensive farming." (32) Again, Wilton does not deduce from this reflection that he, too, is a phantom who will disappear in due course; instead he identifies himself with the economic activity of farming. In other words, he is not a mere person, born today, gone tomorrow, but an enterprise that persists beyond the lives of mortal men.

It is left to Wilton's friend Cedric, whose house is amongst those now mouldering in Wilton's ever-expanding fields, to voice some moment of conscience for the actions that Wilton was committing:

> Banished by the house, Cedric looked out over the assaulted landscape. Could he now, then, look at this dispassionately? It would appear that the fated prime land was about all that was left of the original landscape in the confines of the present panorama spreading northward from the old homestead. The ute sped over the paddock tracks and came

to the fringe of scrub. This remnant of bush, if left unmolested, this at least would be some atonement for the earlier offences against the countryside. (32)

Wilton was not unmoved by the land's beauty and often remarked on the matter, but it was not something that would be enough to change the course of action, the primacy of making the land useful. Utility must prevail over mere sentiment, no matter how beautiful the land may look in the late-afternoon sun. When Wilton's wife leaves him near the end of the story, he is not too shaken. She had surmised correctly that the farm meant more to him than she did. The story leaves a stern judgement on his stance, connecting the indifference he had as a husband to the callous indifference he had in husbanding his land. She had been slowly adjusting to the land and a life on it, but his distance from her prevented the adaptation from continuing:

> Wilton, so absorbed by his increasing productivity, oblivious of what was happening to the countryside, blind to persistence of annihilation of native vegetation and wildflowers and the general depauperisation of the landscape itself, was less noticing still of his wife's dilemma, her desperate effort to gain acceptance in a countryside she was still trying to comprehend—could not even make a gesture of guidance. He was as remote from the "soul" of the landscape as were his own machines... The landscape for him had become a thing inanimate. Its "livingness" no longer touched him. (34)

In the final summation, the story draws on a distinction we first saw with James Pollard in his description of Pete Rodon in *The Bushland Man* in comparison with the farmers—Rodon was of the bush, they were on the land. The formulation in York Main's story is quite close to this. Wilton was a man who "works so frenetically *on* the landscape but failed to become a part *of* it." (34; original italics).

Chapter Nine

Elizabeth Jolley (1923–2007)

This literary history is centred on people who lived in the wheatbelt and wrote creatively about the experience. In this chapter, I bend this rule so as to consider the work of Elizabeth Jolley. Jolley never lived in the wheatbelt, although she was a frequent visitor over many years. Yet it was Jolley who wrote the wheatbelt's most famous novel, *The Well* (1986), which won the Miles Franklin Award that year.[1] And it was she who first captured certain of the wheatbelt's existential qualities. In many ways what she saw in the wheatbelt—a particular vertiginous terror—is a feature that would infuse the works of the younger writers that would appear in the 1980s, Tom Flood and John Kinsella. Jolley arrived in Western Australia in 1959 at the age of thirty-six with her husband, Leonard Jolley, and three small children. Leonard Jolley had been recruited from Glasgow University by Fred Alexander to become the new librarian at The University of Western Australia, a post he would hold until 1979. Elizabeth had been writing creatively since her adolescence and worked on novels and stories throughout her adult life, but her formal literary career can be dated to the late 1960s when she began to have stories published in *Westerly* and *Quadrant*.[2]

In 1970, Leonard and Elizabeth purchased a 5-acre holding in the Darling Range near the town of Wooroloo, about 60 kilometres from

Perth. It was to be a "hobby farm" in the parlance of the day, to which they might retire on weekends, keep poultry and plant fruit trees. The Wooroloo property in the Perth Hills was the bridge between Jolley's life in the well-heeled suburb of Claremont and the wheatbelt, which had begun to exert a fascination on her mind as she traversed it in the mid-1970s. In many ways, such "weekend" farms filled the role of allotments in English towns, allowing city residents to grow and produce food and take time out of otherwise busy lives. Elizabeth Jolley had grown up in the Black Country of the English Midlands. Weekends spent at Wooroloo acquainted Jolley with the very different landscape, flora, climate and texture of rural life in Australia. The property also revealed a very particular relationship in Jolley's life in relation to land—one that translates markedly in her fiction. Indeed, as Chris Prentice noted, "few of Jolley's stories and novels do not touch in some way upon land and landscape."[3] Jolley later published selections from a journal she had kept in the early days at Wooroloo in *Diary of a Weekend Farmer* (1993).[4] Included are entries depicting various trips to inspect properties to find one that would fit their budget and their wishes. The diary entries are interspersed with poems by Jolley written in response to their weekend farming. One element that is significant is the wish to hold "land", or as Jolley terms it, this "strange land hunger" (12). In this, there is the residue of the land-wish that is common to both the migrant experience in Australia and the creation of the wheatbelt, two phenomena which are not unrelated.[5] After missing out on one property because it was too expensive, she wrote: "People like us have no land behind them, even the place where I was born, 'The Beeches' Gravelly Hill Birmingham, no longer exists. How can I buy land!" (14) Land, in this case, becomes the symbol of one's place in the world, a sign that one belongs and is meant to exist, a repudiation of life's ephemerality.

The fact that land can also stand for something more than these things is also freely accepted in Jolley's journal, and is presented in an unusually frank form: "Perhaps we are trying to replace a daughter with a piece of land", she wrote on 29 September 1970 (12). Over the ensuing years, they planted many fruit trees, grew vegetables, beans in particular, kept a range of poultry and a few sheep. It was a family activity, and Elizabeth and Leonard were joined by their children who helped with the planting and repairs. But even so, it was typical of Jolley that the place would occasionally lose its reality, its relation to seasonal activity, and a feeling of estrangement would set in. In February 1973, just a few months before her fiftieth birthday, she wrote:

> Sometimes it is easy to lose the way in the seasons. Not to know what is the next thing to be done. It is then that I can feel aimless and the place, the orchard quickly seems like an alien place to be eaten up again by the bush. It is an alien place resisting or it is retreating from all our human endeavour. And then the doves fly up glowing in the rising sun and the sound from their wings is like a tiny clapping. (83)

The moment is not unlike that in Cowan's first published story, "Living" (1943), in which a grieving farmer can suddenly no longer make sense of any of the workaday activities that once filled and structured his life. The crop was ready for harvest, but he could not bring himself to take it off—"Let the scrub have it", he says to himself and the fields he had cleared. The Jolleys' hobby farm was not in the wheatbelt, but it shows something of the desire that fed the wheatbelt's human lives, albeit in microcosm. Jolley even invested in miniature equipment for her farm—a Victa lawnmower to keep the grass down, a rotary hoe to cultivate her fields and a chainsaw for clearing and chopping firewood.

Jolley had joined the WA branch of the Fellowship of Australian Writers (FAWWA), the organisation formed by J.K. Ewers in 1938. It was through the FAWWA that she met Ian Templeman, then executive officer of the Festival of Perth.[6] Templeman founded the Fremantle Arts Centre in 1972, in the mouldering buildings of the former Fremantle Lunatic Asylum, and began offering a range of activities including creative writing classes. Templeman recruited Jolley to this task and she taught her first class in February 1974. The Arts Centre also coordinated a state-funded program called "Arts Access" which sought to bring arts services to people in rural communities. An initiative in this program was the sponsoring and facilitation of book clubs. The Arts Centre would send out a dozen copies of a book—they had twelve titles to draw on—together with discussion notes. Thereafter, a tutor would visit and host a discussion. Jolley became involved in this, first in the preparation of reading notes, which were xeroxed and bound up in what were called "Travelling Notebooks", and then as well, as a travelling tutor. It was through this program that Jolley came to know the wheatbelt, visiting places such as Dalwallinu, Hyden, Wongan Hills and Kojonup.

> They asked me to write the notes, discussion notes, for these books ... they're sort of light-hearted notes with lots of quotations in them about the books, and these notebooks go out ... [to] the country—for country people who had difficulty in getting books, and I or another tutor would go out and start them off ... I would go out to Hyden or the wheatbelt towns and stay in a motel.[7]

The wheatbelt fascinated her, and she came to call it simply "the wheat", in the same way the one might say "the ocean" or "the desert". For Jolley, "the wheat" was just that, a seemingly endless expanse through which one drove in eerie—but also exhilarating—isolation. It became, for her, a blank screen which her darkly comic imagination would populate with intense personal dramas and relationships. She saw in the wheatbelt a place which was outwardly nondescript and, almost for this very reason, deeply intriguing:

> From 30,000 feet, or whatever height the new planes fly at, the different parts of Australia, seen through the clouds, may well look alike.
>
> But here on the ground, and travelling slowly, there is a constant and subtle variation. A distant township near the rabbit-proof fence seems to be desolate, scattered poverty, a shabbiness of weather-blistered little houses, with stack of poles and empty drums gathered near a closed filling station.
>
> There is also a wheat silo alongside the deserted, overgrown railway. Generators reverberate in a tin shed that stands up against the hotel. Suddenly, after leaving the township, a different landscape is revealed. On both sides of the main road there are endless paddocks with far-off patches of gold where the sun, shining from between distant clouds, catches with its brightness the curve of the land as it falls towards the horizon.[8]

A central element of Jolley's sense of the wheatbelt was its apparent endlessness. The sensation of wheat paddocks extending outwards to the ends of the earth. But, like Barbara York Main, Jolley saw something within this apparent endlessness; tiny fissures of life along the "seams" and these seams—lines of trees or residual bush—were what was joining the landscape together, "mending" it:

> All the miles of wheat in all directions, folded and mended in places, are pulled together as if seamed, by little dark lines of trees, as if they are embroidered with rich green wool or silk on a golden background. In the design of the embroidery are some silent houses and sheds. Narrow places, fenced off and watered sparingly, produce a little more of the dark green effect. At the intervals, there are unsupervised windmills, turning and clicking with a kind of solemn and honest obedience.[9]

Like Cowan, Jolley found a paradoxical relationship between isolation and intimacy, a sealed intensity in which two people could become deeply absorbed in the mutual play of fantasy life. And like Cowan, Jolley thinks of the wheatbelt as something which produces this isolation, the effects of which then determine the lives of those living under these conditions.

"The Long Distance Lecture" (1979)

A rural locality predominates in Jolley's first book, the short-story collection *Five Acre Virgin* (1976), which was also the first work of fiction published by the newly established Fremantle Arts Centre Press.[10] The collection is dominated by an interlinked set of stories that take place, loosely at least, in the hilly Jarrah and Wandoo country of the Darling Scarp, and made up of small holdings not unlike that of the Jolleys' own "five acre virgin" property at Wooroloo. A similar locality is visible in Jolley's first published novel, *Palomino* (1980), which had won the Victorian FAW prize for the best unpublished novel in 1975, but had travelled an arduous path into print.[11] The first story to have a recognisable wheatbelt setting was "The Long Distance Lecture" which appeared in Jolley's second FACP short-story collection, *The Travelling Entertainer and Other Stories* (1979).[12] It is not without significance that the story is centred around a drive.

Jolley did not drive in England, only learning to drive in Australia in her forties. The experience of driving in the wheatbelt thus carries a particular significance for her, a sense—sometimes almost giddy—of being able to author her life's direction.[13] "The Long Distance Lecture" is written in the first-person voice of a man, but clearly recalls Jolley's recent experiences teaching literary appreciation and creative writing in country centres of Western Australia:

> I'm on my way to give a lecture in a country town; an informal lecture, a mixture of fact and imagination from chosen writers and the ways in which they approach death.
>
> That death is a part of living I find unquestionable, and keeping one hand on the skull, like St Jerome, has become a part of my life. There is to me a strange fascination about the ways in which the writer presents the long illness and subsequent death. My lecture is called *The Deathbed and the Chaise Longue.* (176)

The tone is matter-of-fact but the theme, as is already visible, is distinctly macabre. The combination recalls Kafka, and the lecturer is reminiscent of Kafka's fussy, self-justifying, slightly buffoonish protagonists. The story is in the form of an interior monologue, and follows the drift of thought as the lecturer drives towards his destination, a country town where he is to deliver a lecture on literary treatments of death. The various writers that he will touch on during his lecture meander through his thoughts. He recites to himself passages from *Ecclesiastes*, Tolstoy's *Death of Ivan Ilych* and Ibsen's *Ghosts*, particularly the memorable line that we all "sail with a corpse in the cargo"—that we carry our death with us as soon as we are born. The lecturer muses, even more pointedly: "Every pregnant woman carries death as well as birth inside her." (179)

The lecturer had been to the town to give a lecture the previous year, but is taking another route this time because he has had to make a detour to drop another lecturer—the "china painting lady"—at another town, and is now running behind. He had been given directions, but having turned off the main road, he now seems unable to find the next turn-off and is not sure if he has missed it. Nevertheless, the journey is a pleasant one, indeed idyllic:

I'm enjoying the journey. The road is well made and the wheat is standing in that golden stillness just before the harvest. Two girls are on horseback at the side of the road. They look just old enough to be admired. They are part of the landscape with their sun-brown skin and honey-coloured hair. Their horses are this same colour, palomino, cream and gold, well bred. It's a pity their youth can't be part of this afternoon for ever. (176)

The journey is thus also a vehicle for fantasy. The landscape is a blonde one—the straw-coloured wheat, plump and ready for harvest, is answered by the image of the girls also on the cusp of consummation. Even the horses are blonde. The image is a fantasy of sunny fertility limned by its impermanence: "It's a pity their youth can't be part of this afternoon for ever." (176) But darker thoughts intrude, and provide a countervailing image of the reduction of life to certain brute facts. He thinks of the town's motel and how motels all over the world are the same. This dreary sameness is epitomised by the ubiquity of concrete, a material which stands in for death as much as the wheat had stood for life:

> The place where I will have my room has all the qualities which belong to concrete, cyclone-wired enclosures and storehouses on concrete stairways stained blamelessly as if from other innocent imprisonments. It has the cracking associated with concrete and water unable to soak through sluggish drains ... even here in the wheat, all motor hotels are the same. It's hard to remember where you are when you wake up inside this concrete. (177)

After the splendour of the golden wheatfields, the town is a disappointment, a jolt back into the plainness of existence and the grubby demands of mortality:

> I remember, last year the township at dusk seemed to be a desolate scattered poverty; a shabbiness of blistered little houses, stacks of poles and empty drums gathered near a closed petrol station, and a wheat silo alongside a deserted overgrown railway line. The place reverberated with generators in a tin shed up against the hotel. (177)

The concrete and the wheat are juxtaposed domains in the story, standing, more or less, for life and death. And yet they share qualities which suggest that one might, after all, simply be the shadow of the other. For instance, both the wheat and the concrete have a spreading, continuous quality, as belongs to a general state of being, as much as to an entity. Just as blondeness had spread through the entire scene of the girls on horseback, so does concrete spread through the cities and towns of the earth—even the smallest wheatbelt hamlet is beset with it. Both the wheat and the concrete have an oceanic quality, as if they are being endlessly produced, flowing over and coating the entire surface of the earth.

A noted recurring motif in Jolley's imagery of the wheatbelt is the lines of trees appearing as "seams" that join the paddocks together. Another author to see the trees as seams in the fabric of the landscape was Barbara York Main. This domestic image links in with other moments in Jolley's fiction that feature the sewing of clothes or bedsheets:

> This is where I turn off. What a great wide place this is. All those miles of wheat in all directions, folded and mended in places, pulled together as if seamed by little dark lines of trees. Sometimes in these seams there is the darker green of something cherished, growing beside a house. Just now, the wind comes with restraint across the harvest, a gentle sound like the faint playing of a flute being carried on the wind. There is peace here in the ripened corn and the light and warmth of the sun. (178)

It is along one of these "seams" that the lecturer finds himself driving down a "hairline path", and the story begins to take on the qualities of a fairytale, not unlike Hansel and Gretel. He begins to feel affected by the silence and the isolation: "Here in the wheat is solitude and already I am feeling, not afraid exactly, but I feel the silence all around me." (180) And yet it was not entirely unpleasant, indeed he resented his passenger, the woman he had dropped off in another town, because she "stole the solitude" he longed for (180).

As he follows the narrow road, strange things begin to happen. A pungent smell of death becomes noticeable and then a dead heifer, grotesquely distended, is seen at the road's edge. The land, which had seemed relentlessly flat before, has suddenly become precipitous. Clouds descend and the narrator fears he might run off the road and into a ravine. Then the clouds disappear as quickly as they had appeared and the land resumes the flat contours of the wheatbelt, only now these are not pleasantly undulating but menacingly empty and devoid of humanity:

> There's nothing here. No house in sight and no harmony of sheds and farm machinery. All life is withdrawn from this place.
>
> ...
>
> The track moves like a snake; soft, soft, disappearing, merging with the scrub and appearing beyond the scrub. The scrappy salt bushes invade and fill the narrow path, hitting and scraping my car. And all around is an indifference of wheat. (182)

Because the story is an interior monologue, when the lecturer starts to scream in sheer, blind terror, we cannot hear it, we can only hear him commenting on the fact that he is hearing himself scream. The event is so disembodied that he is only able to deduce that he is screaming because he hears a scream but can see no others around:

> Where are you? Was that me calling out? There's no one here to call. It's all around me this quietness and loneliness.
>
> Whose voice was that screaming so terribly? I've never heard such a scream in my life.
>
> There's no one here to scream except me.
>
> ...
>
> I can feel the scream coming in my chest. It's quite without reason. I know there's no reason to scream. I can't go on!
>
> I can't go on screaming out here alone. How strange and uncontrollable this is, this fear of being afraid. I'm not even lost. If this track is not the right one I can go back and try one of the others. There they all are, winding across this empty world. (183)

He comes, late in the afternoon, to a house that reminds him of a distant memory from his childhood, and we are by now no longer sure whether such things are happening in the reality of the story or are being hallucinated. The house is unlike a dusty wheatbelt farm in early summer and more like a house in England, with blue bricks and a path overgrown with "sweet smelling grass". It appears, at this point, that the lecturer is now living out a memory from childhood, where he had grazed his knee and was looked after by grandparents and given biscuits to soothe him. The mixture of memory and present reality has by this point in the story become so tangled that it has largely lost its traction as an event in the world and become a portrait of a delirious inner state. The wheatbelt's iconic landscape, which had punctuated the story, now appears in that stagey, distorted and expressionist form that the Congolese jungle does in Conrad's *Heart of Darkness*.

But the story that most influences Jolley's is Jack London's "To Build a Fire" (1908).[14] In that story, a man attempts a journey to catch up with friends at a camp in the Yukon. It is very cold, too cold to be attempting the journey, but the man is new to the region and eager to meet his friends. He is accompanied on the journey by a dog, and a series of minor mishaps, trivial in other circumstances, become the difference between life and death. This enters into the narrative, brilliantly, as a realisation—a fact known all along but gradually and chillingly becoming ever more real. In the end, the man's life or death is decided by the simple act of building a fire; his hands freeze and he is unable to coordinate them sufficiently to strike a match. This is alluded to briefly in the lecturer's thoughts and we assume that it, too, will form a part of the evening's lecture.

> Another man lost in snow bound country, trying to follow a dark hairline trail, making his journey through life, bargaining for more time, tries to build a fire. The approaching death is heralded by the lack of the sun and by the pall over the countryside. The man's spit freezes and his mouth is clenched firmly shut in his beard, lengthening, amber-coloured with frozen tobacco juice. How will people listening to my lecture be able to imagine, in this sunfilled place, the deep snow and a man contemplating the killing of his dog so that he can thaw his frozen hands inside the carcass of that dog? (179)

London's story is memorable for the tension between the man's cogitation, his determination to keep calm and meet his setbacks logically, and the incipient panic which answers all of this with the simple question—but what if this fails? Of course, the answer is if he fails (to build a fire) he will die. A disconcerting aspect of the story is that when the man does surrender to his fate, his death comes as a relief both to him and to the reader. In other words, at least in this moment, we meet quite vividly the wish for death.

It is exactly these dynamics that prevail in Jolley's own story, so clearly modelled on London's. She is aware of the oddness of this, allowing her narrator to wonder how a story of the icy gloom of the Yukon could ever be understood in the sunny wheatbelt and by the people who live there. The story, in effect, provides a rejoinder to this objection, allowing us to experience in the endless open fields of the wheatbelt, a feeling of vertigo, as if the space itself might evacuate all meaning from any stranger foolish enough to blunder into its limitless expanse. In the lecturer's mind, the emptiness of the wheatbelt is associated with a fundamental uncertainty about the nature of his audience, and even whether it exists: "There's no one here at all, no one in these paddocks and no one on the road. What kind of people will come to my lecture? Will there be anyone there?" (179) In this way, the wheatbelt represents the possibility that no one can hear you speak—it is the possibility that, in spite of one's endless words, one is, for all intents and purposes, mute. Again, we might see in this trepidation the shadow of the work of Peter Cowan, a writer who Jolley knew and admired. Of course, Cowan's writing is completely lacking in the grotesque humour that typifies Jolley's work, but in the authors' underlying apprehension of the uncanny power of silence, they share a bond.

It is not insignificant in this context that the workshops that Jolley gave as part of the Fremantle Arts Centre rural outreach program were met, in fact, with considerable enthusiasm and showed a deep intellectual hunger in wheatbelt residents, particularly women.[15] But the journeys, nonetheless, must have been filled with a certain anxiety over the place of literature in the wheatbelt—that it was a frivolous anomaly in the midst of the no-nonsense tasks of farming. The lecturer remembers the occasion the previous year when he stayed at the local hotel which was filled, at the time, with builders doing work in the town:

Some of the builders are fleshy, filled with food, dimpled, curly and big, and others are slender, with naked waists and long fair hair. Some, in little coloured caps, smile at each other and eat quickly. Others eat their food slowly and never raise their eyes. I think of Beethoven's death in my brief-case and begin again to question if my world can ever meet this world. These notes of mine so carefully prepared from years of studying, whatever can they mean here?

"What are you here for anyhow?" The hotel manager asked me last year, and I couldn't explain. (184)

The question that underpins the story is centred on the double nature of the lecturer's discomfort. In other words, if the lecturer is so uncomfortable giving these lectures, why is he giving them? This points, in turn, to a certain need on his part to be heard, to have his research and rumination expressed, acknowledged, appreciated. In this way the story espouses a dimension of London's story that might be missed in its stark naturalism, in which a man gradually succumbs to the forces of nature, undone by its dumb vicissitudes. Why was he risking the journey in the first place, since he readily admits it was ill-advised? It was so he could be with "the boys", his friends camped further along. The need for fellowship, in other words, has caused him to risk his life. So it is with Jolley's story. It begins with the idea that the lecturer is on a pleasant country drive, but gradually we realise that the lecturer is not driving but *being driven*, and the question of the story becomes, what is driving him?

The answer that the story gives is that he is being driven by memories of elsewhere. We only see glimpses of these memories, that erupt into "the drive" as images and scenes—the dead heifer, the girls on horseback, the house with the blue bricks. In fact, despite the overt setting, it becomes clear that the lecturer is only fractionally present in the wheatbelt of Western Australia and that almost the entirety of his psychic life is transpiring in another scene entirely. "The wheat", as Jolley calls it, is a signifier which allows an almost complete teleporting of the lecturer to an English landscape many decades before where the wheat grows to the sea's edge, which it never does in Western Australia:

I'll drive on to the next horizon and see what lies beyond. I want to come to that place where the wheat drops suddenly into the sea. The place where I am to give my lecture crouches between shorn headlands, half hidden in rain mists and surrounded by that bewilderment of movement where land and water meet. The wheat runs in golden rivers all down that valley and there are sheep on the headlands. Last year I walked alone early in the morning by that rolling, green sea. (184)

It is true of each of Jolley's "wheat" stories—"The Long Distance Lecturer", *Foxybaby* and *The Well*—that the landscape is always doubled in this way.[16] An almost surreal conjoining of a remembered northern European countryside and a currently experienced Australian one. It would be wrong, though, to simply cast this as somehow inauthentic—the usual misreading of Australian conditions by European eyes. To do this would be to miss one of the major arguments in this study, which is the wheatbelt is always the subject of fantasy. The estranging effect of Jolley's wheatbelt merely exposes a fantasy that is at odds with the one we expect to be there—the one given to us by what I have been calling the ideology of wheat.

The Well (1986)

The 1980s were a prolific time for Jolley. As Barbara Milech points out, "after twenty years of the slow hard work of getting published from a regional base, Jolley became a central figure in the distributional and conversational networks of Australian literary production and reception in the 1980s and 1990s."[17] Having gained a national reputation she was now able to find outlets for her work, and novels that she had been working on for years were now reworked and came out in quick succession. She was by this time a tutor in creative writing at the Western Australian Institute of Technology (WAIT, which became Curtin University in 1986). Her fifth novel, *Foxybaby* (1985), begins in a remarkably similar way to "The Long Distance Lecture". A writing teacher, Miss Alma Porch, is driving out to deliver a course in a country town, Cheathem East, somewhere in "the wheat". Again, there is the sensation of innocent pleasure accompanying the journey as she drives through stubbled paddocks, singing to herself, "snug" in her Volkswagen. Occasionally, a shadow falls across the idyll, and her excitement at the feeling of escape is dampened by an anxiety about the kind of students she might have to face: "With failing confidence she thought of the death of Chekhov in her brief case and other unsuitable things remembered and stuffed in at the last moment. She wondered how the students would respond." (11) Along with this similarity, there is also the sensation that the lulling paddocks of wheat and stubble can induce more baroque hallucinations or fancies:

> There are strange things about driving alone on long lonely roads through the wheat. Old, grey, bent men and women wait indefinitely on green misleading corners, becoming part of the bushy roadside undergrowth as soon as the helpful traveller stops to investigate. Comfortable inviting tracks in the twilight, lined with soft sand and leaves, appear to lead off easily to the right as the main road curves to the left. And, as dusk advances, more gnarled old men march in formation, keeping up a remarkable speed, alongside, in the shadowy fringes of the saltbush. Occasionally a solitary driver pulls off on to the shoulder of the road to allow a ship to cross in front of him from one moonlit paddock to another. (13–14)

The dreamy drive is brought to a sudden end as she collides with a stationary bus on a curved section of the road, only to be hit herself moments later by the next car behind her. She realises that the isolation of the wheatbelt is partially an illusion, that people move along its various roads at dynamic equidistance, and one need only stop to realise this: "An uncanny concertina-like closing of the long-distance spacing occurs." (15) After the accident, a tow-truck appears and the victims, unhurt, are placed aboard the bus to be delivered to Cheathem East. Miss Porch drifts into sleep and almost all of the novel is given over to a dream of what occurs when she reaches the school where she is to deliver her classes.

In *Foxybaby*, there is little that we might say belongs to the wheatbelt. Its social texture is completely absent, and so are the rhythms of its seasons, the patterns of its ecology and the histories that condition its existence. Jolley was somewhat bemused to receive

446

a letter from a reader in England thanking her for setting her novel in East Anglia.[18] And yet one can sympathise with this reader because although Jolley insists that it is based in the Western Australian wheatbelt, the novel is strikingly devoid of locality. Having been largely sponsored by a regional Arts centre, Jolley certainly believed in the value of regional identity. In 1978, she was a panellist at the Fremantle Arts Centre's seminar on "Regionalism in Contemporary Australian Literature".[19] But, more than this, as a writer Jolley was remarkable for the tremendous work she did connecting with readers, taking to heart the problems that they might have with her. She wanted to be understood, and strove towards creating environments where this understanding might take place in ways that did not compromise the complexity of the truths she was trying to articulate. She saw a connection, in fact, between autobiographical fidelity and regional distinctiveness:

> My fiction is not autobiographical but, like all fiction, it springs from moments of truth and awareness, from observation and experience. I try to develop the moment of truth with the magic of the imagination. I try too to be loyal to this moment of truth and to the landscape of my own region or the specific region in which the novel or story is set. I have always felt that the best fiction is regional. In Western Australia, in the vastness of this one-third of the whole continent, there are a variety of regions from the seacoast through to the deserts that separate us from the rest of Australia.[20]

But having asserted that her fiction is true to its regional setting she then adds this qualification: "The landscape of my fiction is not to be found exactly on any map but I am faithful to the landscape and I do not make mistakes. I never have water flowing where it could never flow ..." (49; original ellipsis). The curious remark at the beginning of the passage above, that her fiction was "not autobiographical", can thus be seen as a corollary to her insistence that she is "faithful to the landscape"—in both cases she is citing an interceding level of truth, what might be called the truth of fiction, in which the outward facts of a place or of a life are not as important as the inward ones which derive from emotional reality: how something truly feels.

57. Elizabeth Jolley in her studio at Wooroloo in 1986. Photograph courtesy of Christina Wilcox.

All of this needs to be borne in mind when one considers the wheatbelt in Jolley's fiction. In *Foxybaby*, the wheatbelt functions as little more than an enchanted forest through which the protagonist—Miss Alma Porch—can meet herself in the primary fantasies that otherwise lie submerged in her life as a middle-aged, middle-class school teacher. It is quite correct that Jolley's fiction speaks of "the wheat" rather than "the wheatbelt" because what we get is not a place but, as we saw in "The Long Distance Lecture", a signifier which announces the eruption of primal memories and scenes. To enter "the wheat" in Jolley's work is to enter the deep antiquity, not of nature, but of one's own subjective formation in the psychodramas of infancy. This basic axiom holds true in Jolley's most famous novel, *The Well* (1986), although it also portrays the wheatbelt as a social world and an economic enterprise. The protagonist is once again a woman well past the middle of her life, childless and eccentric, fussy and forbidding. We are once again going to be cast into the realm of primary fantasy—the fantasies of childhood which provide the unconscious coordinates of our erotic, adult life—as is signalled by an ominous epigraph:

> "What have you brought me, Hester? What have you brought me from the shop?"
>
> "I've brought Katherine, Father," Miss Harper said. "I've brought Katherine, but she's for me."

At this point, none of the characters have been introduced and we can know nothing more than the intimation that the novel is to be concerned with a contested transaction between a father and a daughter. The novel gradually fleshes out the basic milieu which occasions this exchange:

> Hester Harper was no longer young when her father, old Harper, died. In spite of a lame leg which caused her to walk awkwardly leaning on a stick, and in spite of her own advancing years, she decided that she would continue to run the property.
>
> Following her father's ways and wearing all the keys on a gold chain round her neck she concentrated on wheat and sheep; the sheep being able to feed extensively on the endless stretches of wheat stubble when there was very little else for them to eat.
>
> The keys on their valuable mooring were not an ornament but were more of a reassurance. She wore them hidden beneath the bodice of her dress and was able to feel them, every minute of the day and night (when she was awake), nestling between her rather flat breasts. She did not wear rings or ornaments of any kind. Only the keys. (9)

The farm that Hester had inherited from her father was one of the largest and most prosperous in the district, facts which conferred on her certain privileges. She treats others with short shrift, and refuses to suffer fools gladly. Nevertheless, she is generally respected by her neighbours, if not especially liked. Even before her father dies, she has for some time been running the affairs of the farm. Within the patriarchal expectations of the wheatbelt she has become, as it were, the son and heir.

Despite her wealth, she watches her money carefully and keeps a close eye on her employees, who do the heavy work required to run the farm, now that her father is in his twilight years. All of this changes, however, when on a visit to town she meets Kathy, a teenage girl working for the local shopkeeper Mrs Grossman. Kathy had been sent to work at the shop from an orphanage but Mrs Grossman had found there was not sufficient work to keep her. On a whim, Hester offers to take Kathy to help her around the house and Mrs Grossman agrees. Taking her home, Hester introduces Kathy to her father and the exchange given in the epigraph is repeated, this time with a context that allows us to understand it:

> "I've brought Katherine, father," Miss Harper said, indicating with a toss of her head where Katherine should put the sack of sugar she was dragging across the boards. "But she's for me," she added.
>
> "Let's have a good look at you Kathy," Mr Harper said, "let's see if your legs are good." He poked his stick under her skirt flipping the material up. "Give her a pinch," he said to Mr Bird, "on the bottom," he added. Mr Bird, grinning, leaned forward making a pecking movement with his thumb and forefinger but Kathy, who was nimble, jumped aside. (13)

Like much of Jolley's fiction, there is a distinct folktale sensibility at work in this novel. Kathy is an uncanny figure. Clearly she is at the mercy of her new environment, but she is no fainting Gothic victim. Instead, she shows herself to be more than a match for her new captors. She soon has Hester wrapped around her finger, continuously calling her "Miss Harper, dear" as if it is she, and not Hester, who is the seductress.

When the father dies, Hester loses all interest in running the farm and it begins to decline financially, much to the distress of the family's accountant, Mr Bird. Hester realises that all her interest has become fixed on Kathy and, though she apprehends that this obsession is not in the best interests of either party, she is powerless to stop it. A strange romance ensues:

She treated Katherine with an affectionate though severe generosity. She did not regard herself as a mother or even as an aunt. She did not attempt to give any name to the relationship. She realized quite quickly that she was possessive. She knew she was irritable and restless during the evenings if Katherine was writing a letter to one of the girls she had grown up with at the convent. And if a letter came for Katherine she always expected to be shown the contents. (19)

Katherine also causes a sea-change in Hester's relationship to expenditure. Once dour and miserly, she now became profligate, buying trifles and trinkets, anything that Katherine wants:

> ... after all the years of careful frugal housekeeping, she became extravagant and wasteful. It seemed that whenever she went with Katherine to the city she had to buy everything they saw. She bought clothes, foods, furniture, cassette players and transistors. They were always needing batteries, cassettes, cooking utensils, jewellery, materials and trimmings, oil paints—for they both fancied themselves as artists— guitars—for they thought they could create a group—and they chose a new piano ... Also Katherine coveted gear from a boutique and Italian leather boots, soft and gracefully elegant, two pairs, one pair plum coloured and the other the colour of fresh milk. (30)

Unable to refuse Katherine anything, but aware that the finances of the dwindling farm could not stretch forever, Hester accedes to a proposal from Mr Bird to rent the main house to a nearby farmer, Mr Borden, with a large family, while she would move with Katherine to a small, disused "shepherd's cottage" on a corner ("dog-leg") of the property. Although it was a demotion of sorts, Hester quickly came to enjoy the increased privacy of this new location and the chance for even greater intimacy with Katherine.

The fly in the ointment, of course, was that Katherine began to chafe under these smothering conditions and, now an adult, started to complain about her lack of freedom. She pleaded with Hester to allow a friend, Joanna, to visit and then, also, to be taught to drive. Hester tried to bat away these pleas but in the end, as with everything, gave in to Katherine's demands. Placating Kathy in this way, Hester was able to keep the two of them together in this bower tucked away from the prying eyes of a rural community. Next to the cottage was a well, which appeared to be dry, and was partially covered by a rusted metal sheet. It became the rubbish bin for the two women, and they put all their unwanted things into it. The housework which had once been such a point of pride for Hester and in whose execution she would sternly supervise Katherine, began to lapse: "Any dish which proved too disgusting to clean was simply carried outside and pushed through the hole in the rotting corrugated-iron cover of the well." (52) Hester no longer cared much for the farm that had been the centre of her life for almost as long as she could remember:

> Thinking of her endless paddocks should comfort her. She loved her land but recently had been forced to realize that the years of drought had now become several years. She was relieved that Mr Borden still wanted to live in the farmhouse. She never went across there. Days, weeks, months, years with Katherine made time go by very quickly. The farmhouse seemed a long way away. (59)

With the farm falling into disarray and money continuing to seep away, Mr Bird comes to Hester with a new proposition from Mr Borden—to buy the farm outright. Mr Bird advises that the sum is good and, given her loss of interest in the property, this presented an opportunity to secure her financial independence into the future.

Hester sells the farm and ignores Mr Bird's advice to invest and live off the earnings, opting instead for money in the bank and drawing upon it freely. Meanwhile, to celebrate the acquisition of the plum property in the district, the Bordens announce a big party to be held at the local hotel and invite the whole town, including Hester and Katherine. Hester would prefer not to go, but Katherine is thrilled at the prospect of a big social event at which she could dress up and go dancing. The event was doubly vexing for Hester. Not only was she having to share Katherine with the world, but the party was a celebration, in effect, of her own divestment. She had not just sold her land but, she gradually realised, her standing in the community:

Though the deal had taken considerable time Harper's good reputation was, all at once, overnight it seemed, Borden's. A dull echo resounded in her head, not a headache exactly but a threat of one perhaps; the echo throbbed; Miss Harper's grand champion ewe, Miss Harper's prize-winning ram and Miss Harper's harvest. Harper's Place had become Borden's Place, the property of Mr Borden and his wife, Rosalie. Mr Borden said, she remembered, that he might keep the name of Harper's Place. Hester knew that a place name came from what it is, the place, was known by. She knew at once the place would be called Borden's. In her mind she saw the old house at dusk, closed up and secretive as she had seen it often, raised high on the slope facing west. She wished she had not come. (88)

The Bordens had six sons, all bred to take over farming duties in due course, and it is this patrilineal usurpation that shakes Hester Harper most of all—this and the sheer act of heterosexual reproduction. The continuous, rude "breeding" of the Bordens seemed to pillory her own life choices, but worse than that, threatened to lure Katherine away from the bower she had created:

> Looking across at him Hester could not help thinking of the fleshy shoulders of the mating bulls. Mr Borden gave the impression of setting about the male task of servicing frequently and thoroughly with a view to enriching his property with a number of sons. The Bordens already had six little boys being raised to reward the farm in the way that well-bred cattle reward. Rearing cattle and children, Hester knew, was a part of farming. Her maidenly mind was quite capable of vividly imagining Mr Borden in performance. She did not blush at her own thoughts as Mrs Borden would have done if she had known exactly what was in the mind of her elderly guest who knew too that there was a certain obligation on the part of the new landowner's wife to take care of her during the horrible evening. (91)

The "horrible evening" keeps getting worse for Hester. At one point she is buttonholed by Mrs Borden, who tells her that "it is not right to keep Katherine, a young woman, shut away." Adding: "I mean, she must think of men, a man? Sometimes?" (94)

At last she escapes Rosalie Borden and tries to recover herself by watching Katherine on the dance floor, where she might enjoy the "infinite secret pleasure" it gave her to see "Kathy abandon herself to her own energy" (95). The evening, in fact, boiled down to this. The pure pleasure she obtained from Kathy, which was nothing short of the repayment of all the pleasure she forsook in the cause of her stern standards, was something she could now no longer relinquish. She had lost every element of her previous life—the farm, the fields, the prize sheep, the hard-won reputation; in short, her very name. And she had lost it so as to hold Kathy and, watching her dance, she was in no doubt that it had been worth it.

> In the privacy beneath her strict clothing she knew she was capable of an inner excitement which belonged only to her. It was a solitary experience but she did not mind this, being simply grateful for it. The music, the beat and the rhythm of the dancing filled her with a glow of satisfaction and a realization of deep happiness. She felt as if she had been singing and dancing, moving in time with the music and with other people. She felt as if her hair was loose and as if her clothes were bright and light and as if they moved too, easily with her own rhythm. She felt free of bitterness, jealousy and longing. She was free from anxiety; who minded now, at this moment, about drought or about floods. She forgot she was lame and had always to depend upon a stick. (95–6)

Hester is caught in the bind that holds all who live pathologically through another. They create their object to be the emblem of a freedom they do not feel they possess and then refuse to set them free; in this way they create an image of their real condition, the prisoner. It is also noticeable that the quality of freedom that Hester finds in Katherine on the dance floor—which briefly pushes away the cares of everyday life—is very similar to the sensations of freedom that both the long-distance lecturer and Alma Porch in *Foxybaby* felt when driving in "the wheat".

On the way home, Katherine insists that she will drive and Hester should rest. Hester gives in without much complaint, exhausted by the night's exertions and indignities. It is here that the book restages an event which, like the epigraph, we had already been given at the start of the novel, before we had any context by which to make sense of it. Katherine, in an exuberant mood, is driving the car quickly on the deserted roads back to their cottage. She is driving dangerously fast and a mist has started to form in the lower parts of the country, causing it to take on a strange, unfamiliar aspect:

> The road between the black paddocks was flat and strange as though they had never travelled along it before. Swirls of white mist came towards them and sometimes when there was a dip in the road they were completely enshrouded in a light white endlessly winding garment. The surrounding countryside, Hester said, could seem desolate and frightening for anyone travelling especially if they had no home to go to. Katherine agreed, she for one would not want to drive the road at night. "I'm glad we're together Miss Harper, dear," she said. (102)

The description of the mist swirling in the hollows enshrouding them "in a light white endlessly winding garment" echoes quite forcefully the image that Katherine's yellow dress had formed in the mind of Hester: "The misty quality of the material had been just right." (102) The linkage is quite important, for it is the fatality of Hester's infatuation with Katherine that is the underlying basis for the "accident" that ensues. Coming too fast around the right-angle bend just before the cottage, Hester loses control and hits "something" on the track:

> "Look out! There's something on the track. Look out! Brake Katherine! Brake. Oh look out! Oh God! The bend!" Hester's shriek stopped abruptly as something hit the car with a heavy dull thud. Katherine stopped the car, the engine was still running.
> "I think we've hit a roo." Hester, grabbing her stick, clambered with difficulty from the truck and limped to the front. "It's not a roo," she called in a low voice. "Don't come out. Stay where you are!" She moved slowly round to Katherine's side. "It's horrible," she said, "it's caught up on the bar. It's …" (102)

It becomes clear that they have actually run over a man. With the man's body still gruesomely snared in the roo-bar, Hester instructs

Katherine to drive the car as close as possible to the well next to their cottage. Once there, Hester grimly unhooks the body from the roo-bar and with some difficulty heaves it into the well. By this time, Katherine is crying hysterically and Hester is telling her over and over again that this is the only thing that they can do.

What the event exposes is that the crime was not so much the running over of the man by Katherine, but the disposal of the body by Hester. In taking this measure, Hester cast the two women, once and for all, beyond the reaches of the law. It has grave consequences, because it results in the insanity of Katherine. Only the law could account for the action and that is what Hester refuses to allow into the scene: "If this thing, now called 'the accident' in her own mind, was ever known about everything they had would be disturbed and spoiled. She was determined that the whole thing was to be considered over and done with." (111) The "accident" occurs near the mid-point of the novel, and causes a dramatic shift in tone. Until then the book was in the register of mild satire, and the disturbing features of the scenario—effectively, Katherine's imprisonment—kept in the realm of eccentricity and human foible. Hester is suddenly revealed as a criminal, not because she had run over the man, but because she will go to any length to conceal the crime, what Veronica Brady called her "guilty need for concealment".[21] Concealing the crime, which she rationalises as necessary to "protect" Katherine from her unfortunate action, is in fact the crime itself, because it is motivated by the need to bond her younger companion permanently under the seal of their transgression.

The novel continues to twist in macabre fashion. Upon entering the house, Hester discovers that a large quantity of cash which she had stowed in a cupboard is missing and deduces that the man had in fact stolen it. It must now be at the bottom of the well, still secreted on his person. It was too great a sum to simply let rot in the ground and she formulates a plan to buy rope and send Katherine down to fetch it:

> "Kathy," she said in a cajoling tone, "it will not be at all difficult. I'll get a rope, a good one, today. I'll go to town. Tonight, when it's dark we'll get our money back."

"It's your money, not mine," Katherine said, "and I'm not going down there. I won't go. I can't! It's too horrible. I can't ... I ... "

"Katherine!" Hester said, "do you want us to starve?"

"It's not all the money you've got, Miss Harper."

"That's beside the point. It happens to be our ready money, we need it right away."

"Not ours, it's yours. Yours! I didn't put it down there."

"Katherine, you must surely understand, it's too much to simply lose like that. You will do as I say and go ..."

"I won't! He's dead. I'd have to touch a dead man. I might have to look for the money on him. I'd have to touch him," Katherine began to cry. "I'm going to be sick. Miss Harper he might have it next to his body, next to his skin, I couldn't do it."

"Yes I know he's dead, Katherine," Hester's voice was low and grim, "and I'll remind you who killed him. Now, you stay here today while I go into town for a proper rope." (114–15)

The enormity of the crime is thus gradually revealed. It was not a murder but was made one by the actions after the event. The killing is seized upon opportunistically by Hester as the grounds for blackmailing Katherine into complete obedience. Hester wishes to complete the enmeshment of Katherine in her crime by having her desecrate the body, which would cast her decisively into culpable complicity.

The crime is also linked quite directly to the loss of Hester's land: "She always felt no harm could come to her once she was on her own property." (125) But now the property was not hers, she was no longer able to maintain the illusion of impunity. As she notices, a little later: "The quiet paddocks on either side of her did not provide the usual comfort." (137) In the story, the various events—the loss of the land, the stealing of the money by the man, Kathy's wish to leave, the killing of the man and his disposal in the well—are welded together, forming a tight nucleus of fear and desire, action and consequence, fantasy and nightmare. The common denominator is the exclusion of masculine authority—the law, in short. This is a fact noticed by early critics of Jolley's work such as Veronica Brady and Joan Kirkby. Brady points out that this feature of Jolley's fiction is not just realised at the level of theme, but inflects the form of her work, causing it to cycle back on itself. This is caused, Brady suggests, by the tension in her characters between the wish to exclude masculine agency from their lives, on the one hand, and a need, on the other, to find something of themselves in this masculine agency:

> The painfulness of this suspension is evident. It makes itself felt in the shape of the narratives which are often hesitant and repetitive. Curiously regressive, they circle obsessively around some primal scene which has to do with the lost father, with what Kristeva characterises as "the law unto the name of the father", the dead man in *The Well* and the absent but longed for father in *My Father's Moon*. Both the stories remain inconclusive because he is never found; the self remains perpetually incomplete, in search of this lost authority, which is unattainable. (51)[22]

Kirkby follows a similar line of thought, emphasising that the father is a key symbolic coordinate in Jolley's fiction—notable most particularly for his absence, what one might call a present absence—because "[b]ehind the father of individual history stands the symbolic father, the representative of 'the law'".[23] In Jolley's work, the "wheat" is a place where the "law" is suspended; in other words, it is outside of the law.

Hester's determination to return their lives to normality after the "accident" meets a new and poignant challenge when she is confronted with the news from Katherine that the man is very much alive at the bottom of the well and that they have been communicating. She has sent him down food and he has asked if she could lower a rope so that he might climb out. The alarmed Hester soon concludes that Katherine has started to hallucinate—she can hear nothing from the well. Katherine's fantasy develops quickly and soon she reports that the two have fallen in love and that the man in the well, who is very well-spoken and quite charming, has asked for her hand in marriage and they were already planning their first child. In this way, the man in the well becomes the embodiment of everything that Hester has forbidden for Katherine, and which amount, in fact, to the same thing—a forfeiting of her right to reproduce. It is here that Jolley's novel intersects with one of the long-standing concerns of wheatbelt literature, which is the anxiety over fertility. The theme of fertility joins together the drive of production—in the fields—and the drive of reproduction, the wish that one's lands might be passed on to heirs, who will pass it on in turn to their progeny and thus the "land" will unite both the dream of dynastic succession and the demands of market-driven commodity capitalism.

But the places where we have seen this dynastic dream—most notably in the sagas of Ewers and the stories of Peter Cowan, has typically been a masculine one. This idea of a handing down of land to sons by fathers was the subject of critique, not so much in Hewett, where one might expect to see it, but in the work of Barbara York Main. In Hewett's case, there was instead a complaint directed at the maternal line—her mother and her mother's mother—for emasculating the men in their lives and leaving the "land" desolate and embittered. From the 1960s, it was the image of salt, of secondary soil salinity, that became the sign of this defeat of sexual relations. Jolley's work also uses the land as a sign that all is not well in the field of human reproduction. The slow and steady decline of Hester's farm seems to mirror the slow and steady decline of her father's health and potency. The horrific developments that emerge in the latter half of the novel seem both caused by, and at the same time to cause, a further alienation of Hester from the land in which she had centred her existence hitherto. So, when Katherine begins to rave about the man in the well and how she will marry him and have his child, it fills Hester with terror:

> "Katherine stop! Stop this. At once!" Fear. All the fear which Hester had often imagined could dissipate itself into the light gently moving air if she walked small and safe, low close down to the earth, along the road beneath the immense sky and between endless paddocks was in her voice when she spoke. (150–1)

The terrifying thing for Hester is that it does not matter if she knows the man in the well is dead, her world is ruined for so long as Katherine believes that he is alive.

A stand-off ensues as Katherine plots to get hold of the rope she knows Hester has bought—so she can rescue her new lover—and Hester tries to talk Katherine into giving up her delusional belief, knowing that they would be exposed if she could not prevail. The affair reaches a climax when it begins to rain heavily and the water level in the well starts to rise, carrying the corpse ever upward. Hester was torn between a terror at having the body float back into sight and, as it were, manifest itself, and a hope that in this way she may yet get back the money she had lost. But as she ponders this, she is interrupted by the sight of headlights crossing the paddocks, and she is visited by the new owner of the farm, Mr Borden, who had come to check how she and Katherine were faring in the storm. He notices the damaged well-cover and offers to send someone in the daylight to fix it. This closure of the well's aperture duly takes place the next morning and, with it, the delusion that had gripped Katherine seems to vanish.

The novel ends, therefore, in a minor key—the denouement strangely quiet after the grotesque, hysterical events of the previous evening. Katherine seems to have forgotten about the man in the well, the event now "sealed" by the new well-cover installed by Borden's men. Hester and Katherine return to the preparations they had been making for the visit of Joanna, Katherine's friend, but the atmosphere has changed, somehow cooler and cleaner than before, a distance now between the two women: "Katherine had developed a different way of speaking. Her voice was flat and often she did not look up when she replied to anything Hester said." (214) Again, as the rhythm of domestic activity re-emerges, the alteration in mood is paralleled with a change in the relation that Hester feels towards the land. Significantly, Hester awaits the visit of Mr Bird, who she has not seen for some time now:

> During those few days, during the relentless cleaning of the rooms, the relining of the scrubbed-out cupboards with fresh shelf paper, the airing of more blankets and the sewing of yet another frilled quilt for Joanna's bed, Hester was sure Mr Bird would come. She looked frequently across the paddocks to the rise to watch for his cloud of dust and then remembered, as if stepping into another world, that the

rain had come and there would be no dust. The steady drone of the tractors, sometimes near and sometimes far off, as they crossed and recrossed ploughing the rain-softened earth, enhanced the emptiness and the isolation. (213)

The final sentence in this paragraph could have been written by Peter Cowan, with its quiet repeated phrasings—"sometimes near and sometimes far off", "crossed and recrossed"—and the slight suggestion of melancholy that the scene evokes.

Some days later, Hester and Katherine head into town, and Hester drops Katherine at the markets, no longer afraid that she will "blurt out" the whole hideous story. She goes to visit Mr Bird at his office and finds, to her shock, that he has been taken to the hospital in the city with a haemorrhage. The situation is explained by Mr Bird's assistant, a woman Hester has never met. Hester, who needs to rearrange her affairs, is taken to the books Mr Bird had kept on her property. There, she finds an exercise book listing transactions and balances, and prefaced by an instructional note to her, handwritten by Mr Bird, setting out her investments and advising her how to manage these in simple, straightforward words. Reading Mr Bird's note, Hester finds herself weeping uncontrollably:

> She could not go on reading. The little exercise books were a powerful indication of how she had been looked after and she was ashamed because she had never wanted to know and had never given a glance or a smile of gratitude or a word of thanks. She understood too, at once, that she needed to be looked after, cared for, more than ever. She had never felt so afraid and so alone. (223)

Mr Bird never recovers, dying in hospital. The novel ends with Hester running out of petrol on her way with Katherine to pick up Katherine's friend, Joanna, from the station. It is an annoyance, but nothing more than that. She begins to walk up the road towards the roadhouse:

> Hester is walking at the side of the long straight road low down between the brown paddocks which stretch endlessly on both sides to

far-away horizons. A practical consideration which can bring a human being into perspective, she thinks, is the knowledge that a tiny handful of people produce from the vast landscape enormous quantities of food. The great dome of the familiar sky is above like a never-ending floating roof of light clean air. (225)

The intrusion of this "practical consideration"—the wheatbelt's economic function—had been presaged by the "steady drone of the tractors" in the earlier passage. It is something which exists only fleetingly in Jolley's fiction; but it is there, nevertheless. In a more direct sense, this pressure to produce—which was a steady motif in the fiction, memoir and natural history of Barbara York Main—is embodied in the novel by the Borden family, who, as we have also noted, are the agents of the pressure to reproduce as well. And Hester Harper does bear a resemblance to the aging, eccentric women who are the heroines of York Main's stories "The Pyrophiles" (1970) and "Marginal Country" (1972), holding out in obstinate defiance against the Bordens in their lives.

Against a view of the land based entirely on what it can produce when "worked", Hester and the women in York Main's stories suggest, and it is admittedly a subtle difference, a view of what the land might provide when it is let be:

As she walks she tells herself that she must enjoy the feeling of her own insignificance which is enhanced by the indifference of the land. This silent indifference towards human life can make her feel small and safe. It is a safety which brings freedom for the time being. It is a freedom from fear. As she is able to sift her thoughts and feelings she knows, as she has always known, if there are several fears then there are really none. (226)

Here, though, Jolley moves into territory not canvassed in York Main; the deepest terrors of existence. York Main's writing takes place, for the most part, on the other side of grief—in the calm ache of reality grasped as it actually is. It is from this point that she is able to see ecological loss, in all its dreadful totality, and still find hope. Jolley's writing emerges at the point just prior to grief—in the frantic, final throes of refusal, where the world fills up with sinister intimations and nameless fears, and whose appearance marks the boundary of the ground that must, in the end, be traversed. In this way, *The Well* marks a significant evolution in emotional consequence from the story that might be seen as its earliest predecessor, "The Long Distance Lecture", and, too, from the dream-novel *Foxybaby*. It points, in fact, to the thoroughgoing recapitulation of Jolley's formative experience in the "Vera" trilogy—*My Father's Moon* (1989), *Cabin Fever* (1990), *The George's Wife* (1993)—written in the cool precision of the author's late style, which almost completely abandons the gothic comedy and surrealist grotesqueries of her writing in the 1970s and 80s. In this context, the wheatbelt seems to have acted as a curtain which held the events of her emotional life just out of view, or visible only in its lineaments or basic shape.

The emphasis that is always placed on "the wheat" in her writing—and we see it even in the passage above depicting Hester on the roadside with a petrol can—is upon its endlessness, the fact that it extends in all directions to "far-away horizons". It is this quality which indicates that the wheatbelt exists in Jolley's fiction as the space of escape, which is to say, the space of fantasy. But fantasy does not exist as a stable bubble in the swirl of life without the investment of significant energy and nor is it sensible to think of escape without thinking too of what is being escaped. This is the point which was raised earlier in the context of "The Long Distance Lecture" when the question was asked: *what is driving the driver?* This question is given shape by considering, as one and the same thing, the issue of where the driver is driving *to* and where the driver is driving *from*. What this provides is a model for the way that memory and fantasy are connected, which is through a compulsion to repeat—this is the name given to the phenomenon, so common in horror films, whereby running away from something takes us directly to it. What happens, though, in *The Well,* is that Hester does eventually stop running. The endlessness of the wheat fields brings her a strange gift, which is actually her original fear, but now in a form which she can see and, though it breaks her heart, cope with. Realising that "if there are several fears then there are really none", she knows that to see her fear truly is to realise it in its singularity:

> One fear on its own, is really fear and it is one fear that she has. Out between the apparently deserted paddocks it seems to be dissipated and she can say aloud in a croaking sort of voice, talking to herself, that if Kathy wants to go with Joanna to the city—to America—wherever it is people go these days, she, Hester, must not mind. Of course she minds, she says; she does mind … (226; original ellipsis)

But the difference this time is that although she does not want it to happen, she knows Kathy must leave, and she will not finally oppose it. It was the events in the well that had brought about this change—the encounter with the man's dead body, driven upwards by the swell of the storm, where she forfeits the right to recover her stolen money and allows the other men to re-cap the well. In other words, she allows him to be properly buried. The events in the well are similar in quality and function to the actions of the "night people" in Hewett's *Man from Mukinupin* (1979). These events are the site of excluded thoughts and wishes, and of the dramatic residue of foundational crimes.

Allowing the man in the well to be laid to rest, rather than desecrated, then extends into the affairs of the "day" world with the death of Mr Bird, who never recovers from his aortic haemorrhage. This further news does not crush Hester, because she had already begun to mourn his passing when she read his note to her in his office. She is picked up on the roadside by Mrs Borden in a car filled with her young boys who are talking over each other in the back-seat. They had seen her car stopped further back and Katherine waiting inside, doing some hand-sewing. The boys had noticed that the spotlight on the front of her Toyota had been broken: "under the cover it's all splintery … all smashed and splintery …" (230). Hester had previously checked and thought that the car had escaped, remarkably, without a mark after the accident, but she had not checked behind the spotlight cover. The image of a shattered lens beneath an intact cover is an echo of the broken things that lay beneath the new well cover, and points more profoundly to the state of Hester, and perhaps even further to something like a general condition in human subjectivity. It also alludes to the idea that "the wheat" is a kind of coating across the surface of things, masking a shattered reality. The novel ends with

Hester promising the Borden children to tell the story of how the light had been broken:

> As they drive back with the petrol they can see the gun-metal colour of the Toyota gleaming on the slight rise. The immense landscape dwarfs all human life. Hester is grateful for the smallness of the Toyota. It is not possible from this distance to see the small figure within bent with devotion over her sewing. In a few years Hester thinks they will all be gone, even these children, *as the one dieth, so dieth the other.* Of course she cannot say this aloud and these children are so much alive, their life seems to come through their skin.
>
> "It was one dark night," she tells them, "along this very road only much farther on … something … happened …" (234; original italics)

We are not to know the version of the story that Hester will give to the boys. Because they are not expecting the truth, but simply a story, it is quite possible she could even tell the truth and it would not matter. The novel's closing landscape image is once again one of an immensity that "dwarfs all human life", which on this occasion does not cause fear, but becomes a kind of comfort.

What Jolley offers to the corpus of wheatbelt literature is something quite significant. Though the picture we get is only, perhaps, very partially based on the experience of wheatbelt life, it is nevertheless a picture which captures a key tension in the wheatbelt's imaginative dynamics. This is the fact that the wheatbelt has always been, since its inception, a place of escape, driven by a hope for a "better" life. We saw this in the enthusiasm that Facey's uncle Archie had to finally own land, no matter how primitive and raw the existence it was to give. It was something that infused the poetry of Cyril E. Goode, turning it from exaltation to despair as the prospects for this better life waxed or waned. Cowan's writing, too, to say nothing of his own life, testify to the draw of the wheatbelt as a place where one might seek meaning or regeneration, or simply privacy or anonymity. But Jolley's writing is original in that this movement away and into the wheatbelt does not deliver this change into a simpler order of things, but produces the grounds for the full emergence of the things one sought to leave—the dark memories that condition our inner life and provide its horizons. Jolley, in other words, is the first to produce a Gothic wheatbelt. Hewett, we have seen, was the writer that, in "Legend of the Green Country", imbued the wheatbelt with a tragic dimension, with a world in which the king had died and the land had gone to ruin. This tragic dimension of loss and crime—particularly environmental destruction and Aboriginal dispossession—is then put into a register of uncanny farce in her musical play, *The Man from Mukinupin*, but in none of these works do we feel the element of fear. Fear is the great gift of Jolley's wheatbelt and it is this dimension which dominates the work of the remaining writers in this study—Tom Flood and John Kinsella.

58. Elizabeth Jolley at Wooroloo in 1986. Photograph courtesy of Christina Wilcox.

Chapter Ten

Tom Flood (1955–)

Wickepin (1956)
Beacon (1973)
Marvel Loch (1974)
Esperance (1975)

Dorothy Hewett left Perth with Les Flood in 1948, and the pair lived together in Sydney for eleven years before Hewett returned to Perth in 1959. During those eleven years, Hewett and Flood had three children—Joe, Michael and Tom. As we have seen in our chapter on Hewett, she took all three boys with her back to Perth, and there she met and married Merv Lilley and had two daughters with him—Kate and Rozanne. Three of Hewett's children pursued a life in letters, both of her daughters and her youngest son, Tom Flood, who was born in Sydney in 1955. Of these, Tom has won the greatest acclaim—a reputation based largely on a single, remarkable novel set in the wheatbelt, *Oceana Fine* (1989).[1] The novel won the *Australian/ Vogel's* Literary Award in 1988 for the best novel manuscript by an Australian under thirty-five years of age. The award is co-sponsored by Allen & Unwin, who under the terms of the prize also agree to publish the winning entry. Published in 1989, the book went on to win, in 1990, the Vance Palmer Prize for Fiction at the Victorian Premier's Literary Awards, and Australia's premier literary award, the Miles Franklin. *Oceana Fine* begins as a murder mystery in which a young wheat-sampler is killed in mysterious circumstances at Marvel Loch in the far eastern wheatbelt. The death of this young man is then displaced by a completely different storyline, written in a completely different mode. In this story, we go back to the wheatbelt's origins in the early twentieth century and move forward in time by following the lives of the Cleaver family as they survive and grow their farm through the years until the present. The stories are united as the novel reaches an elaborate, macabre conclusion.

Flood's knowledge of the wheatbelt came from two main sources. The first was his family history, particularly the elaborate wheatbelt mythology evolved by his mother Dorothy Hewett. The second was his own experience working on "the bins" in the outer wheatbelt in the 1970s. After attending Kent Street High School, Flood enrolled at The University of Western Australia in 1973, and that summer worked as a sampler on the wheat bin at Beacon, 42 kilometres north of Bencubbin in the northeastern fringe of the wheatbelt. "Beacon", recalls Flood, was "more of a district than a town": "Head north on the Goomalling Rd, via Cadoux, Burakin, Kulja. It's pretty stark out there. Saltbush, salt lakes, myall scrub, spindly gums, big cleared paddocks of wheat."[2] The following summer Flood worked the bin at Marvel Loch, where *Oceana Fine* is set, also in the outer extremity of the wheatbelt. It was this experience that inspired the novel: "The principal catalyst for *Oceana Fine* was the time at Marvel Loch bin. It was the most striking in my memory, and the most mythical. The first three quarters of Section One [of the novel] are really verbatim from that experience, although there are many more stories from that bin than reflected in the novel."[3] Flood then worked a third summer, the summer of 1975–76 in a bin near Esperance. In 1978 he departed Western Australia permanently and has lived the remainder of his life in New South Wales.

Oceana Fine (1989)

We have already glimpsed the beginning of *Oceana Fine*, which I quoted in the introduction to this book. It begins with a young man driving his battered Holden ute into the wheatbelt on the Great Eastern Highway. The time is somewhere in the early- to mid-1970s. The driver is Finlay "Finn" Torrent, a science student at The University of Western Australia. It is early summer but the landscape is already parched and spreads out endlessly before him as he drives to take up his job at Marvel Loch, on the far eastern edge of the wheatbelt, where he will work as a sampler at the receival bin during the harvesting period. It is night by the time he arrives, but still the massive "A" Class Bin is clearly visible as he pulls into the deserted facility that will be his home for the next few months:

> The small twisting hills flattened out and there before him was the bin. It was big. A giant shed, bigger than any he'd ever seen ... it sat on the land like a great square Buddha, its dwarfed paraphernalia of equipment and storage falling away from vast iron flanks ... [The] low hills he had come through were already deep shadows. Only the bin shone, burnished silver in the last orange rays, brighter than the new moon already risen over the flat plains of wheat sweeping away to the south. (5)

As in Cowan's *Summer* (1964), the bin takes on a Gothic dimension—looming, cavernous, sinister. It is seemingly out of step with nature; light when everything else is dark, outshining the moon, and existing on a scale that belongs to a wholly different order of being. And, as for Henry in Cowan's novel, the work on the bin brings Finn closer to nature, but not quite in the way that he had hoped.

The following morning Finn is rudely awakened by his "senior" on the bin at Marvel Loch, a man in his early twenties, Mark Reynolds. Reynolds begins immediately to initiate Finn into the world of young rural masculinity. He begins by cooking a breakfast of eggs and chops for Finn:

> "Four chops. I'll be sick if I eat all that."
> "Bullshit! Do y'good. Hard day's work, we got, mucking out the grid. Stinkin' job. Eat it, don' be pissweak. I been on the piss all night, spewed me guts out, an' I could eat twice this. Eh, y'seen the barmaid at Bodallin? Tracey, her name is. Tits? Y'can't find 'em, but boy, does she go. Shaggin' all night, we were. Feels like the old boy's been run over by a semi!" (10)

This kind of off-colour banter, largely one-sided, continues more or less relentlessly. Mark subjects Finn to various pranks, including driving him at breakneck speed in the scoop of a front-end loader.

When the bin opens, Finn meets the local growers, who are led by the gregarious, middle-aged Rex Cleaver, who had "something of the clergy in his demeanour, though well hidden by the down-to-earth man-of-the-land cover" (12). Cleaver was the elder-statesman of the district, a one-time shire president and pillar of the National Party. He offers Finn a beer and then a slice of his local bread, which he has named "Heart of Gold":

> "It's the best bread you'll ever taste. And that's got nothing to do with my baking. You try any bread from this area and it'll be just as good. The type of bread may differ but the goodness is inherent." A thick finger pointed at the billowing fields of wheat. "That's the best bread wheat in the world. I guarantee you won't get even one truckload of less than top grade the whole time you're here. All you see is beautiful rich wheat so golden you could mint it." (14)

Finn realises that it is likely that Cleaver is just buttering him up because he is the new sampler and his results would have material consequences for Cleaver and the other farmers. Nevertheless, after a week working side-by-side with Reynolds, it was a relief for Finn to speak with someone who gave some thought to the world around him. The sacramental aspect of wheat—the "inherent" source of bread's goodness—is emphasised by the communion that Cleaver offers, and he encourages Finn to reveal his underlying motivation for his coming to the bin:

> "… that's what I've been waiting for, you see. To be part of the harvest. That's why I took the job. I wanted to see if I could find something in the country. In nature. All of this," he said looking past the other man's shoulder at something he seemed to see halfway to the horizon. "And me part of it." (14)

The simple earnestness of Finn's hope is one that is now familiar to us, evident in the very earliest expressions of wheatbelt literature, such as Ewers's poem "Wheat Men" from 1926. Yet this hope contains, as we have seen, two quite distinct—perhaps irreconcilable—pleas. On the one hand it is to be part of *nature*, and on the other, to be part of *the harvest*.

As the novel develops, this quandary (the conflict between the wish to be immersed in nature and also to capitalise on it) becomes more and more visible. But even at this early point, Finn's romantic desire is quickly, and perhaps a little surprisingly, struck down by Cleaver, who turns to the fields that Finn was gazing dreamily upon and says:

> "See that out there. There's nothing natural out there, boy. That's built by man's hand. The granary of the world. Nature couldn't even begin to do that. It's the biggest factory you'll ever work in, Finlay. A production line of planting and growing and harvesting that Henry Ford would be proud of. It's streamlined to produce the most wheat in the shortest possible time. Those heads of wheat out there, they're ten times the size of wild wheat and they grow so quickly they could never reproduce themselves in that volume. That's Oceana Fine. Machine-planted, man-made, Finlay. An interloper, or thing threatening to it, is poisoned or shot. That's monoculture, Finlay, like the city. It's a city of wheat." (14)

This summation is something quite new in wheatbelt literature. Certainly, there was the awareness of the artifice that the wheat farms had introduced into nature—a fact underscored by Pete Rodon in Pollard's *The Bushland Man* (1926) and Avea Lea in Ewers's wheatbelt saga. And in the natural histories of Barbara York Main, we apprehend the deep division between the emptiness of the rectilinear fields and the density of life in the bushland remnants. But no one had yet gone as far as Flood does here in seeing the wheatbelt as pure economic artefact—one that was obtained and is maintained by ardent and violent control: "An interloper, or thing threatening to it, is poisoned or shot." (14)

In *Oceana Fine*, what we see for the first time is the concept of the wheatbelt as a geo-economic totality; in effect, a massive "factory" spread over the landscape on a scale almost incommensurate with life—and only made possible by industrial fertilisers and sophisticated machinery. And pursued in a manner inimical to all life-forms other than the chosen crops. Cleaver's speech needs to be seen as representing a crucial new phase in the understanding of the wheatbelt. What he declares to Finn, in many ways, predicts the entire oeuvre of John Kinsella's wheatbelt poetry. It is uncertain at this point of the novel whether Cleaver's insistence on the wheatbelt's artifice is made in triumph or in denunciation. In many ways, this crucial ambiguity defines both Flood's remarkable novel and the twenty-first century wheatbelt. The problem is now, for the first time, seen in all its horror: not that the wheatbelt might fail, but that it has succeeded. The beginnings of this position appear in Cowan's fiction and in the vignettes of Barbara York Main, but the full metaphysical implications—that the wheatbelt has destroyed the very hope of natural immersion that helped to found and sustain it—do not fully materialise until this point in the late 1980s.

On the fourth day after the bin had opened, a disturbing incident occurs. Finn finds a severed human finger lying "among the golden grains" (17). The farmers explain that the finger was the result of an accident, caused by a drunken header-driver who had already lost two other fingers in this fashion. Nevertheless, the appearance of the finger is a sign of something more serious. That the finger had appeared in the sample, in the scientific heart of the wheat's harvest, suggests that the instrumental goals of the wheatbelt were no longer to be completely divorced from the carnal world of human passion. Finn's story culminates shortly afterward. He decides to investigate the interior of the bin, which had been closed since its cleaning the previous week. He shimmies up the grain elevator and makes his way into the bin via the ceiling. There he discovers two bodies—a young man and a young woman—hanging in the darkness:

> It was a body. A human body, gone slightly off. He turned away in horror. It had appeared to be strung naked on a piece of wire dangling about four metres off the ground. The wire was passed through the flesh of the ribcage and caught somehow inside. He thought he would vomit. He held his breath and looked again. It was a youngish man, the face obscured by the head hanging down, the chin resting on the chest. Standing under the body was bound sheaf of unthreshed wheat. He looked away and, as he did so, a similar sight on the other side of the catwalk caught his eye, this one a woman. (25)

59. The beginning and the end of the wheatbelt at Ghooli. Marvel Loch is roughly 20 kilometres south of this.

Hysterical with fear, Finn makes his way back outside and down to the ground. His car will not start and so he sets out on foot just as a dust storm begins to darken the skies. Battered by the dust, he finds himself in a wheatfield on his hands and knees and feels he is becoming, in grotesque accord with his earlier wish, a part of nature. Finn dies alone in the field.

Magical Realism

With the death of Finn Torrent, Flood's novel shifts back in time a decade or more to the year 1960. The new section begins enigmatically: "It was another time. A time when the big house still stood. When the family was still known in that district. When the order of our lives stretched back to another country and every day was clearly planned and ruled off, as was the custom, in the big house ledger." (35) The narrator is James Cleaver, the youngest son of Rex Cleaver, the farmer who had espoused the virtues of wheat to Finn at the Marvel Loch bin. In many ways, the novel ends up being the story of Rex Cleaver. James tells us that his father had acquired the property—dubbed "Cleaver's Lot"—at Marvel Loch in 1946. The farm was near a goldmine, which Rex had helped manage during the 1930s.[4] Rex Cleaver had bought the farm from the Agricultural Bank, who had acquired it upon the death of its former owner, Otto Tinkler. Tinkler was an Austrian who had "cleared and partly fenced the land in the tougher days of the 30s and who even managed to eke out a living when most of his neighbours were walking off their places." (46) But Tinkler was interned when World War Two broke out, and the property was confiscated. During his internment, Tinkler died and the property passed back to the Agricultural Bank. Cleaver moved to Marvel Loch with his wife and baby son in 1946 and was eventually joined there by his parents (Ben and Chloe Cleaver) and by his aunt, Grace (Chloe's younger sister), who moved from their farm at Yealering to "Cleaver's Lot" in 1950. James was born, like the author himself, in 1955, and by the time he was five, the 1960s were dawning and would begin to decisively break from the world before: "a decade that would change a whole country: Vietnam, the hippies, conscription, rock music, divorce, satellites, the Pill, TV, drug culture, dollars and cents, mini skirts, 727s, the world was about to invade Western Australia, though there was little sign of it on the face of Rex Cleaver, father, farmer and owner of the Marvel Loch Miracle." (39) James also discloses certain, troubling facts about his own life. For instance, his mother ("Margie") had killed herself immediately after his birth. Also, it seems doubtful that Rex was, after all, his father. James was of a noticeably darker complexion than the other children (his brothers call him "boong-face"), and this was also said to have contributed to Margie's suicide. As a baby, James was also "dropped" at one point, breaking his ankles and leaving him with disfigured feet and a stumbling walk.[5]

James's broken ankles are metaphorical of his traumatic origins, and beyond that the traumatic origins of the wheatbelt itself. In many ways, it is Flood's novel that makes us feel breakage for the first time in relation to the wheatbelt as a literary artefact. This is closely related to the advent of postmodernism, a change in historical consciousness that we will see as a defining feature of the poetry of John Kinsella. We have seen that industrial modernity was present in the wheatbelt from the outset. Indeed, it could not have been developed without railways and industrial fertilisers. But in the 1960s, we begin to enter the post-industrial age. This sensitivity to rupture is the great innovation of Flood's novel and is signalled by a fundamental shift in the form of the narrative itself. With the death of Finn, the novel effectively changes registers. If the opening chapter had resembled a crime novel, the remainder of the book is written in that style, so popular in the 1980s and '90s, known as "magical realism". Its hallmark is a certain playful relation to the facts of the world and to "history". Magical realism is most closely associated with Latin American fiction, particularly the works of the Colombian writer Gabriel Garcia Marquez, but applies as well to writers such as Günter Grass, Angela Carter and Salman Rushdie. It is typical of the magical realist novel that it takes the form of an ironic epic, where history loses its sober hold on reality and is brought back to the level of rumour, innuendo, farce and family mythology.

Like other magical realists, Flood is both captivated and deeply suspicious of history. His novel wants to encompass the epic dimension of the wheatbelt but also to debunk its claims to heroism. This fraught sense of history, so typical of the decades leading to the millennium, seems directly linked to a decline in the legitimacy of the family. Michael Heald's review of the novel for *Westerly* in 1990 astutely noticed that "*Oceana Fine* is in fact a kind of family history".[6] Or, to use the term I have favoured in this study, the novel is a generational saga, a story of the hopes and tribulations of an extended family as it falls through time. It is instructive to compare the Cleavers in Flood's novel with the Leas in Ewers's novels. In both cases, we are reminded that the family is the key social unit of the wheatbelt and the wheatbelt's formation was driven by the particular energies that animate family life. Both Flood and J.K. Ewers rely on the family as the vehicle of history. But whereas Ewers used the Lea family to unify the wheatbelt story, to give it shape and historical direction, Flood uses the ambiguities of family life, its strange mixture of fact and legend, its inconsistencies and telling silences, to evoke a history of the wheatbelt that is anything but unified. Indeed, the name "Cleaver" encapsulates the ambiguity of biography, because cleave means, depending on context, either to join together (to "cleave to") and to split apart (to "cleave in two"). What the novel postulates—and this is true more generally of magical realism—is an equivalence between the problem of knowing history and the problem of knowing the truth about one's family's past. As James puts it: "Childhood histories seem always only partially remembered and largely gleaned from family stories that slowly homogenise as the past recedes, until the reality of events is finally set in a well-rehearsed, widely accepted tale." (42)

However, despite their differing treatments of the family, the novels of both Ewers and Flood retain a special determining role for families. They also each reveal a particular mixture we find in the wheatbelt of bourgeois values—tidiness, prudence, education, improvement, home and hearth—and a more grandiose, dynastic sense of history and succession. Each farm was not just a minor agricultural enterprise, a family business; it was also a historical achievement whose evidence was in the landscape. In this way, each family farm in the wheatbelt could feel itself to have its own history, something that was written into the earth with the blood, sweat and tears of those who went before. This sense of being the product of an epic history and not just of economic necessity is bolstered by the continual linkage of the wheatbelt to the history of the world at large. Again, each farm seems to offer itself as a record through time of the world's great events— wars, economic collapse, gold rushes, technological revolutions. But Flood's novel does not allow this mythologising wish to triumph. The novel asks serious questions about the ideology of wheat and the ideology of family. What, after all, is the self-evident goal of each? When are we supposed to have reached it? Could it be that the passage of time is not a narrative of progress and improvement but something else? Who writes history and why do they do it? Does every history of overt success contain within it a suppressed history of the costs borne by others to make that success possible?

Magical realism is a mode built on these exact questions. In books of this kind, a thoroughgoing uncertainty prevails. Often the narrator does not even know how to begin the story and is beset by a terminal confusion about their own status, origins and place in the order of things. Rushdie's narrator in *Midnight's Children*, Saleem Sinai, is exemplary in this respect and that novel is perhaps the clearest model for the magical realism of *Oceana Fine*.[7] The conflict is between having to begin somewhere, and not knowing where things actually began. As James Cleaver put it:

> I must begin somewhere. I can't seem to find a suitable entry into the whole business. Should it be what happens next or what happened first, or even somewhere in the middle? Does it begin with Franklin Poston, my American great-uncle: or perhaps it follows the long line back from a dago who was not Italian, from Mussolini's Blackshirts and from Aunty Bap and "La Vecchia" in the poverty and superstition of southern Italy's peasantry. (36)

It is also typical of magical realism that the reader is bewildered by names and events that mean nothing at the point in the story they are introduced but whose significance gradually emerges as the novel, as it were, catches up with its events. Facts that would make situations clearer are not revealed until much later, or they are given so early that we are not in a position to grasp their significance sufficiently to store them for the task of interpretation. The characters, too, find themselves in this position. Of one, James Cleaver tells us, that he "would come to know the rest of this story only after the event and by then he was in no position to pursue the shreds" (74). In this way, the basic principles of narration—the sequential disclosure of information constituting a chronology of events—are the very things which go missing in magical realism. It causes the reader to experience the effect of not knowing where one is from—and in this way to put received history into doubt, to cause it to wobble on its pedestal and eventually fall to the ground and break apart. We can understand magical realism's assault on narrative to be a strategy for the "un-writing" of history: what history had patiently stitched together from patterns given to it by prevailing ideology, magical realism just as diligently unpicks on behalf of those who have been excluded. It was the innovation of magical realism that conveyed the fragmentation of history—its true reality, before it has been smoothed out—through the mechanism of a dislocated narrator. Again, as James puts it: "I began out of time and seem never to have been properly put back in place (if indeed I have a place) but have continued in bursts and spasms to defy clocks although now, as the pendulum swings back and times move sideways, they begin to rally against me." (39–40)

Through such means magical realism seeks to challenge the idea that history is a simple causal pattern in which the present emerges inexorably from an unbroken chain of events. The problem with this, if you like, "common sense" idea of history is that it is inherently conservative. It tends to suggest that the present is exactly as it should be because of the past, and the past could not have been otherwise because it has produced the present. In the 1980s, magical realism channelled a broader mood for historical revision. Yet, although magical realism was an international literary trend, Flood's usage also had a very definite national context. The limitations of Australia's schoolbook history—Cook, convicts, explorers, gold, Anzacs—were certainly becoming evident at the time Flood was writing *Oceana Fine*. This was caused, at least in part, by the approach of the Australian Bicentenary in 1988. We have already seen the extent to which the Bicentenary, and the earlier Western Australian Sesquicentenary in 1979, shaped the work of Dorothy Hewett and Jack Davis. Their plays were written almost as a direct answer to the calls upon nationhood and national mythology that these centennial events brought into the public sphere. In both writers we saw that the central action in their plays was disrupted by the emergence of an alternative historical moment. In *The Man from Mukinupin* it was the appearance of the "night people" who bore witness to another kind of history than the one that the town was at pains to narrate about itself. In Davis's plays it was the events of violent colonisation that kept breaking into the surface world of his modern Noongar families. Flood's novel is very much in the same bracket as other Bicentennial novels, amongst them Thea Astley's *It's Raining in Mango* (1987), Kate Grenville's *Joan Makes History* (1988), Peter Carey's *Oscar and Lucinda* (1988) and Tim Winton's *Cloudstreet* (1991), all of which reimagined Australian history in a critical spirit.[8] These novels used the intensification of national self-scrutiny caused by this occasion to raise questions about the accepted versions of Australian history, to put into doubt the stories of origin that the Bicentenary was meant to celebrate.

With this understanding of magical realism as a counter-historical mode, we can also see that in the transformation of *Oceana Fine* from a detective story into a speculative family history, the novel no longer attempts to keep the wheatbelt together as a unified backdrop to the narrative. In short, the rupture in narrative mode signals a rupture in historical continuity, which points to the feature of the wheatbelt I have been underscoring throughout this study: that it was driven suddenly and violently into existence. The significance to the wheatbelt of this change in historicity—a change to the way that time as a causal order is felt and experienced—is that the simple certitudes of development that had for so long prevailed become unmoored and we see before us not a land which must be as it is—a chequerboard of cultivated fields—but something other, something different and anterior. Moreover, Flood's novel even dismisses the presumption held equally by the wheatbelt's critics as by its advocates: that the situation could be assessed in a single sweep. In *Oceana Fine* we experience a wheatbelt that refuses to be totalised, that simply cannot be known from a single perspective and in which to shift perspectives is not to gain a fuller view of the matter but to come up against the problem of knowledge itself. This inherently partial, fragmented and "open" manner of knowing the wheatbelt is the sign that we are now seeing the wheatbelt through the eyes of postmodernism.

Uncertain Origins

After beginning in the 1970s and moving back to the 1960s, the novel shifts backward again, this time all the way back to Federation day—1 January 1901. On this defining day, when Australia became a nation, the Rector of York, John Field, finds a young girl and her baby sister apparently abandoned on the road to Northam. The Rector and his wife Jane adopt the two girls, naming the older one Chloe and the baby Grace. Chloe, precocious even in her first encounter with John Field, quickly outgrows York. In 1911, aged eighteen, she absconds with a magician, Ben Cleaver, who, appearing under the stage name "Mesmer", was visiting York with Sloggett Bros travelling circus.[9] John Field managed catch up with his daughter in Bunbury and a hastily arranged wedding was concluded between Chloe Field and Ben Cleaver. Shortly after this, the younger daughter, Grace, aged eleven, also ran away from home. To escape, Grace had hidden herself inside a barrel, and this had fallen off the carriage on its descent down

Greenmount Hill towards Perth. The barrel and its contents were then picked up by Peter Jorgensen, the son of a Swan Valley vintner. Grace became, for the second time, a foundling, and was once again adopted into a household of complete strangers. She fell pregnant to young Peter Jorgensen, but used this condition to blackmail a wealthy American, Franklin Poston, whom she eventually married (still only twelve years old, although she had lied about this) under the assumed name of Ekaterina Corbera.

This extravagant story would seem to have little to do with the wheatbelt, but it is Grace's marriage to Franklin Poston that leads her to Yealering. (Yealering is, of course, the location of Lambton Downs, where Dorothy Hewett grew up.) Poston, we are told, "had considerable influence in the affairs of the day with his frontier consolidation theories and his rail, industrial and land interests" (75). Poston commences construction on an improbable Jeffersonian marble mansion, "Liberty's Home", in Yealering:

> Franklin had bought the property already partly developed when the land was opened for wheat, part of the government's agricultural drive to expand the State's economy and make use of the huge growth in population caused by the 90s' rush ... The place was financed with an incentive loan from the new Agricultural Bank ... If profit was the motive something must have gone wrong because the spur line that was built in 1909 from Narrogin stopped short at Wickepin and it took the arrival of the beautiful Chloe to entice the rails into Yealering. (77)

This architectural folly and its property became the family home in the years that follow, even though Poston himself was to leave in 1914, pursued by his creditors. The abandoned Grace wrote to her elder sister, Chloe, who comes to her aid, accompanied by Ben, her husband, the former magician. Thereupon they discover that Grace has decided that she will stay on her departed husband's property and "become a wheatgrower":

> This would have seemed like lunacy to anyone but Grace. She had no funds. She was besieged by debtors. She was a woman on her own in a vocation and place that had defeated whole farmfuls of strong men.

She knew almost nothing about farming. She was over thirty miles from the nearest rail siding. And more than all of this, she was only thirteen years of age, though her composure belied this. (79)

The year 1914 also saw one of the worst droughts in the history of the wheatbelt. To survive, Grace sells her husband's fine linen and the silver and buys seed and equipment. When her sister and brother-in-law (Chloe and Ben Cleaver) arrive she is dressed in oversized men's clothes and is steering a three-disc plough over the home paddock. They also employ one of Ben's old circus friends, the former strong-man Willy Sargent, to help with the heavy work of the farm.

As we have already noted, Flood's novel shares some similarities with Ewers's Avea Lea saga. To these we might add that each has at its centre a resilient woman who succeeds after the men around her fail. (In this sense, both Avea Lea and Grace Poston are versions of Lawson's "Drover's Wife".) But in Ewers's book, the founding events are marked by tragic accident, as well as natural and man-made disasters. The young son of Tommy Lea drowns in a dam, Tommy himself falls asleep at the reins and is maimed by his own wheat-cart, the house is destroyed by a storm, the Great War takes the district's young men, rabbits assail, drought strikes, prices fluctuate and then collapse—all these things are cast in Ewers's novel as fated events, beyond the compass and control of the earnest mortals labouring with their simple aspirations for family and a country life in the wheatbelt. In this, Ewers's novel was utterly consistent with the shire histories of the wheatbelt, remembering of course that Ewers's 1959 history of Bruce Rock was amongst the first of these. In Flood's novel, by contrast, the founding events are the antithesis of this wholesome struggle. His characters are quite literally illegitimate, and virtually no one has parents who are actually their parents. Likewise, the acquisition of property is never above board in Flood's novel, but instead comes about through scheming, blackmail, misadventure and questionable inheritance. In this respect, the origins of wheatbelt prosperity in *Oceana Fine* are mired in scandal and secret "histories" of the kind we saw in the work of his mother.

But if Flood's novel is a saga—a form whose key dynamic is generational conflict and continuity—then we must also account for the children. Grace herself, as we have seen, had a son, born in 1913 to Peter Jorgensen but attributed to Franklin Poston. This baby had been secretly deposited in the care of the Benedictine Brothers at New Norcia just before his fourth birthday in 1916, where the Spanish monks renamed him "Jorge". Chloe and Ben Cleaver's son, Rex, was born the year after George, in 1914, and the two boys live parallel lives. In fact, Rex and Jorge are, in effect, "twins" of the type we saw in Hewett's *Man from Mukinupin*, with Jorge as the "night" version of Rex. This is accentuated by the fact that for various reasons Grace, who had abandoned her own son, largely raised Rex, her sister's son. While the existence of Jorge was hidden and repressed, the existence of Rex was celebrated and vaunted. Grace invested her sense of future in Rex, grooming him as her successor to the mining and farming empire that she was building: "Grace saw the growth of the boy and the farm as one." (87) In 1927, she sent the thirteen-year-old Rex Cleaver to Marvel Loch "to learn and take part in the reopening of the Sons of America claim", which she had inherited from her husband. This became a significant asset after the commodity crash of 1929, when gold became a safe haven amidst the general turmoil.[10]

Marvel Loch becomes the setting for the re-emergence of Grace's son, Jorge, who was now in his late teens. He had left the New Norcia mission and begun to earn a living as best he could in the back-blocks of the wheatbelt. Near Marvel Loch, Jorge meets Otto Tinkler, an Austrian migrant getting on in years. Tinkler has rented land from a Henry Reynolds, who was in fact the grandfather (or would be) of the Mark Reynolds that Finn would meet at the bin at Marvel Loch. Tinkler espoused a philosophy of "natural" farming, broadly akin to what we would call "organic" farming today. His oracular speech opposes itself to the scientific farming practices that made broad-acre cropping possible in the conditions found in the semi-arid zones of Australia's wheatbelts. When asked by Jorge why he does not take up land himself, rather than working for Henry Reynolds, Tinkler says that it is because he opposes the "improvements" (mainly clearing and fencing) that were the conditions of land being granted at the generous rates offered by the government:

"Why don't you take up some of this [land] on the government?"

"Government says improve. Their improve is different to my improve. They want big change, all clear, fencing. This I cannot do."

"Why not?"

"Money." The older man smiled through his eyes again but the smoke obscured his expression. "Not only money. Superphosphate is what they say … Henry says he will sell me good land, very good soil, very good price. What do you know about growing? The earth is growing for you and everything that is growing for a reason is there. Good farmer, he learns to go with Nature, to understand each part so life can be going on. Each thing that is of the soil is replenished, even he cannot see immediate the reason … There is more than this sub and super they are all just now talking. Soil cannot stripped become all the time. It will not go on forever. It is fighting Nature when Nature need not be fought. (99–100)

In the way that Otto Tinkler represents an excluded aspect of wheatbelt history—a voice against wholesale and heedless development—he too (along with Jorge) is cast in the same mould as Hewett's "night people" in *The Man from Mukinupin*. Eventually, after working Reynolds's land, Jorge and Tinkler save enough to buy two separate plots from Reynolds and set up a farm at Marvel Loch. Tinkler began to turn his holding more into a nature reserve than a farm, and to revegetate it with native plants. The farming he did do was done stubbornly in the old fashion, mainly by hand, and with a consequently small output. Tinkler is also given a certain Indigenous accent, by living in closer connection with the land. He brews and ferments his own liquors and smears foul-smelling ointment on his skin to protect him from the sun. He bears some resemblance to the ambiguous wild man that figures in Peter Cowan's story "The Tractor" (1964).

Back on the farm at Yealering, the conventional wheatbelt history is also shown to be in motion, with Grace investing in mechanised machinery, such as the tractor that replaces the twelve-horse team. The succession of farming machinery is one of the most powerful iconographies of progress in rural districts, bearing testament to the radical changes in farming practice that have taken place since the nineteenth century. The advent of motor transit made it more feasible for someone like Grace to own shops in multiple towns. The telephone, electricity, and radio are all shown arriving in the wheatbelt. But it is not, after all, this model of history that prevails in Flood's novel. *Oceana Fine* is not premised on a history of incremental advancement, but one of deferred consequence, in which events erupt with the muffled report of a depth charge, and the bodies only wash up much later on the shores of the present.

Ahab in the Wheatbelt

Having moved slowly from 1901 to the beginning of World War Two, the novel fast-forwards to 1968, re-joining the story of James Cleaver on the farm at Marvel Loch. In the story hitherto, Rex Cleaver had only featured in a minor way. He was the mild-mannered patriarch who had briefly taken Finn Torrent under his wing before the latter's demise. And we had seen him as the slightly bullied heir to his Aunt Grace's grand ambitions. With Grace now dead, Rex is the undisputed head of the household and has developed ambitions of his own. We now see Rex Cleaver through the eyes of his son James, who is in early adolescence, and becoming conscious of a certain monstrous dimension not just to his father but to the wheatbelt, with all its grand ambitions. This is something new in the literature of the wheatbelt. We have seen throughout this history that the creation of the wheatbelt and the claims made for it via the ideology of wheat were subject to critique. It had been seen as misguided perhaps, hypocritical and greedy at times, even tragic inasmuch as it had devastated the natural world and deprived the Noongar of their land, but no one had yet cast the activity as diabolical or deranged. It is this idea which begins to take hold in the latter stages of *Oceana Fine*.

This idea is given shape by a comparison made in the novel to Herman Melville's *Moby Dick* (1851).[11] One of James Cleaver's earliest memories was visiting Mandurah in the late 1950s. His father had wanted to see the newly completed Narrows Bridge which now connected Perth to South Perth with a freeway and was a potent symbol of the city's new modernity and post-war prosperity. Yet it was the images from John Huston's 1956 film *Moby Dick*, with Gregory Peck as Captain Ahab, which had remained with James. The film's plot forms an unlikely allegory for his father and his father's wheatbelt dreams, although James cannot say when it first occurred to him that his father "might be seen as some kind of Ahab" (126). Now a teenager, James looks out at the wheatfields in the midst of a storm and recalls the film: "That huge storm-tossed screen seemed to meld with the wind-lashed town to form this dark wild universe that lay, submerged, beneath the sunstruck landscape." (126)

> The wheat, moving restlessly in great slow undulations beneath that massive cuttlebone storm-threatened sky, looked as stained and white as the heaving sides of Moby Dick, and the fenceposts, black as ticks, rode the back of that white leviathan like the harpoons that ploughed red the cream flesh of Ahab's nemesis.
>
> This image is a constant one, the wheat as sea-monster, kraken, serpent, whale—some leviathan moving deep beneath what seem to be placid country lives, something caught in and torn from the picturesque gold and blue shimmer of the landscape, turning up in the white belly of a salt lake, the eyes (burnt out with distance) of a fringe-dweller, the bone crest of a wave of wheat. (125)

The ideology of wheat posited the farm as the stable point of commencement. Owning and working your own land would put you into the rhythm of nature, a cycle from which industrialisation had torn the inhabitants of modernity. However, the association that James makes with Melville's great novel of obsessional mania destroys the settled quality of the wheatbelt landscape and gives to its history the quality of a deranged quest.

In *Moby Dick*, Ahab is trying to avenge the loss of his leg in a previous encounter with the whale. The continuing fascination of Melville's novel might be attributed to the fact that it becomes increasingly difficult to distinguish the monstrosity of Ahab's desire for revenge from the monster itself. Moby Dick, in other words, is Ahab's desire—it is the literalisation of revenge rather than its cause. And Ahab himself admits as much: "That inscrutable thing is chiefly what I hate; and be the white whale agent, or be the white whale principal, I will wreak that hate upon him."[12] The analogy with Moby Dick also forces an uncomfortable comparison between wheat farming and whale hunting. Farming is not generally conceived of as an extractive industry, but of course it does extract resources both from the immediate environment (soil, water) and further afield (fertilisers, machinery, fuel and other "inputs"). As Otto Tinkler puts it: "Soil cannot stripped become all the time. It will not go on forever." (100)

Rex Cleaver's obsession with wheat and restoring the soil's fertility becomes ever more bizarre, grandiose and magical. Assisted by his neighbours the McMillans and the Mazzones, Cleaver begins a program of electrifying the fields by inserting large metal poles—"harpoons"—into his fields to attract lightning during the summer storms that form spasmodically in the wheatbelt:

> His crazy notion was to draw huge bolts of electricity from the electrical storm the bureau had forecast would pass through our area that week, which would supposedly help activate the soil, or, more specifically, the amalgam of fertilising agents that, on his urging, had been dug into the paddocks of a large part of the local area in order to restore and revitalise the growth patterns of the valley. The poles ... [had] been placed at carefully calculated points along the magnetic meridians corresponding closely to what he called the "agonic line" (where the declination of the earth's magnetic field is zero) ... (130)

Although Rex had convinced his neighbours to share his delusion, James realises his father is "as mad as a cut snake" (130). The passage of the storm over Cleaver's fields is watched from a specially constructed "Observatory", a windowed polygon that Rex Cleaver has built into the roof of his farmhouse to survey his farm. When James begins to internally question the sanity of his father he is taunted by his grandmother, Chloe, who says: "You boys, you don't know the half of it." (127) In this way the novel continues to insinuate the existence of an occult history that is hidden by the outward order of agricultural progress.

The Illegible Ledger
The emblem of this dual history—one an official account of the triumph over adversity, the other a record of obscene passions—is the "Ledger" that Grace had kept dutifully through her life. This had been

commenced as a record of transactions in the business of the farm she founded at Yealering, but increasingly came to record her personal reflections. When Grace dies, James resolves to read the Ledger, only to find that it has gone missing. The ten bound volumes of the Ledger are neither in her room, nor in his father's office. Meanwhile, other incidents start to cast into doubt the version of his family's life that James had been given. The girl he likes, Dossie, reveals that they cannot have a relationship because Rex is in fact her father: "The words come out quietly, with a force as vicious as if she'd flung a stone at my head. 'I'm your sister, you dumb prick.'" (141) Then James is given a letter by Jorge, who still lives on the property he had farmed with Otto Tinkler. The letter is from Tinkler to Jorge and was sent from the Internment Camp where he had been incarcerated during World War Two. In it he announces that he now intends to take his own life. Like the Ledger, Tinkler's letter is a document attesting to the existence of an alternative history. In its cryptic, slightly jumbled language, Tinkler indicates that Cleaver had a hand in his removal— certainly that he was a beneficiary in being given access to land he had long coveted: "*I know the land is already taken. I am sorry, my friend. Government, Bank, Cleaver, what is different? There is something to be ashamed.*" (144)

There is, as we have noticed, a distinct resemblance here to the kind of dualistic universe in the work of Flood's mother, Dorothy Hewett. And like the "night people" in *The Man from Mukinupin*, Jorge refuses to be fully repudiated and hovers at the edges of official vision as a persistent emissary of the district's hidden history. When James needs to find out what is really going on, he turns to Jorge as the repository for repressed knowledge. Because the truth he contains is incommensurable with the official story of the Cleavers, Jorge occupies a different order of existence. He is present, in the sense that he lives in the district of Marvel Loch, but not as a farmer or in any accepted capacity. Instead, like other eccentric outcasts we have encountered—the wild hermit in Cowan's "The Tractor" (1964) or the recalcitrant Mr and Mrs Hudleston in York Main's "Marginal Country" (1972), or indeed Hester Harper in Jolley's *The Well* (1986)— Jorge stands in implied critique to the instrumentalist ideology that governs and binds the social life from which they are excluded. Jorge tells James: "They always leave out the juicy bits, these old sods who put histories together." (157) But he also warns James to give up trying to get to the bottom of these things: "You'll never work it out. I haven't and I've been at it for thirty-five years." (161)

It is late at night, and James is drunk on Jorge's homemade mead when he sets out for home through the darkened bush. He is accidently shot in the head—though only "singed"—by the local kangaroo shooter, Tinmouth, and knocked unconscious. When he recovers he finds himself near the abandoned main tunnel of the "Phoenix" goldmine inherited by Grace from Frank Poston and developed by Rex Cleaver during the 1930s. Inside the mine he finds that someone has fashioned a small room with table and chair, and on a shelf he sees all ten volumes of the Ledger. The Ledger is open to the day on which James was born:

20/1/55

A terrible day for all of us. I cannot explain all that has happened except to say that I am not entirely blameless. The child, blessed be, will live but may never walk correctly. There is no doubt it is not his. If there is a God, then all of us must be seen to carry the burden of our guilt, even poor Margaret. The sight of my dear sister is more than I can bear. I shall pay with the rest of my days, my penance here stated: every day to look upon the face of my beloved and receive not even tenderness in return; every day to look upon the two other dear lives and take responsibility in their disfigurement; every day to know I am compromised by my pact with the old woman and to bear that shame silently until she or I am dead. (170)

The central scandal to emerge from the Ledger is that Grace had become involved sexually with her adolescent nephew Rex. The sense that there was an unhealthy closeness between the two was already given in the novel and the Ledger provides the rationale and the substantiation for the unspoken thrall that Grace had over Rex. The Ledger also confirms the earlier observation that illegitimacy is the general condition of *Oceana Fine*. As we have noted, almost no one in the novel has parents who are actually their parents. Grace and Chloe were foundlings. Rex was born to Chloe out of wedlock and then largely raised by Grace. Jorge was born to Grace out of wedlock and deposited in New Norcia mission. James Cleaver, as the Ledger notes above, was not the son of Rex Cleaver, while Dossie was the unacknowledged daughter of Rex. Ironically, this meant that the relationship between James and Dossie would not have been incestuous.

This tortuous family tree is the key to *Oceana Fine*. It is the central mystery and the animating problem of the novel. Again we see a close correspondence between Flood and Hewett on this point, which is perhaps not surprising. From the point of view of the wheatbelt, the effect of these affairs is to delegitimise the enterprise—to suggest that, in spite of outward prosperity and vaunted family values, the origins of the wheatbelt do not bear close scrutiny. This is the effect of the novel at least and one might easily object that it is simply a novel and makes no claim on the actual history of the wheatbelt—and even if it does, the history of the wheatbelt is still separable from the baroque intrigues of this strange family. Yet on this latter point, the problem is that the scrambled family history and the emergence of the wheatbelt are fused together in the novel. The driving forces of the farming enterprise—Grace and Rex—are also the major corrupting influences. To the broader objection that a novel like *Oceana Fine* can in no way posit a critique of the "real" wheatbelt, this would be like saying that *Heart of Darkness* bears no relationship to the history of colonialism in the Congo because Kurtz was not a typical company man. *Oceana Fine* is not a novel in which the wheatbelt is merely a convenient setting. In fact, more than any other work, it sees the wheatbelt as something that existed simultaneously in the planes of family, economics, ecology, history and metaphysics. Despite its magical-realist playfulness it has a firmer grip on the dynamics of the wheatbelt as an unfolding event through historical time than any of the texts we have seen in this study, with the possible exception of the sagas of Ewers. But unlike Ewers, Flood was able to draw on the key breakthrough in his mother's work, which was to apprehend that the wheatbelt was framed by an unconscious history it wished to forget.

James is not quite alone when he begins to read the Ledger in the mine tunnel. He is joined by a mortally wounded wallaby, which (like James) had also been shot that night by the licensed shooter on his nightly rounds. The wallaby had used its remaining strength to find the shelter of the tunnel and was passing its last hours there. The animal dying in quiet agony forms an index in the natural world to the catastrophic confirmation of long-held unconscious suspicions. James's attention wanders between the horrors of the page and the creature *in extremis* nearby, almost as if he is using one to cancel out the claims of the other:

> It was unable to get up and, as I didn't move, it soon stopped trying to drag itself away and settled for regarding me warily from across the cavern. Its ribs, rounded out to a fat barrel by the unusual position it lay in, pumped in and out, nostrils flaring widely. I still could hear only my own much-quietened breathing. Somewhere along the line we must have lost the ability wild animals seem to have—to expel their air silently even under duress ...
>
> It looked at me, eyes like warm cowpats. I riffled through a few pages, trying to concentrate on the book. It jerked its legs in a feeble spasm of escape, but soon fell back. I moved again but this time it ignored me as if to indicate it was in too much pain to bother with games. I turned the pages to the beginning ... (172)

Later, James contemplates whether the right thing to do would be to kill the wallaby and put it out of its misery, but he can think of no way of doing this. He then wonders why he should feel this obligation at all and starts to speak to the animal:

> "What're you looking at?" I said out loud. It lifted the veil from its eyes. "You think you're in a bad way, you should cop some of this. Here's my dad and his old aunty having it off since before I was born and never breathed a word."
>
> The wallaby made the smallest of movements, a kind of body shrug, and then there was a long soft hiss. It was farting. That made me laugh.
>
> "Well, thanks for your concern. I suppose your lot get up to that sort of thing all time."
>
> The laugh hurt my head. The wallaby shrugged again, this time more definite. I waited for it to fart. Then I noticed the blood dripping

from its arsehole. Something rose in my throat but nothing came out. I looked down at the candle. It was almost exhausted. I felt like apologising. To everything. I didn't want look at the eyes. I could feel them on me. I returned to the first ledger and stuck my nose determinedly inside it. (176)

This is the kind of slightly painful gallows humour the novel executes so deftly. On the one hand the kangaroo's flatulence is a perfect answer to the anguish that James is suffering—an overheated drama that exists solely inside the confines of his head—and on the other, the blood issuing from its rectum takes the image beyond comedy and startles us into realising the extremity of the animal's condition. And not just the animal, of course. The animal represents, as suggested above, a living (dying) index of James's own position. The wallaby's presence is to suggest that the hidden wounds of his inadequate familial life may yet be bleeding him to death. There is no guarantee that he will be able to somehow laugh them off and dance merrily into a future. The theme of the novel, and its hypothesis, is that any future is exactly as secure as the past that ushers it into being.

The End of the World

The penultimate section of the novel has us back in the place in time where the novel had begun, and which had previously concluded with the death of Finlay Torrent. The new section follows the story of John Finder, who is looking for his daughter who had disappeared with her boyfriend in the vicinity of Marvel Loch whilst prospecting about three weeks before this point. What we as readers already know, and John Finder does not yet, is that the girl and her boyfriend have been murdered and their bodies crucified and hung inside the "A" Class bin at Marvel Loch. The local police were not especially concerned when Finder raised their disappearance, and he is also given the cold shoulder by the residents of Marvel Loch. Finder hears about the death of the young sampler, which happened at around the same time his daughter had disappeared, and also about the disappearance of another older prospecting couple in the district about three years earlier. He visits the Mazzone farm and is told to go and see Rex Cleaver. He does this, and Rex suggests to him that accidents happen and it is best to let the authorities sort these kinds of things out. The advice is correctly taken by Finder to be a veiled threat. He wakes up from his bush camp site the next morning to find his van incinerated at the bottom of a hill. He is rescued by Jorge who takes him home to his dilapidated house amongst the forest he has planted to feed the bees he keeps. There they are joined by Wally Reynolds, the father of Mark Reynolds, Finn's rambunctious work colleague at the Marvel Loch bin. We learn that with the death of Finn, Mark's behaviour has become increasingly erratic and his father has become concerned enough to travel over from Bodallin to check on him.

Both Wally Reynolds and John Finder push Jorge to tell them what is going on. After a pause, Jorge agrees. He tells him that Rex Cleaver is indeed a "crusader" and he has enlisted the farmers of Marvel Loch in a crusade against a modernity that no longer cares for them. In fact, Cleaver has become a self-styled prophet espousing a religion based on the growth of wheat—a modern fertility cult, conducting services in the "temple" of the A-Class Bin. His preaching galvanises the widespread feeling in the district that the dream of wheat had evaporated in the face of a capitalist system that demanded ever greater efficiency and ever greater alienation from the land. Cleaver's cult sought to re-establish a sacred covenant between the growers and their harvest. As Jorge puts it to Wally and John: "Rex, he is giving back the integrity. He makes the wheat proud again." (207) At the centre of their cult is the new wheat variety, Oceana Fine, which Rex had acquired from Otto Tinkler. Rex, although he had been seen hitherto as something of a scientific farmer, obsessed with yields and maximising production, becomes in this new guise a reincarnation of Tinkler's core principles of putting back into the soil as much as you take out. In this sense, Rex follows the same trajectory as that recorded in the Ledger, which was commenced as a strict record of commercial transactions but slowly became the repository of occult history. Rex refuses to spray chemicals on his crop and convinces sceptical neighbours—like the Mazzones—to follow suit, with ever-increasing fervour. Jorge tells Finder and Wally Reynolds:

> "[Rex] is become the farming fanatic. I am sorry, this is exaggeration. Growing the wheat is, for him, and so many, deep inside. This is like

religion ... no, like faith. It must be Rex who brings religion, if that is what you like."

"What do you mean by religion?"

"I mean nothing, this is others. They say fertility cult, harvest rites ... all this is primitive! ..." (207)

While on the one hand the religion worshipped the new, sacred grain variety—Oceana Fine—on the other it sought to redress the damage done over the years to the soil. The soil needed to be "rejuvenated", to have its lost fertility restored. This was the redemptive, messianic dimension to the religion: the soil needed to be prepared for the arrival of the saviour (Oceana Fine). But Jorge also explains to Finder that the religion is a syncretic combination of old lore and pseudoscience and that they were spreading a magical "compost" containing gold into the soil to restore its vitality. It was, Jorge said, "alchemy ... backwards", turning gold into something baser and more earthy. This magical compound would circumvent the need for chemicals and superphosphate, and reverse the ravages of salinity. It was, in other words, an antidote to everything that was felt to be wrong with modern farming.

The picture that emerges of Rex is not the usual criticism of the farmer who puts production before all things and cares nothing for the collateral damage. We saw both Cowan and York Main mount this critique in the post-war period as environmental consciousness began to register the full cost of the wheatbelt's destruction. Rex is not the cold-minded farming rationalist that York Main depicted in stories such as "A Third Generation Farm" (1971) and "Marginal Country" (1972). Rex, if anything, is on the side of the environment, or at least a version of it. Though he seems to care little for native habitats, he is deeply troubled by the declining fertility of the soil and suspicious of the damage that is being done by chemical fertilisers, herbicides and pesticides. He does not like trail-bikes, pointing to the damage and erosion they cause, and the noise and air pollution they produce. He hates the groups of local youths going on alcohol-fuelled kangaroo "drives", shooting up the countryside. These are the exact same ills that John Kinsella, who we will meet in the next chapter, rails against in his activist poetry.

Hewett's work had touched on an occult worship of fertility, perhaps most memorably in the "Five Man Morris" harvest song chanted by the "night people" in *The Man from Mukinupin*: "Bringin' in the sheaves, bringin' in the sheaves / We'll bless all Mukinupin bringin' in the sheaves." (6) But, in many ways, the kind of cult we see in *Oceana Fine*—led by an enigmatic, charismatic saviour— seems to have its closest parallel in Randolph Stow's *Tourmaline* (1963), where a dying outback town is transfigured by the arrival of a stranger (Michael Random) who reluctantly takes on the role of saviour.[13] Hewett was a great admirer of Stow, and particularly *Tourmaline*, and Flood too seems to have this novel at least partially in mind. (The narrator of Tourmaline also keeps a "ledger".) In *Tourmaline*, the saviour fails to find the water that the town craved. He wanders back into the desert from where he had arrived, leaving a town disappointed but no worse off than he found it. *Tourmaline*, published shortly after the Cuban Missile Crisis, is a post-apocalyptic novel. Some deep catastrophe has destroyed the town and its inhabitants exist in the mode of survivors, eking out the meagrest of existences, and living day-to-day in the scorched remnants of the

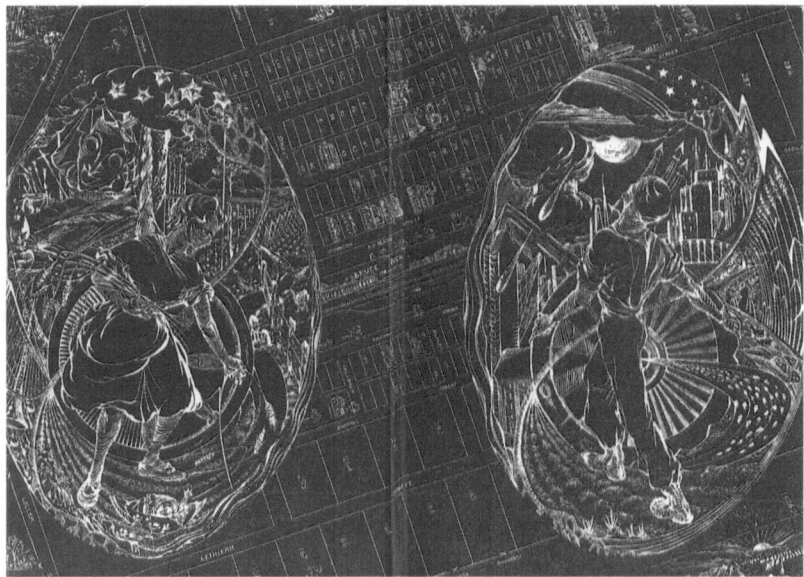

60. End papers from John K. Ewers's *Bruce Rock: The Story of a District* (1959).

earlier world. The quality of hope has atrophied to the point where it is actively resisted, and any movement towards it treated with the gravest caution.

Where *Tourmaline* exists in the wake of catastrophe, *Oceana Fine* takes place in its long prelude. Also, in *Tourmaline* we do not know what has happened to ruin the world and the event that caused it is now closed off from the everyday speech of the inhabitants. In *Oceana Fine*, the catastrophic event, when it happens, is depicted with a slow, terrible inexorability—a deadly chain reaction that once it starts cannot be arrested. There is a gathering at the Marvel Loch bin, a site which had now become suffused with sinister metaphysical significance. Inside the bin, Rex is conducting a service of thanksgiving for the harvest that has been collected. A flat nave has been levelled in the mountains of wheat stored within the bin and a group has assembled to hear Rex Cleaver address them from a catwalk in the roof's superstructure.[14] John Finder ascends the hill of grain and confronts Rex Cleaver. Finder apprehends that his life is in danger but decides to press on. When Rex is apprised of Finder's arrival he realises that Finder now knows that he and his followers are responsible for the death of his daughter:

> "Mr Finder, this, though you may not care, is a temple. A place of worship. It's also a storage bin for the world's finest wheat. The two aren't entirely disconnected. What you're walking on, Mr Finder, is no less than a miracle. Does that seem remarkable to you? It doesn't to these people … They're surrounded by miracles. Theirs is a fairytale, Mr Finder, a fairytale come true—by hard work and guts and courage and most of all by faith." (210)

While this is occurring inside the bin, a cataclysm is beginning to take place outside. In the first instance, a storm is approaching. Farmers rushing to unload wheat have not been able to fix a broken grain conveyor and have removed a sheet of the roof iron so they can shovel it manually into the bin. But the wind blows as much out of the bin as into it, and then a gust takes the sheet off the roof and sends it cartwheeling across the ground and slices through the approaching figure of Wally Reynolds, cutting him in two.[15]

Word of this accident reaches Rex and the others inside the bin and they rush to attend the scene, but as they seek to comprehend what has happened the encroaching storm drives the onlookers back into the bin. There, as Rex tries to calm his followers, they are met with a new problem. Mark Reynolds had found his father's sundered body and sees it as the final outrage of Cleaver's blood cult. From the catwalk he swears vengeance upon those below. Above him, high in the bin's roof-space, he has roughly wired the body of his father together—a grotesque resurrection of the father by the son. As the Mazzone sons try to apprehend Mark, he sets fire to the grain which he has soaked in petrol. Burning grain is dumped onto the mounds below from a conveyor belt and soon the mounds catch alight. Mark has locked the doors and there is nowhere to go as the flames spread through the bin:

> The whole bin had begun to heat up like an oven and the air on the catwalk was difficult to breathe. Most had cloth over the lower half of their faces, some over their whole heads. Even the catwalk felt hot against bare flesh as the whole stack burned inwardly, areas collapsing to expose a core of red-hot, almost molten, seed beneath the surface. To those above, it looked like the landscape of Hell as they had learned it in their childhood. A burning pit. Some fainted and were either wrapped in coats or supported by their neighbours. (228)

The roof is then torn off the bin by the force of the storm and John Finder and two others manage to escape through a "rent" in the wall caused by this. The earlier allusion to *Moby Dick* is revived by the description of "the monstrous sounds of the twisting leviathan", as if the bin has now taken on the role of the fatal whale in that novel.

John Finder survives the inferno but is horrifically burnt. Outside, amongst the devastation of the storm and the conflagration of the bin, a new catastrophe becomes evident. The entire surface of the earth surrounding the bin and as far as the eye could see has been inundated with salt water:

> It was on everything. In everything. Salt.
>   And the water. There was so much of it. Like a flood. But they didn't get floods in Marvel Loch. Not even in miracles. Because it

wasn't raining. Didn't look like it had rained. But there was water on the ground, past the ankles in some bits. Salty water. (229)

The inundation completes the catastrophe by making the destruction permanent and abiding. The new day dawns with a vision of "the wide expanse of uncultivable saltpan that was once the granary of the disease-resistant wheat Oceana Fine" (230).

The Seventh Day

The novel shifts suddenly forward in time once more. Now we are in the present day (the 1980s), reporting on the sad affairs of Marvel Loch from a chastened future. We are told that in the years following the "tragedy at the former wheat bin" both of Rex Cleaver's elder sons—Graham and Frank—had passed away. James, we are also informed, has left for Sydney but would be of little assistance even if he were found since he "had mental problems from his early years, probably inherited from his mother who shot herself during his birth" (230). James returns to narrate the closing of the novel, which involves him returning to the now-barren wasteland of Marvel Loch. His father's farm has been almost entirely consumed by the salt-pan formed by the saline flood that coincided with the burning of the bin. The farmhouse, though, has been preserved on a rise just beyond the reach of the flood. He walks through its various rooms, all preserved as if in some magic bubble. At the centre of the house is the "Dark Room", where Chloe once developed her supernatural photographs and where James's mother gave birth to him and, simultaneously, committed suicide. Directly above the Dark Room—the "womb of the house" (244)—is his father's "Observatory", with its twenty-four glass panels offering a panorama of the property. From the observatory, James glances south towards the fields that used to extend down the valley, once gold with the ripened wheat: "Except it's not there. The gold, the soothing gold, I mean. It's wide and flat and forever—and white. Bare blistering white. A wasteland. A white desert. A lake—shoreless, wheatless, waterless." (235)

He drives over to Jorge's place and find his house has been destroyed with the passage of time and the effects of the elements. His land is now densely overgrown with the trees he had planted.

Nearby, though, Tinkler's hut is in surprisingly good condition, and so is the rainwater tank and the grape vines that it irrigated. But the whole garden is overgrown with morning glory, which has grown to a preternatural size and takes on an uncanny quality of life, heaving itself into existence in amongst the arid country: "There's a quality about this garden, this rusting old tank. Timeless would be the usual word but it'd be more correct to say outside time, a thing that doesn't apply, doesn't respond to modern tools." (238) Peering into the tank, James sees the stem of the vine swollen and twisted upon itself so that it filled the entire cavity and yet was somehow pumping water from deep within the ground. In amongst the stalks there is the preserved skeleton of what would seem to be a man; preserved so that the man and the plant had now become united, interwoven:

> The glory, with its purple blooms distinct on soft green leaves, must have been the pump that fed this timelessness. Was this planned? The tank was Tinkler's—could he have known this? And made use of it? I say it though the word is made useless against such force. The scope, the understanding of the engine of nature that could seek to arrange such perpetuity. As I said, I tried to fathom what I saw but couldn't get to the bottom of it. The glory, the water table, the pull of worlds I didn't perceive, the push of those I may, the garden, the cemetery of such symmetry, the bones, plant and animal strangled together—a coincidence of man and nature? (250–1)

Next, James encounters the furtive, burnt and deranged figure of John Finder, the only survivor of the bin inferno, who is now known in the district as "Yilgarn John". John takes James down into the abandoned mine shaft and there James finds that John now lives in this subterranean world. He has removed all of Rex's books and belongings and they now surround his makeshift abode in a cavern within the mine. Finder, living as an underground hermit in Rex Cleaver's abandoned mine, has been obsessively reading the volumes of the Ledger. It becomes clear that John has now become the repository of the secret story of Marvel Loch. James, though, wonders why Finder is doing all of this, what it is that binds him to this task:

What's he doing down here, hiding beneath the hills like an animal gone to earth, living in my family's warren, existing I don't know how? When I ask him he laughs, says he's atoning for all the rabbits he's terrified or killed in his life; that he's taking himself seriously and really living with the land; that he's looking for the secret of alchemic gold, the gold my father could touch but could never feel (what did he mean by that?); that he's tired and would like to save the world the trouble of burying him or the mistake of burning him. (242)

Wandering around the locality of his childhood, James re-experiences the traumatic memories of growing up in Marvel Loch. In particular, he is confronted once again with his own impossible origin. The desolated landscape literalises the destruction of his own previously imagined past, a past that came crashing down when he discovered that his father had been sleeping with his aunt, and that he himself was the product of an unknown father and a mother who shot herself during his birth. He knows he is not Rex's child, but Rex was the only father he knew. It is the irreconcilability of his condition that causes James to feel as if he is, at times, no more than the medium for the contesting desires of his antecedents: "Sometimes I wonder if parts of mother's head didn't scramble intact through the umbilical in the moment her brains blew across the Dark Room wall." (254) The novel's final image is of James preparing the ink to reinscribe the Ledger.

What are we to make of this strange conclusion to this strange novel? We are told on more than one occasion that this return to Marvel Loch is taking place on the "seventh day"—that is, on the day after the momentous events that created the world. Structurally this alerts us to the fact that this is, after all, the seventh chapter of the book. The previous chapters of the book were organised in the fashion of a nest: Lie of the Land 1; Another Time 1; Histories 1; Histories 2; Another Time 2; Lie of the Land 2. So, this final chapter does stand outside the circle created by that sequence. From this position one sees the world, not as a line of continual advancement, but as a circle, an "Ouroboros" (258), where the snake bites its own tail, and where every attempt to walk towards a goal imperceptibly has you end up where you began. In the pre-dawn light James sees the Mazzone's dam where he had once trysted with Dossie: "It seemed so long ago, in my mind, a circle round a circle going round." (246) The appearance of the "seventh day" would thus seem to offer an opportunity for breaking the cycle. The image of James preparing the ink to write into the Ledger suggests the beginnings of an agency in his life that had not been granted to him hitherto. But the novel offers only a tenuous grasp on this empowerment. The charmed vantage granted to those in the seventh day seems to come at a price. There, you might live beyond the endless repetition of life, but this appears to be purchased by somehow also being outside life. It seems no coincidence that those who inhabit the seventh day—James, Chloe, John Finder—are all deranged. The realm of the seventh day seems not, after all, to be a place where one might live, at least not in any conventional sense. It is rather the unfathomable, perhaps even terrible, zone of life as a brute force rather than a habitat.

History has not been especially generous to Tom Flood's novel *Oceana Fine*. It has enjoyed neither the popularity nor the acclaim that has come to the works of Winton, Carey, Malouf and Grenville. That in itself is not so remarkable—unlike Flood, these other writers have published many novels and their reputation has grown steadily as a consequence. And no doubt there are many cases to be made for neglected novels in Australian literature, or any other literature for that matter. And yet, as we have seen in this chapter, there is a range of reference and imagination in Flood's novel that places it into a rare sphere. Few novels in the history of Australian writing can match this work for sheer metaphysical audacity, to say nothing of the complex deconstruction it instigates of social history and family life. It is, unquestionably, a difficult novel and one really only apprehends its majesty when one re-reads it. There are simply too many internal cross-references for it to be grasped at a single pass. From the point of view of the literary history of the wheatbelt, Flood's novel is unsurpassed. There is no particular reason why there should be a Great Australian Wheatbelt Novel, but with *Oceana Fine* it turns out, in fact, that one exists. Certainly, it has not been taken to heart to the degree that Jolley's *The Well* has; unlike that novel, it is unlikely that *Oceana Fine* will feature on any high-school reading lists, at least not in the near future. Flood's novel is one whose complexity demands a reader that is ready to submit to confusion, to blind alleys and trapdoors and maddening circular corridors. In this way it works powerfully against the telos of the wheatbelt it depicts. Where the ideology of wheat draws upon the image of a golden future, Flood's novel throws us continuously back into the past—insisting that the only way forward is backward.

Chapter Eleven

John Kinsella (1963–)

York (1963–)
Mullewa (1975)
Geraldton (1978–81)
Williams (1991–93)
Toodyay (2009–)

John Kinsella is the most significant writer to emerge from the wheatbelt since Dorothy Hewett and the only one to challenge her in stature and renown, and, for that matter, in controversy. Like Hewett, Kinsella draws on his family connection to the wheatbelt to criticise the enterprise from within. But while Hewett seemed to direct her ire at the hypocrisy of the past, Kinsella's critique is for the most part directed urgently at the present. Kinsella's is a real-time analysis of the challenges he sees everywhere in the wheatbelt—species loss, environmental degradation, chemical poisoning, genetic modification. In this sense, he is a forceful heir to the environmental tradition that we have traced in this history, beginning with James Pollard and running through Peter Cowan to Barbara York Main. More particularly, Kinsella shares with Tom Flood the heightened awareness, so typical of the current epoch, of the wheatbelt's artificiality, of the fact that the wheatbelt is not just a danger to the nature that lies in its path, but to nature as such, threatening to unpick the fabric of natural connection and continuity. For Kinsella, modern technological farming practices imperil the very substance of nature as it subsists genetically and molecularly. Kinsella is also writing from the modern consciousness of Aboriginal dispossession, and his writing attempts to reach out respectfully to the Noongar as traditional owners of the land in the southwest. From a literary point of view, one of the remarkable features of Kinsella's writing is its sheer quantity. He is prolific by every standard and at last count had published fifty-four volumes of poetry, eight volumes of fiction, two volumes of memoirs, along with writing eight plays and editing some seventeen further anthologies, including the influential *Penguin Anthology of Australian Poetry* (2009).[1] Certainly not all of this work deals with the wheatbelt, but a good deal of it does and the wheatbelt provides a clear centre to an otherwise dizzying array of projects, interests, causes and achievements. His career is still very much in progress and this chapter will focus mainly on the first twenty years which fit with the timeline in this study and show the basic stances that Kinsella's later work continued to develop.

John Vincent Kinsella was born in South Perth on 2 February 1963. He was the first child of Wendy and Ron Kinsella, who had married in 1959. Kinsella's mother, born Wendy Jeanette Heywood in 1938, was the major creative influence in his early life. After matriculating from St Mary's Anglican Girls' School in 1952, Wendy Kinsella trained as a secretary at Underwood's Business College and worked for a stockbroking company, and then later, an optical wholesaler. By the time John Kinsella was born in 1963, and his brother Stephen in 1965, the family were living in the southern Perth suburb of Mount Pleasant, near the fork of the Canning and Swan Rivers, and it was here that John first attended Brentwood Primary School in 1969.

His parents' marriage was to break down irrevocably the following year, 1970, and his mother decided to enrol at The University of Western Australia as a mature-age student. She completed her BA in 1974 with majors in English and Ancient History, and then a Diploma of Education in 1975, before commencing her first position teaching English at North Lake Senior High School in 1976. John Kinsella attended Rossmoyne Senior High School, where he completed his first two years of secondary education. Then, in 1978, Wendy Kinsella moved with her sons to Geraldton to teach at Geraldton Senior High School, where John matriculated in 1980. The family returned to Perth in 1981 in time for John to enrol in a Bachelor of Arts degree at The University of Western Australia. He studied there until 1982

61. Ron and Wendy Kinsella, with the infant John, 1963.

when, as with Dorothy Hewett, personal difficulties, in particular a long and difficult battle with addiction, made university study less and less viable and he withdrew.

From this cursory account of Kinsella's upbringing it is not immediately clear how he is connected to the wheatbelt, and why this region would dominate his literary life. The one connection already visible is the years spent in Geraldton. This town in the mid-north is the most northerly of the five export ports for wheat in Western Australia; the others are Kwinana (which replaced Fremantle), Bunbury, Albany and Esperance. Geraldton exports grains and live animals from the northern wheatbelt, and the town is surrounded by wheat and sheep farms, which come to an end just to the north at Northampton. However, it has also been a contention throughout this study that the wheatbelt's particular power is as an idea, so it is useful to trace the genesis of this idea in John Kinsella. Kinsella had been visiting the wheatbelt towns of the Avon Valley from an early age. His mother's sister, Lorraine Heywood, had married the York farmer Gerry Wheeler in 1953. Gerry was one of several Wheeler brothers farming adjoining properties that were once part of the Mount Hardy farm that had been granted to the Wheelers in the early settlement of the Avon Valley. Gerry and Lorraine Wheeler's farm, "Wheatlands", became a home away from home for Wendy's young family and John Kinsella's experience and connection to the wheatbelt derives powerfully from the summer months he spent there in his childhood.

Both Wendy and Lorraine, in their childhoods, had spent time on a wheatbelt farm in Pingrup, south of Lake Grace, owned by friends of their mother. The first trip had been in the May holidays of 1945, travelling by train and spending the night in Katanning. John Kinsella's father, Ron Vincent Kinsella, was born into a forestry family at Jarrahdale in the Darling Scarp. He trained as a mechanic and worked

62. The extended Wheeler family at "Wheatlands" in 1963. Ron, Wendy and John Kinsella are in the centre of the photograph.

for MTT (Metropolitan Transport Trust) in Perth. After the breakdown of the marriage to Wendy, Ron Kinsella returned to the country, heading north to work in the Pilbara before taking on the management of a large-scale wheat farm near Mullewa in 1975. The 30,000-acre farm was owned by the prominent Perth entrepreneur Alan Bond, and Ron Kinsella serviced and maintained its fleet of agricultural equipment—the kind that was by then transforming the broad-acre farming in the flatter outer-districts of the wheatbelt. It is from visiting this farm as a twelve year old with his brother Stephen that John Kinsella first apprehended the industrial dimension of the wheatbelt that sat uneasily with the more bucolic mythology of farm life.

Early Work

The years between 1980 and 1983 mark the first phase of Kinsella's writing career, a period which would culminate in the publication of his first volume of poems, *The Frozen Sea* (1983), which he published under the name, "John Heywood" (his mother's maiden name).[2] The staple-bound chapbook was published by "Zepplin" Press in Perth's St Martin's Arcade and consisted of nineteen poems over sixteen unpaginated pages. Zepplin Press was a short-lived publishing venture run by Digby Knapp, whom Kinsella had met while studying at UWA.[3] The poems in *The Frozen Sea* are subjective lyrics characterised by a lush, late-romantic play of image that gives them a kaleidoscopic or slightly hallucinatory quality. They do not refer directly to the wheatbelt, but they do show a disposition to landscape, and particularly to a landscape in which fertility is marginal, a place that is limned by desert and in which life takes place precariously or under duress:

> i think of thirst,
> the drifting sand does not
> lend itself to description,
> the sketchy border trees
> offer little protection
> from the sun as we negotiate
> the edge and the fine line
> between sand and vegetation.
> ("Links", stanza ii, n.p.)

This poem and others in *The Frozen Sea* have a self-consciously enigmatic quality that is reminiscent of the more Taoist poems of Randolph Stow, as well as sharing Stow's arid-country metaphysics. Kinsella had fallen in love with the poetry of Stow while at high school in Geraldton through Alexander Craig's widely taught anthology of Australian poetry for Jacaranda Press, *Twelve Poets, 1950–1970* (1971).[4] Craig's book also introduced Kinsella to the poems of Les Murray, Francis Webb, Gwen Harwood and Michael Dransfield.[5] In Kinsella's *The Frozen Sea*, the metaphor of "dust" runs through several poems and, as in Stow's work (and indeed in Judith Wright's, another early influence), it seems to carry the significance of ambitions that have been laid to waste—an import that, as we have seen, is carried by the concept of "salt" in the work of Hewett. In due course, salt would become a major signifier in Kinsella's work, as well. The poem "Desert Fruit" is another of the desert poems in *The Frozen Sea*. The images in it bespeak a paradoxical or quixotic appearance of life in the midst of a more general desolation.

> the desert in spring
> edges its way thru two worlds
>
> the fading fruits of spinifex
> and wildflower
>
> the night parrots glide
> thru a night-lilting sky
> and break away to the east
> having crushed this fruit
> over their hard tongue
>
> guided by memory
> and the smell of water
> they settle on the banks of shrinking rivers
> ("Desert Fruit", n.p.)

Another feature of *The Frozen Sea* that will recur in Kinsella's later poems is a referencing of classical myth—to Orpheus and Faust, for instance (see poem 9, "Orpheus & Faust – 2 Legends"). Such references, as well as an archaic diction and syntax, have the effect of situating these subjective memory-poems within a mythic register. Indeed, these two myths in particular—Orpheus and Faust—occupy a structuring centrality to the view that Kinsella will develop of the wheatbelt. On the one hand, the story of Orpheus is about a bard-poet who sings each year for his lost lover (Persephone) and thereby restores the fertility of the land by animating the cycle of the seasons. Against this pastoral pattern there is the Faustian spectre of a contract with forces—capitalism, technology, bio-science—that are inimical to nature but central to production.

Kinsella's first collection of poems for Fremantle Arts Centre Press, *Night Parrots* (1989), marks his emergence as a poet of note, and since then books have flowed at a remarkable rate. *Night Parrots* reprinted some of the *Frozen Sea* poems as the opening sequence; other sequences included the "Lasseter" sequence and the "Nebuchadnezzar" sequence.[6] These figures, the mythic gold-prospector, Lasseter, and the ancient Assyrian king, Nebuchadnezzar, continue the thematic emphasis on desert metaphysics.[7] The figures and action in these poems are marked by a certain historical irony, where the desert sands mock the grandiose ambitions of men in a manner made familiar to generations of school children by Shelley's "Ozymandias". *Night Parrots* also explicitly enters into dialogue with the modernist painter Arthur Boyd, in particular his painting *Red Nebuchadnezzar* (1968–71) which features on the cover of the collection. Kinsella shares with Australian modernism the mythic transposition of the classical world onto the arid centre of Australia. In this way, Australia's emptiness is inverted, becoming a stark existential intensity. Stow's *Tourmaline* is the other major touchstone in Kinsella's early poetic universe. In *Tourmaline*, as we have seen, an enigmatic and reluctant prophet emerges from the desert with the promise—seized on rather desperately by the townsfolk—that he might restore the dying town by discovering water. Kinsella's Lasseter is not too far, in many respects, from Stow's Tourmaline, although in a slightly more puckish vein:

O Lasseter, inheritor
of the shrinking gnamma holes,

what time have retreating waters
for such as you? What images
persist beyond dislocation? (44)

The reason for noting this prevailing motif in Kinsella's early poetry is that his poetry of the wheatbelt, when it begins to emerge, fits quite closely with the thematic palette that has been established.

The poem "Finches", from *Night Parrots*, provides the first real glimpse of the wheatbelt, as a place of memory and material practice, in Kinsella's oeuvre. In four parts, the poem recalls a section of the "Wheatlands" farm affected by salt. We have already seen how salt was a metaphor for hubris in Hewett's poetry, notably in her definitive biographical poem, "Legend of the Green Country". In that poem, Hewett described how her father was an early campaigner to reafforest wheatbelt land to combat salinity. A similar pattern emerges in Kinsella's "Finches", where his cousins had planted tamarisks in a bid to lower the water table.[8] But, there is a distinct new note in Kinsella's treatment of salt-affected land, when compared with Hewett's, and that is the note of uncanny fascination. The poem

63. *Night Parrots* (Fremantle Arts Centre Press, 1989) and the author in his mid-20s.

begins by describing the "Salt Paddocks": "Down below the dam / there is nothing but salt, / a slow encroachment." (25) In the "ring" of tamarisks planted there to contain the spread of the salt, a "colony of finches" have taken up residence. The finches can only be glimpsed now and again, darting about through the dense thicket, and the boys (the "I" of the poem and his cousins) stare on in fascination, wishing somehow, and impossibly, to be part of it, "To join the finch / in his tenuous kingdom / among tamarisks" and in "the hot snow of salt" (26). The closing image of the poem, though, is of a dead finch:

> The dead finch lies on salt,
> tight winged and stretched.
>
> The others shimmer
> loosely in heat
>
> the salt's white mystery
> coveting tin cans, skull of sheep.
> Slowly, death rides this hot glacier
> further and further away. (26)

This little vignette ushers in key elements of what we might designate as the typical "scene" of Kinsella's wheatbelt poetry. It is not exactly a wasteland, at least not in the classic modernist sense that Hewett took from T.S. Eliot. Certainly, it is a devastated landscape, but instead of the mournful traipsing of hollow men amid alienated desolation, there is a furious, but difficult to apprehend, activity of recolonisation—a feral reclamation of lost life. Kinsella's wheatbelt is a paradoxical conjunction of sinister, creeping death ("the salt's white mystery") and frantic, unruly life—here figured by the finches. The other key element to note, again because of its extension through much of Kinsella's later work, is the position of the witness. His is a poetry of witness, and while the register of this witness can modulate significantly—sometimes comic, sometimes desperate, other times inhabiting an almost inhuman, affectless distance—his poems all have the quality of attestation and a plea that someone, everyone, needs to notice what is going on.

Moreover, the wheatbelt that we see in "Finches" is a summer wheatbelt, drawn from memories of childhood summers spent at "Wheatlands". Hot Januaries, where it seems the only things moving are the bored children of farms and their cousins visiting from the city. Water has all but disappeared from the earth's surface and, indeed, the very idea of moisture seems almost impossible to imagine. In the 1970s that Kinsella grew up in, air-conditioning and swimming pools had not yet arrived to offer their significant solace to the wheatbelt, and people sweltered through summers or ran to the coast. It is this hot, dry wheatbelt that ties in so closely with the desert metaphysics of Australian modernism, typified by the paintings of Arthur Boyd, Sidney Nolan and Russell Drysdale, the poets of the Jindyworobak school of the late 1930s and through the 1940s, and the mature literary masterpieces of Judith Wright's *The Moving Image* (1946), Patrick White's *Voss* (1957) and Randolph Stow's *Tourmaline* (1963).

In Kinsella's second volume with Fremantle Arts Centre Press, *Eschatologies* (1991), the wheatbelt takes centre stage, becoming a fully-fledged locus of action and life—a universe in fact.[9] The first section of the volume, subtitled "The Millenarian's Dream", contains eighteen poems about the wheatbelt and initiates a number of the lines of thought that will run through Kinsella's work in subsequent decades. But whereas in Hewett, the wheatbelt was a cipher for the baroque fantasy structure by which she unified her familial network, in Kinsella the wheatbelt emerges in imagistic fragments, much like the way the boys saw the finches darting about in the tamarisk thicket. Also, in Hewett we get to know her cast of family characters, or their various avatars, but in Kinsella's poetry we rarely meet people—at least not in the interior way in which family get known. Hewett's lore is passed down through her forbidding ancestors, and while Kinsella's poems share this quality of hearsay and rumour (i.e. of an amorphous, hidden truth), the revelations come as if from strangers, conversations overheard in pubs, or picked up as asides in more workaday encounters. To the extent that people populate Kinsella's poetry, they do so as figures of pathos, shrunken by guilt or, even worse, by the self-abnegation that comes about when guilt is refused. Instead of actual people, the poems tend to feature the signs of people now gone, as if the perpetrators have fled the scene of the

64. Kinsella as a toddler and playing cricket at "Wheatlands". Kinsella is batting and the Needling Hills are in the background.

crime. In this way he has an eye for the past that is not so far from Barbara York Main's, although she does not share his sense of surreal interconnection. The animate forms of Kinsella's poems are mainly non-human—mammals (feral and native), insects, reptiles, birds; but also, the diverse flora of the wheatbelt is catalogued lovingly through Kinsella's poems, and other kinds of natural phenomena, from the erosion of granite to the explosion of summer lightning.

The opening poem in *Eschatologies*, "Inland", marks a muted entry into the topos. In some ways we see quite a traditional scrub-and-stubble portrait of an Australian rural hinterland.

> On the cusp of summer
> an uncertain breeze
> rises in grey wisps
> over the stubble —
> the days are ashen,
> moods susceptible,
> though it does not take
> long to get back
> into the swing of things
> …
> it's a place of borrowed dreams
> where the marks of the spirit
> have been erased by dust —
> the restless topsoil (14–15)

This idea that the wheatbelt is built on "borrowed dreams", though, is quite scandalous. To say the wheatbelt is built on dreams is one thing (the shire histories are more than happy to affirm this), but to say these dreams are "borrowed" impugns their legitimacy. It puts a distance between the founding ideas and the would-be founders, between the dream (the ideology of wheat) and the pioneer (the "man on the land"). In this way, Kinsella, like Hewett, Flood and York Main (all in slightly different ways), undertakes a critique of the pioneer narrative. Kinsella is more like Flood than Hewett inasmuch as he does not content himself with naming the sins of the father, but proceeds to a present-day analysis of things happening *right now*.

Another persistent feature in Kinsella's work is his interest in non-human life. The identification with animals is one of the strongest continuities in this literary history, something that runs from Facey, through Pollard, Goode, Ewers, Davis and York Main. But animal life in Kinsella's work appears in a way distinct from each of his predecessors. Animals in his poems are either blessed by a strange resilience, something elusive and awkward, or blighted with the symptoms of the wheatbelt's affliction. In this latter guise, they are the horrific undead remainder of a process of destruction that has since been camouflaged by the ordered landscape of the settled wheatbelt. For many of the early writers, the animals conveyed loss—they were the emblems of their own extinction, poignant reminders of the wholesale destruction of habitat that took place when the wheatbelt was "cleared". But in Kinsella's poetry, the animals are also signs of an improbable endurance. Indeed, animals in his poems become a loosely aligned non-human army that begins to reinscribe the present with an alternative future. This sense of an alternative future is the revolutionary component of Kinsella's wheatbelt, one which can easily be missed if one only hears the more overt jeremiad. We have already seen the finches at work in the heart of the salt "snow"; there are many other poems where creatures busy themselves in this way, animating the ruins to which they are indifferent. Amongst the abandoned machinery rusting at the edges of fields, or the abandoned mine-shafts, or the partially collapsed wells dug in earlier generations, animals and plants grow tenaciously and incongruously as if to re-close a wound in the land. Not perfectly, to be sure, and not in a way that might be predicted, but their contrarian spirit seems the only way out of a hideous human impasse. These qualities are visible in the poem "Spontaneous Regeneration", also taking place on salt-damaged land:

> I am here to rekindle
> the moon dying in its race
> for the sun, to break
> the puff and bubble of salt,
> to entertain the legions
> of black-winged stilts

in their long march
to the dam, to harness
the wind dusting
knucklebones of a frayed
and peeling earth, to enter
the season of spontaneous
regeneration
        in company. (21)

The poem places the poet in the position of regenerator. Again, this is not quite the Fisher King of modernist poetry, who will redeem the wasteland of modernism by bringing back the ancient cycles of fertility. Instead, we have the distinctly postmodern acceptance of partial reparation and micro-healing of the kind we saw at the end of Flood's *Oceana Fine*. There is a post-catastrophic reconciliation at work in the vision of the wheatbelt that emerges in Kinsella's poems. They are poems about living in a blighted world, a salinised world. The "black-winged stilts" are the emblems of a certain dumb resilience: awkward, elegant, unbowed. While not the "I" of the poem, these birds "in their long walk / to the dam", are the acting, animate element.

A similar set of avian actors can be seen in the poem, "The Myth of the Grave". In this poem, Kinsella takes up a motif and a theme that were prominent in York Main's work—the motif is the rural gravestone, and the theme is the passage of generations: "A fresh grave that holds three / generations is something you question / on a first encounter." (29) So we have moved ahead one generation from York Main. Her "Third Generation Farm" is about a boy whose grandfather selected the original bush-block. But in Kinsella's poem, a grave containing three generations speaks necessarily to a fourth. Still, the poem is circumspect on the pretension of the monument:

The epitaph is measured
by the size of the plaque,
or is it the plaque that's
measured by the epitaph?

It seems to matter.
Death becomes a question
of economy — the lavish are big
on ceremony, slight on prayer. (28)

This kind of wry epigram is reminiscent of Robert Frost, and his neat summations of country wisdom. Against the incongruous mass of the grave—sitting in the landscape like the A-Class bin that loomed ominously in Flood's novel—the rest of the non-human world continued to enact its cycles oblivious to the human memorialisation in its midst. First, there is "A pair of painted quails" scurrying "across the quills of stubble" and then,

At a distance
sheep leave salt-licks
beside a dam and zig-zag down towards the shade.

Grey gums bend with the tide
of the breeze, the midday sun
would carry their doubles
to the grave and fill the urns.

The ground dries and crumbles,
a lizard darts out of a crack
and races across the paddock.
Do ashes rest easily here? (29)

The quails, the sheep, the grey gums and the lizard form this ancillary lifeworld that darts and scurries about a wheatbelt seemingly scraped clear of its biota. The humans are nowhere, three generations are now buried in a tiny rural plot, but at the same time they are everywhere in the sense that the landscape has been radically remade to serve them. The animals are the survivors of the great extermination, and some—like the sheep—are its introduced servants. If the wheatbelt is characterised by a process of progressive settlement, then Kinsella's wheatbelt poetry is defined by its antithesis: *regressive unsettlement*.

What marks the boundary between modernism and postmodernism in the wheatbelt is the quality of alienation that governs their respective wastelands. In Hewett's modernism, the devastated farm at Lambton Downs is destroyed by all-too-human forces—a woman's greed, a man's cowardice, a child's sin. Betrayal, venal ambition, and the corrupt flesh are at the heart of the problem. In the kind of wasteland that emerges in Flood and Kinsella, the landscape becomes not just inhuman, but unnatural. A radical interruption in life itself has occurred, and no Fisher King can undo it. For Kinsella, the salt-affected paddocks and slowly spreading saltpans are like the extrusion of non-life into the plane of the living. The poem "Pillars of Salt" is the most arresting of the six poems that touch on salt in *Eschatologies*:

> The salt is a frozen waste
> in a place too hot for its own good,
> it is the burnt-out core of earth's eye,
> the excess of white blood cells.
>
> …
>
> Salt crunches like sugar-glass, the sheets
> lifting on the soles of shoes (thongs scatter
> pieces beyond the hope of repair) — finches
> and flies quibble on the thick fingers
> of salt bushes, a dugite spits
> blood into the brine. (34)

This appearance of an eerie, fragile membrane on the surface of the salt-pan is suggestive of the very first dermal accretions in the wake of injury. The land is not quite a raw wound, but, as the "excess of white blood cells" makes clear, a wound in the initial moments of reparation, the merest incipience of a scab. There is a rawness, a stinging hypersensitivity in Kinsella's poetry that contrasts sharply with Hewett's cold fury, and is not quite matched in this regard by any other of the wheatbelt writers. And it is this present-tense suffering that defines Kinsella's work and drives its urgency.

In 1990, between *Night Parrots* and *Eschatologies*, Kinsella founded the literary magazine *Salt*, which he would edit and publish for most

65. A wheat paddock near Yealering; Andrew Wyeth, *Christina's World* (1948).

of the next two decades. The title of this magazine is not surprising because salt, even more than it had been for Hewett, becomes a master-signifier for Kinsella. Salt is more than just a molecule in his work, it is a metaphysical substance that erupts in the fissure between dying and living. Salt means something distinct and ominous in the wheatbelt because of the spread of dryland salinity in its vast cleared areas. It is rainfall, mainly in the form of winter cold fronts, that delivers the salt to the wheatbelt, and it has done so for millennia. Dissolved oceanic salt is contained in the water droplets in these weather systems that sweep in from the Indian Ocean. Because of the flat terrain in southwest Australia, the friable soils and the high evaporation rate, there is very little run-off delivered back to the ocean in rivers. Instead, water either collects in shallow basins (salt-pans) or runs through the soil into the ground. As the rainwater runs through the soil, the salt crystallises there. But the clearing of deep-rooted perennial vegetation in the wheatbelt has caused the water table to rise. Secondary salinity occurs when the water table rises back through the soil and redissolves the salt sequestered there. The first land affected was the lowest land, which in the initial settling of the wheatbelt was also the best land, with the heavier clayey soils. Agricultural technology, though, has allowed the farming of lighter soils and this has offset the loss of productive land due to salinity. Still, it is a massive problem in the wheatbelt. Indeed, dryland salinity is the most significant ecological problem in Western Australia. And yet strangely, and Kinsella's poetry intuits this, the loss of land to salinity has actually been a gain of land for nature. Certainly, it is no longer what it had been—but the primordial condition of the land was lost when it was cleared. However, the fact that farming is no longer possible has allowed saline land to be recolonised by those species in the wheatbelt already adapted to the naturally occurring saline environments. So, the ugly salt "scars" that appear as dead-zones in the patchwork of productive fields are ironically places of significant life and regeneration amid the monocultural desert of the cleared paddocks.

In 1993, Kinsella's third book for FACP, *Full Fathom Five*, was published.[10] Many of the poems in the volume are ekphrastic encounters with paintings by Warhol, Klee, Pollock and others, but, like *Eschatologies*, it begins with a sequence of wheatbelt poems. In *Full Fathom Five*, Kinsella embraces more fully the Gothic mode—here understood as the register of grotesque melancholy and eerie isolation—that had been beginning to inflect the poems in *Eschatologies*. He also starts a process of intertextual identification that would continue hereafter, in which he searches the historical canon of Western high culture for the wheatbelt's genre. In "Wheatbelt Gothic or Discovering a Wyeth", the American regionalist painter Andrew Wyeth (1917–2009) is invoked to convey the atmosphere of remote farmhouses scattered through wide, open fields. In this poem, Kinsella again focuses on a salt-affected pocket of land, a soak and associated well. Soaks were areas of naturally occurring damp ground, often at the edge of granite outcrops. In the settling of the wheatbelt, and going back to the pastoral occupation of the nineteenth century, soaks were often dug out to create small ponds to water stock. With the rise of the water table, these freshwater soaks turned saline as salinised groundwater from neighbouring soil mixed with the freshwater surface run-off that had created the soaks.

> Outflanked by the sheep run, wild oats
> dry and riotous, barbed wire bleeding rust
> over fence posts, even quartz chunks
> flaking with a lime canker, the theme
> chooses itself: *ubi sunti motif*, but the verse
> becomes as deceptive as an idle plough,
> or a mat of hay spread over the ooze
> of a dead sheep that is the floor
> of the soak (blood-black beneath the skin,
> bones honeycombed), crystallised with salt. (13)

The theme of *vanitas* that Kinsella invokes here has been visible throughout this literary history of the wheatbelt, although the precise coordinates of the vanity have varied. Moreover, the dead sheep in the "floor" of the soak is an image of primal sacrifice, or foundational crime, that we see running through many of the modern writers, from Cowan and Hewett, to Jolley and Flood. The stanza in fact concertinas together an array of entropic images that recur throughout

Kinsella's work—discarded machinery, flaking rock, rusting fences, dead wild oats, poisoned wells, and of course, the incipient salt. The apocalyptic grotesquery recalls Bosch and Brueghel with the contorted and abused bodies of dead sheep featuring in a number of the poems, including "Carcass of Sheep in Fork of Dead Tree" (16), where a sheep had been strung up as a target and as bait for birds to be shot.

Postmodernism

With the publication by FACP of *Syzygy*, 1993 also announced a radical swerve in Kinsella's poetry, towards the experimentation associated with the avant-garde American movement clustered around the magazine $L=A=N=G=U=A=G=E$ in the late 1960s and early 1970s.[11] *Syzygy* is Kinsella at his most postmodern, and introduces an alternative vision to the one that emerges in his more realist poems. Even so, these more experimental poems do not completely divest themselves of reference to reality. In fact, Louis Armand has usefully tied Kinsella's experimental poetry to the concept of "traumatic realism" proposed by the American art critic Hal Foster.[12] Foster cites the paradigmatic case of Andy Warhol, whose paintings embody a series of contradictions—they are by turns, Foster writes, "referential and simulacral, connected and disconnected, affective and affectless, critical and complacent."[13] It is this equivocation between representing something and disavowing representation that is characteristic of traumatic realism. For Armand, Kinsella's poetry shares Warhol's traumatic realism inasmuch as it oscillates between the "affective" (Kinsella's passion) and the "affectless" (Kinsella's dissociation). This is a crucial insight because it helps to explain a tonal dissonance that runs through Kinsella's work in which the urgency of the plea for change is partially subdued by the often depersonalised form of the speech. Recognising the traumatic realism of Kinsella's poetry also helps to place him more precisely in the literary history of the wheatbelt. It allows us to make sense of a landscape poet who refuses, from the outset, the very concept of landscape—and to see this as more than mere contrariness. To accept the conventional realism of landscape is, for Kinsella, to accede to the reduction of the non-human world—nature, life, biodiversity—to the status of backdrop. Thus, for Kinsella, conventional realism constantly threatens to eradicate the real. Traumatic realism emerges in deference to this position and sponsors a form of language that proclaims its artifice, indeed proclaims its affinities, with the machinic dimension of modern life.

So, in Kinsella's experimental poetry there is a double articulation to the wheatbelt. On the one hand, its flagrant violations of syntax, its clanging neologisms and interchanging of verb and noun forms, de-unify language and make it appear as jagged, broken wreckage: a linguistic emulation of the devastated landscape. On the other, its valorisation of language as machine gestures towards the wheatbelt as an industrial artefact. And while, on the whole, the wheatbelt does not feature prominently in *Syzygy*, the experiments in that volume do open up new possibilities in Kinsella's writing, which then find their way into subsequent wheatbelt poems. Moreover, vignettes from the wheatbelt do intrude in *Syzygy* on occasion, most notably in the long concluding poem to the collection, "re (con) stru̲ctu̲re ing / damage / control". As the title indicates, a key strategy in this poetry is to use typography to interrupt the linearity of print. So, in the case of the title, the underlining of letters in "structure" allows it double as "suture". Here is an extract from the poem in which the wheatbelt becomes visible in a way that it has never been before:

> quartz or nacre
> lose lustre (less)
> minutiae
> packed & labelled
> analytic & rolling
> fencewire
> plugging gulleys

certain
even
    lichen covered rags
scrunched & welded
ARE dead parrots
sauve-qui-peut
    (!)

The point of impact
fabricates & inde
pend {ates} enhances — a disc plough
or slave cylinder
mixing mediums
with disaster
intra-personally: saltwash,
the creeks are storming
the river
& the crops are
waterlogged — melaleuca & salt scars
collaborate in a bundesfest
discordant
visits politely
call ING music
out-back. the tractor   'wends its way]
no longer bushbashing
but suppurating spray
from soil, frisking
clean air
& tourists
warm in town (296–7)

Clearly poetry written in this mode makes quite significant
demands on the reader, its accumulated violation of linguistic etiquette
prompting protestations: Does this even make sense? Why am I being
addressed like this? What has happened to the basic principles of
grammar? But the text draws you back with its arresting fragments of
lucidity. Again, we have Kinsella moving in a distinctly original way.
So much of what we have considered in this history has been, almost
by definition, a literature directed to location. But here is a poem
about the wheatbelt that is directed towards dislocation, suggesting
a paradox: *the wheatbelt is a dislocated location.* And yet, and this is the
exact point of traumatic realism, we experience a kind of violence
in this poetry that is somehow commensurate with the wheatbelt's
violent formation. By violating grammar, Kinsella's poem makes us

feel, at the very heart of our linguistic being, the violation of land and Indigenous culture that is the inalienable partner of the wheatbelt's foundation.[14] The oddly boxed poetic cliché "wends its way"—which references the desolated saline creeks and eroded gulleys of the wheatbelt—stands off to the side as if to typographically inscribe the hermetic removal from reality enforced by romantic landscape poetry. Instead of the composed middle distance of romanticism, Wordsworth's "emotion recollected in tranquillity", Kinsella's poem attempts to narrate the wheatbelt from the "point of impact". In the poem, this traumatic degree-zero is captured in the simple, seemingly benign image of the "disc plough" incising the soil. And as with much of Kinsella's poetry, we are also contending with a world that is radically desubjectified. The poem aches with the absence of a whole human subjectivity that might contain the destruction. And in fact, it is a broken self—a self in parts—that seems to answer most truly to the broken landscape. Poetic sympathy, the hallmark of romantic poetry, is transformed through the metaphors of the mechanical world. Here, the poet is a "slave cylinder", dependent for its movement on the operation of a "master" cylinder in a hydraulic circuit. But there is no master cylinder named in the poem. Or, if there is one, it seems to be disaster itself, functioning as an implied apostrophe. The poet becomes disaster's avatar, "mixing mediums / with disaster / intrapersonally".

The Silo (1995)

After the experimental effusion of *Syzygy*, Kinsella's next major work—*The Silo* (1995)—returned his oeuvre to the broadly realist lyrical mode.[15] *The Silo* is a major event in the literary history of the wheatbelt, and a major new stage in Kinsella's career. It is his first volume entirely devoted to the wheatbelt and it saw Kinsella fully embrace the role of wheatbelt bard.[16] The success of *The Silo* led to Fellowships from The Literature Board of the Australia Council, and reading tours to Cambridge University, the United States and Canada. Eventually Kinsella took up residencies as a fellow at Cambridge and at Kenyon College in Ohio on the strength of this work. *The Silo* is divided into five sections that correspond to the five movements of Beethoven's 6th "Pastoral" Symphony. The invocation of the pastoral motif is part of a broader deconstruction of rural mythologies that Kinsella has pursued throughout his career. In some ways, one might see Kinsella's whole poetic project as a protracted tarrying with the pastoral ideal.[17] He describes his particular stance as "counter-pastoral", a term he takes from the great Marxist literary critic Raymond Williams. Williams distinguishes, in fact, between the pastoral, the anti-pastoral and the counter-pastoral.[18] The pastoral tradition has been remarkably durable since its classical origins. At its core, the pastoral "idyll" is a fantasy of return to a less complex time and way of life and reflects the division between town and country that features in most agricultural human societies. The anti-pastoral is a mode closely connected to the pastoral, but inverts the valuation, denouncing the very things that pastoral celebrates. So, in the anti-pastoral, simplicity becomes small-mindedness, quietude becomes boredom, and seasonal cycles represent endless stagnation. The third term, "counter-pastoral", was introduced by Raymond Williams to designate literature which sought to critique the basic assumptions of the pastoral fantasy (which the anti-pastoral tends to leave intact, albeit in inverted form), and it is with this critical tradition that Kinsella identifies and to which his work properly belongs.[19]

If we look at *The Silo* we begin to see what counter-pastoralism means. The section titles take their cues from the short descriptions that Beethoven gave for each of the movements of his pastoral symphony. The first movement is glossed by Beethoven in the following manner: "*Erwachen heiterer Empfindungen bei der Ankunft auf dem Lande*" [Awakening of cheerful feelings upon arrival in the countryside].[20] This is the classical beginning of a pastoral idyll—the arrival of the urban refugee into the embrace of rural simplicity. But Kinsella refuses all such automatic consolations. Hence, Kinsella's first section is titled "On Arriving At A Deserted House Deep In The Country", already signalling a rather different kind of arrival, and suggesting a transposition of the pastoral into the Gothic mode. But the arrival is twisted again, when the section title becomes the title of the first poem, but with this addition: "… After Running Over A Rabbit On A Gravel Road, At Night". Here is the poem in full:

The flywire door slams ominously
as the fluorescent starter cracks

and light suggests company
that evaporates, fails

to materialize. An Axminster sofa
eases comfortably, though beneath

the covering you know the springs
are shot, recoiling like bad suspension

as the car grinds to a sluggish halt,
tyres slicked with blood-letting,

fur-coated in summer. Stop damned
flywire, stop! Yes, the front door's

open as well, channelling the southerly
through the kitchen. Mice unsettling.

If not fear then uncertainty
curtains the windows like moon slick

on a densely atmosphered night. Wide-eyed
like a rabbit, I await my brother.

The forest, tidal and moving away,
a dim shadow from the back verandah,

the paddocks grey-blue and dissoluble,
while I, ultramarine, hear voices

tackling the distance, calling
fluorescence into darkness. (12–13)

This arrival poem is reminiscent of the opening scene in Cowan's story "The Unploughed Land", where the protagonist Lee arrives at a fog-bound farm at night. Cowan's story, though, ultimately resolved this uncertain beginning through the (mostly) conventional mechanism of pastoral romance: Lee married Vera, the farmer's daughter (after getting her pregnant), and takes over the running of the farm, thereby securing its generational succession. Kinsella's poems do not go in that direction. People never quite get settled on the land. At best, they acclimatise to their unease. This opening poem from *The Silo* is one which could be used to typify much of the conflict that surrounds location in Kinsella's poetry; the fact that location, in his writing, is constantly transmuting into dislocation and back again. *The Silo* is dedicated to his younger brother Stephen, a shearer who has worked up and down the wheatbelt throughout his life. The poem narrates the arrival of Kinsella at his brother's house near the Williams farm ("Happy Valley") where Stephen is working, and the book owes much to the time that Kinsella spent working with his brother at Happy Valley. But in the poem the house is eerily empty—the knocking of the flywire door in the wind and the sinister crackle of fluorescent tube lighting convey a desolate and uncanny emptiness that is brilliantly captured in the enjambed lines: "light suggests company / that evaporates, fails // to materialise." It is a poem of aphanisis, the eerie disappearance that animates so much of the horror genre by alluding to a primal terror of abandonment. This is what happens to the pastoral trope when the urban refugee flees to the embrace of the country, only to find it an empty, hollow shell. What ensues in the poem is a kind of preternatural reanimation. The uncanny agency now acquired by the electric lights, the doors, the mice, the wind, the "tidal" movement of the forest and the "grey-blue" shadow of the paddocks—all replace a life that is felt to have suddenly disappeared. And mixed into these undead signs is the recollection of a rabbit that was run over, not, apparently, on this particular occasion, but earlier, in the "summer". Reflecting some years later on this poem, Kinsella discloses that,

> [f]or a vegan, the death of the rabbit presented both an ontological, a
> spiritual disaster, as well as an emotional one. It recalled [a] time from
> childhood when I shot rabbits – a memory repugnant to my adult

self, but one I have constantly to confront … [The poem] becomes a confessional, a transference. It opens the book ominously (for me at least), as no journey into the country (the pastoral construct) can be free of guilt by association, at the very least.[21]

This lays bare the basic gesture that so much of Kinsella's poetry enacts, which is to locate the crimes of childhood in the matrix of the broader ecological disaster of the wheatbelt, to unite the "emotional disaster" of infancy and adolescence with the "spiritual" and "ontological" disaster he sees in the wheatbelt. The dead rabbit, whose blood still "slicked" the tyres of his car, is thus like the dead finch in "Finches" and, in fact, the whole charnel house of dead animals that punctuate Kinsella's work. But rather than dead, it is more correct to say that the animals in Kinsella's poems are *undead*, moving with the pathos and quiet incrimination of zombies in the stanzas of his poetry.

And yet, not all the poems in *The Silo* are suffused with horror. There are simple Georgics that describe the gentle rhythms of rural life and the unselfconscious pleasures of bucolic existence. In particular, the middle "movement" of the volume ("Drinking In The Saloon Bar Of A Country Hotel"), celebrates the knockabout life of wheatbelt farmers and workers—new tractors, holidays to Bali, tall-tales at the local pub. And there are also slightly sharper Frostian meditations such as "Harvest" (38–41) or "Rock Picking: Building Cairns" (33–4) which see a certain earthy profundity in the practices of those on the land. These bring Kinsella closer to the poet Les Murray, whose work has also been a major influence. Particularly in the 1980s and '90s, Murray was the leading Australian poet and one whose exploration of a de-romanticised Australian countryside, most particularly that of his native Bunyah in the dairy country of coastal New South Wales, provided a significant example to Kinsella. Several of *The Silo*'s more gothic poems have an equanimity and playful irony about them that are reminiscent of Murray's tonal palette. "Hoppers And Gargoyles" is a Murray-esque poem consisting of two opposing stanzas. The first unfolds with the kind of wry judgement that Barbara York Main displayed in relation to the modern farming practised by her brothers and which was wiping out the remaining vegetation of the wheatbelt in the 1960s and '70s:

> A screw drives the lupins towards the chute,
> lupins spill into the hopper, an auger drags
> them upwards towards the spout, lupins spill
> into the silo. These are the facts, or facts
> as they seem to the farmer who follows
> the tried-and-true procedure, believes
> what his eyes tell him, and is satisfied
> with the end result. These are the facts
> as his father has told him, neighbours. (23)

Like York Main, Kinsella here adopts a relationship of irony to the world of "facts" which others dutifully invoke in the manner of an alibi, fortified by the tonic of common sense. But for York Main, the errors that were committed—the overstocking, the needless clearing, the relentless cropping—were attributable to human greed and short-sightedness, a moral parsimony that was culpable but not hideous or inhuman. In this view, York Main and Hewett share common ground with Pollard and Ewers. But Kinsella's poetry falls within a new and sinister vision of the wheatbelt that first found expression in the prose of Peter Cowan and became much more pronounced in Jolley and Flood, where something deeply hostile to life was seen to emerge in the placid fields of the wheatbelt. So, the second stanza of "Hoppers And Gargoyles" answers the first one like this:

> Another view, another set of facts: the gargoyle
> masquerading as a spout draws all into its mouth
> and spits it back, the hopper—its belly—endlessly
> fuelled by the reaper who, disguised as a farmer,
> cannot be content with endless death, but rather
> gains its pleasure from the neighbours who believe
> what they tell the farmer, who stare at the spout
> and see no more than lupins filling his coffers. (23)

In this way, the instrumental aims of the wheatbelt hide within the plainness and self-evident quality of their facts—the so-called facts of life, at least as they exist in late capitalism—and the "endless death" that is bound to the project. In these sorts of ways, *The Silo* does not offer up the wheatbelt as an unremitting wasteland, but as a place of contradiction, where genuine pleasure and goodwill can be suddenly and uncannily inverted.

There is also a pronounced narrative impulse in *The Silo*, with many poems working as tiny stories or short prose poems. This would reappear later in prose collections such as *In the Shade of the Shady Tree* (2012) and *Crow's Breath* (2015), but is seen in *The Silo* in the prevalence of short narrative poems such as "Brothers Trapping Parrots at Mullewa", which begins[22]:

> Using an old bed base
> propped in one corner
> with a star picket
> and sprung with a length
> of cable from behind
> the superphosphate shed,
> two brothers
> with the blessing
> of their father
> trapped flocks
> of pink and grey galahs,
> red and black tailed
> cockatoos and Port
> Lincoln parrots,
> to take back
> to city aviaries. (14)

The poem then narrates how the birds "eventually / perished in damp hessian sacks / slung in a boot and carried / four hundred miles" south to their mother's home in Mount Pleasant. The enormity of the brothers' actions really only sinks in when they reached Perth and saw the "look on their mother's / face". By now we have become accustomed to this kind of crime poem, where a thoughtless act of destruction is confessed or announced. Such incidents litter Kinsella's writing and, as we have seen, draw on an interplay between the delinquent acts of adolescence and the greater tragedy of the wheatbelt as a region of deep and systematic loss. In this way, there is a certain valuable narcissism in Kinsella's approach, where his poetry's obsession with confessing the crimes of his youth—the shot rabbits, the smothered parrots, the incidental cruelties perpetrated by every child in one way or another—does provide an ethical pathway towards owning the problems of the wheatbelt today. The wheatbelt's problems were collectively caused and need to be collectively addressed, but they are also the product of a multitude of individual actions. Where Hewett heaped blame on her ancestors, Kinsella saves an intimate portion of the guilt for himself. Yet there is also a strong connection between his own acutely felt sense of responsibility and the actions of his forebears. It is significant in this poem that trapping the birds was done "with the blessing / of the father", and equally, that it was the mother's implied revulsion that called the action to account. The scene of the crime was their father's farm (the one he was managing for Alan Bond) at Mullewa, but the scene of judgement was their mother's house in the southern suburbs of Perth. This pattern echoes the decision to publish his first poetry under his mother's name of Heywood. In the metaphors of Kinsella's poetry, the father's name, and the position of the father more generally, are associated with horrifying loss and wanton destruction, while the mother occupies the position of grace.

Paranoia

It is impossible to overlook the theme of death that runs most persistently through *The Silo*. From the opening poem about the rabbit that was run over, to the poem of the parrots dying in the boot of the car, to a long poem called "Shootings" which documents the various animals killed by the poet (parrots, crows, rabbits, sheep) and shot by his family and by young men as part of weekend sport—the book returns again and again to the act of killing. The wheatbelt that Kinsella depicts is one of violence, both historical violence—ecological destruction and Aboriginal dispossession—and a residual present violence, constantly simmering beneath the seemingly placid surface of the wheatbelt. This fear is exemplified in the poem "Falnash" from Kinsella's next volume, *Lightning Tree* (1996). The poem is set in another of his brother's farms, this time in the Great Southern, where bands of dissolute locals come at night to shoot the place up:

sometimes the rednecks come
with their guns & cross-haired telescopics
utes & spotlights & cartons of beer

"Shoot Ferals" their engines
rev & throb, slugs ricocheting
from Falnash's solid walls

& as they race down
the gravel track, their hoots
trailing like exhaust (48)

In a similar vein, another poem from that volume, "Heading South through the Long Paddock", is dedicated to Tom Flood and Dorothy Hewett, and concurs with the view given in *Oceana Fine* of life on "the bins" in the 1970s.

On the last day of November
I journey to see my brother,
the tyres sticky on the asphalt
as the ground thunders
with grain trucks.
The fly-blown carcasses
of kangaroos fester like boils
and I think of the times
I worked on the wheatbins,
two seasons in hell,
trapped in a hut with a bunch
of boys who had to be *boys*
even though they probably
found it hell as well. (34)

The poem is a brilliant, bitter diatribe. It is also one of Kinsella's many "driving" poems where the car's windshield becomes like a cinema screen on which the wheatbelt's shadow history is projected. The emergence of the wheatbelt as something primarily apprehended through the window of a car is a phenomenon that we saw first in Jolley's work, and then again in Flood's, but it is in Kinsella's poetry that the car most fully saturates the sensorium.[23] His driving poems replicate a certain benumbed visuality, where the monotony of the landscape induces a trance-like state of anxious reverie that refills the empty fields. Items from the edge of vision— road-kill, distant agricultural machinery, flocks of parrots, dead trees in fields—hover ever more forcefully towards the centre of consciousness and find themselves joined to the repressed events of earlier painful moments. Thus, in this poem, the dead kangaroos by the roadside precipitate an association with the atmosphere of implied violence on the bins, where "boys had to be *boys*". Driving thus gives birth to a steady-streamed phantasmagoria of infernal images, underpinned by scenes of acute trauma. As the poem continues, it draws an intriguing connection between the collapse of words into images, on the one hand, and the threat of destruction, on the other:

> Here, with only the wind
> rushing through the car window,
> my language is of sight
> and words merely compressions
> of what I see: parrot flocks
> seething on the ragged edge
> of a soon-to-be harvested crop,
> the header comb set low
> and a crew getting ready
> to spot that night. The images
> crash into each other (36–7)

The submerged association here is between the harvester ("the header comb set low") and primal loss (death, castration), an association that was also made in the work of both Peter Cowan and Tom Flood (to whom the poem is dedicated). The poem concludes with the persona hitting a "rupture in the road" that allows the associative spell to be broken, and leads to a crucial epiphany that, in many ways, sums up the basic predicament of Kinsella's wheatbelt:

The wheels hit a rupture in the road.
I struggle to maintain control.
Everything here is like something else
because it is not as it was. (37; emphasis added)

The final couplet speaks to the problem of primal loss. This is what the empty horizons of the cleared wheatbelt signify to Kinsella. Indeed, to him, or at least to his poetic persona, it is as though they are screaming their emptiness. Kinsella's writing is remarkable for the way that it brings the loss of the wheatbelt into a direct relationship with de-centred human subjectivity. The critique of the unified, humanist self is one of the major legacies of postmodernism, and Kinsella, with Tom Flood, are the first to bring this to bear as literary witnesses to the wheatbelt. As well as a diagnosis of the wheatbelt, the final announcement—"Everything here is like something else / because it is not as it was"—is also a precise formula for what it means to be a human animal, which is an animal at the mercy of language. Our entry into the linguistic chain defers meaning (and, with it, our existential substance) to the next signifier. In the world of language, of speaking beings, everything can only be "like something else"— the founding breakthrough of postmodernism was to apprehend that language has no positive substance, but consists entirely of difference. Entering the world of language means consigning our imaginary identifications to the background, where they will re-emerge in daydreams, night dreams, poems, mistakes and all the other artefacts of fantasy. In this way, in Kinsella's work we have the wheatbelt functioning as an allegory for post-humanist despair.

The totality of the loss that Kinsella confronts in his poems is mitigated in various ways, but one of the major strategies is that of paranoid recuperation. This is not a term to be taken pejoratively, but simply as designating a particular psychic response to the presence of a void, that is, to the sensation of there being nothing where there ought to be something. We have seen a little of this in Kinsella's poem about the deserted farmhouse. The abhorrence of an empty house is met—not just by Kinsella, but by each of us—with a wish to refill it. Yet we know it is empty. The only way through this impasse is to have it populated by beings that are not bound by rational knowledge. In other words, our rationality bends slightly to accommodate an even stricter mandate against subjective abandonment. The sinister quality that these "ghosts" will have is partly the sign of the fact that they are illicit, in the sense that they contravene the dictates of common sense. If we accept this explanation, it paves the way for making sense of the paranoid strand that features so strongly in Kinsella's writing and which any assessment of his oeuvre needs to take account of. Already visible in *The Silo*, the paranoid dimension comes to the fore in two other volumes by Kinsella from the late 1990s—*Kangaroo Virus* (1998) and *Visitants* (1999).[24] *Kangaroo Virus* was a multimedia collaboration with Ron Sims, in which Kinsella's poems are accompanied by photos and a soundscape by Sims. The book included a compact disc in its sleeve (a relative novelty at the time) containing sounds recorded in the wheatbelt forests at Dryandra along with Kinsella reciting the poems. The book's introduction explains that the book had been a response to an apparent spate of kangaroo deaths in the wheatbelt around Dryandra:

> I'd not long been back from Cambridge, England, when my partner and I decided to spend a day with my brother in Dryandra Forest near his home in Williams. We visited Congelin dam not far off the York-Williams road. My brother had been there a week earlier and found a number of dead kangaroos through the bush. On arriving, we immediately found a corpse floating in the dam like the rotting hulk of a whale. The dam was built to service the railway that used to cut its way through the forest late last century. Gnarled and petrified corpses in grotesque foetal-like positions were to be found through the bush. My brother recounted how in recent months, kangaroos, not only in this district but throughout the wheatbelt, had been struck down by a mysterious "virus" that left them blind. He'd seen them hopping into fences and ploughing into tractors, dead in their dozens along the roads. We talked about the release of the calici rabbit virus, how it had "escaped" before "release" from Kangaroo Island off South Australia. It seemed like a sick coincidence. (9)

In all likelihood, at least some of these events were coincidental. A significant outbreak of Epidemic Blindness (Chorioretinitis) in kangaroos did take place in Western Australia between April 1994 and July 1996, probably caused by the Wallal virus.[25] There are, however, no known crossovers from the calici virus to other mammals, nor is blindness a typical symptom of the calici virus (it kills through rapid haemorrhaging), though it was a symptom of myxomatosis, the biological control introduced to curb rabbits in Australia in 1950. In this sense, the book is best understood as a kind of metaphor. The effects of European intervention in the wheatbelt have been, without doubt, devastating. The enormity of this devastation means that it is actually difficult to represent it fully. This has been a major theme of my study, and the basis for turning to creative literature in order to locate forms of language that might begin to capture the singularity of this event. In this context, the "virus" that Kinsella's and Sims's book addresses is a metaphor for the radical human intervention that has decimated the wheatbelt's natural systems. Put another way, and this is basically what is being said by Kinsella in the excerpt above: humans are the wheatbelt's virus, killing it with the blind efficiency that the calici virus kills rabbits.

The volume consists mainly of "quatrains" by Kinsella which are paired on opposing pages with photographs from Sims. The opening quatrain is paired with a photograph of a cleared field, with a trench in the middle ground, possibly for drainage, but which Kinsella's

66. *Kangaroo Virus*, photograph by Ron Sims.

quatrain likens to the barrow-graves of Neolithic Britain—the sign in other words of a buried culture, an entire universe vanquished by historical forces and lying just beneath the ground.

> As if in barrow country
> where all interlopers or passers-by
> change on entry, something of them
> taken below — a condition of history. (17)

Other photos depict typical wheatbelt objects, but in ways that isolate and estrange them—close-up black-and-white pictures of lichen, disused fencing, abandoned rail structures, rotting trees. The effect is one of uncanny emptiness or unexplained abandonment. The climactic photographs are of the decomposed carcasses of dead kangaroos:

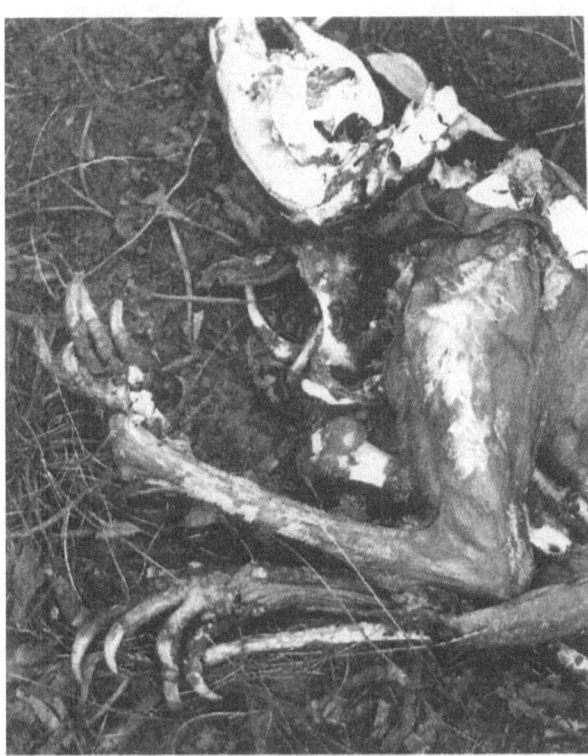

67. *Kangaroo Virus*, photograph by Ron Sims.

The gesture. The fine hand-movements
in the blackout, the down-loading of Hamlet
in the south-west of Australia,
as sharp as the eye is not. Farewell exposure! (61)

This intrusion of the grotesque, one which began with Elizabeth Jolley, signals an important realignment of the wheatbelt within the cultural imaginary. Once the emblem of nature, the wheatbelt becomes, towards the end of the twentieth century, the emblem of something very unnatural—perhaps even the "end" of nature itself. Kinsella's poetics treat the wheatbelt as something that is fatally embedded in modern systems and codes, and sees the poet's role as intervening in these codes, whilst also acknowledging the basic contradiction of fighting symbols with symbols: "Everywhere we look there are the signs of human intervention. Not least, ironically, in our language and image. But what we hear, and what lies before our eyes, can't be ignored. Our visitation is problematic, but we don't want to leave the environment any more disturbed than it already is." (9) Perhaps surprisingly, Kinsella insists that in its basic aims and methods, art is not opposed to science: "As a poet, I explore the data of language for codes and truths. I develop hypotheses and search for answers." (9) In fact, there is a curious mixture of technophilia and technophobia in his writing. One of the virtues of his practice is that he has no time for the cult of purity that can afflict and pervert both modern environmentalism and contemporary eco-poetry. Kinsella's vision is one of feral restoration, of allowing weeds and broken things into the future as the price of new life. Similarly, he does not try to wash technology out of the modern world and live in some hermetic romantic denial. It is a complicated position to maintain, and one not without contradictions, but it is built around an ethic in which killing, eradicating, poisoning, burning and clearing can never be the answer.

In a similar vein to *Kangaroo Virus*, Kinsella's *Visitants* (1999) is a volume of poems which documents an assortment of strange phenomena drawn from anecdotes, personal experience and contemporary rural myth. The title is a gesture to Stow's novel, *The Visitants* (1979), a fantasy novel based on the visit of extraterrestrial life to the Trobriand Islands. Kinsella's *Visitants* narrates various suspicious and paranormal activities, so that the collection is something like a poetic version of the television series *The X-Files* (1993–2002), which was popular in the late 1990s. *Visitants* shares that show's mixture of conspiracy theory (government cover-up) and millennial anxiety. These ingredients are visible in the sequence-poem "Phenomenology", which concludes as follows:

5. keeping your mouth shut – against conspiracy

Area-51 was a place called Nungalloo
just north of Geraldton. The huge
mineral sands processing plants
of Jennings and Allied mutated
out of borderline farmland.
As if a neutral zone, Associated Labs
sat nearby, upwind. Testing
monazite and rutile
late at night a storm hit
the narrative and the x-ray
equipment went wild, the gun
shooting rays outside its alignment,
the telex scripting the electric air,
my flesh spread like an internal horizon –
a chemiluminescent shadow puppet
experimenting with form,
my organs glowed and I watched
the machinery of my fear,
the production of silence. (15)

Again, it makes sense to not necessarily treat these poems as direct assertions of fact. But it would be wrong, too, to stop the poems from engaging with the facticity of the wheatbelt's conditions. The best method for coping with this is to accept them as metaphors, as the creative deployment of analogies and conceits. So, just as the "virus" killing the kangaroos was a way of giving a very particular shape to human-authored environmental destruction in the wheatbelt, the "visitants" (i.e. the alien force) in this volume can be understood as the Europeans who have come, as if from outer space, to a world that had persisted, grown and flourished in complete ignorance of them.[26]

Jam Tree Gully (2012)

This account of Kinsella's poetry is deliberately incomplete, stopping more or less with the end of the twentieth century. Kinsella's investigation of the wheatbelt ramifies after the millennium, producing major new works, modes and motifs. The first of these was his collaboration with Dorothy Hewett, *Wheatlands* (2000), which intersperses poetry with commentary from the two poets who have done most to define the wheatbelt as a literary region.[27] In landmark volumes such as *The Hierarchy of Sheep* (2001), *A New Arcadia* (2005), *Shades of the Sublime & Beautiful* (2008), and *Divine Comedy: Journeys Through a Regional Geography* (2008), the themes we have already seen are given ever greater amplitude.[28] The prose collections, *In the Shade of the Shady Tree: Stories of the Wheatbelt* (2012), *Tide* (2013) and *Crow's Breath* (2015), develop the narrative dimension we have seen in a number of the story-poems in Kinsella's work and marks the most extensive exploration of the wheatbelt in the short-story form since Peter Cowan.[29] In his poetry, a certain slow change of mood is visible and the transit of ideas is best seen if we move ahead to a more recent volume, the acclaimed collection *Jam Tree Gully* (2012), which won Kinsella the Prime Minister's Literary Award in 2013.[30] This volume traces the period in 2009 when Kinsella, together with his wife, the poet Tracy Ryan, and their young son Tim, moved into a small rural property they had purchased the year before. The property was near the town of Toodyay, in the hills that form part of the Darling Range that separates the coastal plain from the plateau of the wheatbelt. This was the first property Kinsella had owned, and the decision to buy it was marked by a distinct ambivalence. For, after all, was he now not joining the land-owning rural class that had decimated the wheatbelt ecosystems and continued to threaten the remaining unspoiled land? It is this dilemma that we see played out in *Jam Tree Gully*.

Many of Kinsella's volumes have cited, as intertextual analogies, works within the pastoral tradition in its broadest sense. As we have seen there was Beethoven's Pastoral Symphony (*The Silo*), but also Philip Sidney (*The New Arcadia*), Edmund Burke (*Shades of the Sublime & Beautiful*) and Dante (*Divine Comedy: Journeys Through a Regional Geography*). *Jam Tree Gully* continues this practice, invoking the spirit of Thoreau's *Walden* (1854). In some ways one might expect Thoreau, the seminal nature writer in the North American tradition, to be a "natural" interlocutor or model for Kinsella. We will recall that in 1979, reflecting on 150 years of literature since the founding of the Swan River colony, Barbara York Main had asked: "Where are our Thoreaus?" However, for reasons already alluded to, the particular form of communion that takes place in *Walden* is not something which can be authentically embraced within the conditions that beset the wheatbelt and press so painfully into Kinsella's vision. Tom Bristow has noted that the relationship with Thoreau in *Jam Tree Gully* is not one based primarily on direct emulation. Instead, Kinsella "mimics" Thoreau's "experimental consciousness" but with a "satirical" inflection.[31] This is a useful way of understanding the postmodern irony in Kinsella's use of allusion. Once upon a time, allusions to classical texts were used to show how the new world had been anticipated by the old. But postmodernism bespeaks a world in such a rapid state of change that it is no longer able to locate itself within tradition and uses irony to decry this alarming detachment. We see this in Kinsella's invocation of Thoreau, where he seems to be suggesting that Thoreau's example is both crucial and absurd.

Jam Tree Gully is a distinctly personal book—almost a diary in poems—as Kinsella attempts to document the difficult decision to live authentically in the wheatbelt. Marked by a new and acute existential urgency—the need, in short, for a home—Kinsella leans more heavily on Thoreau than on the other figures he has appealed to in earlier works. In *Jam Tree Gully* there is, for instance, a notable absence of "driving" poems which had become a major mode epitomised by Kinsella's *Divine Comedy*. But in *Jam Tree Gully*, the poetic persona resists a deeply felt urge for movement and doggedly stays put. In "Arrival: First Lines Typed at Jam Tree Gully", Kinsella surveys the property—or, as he might prefer, performs a kind of *anti-survey*—counting, and excitedly noting what is there and what is not:

> Weebills are here! And mistletoe birds
> have been where mistletoe fruits have prospered,
> have seeded jam trees, where nectar hungry
> birds of many varieties test the flowers
> drooping in swatches from thin, straining necks (22)

Initially, the poem appears to evoke the familiar enthusiasm of nature poetry: its wish to capture nature in harmony with itself. However, Kinsella's habitual move at such moments is to express a sense of disconnection rather than to savour the scene—to feel painfully the sense of his own intrusion and to apologise. The verse continues:

> the parasitic engenders its own chains of being.
> I am not asking to be part of it. With time,
> something will click, I have no idea what. (22)

The "parasitic" mistletoe of the earlier lines is now generalised into "the parasitic" as a foundational category. The parasitic, in this sense, is part of an important thematic strand in Kinsella's work that accents the dynamics of dependency. Just as significant, though, is that the chains of being which "the parasitic engenders"—the ecosystem more generally—are irrevocably cast on the other side of the "I" that observes them. Here we find illustrated a post-Romantic position: where Romanticism makes use of the pathetic fallacy to establish a unity between the natural world and the poetic sensibility, the post-Romantic universe accentuates the profound otherness of the non-human. In contemporary thinking, this may indeed appear to represent a positive ethical move, a welcome corrective to the imperial Romantic ego that grandly subsumes the sky, the mountains, and the entire ecosphere into the ensemble of its moods and ideation. Today's eco-poet studiously avoids any such aggrandisement, adopting a position of humility and deference. But Kinsella's persona goes further still: he represents himself as a perpetrator (or at least, a close relative of the perpetrator) returning to the scene of the crime, daring to show his face to the victims, torn between wishing to make amends and the thought that his very presence can only make things worse.

Returning to the passage above, we observe not only that the persona baulks at asking to be part of the chains of being that hold the natural world together—already, after all, a deep and radical exclusion—but that the speaking voice drops suddenly out of the poetic, aphoristic phrasing used to celebrate the weebills and the mistletoe birds. The idiom falls suddenly into clattering, colloquial prose: "I am not asking to be part of it. With time, / something will click, I have no idea what." This idiomatic collapse appears to compound the expulsion; after all, it is the fact of language that tears us from the chain of being and binds us to the chain of signification.

What seems to be novel in *Jam Tree Gully* is its articulation of the relationship of poetry to bioregional place. In this new kind of encounter, damage meets damage, fragility meets fragility. It is not that Romantic eco-poetry lacks the doubts which pervade Kinsella's work—Wordsworth's *Prelude* (1799) and Whitman's *Leaves of Grass* (1855) are punctuated by misgivings and uncertainties. The post-Romantic position, however, is defined by a nature that no longer provides existential redemption; it is still a stage for human drama, this much stays the same, but what is now staged is fracture, loss, fragility. The comparison of Kinsella to Thoreau amply illustrates this poetic vision of fragility. For Thoreau, the hut he builds at Walden Pond acts as a stable base from which he begins to observe, contemplate, document and extrapolate. By contrast, Kinsella occupies his Toodyay property in the way a cat approaches a new apartment—carefully sniffing each corner, cautiously advancing, casting nervously around for exit points and lines of flight, before eventually disappearing into a dark corner of a cupboard for several days. In the opening poems, we see a series of preliminary explorations of this kind. In "We Spend Days in the House" the title is continued in the poem's first line: "… but not nights" (24), a statement which is repeated four times, at the beginning and end of the first and last stanzas:

> We spend days in this house but not nights.
> We have seen the early morning sunlight
> infiltrate the eucalypts, sunset deflected
> by acacias. We have sweltered at midday.
> We have walked every acre intimately.

The kangaroos recognize us and linger.
We spend days in this house but not nights. (24)

This qualified occupation is in stark contrast to Thoreau's installation of self at the centre of things. Several poems in *Jam Tree Gully* address the fact that one of the first jobs on the property was to remove the fences, both internal fences and the fence that adjoined the nature reserve on one side of the property. This emancipatory gesture is cast as a key first step in restoring the property to life. The presence of the kangaroos, which graze on the fields that until recently had held sheep and horses, is a sign of this shift in disposition.

But time and again the stress of the poems falls on the limits of this rapprochement. Animal meets human, and human must stand back and admit their non-admittance—that however much the human might wish to be a part of this world, they must not presume to enter it. "Eagles at Sunset Stock Epithet", a poem about watching in fascination the flight of wedge-tailed eagles, concludes as follows:

... Night falls and we climb
back down to the house, oversensitised—almost—
to the movements of what the eagles were after,
a transference we're not ready for—true or not,
wishful thinking, hunger for thermal imaging. (30)

In this case the hesitation is not only out of deference to the animal's otherness, but from the fact that a full "transference" would situate the subject as pure predator, a somewhat awkward position for a vegan pacifist.[32] But the key dynamic here is the sudden arrest of fantasy, the collapse of reverie that is the mark of Kinsella's post-Romanticism. In another poem, "Reptile Life", the animal addressed is a blue-tongued skink, "the largest I've seen" (31). But again, the poem does not emphasise an unmediated access to the animal. It is not just a poem about a lizard, but a poem about looking up the lizard in a reptile book. This simple action of consulting a reference work to discover what it is we are looking at is usually never mentioned, forming part of the polite unconscious of nature poetry. The romantic nature poet tends to put forward knowledge of the natural world as somehow *a priori*—as if it springs from the same primary substance as nature itself. Kinsella's work does not obey this pretence, but candidly foregrounds its own ignorance. In this light, Kinsella's blue-tongued skink is a hypertext—a text that refers immediately to another text, in such a way that the subsequent text replaces the former. But in "Reptile Life", the hypertextual action of replacing an image of the lizard with its description, keeps undoing itself:

> A reptile book is a way of saying language
> isn't tired in your hands, looking up a species.
> Photo ID or running a finger down an index.
> Eye, skin, elision. What tongue twists its warning.
> A book of riddles in that old between-the-epochs speech.
> We measure life by their presence—snakes
> and lizards. They ripple gloss across the pages,
> exfoliate granite. Quiet in the biting sun.
> But beneath a boulder, an easement cupping
> A blue-tongue skink, the largest I've ever seen.
> What do we say to that? Nothing in the pages
> to correlate. Brandishing in the shade,
> smoothed to cool and breathing slowly,
> travesty of winter in mid-summer apostasy.
> It watched with one eye and paced its heartbeat.
> Without religion, we make our exegesis
> out of amateur herpetology: those shiny
> pages, measures of scale and thermoregulation.
> Heating or cooling, we exclaim the wonder
> of observation. It fits the picture and outgrows it. (31)

In this poem, the animal's life is translated into the classificatory system by which science recognises it. This act of translation captures the poignancy of Kinsella's writing, pinpointing what makes it, despite its avowed posthumanism, fundamentally human; it strives to make the signifier live, catching the shadow of movement in even the most desiccated language. Here the stationary reptile, cold-blooded and thermoregulating, presents as the exact analogy of the enigma of speech. The blue-tongue lizard is silent and yet it is, both in the poem and in the encounter to which the poem alludes, signifying.[33] This situation offers a variation on the more general project of ecocriticism, which defines environmental writing as oriented to the recognition of nature's otherness—what Lawrence Buell calls "an aesthetics of relinquishment".[34] In this way, ecocriticism upholds the ecocentric ethics of deep ecology.[35] Yet in "Reptile Life", instead of the poem declaring language's incommensurability with nature, the reptile—utterly still and basking on the granite outcrop—comes alive in the pages of the reptile book, to "ripple across its pages". Further still, it seeks to bring the book into the organic world of dynamic change, making the book itself subject to the kind of deep-time processes in which granite takes on its familiar bulbous shape through spheroid erosion. The geological term "exfoliate" captures the organic quality of erosion and alludes, in one of the poem's most electric images, both to the skin shed by the lizard and the pages of the book.

The poems in *Jam Tree Gully* do not immerse John Kinsella in an ecology, even though they are charting the acutely felt process of his trying to be at home in nature. To be in nature, for Kinsella, is not an act of mystical communion, but to be afflicted by nature—to feel its sting. This can be seen in the many poems about bees, wasps and hives in Kinsella's work. For Kinsella, the hive is the emblem of the hostile, fascinating, inassimilable point at the centre of human subjectivity (i.e. that which decentres "us"). In *Jam Tree Gully*, the poem "Hive Liberty" begins with the familiar observational gesture of nature poetry:

> Most of the York gums here are old
> and hollow. Many are dead and collapsed
> open like a star losing its mass. Inside
> one, down in the gully, bees have invested
> an opening, a hollow where a limb has torn
> away and termites have eaten the rings
> of time. It echoes with bees, wild and intense
> through the fissure, fanning flames
> of neologisms because 'feral' doesn't fit. (33)

This speculative moment reaches a strange, and unusually concrete, epiphany. The bees encircle the persona and one stings him; just one sting which announces a boundary. He is not driven away by swarms of angry bees; he is simply stung. The persona then takes this lesson home:

> I will show the rest of the family,
> but warn them to go only so close—
> not as close as I went: curious, arrogant,
> sure I'd make it through and become
> staunch defender of hive liberty,
> co-existence wherein we title our claims. (33)

This last example gives some support to Bristow's characterisation of Kinsella as a satirist. Here, his own ideals are the target: the bees literally puncture and deflate his self-importance. But the poem has a deadly serious message because it is this establishing of a proper distance that is the key psychic operation. Our fantasies, defences and the symbolic itself are geared towards keeping this distance just, as the poem correctly puts it, *so close*.

Another element of the bee poem is the reminder that these kind of hive-based honeybees are in fact "feral" European bees that were brought out with colonisation and have become established in the ecosystems of Australia. The wilderness purist tends to abhor all "introduced" species. Certainly, feral animals (birds, spiders, insects, mammals, toads, fish) and plants (weeds) have caused untold damage to an Australian biosphere whose continental isolation led species to evolve very differently within their unique environment. But Kinsella does not vilify feral species; indeed, they are celebrated. His whimsical poem "Goat" features a wizened goat with one hoof missing, which stands in for a certain guileless genius. Being considered destructive pests, feral goats, like feral pigs, horses, dogs, cats, donkeys, foxes and camels, are subject to culling. But Kinsella cannot reconcile this with an ethics of nature.

> … To us, it is Goat
> who deserves to live and its 'wanton destruction'
> the ranger cites for shooting on sight
> looks laughable as new houses go up, as dozers

push through the bush, as goats in their pens
bred for fibre and milk and meat forage
down to the roots. (27)

There certainly is a particular form of hatred that attaches to feral animals in Australia, a country where the undisputed monarch of feral animals is the European human. The poem continues:

Goat can live and we don't know
its whereabouts. It can live outside nationalist tropes.
Its hobble is powerful as it mounts the outcrop
and peers down the hill. Pathetic not to know
that it thinks as hard as we do, that it can loathe
and empathise. Goat tells me so. I am being literal.
It speaks to me and I am learning to hear it speak.
It knows where to find water when there's no water
to be found—it has learnt to read the land (27)

What is valued in *Jam Tree Gully* is not the idealised synthesis, the homeostatic ecosystem, but the fissure where things disappear and come into existence, a breakage which holds the fragile interface between life and death. "Hive Liberty" is, as we saw, a precise rendering of this logic. The hive had formed in the hollow of a dead tree, a York gum which had "collapsed / open like a star losing its mass". This collapsing star, a singularity, is the point at which things are both most dead and, paradoxically, most alive. For it is here that "bees have invested / an opening", an opening made by another hive creature, termites, that "have eaten away the rings of time", which is to say, the tree's flesh. The bees pour in and out of this hole, "wild and intense / through the fissure" (33).

In a more muted form we see a version of the life-bearing-fissure conceit in a poem called simply "Leak", which describes a leak in a rainwater tank—no small thing for the tinder-dry country of the wheatbelt. In farmhouses across the wheatbelt, many of which have no scheme water, the rain which falls in the winter months from May to September is harvested from the roofs and guttered into tanks for domestic consumption. It must last through the long, dry summer, or water will have to be trucked in. The signs of a leaking rainwater tank, in these circumstances, drag painfully on one's sense of survival. In a world as parched as this, a dripping tap is a crime, a sin against the basic precepts of dry-country living. It is not exactly a matter of life and death—Toodyay is hardly at the ends of the Earth, and in modern conditions, the leak is more an inconvenience than an actual threat. Yet the leak remains as a sign that water is not to be taken for granted, that without some quite essential precautions one could die for the lack of it. This small domestic detail, in other words, opens up onto the precariousness of human life:

> The ninety-thousand-litre rainwater tank
> is concrete and afflicted by cracks—where
> water leaks through, lime and algae react
> with water and air and seals the cracks.
> At present, there is a large fracture
> that won't close over, though layers
> of plant and mineral are building.
> Small birds—probably thornbills—
> grip this formwork and drink
> as if from a slowly dripping tap,
> the trace of water in forty-degree heat
> doubly enhanced by the shade. Pinpoint
> beaks catch a droplet and tilt back
> with a flash that would ignite all around,
> so combustible, so traumatised
> by dryness, the eradication of moisture.
> The leakage is remarkably cool
> as it emerges, so much pressure
> behind it, concrete perspiring
> in the volatile and oily air. (34)

Like "Hive Liberty", this poem is an ode to a very specific form of aperture. It is a secret, at first imperceptible, life-giving fissure. Even in a poem on seepage, there is an electric, incendiary element offered through the conceit of the birds' beaks darting at the droplets. This atmosphere of threat hovers through much of *Jam Tree Gully*.

Although I have emphasised that Kinsella's poetry is, in quite a radical way, about life, I should also clarify that the poems in *Jam Tree Gully* retain the persistent sense of threat that runs through the earlier works. The book is filled with disconcerting discoveries—unexplained bones, noises, gunshots—the gully indeed seems alive with uncanny and ominous signs. But signs of what? Certainly, we are made conscious of the fact that this country is, to recall a phrase from Barbara York Main, "twice trodden ground". The phrase designates not only that the wheatbelt is Indigenous land now occupied by the coloniser, but that it is characterised by a sort of perpetual belatedness, in which one never fully connects with the place as a point of origin, but rather as a latecomer to the scene. This last quality points towards a certain crisis in temporality which makes the wheatbelt symptomatic of the current epoch. The ancient ecosystems have been shattered and now exist in fragments or remnants. The result is a place cleared in large part into the rectilinear allotments of industrialised agriculture and delimited by precise rainfall quanta. But this alienated zone is shot through with the memory of the previous, marvellously intricate living world. This memory exists in the embattled biota of remnant wheatbelt bushland, but also in the enduring lifeways of the Noongar and other Indigenous groups. Kinsella's own heightened sense of the wheatbelt's desecration certainly does not sit easily with his neighbours, as more than one poem attests. The resentment of "greenie" outsiders is often vitriolic and perhaps, in some cases, not entirely without foundation. But to view Kinsella as someone who casts judgement from some Olympian sanctuary is also wrong. The *Jam Tree Gully* poems show a willingness to remain on the ground and in the fray, mired in the reality which continues to emerge.

Epilogue: The Wheatbelt in Deep Time

With any history of a place, one is tempted to offer an ending to the story. But the story of the wheatbelt has not ended. All that my history has been able to do is to suggest something of the forces that drove the wheatbelt into being during the course of the twentieth century, and how these forces were registered in the literary imagination of those living there. I have made a particular claim about the value of literature in the understanding of geography. In this sense, my study is best thought of as an amalgam of literary history, literary sociology and literary geography. There is no exact precedent in this country for what I have done in studying creative writing and the Western Australian wheatbelt, though I am by no means the first to draw a relationship between Australian literature and place.[1] What I have attempted to do here, however, is to treat a settled landscape as a sudden event.[2] This has meant displacing human time into geological time. By doing this I have largely used the writers we have come to know in this study, not as chronicling a long history but as—even though they may stand as much as a century apart—common witnesses to a single event.

While following this approach has implications for the way that the wheatbelt is understood, it also has implications for the way that literature is treated. In particular, rather than presenting the literature as an ensemble of quotations, I have striven to maintain the integrity of each writer as a discrete subject in time and place. This may look at first like a return to a naïve biographical criticism, where an author's work is explained by correlating elements in their writing with elements of their life. Certainly, there is a biographical premise in this study. With the exception of Elizabeth Jolley, I have selected writers who have lived in the wheatbelt for part of their lives. But it is not my intention to mystify this relationship, and a considerable effort has been spent with each writer detailing the ways in which their particular lives intersected with the wheatbelt. Nor has the purpose of treating each writer separately been to quarantine them from criticism. On the contrary, treating them as historically determined subjects has made them directly accountable in ways that are far more exacting than would have been possible if they were quoted in passing or as dimly perceived literary "voices". The paradoxical effect of this is to allow responsibility to flow through each writer into the world that produced them.

Moreover, as important as biography has been to the pursuit of this study, the delineation of genre has been a greater preoccupation. It is this specifying of genre (and attendant concepts such as mode and register) that a training in literature enables. Performing this task allows us to compare wildly different kinds of writing and still ask: what are they saying about the wheatbelt? It is what allows us to account for the generic bias that proceeds from the fact that something is written as memoir, or generational saga, or expressionist drama, or natural history, or historical tragedy, or confessional lyric, to name only a few of the modes we have encountered. This is not just a practical consideration, but one which goes to the heart of knowledge itself. One might think that if only we got rid of genres we could see the wheatbelt as it truly is. But the problem is, whether we realise it or not, that we only know things from within genres. The fact that literature exists in different forms speaks not to an accidental diversity, but to the structural inadequacy of each way of knowing. This is why I have throughout this study emphasised the generative or enabling dimension of each work. Why I have said, for example, that Dorothy Hewett was the first to make the wheatbelt visible as tragedy. Or that

Jack Davis allowed us to see the black wheatbelt for the first time. Each chapter has been premised by this basic underlying question: what is this witness seeing that no one else has? And then, following this: what accounts for the singularity of their work?

The purpose of working in this way has not been to produce an averaged or fully synthesised picture of the wheatbelt, but to do exactly the opposite of this: to shatter the synthesised picture. Instead of creating a general portrait, what I have tried to do through my focus on individual authors is to make their writing available as a repertoire of ways of knowing, to force a reckoning between accounts that shows that each one cannot be entirely subsumed by another. That by forgetting about James Pollard or Cyril Goode or Tom Flood, we would lose an irreplaceable dimension of the wheatbelt as an entity sustained by human imagination—even as its consequences are wrought into the natural environment. And yet, I have also chosen to leave certain writers out of the story so as to give a fuller account of the ones I have included. Arthur Upfield, M.V. Peacock, Colin Johnson (Mudrooroo), Archie Weller, Henrietta Drake-Brockman, Glen Phillips, Caroline Caddy, Olive Willey, Glenyse Ward, William Hart-Smith, Joseph Placid Stokes and Randolph Stow all have claims that have been difficult to refuse. I have, as well, neglected local writing collections and numerous memoirs and shire histories, some of which are very fine indeed. But this has come about as a consequence of the method I have adopted, which is that of detailed treatments of select authors. The authors have been chosen to provide an overlapping sequence that links the end of the twentieth century to its beginning in a way that captures not just changes in the shape and texture of the wheatbelt, but changes in the deepest habits of thought. In this way, it is not just the two world wars and the Depression that passed through the wheatbelt, but artistic modernism which arrived with Cowan and Hewett and disappeared with Flood and Kinsella.

I do not have a final view on the future of the wheatbelt. I accept that it is a crucial farming region, which produces food and fibre that serve humanity and contribute to the local, state and national economies. I accept that the wheatbelt has been and continues to be not just a source of livelihood, but of life for thousands who live and have lived there. I accept, too, that the wheatbelt could not exist without vast clearing. It may be the case that the extent of the clearing exceeded prudent usage and was driven by short-term gain at an unacceptable environmental cost. I hope that this history of the wheatbelt will help us to form long-term views on these matters. If nothing else, what I hope is that by shifting the temporal focus away from the annual production cycle, and even beyond things as seemingly venerable as the passage of human generations, towards a scale of time that is closer to that which had prevailed in the wheatbelt area until comparatively recently, that we might draw on the lessons of the past. Certainly, it is alarming to think there is now pressure to extend the wheat frontier once more, this time into the pristine and priceless Great Western Woodland. This woodland has been made more precious by the fact that the Great "Eastern" Woodland was eradicated to build the wheatbelt. I hope that this study helps in some small way to put an end to the idea of endlessness, at least in the pernicious sense that it was used to justify clearing in the twentieth century by suggesting that there was "always more" bush just a bit further out. I think agricultural efficiency would be better served by accepting fixed limits to the land, of the kind that most settled countries would have no hesitation in accepting and which common sense (fed by bitter experience) tells us must, in fact, exist. Within these limits, hard decisions should be made about those parts of the land where the agricultural production is so marginal and relies on such heavy subsidisation or state underwriting that it cannot reasonably be said to be adding value, especially once a true value is placed on biodiversity and natural heritage. With these modest measures a wheatbelt very much as productive as the one we have now but much more available to natural restitution must be possible.

For a vision of the wheatbelt as a future place I have found no better model than that offered by Barbara York Main in her essay "Living in a Fabricated Landscape" which was given at a workshop on Dryland Research at Tammin in 1992.[3] In it she accepts that the land of the wheatbelt has been changed irrevocably and that some of the worst changes took place after World War Two. We have seen her document these ravages in her natural histories and autobiographical vignettes. But here she is looking forward and what she proposes is in keeping with new thinking about what constitutes restoration. First, of course, there needs to be a willingness to restore. But this can be inadvertently chased away by a too-strict adherence to the idea of pure, untouched landscapes and, as an unintended consequence, "degraded" country which has forfeited its rights of protection against development. For this reason, York Main embraces the wheatbelt as a "fabricated landscape": "Our goal now then, within this concept of fabrication, is to reshape such landscapes so that they both satisfy our physical needs (through the practising of agriculture) and reflect our spiritual visions (which must surely encompass nature conservation and what elsewhere has been termed a 'biocentric' rather than an 'anthropocentric' regard for the landscape)." (39) York Main had the courage to accept the world we are living in now so that we might follow courses of action that redress its wrongs or answer its warning calls. The wheatbelt is a fabricated landscape and the writers in this study have all in various ways emphasised this fabrication. This is not to deny the unique value of the found environment, but to allow us to continue to value and revalue the world we have made.

Notes to the Preface

1   I am indebted to Jeremy Wallace at the CSIRO in Western Australia for fielding my enquiries so fully.

2   The famous "Goyder's Line" in South Australia, drawn in 1865 and variously kept to and abandoned thereafter, is a similar frontier. Janis Sheldrick's history of Goyder and his line captures the ambiguity of a demarcation that is both natural and artificial in the title: *Nature's Line: George Goyder: Surveyor, Environmentalist, Visionary*, Adelaide, Wakefield Press, 2013.

3   See *Environmental Protection of Native Vegetation in Western Australia: Clearing of Native Vegetation, with Particular Reference to the Agricultural Area* (Position Statement No. 2), Environmental Protection Authority, 1990.

4   Ronald Gidgup Senior in *Ngulak Ngarnk Nidja Boodja: our mother, this land*, Centre for Indigenous History and the Arts, The University of Western Australia, 2000, p. 75.

5   Kim Scott and Hazel Brown, *Kayang and Me*, Fremantle, Fremantle Arts Centre Press, 2005, pp. 18–19.

6   Tom Flood, *Oceana Fine*, Sydney, Allen & Unwin, 1989, p. 3.

7   J.K. Ewers, *Men Against the Earth*, Melbourne, Georgian House, 1946, p. 121.

8   I own over thirty of these books, and some are very fine indeed. Amongst the best are J.K. Ewers's *Bruce Rock: The Story of a District*, The Bruce Rock Road Board, 1959; Rica Erickson's *The Victoria Plains*, Perth, Lamb Paterson, 1971; Joseph Placid Stokes's *Cunderdin-Meckering: A Wheatlands History*, Melbourne, Hyland House, 1986; Lyall Hunt's *The Yilgarn: Good Country for Hardy People*, Southern Cross, Yilgarn Shire in association with the Western Australian College of Advanced Education, 1988; and Reg Appleyard and Don Couper's *A History of Trayning*, Crawley, UWA Publishing, 2009.

Notes to the Introduction: Songs of Wheat

1   G.H. Burvill, *Agriculture in Western Australia: 150 years of development and achievement, 1829–1979*, Nedlands, UWA Press, 1979, p. 25.

2   J.M.R. Cameron, *Ambition's Fire: The agricultural colonization of pre-convict Western Australia*, Nedlands UWA Press, 1981.

3   Burvill, *Agriculture in WA*, p. 8.

4   Burvill, *Agriculture in WA*, p. 12.

5   Trollope quoted in Geoffrey Bolton, *Land of Vision and Mirage: Western Australia since 1826*, Nedlands UWA Press, 2008, p. 43.

6   It is worth pointing out that after wheat, the major crop in this era was hay. Until the advent of motor transit, horses were integral to economic life of every kind, and fuelling these beasts was a substantial and ongoing task.

7   Bolton, *Vision and Mirage*, p. 52; The Final Report of the Commission on Agriculture is found in the WA Parliamentary Papers of 1891–2, no. 1.

8   Eva Braid, "Explorer Surveyors' Classification Work", *Early Days: A journal of the Royal Western Australian Historical Society*, vol. 8, 1980, p. 22.

9   In the pastoral era, the nodal points were in fact the sporadic granite outcrops of the plateau, at whose feet were the soaks that provided the only sure source of water through the long summer months, for the watering of stock. In this sense, the pastoral era of the southwest, once it had pushed beyond the Avon valley, followed the patterns of Noongar occupation, whose wells and gnamma holes in the rocks the pastoralists and their servants used extensively for their subsistence and that of the stock animals they husbanded.

10   Burvill, *Agriculture in WA*, p. 19. The goldfields fundamentally changed the shape of the Western Australian "interior". Prior to that the emphasis had been on northward and southward lines of expansion. The Great Southern line to Albany, for instance, was completed in 1886, some years prior to the discovery of gold at Southern Cross.

11   Bolton, *Vision and Mirage*, p. 61

12   Quoted in Bolton, *Vision and Mirage*, p. 61

13   Braid, "Explorer Surveyors", p. 25.

14   J.K. Ewers, *Men Against the Earth*, Melbourne, Georgian House, 1946, p. 38.

15   J.P. Gabbedy, *Yours is the Earth: The life and times of Charles Mitchell*, Nedlands, UWA Press, 1972, p. 65.

16   M. Barnard Eldershaw, *My Australia,* Jarrolds, London, 1939, p. 209.

17   Gabbedy, *Yours is the Earth*, pp. 67–8; 73.

18   Quoted in Braid, "Explorer Surveyors", p. 33.

19   A good illustration of the ambiguity is in the popular agricultural guide produced in Western Australia by the Professor of Agriculture at the University of Western Australia, John Paterson, *Nature in Farming: A discussion of scientific principles in their relation to farm practice*, Perth, Government Printer, 1923. The "nature" in this book refers to the biological conditions of farming not the natural ecosystems that farming supplants.

20   D.W. Meinig, *On the Margins of the Good Earth: The South Australian wheat frontier, 1869–1884*, Chicago, Rand McNally for the Association of American Geographers, 1962, p. 3.

21   C.J. Dennis, "Wheat", *Backblock Ballads and Later Verses*, Sydney, Angus & Robertson, 1918, pp. 23–26.

22   A.B. Paterson, "Song of the Wheat", *Lone Hand*, vol. 17, no. 91, 2 November 1914, p. 403; Reprinted in A.B. Paterson, *Saltbush Bill, J.P., and Other Verses*, Sydney, Angus & Robertson, 1917.

23   C.H. Souter, "W'eat Cartin'", *The Bulletin*, vol. 47, no. 2405, 18 March 1926, p. 22; "Harvestin'", *The Bulletin*, vol. 47, no. 2445, 23 December 1926, p. 22.

24   R.G. Henderson, "The Wheat", *The Bulletin*, vol. 47, no. 2435, 14 October 1926, p. 7.

25   Henry Lawson, "The Drover's Wife", *The Bulletin*, vol. 12, no. 649, 23 July 1892, pp. 21–22; Barbara Baynton, "Squeaker's Mate", *Bush Studies*, London, Duckworth, 1902, pp. 15–43.

26   "Steele Rudd" (Arthur Hoey Davis), "Starting the Selection", *The Bulletin*, vol. 16, no. 790, 6 April 1895, p. 24.

27   "Steele Rudd" (Arthur Hoey Davis), *On Our Selection!*, Sydney, Bulletin, 1899.

28   "Steele Rudd", *On Our Selection*, Stepney, South Australia, Axiom Publishing, 2001, p.14. Subsequent page references are to this edition.

29   Randolph Stow, *A Haunted Land*, London, MacDonald, 1956; *The Bystander*, London, MacDonald, 1956; *The Merry-Go-Round in the Sea*, London, MacDonald, 1965.

30   K.S. Prichard, *Working Bullocks*, London, Jonathan Cape, 1926; *Coonardoo*, London, Jonathan Cape, 1929; *The Roaring Nineties*, London, Jonathan Cape, 1946; *Golden Miles*, London, Jonathan Cape, 1948; *Winged Seeds*, London, Jonathan Cape, 1950.

31   Quoted in Braid, "Explorer Surveyors", p. 32

32   Indeed, the effect of the war in the wheatbelt was significant. In the first instance, it led to its substantial depopulation, as men of eligible age (and many below) joined up in droves. It also led to an increase in agricultural demand as the developed nations of the world moved into an unprecedented situation of total, industrial war. Produce was requisitioned by governments, and prices rose as demand outstripped supply. After the armistice in 1918, there was a renewed push towards developing the wheatbelt, this time with the aid of demobilised, returned servicemen. The cheap land prices, and the liberal lending policies of Western Australia continued to drive internal migration from other Australian states, as well as from abroad, particular from Great Britain.

33   K.S. Prichard, *Child of the Hurricane: An Autobiography*, Sydney, Angus & Robertson, 1963. It is certainly curious that Prichard devoted three pages to her beloved gelding Wyburn and not one word for Cowcowing. The impression given by her account is that after the War, the couple moved to Greenmount in the Perth Hills and stayed there. A brief description of their married life at Greenmount is provided, before the memoir concludes by touching on the suicide that ended Throssell's life in 1933.

34   K.S. Prichard, "Christmas-tree", *Potch and Colour*, Angus & Robertson, 1944, pp. 158–69.

35   Throssell's achievements, personality and connections meant he was never short of work, although these same things also, in a way reminiscent of Lawson's later life, led to a certain self-sabotaging of opportunities. He worked for a while for the Returned Soldiers' Land Settlement Board, a plum job no doubt, but eventually lost it—Prichard felt—because of his outspoken support for communism on both his own account and in defence of his famous wife.

Notes to Chapter One: Albert Facey (1894–1982)

1   A.B. Facey, *A Fortunate Life*, Fremantle, Fremantle Arts Centre Press, 1981.

2   J.B. Hirst, "Facey, Albert Barnett (Bert) (1894–1982)", *Australian Dictionary of Biography*, vol. 17, Melbourne UP, 2007, p. 372. See also, J.B. Hirst, *The World of*

Albert Facey, The History Institute of Victoria in association with Allen & Unwin, St Leonard's, NSW, 1992.

3   Perhaps the most direct predecessor to *A Fortunate Life* was *The Autobiography of John Shaw Neilson* (Canberra: The National Library of Australia, 1978), which was not published until nearly half a century after the poet's death. It describes the poet's life of hardship as an itinerant rural labourer in Victoria's Wimmera in the 1890s and early 1900s.

4   Certain aspects of Facey's war service have recently been brought into serious question by scholars. It now seems clear, for instance, that Facey was not in the first landing at Gallipoli on 25 April 1914, as he claims in *A Fortunate Life*, but with the third reinforcements of 5 May. There are other discrepancies in his account as well, although the basic facts of him being at Gallipoli and evacuated due to injury in 1915 are not in dispute. See Ffion Murphy and Richard Nile, "The Wounded Storyteller: Revisiting Albert Facey's Fortunate Life", *Westerly*, vol. 60 no. 2, 2015, pp. 87–100; James Hurst, "The Mists of Time and the Fog of War: A Fortunate Life and A.B. Facey's Gallipoli Experience", *Melbourne Historical Journal,* vol. 38, 2010, pp. 73–88; and David T. Rowlands, "An Unfortunate Lie? A.B. Facey and the Gallipoli Landing", *Teaching History,* vol. 45, no. 1, 2011, pp. 24–37.

5   Phil Bianchi, Peter Bridge, Ray Tovey, Eds, *Early Woodlines of the Goldfields: The untold story of the woodlines to World War II*, Carlisle, Western Australia, Hesperian Press, c. 2008.

6   The truest heir to the Steele Rudd tradition is Colin Thiele, in particular his classic sketches in *The Sun on the Stubble* (Adelaide: Rigby, 1961), which movingly and often hilariously document the life of the Gunthers, a German farming family in South Australia's wheat-country during the Depression.

7   On this point, see Lorenzo Veracini's analysis, *Settler Colonialism: A Theoretical Overview*, Basingstoke, Palgrave Macmillan, 2010.

8   This was first detailed in Sylvia Hallam's classic study, *Fire and Hearth: A study of Aboriginal usage and European usurpation in south-western Australia*, Australian Aboriginal Studies No. 58, Australian Institute of Aboriginal Studies, Canberra, 1979. A revised edition has recently been published: *Fire and Hearth: Karla Yoorda*, Nedlands, UWA Publishing, 2014.

9   Henry Kingsley, *The Recollections of Geoffry Hamlyn*, Cambridge, Macmillan, 1859; Patrick White, *The Tree of Man*, New York, Viking, 1955.

10   "Steele Rudd" (Arthur Hoey Davis), "Starting the Selection", *The Bulletin*, vol. 16, no. 790, 6 April 1895, p. 24.

11   Laurie Anderson, *Windows on the Wheatbelt*, Bassendean, Access Press, c. 1999, p. 7.

12   Henry Sherar, *South of Nulla Nulla: A story of the Yilgarn*, Swanbourne, Western Australia, H. Sherar, 1983.

13   I am relying here on the revised chronology provided by Murphy and Nile above, and not the dates given in *A Fortunate Life*.

14   Murphy and Nile also question the nature of Facey's injuries, suggesting they were predominantly (perhaps exclusively) of a nervous nature, a fact that might have been covered up by Facey for reasons of shame, and also to preserve his pension. This supposition is based on inconsistencies in the medical reports in his war-service records and also in his accounts of the engagements where he claims to have suffered the injuries.

15   23,347 returned soldier farms had been granted throughout Australia by 30 June
      1924. "Special Article – Settlement of Returned Soldiers 1914–18", *Year Book
      Australia, 1925*, Australian Bureau of Statistics, 1925.

Notes to Chapter Two: Cyril E. Goode (1907–83)

1   Goode was born Cyril Harry Everard Good, but adopted the new spelling as a
      pen-name in his late teens. His first pen-name was "Cyril Everard" and it seems
      a compromise was reached by appending the "e" from the favoured middle name
      to his original surname—thus Good became Goode.
2   Lyall Hunt, *Yilgarn: Good country for hardy people*, Yilgarn Shire in association
      with the Western Australian College of Advanced Education, 1988.
3   Cyril Goode papers (PA 291), Box 1, State Library of Victoria. I am indebted to
      Cyril Goode's daughter, Cathy Culbard, the copyright holder of his papers stored
      at the State Library of Victoria, for her assistance with her father's personal papers,
      and in particular for making available to me the photographs from her personal
      collection that appear in this chapter.
4   John Larkin, "Bush Poet Finds Recognition at Last – in Manilla", *The Age*,
      18 November 1969, p. 2.
5   It is in the literature and accounts of the wheatbelt that the noun "a clearing"
      is brought back into intimate connection with its verb. In settled country a
      clearing exists, but in the early days of the wheatbelt, they were strenuously
      made.
6   G.H. Burvill, *Agriculture in Western Australia, 1829–1979*, UWA Press, 1979, p. 41.
      See also, "Big Scheme: For 3500 Farms: Complete Survey Recommended",
      Canberra Times, 22 April 1929, p. 1.
7   Burvill, *Agriculture in Western Australia*, p. 47
8   "Cyril E. Goode", *Williamstown Chronicle*, 4 August 1950, p. 8.
9   John A. McKenzie, "'Bullant' McIntyre of Southern Cross", *Early Days*, vol. 10,
      no. 6, 1994, pp. 579–91. See also, Larkin, "Bush Poet Finds Recognition at Last –
      in Manilla".
10   Henry Sherar, *South of Nulla Nulla: A Story of the Yilgarn*, Swanbourne, H. Sherar,
      c. 1983. Sherar moved to Noongaar in 1925.
11   *Southern Cross Times*, 8 December 1928.
12   Only the heavy clearing of "forest country" attracted this bounty; the
      scrub-rolling of "light" land was considered part of the normal course of
      "improvements" that were also assessed but did not generate a separate advance
      from the bank. P.T. McMahon, *They Wished Upon a Star: A History of Southern
      Cross and Yilgarn*, Perth, P. McMahon, c. 1972, p. 73.
13   Edward Fitzgerald, *The Rubaiyat of Omar Khayyam: A Critical Edition,* ed.
      Christopher Decker, trans. Edward Fitzgerald, Charlottesville, UP of Virginia,
      1997 [1859], p. 130
14   Many farmers, like Facey's Uncle Archie, came from the goldfields to the
      wheatbelt. Likewise, when his farm collapsed in the Depression, Goode would go
      on to work in the goldmines of Wiluna.
15   *The Rubaiyat of Omar Khayyam*, p. 134
16   The life of a Bank "inspector" comes through vividly in J.P. Gabbedy's biography
      of Charles Mitchell, *Yours is the Earth*, Nedlands, UWA Press, 1972. Mitchell
      commenced as an inspector for the Agricultural Bank, stationed at Narrogin, in

1908, a position he would hold until 1929. He was the brother of premier James Mitchell, one of the architects of the wheatbelt.

17   I am indebted to Alan Pegg, agricultural scientist, consultant and historian, for clarifying this aspect of farming practice.

18   At a nearby farm in Noongaar, Henry Sherar's first encounter with the Depression was the appearance of men from the city looking for work in the winter of 1930. After struggling to find clearers earlier in the year, they were soon inundated in response to an advertisement they had placed in the *West Australian*: "We could not understand why there was such a demand for this clearing contract. We decided to go into Noongaar and inform anyone there seeking the job that it had been let. When we go to the siding we found a dozen men waiting to see us … They were desperate. We did not realise things were so bad and so many people were out of work … This was our first experience of the Depression." *South of Nulla Nulla*, p. 81.

19   Geoffrey Bolton, *A Fine Country to Starve In*, Nedlands, UWA Press, 1972, p. 134.

20   G.D Snooks, *Depression and Recovery in Western Australia 1928'29–1938'39: A Study in Cyclical and Structural Change*, Nedlands, UWA Press, 1974, p. 26.

21   ibid., p. 23.

22   Bolton wrongly calls Goode "an English migrant".

23   I thank Goode's daughter, Cathy Culbard, for lending me this scrapbook, which collects a number of his poems, stories, columns, as well as reviews of his work. The scrapbook has dates handwritten by Goode, and I have relied on these dates, together with the diary held in the State Library, for the chronology of my account.

24   *The Sunday Times*, 7 January 1934.

25   Salmon-gum and morrel were both indicative of the better loamy soils sought after in the settlement of the wheatbelt, although the latter was also generally powdery and prone to wind erosion.

26   *Williamstown Chronicle,* 4 August 1950, p. 8.

27   A later short story by Goode, "The Slav Singer", takes the final four lines of his poem "The Clearer" as its epigraph, and follows the life of the contract-clearer Antonyev "Tony" Markonvitch as he worked on farms in the Yilgarn.

28   A moving account of the end of the horse-drawn era from 1940s Wickepin is Paul Gribble's *Hoofprints: A tribute to the working horses of the wheatbelt*, City Beach, P. Gribble, c. 2007.

29   Cyril E. Goode, *The Bridge Party at Boyanup*, J. Roy Stevens, Melbourne, 1944, p. 16.

30   "Cyril E. Goode", *Williamstown Chronicle*, 4 August 1950, p. 8.

31   ibid.

32   Cyril E. Goode, *Yarns of the Yilgarn*, Melbourne, Oldfort Publications, 1950, and *Stories of Strange Places*, Melbournes, The Hawthorn Press, 1973.

33   *Yarns of the Yilgarn*, pp. 64–67. I have not found the original newspaper in which this story appeared although Goode retained a copy (without publication details) in his scrapbook. Based on the adjoining work it probably appeared in 1934 or 1935. The story was re-published in both *Yarns of the Yilgarn* and *Stories of Strange Places.*

34   Goode's reading list did, however, show a continued interest in the works of Thoreau and, as we have seen, he quoted Thoreau's counsel in his "Turkey Hill Notes" to love the land but "own it not".

35 *Yarns of the Yilgarn*, pp. 50–54.

36 Republished in *Yarns of the Yilgarn*, pp. 28–33.

37 *Yarns of the Yilgarn*, pp. 34–41. Again, I have not found this story as it was published (if it was) in a contemporary journal or newspaper.

Notes to Chapter Three: James Pollard (1900–1971)

1 Stephen Garton, *The Cost of War: Australians at War*, Melbourne, Oxford UP, 1996. Bobbie Oliver, *War and Peace in Western Australia: The Social and Political Impact of the Great War, 1914–1926*, Nedlands, UWA Press, 1995. J.M. Powell, "The Debt of Honour: Soldier Settlement in the Dominions, 1915–1940", *Journal of Australian Studies,* vol. 5, 1980, pp. 64–87.

2 Brady and Cowan note that these novels catered to "a growing number of readers becoming interested in their own country—in fact, in the discovery of it through the novel and stories." Veronica Brady and Peter Cowan, "The Novel", in Bruce Bennett (ed.), *The Literature of Western Australia*, Nedlands, UWA Press, 1979, p. 70.

3 Alice Powell, Letter, c. 1980, MN742, Acc 2846A/1, Battye Library. I have used the word "pillow" as my best guess. In fact, the letter appears to read "under his people".

4 J.K. Ewers, "James Pollard", *Walkabout Magazine*, 1 June 1951.

5 *Listening Post,* vol. 2, no. 2, 19 January 1923, p. 17.

6 Letter from editor of *The Listening Post* to Pollard, 9 May 1922, MN 742 Acc 2486A/84, Battye Library.

7 Ewers, "James Pollard".

8 ibid.

9 His father also opened that town's first private store to run in successful competition with the Farmer's Co-op. J.K. Ewers, *Bruce Rock: The Story of a District*. The Bruce Rock District Road Board, 1959, p. 53.

10 James Pollard, Biographical Notes sent to *Our Rural Magazine*, 1927, MN742, Acc 2846A/99, Battye Library.

11 Letter from J.M. Le Souef, 17 October 1924, MN742, Acc 2846A/85, Battye Library.

12 Letter from Bruce W. Leake, 3 September 1923, MN742, Acc 2846A/85, Battye Library. For Leake's reflections on his life at Kellerberrin during these years, see Bruce W. Leake, *Cardonia*, Carlisle, Hesperian Press, c. 2004.

13 Letter from J.W.H., 24 April 1924, MN742, Acc 2846A/85, Battye Library.

14 Letter from W. Matson, 25 February 1924, MN742 Acc, 2846A/85, Battye Library.

15 He also contributed to *The Emu*, the newsletter of the Royal Australian Ornithologist Union (RAOU). See James Pollard, "The Nornalup Camp-Out", *The Emu,* vol. 27, 1928, p. 163. For a consideration of the importance of this journal and popular Australian ornithology more generally see Libby Robin, *The Flight of the Emu: A Hundred Years of Australian Ornithology, 1901–2001*, Melbourne, Melbourne UP, 2001.

16 The correspondence between Pollard and Jones is found in Pollard's papers at MN742, Acc 2846A/81, Battye Library.

17 ibid., 2 November 1925.

18 ibid., 21 December 1925.

NOTES

20   ibid., 4 December 1925.
21   ibid., 15 November 1925.
22   ibid.
23   Letter from J.M. Drew, 3 January 1929, MN742, Acc 2846A/85–93, Battye Library.
24   Letter from Clarence Eakins, 18 June 1930, MN742, Acc 2846A/85–93, Battye Library.
25   Letter from T.L. Harris, c. 1940, MN742, Acc 2846A/107, Battye Library. Pollard continued to publish in the *School Magazine* until 1964. He also published in Victoria's equivalent, *The School Paper*, between 1954 and 1959.
26   Republished in *The School Paper* in May 1959.
27   Letter from Doris Chadwick, a sometime novelist and friend of the prominent writer Kylie Tennant, n.d., c. 1948, MN742, Acc 2846A/107, Battye Library.
28   Ewers, "James Pollard".
29   Gene Stratton-Porter, *Freckles*, Stillwell, KS: Digireads Book, 2008; originally published by Grosset & Dunlap, New York, 1904.
30   From an anonymous review of *The Bushland Man* for *The Queenslander*, 18 December 1926, p. 8. *The Queenslander* was published in Brisbane between 1866 and 1939.
31   *The Queenslander*, 18 December 1926, p. 8.
32   As with Ewers's sagas, the dynastic dimension of Pollard's novel begins with the death of the patriarch, Michael O'Meare, the father of Rose, and the youngest brother of Joseph.
33   The practice of wheat pickling is reported in *The Western Mail*, 24 January 1896, p. 41. In South Australia, it was pioneered as a method by John Reynell in 1843.
34   James Pollard, "Servants of the Fields", reprinted in Peter Cowan (ed.), *Impressions: West Coast Fiction, 1829–1988*, Fremantle, Fremantle Arts Centre Press, 1989, pp. 272–5.

Notes to Chapter Four: John Keith Ewers (1904–78)

1   J.K. Ewers, "A Writer in Perth", *Westerly*, vol. 4, December 1967, p. 63.
2   J.K. Ewers, "James Pollard", *Walkabout Magazine*, 1951.
3   Letter from J.K. Ewers, 19 December 1924, MN742, Acc 2846A/69, Battye Library.
4   J.K. Ewers, *Long Enough for a Joke*, Fremantle Arts Centre Press, 1983, p. 103. A. Neboiss, "Lyell, George (1866-1951)", *Australian Diction of Biography*, vol. 10, Melbourne, Melbourne UP, 1986, p. 171.
5   Letter from J.K. Ewers, 26 March 1926, MN742, Acc 2846A/69, Battye Library.
6   J.K. Ewers, "A Writer in Perth".
7   See the essay by Amanda Laugesen, "*Aussie Magazine* and the Making of Digger Culture during the Great War" for the National Library of Australia, www.nla.gov.au/pub/nlanews/2003/nov03/story-4.pdf.
8   The bank manager corresponds to the portrait that Gabbedy gave of Charles Mitchell at the Agricultural Bank and also that of Christopher Tregear, the bank manager featured in Katharine Prichard's story "Christmas-tree".
9   David Mossenson, *State Education in Western Australia, 1829–1960*, Nedlands, UWA Press, 1972, p. 124.

10   ibid. The number of schools in Western Australia peaked in the year 1935 before dropping steadily through amalgamation—made possible by better transit—as well as regional de-population, firstly through the Depression and then with the effects of mechanisation. The number of schools fell steadily until by 1952 they were at pre-1910 levels, before beginning to grow once more.

11   ibid., p. 125.

12   The role of Aboriginal women as midwives is also noted in Lawson's "The Drover's Wife".

13   Cyril Ayers, *A Heritage Ingrained: Co-operative Bulk Handling Limited 1933–2000*, West Perth, Co-operative Bulk Handling Limited, 1999, p. 13.

14   In the South Australian wheatbelt, Colin Thiele (born in 1920) was able to recollect these events, nearly seven decades later, with absolute, chilling clarity in his memoir *With Dew on My Boots & Other Footprints*, South Melbourne, Lothian Books, 2002, pp. 98–9.

15   Tim Bonyhady has detailed the relationships between Drysdale's painting and the El Nino drought of the 1940s, with its consequent topsoil erosion and dust-storms. "The Cross of Erosion", *Australian Humanities Review*, vol. 6, June–July 1997.

Notes to Chapter Five: Peter Cowan (1914–2002)

1   Oral History Transcript, Tape 1, Side A, p. 3. Peter Cowan interviewed by Stuart Reid for joint oral history project between National Library of Australia and State Library. Recorded on 4 October 1991 and 3 August 1992. State Library of Western Australia, OH2501.

2   Geoffrey Bolton, *A Fine Country to Starve In*, Nedlands, UWA Press, 1972, p. 186.

3   Oral History Transcript, Tape 1, Side A, p. 2.

4   The situation bears a superficial resemblance to John Shaw Neilson, who subsisted from hand-to-mouth in the earlier depression of the 1890s. Yet Cowan's itinerancy is not quite the same as Neilson's in the Mallee of Victoria at the turn of the century. Neilson, born in the country to farming parents, seems never to have truly imagined a life beyond this, even if the chronic ill health of his later years found him in Melbourne.

5   The personal papers of Peter Cowan were donated by his daughter-in-law, Diana Cowan, to the Peter Cowan Writers' Centre at the Joondalup campus of Edith Cowan University, Western Australia. At the time of writing, the letters and other personal effects had not been catalogued, but I was kindly granted permission to access them by the President of the Centre, Susan Stevens, in January 2013.

6   The letter is dated the "15th" – internal evidence points to 15 April 1933. Held by Peter Cowan Writers' Centre. The spelling of "color" seems to be a sign of the influence of American literature on Cowan.

7   His most serious flirtation with land ownership had been an idea of teaming up with a friend, Roy Brown, to take on an abandoned Group Settlement near Cowaramup in 1935. Cowan had holidayed at his uncle's farm near Cowaramup as a boy in the mid-1920s, so he knew the district well. But, in the end, they did not feel they could make the concern work; the debts they would take on as the cost of acquiring the property would never likely be repaid. This, in miniature, was exactly the situation for much of rural Australia in the 1930s.

8   ibid., c. 15 April 1933.

9   Possibly 1935, in any event, after Waeel, to which he compares this farm.

10   Bennett notes that this made him "the longest serving editor of any Australian cultural magazine." Editor's Notice, *Westerly*, vol. 39, no. 1, Autumn 1994.

11   Letter from Peter Cowan to Edith Howard dated 1 January 1941, held by the Peter Cowan Writers' Centre.

12   The letter is undated, but written on Guildford Preparatory School paper, where Cowan was teaching in 1941.

13   ibid., c. 1941.

14   Bruce Bennett and Susan Miller (eds), *Peter Cowan: New Critical Essays,* Nedlands, UWA Press in association with The Centre for Studies in Australian Literature, The University of Western Australia, 1992. See, particularly, Elizabeth Jolley's "Silences and Spaces", pp. 9–20 and Bruce Bennett's "Peter Cowan's Landscapes of Silence", pp. 89–98.

15   Oral History Transcript, Tape 2, Side A, p. 15.

16   Oral History Transcript, Tape 1, Side B, p. 12. "I think whole English syllabus at the University [of Western Australia] in those years if I speak only of the late '30s, it wouldn't have been different if you went back any other distance, and it was being enlivened in the end of the '30s by people like Alec King. Really it almost didn't acknowledge modern writing to any degree at all, and I think if say Alec King hadn't been there you wouldn't have come across any of the modern English poets of the period; and one wouldn't have known all this was going on."

17   The stories in *Drift* were divided into three sections, three *tenses*, as it were— "Yesterday", "Between" and "Now". The stories in the final "Now" section of the book all reference the impact of the Second World War in one way or another, while the three stories from the "Yesterday" section appear to be set in earlier times, but only slightly. The "Between" stories are stories of a space of time brought into being by 1929, the time "between the wars", and for the most part depict life during the Depression.

18   One can compare the imagery in these passages with an anguished letter he wrote to his wife on 26 August 1943, where, risking the censor's wrath, he described trying to get a release from his RAAF teaching job at Melbourne's Exhibition Buildings: "What a bloody fool use of manpower ... Bugger this stupid bloody crooked capitalistic racket, and its denial of all usefulness and decency." Personal letter from Peter Cowan to Edith Cowan (née Howard) dated 26 August 1943, held by Peter Cowan Writers' Centre.

19   Howard Taylor (1918–2001), born four years after Cowan, moved to Western Australia from Victoria (via South Australia) in 1932 and shares a similar modernist trajectory to Cowan, with his paintings becoming ever more abstract and rarefied, yet in a manner that led to the intensification, rather than the depletion, of their effect.

20   A little as Cowan himself had nearly done with his friend Roy Brown—see footnote above.

21   The first seven stories in *The Unploughed Land* had originally appeared in *Drift*, to which were added five further stories. So, the date of 1958 is a little misleading in terms of the history of the book's composition. Not only were the stories from *Drift* written in the late '30s and early '40s, but the "new" stories were mainly composed—at least earlier drafts of them—in the mid- to late-1940s.

22 Peter Cowan Papers, Scholars' Manuscript MS0117, Box 3, Files 16–22, Scholars' Centre, The University of Western Australia.

23 ibid., File 17.

24 The opening part of this story was originally composed in the first person, and it is changed into the third person in an early revision. The move is consistent with the general reduction of this element of a story's immediacy.

25 Randolph Stow is another to have been influenced by Mackenzie's novel, mentioning it briefly in *The Merry-Go-Round in the Sea*.

26 Cowan had already had his work prosecuted for obscenity in the infamous "Ern Malley" trial. His memories of the 1940s and '50s recall strongly the extent to which it was an era of sexual hypocrisy.

27 Peter Cowan Papers, File 29, Scholars' Centre, The University of Western Australia.

28 ibid., Files 27 and 28. Like many of Cowan's books, though, they often have remnants of much earlier stories in them, often forming the nucleus of the story, or sometimes just a description or episode. Cowan had sent, in 1954, two short novel mss. to Frank C. Betts in London, one entitled "The Tree" and the other "Summer". Betts declined both saying they lacked a discernible plot and contained "far too much loose dialogue". Letter from Betts to Cowan, 10 March 1954, in Cowan's personal papers held by the Peter Cowan Writers' Centre.

29 Oral History Transcript, Tap. 4, Side B, p. 45.

30 ibid., p. 44.

31 The wheat bin does feature in other Australian stories, notably in E.O. Schlunke's "The Man in the Silo", *The Bulletin*, vol. 65, no. 3352, 10 May 1944, p. 4. Schlunke's story is set during the war and concerns a wheat bin on a siding in the Riverina where a mysterious man had decided to camp. Eventually, the town, fuelled by war-time anxiety, tried to capture him but he disappeared, possibly drowned in the wheat.

32 Cyril Ayers, *A Heritage Ingrained: Co-operative Bulk Handling Limited 1933–2000*, West Perth, Co-operative Bulk Handling Limited, 1999, p. 19. See also, Richenda Goldfinch (ed.), *Legends of the Grain Game,* West Perth, Co-operative Bulk Handling Limited, 2003; and Michael Zekulich, *The Grain Journey: The History of the Grain Pool of WA*, Perth, The Grain Pool of Western Australia, 1997.

33 Oral History Transcript, Tape 4, Side A, pp. 40–41.

34 Note by Cowan in Peter Cowan Papers, File 26, Scholars' Centre.

35 The clearest predecessor in Australian literature prior to this was Barbara Baynton, whom Cowan had written on for the *Arts Quarterly* in 1949. "A Note on Barbara Baynton," *Arts Quarterly*, Summer 1949, pp. 8–13.

36 The precedent to all of these works is Arthur Upfield's *Mr Jelly's Business*, Sydney, Angus & Robertson, 1937 [first serialised in 1932]. Upfield's novel was set in 1929 in the wheatbelt town of Burracoppin where the rabbit-proof fence intersects the Great Eastern Highway.

37 Copy of letter of Peter Cowan to Judith Wright dated 13 April 1966, Peter Cowan Papers, Box 6, File 56, Scholars' Centre, The University of Western Australia.

38 ibid. Letter of Judith Wright McKinney to Peter Cowan dated 23 April 1966.

Notes to Chapter Six: Dorothy Hewett (1923–2002)

1   Both Dorothy and her younger sister, Lesley, were born at a small hospital in the well-to-do Perth suburb of Mount Lawley. It was in keeping with the family's relative wealth that they were able to have their children in a private Perth hospital.

2   Hewett has been the subject of considerable critical attention, not all of which can be cited here, but whose occasionally fierce debates have helped me in ways I hope to touch on as I proceed. The starting point for the critical reader of Hewett is the Bruce Bennett (ed.), *Selected Critical Essays*, Fremantle, Fremantle Arts Centre Press, 1995. The collection includes key essays by John McLaren, Barbara Holloway, David Brooks, and others. Also included is Lawrence Bourke's "Dorothy's Reception in the Land of Oz", which summarises the criticism of Hewett's work in Australian books and journals up to 1995.

3   Hewett's mother was known throughout her life as Rene or René, pronounced *Ree-nee*. I am grateful to Hewett's niece, Lucy Dougan, for this and many other points of clarification. And also, to her mother, Lesley, Hewett's younger sister, who met with me in 2012 to discuss the early life of Hewett.

4   Lesley attended Perth Modern School on a scholarship. I am deeply indebted to Lesley for assisting me with this chronology, which has been difficult to piece together. Future scholars will have the benefit of Nicole Moore's biography of Hewett.

5   Dorothy Hewett, *Wild Card: An Autobiography*, Ringwood, Victoria, McPhee Gribble, 1990, p. 236. Unless, otherwise stated the parenthetical page numbers in this chapter refer to *Wild Card*.

6   Hewett's writing is intensely scenic. As her daughter Kate Lilley notes: "Hewett piled image on metaphor in cascading, panoramic catalogues reminiscent of Whitman and Ginsberg, cinematic and sometimes faintly surreal …" (*Selected Poems*, Introduction, p. 4)

7   This poem, along with others from Hewett's childhood and the playscript "The Gipsy Dancer", have been retrieved from Hewett's papers in the National Library of Australia and published under the editorship of Christine Alexander: Dorothy Hewett, *The Gipsy Dancer and Early Poems*, Sydney, Juvenilia Press, c. 2009.

8   The poem reappeared in the anthology *Brave Young Singers*, Melbourne, Melbourne UP, 1938. The book collected poems written by correspondence students in Western Australia, and was edited by the Director of Distance Education, J.A. Miles. See also, Nicole Arnae, "'Brave Young Singers': Children's poetry-writing and 1930s Australia", *History of Education Review*, vol. 43, no. 2, pp. 209–30.

9   Lesley Dougan, "My Sister, Dorothy Hewett", in Glen Phillips and Julienne van Loon (eds), *Lines in the Sand: New writing from Western Australia,* Swanbourne, Western Australia, Fellowship of Australian Writers, WA, 2008, p. 31.

10 The Commonwealth Literary Fund had been started to fund Australian writers living in poverty, and was introduced in 1908 by Alfred Deakin. Deakin was amongst the most lettered of Australian prime ministers and an early supporter of Murdoch, and it was Murdoch who became Deakin's biographer. In 1939, the CLF budget was tripled and this led to the funding of lectures by Ewers and others on the subject of Australian literature.

11   A foundation professor in 1913, Murdoch retired as Chair of English in 1939
      to take up the position of Pro-Chancellor. Alec King (1904–1970) had met
      Catherine Spence Murdoch, the daughter of Walter, while training as a teacher
      in London, and followed her back to Perth where the two married in 1929. At
      Oxford, King had been close to both C. Day Lewis and W.H. Auden, and Day
      Lewis married King's sister Mary. (The chapel at Perth Ladies College in which
      they were married features, coincidentally, in Hewett's play, *The Chapel Perilous*.)
      King had been assistant lecturer at UWA since 1933 and obtained a full-time
      lectureship in 1941. John Hay, "King, Alexander (1904-1970)", vol. 15, *Australian
      Dictionary of Biography*, Melbourne, Melbourne UP, 2000.

12   Indeed, King may well have influenced the choice of Edwards as the new
      chair. For this point, and the history of English at UWA see Leigh Dale, *The
      Enchantment of English: Professing English Literatures at Australian Universities*,
      Sydney, Sydney University Press, 2012, p. 190.

13   Edwards had an enduring influence on the cultural development of the
      University of Western Australia and in the 1960s commissioned the two exquisite
      Margaret Priest works that adorn the "New" Arts Building—the courtyard
      fountain and the weather-vane.

14   The date of Hewett's suicided attempt was given to me by Lesley, Dorothy's sister.
      This is corroborated in a short article, "Writes Prize Poem After Breakdown" in
      The Daily News on 31 May 1945, where it was reported that the young "poetess"
      had written the poem "during her convalescence from a breakdown in December,
      1943". It also notes that "she received news of her win about a fortnight ago, just
      before she went into hospital for an operation" and that she had "returned home
      from hospital three days ago". It does not state what the operation was for. In
      Hewett's autobiographical play *The Chapel Perilous*, there is also a suicide attempt,
      although this occurs in 1945: "POLICEWOMAN: Sally Banner, pay attention.
      On the fourteenth day of August, nineteen forty-five, by mistake did take Lysol
      from a bottle carelessly left unlabelled on a shelf. Sally Banner to do away with
      yourself is a punishable criminal offence. Sally Banner, everything to live for.
      All your life before you. Next time you do it you won't get away with it." (43)
      Both *Wild Card* and *The Chapel Perilous* have Hewett ("Sally Banner") hearing
      the poem read on the ABC whilst at hospital but it is difficult to find a timeline
      which fits this in. Dorothy Hewett, *The Chapel Perilous*, Sydney, Currency Press,
      1973.

15   The acuity of Hewett as a reader and critic is seen at this time in a remarkable
      review essay on the poetry of Edith Sitwell for *The Black Swan*, a literary
      magazine published by the Guild of Undergraduates at UWA.

16   "New Writing is Vital Force", *The Workers' Star*, 22 December 1945; reprinted in
      Selected Prose of Dorothy Hewett, Nedlands, UWA Publishing, 2011, p. 120.

17   This is the date given in *Wild Card*, p. 111. But in the biographical note to *The
      Chapel Perilous* states that Hewett joined the Communist Party at age nineteen
      (i.e. 1942–43) and left in 1968. In Frank Hardy's introduction to *What About the
      People!* (Manly, National Council of Realist Writers Groups, 1963) he states she
      joined the Party in 1945. In *Wild Card*, and elsewhere, she states she was in the
      Party for twenty-three years. This would suggest that 1945 is the correct date,
      and she actually joined the Party at age twenty-two not nineteen.

18 The term "Jindyworobak" was thought to come from the Woiwurrung (the traditional people of the Melbourne region) word meaning "to join, annex".

19 Hewett wrote the poem at UWA, when she was eighteen. *Meanjin*, started by Clem Christesen in 1940 in Brisbane, moved to Melbourne in 1945, where it still remains. Christesen had asked that Hewett visit a fellow writer, William Hart-Smith, in the psychiatric ward of Midland Army Hospital, and the 32-year-old poet was happy to read her poems and offer advice to his 21-year-old visitor: "'You've got to work at them,' he said. 'Hone them down. Don't just let it all gush out.'"

20 Dorothy Hewett, "Empty Streets and Lonely Beaches: Peter Cowan's Moral Universe", in Bruce Bennett and Susan Miller (eds), *Peter Cowan: New Critical Essays*, Nedlands, UWA Press, 1992, pp. 1–7.

21 In a statement concerning her poetics, also from the late 1980s, Hewett again recalls "the excitement of first reading Judith Wright's *The Moving Image* in 1945, when her language and concepts seemed to mirror a new maturity in Australian poetics." She continues: "In prose, Christina Stead's *Seven Poor Men of Sydney*, Kenneth Seaforth Mackenzie's *The Young Desire It*, and the magazine *Angry Penguins* (replacing the spurious invented vitalism of the *Vision* school) appeared to link Australia, however insubstantially, to modernist influences and debate in literature and art." Dorothy Hewett, "The Shape-Changing Muse" in David Brooks and Brenda Walker (eds), *Poetry and Gender: Statements and Essays in Australian Women's Poetry and Poetics*, St Lucia, University of Queensland Press, 1989, pp. 243–52.

22 Dorothy Hewett, "Testament", *Collected Poems, 1940–1995*, ed. William Grono, Fremantle, Fremantle Arts Centre Press, 1995, p. 36. Poems will be quoted from this edition and parenthetical page numbers following poems will, unless otherwise stated, be for the *Collected Poems*.

23 From Hewett's introduction to the 1985 Virago reprint of *Bobbin Up*. Quoted in John McLaren, *Writing in Hope and Fear: Literature as Politics in Postwar Australia*, Melbourne, Cambridge UP, 1996, p. 72. His is the definitive study of this period in Australian letters.

24 Of the eight Jarrabin stories which had become "the first eight chapters" of a larger book going under the title *The Wire Fences of Jarrabin*, a further two found their way into print. "Who's to Remember Sweet Alice?" was originally published in 1962 in Geoffrey Dutton's and Max Harris's journal *Australian Letters* and "Joe Anchor's Rock" was published in *Overland* in 1964. Late in her life, in the 1990s, Hewett again returned to Jarrabin, writing three connected plays called "The Jarrabin Trilogy" which extended over 400 pages and were set in 1920, 1939 and 1947. Originally commissioned by the Melbourne Theatre Company and the Black Swan Theatre Company, neither felt able to stage it. In 2002, a condensed version was prepared and staged by John Clark, the Director of the National Institute of Dramatic Art (NIDA) in Sydney. Hewett died the day before the rehearsals began. See Catherine Keenan, "Talk of the town plucked from too-hard basket", *Sydney Morning Herald*, 16 October 2002. The manuscript of the trilogy is held with Hewett's papers in the National Library of Australia (MS 6184, subseries 4.25).

25 Dorothy Hewett, *A Baker's Dozen*, Ringwood, Penguin, 2001, p. 53. The parenthetical page numbers for the quotations from the story refer to this edition.

26   *Wild Card,* p. 45; Hewett, "Introduction", *A Baker's Dozen,* p. 3.

27   The overall veracity of the picture given in Hewett's story is certainly borne out in Anna Haebich's history *For Their Own Good: Aborigines and Government in the South West of Western Australia, 1900–1940,* Nedlands, UWA Press, 1988.

28   In her memoirs, Hewett regards sending the story she sent to the *Women's Weekly,* minus the strike, as a mistake. *Wild Card,* pp. 247–8.

29   The Pilbara Station Strike is celebrated in Hewett's poem, "Clancy and Dooley and Don McLeod", first published in *Black Swan,* vol. 25, no. 1, October 1946. See discussion of the poem by Maggie Nolan in "'And who the hell are you?': Dorothy Hewett's 'Clancy and Dooley and Don McLeod'", Tanya Dalziell and Paul Genoni (eds), *Telling Stories: Australian Literature and Life 1935–2012,* Melbourne, Monash University Publishing, 2013, pp. 106–112.

30   For an excellent historicisation of the trope of the fence in Australian short fiction, including a consideration of Hewett's story, see Kieran Dolin, "The Fence in Australian Short Fiction: 'A constant crossing of boundaries'?", *Australian Cultural History,* vols. 2-3, no. 28, August–December 2010, pp. 141–53. Dolin argues that in Hewett, Cowan and others, "the fence becomes a symbolic border, a site of transition, holding out the hope of transformed understandings and actions," p. 148.

31   Hewett completed a Master of Arts Preliminary in 1963 (on the novels of Randolph Stow), and began her Master's in 1964 (on the novels of Vance Palmer). In both cases, her supervisor was John Barnes, then a lecturer at UWA. Hewett never completed her Master's, eventually abandoning the academy altogether in 1973 to pursue her writing career. Details of Hewett's career at UWA are preserved in her staff file, and I have made use of three job application letters (1965, 1967, 1971) that appear in this file and in which Hewett recounts her educational history. I am also indebted to John Barnes for confirming the non-completion of the Master's thesis in an email to me on 17 August 2013.

32   Frank Hardy, "Introduction", *What About the People!,* p. 7.

33   Hewett, under her new married name Dorothy Coade Lilley, was a tutor in the English Department from 1964 to 1973.

34   David Brooks, "The Wheel, The Mirror and The Tower: Desire in the Writings of Dorothy Hewett" in Bruce Bennett (ed.), *Selected Critical Essays,* Fremantle, Fremantle Arts Centre Press, 1995, pp. 183–85.

35   This was certainly true at UWA. In 1967, the first-year students that Hewett tutored were advised in an exam that, "W.B. Yeats and T.S. Eliot are perhaps the most important poets of our time", and invited to reveal which one appealed to them more and to discuss at least one poem by their chosen poet to justify their choice.

36   Hewett's other great poetic influence, Tennyson, refers to the Fisher King only in passing in his influential version of the Arthurian cycle, *The Idylls of the King* (1859–1885).

37   In the poem two Perth landmarks are invoked as vantage points for this reverie— the entrance to Fremantle Harbour (protected by the rocks of the north and south mole) and the Horseshoe Bridge that spans Perth's main rail-line.

38   The history of salinity in Western Australia, and particularly the early responses to it, is comprehensively treated in Beresford et al., *The Salinity Crisis: Landscapes, Communities and Politics,* Nedlands, UWA Press, 2001.

39   Judith Wright, "At Cooloolah", *The Bulletin*, vol. 75, no. 3882, 7 July 1954, p. 20.

40   Dorothy Hewett, *The Gipsy Dancer & Early Poems*.

41   Dorothy Hewett, "On the Open Stage", in Ortun Zuber (ed.), *The Language of Theatre: Problems in the Translation and Transposition of Drama*, Oxford, Pergamon Press, 1980, pp. 15–23. Reprinted in Fiona Morrison (ed.), *Selected Prose of Dorothy Hewett*, Nedlands, UWA Press, 2011, pp. 250–59.

42   In 1977, Hewett wrote of the importance of White's plays, and how *The Ham Funeral* was written in 1947, but not staged until fifteen years later at the Adelaide University Theatre Guild in 1961. She notes that: "The play came before Pinter, Ionesco and Becket's Godot. There was a period after the war when expressionism was considered dated. Brecht was virtually unknown." (221) Dorothy Hewett, "The White Phenomena", *Theatre Australia*, August 1977, pp. 1821. Reprinted in Fiona Morrison (ed.), *Selected Prose of Dorothy Hewett*, pp. 219–30.

43   Barry also directed the play, which premiered at the Playhouse on 31 August 1979.

44   Stephen Barry, "Introduction to the Sesquicentennial Edition", Dorothy Hewett, *The Man From Mukinupin*, Fremantle Arts Centre Press, Perth, and The Currency Press, Sydney, 1979, 2nd Edition, p. ix.

45   The name is a play on the name of the real town of Mukinbudin, although it is not in any other way connected to this town.

46   "Editor's Foreword", *The Man from Mukinupin*.

47   Anna Haebich, *For Their Own Good: Aborigines and Government in the South West of Western Australia, 1900–1940*, Nedlands, UWA Press, 1992, p. 143.

48   The "Radio News" column for *The West Australian* on 19 September 1934 advertises Montesole's tour of Western Australia. Hewett mentions Montesole as well in her autobiographical poem, "Father and Daughter" from her collection *Greenhouse*, published in the same year as *The Man from Mukinupin*: "at the picture-show / in the Town Hall Max Montesole / strangles Desdemona." (*Collected Poems*, p. 190)

49   Eek is reading the words of the newly elected Labour prime minister Andrew Fisher, albeit one month before he actually said them.

50   In Kim Scott's *Kayang & Me*, his Auntie Hazel relates that: "Most of my grandmother Monkey's family were massacred some time after 1880 by white people at a place called Cocaranup, a few miles from the Ravensthorpe townsite. Some of Granny Emily's people died there too." Kim Scott and Hazel Brown, *Kayang & Me*, Fremantle, Fremantle Arts Centre Press, 2005, p. 10.

51   This detail derives from Hewett's mother's recollection: see *Wild Card*, p. 19.

52   The verandah is often the "liminal" space of colonial fiction, where two orders, the colonial and the native are complicated. See Tanya Dalziell, "Beyond the Verandah: Elizabeth Jolley's *The Orchard Thieves* and Drusilla Modjeska's *The Orchard*", *Antipodes*, vol. 11, no. 1, 1997, pp. 37–40.

53   In much the same way, Hewett's maternal grandmother, Marie Coade, had been a "professional dressmaker" in South Melbourne: "Eventually she is 'making' for Melbourne's most fashionable clientele." (*Wild Card*, p. 14)

54   Hewett's idol, Katharine Susannah Prichard, had gone on the road with Wirth's Circus in rural Western Australian in the 1920s to research her novel, *Haxby's Circus*, London, Jonathan Cape, 1930.

55   Dorothy Hewett, "Through Different Eyes" in Dorothy Hewett and John Kinsella, *Wheatlands*, Fremantle, Fremantle Arts Centre Press, 2000, p. 9.

Notes to Chapter Seven: Jack Davis (1917–2000)

1   Jack Davis, "Aboriginal Writing: A Personal View" in Jack Davis and Bob
     Hodge (eds), *Aboriginal Writing Today*, Canberra, Australian Institute of
     Aboriginal Studies, 1985, p. 11.

2   As would be expected, the regional dialects of the Noongar language varied
     considerably over the vast country they occupied, and partly due to this, the
     word Noongar is itself spelt in a variety of ways, including Nyungah, Nyoongar,
     Nyungar and Noonga.

3   The seminal archaeological treatise on Aboriginal farming is Sylvia J. Hallam,
     *Fire and Hearth: A Study of Aboriginal Usage and European Usurpation in South-
     Western Australia*, *Australian Aboriginal Studies*, no. 58, Canberra, Australian
     Institute of Aboriginal Studies, 1979. See, in particular, her discussion of yam-
     grounds near Greenough, Gingin–Bindoon and the Victoria Plains, pp. 12–14.

4   Anna Haebich, "European Farmers and Aboriginal Farmers in South Western
     Australia, Mid 1890s-1914" in Bob Reece and Tom Stannage (eds), *European-
     Aboriginal Relations in Western Australian History, Studies in Western Australian
     History*, vol. 8, December 1984, p. 61. Haebich does also note: "However, many
     Aborigines showed an early positive response to the opportunities created by
     agricultural development and a good number were as keen as the new white
     settlers to establish their own farms. A combination of factors prevented them
     from establishing themselves successfully on the land and by 1914 most of the
     farming blocks granted to Aborigines had been resumed."

5   Rica Erickson, *The Victoria Plains*, Perth, Lamb Paterson, 1971, pp. 19, 54.

6   An important predecessor to the Native Settlement was Rottnest Island, which
     was used to incarcerate Aboriginal people from the 1830s until the 1930s, formally
     operating as a prison from 1838 to 1904. Like the Native Settlements, Rottnest
     brought together Aboriginal people from throughout Western Australia. Jack
     Davis draws attention to this parallel, but with an emphasis on the systematic
     destruction it wrought on cultural continuity: "It is coincidental that Rottnest
     and Mogumber figure so strongly in the destruction of Aboriginal society.
     Separation from the district of their birth and the loss of contact with their
     friends and relatives was terrifying to my people, and no single factor had more
     influence in breaking the back of Aboriginal resistance than the establishment of
     the Rottnest penal settlement. The abduction of Aboriginal children throughout
     the state and the isolation of adults at Moore River were so destructive of
     Aboriginal culture and cohesion that it took decades before new leaders could
     begin to emerge." Keith Chesson, *Jack Davis: A Life-Story*, Melbourne, Dent,
     1988, p. 27.

7   Robert Bropho, *Fringedweller*, Chippendale, NSW, Alternative Publishing Co-
     operative with the assistance of the Aboriginal Arts Board, Australia Council,
     1980, p. 41.

8   R.R.B Ackland, *Wongan–Ballidu: Pioneering Days*, Wongan Hills, Wongan-
     Ballidu Shire Council, 1965, p. 44.

9   Examples include Glenyse Ward, *Wandering Girl*, Broome, Magabala Books,
     1987; Eric Hayward, *No Free Kicks*, Fremantle, Fremantle Arts Centre Press,
     2006; Laurel Nannup, *A Story to Tell*, Nedlands, UWA Press, 2006; and Doris
     Pilkington-Garimara, *Follow the Rabbit-Proof Fence*, St Lucia, University of
     Queensland Press, 1996.

10   In one of history's minor ironies, it would be later re-named "Jack Davis House".

11   Chesson, *Jack Davis*, p. 26.

12   Jack Davis, *A Boy's Life*, Broome, Magabala Books, 1991, pp. 120–21.

13   Zamia, technically a cycad not a palm, produce a fruit very popular amongst parrots and cockatoos but fatal to stock.

14   Jack Davis, *A Boy's Life*, p. 119.

15   Chesson, *Jack Davis*, p. 42.

16   Bulk-handling was introduced in 1932–33.

17   Chesson, *Jack Davis*, p. 45.

18   ibid.

19   ibid., p. 127.

20   As Haebich has extensively documented in Anna Haebich, *For Their Own Good: Aborigines and Government in the South West of Western Australia, 1900–1940*, Nedlands, UWA Press, 1992.

21   Chesson, *Jack Davis*, p. 48.

22   These traditional stories also appear in Eddie Bennell's book, *Aboriginal Legends from the Bibulmun Tribe*, Perth, Rigby, 1981. Eddie Bennell was Jack Davis's nephew.

23   Jack Davis, *First-born*, p. xvi.

24   The Depression and a lingering drought meant that life in Carnarvon was difficult. Davis and his brother were "too proud to accept rations", to which they were entitled as Aboriginal people. Instead, they scrounged work as best they could, first building roads and with the money they saved, setting up as kangaroo shooters in the district. During this time, Davis was imprisoned twice for refusing to adhere to the curfew that applied to Aboriginal people within the limits of the town, the first time for a month, and the second time, for four months. Chesson, *Jack Davis*, p. 82.

25   Chesson, *Jack Davis*, pp. 95–96.

26   ibid., p. 103.

27   ibid., p. 121.

28   ibid.

29   In 1967, the AAC opened the Aboriginal Centre at 201 Beaufort Street in North Perth, with a view to meeting, in particular, the needs of Aboriginal youth, but serving more generally as a hub for welfare services and a centre for political advocacy. Davis was soon appointed manager, later managing director—a position he held until 1973.

30   Jack Davis, *The First-born and Other Poems*, Sydney, Angus & Robertson, 1970, p. x.

31   ibid., p. ix.

32   ibid., p. xi.

33   Chesson, *Jack Davis*, p. 63.

34   ibid., p. 111.

35   ibid., p. 112.

36   ibid.

37   Kath Walker, *We are Going*, Brisbane, Jacaranda Press, 1964; and, Kath Walker, *The Dawn is at Hand*, Brisbane, Jacaranda Press, 1966. Kath Walker changed her name to Oodgeroo Noonuccal in the 1980s, but I have chosen to use the name she was using at this time to be consistent with the period I am describing.

38   John Collins, "A Mate in Publishing" in Adam Shoemaker (ed.), *Oodgeroo: A Tribute*, Special Issue of *Australian Literary Studies,* vol. 16, no. 4, 1994, pp. 9–23.

39   Like Davis's brother Harold, Walker's two brothers served in World War Two, and were also imprisoned, although by the Japanese. Walker herself served as a signaller in the Australian Women's Army Service from 1942.

40   *Aboriginal Writing Today*, p. 12.

41   Philip Roberts, "A Time of Innocence", *Sydney Morning Herald*, 31 July 1971, p. 20. Others found them to be compromised by their adherence to European forms—bearing in mind that Australian modernist poetry had for some time been interested in the primitivist possibilities of traditional Aboriginal songs. James Tulip in the *Bulletin* felt that the poems in *The First-born* revealed that Davis was "uncertain in the totemic world of the white man's printed page," speculating that the "medium of poetry ... [was] too heavily involved in the sophistications of western society to let [him] feel at home", James Tulip, "Private Poets", *Bulletin,* vol. 94, no. 4788, 8 January 1972, pp. 34–35.

42   Other early critics sensed this too, including Ronald Dunlop who wrote in a review for *Poetry Australia* that although Davis's verse "lacks, generally, the refined complexity of much modern writing" it had nonetheless a vitality that this same modern writing was often missing. He cites Eliot's description of Blake's verse as fitting of Davis. For Eliot, Blake's visionary poems had "the unpleasantness of great poetry" which was typified by "a peculiar honesty, which, in a world too frightened to be honest, is peculiarly terrifying. "Old Verse", *Southerly,* vol. 31, no. 3, 1971, pp. 227–40; the quote is from p. 232.

43   Kevin Gilbert, *End of Dream-Time*, Sydney, Island Press, 1971.

44   Ronald Dunlop, "Australian Poets at Work: Some Recent Books", *Poetry Australia,* vol. 38, 1971, pp. 61–4.

45   Nene Gare, *The Fringe Dwellers*, London, Heinemann, 1961, p. 54.

46   Ironically, when Bruce Beresford adapted Gare's novel as a film in 1986, and the story was shifted from Geraldton in the late '50s to Queensland in the mid-1980s, Kath Walker (by then, known as Oodgeroo Noonuccal) was employed both as a script-consultant and actor.

47   Robin Smith Walley and Tracie Pushman, *On the Outskirts: Photographs of Allawah Grove Aboriginal Settlement, Perth*, Berndt Museum of Anthropology, Occasional Paper no. 7, The University of Western Australia. See also, Anna Haebich, *Spinning the Dream: Assimilation in Australia, 1950–1970,* Fremantle, Fremantle Press, 2008, especially "Part III: Assimilation in Nyungar Country", pp. 213–300.

48   The final line echoes the final triplet of Kath Walker's poem "Intolerance" from *We Are Going* (1964): "People who say, by bias driven, / That colour must not be forgiven, / Would snub the Carpenter in heaven."

49   See *First-born,* p. xvi.

50   H.C. Coombs, "An Invitation to Debate", in Jack Davis, *Kullark / The Dreamers*, Sydney, Currency Press, 1982, p. x.

51   Kath Walker, "A Plea for Tolerance: Jack Davis: *The First-born and Other Poems*", *Makar,* vol. 7, no. 1, May 1971, pp. 41–2.

52   The pioneering linguistic study of the Noongar language(s) was Wilfrid H. Douglas, *The Aboriginal Languages of the South-West of Australia*, Canberra, Australian Institute of Aboriginal Studies, 1968. A compilation of Noongar words

based on the key colonial sources has been produced by the Western Australian Museum: *A Nyoongar Wordlist from the South West of Western Australia,* Perth, Western Australian Museum, 2002. Recent work on Noongar led by the novelist Kim Scott has turned away from the concept of producing word-lists and focused on the practice of language regeneration through creative community projects, including making use of the recovered sound-recordings made by the American linguist Gerhardt Laves in 1931.

53   Kevin Gilbert, "Black Theatre" in his *Because a White Man'll Never Do It,* Sydney, Angus & Robertson, 1973, pp. 118–22. Gilbert's play was only printed for publication much later: Kevin Gilbert, *The First Written Aboriginal Play: The Cherry Pickers,* Canberra, Burrambinga Books, 1988.

54   Chesson, *Jack Davis,* p. 191.

55   Papers from his time in the Aboriginal Publication Foundation reveal an early draft of *The Dreamers* which takes place in a single act and may well be the script for the 1972 production. I am grateful to Madelon Davis and AIATSIS for allowing me to review part of the Jack Davis papers, which at the time of writing were still in the process of being fully archived. I was not able to locate the original "The Steel and the Stone" script in these papers, but further work is needed once this important archive is made fully available.

56   MS 2782, Aboriginal Publication Foundation, Box 13, Series 11, Jack Davis, AIATSIS Library. Folder 2 contains a typescript draft of *The Dreamers* which is clearly a predecessor to the later play. There is no date, but the papers cover the period 1973–79. The play resembles the beginning of Act One of the later play and takes place in the kitchen of the Wallitch family, although this family name is not used. There is also a "Granny" character (who disappears from the final version) and an "Uncle Wally" character, who will become Worru. In this early draft, Wally (Worru) appears in the kitchen with everyone else. In the final play, Worru is in hospital and only appears in later scenes after they collect him.

57   Jack Davis, *Kullark / The Dreamers,* Sydney, Currency Press, 1982; *No Sugar,* Sydney, Currency Press, 1986. Parenthetical page numbers for quotations from these three plays are to these two editions.

58   Indeed, Davis credits Ross with a number of the crucial technical elements in the stagecraft that helped to bring *Kullark*'s sudden historical shifts into a viable dramatic form.

59   Raymond Williams, *The Country and the City,* London, Chatto & Windus, 1973.

60   Haebich, *For Their Own Good,* p. 304. Haebich's account of this incident and various similar ones documents the broader pattern in which Aboriginal people were dealt with, particularly after the Depression hit and jobs, even the lowly paid casual itinerant work (clearing, fencing, stooking), disappeared from the wheatbelt.

61   As noted above, Worru was named Wally in the earlier play.

62   There is a slight discrepancy in the text surrounding Neal. The superintendent of Moore River at this time was Arthur J. Neal, but the play uses the initials "N.S. Neal".

63   This theatrical concept has recently been developed and used to dramatise life on the Coranderrk Mission in Victoria. See Giordano Nanni and Andrea James, *Coranderrk: We Will Show the Country,* Canberra, Aboriginal Studies Press, 2013.

64   This is deftly caught in a line from *No Sugar* when the exasperated police sergeant mutters to his constable: "Looks like I'm the one that needs protection".

Notes to Chapter Eight: Barbara York Main (1929–)

1   It is already reaching a significant level of sophistication and development in Aldo Leopold's *Sand-County Almanac*, Oxford, Oxford UP, 1949. In Australia, a quite sharp sense of the environment, although without Leopold's far-reaching meditations, is supplied by British biologist Francis Ratcliffe's classic study *Flying Fox and Drifting Sand*, Sydney, Angus & Robertson, 1938.

2   Elyne Mitchell, *Speak to the Earth*, Sydney, Angus & Robertson, 1945; *Soil and Civilization*, Sydney, Angus & Robertson, 1945.

3   *The Australian Environment: Handbook prepared for the British Commonwealth Specialist Agricultural Conference on Plant and Animal Nutrition in Relation to Soil and Climatic Factors, held in Australia, August, 1949*, Melbourne, CSIRO, 1949.

4   Rachel Carson, *Silent Spring*, Boston, Houghton Mifflin, 1962.

5   The double-helix structure of DNA was first documented in 1953.

6   Vincent Serventy, *Australia: A Continent in Danger*, North Sydney, Ure Smith, 1966.

7   Judith Wright, "At Cooloolah", *The Bulletin*, no. 3882, 7 July 1954, p. 20, and *Birds*, Sydney, Angus & Robertson, 1962. Robert Zeller, "Judith Wright's Nature Poetry: The Problem of Living 'Through a Web of Language'", *Antipodes*, vol. 12, no. 1, 1998, pp. 21–5.

8   Xavier Herbert, *Capricornia*, Sydney, Publicist Publishing Company, 1938, and *Poor Fellow, My Country*, Sydney, Fontana, 1975.

9   Barbara York Main, *Between Wodjil and Tor*, Brisbane, Jacaranda Press, 1967, and *Twice Trodden Ground*, Brisbane, Jacaranda Press, 1971.

10 Interview with Gladys Beatrice York (nee Tobias) by Colin Puls, Battye Library Oral History Program, 12 March 1976.

11 ibid.

12 Gladys Froggatt, *The World of Little Lives*, Sydney, W. Brooks, 1916.

13 May Gibbs, *Gum Blossom Babies*, Sydney, Angus & Robertson, 1916.

14 Alice Clucas, *Behind the Hills*, Melbourne, Lothian, 1926.

15 Rudyard Kipling, *The Jungle Book*, London, Macmillan, 1894, and *Just So Stories*, London, Macmillan, 1902.

16 Minnie Smith, *"Granny Smith's" Book: Verse and Legends of the Australian Bush*, Perth, Patersons, 1941.

17 Barbara York Main interviewed by John Bannister, UWA Oral History Project, UWA Historical Society, 22 August 2012, Tap. 1.

18 Barbara York Main, *The Spiders of Australia*, Brisbane, Jacaranda Press, 1964.

19 Henry David Thoreau, *Walden, or Life in the Woods*, Boston, Ticknor and Fields, 1854, and *The Maine Woods*, Boston, Ticknor and Fields, 1864. Gilbert White, *The Natural History and Antiquities of Selborne in the County of Southampton*, London, Benjamin White, 1789.

20 Jack Hyett, *A Bushman's Year*, Melbourne, F.W. Cheshire, 1959.

21 Perhaps inspired by *Wodjil and Tor*, York Main's former mentor Vincent Serventy also produced a calendar of wheatbelt bushland three years later, *Dryandra: The Story of an Australian Forest*, Sydney, A.H. & A.W. Reed, 1970.

22 Nathan McQuoid, *Lifting the Bonnet on Wheatbelt Woodlands: A guide to the connection between landscape and vegetation in Southwest Australia*, Ultimo, WWF-Australia, 2014, p. 22.

23   For a list of these factors see McQuoid, *Lifting the Bonnet*, p. 24. Irene
       Cunningham has also written on the extraordinary diversity of wheatbelt flora:
       The Land of Flowers: An Australian environment on the brink, Otford, Otford Press,
       2005. See also, Stephen Hopper, *Life on the Rocks: The art of survival*, Fremantle,
       Fremantle Arts Centre Press, 1999.

24   Nathan McQuoid, commenting much more recently on the phenomenon of
       the apparent health of wheatbelt woodlands, describes the situation this way:
       "The familiar and typical central Wheatbelt woodlands stand as mostly small,
       dysfunctional groups of old trees in various states of disrepair, having largely lost
       their ability to regenerate. These old stands are sometimes known as the 'the
       living dead', because while the trees are alive and often look quite majestic, they
       cannot self-regenerate. Once they die, they will not be replaced in the landscape."
       Lifting the Bonnet, p. 69.

25   Indeed, York Main does not recall meeting a single Aboriginal person in her
       years growing up at Fairfields farm near Tammin.

26   Sylvia J. Hallam, Fire and Hearth: A Study of Aboriginal Usage and European
       Usurpation in South-Western Australia, *Australian Aboriginal Studies*, no. 58,
       Canberra, Australian Institute of Aboriginal Studies, 1979.

27   J.K. Ewers, *Bruce Rock: The Story of a District*, Perth, Bruce Rock District, Road
       Board, 1959; Frank H. Goldsmith, *The History of Morawa District: The Story of
       Progress*, Morawa: Morawa Shire Council, 1961; F.A. Law, *The History of the
       Merredin District of Western Australia*, Merredin, Merredin Road Board, 1961.

28   As well as "sketches" York Main calls them "essays" and they are within the
       genre we have lately come to call the personal essay, but which does have a
       longer lineage. The fact that these are the author's experiences, and not those of
       a fictional persona, is only something which is implied by her calling them essays.
       In fact, they could just as easily be read as fictional stories since they are singularly
       lacking in proper nouns—we know nothing of the names of the people involved
       and nothing either of the places. Again, this gives to the writing a certain
       Cowanesque abstraction that is—in both writers—in permanent tension with the
       intensity of the regional focus.

29   In this way, just like *Between Wodjil and Tor*, *Twice Trodden Ground* begins with
       the sound of wind at night, albeit a wintry one in this case.

30   G.H. Burvill, *Agriculture in Western Australia: 150 years of development and
       achievement, 1829–1979*, Nedlands, UWA Press, 1979, p. 62. Not all of this was
       taking place in the wheatbelt, but most of it was.

31   ibid., p. 164.

32   ibid., p. 166.

33   ibid., p. 61.

34   Barbara York Main, "Marginal Country", *Westerly*, no. 2, June 1972, pp. 21–36.

Notes to Chapter Nine: Elizabeth Jolley (1923–2007)

1   Elizabeth Jolley, *The Well*, Ringwood, Victoria, Viking, 1986.

2   Brian Dibble, *Doing Life: A Biography of Elizabeth Jolley*, Nedlands, UWA Press,
       2008. Dibble's is now the definitive study of Jolley's life and work. Dibble was
       a long-time colleague of Jolley's at Curtin University. Dibble's partner, Barbara
       Milech, also at Curtin University, wrote a key early study of the emergence
       of Jolley as a writer, "Becoming 'Elizabeth Jolley': The First Twenty Years in

Australia", published in Alison Bartlett, Robert Dixon and Christopher Lee (eds), *Australian Literature and the Public Sphere*, The Association for the Study of Australian Literature, 1999, pp. 132–41.

3   Chris Prentice, "Writing into the Land: The textual mediation of relationships to the land in Elizabeth Jolley's fiction", in Delys Bird and Brenda Walker (eds), *Elizabeth Jolley: New Critical Essays*, Sydney, Allen & Unwin (in conjunction with the Centre for the Study of Australian Literature at the University of Western Australia), 1991, pp. 1–14.

4   Elizabeth Jolley, *Diary of a Weekend Farmer,* Fremantle, Fremantle Arts Centre Press, 1993.

5   Prentice sees this "land hunger" as part of "the post-colonial drive to write the self into the land", "Writing in the Land", p. 2.

6   Dibble, *Doing Life*, p. 169.

7   Transcript of Elizabeth Jolley interviewed by Stuart Reid for the Battye Library collection. Part of a collection of oral history interviews produced by a joint project between the National Library of Australia and the J.S. Battye Library of West Australian History, recorded at Perth, Western Australia, on 10 July to 5 August 1989, OH 2268, Tape Nine, p. 71.

8   Elizabeth Jolley, "A Small Fragment of the Earth" in *Learning to Dance: Elizabeth Jolley, Her Life and Work*, selected and introduced by Caroline Lurie, Camberwell Victoria, Viking, 2006, pp. 177–84. Quote is on pp. 181–2.

9   Jolley, "A Small Fragment of the Earth", p. 182.

10   Elizabeth Jolley, *Five Acre Virgin*, Fremantle, Fremantle Arts Centre Press, 1976.

11   Dibble, *Doing Life*, p. 172. Elizabeth Jolley, *Palomino*, Collingwood, Outback Press, 1980.

12   Elizabeth Jolley, "The Long Distance Lecture", *The Travelling Entertainer and Other Stories*, Fremantle, Fremantle Arts Centre Press, 1979, pp. 56–69. Reprinted in the compilation, *Elizabeth Jolley, Stories: Five Acre Version and The Travelling Entertainer*, Fremantle, Fremantle Arts Centre Press, 1984, pp. 176–89. I have used this later edition and the page numbers correspond to the later work.

13   Transcript of interview of Elizabeth Jolley by Stuart Reid, p. 52.

14   Jack London, "To Build a Fire", *Century Magazine*, vol. 76, August 1908, pp. 525–34.

15   I am grateful to discussion with Brian Dibble, Barbara Milech and Delys Bird for this basic insight into the experience of these country workshops.

16   Elizabeth Jolley, *Foxybaby*, St Lucia, University of Queensland Press, 1985.

17   Milech, "Becoming 'Elizabeth Jolley': The First Twenty Years in Australia", p. 139.

18   Transcript of interview of Elizabeth Jolley by Stuart Reid, p. 77.

19   Milech, "Becoming 'Elizabeth Jolley'", p. 138. Elizabeth Jolley, "Landscape and Figures", Special Issue: "Regionalism in Contemporary Australian Literature", *Westerly*, vol. 23, no. 4, December 1978, pp. 72–73.

20   Elizabeth Jolley, "A Scattered Catalogue of Consolation" in *Learning to Dance: Elizabeth Jolley, Her Life and Work*, North Ryde, Angus & Robertson, 1991, p. 48.

21   Veronica Brady, "'Speaking from where she is not …' *The Well* and *My Father's Moon*", *Elizabeth Jolley: New Critical Essays*, p. 51.

22   Brady here cites the French psychoanalyst of the Lacanian school, Julia Kristeva, in particular her book, *Desire in Language: A Semiotic Approach to Literature and Art*, Oxford: Blackwell, 1980, p. 241. For Lacan, the "law" which mandates our

identity and ratifies our desire is vouchsafed by "the name of the father". This symbolic father is what allows us to conduct legitimate relationships and to conclude legitimate transactions with others.

23   Joan Kirkby, "The Joseph Complex or the Father / Daughter Bond in the Fiction of Elizabeth Jolley", *Elizabeth Jolley: New Critical Essays*, 1991, p. 65.

Notes to Chapter Ten: Tom Flood (1955–)

1   Tom Flood, *Oceana Fine*, Sydney, Allen & Unwin, 1989.

2   Personal email correspondence with Tom Flood, 15 January 2015.

3   ibid.

4   The "Sons of America" goldmine was owned by Rex's aunt Grace Poston through the family company "Poston Perseverance Ltd". The name of the mine alludes to the "Sons of Gwalia" mine near Wiluna that was managed during the late 1890s by Herbert Hoover, the future United States president. The Sons of Gwalia company also owned a mine at Marvel Loch. Goldmining re-emerged during the Depression years as a profitable enterprise, with gold's value increasing as other commodities, including wheat of course, crashed. Marvel Loch, and the Yilgarn more generally, was thus a zone that was able to move between gold and wheat as prices varied. We have already seen this in the case of Cyril Goode, who after his farm failed in the early '30s spent much of the remainder of the decade working in the goldmine at Wiluna.

5   The household thereafter consisted of James's father, Rex Cleaver, Rex's parents Chloe and Ben ("Jam"), and Rex's aunt Grace, who is Chloe's sister and the driving figure of the household. There is also an Italian housekeeper known as "Bap" (Baptista), and two significantly older brothers, generally referred to as "The Brothers" (Graham and Frank). We can again see echoes here of the author's own family and its potent mixture of myth and trauma.

6   Mike Heald, review of Tom Flood, *Oceana Fine*, *Westerly*, vol. 3, September 1990, pp. 93–94.

7   Salman Rushdie, *Midnight's Children*, London, Jonathan Cape, 1981.

8   Thea Astley, *It's Raining in Mango: Pictures from the Family Album*, New York, P. Putnam's Sons, 1987; Kate Grenville, *Joan Makes History*, St Lucia, University of Queensland Press, 1988; Peter Carey, *Oscar and Lucinda*, St Lucia, University of Queensland Press, 1988; and Tim Winton, *Cloudstreet*, Melbourne, McPhee Gribble, 1991,

9   The motif of the circus was something we saw in *The Man from Mukinupin*, with the ex-tightrope walker, Miss Clemmy Hummer. Clemmy Hummer, in turn, might be seen as a nod to Hewett's idol Katharine Susannah Prichard whose novel *Haxby's Circus* (London, Jonathan Cape, 1930) was based on a period Prichard spent touring with Wirth's Circus in the southwest.

10   The Depression years are treated with characteristic irreverence: "Out on the far side of the rabbit-proof fence, people were abandoning the farms they'd scratched out through the fat years of the 20s, going under to debt and the dry perimeter. Others, sick of dryblowing a dream east of Southern Cross, walked west to take their place. Sheep committed suicide from desolation and the golden grain just wasn't worth growing that far from anywhere." (96)

11   Herman Melville, *Moby Dick: The Whale*, New York, Harper & Brothers, 1851.

12   Melville, *Moby Dick*, ch. 36.

13   Randolph Stow, *Tourmaline*, London, MacDonald, 1963.

14   The service is not especially solemn; in fact, it is comically banal in many respects. Nevertheless, the ceremony represents a perversion of the Christian communion. Instead of taking bread in remembrance of Christ's body, the wheat becomes the messianic agent, with sacrificial human bodies used to power it. In other words, Cleaver's cult is a reinstatement of the human sacrifice that Christ's death had meant to cancel out for all time. Rex intones: "The Miracle that has called this flock together and given us the fruit of His goodness, the means to cast off the stranglehold of Finance, the way to ensure His land that is promised be saved from the mineral rape of the pharisees, restored for the health and well-being of all, the golden nature, the true way of Oceana Fine. This is … nature's way and nature is good because she is the daughter of God." (217)

15   This horrific image—of a man severed in two—is in fact one that is repeated at key points in the novel, most significantly with the sundering of Willy Sargent by an unknown assailant. It also links to a motif of severance that began with the finger that Finn Torrent found in the grain sample and continued in other severed fingers and hands encountered in unexpected places by others in the novel.

Notes to Chapter Eleven: John Kinsella (1963–)

1   John Kinsella (ed.), *The Penguin Anthology of Australian Poetry*, Camberwell, Penguin, 2009.

2   John Heywood, *The Frozen Sea*, Perth, Zepplin Press, 1983.

3   Knapp accidentally misspelled Zeppelin and then decided to keep the name "Zepplin" for his press.

4   Alexander Craig (ed.), *Twelve Poets, 1950–1970*, Brisbane, Jacaranda Press, 1971.

5   John Kinsella, "Towards a Contemporary Australian Poetic", *Poetry*, vol. 169, no. 1, October-November 1996, pp. 94–107. Reprinted in John Kinsella, *Spatial Relations*, vol. 1 (2 vols.), Gordon Collier (ed.), Amsterdam and New York, Rodopi, 2013, pp. 38–50.

6   John Kinsella, *Night Parrots*, Fremantle, Fremantle Arts Centre Press, 1989.

7   For a discussion of the Lasseter sequence from *Night Parrots*, see Andrew Duncan, "National Geosophical Lexison: The Lasseter Sequences" in Rod Mengham and Glen Phillips (eds), *Fairly Obsessive Essays on the Works of John Kinsella*, Nedlands, Centre for Studies in Australian Literature (at the University of Western Australia) and Fremantle, Fremantle Arts Centre Press, 2000, pp. 53-66.

8   Tamarisks are now a significant weed in the Avon Valley, and have been found to be counter-productive in reducing salinity.

9   John Kinsella, *Eschatologies*, Fremantle, Fremantle Arts Centre Press, 1991.

10   John Kinsella, *Full Fathom Five*, Fremantle Arts Centre Press, 1993.

11   John Kinsella, *Syzygy*, Fremantle Arts Centre Press, 1993. I have relied on *Syzygy* as it appears in John Kinsella, *Poems 1980-1994*, Newcastle-upon-Tyne, Bloodaxe, 1997. The page numbers in my text refer to this later edition.

12   Louis Armand, "'Ground Zero Warholing': John Kinsella and the Art of Traumatic Realism", in *Fairly Obsessive Essays*, pp. 119–43.

13   Hal Foster, *The Return of the Real: The Avant-Garde at the End of the Century*, Cambridge, MIT Press, 1996, p. 130. Quoted in Armand, "Ground Zero Warholing", p. 119.

14   As Kinsella writes: "LANGUAGE poets do not separate the political from the language. And in a sense all language is political." John Kinsella, "The Language Poets" (1995), *Spatial Relations*, vol. 1, ed. Gordon Collier, 2 vols., Amsterdam, Rodopi, 2013, vol. 1, p. 413.

15   John Kinsella, *The Silo: A Pastoral Symphony*, Fremantle, Fremantle Arts Centre Press, 1995.

16   *The Silo* became the first volume in Kinsella's "pastoral trilogy", which also included *The Hunt* (Fremantle, Fremantle Arts Centre Press, 1998) and *The New Arcadia* (Fremantle, Fremantle Arts Centre Press, 2005). In some ways, bracketing Kinsella's work in this way is a little arbitrary, since he continued to write copiously about the wheatbelt, and interrogate the pastoral, in volumes that intervene between these, and in the many works he has published since 2005. Nevertheless, it is useful to select these three works because the author himself conceived them as related to each other and because they epitomise his wheatbelt poetry. *The Hunt* won *The Age* Book of the Year "Dinny O'Hearn Poetry Prize" as well as the Western Australian Premier's Book Award for Poetry in 1998, and in the wake of this Kinsella was made a Fellow of Churchill College at Cambridge University. *The New Arcadia* won the Judith Wright Award for Poetry and the Queensland Premier's Literary Award for Poetry in 2005. So, the trilogy is certainly amongst Kinsella's most celebrated work. See Liu Pingping and Glen Phillips, "Radical Pastoralism: John Kinsella's Great 'Pastoral Trilogy'", *Landscapes*, vol. 3, no. 1, 2009, pp. 1–12.

17   The critique of the pastoral theme has also been a significant project in Kinsella's critical writing, featuring in important essays such as "Pastoral and Political Responsibilities of Poetry" (1996), *Spatial Relations*, vol. 2, pp. 69–75; and "Is there an Australian Pastoral?" in John Kinsella, *Contrary Rhetoric: Lectures on Landscape and Language*, Glen Phillips and Andrew Taylor (eds), Fremantle, Fremantle Press, 2008, pp. 131–61. For a view on Kinsella's relationship to the pastoral, see the separate contributions of Haskell, Larkin, Phillips and Vickery in *Fairly Obsessive Essays*.

18   Raymond Williams proposed the counter-pastoral in chapter 3 of *The Country and the City*, London, The Hogarth Press, 1973. An early and slightly truncated version of this chapter first appeared as "Pastoral and Counter-Pastoral", *Critical Quarterly*, vol. 10, no. 3, September 1968, pp. 277–90. The counter-pastoral designated a counter-tradition in rural literature in which the enabling illusions of the pastoral topos are disrupted by the exposure of certain "real" conditions. For Williams, it is the real of rural labour.

19   In an autobiographical essay from 2005, Kinsella begins: "The basis of my work is the pastoral – or counter-pastoral." "Exhuming Autobiography" (2005), *Spatial Relations*, vol. 2, p. 307. *Counter-pastoral* (Sydney, Vagabond, 1999) is also the title of a chapbook by Kinsella, which begins with an epigraph from Raymond Williams's *The Country and the City*. Williams's book is the most sustained critique of the pastoral tradition, and one to which my own study is heavily indebted.

20   The second movement of Beethoven's symphony is imagined as a scene by a brook. In *The Silo*, part 2 is titled "Why They Stripped The Last Trees From The Banks Of The Creek". Beethoven's "merry gathering of country folk" in the third movement becomes "Drinking In The Saloon Bar Of A Country Hotel"

and the storm in the fourth movement becomes "The Fire In The Tail Of The Cyclone". The Shepherd's song of Beethoven's fifth movement is simply called "Rites of Passage" in *The Silo*.

21 John Kinsella, "Myths of the Wheatbelt", *Contrary Rhetoric*, p. 194.

22 John Kinsella, *In the Shade of the Shady Tree*, Athens, Swallow Press / University of Ohio Press, 2012, and *Crow's Breath*, Melbourne, Transit Lounge, 2015.

23 The mixture of driving and poetry is most explicit in Kinsella's *The New Arcadia* (2005), which is the third volume in the pastoral trilogy that also includes *The Silo* (1995) and *The Hunt* (1998). In *The New Arcadia*, each of the five "acts" (these correspond to the five books of Sir Philip Sidney's Arcadia written at the end of the sixteenth century) begins with reciting the drive from Perth to York, and the archetypal entry into the wheatbelt for many Western Australians.

24 John Kinsella, *Visitants*, Newcastle-on-Tyne, 1999 and *Kangaroo Virus*, Fremantle, Fremantle Arts Centre Press, 1998.

25 PT Hooper et al., "Epidemic of blindness in kangaroos: Evidence of a viral aetiology" in *Australian Veterinary Journal*, vol. 77, no. 8, August 1999, pp. 529–36.

26 In this sense, the poems are actually in a certain way more precise than those poems which see the wheatbelt as alien. They correctly locate the "alien" element in the wheatbelt, not in the spooky or eerie dimensions of its evacuated landscape, but in the agents of capitalistic alienation (the farming enterprise as such) that arrived to remake this landscape for their own ends.

27 Dorothy Hewett and John Kinsella, *Wheatlands*, Fremantle, Fremantle Arts Centre Press, 2000.

28 John Kinsella, *The Hierarchy of Sheep*, Fremantle, Fremantle Arts Centre Press, 2001; *A New Shades of the Sublime & Beautiful*, Fremantle, Fremantle Arts Centre Press, 2008; and *Divine Comedy: Journeys Through a Regional Geography*, St Lucia, University of Queensland Press, 2008.

29 John Kinsella, *Tide*, Melbourne, Transit Lounge, 2015.

30 John Kinsella, *Jam Tree Gully: Poems*, New York, Norton, 2012.

31 Tom Bristow, "International Regionalism as American-Australian Dialogue: The Literary and Psychological Terrains of William James and Henry David Thoreau in John Kinsella's Jam Tree Gully: Poems", *AJE: Australasian Journal of Ecocriticism and Cultural Ecology*, vol. 2, 2012/2013, p. 59. Another Australian ecocritic, John Ryan, has considered the role of Thoreau in Australian nature writing. See, "Recalling Walden: Thoreau's Embodied Aesthetics and Australian Writings on Place", *Journal of Ecocriticism*, vol. 3, no. 2, July 2011, pp. 43–57.

32 Kinsella shares a blog with his wife, the poet Tracey Ryan, under the banner: "Mutually Said: Poets Vegan Anarchist Pacifist" poetsvegananarchistpacifist. blogspot.com.au/.

33 An early ancestor of this hypertextual lizard is the Echidna in his poem "Zone (Echidna)" from the chap-book *Counter-Pastoral*.

34 Lawrence Buell, *The Environmental Imagination: Thoreau, nature writing, and the formation of American culture*, Cambridge, Harvard University Press, 1995, p. 143.

35 Buell proposes that an "environmentally oriented work" will display the following qualities: "1. The nonhuman environment is present not merely as a framing device but as a presence that begins to suggest that human history is implicated in natural history ... 2. The human interest is not understood to be the only legitimate interest ... 3. Human accountability to the environment is

part of the text's ethical orientation ... 4. Some sense of the environment as a process rather than a constant or a given is at least implicit in the text." ibid., pp. 7–8.

Notes to the Epilogue: The Wheatbelt in Deep Time

1   Rosslyn Haynes's works on Australia's "red centre" and on Tasmania are detailed considerations of the relationship between works of culture (film, literature, television, visual arts) and specific (iconic) Australian places. Paul Carter and Ross Gibson pioneered a post-structuralist "spatial history" of Australian regions. See, Rosslyn Haynes, *Seeking the Centre: The Australian Desert in Literature, Art and Film*, Melbourne, Cambridge UP, 1999, and *Tasmanian Visions: Landscapes in Writing, Art and Photography*, Sandy Bay, Tasmania Polymath Press, 2006; Paul Carter, *Ground Truthing: Explorations in a Creative Region*, UWA Publishing, 2010; and Ross Gibson, *Seven Versions of an Australian Badland*, St Lucia, University of Queensland Press, 2002.

2   In this respect, at least, perhaps the closest analogue, and no doubt one of the guiding inspirations behind this study, was Eric Rolls brilliant account of the "creation" of the Pilliga forest, *A Million Wild Acres: Two Hundred Years of Man and an Australian Forest*, Melbourne, Nelson, 1981.

3   Barbara York Main, "Living in a Fabricated Landscape—The Look of the Land" in *Visions for Agriculture: Proceedings of a Workshop Held at Tammin by the Merredin Dryland Research Institute's Research Advisory Committee, 22–23 October 1992*, Department of Agriculture, 1993, Perth, Western Australia, pp. 39–43.

Acknowledgements

This has been a lengthy project and many people have assisted me in it over the years. Several authors have been very generous in their time and interest in the research that went into this book. John Kinsella has been unstinting in his support, and I've enjoyed the various drives to the wheatbelt we have taken together over the years. His mother, Wendy Kinsella, and wife, Tracy Ryan, have also lent me photographs and fed me vegan snacks (respectively). Barbara York Main kindly took me on a trip to visit 'her spiders' in the country between Wodjil and Tor and submitted herself to extensive interviews about her family and life growing up in the wheatbelt between the wars. Tom Flood was good enough to answer my emails with a lengthy account of his experiences of the 'bins' in the 1970s.

For the writers who were no longer living I have been assisted by their surviving family. Cyril Goode's daughter Cathy Culbard has been very kind in making available his diaries and photographs and that chapter could not have been written without her assistance. Trisha Kotai-Ewers read the chapter on her father J.K. Ewers and provided valuable insight into his career. I was fortunate with the chapter on Dorothy Hewett to be able to interview her sister, Lesley Dougan at the home of her daughter Lucy Dougan. Lucy, my colleague at *Westerly Magazine*, has also kindly run countless queries past 'Mum' as I struggled through the labyrinth of Hewett's life. I am grateful to Hewett's literary executor and daughter, Kate Lilley, for permission to reproduce photographs that appeared in *Wild Card* and the poems I quote. I also want to thank Hewett's daughter Rozanna Lilley for reading an early draft of the Hewett chapter and for her insights into her late father, Merv Lilley. Although her biography will arrive too late to help me, I am very grateful to Hewett's biographer Nicole Moore, who also read my work and noticed errors. The expedition to see the remains of Lambton Downs with Nicole, Lucy and her family was especially poignant and memorable. Jack Davis's widow, Madelon Wilkins, allowed me to view papers held at AIATSIS that contained the early work of the playwright. With the Jolley chapter, I was graciously assisted by Brian Dibble, Barbara Milech and Delys Bird. The Peter Cowan Writers' Centre were very helpful in making available their newly donated, and completely uncatalogued, boxes of Peter Cowan's papers. Fellow scholars have been generous in their time and interest and I would particularly acknowledge the exchanges I had with Laurie Smith (on James Pollard), John Barnes (on Peter Cowan), Bill Dunstone (on Dorothy Hewett) and Liana Joy Christensen (on Barbara York Main).

I have also been fortunate to receive institutional support. Most particularly, the University of Western Australia has provided funding and resources, and I also received an ARC Discovery Grant which allowed me to reduce my teaching at key junctures at UWA. My colleagues at UWA, particularly in the School of Humanities, have been a tremendous source of scholarly and moral support. I would particularly like to thank Kieran Dolin, Judith Johnston, Jeremy Martens, Philip Mead and Andrea Gaynor, but there have been many others. Matthew Chrulew and James Quinton were excellent as research assistants and astute editors. I have benefited from a close association with the Westerly Centre at UWA and thank everyone connected to it. The Westerly Centre has been an important host for this research. In recent years I have been involved in teaching UWA postgraduate students studying development in the wheatbelt, and thank the team—Carolyn Oldham, Chantal Bourgault du Coudray, Matthew Tonts and Fiona Haslam-McKenzie—that initiated this innovative program for inviting me to participate. Thanks also to Grant Arthur of the Wheatblelt Development Commission.

The final step to publication has been made very pleasurable by the good and efficient people at UWAP. Particularly, I thank Terri-ann White and the publication committee for supporting this book, and the Staples Bequest for helping to fund it. Kate Pickard and Charlotte Guest at UWAP have also been terrific. Of course none of this would have been possible without my family and I especially thank my parents and my wife, Wai Sum Woo, for their support.

Portions of this book, in earlier incarnations, have appeared in various publications over the years. In particular:

- "Spinning *The Dreamers*: Jack Davis and the Drama of Assimilation", *Westerly* 60.1 (2015) 24–39.
- "The Fissured Future: John Kinsella's *Jam Tree Gully*", *English Academy Review* 31.2 (2014) 138–155.
- "Salt Scars: John Kinsella's Wheatbelt," *Australian Literary Studies* 27.2 (2012) 18–31.
- '"Denizens of the Bush": James Pollard and Popular Naturalism', *Studies in Western Australian History* 27 (2011) 45–61.
- "Islands of Yesterday: The Ecological Writing of Barbara York Main", *Westerly* 54 (2008) 12–26.
- "The Shadow on the Field: Literature and Ecology in the Western Australian Wheatbelt" in CA. Cranston and Robert Zeller, eds., *The Littoral Zone: Australian Contexts and their Writers.* Amsterdam and New York: Rodopi 2007. 45–70.

I acknowledge the image owners of all the images used in this book and reproduce these images with their permission. The sources of images are detailed in the list of illustrations but I would also like to acknowledge the assistance and courtesy of the following people and organisations. Peter Hocking, the archivist at New Norcia and acknowledge the archives of the Benedictine Community of New Norcia for granting me permission to reproduce the image of New Norcia in the Introduction. The images of burning and clearing in Chapter 1 are sourced from the collections of the State Library of Western Australia and reproduced with the permission of the Library Board of Western Australia. I warmly thank Cathy Culbard, the daughter of Cyril Goode, for permitting me to reproduce her father's photographs in Chapter 2. The cover image from *The Listening Post* in Chapter 3 was approved for reproduction by Philip Orchard, the CEO and State Secretary of The Returned & Services League of Australia, WA Branch. The photographs of and by Peter Cowan and caricature of the author in Chapter 5 are reproduced with permission from Vicki Clark of the Peter Cowan Writers' Centre from Peter Cowan's papers held by the Centre. The photographs of the 'A-Class' bin in Chapter 5 are reproduced with the permission of Cooperative Bulk Handling Ltd and appear in their book, *Legends of the Grain Game* (2003). The illustration from the *Australian Woman's Weekly* in Chapter 6 is reproduced by courtesy of the magazine. The photographs of Dorothy Hewett and the cover images of her books in Chapter 6 are made with the permission of her executor, Kate Lilley. The cover image of Kath Walker's (now known as Oodgeroo of the tribe Noonuccal) *We Are Going* (1964) is reproduced by permission of John Wiley & Sons Australia. The two photographs of Elizabeth Jolley are reproduced with the permission of Christina Wilcox and come from the documentary 'The Nights Belong to the Novelist', produced and directed by Christina Wilcox. The reproduction of Wyeth's *Christina's World*, held at MOMA, was made available through Scala Images. The covers of John Kinsella's books *Night Parrots* and *The Silo* were made available to me by the publisher Fremantle Press.

Index

www.ingramcontent.com/pod-product-compliance
Lightning Source LLC
Chambersburg PA
CBHW021934110726
47901CB00003B/828

* 9 7 8 1 7 4 2 5 8 9 2 4 4 *